CLASSICAL MYTH

SEVENTH EDITION

BARRY B. POWELL

UNIVERSITY OF WISCONSIN–MADISON

with translations
by Herbert M. Howe

Pearson

Boston   Columbus   Indianapolis   New York   San Francisco   Upper Saddle River
Amsterdam   Cape Town   Dubai   London   Madrid   Milan   Munich   Paris   Montreal   Toronto
Delhi   Mexico City   São Paulo   Sydney   Hong Kong   Seoul   Singapore   Taipei   Tokyo

In memoriam, Herbert M. Howe (1912–2010), teacher and friend

FLIP

Senior Acquisitions Editor: Vivian Garcia
Editorial Assistant: Heather Vomero
Executive Marketing Manager: Joyce Nilsen
Senior Supplements Editor: Donna
   Campion
Production Manager: Denise Phillip
**Project Coordination, Text Design, and
   Electronic Page Makeup:** Laserwords
Senior Cover Design Manager: Nancy Danahy

Cover Designer: Nancy Sacks
Cover Art: Heracles in the cup of Helius,
   interior of an Attic wine cup, c. 480 BC
   Vatican Museums, Rome, Italy
Senior Manufacturing Buyer: Dennis J. Para
Printer/Binder: Edwards Brothers Malloy

Cover Printer: Edwards Brothers Malloy

Credits and acknowledgments borrowed from other sources and reproduced, with permission, in this textbook appear on the appropriate page within the text and on p. 717.

Library of Congress Cataloging-in-Publication Data

Powell, Barry B.
  Classical myth / Barry B. Powell; with translations by Herbert M. Howe. —7th ed.
    p. cm.
Includes index.
ISBN-13: 978-0-205-17607-6
ISBN-10: 0-205-17607-0
1. Mythology, Classical—Textbooks. I. Title.
BL723.P68 2012
292.1'3–dc23

2011016915

10 9 8 7 6 5 —EBM—14 13

www.pearsonhighered.com

ISBN 13: 978-0-205-17607-6
ISBN 10:   0-205-17607-0

CONTENTS

Part III
Legends

Part IV
Roman Myth

Part V
Interpretation

LIST OF PERSPECTIVES

MAPS

CHARTS

PREFACE

What does our great historical hunger signify, our clutching about us of
countless cultures, our consuming desire for knowledge, if not the loss of
myth, of a mythic home, the mythic womb?

FRIEDRICH NIETZSCHE, *The Birth of Tragedy*, 1872

The category "classical myth" exists more in the minds of contemporary teachers
than it did in the ancient world itself, but it nonetheless serves a useful pedagogi-
cal purpose. For some time now, courses bearing this or a similar title have been a
vehicle for introducing college students to the cultures of the ancient Greeks and
Romans, hence to the roots of Western civilization. By studying the myths of the
ancients primarily through the literary works in which they are preserved, students
are exposed to important classical authors, as well as to stories and figures that have
sustained interest and kindled imaginations throughout the history of Western culture, and continue to do so today.

The present text began as a modern introduction to classical myth at the
University of Wisconsin–Madison, a comprehensive and flexible resource for a
college-level course that would reflect the best recent scholarship in the field. The
fact that the first six editions have been used in many such courses throughout
the United States and in Canada and in Australia, New Zealand, and even Taiwan,
by instructors with different academic backgrounds teaching in a wide variety of
educational settings, has deeply gratified my sense that a book of this type was
needed. In many ways I see it as a summary of my own intellectual career, because

I remember when and usually where I first brushed up against the many figures of myth, when they first became important to me. In this respect this book is more personal than it reflects any objective standard of "what is classical myth," and in many ways my purpose is to share with the reader my own excitement at the discovery of our classical past.

In this seventh edition, I have made many improvements to the book—rearranged some material, corrected expression, streamlined it somewhat, and added perspectives, maps, and illustrations—all changes based on suggestions from instructors who have used the earlier editions in their classes, as well as on my own experience in teaching with the book. I have added links to a modern online version of translations of complete ancient texts, so that the interested reader can easily expand knowledge of a given topic without having to purchase auxiliary texts. But the central goals remain unchanged. The first six editions were unique among texts on classical myth in their *contextual approach,* which emphasizes the context in which ancient stories were told. In the seventh edition I have continued my efforts to place the myths in their anthropological, historical, religious, sociological, and economic contexts. In this edition I have preserved the same order of chapters as in the last, except that I have divided the former Chapter 7 into two chapters, for a total of twenty-five chapters.

The first six editions emphasized the historical development of classical myth and I have maintained that approach here. Only when we see how myth changes over time, yet somehow remains the same, can we grasp its essence. It is important to remember that the versions of myth I present in the text represent only one version of the many disparate, often contradictory, stories that the Greeks told about their gods and heroes. For this reason, at the end of each chapter I cite ancient sources for the myths, which will lead the student to disparate accounts. A complete inventory is, of course, far beyond the scope of this text, but these suggestions can serve as a starting point for those wishing to explore the mythical background more fully.

Many original Greek and Latin sources (which can be complex) are also listed in Edward Tripp's *Meridian Handbook of Classical Mythology* and in the *Oxford Classical Dictionary* (3rd ed., Oxford, UK, 1996), or simply do a Google search on the Internet, whose resources for learning are astounding. There are numerous sites (Google "classical myth") that give ancient sources for even minor figures in myth. You can always Google a name or a place to receive an abundance of information and hundreds of images, too. The computerization of knowledge and its dissemination on the Internet is a profound advance in culture, and students of myth are as much the beneficiaries as anyone. The entries in Wikipedia are also often excellent, containing illustrations, bibliographies, and links to related material.

This book also has its own Companion Website™ located at http:// www.pearsonhighered.com/powell7e, which provides a vast array of resources relevant to the study of classical myth. The Companion Website™ also offers a comprehensive interactive study guide with self-scoring quizzes and other resources designed to assist students in mastering the material.

Many of the passages from ancient literary works quoted here are from well-known sources, but I have not hesitated to present lesser-known passages when that seemed appropriate. Whenever possible I have used Greek sources rather than Latin, but I have included numerous selections from Ovid's highly influential Latin retelling of the Greek myths (and other Latin writers) when the myth is found in no other ancient literary source. The complete text of Ovid's *Metamorphoses* will form a natural, though not necessary, adjunct to this text, as will complete translations of Greek tragedies (many of these texts will be found at the links cited in the text). Pearson Education has made possible the purchase of these and other auxiliary Penguin titles at a much-reduced cost, shrink-wrapped with this text, if the instructor prefers hardcopy to online resources. (Instructors: Please contact your local Pearson Education representative if you wish to order such a packet.)

Like the first six editions, the seventh stresses the importance of interpretation in the study of myth, although without relying on a single perspective. No one approach to interpretation can be adequate to the enormous range and complexity of classical myth. I briefly introduce the subject of interpretation in Chapter 1, and throughout the text I offer interpretive comments on individual myths—a basis, I am sure, for objection as much as agreement! I postpone an in-depth examination of myth interpretation to the last chapter, "Theories of Myth Interpretation," when the student will be familiar with various examples of myth. Many instructors may prefer to introduce this topic earlier, of course, and the chapter can be read at any time without loss of coherence.

The seventh edition remains committed to the principle that when we study classical myth, we also study the roots of Western culture. Ancient works of art play a valuable role in helping students visualize mythical figures and events as the ancients themselves did, and therefore I have included many illustrations from classical sources—more than two hundred reproductions of vase paintings, sculptural works, architectural monuments, and other works of art from the ancient and modern worlds, several new to this edition. In general the maps on the front and back covers have all the important places mentioned in the myths, but for this edition I have included new maps in the chapters that focus on places important in that chapter. When a place is found on a map within a chapter, I put that name in SMALL CAPS when it first appears.

As in the first six editions, chapters also include "Perspective" boxes that examine the uses of classical myth in the medieval, Renaissance, or modern periods. I have added new examples for this edition. Many of the Perspectives incorporate excerpts from or reproductions of literary and artistic works. My intent is to help students see how stories and figures from classical myth were appropriated and interpreted at later stages of history, including the modern period, often for purposes very different from those found in the ancient world itself.

The study of classical myth inevitably presents students with hundreds of new and unfamiliar names. To assist students with pronunciation, I have provided an English pronunciation guide the first time each difficult name appears in the text. The pronunciation guides are repeated in the Index. I have also used **bold** letters to highlight names of greatest importance, those that one really ought to know to claim competence in the topic. These names are repeated in a list of important terms at the end of each chapter, with page numbers where the term first appears. I leave names of lesser importance in ordinary type, although in many cases I give pronunciations for these as well. In the Index I have included a capsule identification for important names, so the Index also serves as a glossary. You can also hear the names pronounced on the Companion Website™ at http://www.pearsonhighered.com/powell7e.

ACKNOWLEDGMENTS

This book grew out of a course in classical myth offered for many decades without interruption at the University of Wisconsin–Madison. The course, one of the first of its kind, began in the 1930s with the labors of Walter "Ray" Agard, whom the famous educator Alexander Meiklejohn brought to Madison from Amherst in 1927 to teach in the Meiklejohn Experimental College. Ray passed it on to **Herbert M. Howe**, who did most of the translations for the book, and Herb to me. Herb died in 2010 at age 98, a superb, even magical, teacher and a world-class swimmer, and I have dedicated this book to him. My long friendship with him was always a treasure. The course continues to be taught today as one of the most popular in the undergraduate curriculum.

I want to express my gratitude to my editor Vivian Garcia, who with great cheer and energy has helped to craft this new edition. Many others have helped, and I am grateful to them, especially **William Aylward**, whose advice has proved invaluable and who has contributed important material to the chapters on Roman myth. William teaches the course today. I also want to thank Dale Grote for his continued superb labors on the Web site, which has so greatly enhanced the value of the text.

I am responsible for the translations from Akkadian, Egyptian, and modern Greek. In our translations we have sought a modern idiom, unrhymed, with a regular beat in the poetic lines. The translator can only try to recreate in modern language thoughts and manners distant from our own. In the preparation of my own English versions of Mesopotamian and Egyptian literary texts, I owe a general indebtedness to the following translations: James B. Pritchard, editor, *Ancient Near Eastern Texts Relating to the Old Testament* (Princeton, NJ, 1969); A. Heidel, *The Gilgamesh Epic and Old Testament Parallels* (Chicago, 1949); Thorkild Jacobsen, *The Treasures of Darkness* (New Haven, CT, 1976); Samuel Noah Kramer, *Sumerian Mythology* (New York, 1961) and *The Sumerians: Their History, Culture, and Character* (Chicago, 1963); and Stephanie Dalley, *Myths from Mesopotamia* (Oxford, UK, 1989). I thank Frederick W. Schwink for his translation of the Hittite "Kingship in Heaven." I also thank Random House for permission to quote "Musée des Beaux Arts" from *The Collected Poems of W. H. Auden* (2007); Simon & Schuster, to quote "Leda and the Swan" from *W. B. Yeats's Collected Poems* (1996); and New Directions Publishing Corporation to quote "Adonis" from *Collected Poems 1912–1944* by H. D. (1986). We also wish to thank the museums, libraries, galleries, and other collections that have kindly allowed reproduction of items in their collections and have provided the necessary photographs. Photographs from these and other sources are gratefully acknowledged in the text.

I welcome comments on this edition from instructors and students who have used it, as these will help plan improvements for future editions. I can be contacted at the e-mail address below.

—*B. B. P.*

Barry B. Powell
Halls-Bascom Professor of Classics Emeritus
University of Wisconsin–Madison
e-mail: bbpowell@wisc.edu

CHAPTER 1

THE NATURE OF MYTH

The longer I occupy myself with questions of ancient mythology, the more diffident I become of success in dealing with them, and I am apt to think that we who spend our years in searching for solutions to these insoluble problems are like Sisyphus perpetually rolling his stone uphill only to see it revolve again into the valley.

SIR JAMES G. FRAZER (1854–1941),
author of *The Golden Bough*

THE WESTERN ROMAN EMPIRE ended more than fifteen hundred years ago, but the stories of classical gods and goddesses, of Greek and Roman warriors and leaders, live on in their ancient vigor. Zeus, Venus, Helen, Odysseus, Achilles, Aeneas—these familiar names stood in the background as later Western art and literature advanced, and they stand there still today. They were bequeathed to us in the writings of the Greeks and Romans, but their names and stories are much older than the written word. They go back before the introduction of writing, an era when classical myth first took a shape we can recognize.

Later chapters examine specific myths that have come down to us from the Greeks and Romans, but in this chapter we limit ourselves to some preliminary questions essential to a clear understanding of classical myth. We discuss the definition of myth and the three main types of myth: *divine myth, legend,* and *folktale.* We also look briefly at some aspects of the study of myth.

WHAT IS A MYTH?

Human beings have told stories from time immemorial, for stories are a natural product of spoken language, an outgrowth of the imaginative power that clearly separates us from our animal cousins. The story is a universal ingredient of human culture, bringing relief from the tedium of everyday labor and reminding listeners of their own values, beliefs, and history.

This book is concerned with a certain type of story known as *myth.* The term *myth* is hard to define, in part because of the enormous variety of stories gathered from many cultures by ethnographers, anthropologists, and literary historians. Originally, the Greek word *mythos* simply meant "authoritative speech," "story," or "plot," but later writers used the term *myth* in more restricted ways. Some recent authorities, exasperated by the complexity of the phenomena, deny that the term *myth* expresses a coherent concept at all. A definition widely agreed on is that myth is *a traditional story with collective importance.* We can accept this definition, but we must consider carefully what it means.

To say that a myth is a story is to say, first, that it has a plot, a narrative structure consisting of a beginning, middle, and end. In the beginning of a typical story, we are introduced to characters in a certain situation, usually one involving conflict with other characters, with misfortune, or with themselves. The word *character* comes from a Greek word meaning "a certain mental imprint." Hamlet cannot make up his mind, Macbeth is ambitious, King Lear is blind to the character of others. Character is the sum of the choices one makes. In myths, the characters may be gods, goddesses, or other supernatural beings, but they may also be human beings or even animals that speak and act in the manner of human beings.

In the middle of a typical story, the situation grows more complex, and tension and conflict develop. In the end, the tension is somehow resolved. Today we might find an example of this basic structure in the plot common to ten thousand novels and feature films: Girl meets boy (the beginning), girl loses boy (the middle), girl finds boy (the end). Plot is an essential feature of myth. Without a beginning, middle, and end, there can be no story and hence no myth. In casual speech we sometimes say that the Greek god Zeus, for example, is a myth. However, strictly speaking, Zeus is not a myth, but a character in myth, in the plotted stories that tell of his exploits. Belief in the existence of a particular god, the observance of a ritual in a god's honor, and religious symbols are not myths.

Another element of myth is setting. The setting is the time and place in which the action of the story unfolds. Myths are never set in the present or the recent past; the action always takes place in the distant past or in a shadowy time altogether outside human chronology. The setting of myths may be in an actual city, such as Athens or Thebes, or some other location familiar to the audience. In other myths, the setting is an obscure place: the underworld, which no one in the real world ever visited; Mount Olympus, which really exists but in myth is the home of the gods; or Crete of a very long time ago.

Thus, like all other stories, myths have plot, characters, and setting. However, a myth is not just any story, but a certain kind of story that we describe as traditional.

Our word *traditional* comes from Latin *trado,* "hand over," and a traditional story is one that has been "handed over" orally from one storyteller to another without the intervention of writing. In societies that do not use writing, stories must be handed over verbally, so traditional tales are the vehicle for transmitting one generation's thought to another. In this way traditional tales maintain contact with the past (about which little real is known) and pass inherited wisdom on to the future. They explain a society to itself, promulgating its concerns and values.

From this function derives myth's "collective importance"—myths hold meaning for the group, not just the individual. They describe patterns of behavior that serve as models for members of a society, especially in times of crisis. For example, in Homer's *Iliad* (written down in the eighth century BC), Achilles tries to persuade King Priam of Troy to eat at a time when Priam is heartbroken for his dead son Hector, killed by Achilles. Achilles tells the story of Niobê, a Theban princess: Although Artemis and Apollo had killed her seven sons and seven daughters, still she ate, and so should Priam. Four hundred years later, when the philosopher Socrates was on trial for his life, he defended his insistence on telling the truth in spite of threats against him by recalling the example of Achilles, who was ashamed to live as a coward and chose to die bravely before the walls of Troy.

Because they are traditional, myths are also anonymous. In contrast to such modern forms of storytelling as Leo Tolstoy's *War and Peace,* J.R.R. Tolkien's *Lord of the Rings,* J. D. Salinger's *Catcher in the Rye,* or George Lucas's film series *Star Wars,* myths never have identifiable authors. Literary works based on myth may have authors, but not the myths themselves. The Greek dramatist Sophocles wrote a play about Oedipus the king, but the *myth* of Oedipus existed long before, and no one can say who created it.

This anonymity helps us to understand why the Greeks, following the lead of the philosopher Plato, eventually came to contrast *mythos,* "story" or "myth," with *logos,* "account." The teller of a *logos* takes responsibility for the truth of what is said. A *logos* is a reasoned explanation of something that emphasizes a continuing causal sequence, as in the proofs of plane geometry. We still use the suffix *-logy* to indicate a reasoned inquiry into a topic, as in anthropo*logy,* "study of human beings"; bio*logy,* "study of life forms"; or even mytho*logy,* "study of myth" (although *mythology* often is used as a synonym for *myth*). By contrast, the teller of a *mythos* does not claim personal responsibility for what is said. After all, the teller did not invent the story, but only passed it on.

PERSPECTIVE 1.1

THE "MYTH OF ATLANTIS"

In his dialogue *Timaeus,* Plato puts into the mouth of the Athenian lawgiver Solon (c. 638–c. 559 BC) an account of Solon's trip to Egypt, where he learned of a utopian* kingdom that once existed on an island in the western seas somewhere beyond the Pillars of Heracles (Gibraltar). The island was larger than Libya and Asia together. A powerful, highly civilized people once lived on this vast island until in a single night earthquake and flood destroyed everything; the continent sank beneath the waves. In another dialogue, the *Critias,* Plato gives a still more detailed account of what he now calls Atlantis ("the realm of Atlas," the Titan thought to support the world).

There is no evidence for this story before Plato, who seems to have modeled it on the story of the Hesperides ("nymphs of the West"), the protectors of a magic tree on an island beyond the Pillars of Heracles. The story is not a myth as we have defined the term, because it is not a traditional tale but an artificial construction devised by Plato to make certain points about ideal government. For a long time "Atlantis" was used as equivalent to a utopian state. Francis Bacon (1561–1626), a philosopher and literary figure during the reign of Queen Elizabeth I, wrote *The New Atlantis* about a utopian world.

The modern search for a real Atlantis buried beneath the Atlantic Ocean, or someplace else, goes back to 1882 with publication of *Atlantis: The Antediluvian World,* by one Ignatius Donnelly. Donnelly argued that Plato's description was literally true. On the lost island of Atlantis first appeared human civilization, he thought, which then spread outward over the earth. Stories of the Garden of Eden, the Elysian Fields, and the like are reminiscences of Atlantis, whose kings and queens became the gods and goddesses of the Greeks, Phoenicians, Hindus, and Scandinavians. The original religion of Atlantis was sun worship, preserved in Egypt and Peru. Remnants from the high civilizations of the so-called Bronze Age are really remnants of the Atlantean civilization, which spread to the mainland, bringing with them stories of the Great Flood.

Recent discoveries that the island of Thera, the southernmost of the Cycladic islands in the Aegean Sea, blew up in an enormous volcanic explosion revived hopes of explaining the origin of Plato's story in prehistory (Perspective Figure 1.1).

It seemed that the explosion might have caused the collapse of the civilization on Crete about 1450 BC. However, in 1991, with the help of the radiocarbon dating of ice cores from Greenland and evidence of frost events in tree rings, the explosion was shown to have taken place about 1620 BC, far too early to have destroyed the Cretan civilization.

---

*The word *utopia,* a Greek word meaning "nowhere," was coined by Sir Thomas More (1478–1535), an advisor to Henry VIII (who beheaded him), for an imaginary perfect state.

PERSPECTIVE FIGURE 1.1 The caldera in the center of the Cycladic island of Thera; before the huge explosion c. 1620 BC, the largest known in the geological record, this was solid land.   (© Mikel Bilbao Gorostiaga / Alamy)

Though not a "myth," the same methods used to explain traditional myths have been freely applied to the story of Atlantis. Always at the edge of a definition stand exceptions that do not fit. Scholars emphasize Plato's transitional role as a thinker who stood between the oral world from which myth came and the literate world in which we live today.

During oral transmission, a traditional tale is subject to constant change. Different narrators of a story have different motives and emphasize or embroider on different aspects. The story of Niobê could easily illustrate the dangers of self-assertion (Niobê bragged that she had more children than the mother of Apollo and Artemis), but Achilles uses the story to prove that eating food can lessen grief. Homer describes Achilles' anguished choice between a short, glorious life and a long, inglorious one, but never presents the choice as between courage and cowardice. In the written works in which Greek myths have been preserved, we often find strikingly different versions of the same myth. The poets Homer and Sophocles both report that Oedipus, king of Thebes, killed his father and married his mother, but in Homer's account Oedipus continues to rule after the truth comes out, whereas in Sophocles' play he pokes pins in his eyes and leaves the city, a wretched wanderer. Neither is the "true" version of the myth, of which the other is a variant. The myth of Oedipus contains *all* the variants.

A retelling of every variant of every Greek myth would require a book of enormous length, or a very ambitious Web site, and would present its own false picture of the tradition. After all it is not the multiplicity of versions that attracts our attention, but the best-known variants, often those of some great literary work. For example, Sophocles' version of the myth of Oedipus is far better known than is Homer's passing reference. Virtually every group of humankind has its store of traditional narrative, but in this book we limit ourselves to the myths of Greece and Rome, only occasionally referring to earlier and parallel traditions, especially those from the ancient Near East, from where much Greek myth came.

TYPES OF MYTH

Modern scholars like to distinguish between several types of myth based on the nature of the principal characters and the function that the story fulfilled for the listener and the teller. **Divine myths** (sometimes called true myths or myths proper) are stories in which supernatural beings are the main actors. Such stories generally explain why the world, or some aspect of it, is the way it is. **Legends** (or sagas) are stories of the great deeds of human heroes or heroines. Legends narrate the events of the human past. The word comes from Latin *legenda,* "things that should be read," that is, originally, morally uplifting stories about Christian saints. **Folktales** are stories whose actors are ordinary people or animals. Folktales entertain the audience and teach or justify customary patterns of behavior.

The more we learn about myth, the more we discover how difficult it can be to separate one type from another. For example, stories that appear to be legends often incorporate elements of folktales or explain the nature of things, as do divine myths. Such distinctions are nonetheless valuable because they allow us to isolate and study various aspects of myth. Let us look more closely at each type.

Divine Myth

The supernatural beings who are the principal characters in divine myth are depicted as superior to humans in power and splendor. Sometimes they take on human or animal shapes at will. They control awesome forces of nature: thunder, storm, rain, fire, earthquake, or fecundity. When these beings appear in their own form, they can be enormous and of stunning beauty or ugliness. Conflicts among them can take place on an immense scale and involve whole continents, high mountains, and vast seas.

Sometimes the supernatural characters in divine myth are little more than personified abstractions without clearly defined personalities. In Greek myth, for example, Nikê (**nī**-kē), "victory," is just the abstract concept (Figure 1.1).

In other cases, the supernatural beings are gods, goddesses, or demons with well-developed and distinctive personalities of their own. Zeus, the sky-god in Greek myth, is much more than a personification of the sky; he is depicted as a powerful father, an often unfaithful husband, and the upholder of justice in human communities.

FIGURE 1.1 Stars descend before Sun. The stars, represented as boys, leap into the sea before the approach of Helius in his horse-drawn chariot (the nimbus around his head is one origin of the medieval halo around the heads of saints), on an Attic wine bowl, c. 435 BC. As the goddess Nikê personifies an event, the stars and Helius personify natural forces. (© Trustees of the British Museum / Art Resource, New York)

The events of divine myth usually take place in a world before or outside the present order where time and space often have different meanings from those familiar to human beings. For example, one Greek myth explained how Zeus came to rule the world: He fought against the Titans, an earlier race of gods,* defeated them in a terrible battle, and established his empire on the ruin of theirs. It would be pointless to ask when these events occurred, even within the context of the story, because they are set in a time before human chronology has meaning. Moreover, many divine myths of the Greeks are set in a place far removed from the familiar world of human beings—on Mount Olympus, far away and unapproachable.

Understandably, many of the gods about whom traditional tales were told were both actors in the stories and objects of veneration in religious cult. Zeus is a character in Greek myth, but he was also a god for whom the Greeks built temples, carried out sacrifices, and celebrated festivals. Because of this double function of the gods, divine myth is easily confused with religion, but the two must be clearly distinguished. Myths are traditional stories; religion is belief and the course of action that follows from belief. *Belief* is best defined as "what you accept (with or without proof) as a basis for action." For example, the Greeks believed that Zeus caused the rain to fall. Therefore, they sacrificed animals in times of drought to persuade him to bring rain. Myths often justify a religious practice or a form of religious behavior, but we can retell a myth, even a myth about divine beings, without engaging in religious behavior. The relationship between myth and religion is complicated, and we will have more to say about it later, but we

---

*The word *God* (capital *G*) should be limited to a single all-powerful being in any religion—Jewish, Christian, Muslim, or other. A small *g* shows that you are talking about one of many divine powers. A *demigod* is the offspring of a god and a human; sometimes a demigod becomes a god at death. The word *deity* is a general term that can refer to God or gods.

must remember that myth is a traditional story with collective importance, whereas religion is a set of beliefs that motivates a course of action.

Divine myths served a function in ancient cultures analogous to that of theoretical science in our own: They explained why the world is the way it is. Many of these myths tell of the origin and destruction of grand things: the universe, the gods, and ourselves; the relations of gods with one another and with human beings; and the divine origin of such human economic and social institutions as the growing of crops, the cycle of the seasons, the making of wine, and prophecy and oracles. Many divine myths deal with limited matters, such as the origin of local customs and practices.

In more technical language, we can describe such explanatory myths as etiological, from the Greek word *aition*, "cause." A creation myth is an example of an **etiological tale** because it explains the causes that brought the world into existence. An etiological myth explained the origin of Mount Etna, a dangerous volcano in Sicily. Beneath it Zeus imprisoned the fire-breathing monster Typhoeus, who continued to spew forth smoke and lava. Another example is the myth of Persephonê, daughter of the wheat-goddess Demeter. Persephonê must spend four months of the year in the underworld, and Demeter refuses to let anything grow during those months—the hot, barren summer. The change of seasons is "explained," according to many, by the myth. The etiological tale expresses a conjecture about the cause of something that existed long before the explanation.

Both divine myth and modern science offer explanations of why the world is the way it is, but they do so in very different ways. Scientific explanations are based on impersonal general laws and statistical probabilities discovered, or at least verified, by repeatable quantitative experiments, whereas mythic explanations, expressed in traditional tales, assume that supernatural beings control the world through the exercise of personal will. Assigning human qualities, especially unpredictability, to the forces that stand behind the world is characteristic of the worldview we find in myth. Thunder is an expression of Zeus's anger, not the necessary result of impersonal physical forces. Greek myth could thus blame sudden and puzzling deaths on the will of the gods, as in the story of how, out of spite, the gods Artemis and Apollo struck down the fourteen children of Niobê. Modern scientists may be puzzled by death from cancer, but they do not blame such death on a divine and irrational agent. The modern world was born from the struggle of scientific thought against traditional explanations for why and how things happen in the world, a struggle by no means concluded today.

In Part II of this text we examine more closely the divine myths of the ancient Greeks.

Legend

If divine myth in oral cultures is analogous to science in modern, literate Western society, legend is analogous to history. Both legend and modern historical writing attempt to answer the question, "What happened in the human past?" Because the past explains and justifies the present, the telling of legends was an important activity in the cultural life of many ancient peoples, and never more so than among the ancient Greeks. In legends, the central characters are human beings, not gods and goddesses.

Although supernatural beings often play a part, their roles are subordinate to those of the human characters. In the legend of Orestes, the god Apollo orders Orestes to kill his mother, but the emphasis of the story is on Orestes' carrying out the order and facing its terrible consequences.

The principal actors of legend are heroes and heroines. Drawn from the ranks of the nobility, they are kings and queens, princes and princesses, and other members of an aristocratic elite. They have extraordinary physical and personal qualities and are stronger, more beautiful, or more courageous than ordinary people. Most Greeks had no doubt that such legendary figures really lived, and members of important families regarded themselves as descended from them. Whereas divine myth is set in a different or previous world-order, legendary events belong to our own order, although they took place in the distant past, at the very beginning of human time when mighty heroes and heroines lived on earth, great cities were founded, difficult quests undertaken, fearful monsters slain, and momentous wars waged.

Most ancient Greeks, then, did not doubt that such events as the Trojan War really did occur, and they pointed out the tombs of legendary figures and the actual sites of their exploits. But the Greeks had no way to compare their traditions with historical reality. Today, armed with the insights of archaeology and techniques of historical investigation, modern scholars recognize that the oral transmitters of traditional tales had little respect for historical truth, or even any concept of it. Greek myth tells us more about the circumstances and concerns of its transmitters than it does about life in the distant past.

Still, legends can contain an element of historical truth. Modern scholars have long thought that Greek legend does reflect, however dimly, major events and power relations of a historical period now known to us through archaeological remains. Many or most of the figures in Greek legend probably did live at some time, most likely in the Mycenaean civilization of the Late Bronze Age (c. 1600–1150 BC). Their very names provide one bit of evidence. For example, the name of Menelaüs, the legendary husband of Helen of Troy, means something like "upholder of the people." This distinctive name is appropriate to the aristocracy that certainly existed during this period, and similar names appear in written documents of the time (the Linear B tablets, the writings of the Mycenaeans, discussed in Chapter 2).

Archaeology provides further evidence. Excavation has shown that many of the places associated with important legendary events were great centers of civilization during the Late Bronze Age. Troy, for example, was a settlement of considerable importance until it was destroyed about 1230 BC. Although we have no proof that it was destroyed by Greek warriors, as Greek legends assert, there remains a tantalizing correspondence between the legend and the archaeological evidence (Figure 1.2).

Like divine myths, some legends also served a specific etiological function. Thus, one Greek story explained why, at the spring wine festival, Athenians brought their own wine jugs, although at other festivals they drank from a communal bowl. According to the legend, the Mycenaean prince Orestes, who had killed his own mother to avenge her murder of his father, came to Athens at the time of the festival. The king of Athens did not want to send Orestes away impolitely, but neither did he want the Athenian people to be polluted by sharing a bowl with a man who had murdered his mother, so the king had every man fill his cup from his own jug. In reality

FIGURE 1.2 The walls of Troy. The earliest settlement at Troy can be dated to about 3000 BC, but the citadel walls shown here belong to the sixth level of occupation (Troy VI), built around 1400 BC and destroyed around 1230 BC. Constructed of neatly cut blocks of limestone that slope inward, the citadel wall had at least four gateways, two of them protected by towers. Either Troy VI or its much poorer successor Troy VIIa, destroyed about 1180 BC, could have inspired Greek legends of the Trojan War.   (Author's photo)

the use of separate jugs seems to have arisen from a fear of contagion from ghosts, thought to be abroad at this season. The practice had nothing at all to do with a visit from Orestes, and the story was invented well after the custom was established. Such is often true of etiologies in myth.

We examine the legends of the ancient Greeks and Romans in detail in Part III of this text, with further remarks on general patterns in heroic myth (Chapter 12).

Folktale

Folktale is more difficult to define than is divine myth or legend because of the variety of traditional stories grouped together under this heading. Some scholars describe folktales as any traditional story that is not a divine myth or legend. This category would encompass such familiar fairytales as "Cinderella" and "Snow White," among the many German stories written down from oral sources in the early nineteenth century by the brothers Jacob and Wilhelm Grimm. Likewise, the beast fables attributed to the Greek writer Aesop (sixth century BC), such as "The Tortoise and the Hare," we might also consider folktales, as could a story such as

"Sinbad the Sailor" from the *Arabian Nights* and most oral tales recorded in North America and Africa during the last two hundred years. In the "myths" of many cultures there is scarcely any divine myth or legend, but all is folktale.

Within this diversity we can still discern common traits. As in legend, the central characters in folktales are human beings, even though gods and spirits appear and play important roles. But in folktales the main characters usually are ordinary men, women, and children rather than kings and queens and others of exalted personal qualities or social status, hence the term *folktale*, a story about common people. Even in fables, a kind of folktale in which the characters are animals, the animals speak and act as though they were ordinary humans. (The fable is the only category of tale for which the Greeks had a specific word, *ainos*, from which comes our *enigma*, "like a fable").

Unlike legends, folktales do not pretend to tell us what happened in the human past. No one believes that Snow White, Cinderella, Hansel and Gretel, or the American Indian trickster Crow really existed, as the Greeks believed that Achilles, Helen, and Orestes did. Often the main characters in folktales have low social status, at least at the beginning of the story, and are persecuted or victimized in some way by other characters. The folktale hero may be an outcast whose intelligence and virtue are not recognized by those in power. The hero often is the youngest child of three brothers or sisters, abused by siblings or by a wicked stepmother. Very often the end of the story brings a reversal of fortune, the happy ending for which folktales are well known. Initially taken to be stupid or ineffectual, the folktale hero triumphs over all obstacles and receives an appropriate reward. The trickster, who gets what he wants by unexpected means, is common in folktale.

Whereas divine myths explain why the world is the way it is and legends tell what happened in the human past, the primary function of folktales is to entertain, although they may also play an important role in teaching and justifying customary patterns of behavior. Folktales draw on such universal human experiences as the child's place in the hierarchy of the family. They appeal to such universal human instincts as the belief that good is eventually rewarded and evil punished. In modern literate culture the novel and the feature film have functions analogous to that of the folktale in oral society. For this reason feature films almost without exception "end happily."

Although curiously few pure folktales have come down to us from the Greeks and Romans, this category of traditional tale is of central importance to the study of Greek myth. To understand why, we must take note of a distinctive aspect of the folktale: the regular appearance of identifiable **folktale types,** even in stories from cultures widely separated in space or time. Scholars recognize more than seven hundred folktale types in traditions around the globe. Sometimes a folktale type is named after a famous example. The "Cinderella type," for example, is any story in which an abused younger sister, assisted by a spirit, appears in fancy dress at a ball, disappears from the prince's admiring glance, then is recognized and marries the prince.

Folktale types are made up of smaller elements called **folktale motifs** that can be recombined in endless variety. A type may occasionally consist of a single motif, but folktales usually have several motifs, and we might think of folktale motifs as the cells that make up the body of a tale. A folktale type is thus a constellation of motifs that constitutes an independent story, that is, a story that makes sense in itself and does not depend on its relation to some larger story. Some motifs making up the "Cinderella type" would be "the abused younger sister," "the spirit helper," "the glass slipper as a token," and "marriage to the prince." Different types may share the same motifs. For example, in any number of folktales the hero grows up and goes off into the world to seek his fortune. This motif by itself could hardly define a type. What defines a type is a recurring constellation of motifs.

PERSPECTIVE 1.2

THE BROTHERS GRIMM

Everyone has heard of "Grimms' Fairy Tales" (*Kinder- und Hausmärchen* = "Child and House Tales"), a collection that reached its familiar form in an edition of 1857, but took fifty years to assemble. Already in the short first edition of 1812–1815, Jacob and Wilhelm Grimm gathered together tales that represent virtually every folktale type found in Germanic countries. From the great work of the Grimm brothers come all later divisions of folktales into certain types and motifs.

Where did the Grimm brothers get these world-famous stories? Their sources were not printed documents. They claimed that their best storyteller was a "peasant woman" who told "genuine Hessian [west-central German] tales." We know, however, that this woman was a tailor's wife from a French Protestant family and that the Grimms' informants were never peasants, but in general educated women, sometimes of high social status. According to the romantic temper of the times, however, the Grimms wanted their stories to come from "the folk," thought to be a repository of uncorrupted truths.

In studying traditional tales, we always face the problem of the relation of our written version with a version that might have really appeared in an oral environment. The Grimms were scientists, yet saw no objection in refining and even recreating whatever might have been their original source. For example, in the first edition of 1812–1815, "The Frog King" opens like this (in English translation):

> Once upon a time there was a king's daughter, who went out into a wood and sat down beside a cool spring. She had a golden ball, her favorite toy, which she threw up high and caught it again in the air and enjoyed herself in this way. (*Kinder- und Hausmärchen*, 1812–1815, 1:1)

In subsequent editions the scene kept growing until in the last edition of 1857, edited by Wilhelm Grimm, the story opens as follows:

> In ancient times, when wishing still did some good, there lived a king whose daughters were beautiful, but the youngest was so beautiful that the sun itself, which has seen so much, was astounded at her when he shone upon her.

Nearby the castle of the king lay a huge dark wood, and in the wood under ancient Lindens was a spring. If the day were hot, the child of the king would go into the wood and sit down at the edge of the cool spring. And if she was bored, she took a golden ball, threw it in the air and caught it again. That was her favorite game. (*Kinder- und Hausmärchen, Ausgabe letzter Hand,* 1857, 1:29)

The words of the story, then, are those of the Grimm brothers, not of a "peasant" from the folk or even an educated and aristocratic informant. Wilhelm Grimm did not think of his embellishments of style as violating his mission to record German "Child and House Tales," because in his view the tale consisted of a constellation of motifs that remained the same in spite of the actual words used to tell it. Probably most myth tellers would agree.

Folktale motifs are not commonplace events, people, or incidents, but are always distinctive or unusual in some way. A "sister" is not a motif, but "an abused youngest sister of three" is. "The woman went to town" has no motifs, but "a hero put on his cap of invisibility, mounted his magic carpet, and flew to the Land Beyond the Sun" has four motifs: "the cap of invisibility," "the magic carpet," "the magic flight through the air," and "the wondrous land." Other common motifs are "the dragon that guards a spring" or "a magic object that protects against attack." Modern scholars have exhaustively described and organized the bewildering variety of folktale motifs, which number in the thousands, so that you can look up a given motif and find where else it occurs throughout world folklore.

A general folktale *type* often found in Greek myth is the quest. In the quest, the folktale hero, compelled to seek some special object, journeys to a strange, terrifying, or wonderful land. There he must face a powerful antagonist: a dragon, monster, ogre, or thoroughly wicked man. To overcome his antagonist, the hero needs the assistance of animals, ghosts, divine beings, or magical weapons or devices. The hero is often a clever trickster, whereas his adversary is brutish, stupid, and cruel. The adversary succeeds in imprisoning, enchanting, or even killing the hero, but at last, often through a trick, the hero escapes, overcomes the enemy, and dispatches him in some cruel or gruesome way. Taking the object he sought, the hero returns to his native land, where his reward is marriage to a princess, or a part of the kingdom, or a great treasure.

Many of these motifs appear in the Greek story of Perseus (see Chapter 14), who was sent on a dangerous journey by an evil king who wanted to marry Perseus' mother. Assisted by nymphs, the goddess Athena, and an array of magical objects, Perseus went to the ends of the earth and slew the deadly Gorgon. On his return journey, carrying the Gorgon's death-dealing head in a pouch, he killed a sea monster that threatened a young woman chained to a rock. He took the woman back to Greece, married her, and killed the wicked king. This story illustrates the way Greek myth can use folktale motifs to elaborate on what would otherwise be considered a legend. About Perseus, for example, we are also told that he was born in the town of Argos and brought up by a poor fisherman on the island of Seriphus, that he accidentally killed his grandfather Acrisius in the town of Larissa, and that he moved to Tiryns and founded Mycenae, where his children later ruled. These are details appropriate to a widespread legend. The myth of Perseus, then, is neither pure legend nor pure folktale, but a mixture of the two.

In general, we may describe much of Greek myth as legend strongly colored by folktale. The main characters in these stories often have names appropriate to men and women who might really have lived, members of a social elite whose stories are attached to prominent Greek towns. Yet their adventures are of a sort we expect to find in folktale. The distinctions we have drawn between types of myth are of great value in organizing our thinking about myth, but we should remember that our distinctions are the results of intellectual analysis; they were not recognized by the ancient Greeks themselves.

THE STUDY OF MYTH

The word *mythology* should mean "the study of myth" (by analogy with *biology, anthropology*), but in common usage *mythology* typically refers more loosely to the myths themselves, or to a particular group of myths, not to the study of myth. Such statements as "I like mythology" are therefore taken to mean "I like myths as such," and the myths of Greece and Rome are often called "classical mythology." To be clear, we avoid the ambiguous term *mythology* altogether, using instead *myth* or *myths,* on the one hand, and the *study of myth* on the other.

The study of myth is multifaceted. There are many different ways in which modern scholars approach the study of myth, but they can be grouped into four general categories:

- The recording and compiling of a given culture's myths
- The analysis of the role that specific myths play or played within the culture
- The study of how one culture's myths are related to those of other cultures
- Assessment of the lasting human significance of specific myths or groups of myths

Let us first discuss the recording and compiling of a given culture's myths. The spread of alphabetic literacy in the modern world, and now communication by the Internet, has greatly reduced the degree to which myths serve as a guide to everyday life, but many cultures still maintain a vital oral tradition. One task undertaken by anthropologists and others who study such cultures is to record, in writing or by other means, the oral tales that are still passed on from generation to generation.

For ancient cultures like those of Greece and Rome a direct recording of oral tales is of course no longer possible. We can only study the myths of these cultures that have been recorded already. Typically the ancient myths were recorded not by scholars studying the myths for their own sakes, but by men (almost never women) who had other goals. In addition, oral tales exist in many different variants; the variant recorded on one occasion could be very different from that recorded on another. As a result, the records that have come down to us are contradictory, confusing, and incomplete. Careful study and considerable experience are needed to move from existing records to a coherent picture of any one myth.

The principal source for the study of ancient myths is works of literature. A literary work can take the form of a narrative and thus have the same structure as an oral tale (beginning, middle, end; plot, character, setting). Literary works, encoded in writing, take their concepts of structure directly from oral tales. Therefore, the study of myth has much in common with the study of literature. However, the structural similarities between the original oral tale and the written work of literature in which it is recorded can be deceptive. The literary work typically is the creation of a single person whose name we often know, whereas myths are anonymous. While creating one's own version of a given myth, the author of the literary work introduces variations not present in the different oral retellings of the tale. Moreover, the author may not have taken the myth directly from the oral tradition at all, but may have worked from versions recorded in previous literary works. We know of many such instances in classical culture, so that often we are not sure whether we are dealing with the study of myths or with the study of literature.

Another valuable source of information about the myths of ancient peoples is the archaeological record. Painting, sculpture, and other nonliterary artifacts can provide valuable clues about variants not contained in the literary record and about who told particular myths, and where and when they told them and why they told them. The art of Greece and Rome is particularly useful for reconstructing ancient myth, but a picture is not by itself a story. At most a picture can represent a character or scene from myth. Still, much can be learned about a culture's mythic traditions by correlating artistic depictions with tales known from other sources. It is often difficult to identify positively a mythical scene or character in art, but in some cases figures are identified by labels or attributes that make possible correlation with other sources. In other cases, inference and educated guesses are the best we can do. A major problem in the study of mythical representations in ancient art is determining whether such images were inspired by written or unwritten sources. In any event, we have a great number of mythical representations from ancient Greece and Rome, and much has been learned through study of them. For that reason, this book contains abundant illustrations from Greek pottery and other artifacts.

A second way in which scholars approach the study of myth is to examine the functions of specific myths in the context of a given society. In a society with a living oral tradition, myths are told by someone to someone on some occasion. Both the tellers of tales and their audience have a certain identity and status within the culture. They are male or female, wealthy or poor, powerful or not. To understand the myth fully, we need to know how it functioned for the people who took part in its retelling. We have already mentioned that myths can be etiological, offering an explanation for beliefs or existing practices. But a myth can function in other ways. Did it enhance the prestige of those who told the tale or heard it told? Did it justify the existing distribution of power and wealth or perhaps express a protest? Did it strike a chord in the universal desire to know the meaning of action and of human life? Just what was so interesting to the people who listened to this tale?

A third way in which scholars study myth is to trace relationships between the myths of one culture and those of others. We have already mentioned that many folktale motifs are found in the same or similar form in many different cultures around the world. We can also look at the way that specific myths have migrated from one culture to another but were transformed to suit the adopting culture's needs and traditions. The migration of myths from the ancient Near East to Greece is an event of extraordinary importance in the history of civilization, and we spend some time on this problem.

Finally, some scholars involved in the study of myth are concerned above all with the assessment of myths. What is the deeper human significance of these old tales? Why have they fascinated so many for so long, even after the culture that produced them ceased to exist? Is there some sense in which deep truths reside in these fantastic tales?

Questions of the deeper meaning and truth of myth have played an important role dating back to antiquity. Some have sought to find philosophical or psychological truth in myth by moving beyond the obvious surface meaning to a hidden, less apparent meaning. But to say that this or that is the genuine meaning of a myth is always a matter for dispute. Although some interpretations can be more successful than others, it is never possible to offer conclusive proof. Still, good interpretations require sensitivity and insight, knowledge of the society that produced the myth, and knowledge of one's own mind, which likes to see what it wants, unaware of its own prejudgments. In studying the history of the interpretation of myth, we truly study more how people's prejudgments have changed than we study myth itself. For some scholars, nonetheless, the assessment of a myth's meaning is the most important aspect of their study, and in this book we offer many interpretations as a basis for discussion. Chapter 25 is devoted solely to an examination of the interpretation of myth and the many different theoretical frameworks.

CLASSICAL NAMES: PRONUNCIATION AND SPELLING

The pronunciation of classical names can be one of the most frustrating aspects to our study of classical myth, and it is important that we have a sense of what the rules are.

Proper names of classical myth are mostly Greek in origin and were later transliterated into the Latin alphabet, which is somewhat different from the Greek. Latin presently broke up into the Romance languages (Italian, French, Spanish, Portuguese); each had its own peculiarities of spelling and pronunciation of originally Greek names. English is not a Romance language, but its speakers were members of the western Christian church, which—in its Roman Catholic branch—used Latin for its liturgy and for almost all its business down to the mid-twentieth century. In consequence, throughout Western Europe Latin was a universal second language for educated classes for about fifteen hundred years. For this reason the most familiar spellings of the proper names of classical myth are Latinized forms of Greek names, sometimes further altered in standard English. Because of their familiarity, these are the forms used (mostly) in this book. (The Index includes the Greek forms of names often encountered in translations.)

The value of the sounds of names in classical myth as pronounced in English, especially those of vowels, is a topic on which people agree to disagree. Certainly an ancient Greek would be astonished at the ordinary English pronunciation of his or her name. So one often hears the name of the Athenian playwright pronounced as *E*-schylus or *Ē*-schylus or sometimes *Ī*-schylus. Is the famous king of Thebes called *E*-dipus or *Ē*-dipus? Professional classicists may use any of these versions without embarrassment. Still, the correct pronunciation should be *Ē*-schylus and *Ē*-dipus according to the following key for the pronunciation in English of long vowel sounds in words of Greek or Latin origin:

ā = p*ay*
ē = b*e*
ī = w*ife*
ō = n*o*
ū = c*ute*

Consonants arouse less uncertainty and tend to follow rules governing the English pronunciation of all words Latinized from the original Greek (!), including of course classical names. Here are the rules:

- The letters *c* and *g* are "soft" before *e* and *i* sounds (not necessarily letters) and "hard" before *a*, *o*, and *u* sounds in words of Greek or Latin origin: for example, *c*enter, *C*aesar, *c*ivic, *c*ycle; *g*entle, Eu*g*ene, Ar*g*ive, but *c*ategory, *c*ooperate, *c*uneiform; *g*arrulous, *g*onad, *g*usto. Notice the requirement "in words of Greek or Latin origin": "get" and "give" are of Germanic origin and do not follow the rule.

- The Greek letter *chi* (*x*), written *ch*, represented a sound like *k* but pronounced back in the throat. In English it is pronounced like the "hard" *c* in "*c*ard," not like the *ch* of "*ch*icken."

- A final *e* must be pronounced as a separate syllable: Daph-n*ē*, Cir-c*ē*. To remind the reader of this rule, I place a circumflex over the *ê* in such syllables (except for the common Aphrodite): Daphnê, Circê. A final *es* is also pronounced as a separate syllable, as in Achill-*ēs*.

Another problem is accent—where to stress the word? Greek relied chiefly on pitch and quantity, whereas English depends on stress. Quantity is the length of time it takes to pronounce a syllable; pitch is the register of the voice. Because of the influence of Latin on Western culture, the English accent on proper names of Greek and Latin origin follows the rule that governs the pronunciation of Latin itself: *If the second-to-last syllable of the name is "long," it is accented; if it is not "long," the third-to-last syllable is accented.* How do you know whether a syllable is "long" or "short"? *If the second-to-last syllable is followed by two consonants, or if it contains a diphthong (ae, oe, au, ei), or if it contains a vowel originally long by nature, it is "long" and must be accented. Otherwise, the accent goes on the third syllable from the end.*

Hence Patroclus = pa-**trok**-lus (because the second-to-last syllable is followed by two consonants); Actaeon = ak-**tē**-on (because the second-to-last syllable contains a diphthong *ae;* all diphthongs are rendered as long vowels). Unfortunately, only by knowing Greek and Latin well can you know whether a vowel is long by nature. For example, the goddess Demeter is de-**mē**-ter because the *e* in the second-to-last syllable is long by nature, but you have to know Greek to know why.

A further complication arises from the fact that the combinations of vowels *ae*, *oe, au*, and *ei* are not always diphthongs (two vowels pronounced as one), but are sometimes pronounced separately. In these cases I place a dieresis (two superimposed dots) over the second vowel. The mother of Perseus was Danaë, pronounced **da**-na-ē (accent is on the third-to-last syllable because the *a* in the second-to-last syllable is short by nature).

These rules are useful but complex. For many it will be easiest simply to consult the pronunciation given after each name in the text and in the Index, where the syllable to be accented is printed in **bold** characters, or simply to listen to the pronunciation on the Web site at http://www.pearsonhighered.com/powell7e.

KEY NAMES AND TERMS

divine myth, 6	etiological tale, 8
legend, 6	folktale types, 1 1
folktale, 6	folktale motifs, 1 1

FURTHER READING CHAPTER 1

Aarne, Antti, and Stith Thompson, *The Types of the Folktale: A Classification and Bibliography*, 2nd rev. ed., trans. and enlarged by Stith Thompson (Helsinki, 1961). The standard work on folktale types.

Grimms' Fairy Tales. Collection of eighteenth-century German folktales by Jacob and Wilhelm Grimm; established, more than any other book, what we think of as a folktale. There are many editions, most on the Web at http://worldoftales.com/fairy_tales/Grimm_fairy_tales.html

Hansen, William F., *Ariadne's Thread: A Guide to International Tales Found in Classical Literature* (Ithaca, NY, 2002). Exhaustive study of world folklore found in classical myth.

Mayor, Adrienne, *Bibliography of Classical Folklore Scholarship: Myths, Legends, and Popular Beliefs of Ancient Greece and Rome*, in Folklore, April 2000, on the Web at http://www.worldagesarchive.com/Reference_Links/Myth_Bibliograpgy.htm

Thompson, Stith, *The Folktale* (New York, 1946; reprinted Berkeley, CA, 1977). Still the standard survey of the nature and forms of the folktale, by the most distinguished modern scholar of the folktale.

_____, *Motif-index of Folk-literature*, 6 vols. (Bloomington, IN, 1993). The basic reference work for folktale motifs throughout the world. The index to the *Index*, the sixth volume, is 893 pages long! On the Web at http://www.ruthenia.ru/folklore/thompson/index.htm

For bibliographic items dealing explicitly with the interpretation of myth, see the list at the end of Chapter 25.

CHAPTER 2

THE CULTURAL CONTEXT
OF CLASSICAL MYTH

Is there anyone to whom you entrust a greater number of serious
matters than your wife? And is there anyone with whom you have fewer
conversations?

SOCRATES TO CRITOBULOS, IN XENOPHON'S
Oikonomikos 3.11–13

MYTHS REFLECT THE SOCIETY that produces them. In turn, they determine the
nature of that society. They cannot be separated from the physical, social, and
spiritual worlds in which a people live or from a people's history. In this chapter we
consider the background of the Greeks (and, briefly, the Romans), the nature of
their land, their origins and history, how they lived as groups and individuals, and
something about their values—what they hoped to achieve in life and how they
hoped to do it. Later, when we turn to Roman myth (Chapters 23, 24), we discuss
that world in greater detail, which was rather different from that of the Greeks.

GREEK GEOGRAPHY

Greece was a poor country, then as now, barren and dry. Greece today supports eleven
million people, two million fewer than in the greater Los Angeles area. Unlike the
rich river valleys of Egypt and Mesopotamia, the rugged Balkan Peninsula, the south-
easternmost extension of Europe, does not seem to be a likely setting for the ancient

civilization it produced (see Map I, inside front cover). Its rivers are too small to be navigable, and they dry up in the blazing heat of the mostly rainless summers. High mountains dominate the Greek landscape and occupy about three-quarters of the land. The towering Pindus range runs down the center of the Balkan Peninsula, then continues into the sea, where peaks appear as dry, rocky islands. The Pindus is intersected by other ranges, which cut across the peninsula. Between these ranges lie a series of small, isolated plains, the only places in Greece suitable for agriculture. Here, in these pockets nestled between the mountains and the sea, Greek civilization developed.

To the northeast on the Balkan Peninsula lie the plains of Thessaly and Macedonia (see Map XIII, inside back cover). To their south lies the plain of **Boeotia** (be-**osh**-a "cow-land"), in which the principal settlement in ancient times was the city of Thebes. Southeast of Boeotia lies the plain of **Attica**, with Athens as its capital. Farther south, on the smaller peninsula known as the **Peloponnesus** (pel-o-pon-**nē**-sus; see Map II, Southern and Central Greece), connected to the mainland by a thread of land called the Isthmus, are other cultivable plains. Argolis in the Bronze Age had Tiryns and Mycenae (mī-sē-nē) as its principal settlements and later, in the Classical Period, the city of Argos. **Laconia**, also called Lacedaemon (la-se-**dēm**-on), is the territory around the town of Sparta. Messenia (mes-**sēn**-i-a) lies across high mountains to the west, with its important settlement of Pylos. North of that lies the plain of Elis, site of the Olympic Games. All of these places are important in Greek myth.

On these small plains the ancient Greeks grew wheat and barley, planted early in winter when the rainy season began, and harvested in May. The olive, whose small, compact gray leaves resist the ferocious summer sun, grew abundantly in the lowlands and provided a delightful light oil for cooking, cleansing and anointing the body, and burning in lamps. Even now Greek olive oil is the finest in the world. Wine grapes grew on vines planted on the slopes that surrounded the plains. Goats, sheep, and pigs were kept for wool, milk, cheese, leather, and meat, but cattle were few because of the lack of forage. Horses were also scarce and highly valued. They were a source of great prestige, the pride of the ruling class.

As cultivable land was limited in Greece, so were other resources. There was some gold in Thrace (far in the north), but none in Greece proper. There were a few deposits of silver (one of them, at Laurium in Attica, contributed to Athenian economic and military power). Most iron was imported, although important iron deposits in Laconia contributed to Spartan military supremacy. Greece imported copper from Cyprus. The source of tin, alloyed with copper to produce bronze, is unclear.

The Greeks did have access to excellent deposits of limestone and clay. The best limestone was found on the island of **Euboea** (yū-**bē**-a), just east of the mainland not far from Athens, on several smaller islands, and in Thessaly. Under high pressure, limestone crystallizes into marble, a lovely, workable stone used by the Greeks for sculpture and for the finest temples, such as the Parthenon in Athens that celebrated the goddess Athena. Important deposits of marble also occur on Mount Pentelicus very near Athens (Figure 2.1) and on the islands of Naxos and Paros.

The finest clay, especially that found near Athens and Corinth, provided material for pottery, which the Greeks produced in great abundance and variety. Once fired, ceramic material is breakable, but its fragments are virtually indestructible.

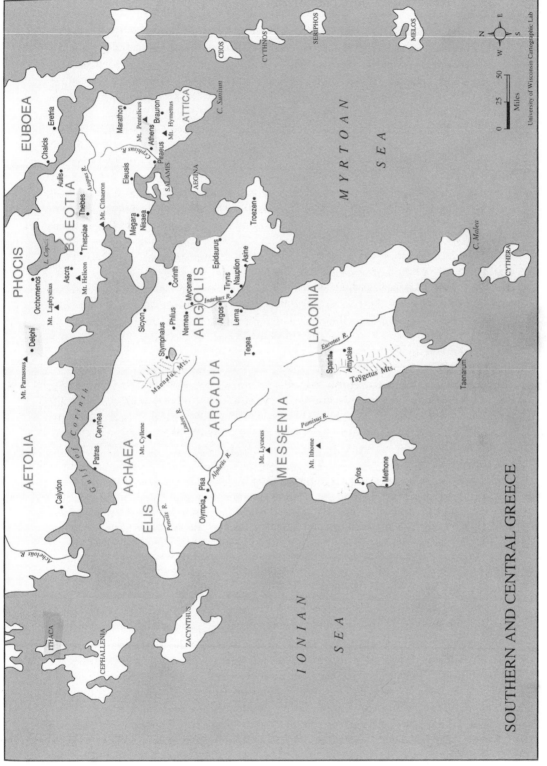

SOUTHERN AND CENTRAL GREECE

MAP II Southern and Central Greece

FIGURE 2.1 Athens, from the west. To the left, the Parthenon, "temple to the virgin," stands on the summit of the Acropolis, a high limestone outcropping. The small temple to Nikê, "victory," and the elaborate entranceway to the Acropolis are just visible at the very edge of the photograph. Below the Parthenon lies the valley of the agora, where Socrates taught and Athenian business was conducted. The rise in the foreground leads to the steps of the Pnyx, a hillside (off the photo to the right) where the people of Athens met to decide issues of peace and war. In the hazy distance is Mount Pentelicon, where the marble for constructing the Parthenon was quarried. This photo was taken in the 1940s, before urban sprawl engulfed modern Athens.   (University of Wisconsin–Madison Photo Archive)

Exquisitely decorated Greek pots have been found all over the Mediterranean world and especially in Etruscan graves in Italy. Such pots were often made expressly for use in burials, where they have been found in modern times. The pictures painted on these pots (many reproduced in this book) provide us with vivid illustrations of Greek myths and wonderfully illuminate many details of Greek social life.

But perhaps the greatest Greek natural resource was the sea. The **Aegean** (ē-jē-an) **Sea** between the Balkan Peninsula and Asia Minor (modern western Turkey) played a central role in the life of the ancient Greeks. Most of them lived near the sea and took from it the fish that were a staple of their diet, although Homeric heroes preferred to eat only flesh. The sea was an avenue of communication with the world beyond the mountains that enclosed the isolated Greek communities.

Because of the islands scattered across the Aegean Sea, a sailor is almost never out of sight of land, and the Greeks learned early to travel long distances in small open boats. Several large islands dominate the others. Crete, the southernmost Aegean island, had an especially important role in the early history of Greece, but Euboea, Rhodes, Chios, Samos, and Lesbos also stand out. There are two principal groups of islands: the **Cyclades** (**sik**-la-dēz, "circle islands"), placed in a rough circle around the tiny central island of Delos, which is sacred to Apollo and Artemis; and the Sporades, "scattered islands," which extend along the coast of Ionia, the western coast of Asia Minor. Curiously, the Ionian Sea and the Ionian Islands are to the west of Greece, far removed from Ionia itself.

The paucity of cultivable land and natural resources led the Greeks to trade with other nations. A mastery of the sea allowed them to transport goods to and from foreign lands. They exported wine, olive oil, and pottery and brought back the metals and other goods they needed, especially grain and prestige items of exquisite quality. Later, they established colonies across the sea, on the coasts of Asia Minor to the east, in Italy to the west, in southern France, around the Black Sea, and even in northern Africa.

The geography of the Balkan Peninsula influenced both the history and the myths of the Greeks. The extremely mountainous terrain discouraged communication by land and favored political independence. Through most of ancient Greek history, the various cities, raised on small isolated plains, remained autonomous political entities. Many Greek legends told of the great deeds of the founders and early rulers of these cities, and I have organized by geography the many cycles of Greek legend. Myths also reflect the fact that the Greeks were the greatest seafaring people of the ancient world (together with the Semitic Phoenicians), as exemplified by the story of Odysseus, whose perilous sea journey home from the Trojan War lasted ten years.

GREEK HISTORY

Greece was occupied even in the Paleolithic (Old Stone) Age, before 7000 BC, but almost nothing is known of these early inhabitants. From the Neolithic (New Stone) Age, 6000–3000 BC, survive foundation stones of houses, pottery, stone tools, and graves. These peoples lived in settled communities and practiced a rudimentary agriculture. Our evidence becomes richer with the advent of the Bronze Age around 3000 BC, after which we divide the archaeological and historical record into the following periods:

Early/Middle Bronze Age	3000–1600 BC
Late Bronze Age (or Mycenaean Age)	1600–1150 BC
Dark Age	1150–800 BC
Archaic Period	800–480 BC
Classical Period	480–323 BC
Hellenistic Period	323–30 BC

These dates are associated with the appearance of civilization ("life in cities," in the presence of writing), c. 3000 BC; the ascendancy of mainland Greeks, c. 1600 BC (the Mycenaeans); the sack of cities and the international disruption of trade, c. 1150 BC; the invention of the Greek alphabet, the principal technology of modern Western civilization, c. 800 BC; the Persian attack and defeat at Marathon in 490 BC and at Salamis in 480 BC; the death of Alexander the Great in 323 BC; and Rome's conquest of Cleopatra's Egypt in 30 BC. The dates are conventional, and to some extent arbitrary, but provide a useful framework for discussion. (See Chronology of the Ancient World at the end of the book, before the Index, for a detailed chronology of the times and people important to this book.)

The Early/Middle Bronze Age (3000–1600 BC): The Origin of the Greeks

We do not regard the inhabitants of the mainland during the Early Bronze Age as Greeks because their cultural traditions were very different from those of the people who eventually became known by that name. We know nothing of their race or the language they spoke. They seem to have been modest farmers who worshiped goddesses of fertility to increase the yield of their crops, a religion still vital among later Greeks and reflected prominently in some Greek myths.

We are far better informed about the inhabitants of the island of Crete, called Minoans after Minos, the legendary Cretan king, although again we know nothing of their ethnic affinities or language. From c. 2200 BC into the Mycenaean Age, c. 1450 BC, the Minoans built elaborate and wealthy palaces. The bull was important in their religious ritual, as was the double ax, or *labrys* (hence "labyrinth"), presumably the special tool by which bulls were sacrificed. They also worshiped a goddess of fertility. The Minoan palaces were not encircled by defensive walls, a fact that lends support to the remark by the Greek historian Thucydides (c. 460–c. 400 BC) that the mythical "kingdom of Minos" dominated the seas. Therefore they feared no enemies.

The people later called the Greeks belonged to a cultural and linguistic group known as the **Indo-Europeans**, whose original homeland apparently was in central Asia, perhaps east of the Caspian Sea. Beginning in the fourth millennium BC, the Indo-Europeans migrated in all directions into Europe and Asia, bringing with them their linguistic and cultural traditions. The exact date of their arrival in Greece cannot be established definitively, but the destruction of existing settlements around 2100 BC, at the transition from the Early to the Middle Bronze Age, suggests the arrival of a new people. From about the same time we find the first evidence in Greece of the domestic horse, an animal elsewhere associated with the Indo-Europeans.

Much of what little we know about the Indo-Europeans today is inferred by scholars from a reconstruction of the language they spoke, called proto–Indo-European. Although we have no written record or other direct evidence of this long-extinct hypothetical language, some of its vocabulary, and even some of its grammatical structure, can be deduced from the many ancient and modern languages descended from it. Every language spoken today in Europe (except Basque, Finnish, Hungarian, and Estonian) belongs to this family. Today more than 1.8 billion people, on every continent, speak or at least understand Indo-European languages. Europe's colonial expansion into the Americas, Africa, Asia, and Australia carried English, Spanish, Portuguese, Russian, and French into new lands, where today they continue to absorb and replace native languages. The spread of the Indo-European language family, now further assisted by the Internet, is one of the most remarkable events in the history of the human race.

According to the elusive evidence, Indo-European society may have been divided into three groups whose membership was determined by birth: kings and priests, warriors, and food producers. They had a highly developed family life, and they were devoted to war. Some think that some basic patterns in Greek myth go back to the Indo-Europeans.

The Greek language of later eras was not the tongue of the early Indo-European immigrants but developed over the centuries after their arrival. The basic vocabulary of Greek is derived from the hypothetical proto-Indo-European parent language, but many words—particularly those for places, plants, animals, and gods—seem to have been taken from the language of the earlier inhabitants, just as in America the names Manhattan, Chicago, and Wisconsin were taken from languages of pre-European inhabitants. There were also many Semitic words in Greek, reflecting the Greeks' enormous debt to earlier Semitic culture.

The Late Bronze Age (Mycenaean Age) (1600–1150 BC)

We have little archaeological evidence from the Early and Middle Bronze Age in Greece, but spectacular ruins and written documents survive from the **Late Bronze** or **Mycenaean Age**, named for the enormous stone citadel of Mycenae in the Peloponnesus (compare Figure 14.1). Greek-speaking Indo-Europeans took over the site about 1650 BC. Immensely wealthy tombs from about 1600 BC prove its richness and importance and provide a convenient date for the beginning of the Mycenaean Age.

In the Mycenaean Age, powerful kings ruled the Greeks. The kings and their retainers constituted a military and an aristocratic elite. They were lovers of war who used bronze weapons, rode to battle in horse-drawn chariots, and concentrated great wealth. Independent kings built impressive strongholds from which they supervised highly controlled and centralized, although local, economies. Their greatest centers of power, in addition to Mycenae, were Thebes and Orchomenus in Boeotia, Athens in Attica, Pylos in Messenia, and a site near Sparta in Laconia. All these centers (except Orchomenus) figure prominently in Greek myth, and we encounter them repeatedly in the following chapters. Unlike the Minoan settlements, Mycenaean palaces were strongly fortified. The Mycenaean Greeks may have called themselves **Achaeans** (a-kē-anz), a word Homer uses to describe the men who attacked Troy.

In about 1450 BC the Minoan civilization was destroyed and the palaces burned, evidently by Mycenaeans from the mainland, who occupied and rebuilt the principal palace at Cnossus. The palace was destroyed again around 1400 BC by an unknown agency, never to be rebuilt. In the ruins we have found documents written in Greek in a nonalphabetic script called **Linear B**. Minoan art and religion made a deep impression on the Mycenaean Greeks and, through them, on subsequent European culture.

In 1952, English architect Michael Ventris deciphered Linear B script, the form of writing used by the Mycenaeans, one of the great intellectual achievements of the twentieth century. Ventris proved that the writing consisted of about eighty nonalphabetic signs, each of which stood for a syllable. In addition to the tablets found at Cnossus and other sites in Crete, documents in Linear B have also turned up at Pylos, Mycenae, Thebes, and elsewhere on the mainland, proving the cultural uniformity of the Mycenaeans. Linear B script, preserved on clay tablets, originated as a modification of the earlier, undeciphered Cretan Linear A writing, which may have preserved pieces of the Minoan language, evidently unrelated to Greek. Linear B script (and Linear A, mostly) was used only for keeping economic accounts. Although these records give us a great deal of information, the ambiguous Linear B script was not used for creating literature.

The coincidence between centers of power in Mycenaean times and important locations in cycles of Greek legend—the Mycenae of Agamemnon, the Tiryns of Heracles, and the Thebes of Oedipus—suggests that many Greek legends originated during the Mycenaean period. In the absence of some form of writing suitable for recording them, however, such tales could only be transmitted orally from one generation to the next. Sometimes non-Greek cities, Cnossus in Crete and Troy in Asia Minor, were provided with cycles of legend, but always as seen through Greek eyes. Of native traditions from Cnossus and Troy, we have no direct information.

There were nine levels of habitation at the site of Bronze Age Troy (see Figure 21.6). When Troy VI was destroyed by human hands about 1230 BC, the people then occupying the site were raising horses and using pottery similar to that found in Greece. Were there Greeks living at Troy at this time? A recent find in the ruins of a tiny bronze seal with Hittite writing on it suggests to some that the Trojans were Hittites, a powerful inland Indo-European people whose capital was near modern Ankara, Turkey, or at least the site was subject to the Hittites. In fact, we do not know who the Trojans were. By 1150 BC fire had destroyed most of the Mycenaean palaces on the mainland. Linear B writing, which supported the palace economies, disappeared forever. Greece sank into a **Dark Age** that lasted nearly four hundred years.

The Dark Age (1150–800 BC)

Later Greeks attributed the destruction of the Mycenaean world to an invasion by Greek-speaking peoples from northwest Greece whom they called the Dorians. The Dorians were equated with the Sons of Heracles in Greek legend, about whom important stories were told. They spoke a distinct dialect. Although modern scholars cannot confirm the Dorian invasion, the explanation seems plausible. Dorian Greeks, whether or not descendants of Heracles, apparently overthrew the Mycenaean Greeks, who earlier dominated Greece, except for remote and mountainous central Arcadia in the Peloponnesus. They then pushed across the Aegean to Crete and other nearby islands and to the southern strip of Asia Minor, where in classical times a Dorian dialect was spoken.

Of the mainland settlements, Athens alone withstood the invaders, according to tradition. Many Greeks from other regions migrated eastward and resettled the Aegean islands. Refugees from the Peloponnesus, passing through Athens and now called Ionians, took possession of the central islands of the Aegean and the central sector of the western coast of Asia Minor, henceforth known as **Ionia**. Its greatest center was at Miletus (see Map XIII, inside back cover). Other refugees, the Aeolians, crossed from Thessaly in the north of mainland Greece to the island of Lesbos and to the northern portion of the coast of Asia Minor near Troy, henceforth called Aeolis. By 900 BC, the map of Greece had been completely redrawn.

Very few archaeological remains survive from the Dark Age, a time of profound social disorganization, depopulation, and impoverishment. Petty kings with only local authority replaced the great monarchs of the Mycenaean Age. Many settlements were split by tribal and family feuds and, in the Dorian areas, by a great gulf between masters and subjects. What civilization remained seems to have centered on the long island of Euboea, just east of the mainland, where recent excavations have revealed a spectacular grave from c. 1000 BC containing a warrior and his wife, with many rare and valuable objects, some gold. Euboean settlements were the only Greek towns to carry on direct trade with the Near East throughout the Dark Age, relations that were to play a central role in the revival of Greek culture. The Greek alphabet first appears on Euboea, where the poems of Homer and Hesiod may have been written down, inaugurating the Archaic Period.

The Archaic Period (800–480 BC)

About 800 BC, someone familiar with Phoenician writing, probably a Semite, invented the Greek alphabet by requiring that a rough indication of the vowel accompany each consonantal sign (Figure 2.2). Phoenician writing had signs only for consonants and could not be pronounced except by a native. It was an odd but purely phonetic syllabary (as was Linear B), with around only twenty-two signs. The Greek alphabet was the first writing that encoded an approximation of the actual sound of the human voice, hence a script potentially applicable to any human language. It is the most important invention in the history of culture after the invention of writing itself and the basis for Western civilization. Except for minor changes, it was the same system of writing that appears on this page. In its Roman and related forms, the Greek alphabet is today found everywhere.

Within a generation, the revolutionary alphabetic technology had spread throughout the Greek people. At the same time, under Euboean leadership, the Greeks sent out colonies to the west, to southern Italy and Sicily, where they built prosperous cities. The period of political and cultural revival that began with the invention of the alphabet marks the beginning of a new era in Greek history, the **Archaic Period** (800–480 BC).

The Archaic Period witnessed the emergence of the Greek *polis*, the politically independent city-state. Unlike the villagers of earlier eras, who defined their position by family relations, the members of a *polis* owed their allegiance to a social group defined by geography. In the *polis* appeared for the first time the explicit concept of citizenship ("city-membership"), so important to the modern state. Only men were citizens and could participate in political affairs; women lived in a separate world, as in Islamic societies today. Within the *polis*, the Greek citizen was in relentless competition with his neighbor. Greek cultural values depended on the

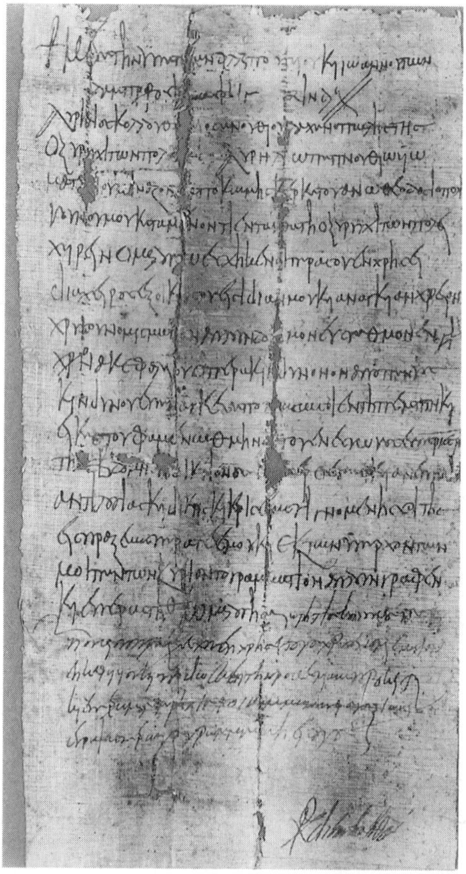

FIGURE 2.2 Greek papyrus. A contract for the loan of money with signature of the notary at the bottom, from the fifth century AD. All ancient Greek literature was recorded on papyrus, made of thin strips of the papyrus plant laid in two cross-grained layers and pounded together. When complete, the papyrus was rolled (hence our word *volume* from the Latin *volumen*, "a thing rolled"), making it difficult to look anything up. Tens of thousands of papyri have survived in the dry sands of Egypt, including most of what we possess of early lyric poets. A new poem by Sappho, preserved on papyrus, was published in 2005.   (From "The Wisconsin Papyri," no. 76, vol. 1, no. 10, 468 AD. University of Wisconsin–Madison Photo Archive)

spirit of male competition (unlike in Egypt, where cooperation was a high social value), and these values permeate the myths they told.

Another important development during the Archaic Period was the rebirth of commerce, which had ebbed throughout the Dark Age. The Greeks' dependence on the sea for commerce, transportation, and food was essential to the formation of their character and had a direct influence on their social structure. Greece was never socially stratified in the fashion of the heavily populated and extravagantly wealthy river monarchies along the Nile and in Mesopotamia, between the Tigris and Euphrates rivers. The Greeks' dependence on the sea further reduced class distinctions. The sudden dangerous storms of the Aegean threatened captain and crew alike. Claims to good birth and upbringing had no survival value. Seafaring encouraged extreme individualism and offered rich rewards to the skilled adventurer willing to take risks. Seafaring was practiced almost entirely by free citizens, and in the *Odyssey* the Greeks invented the world's first tale of danger and wonder on the high seas, a journey that came to symbolize the quest for knowledge itself.

In the sixth century BC commerce received an enormous stimulus from the introduction of coinage, universally accepted weights of portable, indestructible metal certified by civic authority. Before this time, money as we think of it did not exist. Coined money made possible capitalism and the enrichment of new social classes, many of humble birth, by commerce. The traditional aristocracy looked down on and bitterly opposed these upstarts, skillful only at accumulating wealth, and called them *kakoi,* the "bad men," while calling themselves *aristoi,* the "best men" (hence our "aristocrat"). Despite the scorn of the *aristoi,* economic and political power fell more and more into the hands of the *kakoi.*

Between 650 and 500 BC, many Greek city-states were ruled by strong men known as *tyrants,* who represented the interests of the commercial class against the traditional aristocracy. The word *tyrant* comes from a non-Greek language of Asia Minor and originally meant something like "ruler," but by the sixth century BC it referred to a leader who had taken power by "unconstitutional" (that is, nontraditional) means. In the eyes of their aristocratic opponents, the tyrants were arbitrary despots, but tyrants often did much to enhance the wealth and power of the cities they ruled. Rarely did a tyrant give up power voluntarily.

In cultural matters, however, the aristocracy clung to power. As the most literate citizens, its members were creators or sponsors of most Greek literature, art, and philosophy. They gave to *tyrant* the pejorative meaning it has today. When speaking of Greek culture, we refer, with few exceptions, to the literary monuments produced by and for the *aristoi,* the free male citizens descended from old families. About the *kakoi*—the poor, slaves, women, and other noncitizens, who were mostly illiterate—we have little direct information.

During the latter part of the Archaic Period, Greece was threatened by a powerful rival from the East. The Persians, an Indo-European people living on the Iranian plateau east of Mesopotamia (modern Iraq), had developed into a dynamic warrior state under the leadership of Cyrus the Great (600?–529 BC). Conquering and absorbing first the Semitic states of Mesopotamia, then Egypt, and finally advancing into Anatolia (modern Turkey) and southern Russia, Persia became the greatest empire the world had seen. Soon Persia absorbed the Greek colonies on the western coast of Asia Minor.

The Classical Period (480–323 BC)

In 508 BC, in Athens, a remarkable development took place: the emergence of the world's first democracy ("rule by the people"; *dêmos* = "people"), an outgrowth of the centuries-long dispute between *kakoi* and *aristoi.* Under the leadership of one Clisthenes (**klīs**-the-nēz), the social and political basis of the Athenian *polis* was completely reorganized so as to place decision making in the hands of all adult male citizens, who may have numbered about twenty-five thousand. Citizens lived both in the countryside and in the city. Henceforth, authority in government came not from inherited wealth and family prominence, but from one's ability to persuade the large, unruly assembly of citizens.

From this unique political climate emerged many of the forms of civilization familiar to Westerners today: rule by written law, reason supported by evidence as the basis for decisions, and the separation of religious and political institutions. In this environment arose historical writing, science, and philosophy. In Athens, ancient myths were recast as a new form of entertainment and instruction in the annual presentations of Athenian tragedy. Democracy made the ordinary citizen feel he had responsibility for his own destiny.

The Persian army discovered, to their sorrow, the explosive power of this new form of government when they invaded mainland Greece in 490 BC. In a tremendous battle near the village of Marathon, about twenty-five miles northeast from Athens, Athenian citizen-soldiers smashed the professional Persian army and drove the invaders into the sea. "This proved," wrote the fifth-century BC historian Herodotus, "if there were need of proof, how noble a thing is freedom" (*Histories* 5.78). An even greater Persian campaign launched ten years later, in 480 BC, had a foretaste of disaster in the bravery of the three hundred Spartans who fought to the last man at the pass of Thermopylae, then met with catastrophe, first in a naval battle off the island of Salamis near Athens and then on land (479 BC) near Plataea in Boeotia (Figure 2.3; Perspective 2).

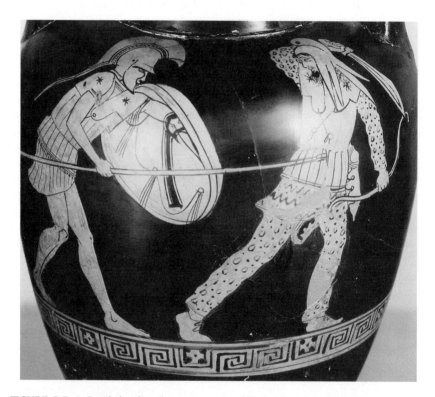

FIGURE 2.3 A Greek hoplite (heavy-armed soldier) drives his spear into a Persian enemy on this Attic water jug, c. 480–470 BC. Note the Greek's bronze helmet, linen cuirass (body protector), and bronze shield held by an arm strap and handgrip. In real life the hoplite also covered his feet and calves with bronze. The Persian, wearing long pants, a shirt, and a leather cap with tassels, is armored only with a linen cuirass. He carries a sword and a bow; a quiver of arrows rides on his hip. Later, Amazons were portrayed in the same garb and identified with the Persian enemy. The Athenian's love of freedom, as well as his superior armor, contributed to his military victory over the Persians in 490 and 480/479. (The Metropolitan Museum of Art, New York. Image copyright © The Metropolitan Museum of Art / Art Resource, New York)

PERSPECTIVE 2

FRANK MILLER'S *300*

The 2007 American action film *300* grossed about $500 million. The film's opening was the twenty-fourth largest in box office history and the third biggest opening ever for an R-rated film. Adapted from a graphic novel by Frank Miller (b. 1967), it is a fictionalized retelling of the Battle of Thermopylae. King Leonidas (Gerard Butler) leads three hundred Spartans into battle against the Persian king Xerxes (Rodrigo Santoro) and his army of more than one million soldiers. The film is a shot-for-shot adaptation of the comic book using the "bluescreen" technique, whereby the actors stand before a blue screen later replaced with background footage. More than fifteen hundred special effects shots were incorporated into the film in this way.

Dilios, a Spartan soldier, narrates the story of Leonidas from childhood to his being crowned king of Sparta. A Persian messenger arrives at Sparta demanding submission to the Persian king Xerxes. Leonidas and his guards throw the messenger into a pit. Knowing a Persian attack will come soon, Leonidas visits the Ephors—ancient priests stricken with leprosy, whose blessing he needs before the Spartan council will authorize war. He proposes that they meet the immense army of Persians up north at Thermopylae ("hot gates"). The Ephors consult an oracle, who decrees that Sparta must not go to war during their religious festival. Two agents of Xerxes appear who bribe the corrupt Ephors with whores and gold.

Leonidas follows his plan anyway, setting out with only three hundred soldiers. He knows that he is on a suicide mission, but hopes his sacrifice will spur the council to action. On the way, other Greeks join the Spartans. At Thermopylae, they build a wall across the pass. Leonidas meets Ephialtes of Trachis, a hunchbacked Spartan in exile whose parents fled Sparta to spare him from infanticide. He asks to join the fight and warns Leonidas of a secret path by which the Persians could outflank them. Leonidas turns him down. Ephialtes cannot hold a shield properly, and he would compromise the Spartan phalanx.

The Persians arrive and demand surrender. Leonidas refuses. Advancing in a tightly knit phalanx, the Spartans use the narrow terrain to knock back the Persian army. Xerxes parleys with Leonidas, offering him wealth and power in exchange for surrender. Still Leonidas declines. Xerxes sends the feared Immortals, his elite troops, to attack the Spartans, but the Spartans finish them off. Xerxes then sends black powder bombs and giant war beasts at the Spartans, but all attacks fail.

Angered by Leonidas' rejection, Ephialtes tells the Persians about the secret path. When they realize that Ephialtes has betrayed them, the Greek allies retreat. Leonidas orders Dilios to return to Sparta to tell the council what is about to happen.

In Sparta, the treacherous Spartan Theron demands that Gorgo, Queen of Sparta (Leonidas' wife), have sex with him in exchange for persuading the Spartan council to send reinforcements. She complies, but Theron then argues just the opposite. Gorgo kills him, repeating his own words as he raped her, "This will not be over quickly!" Her dagger pierces his purse. Persian coins spill from his robe, revealing he is a traitor. At last the council agrees to unite against Persia.

Meanwhile at Thermopylae, the Persians use the goat path to outflank the Spartans. Leonidas hurls his spear at Xerxes, cutting the king on the cheek. Disturbed by his own mortality, Xerxes watches as all the Spartans are slaughtered by a massive barrage of arrows. Moments before his death, Leonidas pledges his love to Gorgo.

Concluding his tale before an audience of Spartans on the edge of the battlefield a year after Thermopylae, Dilios relates how the Persian army was long baffled by the bravery of a mere three hundred Spartans. Word of their valiant resistance spreads across Greece, inspiring the city-states to unite against the Persians. Now the Persians face ten thousand Spartans leading thirty thousand free Greeks. Dilios then leads the Greeks in a successful charge against the Persian army in the Battle of Plataea.

The film has been praised for portrayal of the Spartans' heroic code, but decried for the portrayal of the Persians as a monstrous, barbaric, and demonic horde. Officials of the Iranian government, including President Mahmoud Ahmadinejad, denounced the film: The film was banned in Iran. There is no doubt that *300* was meant to reflect on current political issues. Just prior to its release, the creator of *300*, Frank Miller, said, "For some reason, nobody seems to be talking about who we're up against and the sixth-century barbarism that they actually represent. These people saw off people's heads. They enslave women. They genitally mutilate their daughters. They do not behave by any cultural norms that are sensible to us. I'm speaking into a microphone that never could have been a product of their culture and I'm living in a city where three thousand of my neighbors were killed by thieves of airplanes they never could have built."

This second stunning victory over the Persians, under Athenian leadership at sea and Spartan on land, is a convenient dividing point between the Archaic Age and the brief **Classical Period**. The unexpected victory fired the Greeks, and especially the Athenians, with an unprecedented self-confidence and eagerness to try out new forms of thought, social organization, and artistic expression. These amazing victories inspired the study by Herodotus, who coined the word *history*, which means "inquiry." In this case he wished to inquire into the causes of the Persian defeat. The popular modern marathon race was inspired by the Athenian victory of 490 BC. After the Persian defeat, a runner reportedly ran the twenty-five miles to Athens, announced the victory, then dropped dead from exhaustion.

During the Classical Period, the Golden Age of Greece, worked many of the most influential thinkers, artists, and politicians who ever lived: historians Herodotus and Thucydides; tragedians Aeschylus, Sophocles, and Euripides; comic dramatist Aristophanes; statesman Pericles; philosophers Socrates, Plato, and Aristotle; Ictinus, architect of the Parthenon; sculptor Phidias; and orator

Demosthenes, to name only the most prominent. All these men were residents of Athens (and most of them were born there), a testimony to the city's cultural supremacy fostered by its radical democracy. From other cities during the Classical Period came the poet Pindar; Democritus, who fashioned the atomic theory of matter; and Hippocrates, "the father of medicine."

During the Classical Period the *polis* reached its greatest effectiveness but also showed its worst faults. Some of the tragedies of this era illuminate the violent tensions many citizens felt between ancient loyalty to the family and current loyalty to the political state. Still, the *polis* triumphed as the ideal of social life. In the fourth century BC, Aristotle described the *polis* as the perfect and natural fruit of a long social evolution. According to him, "man is by nature a political animal," that is, a being who reaches full potential only by living in a *polis*.

Although the proud and politically independent city-states struggled constantly and murderously against one another, the Greeks nonetheless maintained the sense of being a single people. They spoke a common language, used a common technology of writing, and called themselves Hellenes (**hel**-ēnz), implying a common descent from the legendary Hellên (**hel**-lēn) (not to be confused with Helen of Troy!). The term *Graioi*, "Greeks," comes from the Romans, who took it from a northwestern Greek tribe living in Epirus, the backward territory across the Ionian Sea that separates Italy from Greece. Greeks worshiped the same pantheon of gods and participated in all-Greek religious and athletic festivals, especially at Olympia. Such regional events as the annual Panathenaic ("all-Athenian") festival in Athens gave the Greeks a sense of ethnic community.

But political unity was beyond the reach of the freedom-loving Greeks. In the crisis of the Persian wars they combined briefly against the barbarian invader. Once the Persian threat receded, they settled into two loosely organized rival leagues, one led by Sparta, a military state ruled by an old-fashioned aristocracy, the other by democratic Athens (Figure 2.4). From 431 to 404 BC, these leagues fought each other in a ruinous conflict known as the **Peloponnesian War**. Greece never recovered.

The Classical Period saw the development of Greek philosophy and history as powerful intellectual rivals to traditional myth. Such physicians as Hippocrates and philosophers like Protagoras and later Plato and Aristotle challenged mythic accounts of the origin and nature of the universe, and the historian Thucydides rejected the conviction, heretofore universal, that gods determine the outcome of human events. The stories of gods and heroes were the common birthright of all Greeks and were celebrated in painting, sculpture, song, and drama, but they were given new meanings in the intellectual ferment of this extraordinary age.

The Hellenistic Period (323–30 BC)

The social and political system based on the *polis* was crippled in 338 BC when Philip II of Macedon, a region to the north of Greece (see Map XIII, inside back cover), overran the Greek city-states and imposed his will on them. The Macedonian state was a monarchy and altogether unlike the Greek *polis*. Although

FIGURE 2.4 The modern village of Sparta in the plain beneath towering Mount Taygetus. Little remains of the ancient city, proving the wisdom of the Greek historian Thucydides, who remarked in his history of the Peloponnesian War (1.10.2), "If the Spartans should abandon their city, and leave behind their temples and the foundations of their permanent structures, no doubt after a considerable time had elapsed posterity would be very skeptical indeed about their power . . . since they do not live in a real city and do not have any rich or beautiful shrines and public buildings, but dwell in scattered villages in the ancient Greek style . . . On the other hand, if the same thing happened to Athens, the visible evidence would lead people to estimate the city's power at twice its true value." (University of Wisconsin–Madison Photo Archive)

Philip admired Greek intellectual culture and Greek economic enterprise, he had no patience with the endless squabbles conducted in the name of "freedom." When he was killed in 336 BC in a palace intrigue, his twenty-year-old son Alexander inherited the throne.

Moved by legends of the Trojan War and seeing himself as a latter-day Achilles, Alexander attacked the enormous Persian empire, ostensibly to avenge the Persian invasions of 490 and 480 BC a century and a half earlier. In a series of brilliant battles, Alexander destroyed the Persian empire and occupied its vast territories. He was by far the greatest field commander who ever lived. His ruthless and bloody conquests took him even beyond Persian domains into India. From 323 BC, when

Alexander died of a fever in Babylon (or was poisoned by rivals) at age thirty-two, we date the **Hellenistic Period** of Greek history. *Hellenic* refers to anything Greek (from the legendary Hellên, founder of the Greek race); *Hellenistic* refers to the historical period that began with the death of Alexander the Great.

After his death, Alexander's empire quickly broke up into separate and hostile kingdoms, but Greek culture became world culture. Everywhere throughout the ancient East—in Syria, Mesopotamia, Palestine, and Egypt—cities were established on the Greek model, decorated in the Greek style, and ruled by Greeks and speakers of Greek. The cultural capital shifted from Athens to Alexandria, a city that Alexander himself had founded in the western delta of Egypt.

In 146 BC, Rome conquered the Greek mainland. Other centers of Hellenistic culture soon met a similar fate. We can date the end of the Hellenistic period to 30 BC, when Alexandria fell into Roman hands after the suicide of Cleopatra VII, the last ruling descendant of a general of Alexander (Ptolemy). But Roman society and culture were in many ways a continuation of Greek Hellenistic culture.

GREEK SOCIETY

Greek myths reflect the society in which they were transmitted, and to understand them we need to know something about the social life of ancient Greece. Unfortunately, our knowledge is limited. About conditions in the Bronze and Iron ages we have archaeological evidence, but no written information except the accounting documents in Linear B script. For the Archaic Period, we have the long poems of Homer and Hesiod, who probably lived in the eighth century BC, but almost nothing after them. We know more about Greek society in the Classical Period, largely because of the tragedies and other literary works from this era. Even here information is scanty. Almost all literary sources are Athenian, and almost all composed by aristocratic males. Most so-called descriptions of Greek social life, based on surviving evidence, are really descriptions of Athenian social life of the fifth and fourth centuries BC, where evidence is most abundant. Although Athens was in many ways a unique community in ancient Greece, in this section we nonetheless attempt to describe the general aspects of Greek society reflected in myth, especially those that seem to us most foreign and distant.

Males

Much of Greek social life revolved around the free males who were dominant in both the private and the public spheres. In classical Athens, there were about twenty-five thousand such men out of a total population of around two hundred thousand. They held final authority over their wives and the other members of their households. They alone were obligated to fight in wars, and they alone were eligible to become citizens of the *polis*.

An education from early childhood prepared them for these roles. They not only learned to read and write but also to be athletic, in rigorous control of their appetites, and fearless in battle and the hunt. They grew up in a small, tightly knit, relentlessly competitive community in which everyone knew everyone's worth and there was no forgiveness for failure. An individual was celebrated for victories over his enemies in war and politics and for his wit and ability to entertain at the all-male *symposium,* "drinking party," the Greek male's principal form of social life and principal setting for the telling of Greek myths in the Archaic and Classical periods.

In the Classical Period, when a boy was born, his father was at least thirty years old. Between ages six and thirteen the boy received instruction from a *pedagogue* ("trainer of boys"), who taught him how to read, write, and memorize the poetry of Homer and other poets from written texts, which he could recite before his male friends. The boy still lived in the women's quarters of the house, but every day he exercised naked with his friends to harden his body against the day when, in defense of the *polis,* he would put on armor and stand against the enemy.

Isolated from the female sex, men in their twenties gathered at the exercise ground to admire the prepubescent boys and to court them through gifts and poetry, a practice called **pederasty**, "love for boys." Greek pederasty has no good modern counterparts, and no other facet of ancient Greek social life seems more odd, a measure of our enormous distance from the Greeks of the Classical Period. Teenage boys also attended the symposium as cupbearers, where such courtship could continue. If the boy accepted a suitor's attentions (he need not), he would submit to kissing and fondling and, eventually, to copulation from the front between the boy's thighs, or even anal penetration (Figure 2.5).

FIGURE 2.5 Pederastic scene on an Attic two-handled drinking cup from the sixth century BC. The mature man fondles the genitals of the boy, who reaches up affectionately to touch the man on the chin. The grapevines on either side refer to the wine drunk from the cup. Such erotic scenes, homosexual and heterosexual, are common on Greek pottery used in the symposium. No other artistic tradition, except that of Japan, rivals the Greek in the explicit portrayal of lovemaking. (Photograph © 2011 Museum of Fine Arts, Boston)

The boy was expected to derive little or no physical pleasure from his lover's attentions, in keeping with Greek moral education in self-control. In the many surviving pederastic illustrations on pots, the boy, always beardless, is never shown with an erection, whereas the man, always bearded, often has one. We learn of few instances of homosexual activity between adults (though Alexander had a male lover), a practice held up to savage ridicule by the Greek comic poet Aristophanes (c. 450–338 BC). Pederasty was an aspect of Greek preparation for manhood and war and was thought to refine the moral qualities of loyalty, respect, affection, and courage.

At age eighteen, when half the boys had lost their fathers in war, a male in Athens became a citizen, a "member of the city," able to vote in elections and speak in public. Between eighteen and twenty he was called an *ephebe* (**ef**-ēb), "one who has come of age," and in an initiatory rite of passage he spent time outside the city practicing military procedure and honing his hunting skills. In one ephebic festival dedicated to the hero Theseus, men dressed as women, a common practice in many tribal cultures to mark the transition from youth to full manhood. Apparently the purpose of the ritual was to identify with the female sex that had heretofore controlled the young boys, then, by disrobing, to break from women's ways forever. At this same time the boy prepared to leave the women's part of the house.

When in his early twenties the young man sought out prepubescent boys for friendship and sexual pleasure, his marriage was still ten years away, and even when he married, pederastic attachments might continue. No longer a cupbearer at the symposium but an equal participant in it, the young citizen reclined to eat and drink on one of the seven or nine couches placed around the walls of the *andreion*, the "men's room," which had a separate entrance from that into the rest of the house. Here he competed in wit and poetry with his friends, many of whom he had grown up with.

The symposium is the setting for the famous dialogue of Plato (427–347 BC), the *Symposium*, where drunken companions attempt to define the nature of *eros*, "sexual desire." The topic is suitable because in addition to the handsome boys who served wine at the symposium, female courtesans called *hetairai*, "female companions," offered every kind of sexual service for pay. *Hetairai* also sang and danced and are often represented on Greek pottery designed to be used at the symposium. They seem often to have been foreign women or slaves and had no standing in respectable society (Figure 2.6).

War was of paramount concern for every Greek male, who could expect at some time, or many times, to face the enemy in hand-to-hand combat. Throughout his life he prepared for that moment. Warfare was constant and half of Greek males would die by the sword. In the Bronze and Dark Ages warfare seems to have been conducted between unorganized gangs from which some hero might emerge, an Achilles eager for glory and reputation, to challenge the best fighter from the other side; men fight this way in Homer's *Iliad*. In the Classical Period, by contrast, a citizen fought as a member of a team, for the glory of the *polis*.

Such warfare was conducted on open plains between opposing lines, as many as sixteen ranks deep, of heavily armed men called **hoplites** (see Figure 2.3; *hoplon* = "shield," "armor"). Each man had to pay for his own equipment, which was often

FIGURE 2.6 The symposium ("drinking party"). On a fifth-century BC Attic vase a nude *hetaira* entertains the male diners by playing on the double flute, really a kind of oboe. Her short hair identifies her as a slave. On the far right a diner plays the game of *kottabos*; the idea is to twirl the large, flat drinking cup called a *kylix* on the forefinger, then fling the dregs of the wine across the room to knock down a small statuette, usually of a satyr, perched atop a stand. The diner to his left reaches out to the *hetaira*, while on the far left two elderly men are deep in their cups; one holds two *kylikes*. This very scene is painted on the outside of a *kylix*. Note the lyre on the wall, used to accompany the poetry sung at the symposium.   (Corpus Christi College. Reproduced by permission of the master and fellows of Corpus Christi College, Cambridge, U.K.)

artistic and beautifully made. The principal weapon was the thrusting spear, but a fighter also carried a one-edged sword for slashing in close encounters. Advancing in tight ranks called a phalanx, overheated in heavy armor with limited visibility, with little command structure but the instinct to prove one's worth in the eyes of one's companions, relying on training and a lifetime of discipline, the front line of one formation threw itself against the front line of the opposition. Fighters further back than the third or fourth row played no direct role at first except to push on the man in front, while himself being pushed from behind. As those in front fell, the back rows entered direct combat.

Eventually one of the formations broke up and the battle was over. A truce was called, the dead buried, and a trophy set up by the winning side at the place where the losing phalanx broke (*tropaion* = "place of turning," our "trophy"). In Homer the heroes go into battle in chariots, then jump down and fight on foot, but hoplite formations did not use chariots. Nor was cavalry—warriors mounted on individual horses—important in Greek warfare until the Hellenistic Period. Even then the lack of saddle and stirrup, introduced to Europe from China in the Middle Ages, and the small size of ancient horses limited the cavalry's effectiveness.

Social institutions encouraged the cultivation and refinement of the warrior's spirit. In the *gymnasium* (from Greek *gymnos,* "naked"), the Greek male practiced nonlethal forms of war. Our tradition of athletics (from Greek *athlos,* "contest") began in Greece (Figure 2.7).

As sport to the Greek was practice for war, war was a kind of sport, and strict rules governed the behavior of the citizen hoplite armies. Competitive rules similar to those regulating Greek warfare extended off the battlefield into every realm of social life.

In the Archaic and Classical periods, a man divided his social relations into clear camps of friends and enemies. A man was measured by the richness of gifts to his friends and the thorough punishment given to his enemies. In Athenian tragedy, poets recast ancient myths to reflect contemporary concerns as they themselves competed vigorously for first prize under the critical gaze of their fellow citizens. In Athenian law courts, one sought not justice, but victory. The notion of "natural rights" to life or property or happiness or anything else, so prominent in our own thinking, simply did not exist.

FIGURE 2.7 A footrace on an Athenian amphora (two-handled jar), c. 530 BC, offered as a prize for victory in the athletic games held every four years during the Panathenaic festival. Homer calls Achilles "swift-footed," as a successful warrior had to be.   (The Metropolitan Museum of Art, New York. Image copyright © The Metropolitan Museum of Art / Art Resource, New York)

Females

Although our lack of sources hinders the study of all aspects of ancient Greek society, we find it particularly difficult to form an accurate picture of the lives of women. Males who composed almost all our literary sources may present a biased, unsympathetic, and contradictory picture. On the one hand, these sources suggest, the ideal Greek woman was tall, beautiful, submissive, fertile, chaste, and silent, virtually invisible to those outside the home. As the statesman Pericles told the widows of soldiers killed in battle, "Your reputation is great when you do not prove inferior to your own nature and when there is the least possible talk about you among men, whether in praise or in blame" (Thucydides 1.45.2). The sources also imply that women were likely to behave in ways that contrasted sharply with this ideal. Fired by an insatiable sexual appetite, the women depicted in literature often are ready to lie and scheme to achieve their selfish aims. It is difficult to distill the truth about women's lives from the sources that are available to us, but we can make at least some observations with a reasonable level of confidence.

In the Classical Period, a little girl of good birth learned the values of modesty, obedience, and restraint in the care of a nurse as she grew up in the *gynaikeion*, "women's quarters," located in the back of the house or on an upper floor. In the *gynaikeion* she also learned the female arts of spinning wool and making cloth, a woman's principal occupation throughout life, except for childbearing and care of the dead (Figure 2.8).

Only rarely did women learn to read and write. In the inner rooms of the *gynaikeion*, women met with other women friends and entertained one another with conversation and music. Although a single reference in Plato's *Republic* (2.376c) suggests that women told stories to their children, we have no direct evidence about the content of such stories. Indirect evidence suggests that they were fables like those of Aesop, or tales of the bogey-man variety. Greek myth, like Greek literary education, appears to have been the province of males, a fact of paramount importance in our attempts to understand it.

A Greek proverb noted that a woman knew two great moments in her life: her marriage and her death. Unlike other ancient peoples (except possibly the Etruscans), the Greeks were monogamous; that is, offspring from one wife at a time were the man's legitimate heirs. The origins of Greek monogamy are unknown, but no other social practice affected more deeply the way Greek men and women behaved toward one another.

Marriage was not based on mutual affection, but arranged between families on political and economic grounds. Even the Athenian *polis,* despite the institutions of democracy, was governed by its leading families. The family provided the woman with a dowry, which allowed the bride's family to retain some control even after marriage. In case of divorce, the husband was compelled to return the dowry intact. The bride may never have set eyes on her husband until the wedding day.

The groom was a mature adult, usually in his thirties, with wide experience of life and war; the bride was a girl in her teens, around fourteen years old, who offered her dolls in a temple as her last act before marriage. The husband had wide

FIGURE 2.8 Greek village women, from about 1920, spinning wool. The women represent all age groups: on the far left, standing up by the tree, a woman whose face is obscured by the wool on her distaff, and a small child; then a woman and her young daughter, also spinning; then a teenage girl; then two older women flanking a prepubescent girl, all with distaffs; another girl stands behind at a higher level. The distaff, held under the right arm, supports a mass of wool, leaving the hands free. With their right hands, the women detach the wool while the left hand guides the thread to a spindle that spins like a top, dropping gradually to the ground as the thread lengthens. Then the spinner must stop and wind the thread around the spindle's shaft. Ancient spinning was done in precisely this fashion. Seven-tenths of the time needed to produce woven cloth is taken up by spinning, woman's archetypal activity until modern times. The women are dressed in dark colors and cover their heads. Their activity and dress are remarkably similar to those of women in ancient Greece.   (University of Wisconsin–Madison Photo Archive)

sexual experience, sometimes orgiastic, with women and boys; the bride was a *parthenos,* "virgin" (Figure 2.9).

No respectable man would knowingly marry a young woman who had prior sexual experience, and a father could sell into slavery a daughter guilty of it, even if she were the victim of rape. For these reasons Greek girls were married off as soon as possible after first menstruation.

FIGURE 2.9 Statue of a *korê*, "maiden." Such statues stood on the Acropolis, where wealthy citizens dedicated them in honor of their daughters, presumably so that by magical sympathy the young women could stand in Athena's protection. The *korê*'s hair is made into elaborate tresses and falls over a linen dress called a *peplos*. The statues, made of marble, were brightly colored. Her "archaic smile" is characteristic of Greek statues from the late sixth century BC. Statues like this one have survived because when the Athenians cleaned up the Acropolis after the Persian sack of 480 BC, they threw the broken statuary into a pit, where it has been found in modern times. (Acropolis Museum, Athens; author's photo)

The period between first menstruation and marriage was one of great danger to the girl, her family, and society itself. As a *parthenos*, the girl was thought to be wild and dangerous, like the goddess Artemis, to whom the *parthenos* was often compared and whose cult young girls served. Most heroines of Greek myth are *parthenoi*, in a momentary position of freedom to do immense harm or bring great advantage to her people. In marriage a woman could gain *sophrosynê*, "self-control." Tamed by the authority of her husband, in willing submission to the weighty demands of pleasing her husband sexually and bearing him children, a woman could overcome her natural weakness and live a modest and silent life away from the scrutiny of others.

The wedding, the high point of a girl's life, ordinarily was held at night, when the new bride moved out of her mother's *gynaikeion* into the house of her mother-in-law, where she first experienced intercourse, bore children, and lived until she died, often in childbirth at a young age. The myth of the abduction of Persephonê (Chapter 10) must reflect the male's perception of the young Greek girl's psychological experience on the wedding night. Terrified when snatched up by Lord Death as she played with her virgin friends, she soon accepted her changed condition in life.

The groom traveled to the bride's house in a cart, where he took her wrist in a special gesture implying a staged abduction (Figure 2.10). At this moment she left behind the authority of her father and entered within the authority of her husband and her husband's mother. To the accompaniment of music, dance, song, and crackling torches the cart made its way to the house of the groom. A song, sometimes

FIGURE 2.10 A Greek wedding, on an Attic wedding vase of special shape (*loutrophoros* = "ritual water carrier"), which held the water by which the bride purified herself, 430–420 BC. The bridegroom moves to the right, having clasped the bride by the wrist; the Greek wedding was a mock abduction. He gazes at the bride, whose face has just been revealed. Over his head is written the Greek word for "handsome." The bride inclines her head slightly in the expected attitude of modesty. Cloth covers her head (compare Figure 2.8), and she wears a bridal crown. Two cupids, called *erotês* (singular, *eros*), flutter about her head, symbolizing sexual desire. Women attendants stand on either side. A column on the right (off the edge of the picture) represents the bridal chamber, where the groom is leading the bride. The bride appears again on the stem of the vase carrying a *loutrophoros* like this one in one hand (invisible here), to cleanse herself, and a necklace, to adorn herself.   (Photograph © 2011 Museum of Fine Arts, Boston.)

with sexual content, might be sung outside the marriage chamber (the famous poet Sappho wrote such songs in the seventh century BC). In the morning, the girl's friends visited her in the bridal chamber and brought gifts (Figure 2.11).

As a virgin, or *parthenos*, the Greek girl was called *korê* (an alternate name for Persephonê). After marriage and intercourse she was a *nymphê*, "bride" (hence our word *nymph*). Not until she bore her first child did she become *gynê*, "woman" (as in *gynecology*), when she assumed full authority over the *oikos*, "family," which included not only the female and young unmarried male members of the household, but also the slaves and domestic animals, the house itself, and its inner storeroom filled with storage vessels. (From *oikos* comes our word *eco*nomy, "management of the family," and *eco*logy, "study of the habitat.") In myth, women are closely associated with vessels, as they are with textiles. By her late teens a Greek woman was a mother and by age thirty-five a grandmother. By age fifty she could be a great-grandmother, if she lived that long, but few did.

A Greek wife did not even eat with her husband. Nonetheless, monogamy placed enormous power in her hands (about which we hear endless complaints in Greek

FIGURE 2.11 The day after the wedding, in the women's quarters, from a fifth-century BC Attic red-figured *epinētron*, an odd ceramic object with roughed upper surface to serve as a knee-cover for wool-working. On the right, the bride rests against a couch. Behind her, the double doors of the bridal chamber stand open. The pillar in front of her indicates that this is an interior view. Outside, friends of the bride bring gifts. One woman talks to a dove, the bird of Aphrodite. Their names are written above them. At the left, a woman arranges myrtle in a *loutrophoros* (see Figure 2.10).   (Photograph © 2011 Museum of Fine Arts, Boston)

myth). Monogamy also isolated her in a way unknown within the polygamous societies of the rest of the ancient world, in which women of the harem had constant companionship, although colored by intense rivalries. Increased prosperity heightened still more the isolation of Athenian women of the Classical Period, for whom abundant slaves performed such menial but social work as gathering water and nursing children. Ordinarily a respectable woman went outdoors only during certain religious festivals, when she averted her eyes from the gaze of men and covered her head.

Several festivals were restricted to women alone, and close study of their symbols and rituals shows how in these festivals the fertility of the earth, and by extension the well-being of the community, was connected closely to the woman's ability to bring forth from her body new life. Childbirth was a moment of personal crisis because many women died from it, but also of enormous pollution, called **miasma**, because of the blood and other fluids that accompany childbirth. No man would come close to a woman in labor.

Women's ability to purify the chamber and the child after birth extended to their care of the dead. Only women could touch a dead body to clean it for burial. After burial they tended the family graves, pouring offerings and tying ribbons around gravestones. Myths are filled with events surrounding birth and death and the special power of women to withstand and control the two crises through which every human being must pass.

Our evidence about family size from the Classical Period is poor, but in the Hellenistic Period an average Greek family consisted of three children, preferably two boys and one girl: one boy to die in the endless wars, another to carry on the family line, and one girl to assist in the formation of interfamilial alliances. Girls were disadvantageous because they required a dowry and did not carry on the family name. Additional children were often exposed, abandoned in the wild. Most died, but some were found and raised as slaves or prostitutes. There are famous foundlings in Greek myth, including Oedipus of Thebes and Paris of Troy.

Athenian women had probably fared somewhat better in the Archaic Period, when great families were in power, than in the Classical Period under the democracy, when citizenship became all-important. To be a citizen meant not to be a woman, slave, or foreigner. In affirmation of the solidarity of the group, Athenian males met together every year in a gigantic civic symposium, the festival of Dionysus, god of wine, where they witnessed the tragedies and lighthearted satyr plays, for which the chorus was dressed as sexually excited horsy creatures. Although no clear evidence shows whether women were present at the festival of Dionysus, their presence would have nullified the all-male esprit that the citizen festival affirmed and would have violated feminine modesty. For this reason most scholars think that only males were present in the audiences for Greek tragedy.

Although powerful women often appear in Greek plays, their fascination emerges directly from the shocking reversal of ordinary roles. In Aeschylus' tragedy *Agamemnon*, the adulteress Clytemnestra ruled the city of Mycenae while her cuckold husband, Agamemnon, fought at Troy. On his return she murdered him. In Aristophanes' comedy *Lysistrata* (lī-**sis**-tra-ta), the women of the Greek cities banded together, went on a sex strike, and took over Athens. To the male audience, this amusing reversal seemed as absurd as if the birds in the sky were to conquer the world—as in fact they do in another of Aristophanes' plays!

Although social tensions between Greek men and women were high and never resolved, the sexes were capable of genuine affection toward each other. Helen's infidelity, so the story went, caused the Trojan War, but Odysseus' longing for home and family led him to abandon an offer of immortal life with a nymph far more beautiful than his wife. Among the most touching works of Greek art are sculptured gravestones showing the deceased in loving company with husbands, wives, or children. In rare cases, women even participated in public life. Aspasia from the city of Miletus, friend and mistress of Pericles, was highly cultivated, knew powerful people, and advised Pericles on foreign policy.

Slavery

Without slaves, ancient civilizations could not have existed. Tribal societies kill captives taken in war or sometimes adopt the women and children, but the ancient Mediterranean civilizations of Greece and Rome were sufficiently wealthy to support vast numbers of slaves, on whom their economies depended. Slaves made up one-fourth or one-third of the workforce in classical Athens, and even men of modest means owned them. They made possible the leisure essential to Athenian democracy, allowing the citizens to argue in the law courts, debate public policy in the assembly, fight their enemies on land and sea, and practice the arts of rhetoric, philosophy, history, and science (Figure 2.12).

Slaves were chattel property and had no enforceable rights. They could be killed or sexually used with impunity. In one of his adventures, Heracles is sold as a slave to a foreign queen to serve as her sexual playmate. Slaves had no legal families of their own. They served in the household, but male slaves also performed work outside it, doing the same tasks as free men, with whom they often worked side by side on farms and in factories. Most unfortunate were those who worked, in atrocious conditions, in the Athenian silver mines at Laurium. Slaves could receive salaries and often saved

FIGURE 2.12 Miners digging clay for making pots on a sixth-century BC black-figured plaque from Corinth dedicated to Poseidon and his consort Amphitrite. Most miners in ancient Greece were slaves. The slaves in Greece were often captured in Thrace or farther north in the Danube region, or they came from Asia Minor, sold into Greece by slave-traders. A pot for drinking water hangs in the center of the plaque. (bpk, Berlin /Staatliche Museen) / Juergen Liepe/ Art Resource, New York)

up enough money to purchase their freedom. In Roman civilization, freedmen—those born as slaves who had purchased their freedom—formed a powerful social caste and were highly influential in the governance of the Roman empire.

Religion

Christians, Jews, and Muslims believe that there is one God who made the world. He stands outside it, yet dwells in the human heart. He works for good in the world. His nature may be love. His plan for humans is revealed through sacred writings, which specialists (priests, rabbis, and mullahs) interpret to the masses within buildings set aside for this purpose (churches, synagogues, and mosques). God demands of his followers love, faith, and adherence to a strict code of moral behavior, including sexual behavior. These religions once had, and to some extent still have, important social and political missions.

The Greeks, by contrast, had many gods, who did not make the world but dwelled within it. Zeus was their leader, but Void (Chaos), Earth (Gaea), Night (Nyx), and other gods existed before him and his brothers and sisters. They continued to exist even after Zeus, by force, achieved ascendancy. No Greek god was all-powerful; rather, each controlled a sphere of interest, which sometimes overlapped with that of other gods. The Greek gods had personalities like those of humans and struggled with one another for position and power. They did not love humans (although some had favorites) and did not ask to be loved by them. They did not impose codes of behavior. They expected respect and honor but could act contrary to human needs and desires. They did not reveal their will in writing. Their priests, having no writings to interpret, were required only to perform appropriate rituals. Because there were male and female gods, there were male and female priests to perform such rituals.

The appropriate ritual was always a form of sacrifice: the killing of an animal or many animals or the offering of foodstuffs. Although human sacrifice is often mentioned in Greek myths, it appears to have been highly uncommon during the historical period, and archaeology has produced only two clear examples from the Bronze Age (from Crete). The underlying logic of sacrifice was always the same: In order to gain the god's goodwill, destroy what you value most. That will place the god firmly in your debt.

Sacrifice was performed outside the god's house on an altar, usually to the east of the temple. The temple was not itself a place of worship. There was no official priestly organization with social or political missions. Priests and priestesses came from local families or were sometimes chosen by lot. When one wanted to know the god's will, one went to a seer or to an oracle. Religious activity—appropriate sacrifice—could help in this life, but had no effect on one's lot in the next world (the mysteries at Eleusis were a notable exception; see Chapter 10). Notions of guilt or sin, which arise from disobeying God's rules of universal application, were unknown. There were no such rules to obey.

The Greek gods were capricious and terrifying, not to be taken lightly. Yet the Athenian comedians made fun of them, and Greek intellectuals criticized them for the immoral behavior reported in Greek myths. A small minority of Greeks even questioned the existence of the gods and sought other than divine causes behind the phenomena of the world. The thinking of these radical intellectuals led to the proposition that gods do not fashion human misery or happiness, success in war or love, or anything else. Humans make their own world, a fundamental principle of what we think of as Western civilization.

Beliefs and Customs

Underlying many Greek myths is a way of thinking about the world that many today would reject, at least in principle. To comprehend these myths, we must make an effort to understand their worldview, one shared by all preliterate societies throughout the world.

One aspect of this view is a belief in magic. We have already mentioned, in our discussion of divine myth, the attribution of human qualities to natural forces. Although modern science rejects this notion, it was present in virtually all ancient societies and even now has wide appeal. Still today we speak of Mother Nature and Father Time. Modern science rejects the theory that we can manipulate the outside world by means of rituals and spells, but ancient peoples (and many modern ones) were certain that magic was effective. Myths talk endlessly about magical objects: amulets, a necklace that bears a curse, or such fanciful objects as a hat that makes the wearer invisible, sandals that enable one to fly, or a fruit that gives everlasting life.

Today we consider words to be unconnected to the objects or ideas that they represent (so that the same thought can be expressed in different languages), but magical practice assumes that words embody creative and effective power. If one commands emphatically that this or that take place, it will take place. Curses on the lips of the dying are extremely dangerous. The word or the name is the thing itself, its essence or soul (hence the biblical commandment, "You shall not take the name of the Lord in vain").

Closely related to the belief in magic is the conviction that the world is inhabited by spirits, the ghosts of the dead (see Chapter 12). From the fear of ghosts comes the belief in blood guilt, which the Greeks called *miasma*, "pollution," the same word used to describe the pollution of childbirth. *Miasma* was thought to afflict a murderer because he was pursued by the spirit that lived in the spilled blood. For this reason murderers were very dangerous company. Their misfortune, certain to come, could afflict those around them. Fortunately, spirits and ghosts could be coerced by means of ritual or spells or persuaded by sacrifice or prayer.

We divide the human world sharply from the natural, but to the ancient Greeks such distinctions were not obvious. Animals may have human qualities, including the power of speech. For example, in Homer's *Iliad* the horses of Achilles speak to him at a critical moment, warning him of his impending death. A human may be born not of woman, but of something in the natural world. The handsome Adonis was born from a tree. Animals may raise humans, as in the story of the twins Romulus and Remus, the founders of Rome; abandoned as infants, a wolf suckled them. Transformation of humans into animal or natural forms (rocks, trees, mountains, or stars) is common (Figure 2.13).

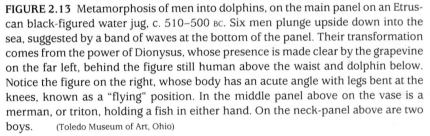

FIGURE 2.13 Metamorphosis of men into dolphins, on the main panel on an Etruscan black-figured water jug, c. 510–500 BC. Six men plunge upside down into the sea, suggested by a band of waves at the bottom of the panel. Their transformation comes from the power of Dionysus, whose presence is made clear by the grapevine on the far left, behind the figure still human above the waist and dolphin below. Notice the figure on the right, whose body has an acute angle with legs bent at the knees, known as a "flying" position. In the middle panel above on the vase is a merman, or triton, holding a fish in either hand. On the neck-panel above are two boys.   (Toledo Museum of Art, Ohio)

A famous story was told about **Narcissus** (nar-**sis**-sus), a youth of tremendous good looks. His parents wanted to know whether their son would have a long life. "Very long," a prophet replied, "if he does not look at his own face." When Narcissus was grown, he saw his face reflected in a spring. Reaching for the beautiful figure, he fell in and drowned (hence our term *narcissism*, meaning "self-love"). His body was changed into the flower that still bears his name.

Similarly, the supernatural world mixes easily with the human. A human being may be born of a god or spirit. Achilles' mother was Thetis, a sea nymph. Male gods commonly have intercourse with mortal women, who bear them mortal but superior human children. Far less often, goddesses have intercourse with mortal men. The line between human and divine is just not firmly drawn. Although Heracles was born a mortal, he became a god at death. Dionysus and Zeus were both gods, but both had tombs where their spirits were honored as those of dead mortals.

We think of the world as a complex machine, governed by the laws of physical nature, through which we wander, dodging misfortune and doing the best we can. God may have made the world, but appears not to intervene directly in it (although in Christian doctrine God sent his only Son). However, the theory of natural law is a Greek invention of the fifth century BC. It did not exist when Greek myth was formed and probably was never accepted by most Greeks.

According to traditional Greek views, there are no chance events. Every event in the world is connected with every other, if only we could see how. At remote Dodona (do-dō-na) in northwestern Greece, servants of Zeus and his consort Dionê (di-ō-nē) could interpret the rustling of the wind in an oak to answer questions written on lead tablets; some of these tablets have survived. Especially important among the Etruscans and later the Romans was information drawn from examining the entrails of sacrificed animals and from observing the flight of birds (*augury*, hence our word *inauguration*, when omens are taken). Professional prophets and seers play a central role in Greek myth.

Dreams were another way to discover hints of the future, for in sleep the spirit is loosely attached to the body and in communication with the realms of Apollo, lord of prophecy. When Hecabê, queen of Troy, was pregnant, she dreamed that she gave birth to a bundle of sticks from which emerged fiery serpents that set fire to Troy. A Trojan seer explained that the child would bring destruction to the city. He ordered the baby exposed on the mountain. Rescued by a shepherd, the child grew up to be Paris, who caused the war that destroyed Troy.

Greek myths often refer to social mores that, although common in preliterate societies, differ sharply from those of classical Greek society itself. Cannibalism, human sacrifice, cattle rustling, wife-theft, and blood-vendetta as the ordinary response to homicide are prominent in Greek myth. For example, Thyestes, a prince of Mycenae, ate his own sons cooked in a stew. His nephew Agamemnon killed his own daughter, Iphigenia, to appease the goddess Artemis. One of Heracles' labors was to rustle the cattle of the monstrous Geryon. The Trojan War began when Paris abducted Helen, wife of Menelaüs. Orestes, son of Agamemnon, killed his mother to avenge her murder of his father. Such practices were not characteristic of Greek society in the Archaic and Classical periods. Cannibalism had long since disappeared in Greece, if it ever existed, and blood-vendetta and human sacrifice were quickly disappearing. Of course, a gory description of an outmoded or outrageous social practice is a good way for a storyteller to attract attention from a restless audience, as makers of modern horror films well understand.

GREECE AND ROME

Classical myth comprises not just the stories of the Greeks, but also Roman versions of those stories and some stories native to Rome. The Romans remade Greek culture in their own image, and they, not the Greeks, passed the classical tradition to modern Europe.

When Alexander "conquered the world" in 336–323 BC, he did not conquer Italy or any other region west of the Adriatic Sea. The western lands were still remote, although Greek cities had flourished in Italy and Sicily since the eighth century BC. But even in Alexander's day a small tribe of Indo-European speakers south of the Tiber River, living in and near the city of Rome and possessing a superior political and military organization, had begun a course of relentless expansion without parallel in human history. Controlling perhaps a few hundred square miles in the sixth century BC, by the time of Christ the Romans governed virtually the entire Mediterranean world and large territories to the north, east, and south of the Mediterranean. Greece itself became a Roman province in 146 BC, as did Asia Minor in 133 BC and Syria in 63 BC. The **Roman Period** in ancient history, as distinguished from the Hellenistic Period, may conveniently be dated from 30 BC, when Egypt, the Hellenistic cultural center, fell into Roman hands. The Western Roman empire crumbled in the fifth century AD, but its Greek-speaking eastern part lasted until AD 1453, preserving virtually all the records we have of ancient Greece.

As Rome was in early times surrounded by hostile peoples speaking different languages, so it was isolated by geography. Greece is made up of innumerable islands, large and small, and, on the mainland, coastal pockets suited to seaborne commerce and international exchange with the East and its extraordinary cultures. Italy, by contrast, is a long boot-shaped peninsula, split down the middle by the rugged Apennine range that cuts off Italy from the East (see Map X, Chapter 23). Seas to the east and west of the Italian peninsula are noted for their sudden storms, and the whole peninsula had few good harbors, only one on the coast facing Greece. To cross Italy from east to west, you had to go over high, bandit-ridden mountains. Traffic from north to south by land was slow and dangerous until the construction of the famous Roman military roads. The first, the Appian Way, was not built until 312 BC. We need not be surprised, then, that Italy remained so long on the periphery of ancient Mediterranean culture.

Italy was a melting pot of diverse peoples who spoke many languages. The Romans spoke Latin, an Indo-European language, but there were many other Indo-European dialects in Italy whose speakers could scarcely understand each other. North of Rome lived the powerful and influential **Etruscans** who, like the Greeks, resided in independent city-states. They spoke a language completely unrelated to Greek or Latin. The modern name of Tuscany is derived from the ancient name Etruria. Their origin is unknown, but some think they emigrated from Asia Minor sometime in the twelfth century BC. Although the culturally powerful Etruscans spoke a non–Indo-European tongue of unknown affiliation, they took over the Greek alphabet within decades of the alphabet's invention around 800 BC, from Greeks living near the Bay of Naples. The Etruscans gave this writing to the Romans, who gave it to us. With the alphabet came the riches of Greek culture, and above all Greek myth.

The Etruscans ruled the city of Rome during the sixth century BC, bequeathing a rich legacy to Roman society, government, and religion (although the name *Roma* appears to be Greek, meaning "strength"). The Roman gladiatorial games developed from Etruscan funeral games in which prisoners were killed in honor of the dead as a form of human sacrifice. The unique genius of the Roman people was to absorb cultural achievements from foreign peoples and yet remain Roman. In the fourth century AD they even took over the Christian church, of Jewish origin. Whereas other peoples made things of beauty, the Roman destiny was to rule efficiently and justly, as the Romans often explained to themselves.

In early times Rome was an oligarchy, ruled by a council of aristocrats, the Senate ("body of old men"). This period is called the *Republic* (from the Latin *res publica*, "public business"). The Republic broke down after a hundred years of civil war between competing factions within the oligarchy, and Augustus Caesar, the grand-nephew of Julius Caesar, defeated his rivals and took power about the time of Christ. Augustus, pretending that the Republic still existed, modestly called himself *princeps*, "first citizen" (the source of our *prince*) and *imperator*, "commander" (or "emperor"). Henceforth Rome was in reality a monarchy, ruled by one man.

Although the Romans had their own religious heritage, they seem to have had few traditional stories, as far as we know. They happily adopted Greek legends, which they learned mostly from Greek poets of the Hellenistic Period. No legend was more important than the story of Aeneas, a Trojan hero in Homer's *Iliad*. By accepting Aeneas as their actual progenitor, the founder of their race, the Romans aggressively laid claim to the rich and prestigious cultural tradition of Greece. Still, as we will see in Chapters 23 and 24, myth functioned rather differently among the Romans than it did among the Greeks.

KEY NAMES AND TERMS

Boeotia, 20

Attica, 20

Peloponnesus, 20

Laconia, 20

Euboea, 20

Aegean Sea, 22

Cyclades, 23

Indo-Europeans, 24

Late Bronze Age, 25

Mycenaean Age, 25

Achaeans, 25

Linear B, 25

Dark Age, 26

Ionia, 27

Archaic Period, 27

polis, 27

Classical Period, 32

Peloponnesian War, 33

Hellenistic Period, 35

pederasty, 36

hoplites, 37

parthenos, 41

miasma, 44

Narcissus, 49

Roman Period, 51

Etruscans, 51

FURTHER READING CHAPTER 2

HISTORY AND ARCHAEOLOGY

Chadwick, John, *The Mycenaean World* (Cambridge, UK, 1976). Overview with good illustrations. Chadwick collaborated with Michael Ventris, the decipherer of Linear B.

Drews, Robert, *The Coming of the Greeks* (Princeton, NJ, 1988). Discusses the arrival of the Indo-Europeans in the Aegean and the Near East.

Finley, M. I., *The Ancient Greeks* (New York, 1987). A readable summary by a leading historian.

Mallory, J. P., *In Search of the Indo-Europeans: Language, Archaeology and Myth* (London, 1989). The best book on the topic.

Morris, I., and Barry B. Powell, *The Greeks: History, Culture, Society*, 2nd ed. (Upper Saddle River, NJ, 2008). Widely used text presenting general study of who the Greeks were, what they did, and why it is important, with many illustrations.

Murray, Oswyn, *Early Greece* (Stanford, CA, 1983). Shows how we can reconstruct Homer's own time from the *Iliad* and *Odyssey*.

Snodgrass, A. M., *Archaic Greece: The Age of Experiment* (Berkeley, CA, 1980). Analysis of the formative period of Greek classical civilization.

RELIGION

Burkert, Walter, *Greek Religion*, trans. John Raffan (Cambridge, MA, 1985). The standard comprehensive scientific description of Greek religion.

Mikalson, Jon D., *Ancient Greek Religion* (Oxford, UK, 2005). A fine introduction pitched to the beginning student.

Nilsson, Martin, *A History of Greek Religion*, 3rd ed. (New York, 1980). An English-language compressed version of his authoritative (and enormous) study in German; Nilsson was one of the great scholars of Greek religion.

GENDER AND SEXUALITY

Dover, K. J., *Greek Homosexuality* (Cambridge, MA, 1978). Scientific treatment of a difficult topic.

Fantham, E., H. P. Foley, N. B. Kampen, and S. B. Pomeroy, *Women in the Classical World* (Oxford, UK, 1994). Superior review of artistic and literary evidence, clear and jargon-free.

Larson, Jennifer, *Greek Heroine Cults* (Madison, WI, 1995). Best book on the topic, with a catalogue of heroines.

Lefkowitz, Mary R., *Women in Greek Myth* (Baltimore, MD, 1990). The types of women in Greek tragedy and their relationship to real Greek women, by a leading scholar; good on the Amazons.

Peradotto, J., and J. P. Sullivan, eds., *Women in the Ancient World* (Albany, NY, 1987). Essays from a feminist perspective.

Pomeroy, Sarah, *Goddesses, Whores, Wives, and Slaves* (New York, 1975). A pioneering survey of the roles assigned to women in ancient Greece.

Stewart, Andrew, *Art, Desire and the Body in Ancient Greece* (Cambridge, UK, 1997). Social, ideological, and sexual aspects to ancient Greek art.

SOCIETY

Golden, Mark, *Sport and Society in Ancient Greece* (Cambridge, UK, 1998). Systematic review of the role of athletics in ancient Greece.

Vernant, Jean-Pierre, *Myth and Society in Ancient Greece* (New York, 1988). Opposing older notions, this leading French scholar exposes the realities of ancient slavery, blood sacrifice, ritualized warfare, ceremonial hunting, and ecstasy.

CHAPTER 3

THE DEVELOPMENT
OF CLASSICAL MYTH

Men imagine not only the forms of the gods but their ways of life to be like our own.

ARISTOTLE,
Politics 1252B

MYTH BEGINS IN THE primordial past. It is possible (although unprovable) that features of myth found in the Classical Period first appeared ten thousand or even a hundred thousand years ago, long before the Greeks and Romans existed. In thinking about the beginnings of classical myth, we can try to peer beyond our earliest written records to reconstruct myths, or religious beliefs, that may have been current in prehistoric times. Comparative material, archaeological and linguistic, offers some opportunity to do this, as does the study of how myth was transmitted before writing. In this chapter we review the earliest information we can infer about the history of myth, then review how myth developed through the historical periods in the pre-Hellenic cultures of the ancient Near East and in Greece and Rome themselves. Surprisingly, the Greeks seem to have owed little to the indigenous cultures of the southern Balkans that they occupied, and a great deal to the distant Mesopotamian culture. More and more, scholars view Greek culture as an offshoot of the Mesopotamian culture rather than as an independent development, in the same way that Roman culture is viewed as an offshoot of Greek culture.

THE BEGINNINGS OF GREEK MYTH

Conspicuous in the museums of southeast Europe and the Near East are figurines that have exaggerated sexual organs and plump buttocks and breasts. Such objects are the oldest freestanding sculptures in the world. Male figurines, often with an erect penis, are also found, but in far fewer numbers. Many wish to connect such figures with goddesses and gods of fertility known from the historical period and prominent in myth.

Figure 3.1 shows one of the best known of these small statues, several inches high and made c. 6500–5700 BC in Çatal Hüyük (**cha**-tal **hu**-yuk), in south central Turkey, the oldest known agricultural community in the world. While seated on a throne, a naked woman but wearing a cap, with exaggerated breasts, is giving birth. The infant's head is just visible as it emerges. Leopards, on which she rests her hands, crouch on either side. Another type of European female figurine comes from the Aegean islands of the Cyclades (Figure 3.2), carved in local marble during the third millennium BC.

Sharp angles intersect pleasingly with plane surfaces. Nose and breasts are reduced to protrusions, and the pubic triangle is large and clearly marked with incisions and, once, paint. Although most such figures are small, this one is lifesized. Rediscovered in modern times, the Cycladic idols had a strong influence on European sculptors of the early twentieth century.

We have neither names to apply to these figurines, made before the introduction of writing, nor information about their purpose. Most examples in museums come from illicit excavations, or are modern fakes, but archaeologists have found

FIGURE 3.1 Goddess giving birth, statue from Çatal Hüyük, c. 6500–5700 BC, 16 inches high.   (Museum of Anatolian Civilization, Ankara, Turkey)

FIGURE 3.2 Cycladic mother figurine, c. 3000 BC. At five feet in height, this is the largest example known. (The N. P. Goulandris Foundation, Museum of Cycladic Art, Athens; author's photo)

some in graves of both men and women. We can guess that they had a magical power to produce new life, which somehow enhanced the ghost's well-being. Because fertility is a permanent concern among human societies, we may also assume that gods of fertility were important in this period, too.

Figure 3.3, from a Greek vase of the sixth century BC, was made six thousand years after the figurine from Çatal Hüyük, but is similarly placed between two wild animals. She holds a spotted panther in her right hand and a stag in her left. The Greeks called this figure of Artemis *Potnia Thêrôn*, "lady of the beasts," whose role in Greek religion was to promote the abundance of game. In this case, the historical religious cult of the goddess Artemis, who protected wild game, appears to be many thousands of years old. Perhaps elements of her myths also reach back into the very distant past. Unfortunately, we can never be sure which details in the stories preserved to us are old and which are recent. The relationship between the archaeological and written record is always difficult, but never more so than when dealing with prehistoric myth and religion.

Another way of trying to reconstruct prehistoric myths is by comparing the myths of different Indo-European peoples. The Indo-Europeans must have had their myths and their religion, which they brought with them as they spread from their homeland into and across Europe, and perhaps through comparative means we can learn something about them. From their linguistic roots, we know that the names of the Greek god Zeus and the Roman god Jupiter are descended from the same Indo-European word, which meant something like "shine," and most would agree that the Indo-Europeans did worship a sky-god, for which "shiner" might be a suitable name. Unfortunately, we cannot go much further than that.

FIGURE 3.3 Artemis *Potnia Thêrôn,* c. 570 BC, on the handle of the famous François Vase in Florence. In one hand she holds a stag, in the other a panther. Her wings indicate her divinity, according to a Near Eastern artistic convention. (Museo Archeologico Nazionale, Florence)

Gods change their nature. We cannot be sure what role such a god played in Indo-European society.

Because several figures in the myths of Indo-European peoples have a name that seems to mean "twin," and because in classical myth we find stories about twins, some scholars speculate that Indo-European myth included a story about twins. They even speculate about an early cultural dualism between the left (dangerous, evil) and the right (lucky, good), and about a primordial war between two of the social orders, the priests and warriors, against the third social order, the food producers (the myth of the Trojan War could be a classical descendant). However, so much is left to hypothesis and imagination in these reconstructions, and so contradictory is the evidence or explicable in other ways, that few scholars have accepted them. In fact, it is striking how few traces of Indo-European culture we find among the Greeks (for more on Indo-European myth, see Chapter 25).

Of great interest to students of the origins of classical myth are names of numerous gods found on Linear B tablets, listed as the recipients of offerings, some familiar from later Greek literature: Zeus and Hera, Poseidon, Athena, Artemis, Hermes, among others, are found. Dionysus, a god long thought to have entered Greek religion after the Bronze Age, is also mentioned. *Potnia,* "lady," as in *Potnia Thêrôn* or as a common classical epithet of Athena, seems to be a separate deity, perhaps the name of a Mycenaean mother-goddess. Deities completely unknown in classical times also appear.

We may be sure, therefore, that some of the classical Greek gods did exist in the Mycenaean Age, but as far as we know only as objects of religious cult. We have no stories or hints of stories preserved in the Linear B records. Although interesting frescoes representing a sea battle and a procession have been found on the island of Thera in the Cyclades, perhaps a Minoan outpost, we cannot identify a single

Minoan or Mycenaean myth in these frescoes. Either the myths did not exist then, or there was no artistic means to represent them.

Perhaps the best approach to understanding the beginnings of Greek myth is found not in the substance of the myths themselves, but in the means by which myths must have been transmitted before writing. On the basis of comparative evidence gathered in modern times, we now think that in prehistoric Greece and on through the Archaic Period illiterate singers called *aoidoi* (a-**oi**-doi, related to our "ode") entertained in aristocratic courts and perhaps in public at festivals. We usually translate *aoidos* (the singular form) as "bard" or "oral poet" (Figure 3.4). Early in life an *aoidos* learned through association with a master, through unconscious absorption, a special language of poetic composition. As ordinary language is shaped by unconscious grammatical patterns, this one was shaped by an unconscious rhythm, which we analyze in written versions as a poetic line called dactylic hexameter. The special language contained many preset rhythmical phrases, such as "swift-footed Achilles," which helped the *aoidoi* to compose a poem even as they sang it to the accompaniment of a lyre.

Homer was such a poet and Hesiod was another. Homer himself gives us an account of a blind *aoidos* named Demodocus (de-**mod**-i-kus, "received by the people") in Book 8 of the *Odyssey*. At an assembly in the morning, the king tells a messenger, "Summon the glorious *aoidos* / Demodocus, on whom a god immortal has poured great skill at reciting. / His song will surely delight us, whatever subjects he fancies." In the course of the festivities, Demodocus sings and plays several times: "They stretched out their hands for the dinner which lay on the table before them; / then, when they all were content and their hunger and thirst were both satisfied," the Muse reminds the *aoidos* of a song, the quarrel between Odysseus and Achilles (about which we know nothing), which he sings. After an interval, Demodocus accompanies a group of expert young men as they dance; he is evidently a skilled musician as well as a singer of songs. He now sings the racy story of adulterous Ares and Aphrodite, trapped in bed as they are having intercourse (see Chapter 8). Odysseus gives him a token of honor and requests a new song. Demodocus again invokes the Muse and sings of the Trojan Horse.

FIGURE 3.4 An *aoidos* sings to a lyre on an Attic cup, c.515 BC. He wears his hair in a curious turban and has a cloak thrown over one shoulder. Meaningless letters spill from his mouth to represent his song, by now equated with alphabetic writing.   (Chazen Museum of Art, Univesity of Wisconsin-Madison)

Many think that in Demodocus Homer gives us a self-portrait, and most of what we know about the social context of Homer's singing comes from these descriptions. Although making use of traditional stories and motifs, *aoidoi* must always have spoken to contemporary concerns and, of course, had no concept of history. The *aoidoi* were the myth-makers of early Greece. In this book, we study many of the stories that they and their direct successors told. Real warriors are interested in hearing about real wars, especially if they themselves fought in them or their fathers or grandfathers did. For this reason it is likely that the great cycles of myth surrounding the Trojan War and the war against Thebes do go back to campaigns waged in the Bronze Age, rumors of which were passed on by generations of oral poets.

THE INFLUENCE OF NEAR EASTERN MYTH

Whereas such myths as those of the Trojan War appear to be Greek in origin and to go back to the Bronze Age or earlier, other very important stories had their beginnings not in Greece, but in the non–Indo-European Near East. Ancient **Mesopotamia**, the "land between the rivers," which occupies the region of the Tigris and Euphrates rivers in what is today Iraq (see Map I, inside front cover), was a particularly important source. The Greek myth of the origin of the present world-order in a battle of the gods, for example, was certainly of Mesopotamian origin. Such stories may have come to Greece in the Bronze Age, but far more likely were imported from Eastern ports in the late Dark Age at the same time that the Greeks invented the alphabet on the basis of the earlier Phoenician writing (c. 800 BC), or they may have been learned from Semitic peoples living in Greece at this time.

Until about three hundred years ago, western Europe knew next to nothing about the ancient Near East, and most of what was known came from the Old Testament, preserved in its original Hebrew and Aramaic (closely related to Hebrew) and in translations into Greek (c. 300 BC) and Latin (c. AD 400). There are also many references, usually inaccurate, to the Near East in Greek and Latin authors and in the fathers of the Christian church. But in the seventeenth century, European travelers began to enter the lands of the ancient Near East and bring back firsthand reports. Pietro della Valle (1586–1682), an Italian nobleman, journeyed to Constantinople, Egypt, Palestine, and Syria, and in Persepolis, the ancient capital of Persia (559–332 BC), copied from the palace doors several inscriptions written in three different forms of an unknown script. In 1700 an Oxford scholar, although unable to read the script, named the writing *cuneiform* ("wedge-shaped," Figure 3.5).

From this time onward a stream of archaeological material from the Near East poured into western European museums, including many inscribed clay tablets, and the ancient languages of the region were gradually deciphered. In 1872 British scholar George Smith deciphered a tablet describing a universal flood that destroyed all humankind. The next year, in Mesopotamia, Smith found the text of the Babylonian story of creation (*Enuma elish*). The much later composer of Genesis, the biblical book of creation, evidently borrowed from such stories to fashion his account. Many wondered how they could continue to regard Genesis as an

FIGURE 3.5 Clay tablet with letter from Burna-Buriash to Akhenaten, pharaoh of Egypt, found in Amarna (middle Egypt) in 1887, c. 1359–c. 1333 BC. It is written in Mesopotamian Akkadian (Eastern Semitic), the diplomatic language of the period. Burna-Buriash was a king of Babylon.   (British Museum, London; © The Trustees of the British Museum / Art Resource, New York)

original and divine revelation. Not surprisingly, these and similar discoveries forced a reconsideration of the importance of myth.

The Near Eastern background for prominent Greek myths is so important that we must now say something about these stories that leaped cultural and linguistic barriers to influence the Greeks and, through them, the entire Western world.

Sumerian Myth

Not until World War II did reliable information about Sumerian myth come to light. Few stories have come down to us complete, and those must be inferred from cryptic texts inscribed on badly broken clay tablets in a difficult script recording a dead language that is poorly understood. We must depend heavily on reconstructions by a few scholars, whose translations are not so much a literal rendering of the meaning of original texts as conjectures about possible meanings.

The **Sumerians**, of unknown racial stock, spoke a language unrelated to any other known language. They lived close to the Persian Gulf in the treeless and stoneless mudlands near the estuary of the Tigris and Euphrates rivers (see Map III, The Ancient Near East). Their culture appeared suddenly, with few antecedents, about 4000 BC. According to their own traditions, they came from somewhere outside Mesopotamia, perhaps from Iran (Persia) or India. Supported by irrigation agriculture, which they

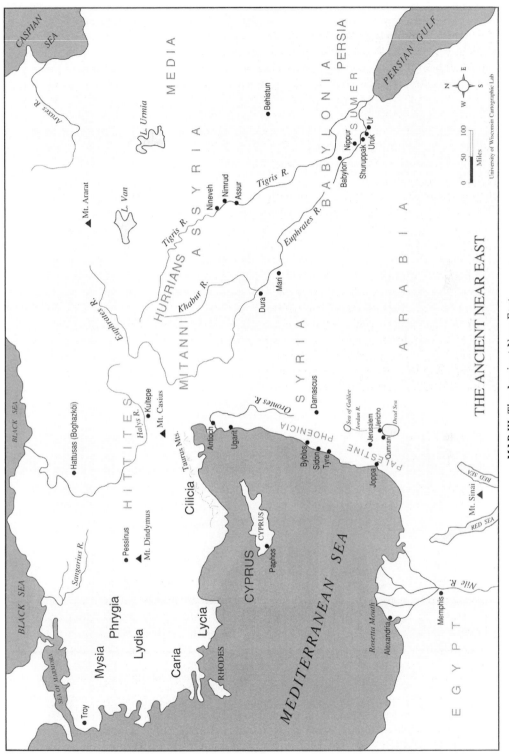

MAP III The Ancient Near East

invented, the Sumerians created the first known full-fledged city-states by 3000 BC, each with as many as forty or fifty thousand inhabitants. Such concentrations of human beings had never before appeared on this planet, as far as we know.

Each Sumerian city had its own protective deity who was closely bound to the city's fortunes, and one city's military triumph over another represented a victory of the local deity. The deity lived in a temple in the city's center, often at the top of a tall, terraced pyramid of successively receding stories known as a ziggurat (Figure 3.6). Times of prosperity brought slaves, gold, animals, exotic clothes, and spices, but some great cities, such as Ur, sank into desolation and disappeared.

Irrigation agriculture greatly increased the food supply, but it demanded social cooperation. The ruling elite's most powerful tool was cuneiform writing (c. 3400 BC), the first known system of graphic markings with a predictable attachment to elements of human speech, that is, the first true writing (see Figure 3.5). Writing appears in Egypt only slightly later, apparently inspired by the Mesopotamian example. Despite its immense complexity, cuneiform writing was the most widely used system of writing in the ancient world before the Greek alphabet and recorded many languages, some unrelated, during its astonishing three-thousand-year history. The earliest myths on earth are recorded in cuneiform writing.

As in all polytheisms, there were dozens, even hundreds, of gods and goddesses in the Sumerian pantheon, but some stand out above the others. **An,** "sky," was god of the infinite expanse of the dome above us, across which the sun travels and from which the rain falls. He was originally the supreme authority, the source of order

FIGURE 3.6 Built of mud-brick, the ziggurat at Ur was built by Ur-Nammu c. 2050 BC during the Third Dynasty of Ur and dedicated to the moon-goddess Nanna. The massive structure is 210 feet in length, 150 feet in width, and of unknown height. It was massively restored under King Nabonidus in the 6th century BC.   (World Religions Photo Library/Alamy)

in the worlds of gods above and humans below. *Anitu,* "Anu-ship," the institution of human kingship that made Mesopotamian civilization possible, came down from the sky: Kingship came from heaven. *An* began as an important figure in myths of creation, then shrank to a remote being with little influence on human affairs, very much like Uranus, "sky," in Greek myth.

Often said to be An's daughter, **Inanna** (in-**an**-na), "queen of heaven," was goddess of sexual love and, curiously, war. Her lust was insatiable, all-consuming, and exceedingly dangerous. One Sumerian text notes that 120 lovers could not satisfy her! Inanna (Semitic Akkadian Ishtar) is like Aphrodite in Greek myth, and somehow their names seem to be related.

As An embodied divine authority, **Enlil** (en-lēl), "lord of the storm," embodied force, power, the unruly violence of a thunderstorm. But he was also a king, An's agent on earth, and was personally involved in earthly events. He possessed the inscribed Tablet of Destiny by which the fates of gods and humans were decreed (a reflection of the power of cuneiform writing within Sumerian society). He could be beneficial, the bringer of fertilizing rain, or destructive, the drier-up of the flood waters, the bringer of locusts and the wild, destructive hordes of hill men eager to prey on the lowland cities. Enlil's position was similar to that of Zeus in Greek myth.

Enki, "lord of earth," was so named because he ruled the sweet groundwater found beneath the soil (see Figure 3.7). He was the active fertilizing principle. As water wends its devious path beneath and around obstacles, Enki was the clever, crafty god, the

FIGURE 3.7 Akkadian seal-impression, c. 2360–2180 BC, showing in the center Shamash (Sumerian Utu), the sun-god, rising from the eastern horizon, rays springing from his shoulders. He holds a saw in his hand, evidently so he can cut through the mountains (or symbolic of his role as judge). To the left of Shamash stands Ishtar (Sumerian Inanna) beside a tree and, perhaps, the hero Gilgamesh with his bow and a lion. Above to the right of Shamash is a bird (perhaps Anzu, which, according to one story, stole the Tablet of Destiny) and Ea (Sumerian Enki), his watery nature indicated by fish-filled streams that pour from his shoulders. To the right of Ea is the two-faced messenger-god, Isimud. In the upper left is a personal name and title in cuneiform script.

trickster of Sumerian myth. He was also the god of wisdom and magic who instructed humankind in all the arts and crafts. Enki has much in common with Hermes but also shares features with Hephaestus, Prometheus, Poseidon, and Dionysus.

The mother-goddess of the Sumerians had many names, and sometimes was just Ki, "earth." She was always Mother Earth, the rich silt built up from the river floods, who united with Enki to produce the first vegetation. In some ways she is similar to the Greek Demeter. Ereshkigal (er-esh-**kē**-gal), "queen of the great below," the Sumerian goddess of death, is an aspect of Ki, the dark soil into which the bodies of the dead were laid. Ereshkigal is like Persephonê in Greek myth.

Mesopotamian myths are vague about the physical appearance of the gods. Many "mythical" representations survive on objects, but they rarely give a clear idea about what is shown (Figure 3.8). However, all the Sumerian gods are anthropomorphic, "human-shaped" in both appearance and behavior. Their society resembles that of humans, with an assembly of elders presided over by an executive leader, a king. They are related to one another in a large family (just how is not always clear). In Sumerian literary accounts, the gods are devoted or capricious, like humans, and are susceptible to human passions, including ambition, anger, and lust. They gossip, scheme, give speeches, win victories, lament defeats, and constantly struggle among themselves, as did the cities they protected.

FIGURE 3.8 Mesopotamian terracotta relief from Khafaje, Iraq, c. 1700 BC, showing a god cutting a one-eyed female demon down the middle. Rays come from her head and her hands are tied behind her back. As so often in Mesopotamian art, which rarely illustrates known myths, we cannot be sure of the identity of either god or monster.   (Scala/Art Resource, New York)

The Sumerian gods figured in an important cycle of legends about the hero Gilgamesh (see Figure 3.7; Chapter 13). However, most Sumerian myths are divine myths, stories of the doings of superhuman beings. Their themes range from the creation of the universe and underworld to the creation of humankind and the universal flood. Somehow all these story patterns traveled from Mesopotamia to the Mediterranean, where they formed part of our own cultural heritage.

Semitic Myth

By 2300 BC Sumer had fallen under the control of **Semites,** seminomadic peoples who inhabited the steppe at the fringes of the Arabian desert and pushed constantly against the river cultures of Mesopotamia. The Semites were not a united people or race. The term is modern, taken from the Hebrew Bible (Genesis 10.21–31), where Shem (hence "Semite"), the son of Noah, is called the father of Ashur (hence the "Assyrians," another Semitic people), Aram (the Semitic "Aramaeans," who lived in Damascus), and Eber (the Semitic "Hebrews"). *Semitic* designates both a linguistic group and its associated cultural patterns.

Led by the great Sargon (c. 2340 BC), the Semitic **Akkadians,** named after their capital, Akkad, whose ruins have never been found, took over the southern Sumerian cities and adopted Sumerian culture. Identifying the Sumerian gods with their own deities (see Chart 3.1), the Akkadians appropriated Sumerian myths, refashioned them, and preserved them in cuneiform script on clay tablets. The Sumerian language itself disappeared as a living, spoken language by 2000 BC and henceforth, like Latin in recent times, was used only by scholars and priests, often to record myths.

Later, in the geographically ill-defined Mesopotamian river basin, a reorganization of power led to the ascendancy of the Semitic Babylonians, whose capital was the famous city of Babylon. Under their leader Hammurabi (1750 BC), whose collection of legal decisions has survived on a column with 3,600 lines of cuneiform writing, the Babylonians fashioned a temporary political unity from the scattered city-states of southern Mesopotamia. After Hammurabi's death, the empire succumbed to attacks from the nomadic and seminomadic mountain dwellers to the east. The biblical story of the Tower of Babel (**bā**-bel, "gate of God") may have been inspired by the great ziggurat in Babylon, built by Hammurabi. From Babylon comes one of

Sumerian Name	Akkadian/Babylonian Name	Concern
An	Anu	sky-god
Inanna	Ishtar	goddess of sexual love, war
Enlil	Enlil, Marduk	storm-god
Enki	Ea	god of sweet water, wisdom, magic
Ninhursag, Ki	—	goddess of earth
Ereshkigal	—	goddess of death
Utu	Shamash	sun-god

CHART 3.1 Near Eastern Gods and Goddesses.

our most important pre-Greek myths, the epic poem of creation called *Enuma elish,* from its first two words meaning "When on high . . ." Most Mesopotamian cunei-form documents were written by scribes to educate other scribes, but the *Enuma elish* appears to have been read aloud at the annual New Year's festival. The cult hymn recounts a divine myth, the making of the world and its present arrangement. We will study it when discussing the Greek account of creation.

The **Hebrews**, the best known of the Semitic peoples, traced their ancestry back to Abraham (c. 2000? BC), who came from "Ur of the Chaldees" in southern Mesopotamia, that is, from Sumer (the biblical reference to the Chaldeans, a later Semitic group, is an anachronism). According to the tradition, Abraham migrated to Canaan (present-day Israel and Jordan) after God promised that he would become the father of a mighty nation destined to possess this land. Abraham's descendants drifted into Egypt, where they became slaves to pharaoh, remaining there for several centuries. This tradition remains today a basis for Jewish self-explanation.

The great teacher Moses (c. 1200? BC), perhaps inheriting teachings of the Egyptian monotheistic pharaoh Akhenaten (fourteenth century BC), led the Hebrews out of Egypt and, in the Sinai peninsula, gave them the Ten Commandments, the ethical foundation of Judaism. The first of God's commandments to the Hebrews was "You shall have no other gods before me." Moses insisted that his people put aside the polytheistic practices characteristic of Egypt and Mesopotamia and devote themselves exclusively to the powerful God called Yahweh (he had other names), who had delivered them from Egyptian bondage. Moses' monotheistic vision pre-vailed, but many of the stories that the Hebrews told about their ancestors and their God—for example, the story of creation and the story of the universal flood—were adapted from Mesopotamian myth.

Under Moses' successors, the Hebrews invaded Canaan and waged a successful war for control of the land against the Philistines, evidently Mycenaean Greek refugees from Crete who lived in five cities along the coast (near modern Tel Aviv). The acme of Hebrew political power came about 1000 BC under Solomon, who built the first temple at Jerusalem. In 586 BC the Chaldeans, a Babylonian dynasty led by the famous Nebuchadnezzar, captured Jerusalem (this historical fact led to the confusion about Abraham, said to be "of the Chaldees"). He destroyed Solomon's temple and deported the Hebrew leaders to Babylon, where they and their descendants remained for almost fifty years, under the spell of Mesopotamian culture.

The Babylonian Captivity was a time of soul-searching for the Hebrews. Asking why Yahweh had abandoned them, the Hebrews took stock of their ancient tra-ditions, many preserved in written texts dating back to 800 BC or earlier. They combined these texts with Babylonian myths to create a coherent but sometimes mythical and sometimes legendary account of the Jewish past, extending all the way back to the creation of the universe. To this account Hebrew scholars added translations from the Egyptian (for example, portions of Proverbs and Psalms) and admonishments by "prophets" written down at different dates, and in different original languages, to form the books that much later, around AD 90, became the Hebrew Bible (or Old Testament, as it is known to Christians).

The writing system used by the Hebrews is often called the Phoenician alphabet, but is really a highly condensed syllabary of twenty-two signs, each of which stood for a single syllable in which only the consonant was specified. Phoenician writing was a great advance over the clumsy cuneiform and was widely used to record many Semitic languages after about 1000 BC. Because the vowels were not specified, however, Phoenician writing was not easy to read. The difficult modern Arabic script, used in many countries today, is a slightly modified form, and the revolutionary Greek alphabet, which specified two kinds of signs, one consonantal and the other vocalic, was adapted from the Phoenician syllabic system.

Other Sources

Some related myths, but with their own innovative features, come from the non-Semitic **Hittites,** one of the most powerful and important peoples of the Late Bronze Age, who controlled central Anatolia (Asia Minor) from about 1600 to 1200 BC. Their myths were preserved on clay tablets in cuneiform writing, but Hittite language, from the thirteenth century BC, found in the archives at their capital city of Hattussas in modern north central Turkey. Although the Hittites were Indo-European speakers—the earliest attested—they inherited cultural traditions first formulated among the Sumerians and later refined by the Sumerians' Semitic successors.

The Egyptian language is similar in structure to Semitic languages, but shares almost no common vocabulary. Scholars include both Egyptian and Semitic languages under a larger category called Afro-Asiatic. Ancient Egypt had few myths. Literary texts from Egypt are mostly collections of wise sayings (whence come many of the Hebrew Proverbs), reports of a man's important achievements, hymns that praise gods (without telling stories), and sophisticated and amusing tales for scribal instruction and entertainment. The most important myth by far in ancient Egypt told of the murder of the god Osiris and his resurrection through the magic of his sister Isis, but nowhere do the Egyptians themselves tell this story; we must depend on an account in Greek.

We examine specific ancient Near Eastern myths in subsequent chapters as we investigate the Greek myths that depend on them.

GREEK MYTH IN THE ARCHAIC PERIOD

Although many Greek myths may have taken shape during the Mycenaean Age and the Dark Age of Greek history and even earlier, it was not until the Archaic Period that myths were committed to writing. Consequently, we derive most of our knowledge of Greek myth from writings of this and later periods. Additional information from the Archaic and Classical periods also comes to us from the fifty thousand pictured Greek vase paintings that survive and occasionally from sculpture. Scholars estimate surviving pictured vases to represent about one percent of the original production, giving us some idea of the explosion of images that flooded ancient Greece and Italy in this period, for which there is no parallel in the ancient world.

Many images on Greek pots represented myths, often inspired by literary accounts, and some are reproduced in this book.

Earlier we discussed myths as being traditional oral tales that eventually were taken down in writing. The earliest Greek literature is the poems of **Homer,** the *Iliad* and the *Odyssey*. We know nothing for certain about Homer's life. Later tradition has him born somewhere in Asia Minor, perhaps in the city of Smyrna or on the island of Chios, but his poems show wide knowledge of the Aegean and Greece. He must have lived just at the moment that the alphabet was introduced into Greece, for (with one exception) Homer's stories never refer to writing. He is unaware of the revolutionary effects alphabetic writing had on social behavior. The absence of descriptions of writing in Homer is one of the principal reasons for placing him in the eighth century BC, when the alphabet was new and unfamiliar. It would have been impossible to record Homer in the earlier Linear B or Phoenician syllabic scripts because the complex rhythms of his poetic line depend on the alternation of long and short vowels, which these scripts were incapable of notating. The extraordinary Greek alphabet made possible the writing down of Homer's poems, and, according to one theory, someone invented the alphabet expressly in order to record Homer's poems.

The *Iliad,* a long poem (about sixteen-thousand lines), is set in a period of several weeks during the tenth year of the Trojan War. Its principal theme is the wrath of Achilles, his anger over being mistreated by the leader of the expedition, Agamemnon. Within this frame Homer includes a wealth of subordinate myths. The *Odyssey* (about twelve-thousand lines) narrates the return of Odysseus to his home after an absence of twenty years. The *Iliad* and the *Odyssey* define what we mean by **epic** (*epos* = "song"): a long narrative poem celebrating the deeds of heroes. Under what conditions Homer may have sung songs as long as the *Iliad* or *Odyssey* remains unclear. These poems probably were never presented in the form in which we have them. The poems we possess are the result of artificial conditions created by the writing down of the poems, when the poet was no longer forced to sing rapidly and had no audience to entertain and so could greatly expand his narrative.

But the Homeric poems are mysterious. In spite of hundreds of years of analytical and historical scholarship, no one has explained what was their purpose. The many problems surrounding the genesis of the Homeric poems, still hotly debated, are called the Homeric Question.

Views differ widely about the reality of the world Homer portrays. The famous archaeologist Heinrich Schliemann, who in 1876 claimed to have found the ruins of Troy in northwestern Turkey, thought they were literal descriptions of the Bronze Age, and we have given reasons for thinking that the stories of the Trojan War may in fact go back to this period. In other respects, however, Homer knows little or nothing about the Bronze Age. For example, in Homer the dead are cremated on a large pyre, then their ashes gathered and buried in an urn. But the Mycenaean Greeks interred the bodies of the dead in graves lined with stone slabs or, if royalty, in enormous underground beehive-shaped tombs. Homeric society consists of petty chieftains, each ruling a small territory; in the Bronze Age great centers of power kept careful watch over a controlled economy by means of a professional literate bureaucracy. Although Homer mentions a certain kind of helmet made of boars' tusks and several other objects familiar only in the Bronze Age, such objects may have been preserved as heirlooms long after the destruction of Mycenae. Others think that the conditions Homer describes are those of the Dark Age, or that Homer's world is an imaginary mixture of details from different periods. On balance, it seems most plausible that Homer incorporated various features from earlier periods preserved through the oral tradition, but that his poems, and especially the social and religious values that move the actors, reflect Homer's own age, the eighth century BC.

Although we do not know the purpose of Homer's poems, their influence on Greek and later culture is inestimable. Less influential but perhaps more important to the study of myth is his near or virtual contemporary **Hesiod** (750–700? BC). Unlike the anonymous Homer, who conceals his personality, Hesiod tells us a little about himself in his two surviving poems, the *Theogony* ("origin of the gods") and *Works and Days,* a sort of combination moral treatise and almanac.

His father had lived in Asia Minor, Hesiod tells us, then moved to mainland Greece to a small forlorn village at the foot of Mount Helicon near Thebes, where Hesiod lived. Like Homer, he became an *aoidos.* According to the opening lines of the *Theogony,* the Muses, inspirers of poetry, came to him in a vision while he was tending his flocks on Helicon. They gave him the power of song (thus "Helicon" is synonymous with "poetic inspiration" in the Western literary tradition). Hesiod's remarkable description of the Muses and his meeting with them contains many unfamiliar names, which we examine later in this book, but is worth quoting here because the description identifies Hesiod as the first European author (Homer never identifies himself), gives the first definition of a *poet* ("maker," that is, of the story), and explains why a poet can speak with authority about past, present, and future: because he is inspired by the Muses with a mission divinely ordained. Hesiod begins his song with the Muses, whose own song celebrates a long list of gods—it was these Muses who gave to Hesiod his power of song (= *aoidê,* hence *aoidos*) (Figure 3.9):

[1]   Let us begin our song with the Muses of Helicon,
       who dwell upon the great and rugged mount of Helicon
       and dance with gentle feet around the indigo spring
       and around the altar of Cronus' mighty son.
5   When they have washed their tender bodies
       in Permessus, or in the Horse's Spring, or holy Olmeius,
       they make lovely, longing dances on the top of Helicon
       and move with thumping feet. From there they rise, go forth by night,
       veiled in dark mist to utter their song in darling voice,
10   singing of Zeus who holds the aegis° and mistress Hera
       of Argos, who walks on golden sandals,
       and of the blue-eyed Athena, daughter of Zeus the aegis-holder,
       and of Phoebus Apollo, and Artemis who thrills to the arrow,
       and Poseidon, who holds the earth and shakes it,

10. *aegis:* A magic shield.

FIGURE 3.9 The Roman poet Vergil sits between the muse of poetry on his right, holding a papyrus scroll (Calliopê, "pretty-voiced"), and the muse of tragedy on his left, holding a tragic mask (Melpomenê, "singer"). With his left hand Vergil holds on his lap the *Aeneid*, where he invokes the Muses (lines 8–9). The Latin reads *Musa, mihi causas memora, quo numine laeso quidve,* "O Muse, tell me the cause, how she [Juno] was offended in her divinity, how was she aggrieved . . ." Vergil was no oral poet, but the Muses have become synonymous with poetic inspiration. Mosaic from Sousse, Tunisia, AD third century.   (Musée National du Bardo, Tunis, Tunisia; Gilles Mermet/ Art Resource, New York)

15   and honorable Themis [Law] and glancing-eyed Aphrodite
      and Hebê [Youth] with crown of gold and beautiful Dionê,
      Leto, Iapetus, and Cronus of crafty counsels,
      Eos [Dawn] and great Helius [Sun] and bright Selenê [Moon],
      Earth too, and great Oceanus and dark Night
20   and the sacred race of all the other ones who never die.
      One day they taught Hesiod glorious song [*aoidê*]
      while he was shepherding his lambs under holy Helicon.

Now Hesiod offers the first speculation in the history of European literary criticism, one that has obsessed commentators ever since: How much truth do myths contain?

Here is the first word [*muthos*, hence "myth"] the goddesses said to me—
the Muses of Olympus, daughters of Zeus who holds the aegis,
25 "You stupid rustic shepherds, bellies and nothing more,
we are the ones who can tell you lies that look like truth.
We can also, if we please, proclaim what indeed is true."
So spoke the trustworthy daughters of mighty Zeus
and gave me a leafy branch of laurel to pluck for a staff.
30 Then into me they breathed the inspired art of the poet,
to sing of things of the past and those that are yet to be.
They told me to sing of the blessed immortal race of the gods,
always beginning and ending my song with the Muses themselves.

HESIOD, *Theogony* 1–33[*]

Poetry, and its burden of myth, can be true or not true, and it can be hard to tell the difference. This sobering reality is always before us when we attempt to reconstruct the truth about the past from literary documents.

The *Theogony*, a description of the creation of the present world-order, owes a great deal to Mesopotamian myths. It tells how Zeus overcame an earlier generation of gods and monsters in battle and established his own power. The *Theogony* is one of the most important mythical texts to survive from antiquity, and we devote the next chapter to it. Hesiod's other surviving poem, *Works and Days*, describes a bitter dispute between Hesiod and his brother over the disposition of their father's property, a theme that allows Hesiod to range widely over issues of right and wrong, which he illustrates by telling such myths as the story of Pandora. We call this kind of literature "wisdom literature," a well-established genre in the Near East, two thousand years old by the time of Hesiod, and another sign of Hesiod's closeness to Eastern sources. In *Works and Days* Hesiod also tells us that he sang at funeral games in honor of a dead prince on the nearby island of Euboea, a detail that may explain how poems by this oral poet came to be written down: The Euboeans were the earliest possessors of the Greek alphabet.

We know that many other epic poems, now lost, were written down during the Archaic Period and that they contained many myths. Commentaries surviving from a later date summarize their contents. These post-Homeric epics are called the Cyclic Poems because later commentators saw them as constructed in a circle (*kuklos* = "circle") around the *Iliad* and the *Odyssey*, telling parts of the Trojan War story not covered in Homer. The Cyclic Poems had an enormous influence on Greek art and on the Athenian tragedians of the fifth century BC. Another important source from the Archaic Period is a collection of poems known as the **Homeric Hymns**. Like the poems of Homer and Hesiod, they were composed orally and, in antiquity, were believed to be by Homer himself. In fact, they are from a later date, mostly from the seventh and sixth centuries BC. Four are several hundred lines long: to Demeter, Apollo, Hermes, and Aphrodite, and we will quote substantial portions of each of these poems.

[*]The first line number in the English translations corresponds to the line number in the original Greek, after which the English and Greek numbering may diverge. The numbers given at the end of a passage refer to the original Greek or Latin text.

A hymn is a metrical address invoking a god or goddess by listing cultic names and telling an important story about the deity. The Homeric Hymns are a literary elaboration of an old religious tradition but very unlike Near Eastern hymns in their focus on mythic narrative, on the story about the god. Whereas epic seems to have been performed before elite male audiences, hymns were probably performed in public places, at festivals that may have included women and a broader range of social classes. Still, like epic, versions of the Homeric Hymns were composed in performance by specially trained *aoidoi.*

In Homer's poems, action is always described in the third person. From the seventh and sixth centuries BC comes a once large, now tiny body of personal lyric poems (including the famous fragments of Sappho), on a wide variety of topics but celebrating notably the individual's pain in love and the uncertainty of war. Many of these poems touch on mythical themes. Unlike the Homeric, Hesiodic, and Cyclic poems, however, this poetry was not composed in performance and recorded by dictation, but was composed directly in writing, meant to be memorized by others and represented orally. This shift in the way literature was created was to have epoch-making consequences.

GREEK MYTH IN THE CLASSICAL PERIOD

We must remember that there never was an agreed-upon version of any Greek myth, because there was no text (like the Bible) with sacred authority and no organization (like the Christian church) to establish an official version. As the Muses in Hesiod explain, the Muses are capable of disseminating lies as easily as the truth. The gods were not necessarily a source of truth. This Greek cultural prejudgment led eventually to the Greek invention of *ethics,* a way to tell right from wrong without divine authority, and *secular law,* where rules of behavior, and punishment for infringements, depend on human invention and not divine revelation. Ethics and secular law together are the heart of **humanism**, a value central to Western civilization. The poets gave form to Greek myths, but no one poet, not even Homer, could claim to promulgate an official version.

Those adept at the memorization of written epic and at the effective public delivery of such memorized texts were called *rhapsodes,* who performed while leaning on a staff (whence our word "rhapsody"). "Rhapsode" seems to derive from the Greek *rhabdos,* "staff," because they held a staff while performing. They were not themselves poets. Oral poets, *aoidoi,* were like jazz musicians who do not use a written score and never play a given tune the same way twice; rhapsodes were like classical musicians who re-create from a written score someone else's invention. Rhapsodes may be as old as the alphabet itself, which made them possible, and they were still a conspicuous feature of Greek life in the fourth century BC, when Plato loudly complained about their pretensions to "knowledge." Certainly rhapsodic performance of epic song rapidly popularized Greek myths, previously confined to the immediate small male aristocratic audiences of *aoidoi,* who could never have been many in number.

The *aoidoi* continued to exist in Greece through the Archaic Period and continued to perform in public and occasionally to dictate their songs to recorders, but by the early fifth century BC, when composition in writing had become the rule, the *aoidoi* had disappeared. In addition to lyric poetry, the new technique of composition in writing made possible **choral song**, memorized for public presentation by a group of twelve or more boy or girl dancers (Greek *choros* = "dance"). Greatest of the choral poets was Pindar (c. 522–443 BC), whose surviving odes ordinarily contain a myth that reflects on the glory of the athlete being praised. Other early versions of Greek myths are found in surviving choral song by Pindar's contemporary Bacchylides (ba-**kil**-i-dēz), whose poem on Perseus we later quote.

By far our most important source from the Classical Period is the tragic plays, performed in Athens during the fifth century BC. The origin of **tragedy** is obscure. The word *tragoidia* means "goat song." Because the goat was an animal associated with Dionysus, at whose spring festival in Athens tragedies were staged, the name may be taken from the song sung during the sacrifice of a goat in the god's honor. Composed in writing, the script of a tragic play was not meant to be read but to serve as a prompt book for a live performance. Although afterward the texts were studied by students and quoted by intellectuals, all of Greek literature was meant to be heard, not read silently as we are reading this book and the literary selections within it.

The actors were always male (as the audience probably was) and, curiously, never more than three in number. They wore masks with stereotypical features to distinguish their roles (for example, old man, young girl, or king). They could communicate emotion only through the use of words and gestures, not by facial expression (Figure 3.10).

Tragedy was a form of popular entertainment directed to the complex concerns of the Athenian male citizen, including his taste for patriotic propaganda, horror, violence, and conflict between the sexes, themes that still command an attentive audience. Dionysus, the divine patron of tragedy, was a god of the *dêmos*, the "people" (that is, the male citizens). Pisistratus, an Athenian tyrant of the sixth century BC, encouraged production of the plays, no doubt to favor the emerging mercantile class who had placed him in power.

In the fourth century BC, Aristotle, the first systematic literary critic, attempted to explain the function of the violent plots of many tragedies by suggesting that, in beholding the dramatization of the destruction of a noble man or woman, the audience was cleansed "through pity and fear" (*Poetics* 6.2): pity for the protagonist ("first actor") and fear that the same fate might become one's own. Tragedy allowed the audience to experience intense, sometimes disturbing emotions that could not be experienced in real life without terrible cost. Tragedy painlessly expanded one's experience as a human being. No more effective answer has ever been offered to the censors who, throughout human history, have policed public entertainment to make it conform to preconceived notions of what is proper.

Aristotle also discussed the structure of Greek tragedy, noting how the protagonist is greater than we, rises to high fortune, then in a "turning around" (*peripeteia*) comes

FIGURE 3.10 A mask from tragedy, on the left, and one from comedy, on the right, perched on a ledge. The tragic mask is of a young woman, with large pins stuck in her coiffure. The comic mask wears the vines and grapes of Dionysus and may designate a satyr. Roman mosaic from Pompeii, c. AD 70.
(Museo Archeologico Nazionale, Naples; © Bettmann/CORBIS. All Rights Reserved)

to a "down-turning" (*katastrophê*, our word *catastrophe*) as the result of a "missing of the mark" or "mistake" (*hamartia*). The Greek word *hamartia* was early mistranslated as "flaw," leading to a misunderstanding of Greek tragedy that is still encountered today whenever anyone speaks of "the tragic flaw." Other explanations of the protagonist's misfortune attribute it to *hubris,* also often mistranslated as "pride," but really *hubris* means "violence" and only by extension the thoughtless behavior that encourages violence. Surely *hubris,* "violence," is punished in Greek myth—Clytemnestra killed her husband Agamemnon because he had killed their daughter Iphigenia, and the gods hated him because he had burned the temples of Troy—but neither "tragic flaw" nor "pride" is a useful category for understanding Greek tragedy and the myths it contains.

Aeschylus (525–456 BC) is the earliest tragedian whose works survive. We have seven plays of the more than eighty he wrote. Aeschylus loved long and elaborate descriptions, especially of foreign lands, and high-flown metaphorical language. He used myth to explore such grand moral issues as the conflict between individual will and divine destiny, and his characters tend to be types or to embody some principle.

Aeschylus lived when Athens basked in its greatest glory, and in his epitaph, which he himself composed, he mentioned only he fought at Marathon. Aeschylus' play, the *Persians,* about events of his own time, is the only surviving tragedy that does not have a mythical theme.

The career of **Sophocles** (c. 496–406 BC) exactly coincides with the political and cultural dominance of Athens. Born six years before the battle of Marathon, he died two years before Athens' humiliation by Sparta at the end of the Peloponnesian War. Of the 123 plays he wrote, seven survive. The vivid characters of his tightly plotted dramas typically are locked in bitter conflict. Sophocles likes to show the dignity of human beings in conflict with superior, often divine forces, a noble person caught in an overwhelming crisis. His heroes are lonely and unbending. They learn too late how they should act. He is deeply influenced by folklore, especially by the theme of the fulfillment of an oracle: In all his plays a prophecy or oracle predicts an unexpected outcome.

From **Euripides** (c. 484–406 BC) more plays survive than from Aeschylus and Sophocles combined, nineteen from the more than ninety he wrote. Euripides was a poet of great range who subjected the traditional myths to rigorous scrutiny and sometimes severe criticism. His characters are often deflated heroes, mere mortals caught up in some all-too-human squabble. His characters often veer off into abnormal mental states. Aristotle remarked that Sophocles showed men as they ought to be, but Euripides showed them as they really are. He reflects contemporary Athenian rhetoric; most of his plays center on a long debate. He has been called an irrationalist because he likes to celebrate the power of emotion over reason.

In Aeschylus, the inherited curse and divine will motivate the action; in Sophocles, fate stands behind events; in Euripides, passionate, often erotic, and especially female emotion drives the action. He is the most modern of the tragedians. His plays were often revived in antiquity and are commonly performed today. Euripides loved sensational bloody scenes and was not above happy endings.

The myths in tragedy are a web of interlocking family histories. Of the thousand tragedies performed between the end of the sixth century BC and the end of the fifth, not a single one was concerned exclusively with the doings of gods and goddesses, as far as we know, with what we have called divine myth. Tragedy shows little interest in the large mythic cycle that Hesiod describes, of creation, the battles of Titans and Olympians, and the births and loves of the gods (the *Prometheus* of Aeschylus stands almost alone). Although gods and goddesses appear on stage and have important roles, the focus is always on the men and women of the Greek legendary past and often on the passions and horrors of family life.

No possibility is omitted: Sons kill their mothers, wives kill their husbands, sons kill their fathers, mothers kill their children, a father kills his daughter or son or all his children, a daughter kills her father, brothers kill each other, sons kill their stepmothers, mothers expose their infants to die, men and women kill themselves. Every chord is struck on the theme of sexual trespass: A son sleeps with his mother, a father rapes his daughter, adultery is rampant, lustful women seduce honorable men (never the reverse), husbands desert their wives and mistresses. Complementing such extreme dishonesty are family relations characterized by intense love and devotion: between brother and sister, brother and brother, father and son, husband and wife, father and daughter.

In their loves and hates, the characters in Attic drama can be extreme cases, and in no sense do such tales reflect ordinary life. Yet the audience must have experienced corresponding emotions, although muted, in their own lives, even as we experience the same emotions today. At precisely the same time as the tragedies were being performed, with their gory scenes and exaggerated emotions, Greek philosophy and Greek science were coming into being. Some intellectuals, such as Anaxagoras (c. 500–428 BC), already subjected myth to a rigorous criticism, denying its validity as a means to achieve understanding (for the rise of rationalism and the critique of myth, see Chapter 25).

GREEK MYTH IN THE HELLENISTIC PERIOD

The conquests of Alexander the Great spread Greek culture throughout the eastern Mediterranean and deep into Asia. In 331 BC he founded Alexandria in the western delta in Egypt. Ironically, for the next three hundred years the center of Greek culture was to lie outside Greece. At Alexandria was established the first real library, the *Mouseion*, "Hall of the Muses," where the classics of Greek literature were gathered together and edited in standard editions. For the first time scholars appeared in the modern sense. They established critical principles to determine the original form of texts corrupted through repeated copying. All Greek texts that survive today passed through the hands of the Alexandrians, who pursued many other branches of learning, especially mathematics, astronomy, and medicine.

While *aoidoi* composed their poems in performance, and rhapsodes and tragic actors memorized their parts from a written prompt to display in public, literature in the Hellenistic Period seems to have been read aloud from the actual papyrus scroll, probably to a small audience of friends. (The practice of silent reading so familiar to us is scarcely attested until the fourth century AD.) The psychological effect of this shift was enormous. Literature was now written to be read, not performed. As a result, it became more self-conscious and learned. It was sometimes extremely abstract and difficult.

The Alexandrian librarian-scholars, keenly interested in myth, produced highly complex poems on mythical topics. One such poem, the *Alexandra* (= the Trojan princess Cassandra) by Lycophron, contains about three-thousand words, of which 518 are found nowhere else! Such learned, allusive poetry is called Alexandrian. The great scholar Callimachus (c. 305–240 BC), author of the first scientific history of literature, wrote mythical poetry of this kind. Although most of his work is lost, Callimachus profoundly influenced the Roman poets, and through them all subsequent Western literature. Another example is his learned pupil **Apollonius of Rhodes** (third century BC), who wrote an epic poem on Jason in the style of Homer, the *Argonautica,* our most important treatment of this myth, and the poem on which we base our own account (Chapter 19).

The Hellenistic Greeks were also keenly interested in the essential truth of myth. Influenced by the philosophical school of Stoicism founded by Zeno of Citium (a town in Cyprus), they refined the allegorical method of interpreting the ancient stories (see Chapter 25). As early as the fifth century BC, Greek scholars called mythographers, "myth-writers," began to gather into collections traditional stories about the doings of gods and heroes. In the Hellenistic Period these efforts increased.

The most important survivor is the *Library* **of Apollodorus** (c. AD 120), which is not a work of art, but a straightforward account of mythical events from the creation of the world to the death of Odysseus. It is one of our best sources of information about many Greek myths, especially those told in the lost Cyclic Poems. The great geographical survey of Greece by Pausanias (c. AD 150) also preserves much mythical material otherwise unknown. One of the founders of modern anthropology, classical scholar Sir James Frazer (1854–1941), author of *The Golden Bough* (see Chapter 25), derived many of his theories about myth from his study of Pausanias, on whom he wrote a famous commentary. A Latin handbook compiled from Greek sources by one Hyginus, from the second century AD, sometimes preserves variants unknown elsewhere.

THE ROMAN APPROPRIATION OF GREEK MYTH

Being careful students of Greek culture from an early date, the Romans eventually took over the whole body of Greek myths, with minor modifications, substituting similar Roman divinities for the Greek gods and goddesses (see Reference Chart, The Greek and Roman Pantheon, at the end of the book before the Index). Catullus (84–54 BC), a contemporary of Julius Caesar, is best known for his love poems but also wrote on mythical themes. **Vergil** (70–19 BC, sometimes spelled Virgil), the greatest Roman poet, told the story of Aeneas in his epic the *Aeneid.* This poem has one of our fullest descriptions of the underworld and our most vivid account of the sack of Troy. The poem also preserves the legends of Dido, queen of Carthage, and of Hercules' (Heracles') battle against the monster Cacus.

The poetry of the Roman **Ovid** (c. 43 BC–AD 17), a generation younger than Vergil, is our most important source from the period of the early Roman empire. Ovid was a man-about-town in Rome, of good birth, famed for his clever and witty verse. He moved in the highest society. Implicated in a sexual scandal that touched the emperor Augustus' own house, he was exiled in AD 8 to the town of Tomis on the Black Sea—remote, lonely, and cold—and there he died.

Ovid left behind a large body of poetry, but none more influential than the *Metamorphoses* (met-a-mor-**fōs**-ēz), by far the most substantial and influential repertory of Greek myth. This highly original work is a handbook in its own right, a compendium of more than two hundred stories ingeniously united by the theme of the transformation of shape. The poem is itself ever-changing, beginning with the transformation of chaos into cosmos and ending with the transformation of Julius Caesar, Augustus' great-uncle, into a star.

But in Ovid's literate and urbane retelling the old Greek tales have lost their religious overtones. Almost every story he tells is a love story, appealing to the refined, good-humored taste of the powerful, but often idle, Roman elite. Clever, engaging, irreverent, sometimes salacious, his *Metamorphoses,* more than any other single work, defines what the world thinks of as classical myth. Ovid wrote much love poetry besides the *Metamorphoses* that also alludes to myth. For centuries, from the Roman Period through the Middle Ages and the Renaissance, Ovid was the most important source of classical myth for artists, writers, and others. His influence has been incalculable, and every art museum has pictures inspired by his stories.

The Roman historian Livy (59 BC–AD 17), Ovid's contemporary, wrote an enormous work describing the history of Rome from the beginning down to his own time, about a fourth of which survives. The early books of Livy give legendary accounts that belong more to the study of myth than to history, and we examine them in Chapter 24. Seneca, tutor to the emperor Nero (ruled AD 54–68) and defender of Nero's crimes before the Roman senate, wrote voluminously, including several tragedies on mythical subjects. Characterized by extreme violence and savage emotion—hence we speak of "Senecan tragedy"— these plays made a deep impression on the literature of the Renaissance and on Shakespeare above all.

As long as myths were transmitted orally, they were subject to endless change and local variation. Written versions also introduced change to fit the concerns and conditions of the day. Eventually, however, and certainly by the Hellenistic Period, standard versions began to emerge of certain myths because of their treatment by such poets as Homer or Sophocles.

A difficulty we face in studying Greek myth is to separate the myth from the work of literature that embodies it. A focus on the myths alone would give us a bare-bones list of all the extant variations of, say, the story of Oedipus. A literary analysis, on the other hand, might concentrate on how Sophocles portrays character in his play *Oedipus the King.* Although this book is primarily about myth, which exists independently of any specific version, we touch on literary features of works that have made some myths better known than others. After all, we care about Achilles not because he fought at Troy, but because Homer described his personal torment in a way that speaks to us all as human beings.

This book has more in common with the method and intellectual interests of the Hellenistic mythographers than it does with the literary sources for myth, especially of the Greek Archaic and Classical periods. When we piece together, for example, the "myth of Dionysus" from different sources widely separated in time, interest, point of view, and even language (see Chapter 11), we present a special version of the myth that was never part of the direct experience of anyone in the ancient world. But such has always been the fate of myth: to be recast and reformed according to the needs of the day. The real mystery is why such stories continue to be so interesting!

KEY NAMES AND TERMS

Potnia Thêrôn, 56
Mesopotamia, 59
Sumerians, 60
An, 62
Inanna, 63
Enlil, 63
Enki, 63
Semites, 65
Akkadians, 65
Hebrews, 66
Hittites, 67
Homer, 68
epic, 68

Hesiod, 69
Homeric Hymns, 71
humanism, 72
choral song, 73
tragedy, 73
Aeschylus, 74
Sophocles, 75
Euripides, 75
Apollonius of Rhodes, 76
Library of Apollodorus, 77
Vergil, 77
Ovid, 77
Metamorphoses, 77

FURTHER READING CHAPTER 3

MOTHER-GODDESS

Gimbutas, Marija, *The Language of the Goddess* (San Francisco, 1989). Of value, according to Joseph Campbell, who wrote the introduction, to serve the "need in our time for a general transformation of consciousness," but many reject such unhistorical approaches to the study of myth.

Goodison, Lucy, and Christine Morris, *Ancient Goddesses: The Myths and the Evidence* (Madison, WI, 1999). Essays by various scholars arguing that the "Great Mother-Goddess" is a fiction of modern times. Critical of Gimbutas (above).

NEAR EASTERN BACKGROUND (SEE ALSO FURTHER READING FOR CHAPTER 13)

Frankfort, H., et al., *The Intellectual Adventure of Ancient Man* (Chicago, 1946). Exciting and penetrating account of myth and culture in Egypt, Mesopotamia, and Palestine in the Bronze Age. See also *Before Philosophy* (New York, 1949), a shortened edition of the same book. A classic.

Friedman, Richard Elliott, *Who Wrote the Bible?* (New York, 1989). Lucid summary of two hundred years of biblical scholarship, reconstructing how our present text came into being.

McCall, Henrietta, *Mesopotamian Myths* (Austin, TX, 1990). Excellent short introduction to the topic.

Pritchard, James B., ed., *Ancient Near Eastern Texts Relating to the Old Testament*, 3rd ed. (Princeton, NJ, 1969). The standard collection of translations by many experts, with commentary, of original texts written in the many languages and scripts from the ancient Near East; a book of incomparable scholarly value.

West, M. L., *The East Face of Helicon: West Asiatic Elements in Greek Poetry and Myth* (Oxford, UK, 1997). Argues that Greek literature is Near Eastern in origin.

GENERAL STUDIES OF GREEK MYTH

Gantz, Timothy, *Early Greek Myth, A Guide to Literary and Artistic Sources* (Baltimore, MD, 1993). A modernization and English-language rewrite of the nineteenth-century German *Griechische Mythologie* by Carl Robert and Ludwig Preller. This invaluable handbook traces the historical development of each myth in detail, giving ancient sources for variants and including references to ancient artistic representations.

Graf, Fritz, *Greek Mythology, An Introduction,* trans. Thomas Marier (Baltimore, MD, 1993). Readable and learned overview; one of the best short books on Greek myth.

Powell, Barry B., *A Short Introduction to Classical Myth* (Upper Saddle River, NJ, 2002). A shortened version of *Classical Myth,* with new material on definition, art, and folklore.

Smith, R. Scott, and Stephen M. Trzaskoma, *Apollodorus' Library and Hyginus' Fabulae. Two Handbooks of Greek Mythology* (Indianapolis, IN, 2007). Good recent translations of these important ancient sources.

Tripp, Edward, *The Meridian Handbook of Classical Mythology* (New York, 1974). Desktop reference to Greek myths if you just want to know the stories. Useful references to primary sources.

EPIC AND ORAL THEORY

Foley, J. M., *The Theory of Oral Composition: History and Methodology* (Bloomington, IN, 1988; reprint 1992). Balanced survey of current thinking, by a leader in the field.

Huxley, G. L., *Greek Epic Poetry* (Cambridge, MA, 1969). Reconstructs the contents of the lost Cyclic Poems.

Lord, Albert, *The Singer of Tales,* 2nd ed., S. Mitchell and Gregory Nagy, eds. (Cambridge, MA, 2000). The theory that Homer was an oral poet who composed without the aid of writing, by a student of Milman Parry. One of the most influential works of literary criticism of the twentieth century, this reprint of the 1965 edition contains a CD-ROM with Parry's photos and film clips and recordings of South Slavic oral poets.

Powell, Barry B., *Homer and the Origin of the Greek Alphabet* (Cambridge, UK, 1991). Gathers the complex evidence supporting the thesis that a Euboean invented the Greek alphabet c. 800 BC to record the poems of Homer.

———, *Writing and the Origins of Greek Literature* (Cambridge, UK, 2002). Ties the nature of Greek literature to the technology that makes it possible.

Shelmerdine, Susan, *The Homeric Hymns* (Newburyport, MA, 1995). Good translations and extensive notes to all the hymns.

TRAGEDY (SEE ALSO FURTHER READING FOR CHAPTER 11)

Baldry, H. C., *The Greek Tragic Theatre* (New York, 1973). What the Athenian stage looked like, how the actors performed, the Athenian tragic contests, and other topics.

Easterling, P. E., ed., *The Cambridge Companion to Greek Tragedy* (Cambridge, UK, 1997). Essays by different scholars on performance and reception, with discussion of productions of tragedy on stage and in film since the Renaissance.

Lesky, Albin, *Greek Tragedy* (London, 1976). Literary analyses of the surviving plays, by a distinguished modern scholar.

Lewis, David M., and Arthur Pickard-Cambridge, *The Dramatic Festivals of Athens,* 2nd ed., ed. John Gould (Oxford, UK, 1989). The standard scholarly study of the festivals at which tragedy was performed, tragic costume, how the prize was awarded, makeup of the audience, and training of actors.

Storey, I. C., and A. Allan, *A Guide to Ancient Greek Drama* (Malden, MA, 2004). Fine survey of drama, tragedy, satyr-play, and comedy, with discussion of theoretical approaches and plot summaries.

OVID

Bogel, B., ed., *Brill's Companion to Ovid* (Leiden, Netherlands, 2002). Up-to-date collection of essays.

Galinsky, G. Karl, *Ovid's Metamorphoses, An Introduction to the Basic Aspects* (Oxford, UK, 1975). The best general book on Ovid's poem, with excellent analysis of the differences between Greek and Roman myth.

Hardie, Philip, ed., *The Cambridge Companion to Ovid* (Cambridge, UK, 2002). A second collection of essays (after Bogel, above).

MYTH AND ART

Carpenter, Thomas H., *Art and Myth in Ancient Greece* (London, 1991). The representation of Greek myths in Greek art, arranged by subject, with many illustrations.

Lexicon Iconographicum Mythologiae Classicae (LIMC) (Zurich, 1981–1999). Massive multivolume compilation of every representation of every myth, with scholarly commentary, in several languages (but mostly English). The single leading resource for the study of myth and art in the ancient world, an invaluable resource but available only in research libraries.

Woodford, Susan, *Images of Myths in Classical Antiquity* (Cambridge, UK, 2003). Up-to-date review.

WEB SITES

The *Bryn Mawr Classical Review* at http://bmcr.brynmawr.edu/, eds. R. Hamilton and J. J. O'Donnell. A searchable archive of recent publications pertaining to the classical world. The leading review journal of classical studies.

The *Perseus Project* at www.perseus.tufts.edu, ed. G. Crane and others, has thousands of links to texts, works of art, maps, lexica, and other aids to understanding myth and the classical world. Many of these links can be reached directly from www.prenhall.com/powell.

CHAPTER 4

MYTHS OF CREATION

THE RISE OF ZEUS

Sing all this to me, Muses, you who dwell on Olympus: from the beginning tell me, which of the gods first came to be.

HESIOD, *Theogony* 114–115

ALTHOUGH IN CLASSICAL MYTH there are always different or even contradictory versions of a story, to the question "Where does the world come from?" the poet Hesiod gave the answer best known to the Greeks who lived after him. In contrast to the familiar story told in the biblical book of Genesis (see Perspective 4.2), where God stands outside of the creation and exists before it, Hesiod tells of the origin of the universe through succeeding generations of gods. **Cosmogony**, a story that explains the "origin of the world" (*kosmos* = "world"), is for Hesiod the same as **theogony** (*theos* = "god"), a story that explains the "origin of the gods" and their rise to power. Hesiod's thousand-line poem, the *Theogony*, composed in the eighth century BC, is in external form an elaborate hymn to Zeus, the Greek version of the Indo-European sky-god, and we have already examined Hesiod's invocation to the Muses, who grant him the power to sing this song. To explain Zeus's supremacy in the world Hesiod must go back to the beginning of all things, to the generations of **Chaos** (kā-os), "chasm," **Gaea** (jē-a), "earth," and **Uranus** (yūr-a-nus), "sky." **(For a complete version of the *Theogony*, go to http://www.sacred-texts.com/cla/hesiod/ theogony.htm)**

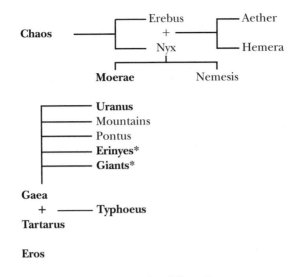

*From blood of Uranus that fell on Gaea.

CHART 4.1 The First Generation of Gods

THE CHILDREN OF CHAOS

Hesiod begins his account thus (see Chart 4.1):

[116]   Chaos was first to appear, then Gaea, Earth, the broad-bosomed,
unshakable base of things, then Tartarus, windswept and dark,
deep in the caverns of broad-wayed earth. And Eros, the fairest
of all the immortals, arose, who frees us all from our sorrows,
but ruins our hearts' good sense, breaking the wisest intention
of gods and mortals alike. From Chaos came Erebus, darkness,
and Nyx, night, mother of Aether, radiance, and Hemera, day;
these Nyx conceived by uniting with Erebus, gloomy and somber.

HESIOD, *Theogony* 116–125

Hesiod's cosmogony is hard to understand, and its meaning is still debated.
Certainly first came Chaos, a being of some kind that was not always there. Where it
comes from Hesiod does not say, and we are not sure what Hesiod meant by it. Chaos
is related etymologically to our words *gap* and *yawn*; we might translate it as "chasm,"
and some understand it as the opening from which the other primordial beings arose.

Implicit in the word is the separation of two things to make a gap in the middle.
After Chaos came Gaea, Mother Earth, the personification of the earth beneath us, the
solid, sure foundation of the world. Tartarus, a name of unknown meaning, is usually
some place below Earth and often confused in Greek myth with the abode of Hades,
but Hesiod personifies Tartarus as one of the primordial creatures by which Gaea
later has offspring. Hesiod is struggling to delineate space in mythical terms, working
toward the scheme Olympus/topmost, Gaea/middle, and Tartarus/bottommost.

After Chaos also appeared **Eros**, "sexual love" or "attraction," the source of motion that brings sexual beings together to produce still more offspring. Eros is a being as well as the force that drives Hesiod's complex genealogies. Hesiod does not say that Gaea, Tartarus, and Eros sprang from Chaos, and some think that he meant the four to represent independent aspects of the primeval stuff from which the world emerged: a gaping (Chaos); the foundation of all that is (Gaea); the underside of that foundation (Tartarus); and the principle of sexual attraction, which ensures future generation and change (Eros). Although I follow this interpretation in Chart 4.1, Hesiod's statement that Erebus (**er**-e-bus), "darkness," and Nyx (nux), "night," came from Chaos may imply that the other primeval beings did too; the Near Eastern myths on which Hesiod bases his account had in fact sought for a single origin to the multiplicities of the world.

The Children of Gaea: The Titans and Their Cousins

From Earth, the foundation of all that is, sprang a host of beings, bewildering in their complexity and in the obscurity of their origins and nature. Most important were the **Titans** (**tī**-tans), but the monstrous **Cyclopes** (sī-**klō**-pēz) and the even stranger **Hecatonchires** (he-ka-ton-**kī**-rēz) had important roles to play in the world's early days (Chart 4.2).

The Titans

According to Hesiod, then, Gaea first bore, asexually, Uranus ("sky"), and the Mountains on her upper side that rise into the sky. Then she bore her watery doublet, Pontus ("sea"). Then in sexual union with her son Uranus/Sky, Gaea/Earth produced the six male and six female Titans, a word of unknown meaning (Chart 4.2). **Cronus** (**krō**-nus), who will contend with Uranus for power, is named as the last born. The Titans rarely are represented in art and do not often play a role in later stories or in religious cult. However, their unions were to produce a whole cycle of divinities:

[126]   The first of the children of Gaea, equal in size to herself,
      hiding her body completely, was Uranus, star-studded heaven.
      The blessed gods needed solider ground to support their feet;
      she bore long ranges of Mountains, pleasant haunts of immortals.
130   Pontus she bore, the unharvested sea with its raging swell,
      without the pleasure of love. Thereafter Gaea was bedded
      with Uranus, lord of heaven, and bore deep-swirling Oceanus,
      Coeus, Crius, Hyperion, Iapetus, Theia and Rhea, Themis,
      Mnemosynê, gold Phoebê, and fair-featured Tethys.
135   Last of all she gave birth to Cronus, that scheming intriguer,
      cleverest child of her brood, who hated his lecherous father.

HESIOD, *Theogony* 126–138

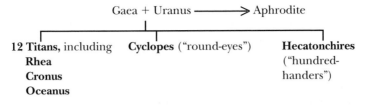

CHART 4.2 The Offspring of Gaea and Uranus

Uranus evidently was the same size as Gaea and covered her completely, as if locked in perpetual sexual embrace (Figure 4.1). The birth of Pontus, "sea," reminds us of the watery nature of the primordial element in the Mesopotamian myths that we examine later in this chapter. Although the oppositions of up/down, Sky/Earth have now appeared, the separation of the primal opposites is yet to be fixed and made permanent.

Two notable Titans are the watery male **Oceanus** (ō-sē-a-nus) and female Tethys (tē-this). According to a passing reference in Homer, Oceanus and Tethys themselves gave birth to all the gods: a good example of a different cosmogony parallel to Hesiod's. Oceanus is a river that encircles the world, where the dome of the sky

FIGURE 4.1 Sky and Earth, from the Egyptian Papyrus of Tameniu, c. 1000 BC. The notion that Sky and Earth are beings once united in sexual embrace, separated at the moment of creation, was widespread in the ancient world, as in this representation, which shows Sky as a woman (= Nut, pronounced "noot") and Earth (= Geb) as a sexually excited man, longing to be reunited with his mate. Other ancient peoples, however, thought of the earth as female and the sky as male, but the Egyptians, as the Greek historian Herodotus remarked, "did everything backwards." To the right, the air-god Shu, who separates Sky from Earth, shows adoration to his parents. The hieroglyph in front of him means "the West," where the sun sets, thus guaranteeing its rising in an eternal cycle. The animal-gods on the left stand for creative power: The ram is probably a creator-god and the goose is "the great" cackler ("great" is written in hieroglyphs) who greeted the world at its rising. (British Museum, London;

touches the flat surface of the earth. All the waters that emerge from wells, springs, fountains, and rivers are also fed by the flow of Oceanus. The pair united to give birth to the six thousand Oceanids (ō-**sē**-a-nids), spirits of the sea, rivers, and springs.

Coeus, Crius, and Theia, "divine," are scarcely more than names. Phoebê, "brilliant," must have something to do with the light of the sky, as Themis, "law," refers to the earth, that which is fixed and settled, like the oracles delivered in her name. The oracular shrine of Delphi belonged to Themis before Apollo took it over. Themis will bear children to Zeus, as will Mnemosynê (nē-**mos**-i-nē), "memory." The name of Iapetus seems related to that of the biblical Japheth, the son of Noah and, in the biblical account, the ancestor of Europeans. Cronus and **Rhea** (**rē**-a), doublets for Uranus and Gaea, are parents or grandparents of the twelve Olympians, including Zeus, the king of the gods and the central subject of praise in Hesiod's poem.

Cyclopes, Hecatonchires

In addition to the Titans, Gaea bore, after union with Uranus, three Cyclopes, "round-eyes," and the mighty Hecatonchires, the "hundred-handers." Sometimes we can understand the meaning of their names, usually allegories, but not always, and they have little role to play as individuals in Greek myth:

[139]   Then Gaea gave birth to Cyclopes, strong and abrupt of emotion,
140   Brontes, Steropes, Arges, stubborn, determined of spirit,
        forgers of thunder for Zeus and makers of bolts of his lightning.
        For the most part, they resembled in features the other immortals,
        but each had only one eye, in the middle part of his forehead.
        Violence, power, and shrewdness attended each of their actions.
145   Still other children were born to Uranus, bedded with Gaea:
        three huge powerful beings, whose names can scarcely be spoken,
        Cottus, Briareus, Gyes, offspring of terrible power.
        A hundred terrible arms hung down from their muscular shoulders,
        and fifty heads surmounted their mighty necks and their limbs.
150   Invincible terrible power glared out from each of the monsters.
        Of all the children descended from Uranus, husband of Gaea,
        these their father most hated, from the very day of their birth.

HESIOD, *Theogony* 139–155

Unlike the famous shepherd Cyclops Polyphemus, son of Poseidon, who imprisoned Odysseus in his cave (see Chapter 22), Hesiod's Cyclopes combined the wisdom of the metallurgist with great strength. They were the clever smiths of the gods. Taking raw iron from the depths of earth, their mother, they made the irresistible weapon of victory: lightning. Their names Brontes (**bron**-tēz), "thunderer," Steropes (**ster**-o-pēz), "flasher," and Arges (**ar**-jēz), "brightener," reflect the noise and brilliance of their marvelous weapon.

Finally, Uranus and Gaea bore the three Hecatonchires, who each had a hundred arms that shot from their shoulders, as well as fifty heads, beings who can easily crush any opponent in their mighty hands.

Hyperion's Children: Sun, Moon, Dawn

The Titan Hyperion ("he who goes above") is a sun-god, father to the better-known **Helius**, also a sun-god (see Figure 1.1); to Selenê (se-**lē**-ne), the moon; and to **Eos** (**ē**-os), the dawn. A *Homeric Hymn to Helius* portrays the journey of Helius across the sky in his chariot, an image familiar in the history of art. A story made famous by Ovid is told about **Phaëthon** (**fā**-e-thon), a son of Helius and Clymenê (**klī**-men-ē), an Oceanid. It is a good example of how, in the hands of the urbane Roman Ovid, descriptions of the world's early days became a prettified fantasy embodying the teasing morals, "Don't be too curious about your origins, and don't get too big for your breeches!"

Although Phaëthon's mother was married to the king of Ethiopia, she assured her son that his father was the sun. Overhearing a companion doubt his parentage, Phaëthon begged his mother for confirmation. She urged him to journey to the house of Helius himself and there present himself to his father.

The boy wondered at the sun-god's shining palace and its brilliant columns. Helius set aside the crown of rays coming from his head so that he might embrace his son. To prove that he was truly Phaëthon's father, Helius gave him one wish, anything he desired. To Helius' horror, Phaëthon asked that he be allowed to drive the chariot of the sun across the sky.

Helius warned Phaëthon of the danger, but he could not go back on his promise. At first Phaëthon drove carefully along the paths of the sky, but soon the four horses sensed the unsure hand on the reins and leaped from their accustomed path in the heaven. Frightened by the animals of the zodiac blazing above him, Phaëthon lost control of the car, and the horses dashed down close to earth, nearly setting the world ablaze. Libya, a desert today, was scorched and seared and the skin of the Ethiopians burned black. Then the horses soared high toward the stars. To save the world, Zeus blasted the boy from the car. He fell into the river Eridanus (the Po, in northern Italy).

Only one story was told of Selenê, the moon, a favorite with love poets both ancient and modern. Having fallen in love with the handsome shepherd Endymion (en-**dim**-i-on), Selenê seduced him while he slept in his cave and eventually bore him fifty daughters. At Selenê's request, Zeus placed Endymion in an eternal sleep, so that he might never grow old.

Eos, the dawn, was even more lascivious than Selenê and had many love affairs. Above all she loved **Tithonus** (ti-**thō**-nus), a Trojan prince. Tithonus received a boon like Endymion's, but with a less serene outcome. The story is told as an aside in the *Homeric Hymn to Aphrodite* (perhaps from the seventh century BC; the rest of the hymn appears in Chapter 9):

[218]   So too golden-throned Eos abducted the noble Tithonus,
another man of your race,° and one who resembled the gods.
220   She went to beg for a favor from Cronus' dark-clouded son,
that Tithonus should be an immortal, living on forever and ever.
Zeus nodded assent to her prayer. But Eos, poor foolish lady,
neglected to ask that her lover might never be subject to aging.
As long as the springtime of life continued, a happy Tithonus

219. *your race:* The Trojans.

225   rejoiced with his Eos the golden-throned, the early-born goddess.
       But when gray hair appeared on Tithonus' cheeks and his temples,
       more and more Lady Eos avoided their once happy bed.
       She attended him still in her house, rendering all her affection,
       giving him food and ambrosia and clothing his chilly old body.
230   But finally gloomy old age laid its ponderous burden upon him.
       No more could he lift his bones to totter, decrepit and feeble.
       At last the goddess agreed on this as the plan she must follow:
       She closed him up in his room, and locked up the glorious portal.
       Inside, his piping old voice droned endlessly. Gone is the vigor
235   he used to enjoy, and the use of limbs once handsome and supple.

Homeric Hymn to Aphrodite 218–238

Later versions report that Tithonus shriveled up and turned into a cicada, chirping uselessly in the wind.

CRONUS AGAINST URANUS

Although Uranus and Gaea bore many children, none could come forth into the light, for Uranus/Sky hated his own offspring:

[156]   As soon as each child was conceived, Uranus kept it well hidden,
        refusing it access to light, deep in the womb of the earth,
        and gloated over his action, while Gaea groaned in her travail.
        But she planned a treacherous scheme. First inventing gray steel°
160   (till that day unknown), she fashioned a terrible sickle.
        She told her children the plan, hoping to stiffen their courage,
        though sorely disturbed herself. "O children, you whom I bore
        to a wicked and terrible father. If you will only support me,
        we can avenge the shame and disgrace he has loaded upon you.
165   For he it was who first devised such hideous actions."
        At that fear silenced them all. Nobody dared give an answer,
        till the wily Cronus bravely replied to the lady his mother.
        "Mother, I am quite ready to carry through with this matter,
        for I scorn our accursed father, who plotted such terrible things."
170   So he spoke, and the heart of Gaea leaped up in delight.
        She hid him, couched in an ambush, and into his hands she delivered
        the sickle, toothed like a saw. Her plot worked out as she planned it.
        When Uranus came to her presence, bringing with him the darkness,
        and, panting with lust, embraced the mighty body of Gaea,
175   from ambush Cronus' left hand seized the genital parts of his father.
        He reached out his right with the sickle, saw-toothed, deadly, and sharp.
        Like a reaper, he sliced away the genitals of his own father,
        flinging them over his shoulder, to roll wherever chance sent them.
        But they did not fly from his hand down to the earth, ineffective,

159. *steel:* The sickle is actually said to be *adamantine,* "invincible," a mythical hard substance often translated "steel," which it probably was not. The word is the source of our *diamond.*

180   for Gaea absorbed the gory drops that rained down upon her,
          and after a year had passed she bore the frightful Erinyes,
          the Giants gleaming in armor, holding long spears in their hands,
          and the Melian Nymphs, whom mortals reverence all the world over.

HESIOD, Theogony 156–187

Although Hesiod speaks of Uranus "bringing with him the darkness and panting with lust," the meaning of the story depends on an image of Uranus/Sky and Gaea/Earth as locked in perpetual intercourse. Uranus/Sky lay constantly across Gaea/Earth, fecundating her but never allowing his children to emerge from the mother's body. There is no space where the activity of the world can take place. By slicing away his genitals, Cronus broke away Sky, allowing him to rise to the place where he belongs. A provisional separation of the two primal elements is now made permanent. The world has reached its proper configuration, Sky above and Earth beneath, with Tartarus attached somewhere below. All around flows Oceanus, the primordial water.

But the permanent separation of the first elements is bought at the high cost of deceit and violence of son against father. Uranus/Sky mightily cursed his treacherous son Cronus. Fecundated by the drops of blood that fell from the ghastly wound of Uranus/Sky, Earth gave birth to the **Erinyes** (e-**rin**-i-ēz), the Furies, ferocious female spirits who haunt anyone who sheds kindred blood, driving them into madness. The Erinyes are especially malignant because kindred blood is, in a sense, one's own. From other drops of the bloody gore sprang up the **Giants**, "earthborn ones," beings of enormous strength and unbridled violence, who one day will bring their power to bear against Zeus and his Olympian brothers and sisters.

The Birth of Aphrodite, Monsters, and Sea Deities

Hesiod goes on to describe the birth of Aphrodite:

[188]   As for the genitals, slashed away by the sickle of steel,
        their impetus carried them out from shore to the tide of the sea.
190   For years the waters swirled them about, as white foam kept oozing
        from out the immortal flesh. Within it there grew up a maiden
        who drifted first to holy Cythera,° then on to Cyprus.
        There she emerged from the sea as a modest and beautiful goddess
        around whose slim-ankled feet arose all the flowers of springtime.
195   Gods and mortals alike call her Aphrodite, the Foamborn,
        or else Cytherea, to honor the island where first she was seen.
        Eros walked by her side, and fair Desire came after
        as she joined the race of the gods. These are the honors she holds:
        giggling whispers of girls, the smiling deceptions they practice,
200   as well as the honeyed delights and all the allurements of passion.

HESIOD, Theogony 188–206

192. *Cythera*: An island off the southeastern coast of the Peloponnesus, where there was an early temple to Aphrodite.

The blood fell on the earth, but the genitals themselves fell into the sea. The sea foam, mixed with semen oozing from the organ, sloshed around them until from the "foam" (Greek *aphros*) appeared a being of dreadful power, Aphrodite, goddess of sexual love (Figure 4.2; compare Perspective Figure 9a). Born from the bloody genitals of a cosmic deity, Aphrodite represents the universal force of irresistible sexual desire, a fruit of mutilation and violence. The destructive power of sexual attraction is a central theme in Greek myth.

The Titans, the Cyclopes, and the Hecatonchires were born of Gaea's union with her son Uranus, but she also had sexual relations with Pontus ("sea"), another of her sons. From this union came a host of other offspring (Chart 4.3), who mostly have little importance in later myth or make only a brief appearance in heroic legend. Some are notable for their monstrous shape or, like the sea that begot them, are changeable in appearance.

Etymologically, *monster* means "that at which you point in surprise," and in Greek art the monstrous descendants of Sea and Earth were most often represented as mixtures of animal and human parts. This tradition derives from Mesopotamian and Egyptian art, but the Greeks changed the meanings of the fabulous creatures whose forms they copied. For example, the Egyptians represented the souls of the blessed dead as human-headed birds. Being ghosts, they could fly where they pleased and enjoy the pleasant gardens in front of

FIGURE 4.2 Aphrodite rising from the sea, from the so-called Ludovisi Throne, c. 465 BC. The relief, found in Rome during the Renaissance, seems once to have decorated an altar in a Greek city in southern Italy. The goddess wears a simple see-through chiton (a type of dress). Two women, probably Horae, "seasons," standing on a pebbled shore, help to lift her from a deep pool between two rocks.   (Museo Nazionale delle Terme, Rome; author's photo)

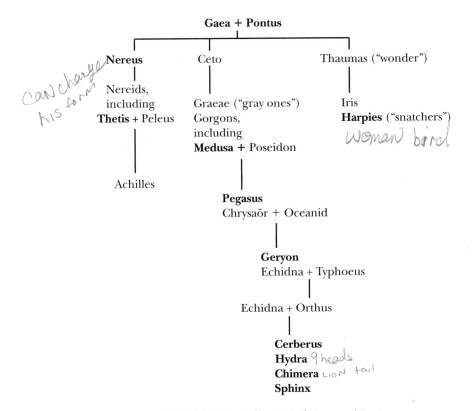

CHART 4.3 The Offspring of Gaea and Pontus

their tombs and the offerings placed there by pious relatives. But in Greek art, human-headed birds became the Harpies, "snatchers," grandchildren of Gaea and Pontus, hostile spirits of storm who appear from nowhere to carry away the living (Figure 4.3).

The Sirens, who lured sailors to their deaths, were shown in the same way, although the Sirens were not descended from Gaea and Pontus (see Figure 22.3). Another example is the **Sphinx**, also a descendant of Gaea and Pontus. The Egyptians symbolized the beneficent and divine power of Pharaoh as a human-headed lion, and in this form Pharaoh watched over Egypt in death as in life. The Greeks changed the Sphinx's sex from male to female, added wings, and explained the name as meaning "strangler," a deadly spirit of plague who in Greek myth besieged the city of Thebes (see Figure 18.3, Perspective Figure 18.1).

The Greeks also invented their own ways to portray monsters in their art, although they preserved the Near Eastern practice of combining parts from different creatures or simply reduplicating normal parts. The Gorgons had a woman's body to which wings were attached, snakes instead of hair, and boar's

FIGURE 4.3 Relief panel from the Harpy Tomb in Lycia, south side, at Xanthos in southern Turkey. The Lycians were not Greeks but were heavily influenced by Greek myth. Between the harpies on either side, carrying away the soul of the deceased, shown as a small person, is a seated figure of uncertain sex receiving a dove from a standing female. The seated figure is holding a pomegranate in the left hand and an unidentified object (possibly fruit or an egg) in the right hand. Limestone, c.480–470 BC.   (British Museum, London; © Trustees of the British Museum / Art Resource, New York)

tusks for teeth (see Figure 14.7). Geryon (**jer**-i-on), an enemy of Heracles, had three bodies joined at the waist; his dog Orthus had two heads. Echidna was an ordinary woman from the buttocks up, but a serpent below, "a glimmering flesh-eater in the inky caverns of hallowed earth," as Hesiod puts it. **Cerberus** was a fifty-headed (or three-headed) hound who guarded the gates of Hades' realm (Figure 4.4).

The water-serpent Hydra, "watery," sometimes had seven heads. Most bizarre was the **Chimera** (ki-**mē**-ra), "she-goat," a lion with a snake's tail and a goat's head growing from its back (Figure 4.5). The shapes of the descendants of Gaea and Pontus could also be drawn from nature, although they possessed extraordinary powers. Ceto (**sē**-to), "sea monster," was a whale or enormous fish. The Graeae (**grē**-ē), "gray ones," were "fair-cheeked hags, gray from birth," as Hesiod describes them. The Nemean lion looked like a lion but could not be killed by ordinary means (see Figure 15.2). Nereus (**nē**-rūs) was the wise Old Man of the Sea, a prophetic deity, as are many sea-gods. Ordinarily he had a human shape, but he could also change his shape at will into fire, a leopard, a serpent, or a tree. He sired the fifty-two Nereids (**nē**-re-idz), a group of sea-spirits hard to distinguish from their cousins the Oceanids but far fewer in number (the suffix -*id* means "daughter" or "descendant"). The Nereids live at the bottom of the sea seated on golden thrones

FIGURE 4.4 Heracles and Cerberus. The tyrant Eurystheus compelled Heracles to perform twelve contests, the last being to capture Cerberus and drag him to the upper world. Here Heracles shows the beast to the cowardly Eurystheus, who raises his hands in terror and stands in a bronze pot for protection. Heracles has the dog on a leash; he raises his club in his other hand. Snakes spring from Cerberus' forelegs and head. This pot was found in Cerveteri in Italy (ancient Etruscan Caere) and was either made there by a Greek immigrant, c. 530 BC, or imported from a Greek city in Asia Minor.   (Musée du Louvre, Paris; Reunion des Musees Nationaux/Art Resource, New York)

FIGURE 4.5 The Chimera, an Etruscan bronze from the fifth century BC, with a lion's body, the head of a goat protruding from its back, and a serpent's tail. According to a variant on the folktale type called "Potiphar's Wife," the hero Bellerophon killed the Chimera (see Chapter 16). The Chimera seems to originate among the Hittites in central Anatolia (Turkey).   (Museo Archeologico Nazionale, Florence; University of Wisconsin–Madison Photo Archive)

and embody the lovely, gentle aspect of the sea. The best-known Nereid was **Thetis** (**thē**-tis), mother of Achilles. Like her father, Thetis could change her shape at will (see Figure 20.3).

ZEUS AGAINST CRONUS: THE BATTLE WITH THE TITANS

Hesiod tells how Uranus tyrannized Gaea with his sexual demands, smothering her and keeping her and all else down. With the overthrow of Uranus, Cronus became the first king of the world. He ruled over a complex realm filled with many new beings. He had to be underhanded, violent, and suspicious to maintain his power. Told by his parents that he would fall victim to one of his children, Cronus feared his children and swallowed them as fast as they issued forth from his wife and sister, Rhea. These children were Hestia, Demeter, Hera, Hades, Poseidon, and Zeus, six gods who would one day divide the power of the world among themselves:

[453]   Rhea, submitting to Cronus, bore to him wonderful children:
         Hestia, gold-sandaled Hera, Demeter, and Hades the mighty,
455   implacable, him whose dwelling is under the earth in the darkness;
         Poseidon, thundering shaker of earth, and Zeus the wiliest schemer,
         father of gods and men, whose thunder shatters the cosmos.
         Each of them Cronus devoured as they came from the holy womb
         to the knees of Rhea. All this, lest she bear him a lordly successor,
460   to hold high honor and rule in heaven among the immortals.
         For his fate, as starry Uranus told him, and Gaea, his mother,
         was one day to fall from his throne, displaced by one of his children,
         in spite of the power he held, through the plottings of great Zeus.
         He therefore kept vigilant watch, and lay in wait to devour
465   each of his children at birth. Rhea mourned, but she never forgot.

HESIOD, *Theogony* 453–467

Rhea went to her parents, Gaea and Uranus, for advice. They instructed her to journey to Crete and there to bear her youngest child, Zeus. This she did, then hid him in a mountain cave, where he was brought up by nymphs on milk from the goat Amalthea (am-al-**thē**-a) and honey from Melissa, the "bee." His infant cries were drowned by the clashing cymbals of the Corybantes (kor-i-**ban**-tēz), perhaps "whirlers," also called Curetes (ku-**rē**-tēz), "young men," or warriors. When Cronus asked for the latest child, she gave him a stone wrapped in swaddling clothes. Stupid Cronus gulped it down. In this way Zeus was saved and grew into manhood.

Hesiod is strangely silent about what happened next, noting only that Zeus eventually forced Cronus to vomit up the children, Zeus's brothers and sisters. Later sources say that the Oceanid Metis, "cleverness," gave Cronus an emetic potion and that Cronus vomited out the children in reverse order to his swallowing them. The stone came out too and was later displayed for all to see in

Apollo's shrine at Delphi. Conical and decorated with carving, this stone was called the *omphalos,* "navel." Priests poured oil on it every day, and unspun wool decorated it during festivals (see Figure 7.5).

Now Zeus became king of the gods, and he and his brothers and sisters took up their abode on Mount Olympus (except for Hades, who ruled the underworld). But the Titans resented their rule. They banded together and attacked the Olympians in the stupendous **Titanomachy** (tī-tan-**o**-ma-kē), "battle of the Titans" (*machê* in Greek means "battle"). Only the Titan Themis and her son Prometheus (prō-**mē**-thūs) dared side with Zeus in the gruesome conflict:

[629] For a long time the Titans and the other gods sprung of Cronus
630 savagely battled each other. The lordly Titans came charging
  down from the heights of Othrys°; the gods, bestowers of blessings,
  whom fair-haired Rhea had borne, bedding in union with Cronus,
  counter-attacked from Olympus.° For ten full years did they battle,
  no rest, no truce in the strife, no victory crowning their efforts.

HESIOD, *Theogony* 629–638

631. *Othrys:* A mountain south of the plain of Thessaly, in northern Greece. 633. *Olympus:* North of the Thessalian plain.

Zeus learned from Gaea that he could win the battle only with the help of the three Hecatonchires, the hundred-handers. He released them and the Cyclopes from Tartarus where Uranus, fearing their power, had imprisoned them. Weakened from long confinement, the Hecatonchires partook of a mythical drink called *nectar* (perhaps meaning "that which overcomes death") and an equally mythical food known as *ambrosia* ("deathless stuff") and soon regained strength. In gratitude, the Cyclopes, wonderful smiths, made for Zeus the thunderbolt, his special weapon:

[666] On that very day the immortals began their terrible contest,
  male and female, the Titans and those descended from Cronus,
  and those whom Zeus had freed from Erebus,° deep in the darkness,
  back to the light of day. A hundred hands, strong and brawny,
670 grew from the shoulders of each, with fifty heads in the middle.
  Forward they marched to war with the Titans, giving no quarter,
  each one brandishing broken-off fragments of cliff as his missiles.
  Against them advanced the Titans, each one urging his fellows,
  each side eagerly vaunting the strength and skill of its ranks.
675 The mighty sea howled around, and the earth resounded beneath them.
  Broad heaven trembled above, and the roots of Olympus were shaken
  by the clash of immortals, resounding louder than echoing thunder,
  as far as windy Tartarus—rushing of feet as they hurried,
  screaming darts in their flight, shouting cries as they rallied.
680 All this rang to the stars as the two sides clashed with each other.
  Now Zeus no longer held back his might. From now on his spirit
  seethed in his rage as he showed the full extent of his power.

668. *Erebus:* "Darkness," used here for Tartarus.

PERSPECTIVE 4.1

GOYA'S SATURN DEVOURING HIS CHILDREN

Francisco de Goya (1746–1828), a Spanish artist of eccentric vision, stood apart from his contemporaries in his perception of demonic forces and the terrors of the human experience. Late in life, suffering from deafness, witness to many horrors, he retired to his house and covered the walls with nightmarish devil-worshipers, subhuman monsters, and other haunting images, including a representation of Saturn devouring his children (Perspective Figure 4.1).

Saturn ("the sower"), an Italian spirit of the harvest, appears in Latin authors as the ruler of Italy in the Golden Age, but also as a cynical old man (giving us

PERSPECTIVE FIGURE 4.1 Francisco Goya (1746–1828), *Saturn Devouring His Children* (detail), 1819–1823, oil on plaster transferred to canvas.   (Museo del Prado, Madrid; University of Wisconsin–Madison Photo Archive)

the English word *saturnine*, "gloomy"). He was the Latin equivalent of "crooked-counseling Cronus," whom Greek intellectuals had equated with *Chronos* ("time"). In this way, the myth of Cronus eating his children could be explained as an allegory for "time devours all things" (see Chapter 25); the scythe of our Father Time, hence of a popular representation of Death, is the sickle whereby Cronus = *Chronos* severed his father's genitals. Hesiod tells us that Cronus swallowed his children whole, as if in one gulp, but Goya heightens the horror through an exaggerated fantasy of Saturn as a ghastly cannibal giant, chomping up one child—male or female, we cannot tell—bit by bit. Even so does ravenous, unforgiving Time destroy all in its bloody, grinding jaws: Even so do the demonic forces in human nature, reflecting savage nature itself, destroy all that is childlike and innocent.

Down from the heaven he rushed, from the highest peak of Olympus,
hurling in endless showers the flashing bolts of his lightning.
685   Forth from his mighty hand flashed glare commingled with thunder,
ceasing for never a moment. Earth, giver of life, could but cower,
tormented and scorched by her burns. Great forests choked in the fire,
as the water of earth boiled off, and the surging tides of the ocean,
even the harvestless sea. The fiery blast soared on upward
690   to the quiet expanse of the heaven, and down to the arrogant Titans,
shriveling sight from their eyes.

HESIOD, Theogony 666–698

The tide of battle turned. Helped by the three Hecatonchires (Hesiod names them), Zeus cast the Titans into black distant Tartarus:

[713]   Leading the bitter struggle were Cottus, Briareus, Gyes,
lusting for battle, each hurling a good three-hundred terrible boulders
715   in fire so rapid the stones quite overshadowed the Titans.
Some they hurled to their ruin, down under the wide-wayed earth
as far underground as earth itself is lower than heaven,
where they bound them in biting chains, curbing their arrogant spirit.
Drop an anvil from heaven; it falls nine days and nine nights,
720   reaching the earth on the tenth. Just so a great brazen anvil,
if dropped from the earth, for an equal time would go hurtling downward,
and would land at last on the tenth day, deep in Tartarus' depths.
Round Tartarus runs a wall of brass, at whose narrowest portion
threefold night gushes out. Below are the roots of the earth,
725   and those of unharvested sea. Within it the Titans are buried
by design of Zeus who assembles the clouds. No way of escape
lies open, for mighty Poseidon set gates of bronze, and around them
the wall hems them in on both sides. There Cottus, Briareus, Gyes,
mighty of heart, all dwell,° strong henchmen of Zeus of the aegis.

HESIOD, Theogony 713–729

729. *all dwell:* As jailers.

Atlas, either a Titan (a son of Uranus) or a Giant (son of Iapetus and an Oceanid), was condemned by Zeus to live at the edge of the world, where he held up the heavens (see Figure 5.1), ensuring the continued separation of Sky and Earth. Later, Atlas was equated with a mountain range in Morocco near the Atlantic Ocean (whence comes its name) and gave his name to the fanciful continent Atlantis, said by Plato to lie in the far west beyond the Pillars of Heracles, that is, the hills of Gibraltar on the northern (Spanish) side and, on the other, of Ceuta in Morocco (see Perspective 1.1).

ZEUS'S BATTLE WITH TYPHOEUS

But Zeus's struggles were not ended. Gaea, who had advised Zeus to summon the Hecatonchires in his struggle against her own children the Titans, for some reason now resented Zeus's victory. She became his greatest enemy. Coupling with Tartarus, she gave birth to the monstrous **Typhoeus** (tī-fō-ūs), also called Typhon (**tī**-fon):

[820] When Zeus had driven the Titans out of the sky into exile,
mighty Gaea gave birth to the last of her children, Typhoeus,
born of Tartarus' lust and the wiles of gold-haired Aphrodite.
Typhoeus had muscular arms, fit for laborious action,
and the tireless feet of a god of might. Surmounting his shoulders
825 sprouted the hundred heads of a terrible serpentine dragon,
flicking their dark livid tongues. The eyes of each sinister forehead
spat out a jet of flame from under its shadowing eyebrows,
and each indescribable mouth had a voice of ineffable volume,
uttering words only gods can know: now the arrogant cry of a bull,
830 a lordly bellow of strength, now the terrible roar of a lion,
shameless and angry. Again, the eager bark of the mastiff,
or the hunter's echoing whistle that makes the mountains resound.
No defense could be found from the day of birth of the monster,
and Typhoeus would soon have been despot alike of gods and of humans,
835 had not the wit of the father of mortal men and immortals
seen through the threat and sounded his irresistible thunder.
All earth quaked at the sound, and the wide-flung arches of heaven,
the springs of Ocean, the seas, and the gloomy depths of the earth.
Under the thundering tread of its monarch marching to battle,
840 huge Olympus was shaken, and all earth trembled and whimpered.
The purple face of the sea was seared by the flames of both rulers,
by Zeus's thunder and lightning, by fire that flashed from Typhoeus:
the lightning bolts of the one, the scorching winds of the other.
All earth boiled, and all heaven. The sea surged over its headlands,
845 its crashing waves driven up and around by the blast of the powers.
Uncontrollable shaking seized all the earth and the heavens,
and even Hades, the lord of the lifeless shades, shook in terror,

and the Titans, buried in Tartarus, huddled together with Cronus.
Now Zeus kindled his rage and eagerly snatched up his missiles,
850   thunder and lightning and fire from heaven, crashing and blazing.
He bounded forward and shot from the lofty top of Olympus.
The fiery blast ignited the marvelous heads of the monster.
Typhoeus, scourged and shattered by Zeus's terrible weapons,
hamstrung, sank to his knees as the mighty earth groaned in despair.
855   From the fall of the stricken ruler, blasted by heavenly lightning,
flames leaped out like those in the woods of rugged Mount Etna,
when it too is struck. For miles the whole great earth was enkindled
by the blast of heavenly wind. It melted like wax in a ladle
worked by a brawny-armed smith, or iron, toughest of metals,
860   smelted in mountain forests and worked in the heat of a forge.
Just so the earth was melted in the white-hot gleam of the fire.

HESIOD, Theogony 820–867

Apollodorus, author of the oldest surviving "handbook of Greek myth" (second century AD), adds interesting details to this account of Hesiod. Typhoeus, he says, was born in Cilicia (the southern coast of modern Turkey) and was so huge that he towered above the mountains, and his head struck the stars. One hand reached the western horizon, the other the eastern. From the waist down he was a tangle of hissing vipers. He had majestic wings, and shaggy hair covered his body (Figure 4.6). Typhoeus hurled fiery rocks at heaven, then charged, hooting and spewing fire from his mouths. The Olympian gods fled to Egypt and disguised themselves as various animals—that is why Egyptian gods have animal shapes! Zeus charged, pitching thunderbolts and brandishing the very sickle with which Cronus had castrated Uranus. Hotly pursued, Typhoeus fled to Mount Casius in north Syria (today in southeastern Turkey). Zeus threw down his sickle and grappled with the monster hand to hand, but Typhoeus caught Zeus in his coils, seized the sickle, and sliced out the sinews of Zeus's hands and feet, which he stored in a jar. He carried the god, limp as a rag doll, to a cave in Cilicia, threw him in a corner, hid the sinews under a bearskin, and placed a dragon to guard the cave.

Fortunately, Zeus's son Hermes and a goat-shaped woodland spirit named Aegipan ("goat-pan") slipped past Typhoeus, took the sinews from the jar, and restored them to Zeus, who mounted a glorious chariot drawn by winged horses. He pursued Typhoeus across the earth, flinging thunderbolts. In Thrace the monster took his stand, ripped out whole mountains, and threw them. Zeus caught and threw them back, badly wounding Typhoeus, whose blood covered an entire mountain, henceforth known as Mount Haemus ("bloody").

Zeus finally ran Typhoeus down in the far west and buried him beneath Mount Etna in eastern Sicily. When today the mountain smokes, it is from the fusillade of lightning that Zeus poured upon the beast, or it may be the fire of Typhoeus himself, escaping from the earth. **(For Apollodorus' account, see http://www.theoi. com/Text/Apollodorus1.html)**

FIGURE 4.6 The **Typhonomachy**, from a vase found in Etruria but probably painted by a Euboean Greek living in Italy, c. 525 BC. Zeus brandishes his thunderbolt in his right hand while he takes aim with his left. Typhoeus is winged with snaky limbs beneath the waist, a full beard, gnarled nose, and pointy ears. Zeus's name is written in front of him.   (Staatliche Antikensammlungen und Glyptothek, Munich; Hirmer Fotoarchiv, Munich)

ZEUS'S BATTLE WITH THE GIANTS

Although he had won wars against the Titans and Typhoeus, Zeus's reign was not secure. The logic of the **succession myth**, which had governed the earliest generations, seemed to demand that Zeus too be overthrown. Cronus was more clever than Uranus, and Zeus more clever than Cronus, but who would be more clever than Zeus? To forestall prophecy, and to establish his rule forever, Zeus married cleverness herself, the Oceanid Metis (**mē**-tis), "cleverness." Metis, who had given the emetic to Cronus and forced him to vomit up the children he had swallowed, was the first of Zeus's seven consorts (see Chart 6.2). Metis was already pregnant with Athena when Zeus learned from Uranus and Gaea that his wife's next child, after Athena, would depose him. Uranus had attempted to preserve his power by keeping his offspring down in the body of the mother; Cronus swallowed his children; Zeus, craftiest of all, swallowed the mother herself before the child was born. Thus did Metis, "cleverness," become part of his own being, inaccessible except through Zeus himself.

Later, suffering a severe headache, Zeus cried out for assistance. Either Prometheus or Hephaestus struck his head with an ax. Out sprang Athena, fully formed, fully armed, screaming the war-cry (Figure 4.7). Thus Athena was the child of Zeus alone, his agent and supporter, female in sex but virgin in body and masculine

FIGURE 4.7 The birth of Athena from the head of Zeus on an Attic cup, c. 560 BC. Hephaestus, who has just struck open Zeus's head with his ax, turns to run, startled at the result. Athena springs forth, armed with shield and spear, while an indifferent Zeus holds a thunderbolt aloft in his right hand.   (British Museum, London; © Trustees of the British Museum/Art Resource, New York)

in thought and behavior. The child who would have overthrown him was never born. The mighty and the brilliant Zeus defied the prophecy by thwarting the biological logic according to which only females give birth.

Hesiod does not tell it, but very popular in classical art was the story of another enemy who rose against Zeus. The Giants, conceived from the blood of Uranus' severed genitals and urged on by Gaea, attacked the Olympians in the **Gigantomachy** (jī-gan-**tom**-a-kē), "battle of the Giants," hurling rocks and burning trees into the sky. Literary accounts and artistic representations pair individual gods with individual Giants. The Giants were shown as enormous and bearded, often with snaky legs and long, disheveled hair (Figure 4.8). The mortal Heracles, son of Zeus, joined the Olympians in the war, for an oracle declared that the gods could not win without a mortal's assistance. The chronology of the world's childhood is vague, yet Heracles' presence indicates that the Gigantomachy was considerably later than the primordial events of the Titanomachy and the Typhonomachy.

The Giants at last were overcome. Now the three male gods, Zeus, Hades, and Poseidon, cast lots to divide the world among them. Zeus took heaven, Poseidon the gray sea, and Hades the dark mist at the world's end. But the earth and the heights of Olympus were common to all.

FIGURE 4.8 Battle of the gods and Giants, from the Great Altar at Pergamum in Asia Minor, east frieze, third–second centuries BC. A Giant with snaky tails attacks Hecatê, goddess of the crossroads, who attacks him with a torch. A head of one of the Giant's snaky tails seizes Hecatê's shield. On the right, another Giant, standing over a fallen snaky-tailed companion, attacks the goddess Artemis (off the picture). The contorted features and writhing, violent postures are typical of Hellenistic art (compare Figure 20.4).   (Staatliche Museen, Berlin; Bildarchiv Preußischer Kulturbesitz/Art Resource, New York)

PROMINENT THEMES IN THE GREEK CREATION STORY

The Greek story of the creation of the world and of the gods as told by Hesiod and Apollodorus is an example of what we have called divine myth; its subject is the actions of gods and the description of grand events and their consequences. Yet the narrative patterns underlying the story owe much to folktale. Here gods act as ogres (Uranus, Cronus) and tricksters (Cronus, Zeus); goddesses behave as sexual victims (Gaea, Rhea), as dangerous enemies (Gaea), and as beneficent protectors (Gaea, Rhea). Typhoeus is a dragon; Zeus is his enemy. Vicious family conflict drives the action: Wife plots against husband (Gaea against Uranus), son against father (Cronus against Uranus, Zeus against Cronus), and father against children (Uranus against the Titans, Cronus against the Olympians). Ancient traditional material has been remodeled to make an exciting tale that answers the question, "How did Zeus come to rule the world?"

The universe portrayed by Hesiod is no static creation, spoken into existence by God once and for all, but comes from successive growth and change, from progressive proliferation and differentiation away from original unity. First was Chaos/Chasm, from which emerged Night and Darkness, primal entities that generate their opposites, Day and Radiance. Then Gaea/Earth appeared, who was the first really animate being, female in nature, who nonetheless gave birth without sexual intercourse to Pontus/Sea and Uranus/Sky. But Eros/Love propelled the expanding creation, and later Gaea/Earth had intercourse with her own children. Henceforth, with few exceptions, reproduction is by sexual means.

The Greek cosmogony/theogony is a tale of the gradual ascent to power of male over female. In the beginning was female Gaea/Earth, mother of all; in the end the male Zeus rules the universe. At the beginning of the evolutionary development, Gaea produced children asexually; at the end, Zeus does the same when Athena springs from his head. For the Greeks it seemed natural to suppose that an orderly universe, like an orderly household or city, would be ruled by a clever and powerful male; this was the social ideal. But the power of Gaea/Earth can never be removed completely. She is the ultimate base on which depends the whole world.

Gaea, although wife and mother to Uranus/Sky, conspired with her son, clever Cronus, to mutilate Uranus and ruin his power. Uranus was an ogre; he opposed life and the future and cared only for his own lust. Like a hero in folktale, wily Cronus sprang from an ambush to destroy the dragon who sexually threatened the woman. Cronus castrated his father with a steel sickle, a special weapon of the sort folktale heroes use to overcome their enemies. As in so many folktales, the story is set within the contradictions of the family. A father begets a son in the hope that one day the son may replace him, not destroy him!

Uranus was a bad father and deserved his fate, but Cronus was hardly better. Uranus kept his children in Gaea's womb. The cannibal Cronus swallowed them into his own stomach (the Greek word *nêdus* means both "womb" and "stomach"). Uranus and Gaea then worked together, advising Rhea how to outwit her husband. The once clever Cronus himself becomes a stupid ogre when he mistakes a stone for his own child. Rhea, a doublet of Gaea, carried her child to a cave, earth's womb, on the island of Crete, where a new champion, the clever Zeus, grew to manhood.

In the detail of Zeus's rearing on Crete, folktale is influenced by historical religion. On Crete flourished an ancient cult of a young male god, perhaps the consort of an ancient Cretan mother-goddess worshiped deep in caves. When the encroaching Indo-Europeans encountered the male god of the indigenous inhabitants of Crete, they seem to have identified him with their own male god, Zeus, although as a dying god of nature (see Chapter 11) the Cretan god was utterly unlike the Indo-European god of storm. The Greeks sometimes called this god "the Cretan Zeus" to distinguish him from the Olympian; islanders could point out the tomb of the Cretan Zeus. According to Cretan tradition, Rhea handed over the infant Zeus to the Curetes ("youths"), who did a war-dance, loudly banging spears against their bronze shields to hide the infant's cries from Cronus. In historical times on Crete, men called Curetes were in fact orgiastic worshipers of a mother-goddess.

The Titans, whatever their origins, came to represent the untamed forces of nature in general. Their offspring were the seas, rivers, and heavenly bodies. Clever

Zeus, the fully anthropomorphized god of historical Greece, could not defeat them unassisted, by raw force alone. Forging a new system of power, he acted as statesman, righting the wrongs of the past and releasing the Cyclopes and the Hecatonchires from Tartarus, where Cronus had imprisoned them. The Cyclopes became Zeus's armorers, who made the thunderbolt. The Hecatonchires served as his mercenary soldiers, and only with their assistance was he able to cast the Titans into darkness.

The ambivalence of the female is prominent in the Greek story. Gaea at first favors progressive change, then, resentful of the overthrow of the Titans, opposes it. She bears Typhoeus, enemy of the new world-order. Later, Gaea/Earth also incites the Giants to revolt. Although born of Uranus' blood, the Giants are her children and represent her interests, in this case malevolent.

In Apollodorus' version of the Typhoeus story, Zeus's special weapon, following the folktale pattern, is the same steel sickle by which Cronus castrated Uranus. Like many folktale heroes, in this version Zeus is temporarily overcome. Paralyzed, without sinews, he lies in the darkness of the womblike, tomblike cave. Thanks to Hermes, the messenger-god who connects this world with the next, and Aegipan, "goat-pan," god of natural vitality, Zeus returns to life. He cannot quite kill Typhoeus, any more than he can overcome Gaea/Earth herself, so he imprisons him beneath Mount Etna, from which emanates irresistible volcanic fire. In Hesiod's version, Typhoeus is still present in our world in the violent winds that rock the sea. (Our word *typhoon*, from the Chinese term *tai fung*, "violent wind," derives its form by analogy with "Typhon"; *typhus* and *typhoid* fever also come from the Greek monster, because both arouse a wild delirium in the patient.) As his reward for overcoming the dragon, Zeus becomes king, takes a wife, and bears many children.

In the cycle of Greek creation myths, the motifs of separation, succession, and dragon-combat are ingeniously melded to tell the story of the fashioning of the ordered and diverse world from the disordered and homogeneous one that preceded it.

EASTERN CREATION STORIES

Scholars once thought that the story of Zeus's war against the Titans might reflect a historical conflict between Greek Indo-European invaders with their new gods (especially Zeus) on one side against the indigenous peoples with their (mostly female) deities on the other. However, the recovery of ancient Near Eastern myths leaves no doubt that the story of war in heaven and other features of the Greek account are taken from earlier Eastern cultures; the story's origin is not historical (at least not in Greece). We are not sure how Eastern stories crossed barriers of language and culture to enter Greece, but cross they did.

The Babylonian *Enuma elish*

The best example of Mesopotamian creation myth is the Babylonian poem the *Enuma elish*, "When on high," recited on the fourth day of the New Year's festival in Babylon in honor of the god of the city, Marduk. The text reached its present form before 1100 BC, although it preserves far older material. Telling of the first days of the creation, the story had the magical power to renew the world at the critical joining of one year with the next. There is little drama or suspense in it, our best example from Mesopotamia of a myth we know to have been told during a religious ritual.

The poem opens with the gods of the primordial waters, male Apsu, freshwater, and female **Tiamat** (tē-a-mat), saltwater, mingled together in an indeterminate mass:

> When on high heaven was not yet named,
> nor was the hard ground below called by name—
> there was nothing but primordial Apsu, the begetter,
> and Mother Tiamat, she who gave birth to everything.
> The waters of Tiamat and Apsu were mingled together as a single body.
> No one had woven a reed hut. There was no marsh land.
> It was a time before the gods had come into being,
> or were called by name, or their destinies determined—
> this was when the gods took form within them.°
> Lahmu and Lahamu° were brought forth,
> called by their names before they had grown.
> Anshar and Kishar° took form, greater than the others.
> They made the days long, added on years.°
> Anu was their heir, rival to his own fathers.

within them: That is, the waters of Apsu and Tiamat. To name is to create; the essence of a creature resides in the word that designates it. *Lahmu and Lahamu*: The primordial slime. *Anshar and Kishar*: Probably Heaven and Earth, Up and Down, to judge from the roots An ("sky") and Ki ("earth"). *added on years*: Time passed.

With Lahmu and Lahamu, "Mr. and Mrs. Mud," the creation began even as Gaea, "Earth," appeared after Chaos in the Greek account. Anshar and Kishar are apparently Heaven and Earth. After **Anu** ("sky" = Sumerian An) is begotten in the fourth generation, many other gods appear, **Ea** (ē-a) (= Sumerian Enki) among them. Eros, who is attraction or the notion of first motion, accompanied Gaea, Tartarus, and Chaos; in the *Enuma elish* the new gods came together "and their clamor reverberated." The activity and noise disturbed Apsu's rest, and with his officer Mummu, Apsu went to Tiamat to complain:

> I cannot stand their ways!
> The day brings no respite, and the night no rest.
> I will ruin their ways and drive them away!
> Then may peace come again, and sleep!

Although the loving mother Tiamat vigorously opposed Apsu's wish to destroy their troublesome offspring, the officer Mummu urged it, and his advice so pleased Apsu that Apsu's face grew radiant and he kissed Mummu.

When the younger gods heard of the plan to destroy them, they fell into a panic. Only Ea, "who knows everything, the skillful, the wise," kept his head. He cast a spell over Apsu and Mummu, sending them into a deep sleep. Then he killed Apsu and strung a rope through Mummu's nose, imprisoning him. On top of the dead Apsu, Ea built his house, into which he moved with his wife.

She soon gave birth to the real hero of the poem, **Marduk**, god of Babylon, in every way an extraordinary being:

> He sucked from the teats of goddesses.
> His nurse filled him with glory.
> His body was charming, sparkling his eyes.
> He was born fully developed, mighty from the start.
> When his father Ea looked upon him,
> he rejoiced and beamed, his heart was gladdened.
> He made him perfect, a god twice over.
> Exalted above them all, he was superlative in every way.
> His limbs were well made, impossible to describe,
> beyond comprehension, hard to perceive.
> Four were his eyes, four were his ears.
> When he opened his mouth, fire shot forth.
> His four ears were huge,
> his four eyes saw all that was.
> His limbs were immense,
> he was enormously handsome.

Marduk's grandfather Anu was so proud that he fashioned four winds for Marduk's plaything. The winds blew constantly to and fro, once more stirring the waters of Tiamat, and again the older gods complained. Tiamat, who earlier defended the younger gods, was now (like erratic Gaea in the Greek story) determined to destroy them, and she begot an army of monsters to help her:

> She set up the snake with horns, the dragon,
> the *lahmu*-hero,° the lion demon, rabid dog,
> and scorpion-man,
> savage *ûmu*-devils,° fishman, bullman.

lahmu-*hero*: Not clear what is meant. ûmu: A word of unknown meaning.

To lead the horde, Tiamat chose a new husband, Kingu, "her only lover." She placed him on a throne and armed him with the mysterious Tablet of Destiny, which gave power over the universe.

When Ea heard of the fresh preparations, he lost his nerve and ran to the god Anshar. In consternation Anshar bit his lip and slapped his thigh and demanded that Ea war against Tiamat. At this point the tablet is broken, but apparently Ea was unsuccessful, for when the text resumes, it is Anu who attacks Tiamat. But Tiamat put her hand against him, and Anu ran away in terror. At the moment of crisis, the gods lost all hope and sank into despair, as they do in many Mesopotamian myths.

Then Anshar remembered Marduk, whose moment had come. He kissed Marduk on the lips, and Marduk agreed to fight Tiamat and her army of monsters, but only on the condition that he be given absolute power as reward:

> "My word alone shall establish fate, not yours!
> What I fashion shall last forever!
> What my lips decree, shall never be changed,
> never altered!" Hastily, the gods agreed.

They gave him a scepter, a throne, a royal robe.
They gave him relentless weapons to overwhelm the foe:
"Go slice the throat of Tiamat!
Let the winds bring her blood, tidings of joy!"

Taking bow and arrows, a mace and net, with lightning flashing before him, with seven winds at his back, Marduk mounted his chariot—the image of a thunderstorm. The chariot's team were named Killer, Ruthless, Racer, and Flyer, and their teeth dripped poison. Radiant with power, he roared down the road toward Tiamat, but when he saw her, he (like Ea and Anu before him) lost his nerve and had to endure the taunts of Tiamat. But he soon regained his courage and rebuked her, so that she was seized by uncontrollable rage, let out a roar, and attacked:

Tiamat and Marduk, the wisest god, locked together.
They tangled in the hand-to-hand, clasped in battle.
Marduk spread out his net to catch her.
The storm that followed behind him, he splashed in her face.
When Tiamat opened wide her mouth to swallow him,
he drove down the storm so she could not close her lips.
The savage winds swelled her belly,
her body puffed up and her mouth opened wide.
He fired his arrow, it burst her belly,
carved through her guts and split the heart,
wrecked and extinguished her life.
He threw down the corpse and trod upon it.

The army of monsters tried to flee, but Marduk caught them in his net, fixed them with nose-ropes, and bound their arms. He imprisoned Kingu, Tiamat's lover, and took control of the Tablet of Destiny. Then (Figure 4.9):

Marduk trod on Tiamat's legs.
With his mighty mace he smashed her skull.
When he had sliced open the arteries of her blood,
the North Wind bore it to places unknown.
When the gods saw what had happened,
they were joyous, radiant.
They brought gifts of homage to Marduk.
But the lord paused to look at her corpse,
so that he might divide the monster and fashion clever things.
He split her like a clamshell into two parts.
Half he raised up high, calling it sky.
He lowered the bar and set up watchmen.
He commanded them never to let her waters escape.

On top of the corpse Marduk built a large temple and cult centers for Anu, Enlil, and Ea. He made the constellations, set up the calendar, put the North Star in its place, and brought forth the sun and moon. From Tiamat's spittle he made the surging clouds, the wind, the rain; from her poison, the billowing fog. He heaped a mountain over her head and pierced her eyes, from which flow the rivers Tigris and

FIGURE 4.9 Bronze statuette of a four-faced god who steps on a ram, from Ischali, Iraq, c. 1800 BC. The god wears a long, flounced dress and carries in his right hand a sickle-ax. The god's identity is unknown, but some think he may be Marduk and the ram Tiamat, embodiment of chaos.　(Oriental Institute of the University of Chicago)

Euphrates. Other mountains he heaped over her breasts, then bent her tail into the sky to make the Milky Way. With her crotch he held up the sky.

Marduk returned home in triumph, delivered the Tablet of Destiny to Anu, and presented his captives before the gods. He washed off the gore of battle, dressed in royal attire, and sat on a high throne to receive homage from the gods. He proclaimed that he would build a great temple, a luxurious dwelling for himself and for all the gods, when they came to visit. He announced another plan:

> "I will mash blood together and bones
> and make a primeval human: Human shall be its name.
> Their purpose will be to serve the gods,
> that they might be at ease!"
> He brought the rebel Kingu before the assembly.
> They tied him up and dragged him in before Ea.
> They carried out the execution, severed his arteries.
> From his blood they made humans.
> Ea made labor to be a human's lot,
> but the gods he set free.

Marduk then divided the gods into those who live in the sky and those beneath the earth. The grateful gods eagerly began to build the palace of which Marduk had spoken, and after two years they completed the great ziggurat of Babylon (see Figure 3.6). They held a banquet and proclaimed Marduk lord of the universe. The story ends with a long list of the fifty names of Marduk (more than one-fourth of the poem), with detailed explanations of each name. In this way was the world made, and the same order of kingship was established among the gods as in Babylon itself.

Observations: Cosmogony and Dragon Combat

In the *Enuma elish* and other Mesopotamian myths, the original creative element is watery, feminine, and ambivalent, both life-giving and life-destroying. Above the earth the waters may descend as life-giving rain, but below the earth they bound the land of the dead. The same ambivalence as that of the original, primeval element of the universe is displayed by female deities, who both nurture and destroy. The dangerous, chaotic waters are represented by a monster or dragon that a hero overcomes to fashion the cosmos. There is a complex association between water, chaos, monsters, the female, and death: In myth, dragon combat and cosmogony can be one and the same. The male hero establishes the world-order and his own permanent reign over the corpse of the she-monster.

Mesopotamian divine myths, like Hesiod's story, envision the formation and organization of the world and of human society as process and change. The world has not always been as it is now. Its initial unity in the primeval waters has moved to diversity. Creation arises not from nothing but, as in Hesiod, from a primordial chaos by means of sexual reproduction and a series of successively more powerful generations. A younger generation opposes, overcomes, and controls or destroys an older generation, until the present world-order comes into being.

The Hittite Kingship in Heaven

Other Eastern myths important to the later classical tradition come from the mighty Indo-European Hittites, who ruled the central Anatolian plain (modern central Turkey) in the Late Bronze Age. Their powerful capital was near modern Ankara, and their art and culture were strong well into the eighth century BC in what is today southeastern Turkey and northern Syria. Only small portions of a poem called *Kingship in Heaven* survive, but the myth has clear relevance to the Greek cosmogony:

[1]   In earlier years, Alalush was king in heaven.
      Alalush sits there on his throne.
      And strong Anush [= Anu], first of the gods, is his servant.
      He bows to him at his feet.
5   He always gives him great cups
      to drink into his hand.
        For nine years of rule, Alalush was king in heaven.
      After nine years, Anush made war against Alalush.
      He defeated Alalush
10   who fled under the dark earth,
      but Anush sat on the throne.
      Anush is there on his throne

and strong Kumarbi always gives him food to eat
and he always bows at his feet
15   and always gives him great cups into his hand.
    For nine years Anush ruled as king in heaven.
In the ninth year, Anush made war with Kumarbi.
The eyes of Kumarbi he could not defeat.
He slipped from Kumarbi's hand and fled.
20   Anush the eagle flew in the sky
and Kumarbi closed in behind him,
grabbed his feet
and pulled him down from the sky.
He [Kumarbi] bit off his [Anush's] genitals.
25   His sperm went into Kumarbi's stomach.
He swallowed Anush's sperm
and was happy and he laughed.
    And Anush turned back to him
and began to speak to Kumarbi.
30   "You are really pleased about your stomach.
It swallowed my sperm.
You should not rejoice!
I have placed a load in your middle.
First, I have made you pregnant with the storm-god;
35   second, with the river Aranzakh;°
third, with the heavy Tasmishu.°
And I placed the burden, the terrible gods into your middle!
You will perish, hitting your head on the mountain Tashshu!"
    When Anush finished speaking, he disappeared.
40   Then Kumarbi went high into the heavens.
He spit from his mouth.
The stricken king spit from his mouth upwards.
That which had been ingested, Kumarbi spit out.

35. *Aranzakh*: The Tigris.   36. *Tasmishu*: An attendant of the storm-god.

There the tablet breaks off. When it resumes, we learn that Anush argued with the storm-god, still within the body of Kumarbi, over how the storm-god should escape from Kumarbi's body. Kumarbi felt dizzy and asked Aya (= Ea) for something to eat. He ate something that hurt his mouth. At last the storm-god, warned not to come forth through various openings, especially not through Kumarbi's anus, came out of the "good place," apparently Kumarbi's penis. The rest is lost, but somehow the storm-god Teshub escaped from Kumarbi's body, overthrew him, and became king of heaven.

Observations: The Succession Myth in Hesiod and the Near East

In the *Enuma elish*, first came a theogony, the generation of Apsu and Tiamat and their descendants. These new gods bring a principle of movement into the world (their activity and clamor), which contrasts sharply with the older forces of chaos, which stand for inactivity and inertia (symbolized by their desire to sleep). The primordial gods' resistance to change leads to a battle in which newer gods overthrow the older. This succession motif, as we have seen, is central in Greek myth as well.

In the first round of the battle of the gods, the wise and clever Ea overcomes wicked Apsu by a spell; his magical power resides in the spoken word. Ea's wisdom and cleverness are contrasted with Apsu's brutish lust to destroy, a common folktale motif: The dragon-slayer is clever and tricky, his opponent dull and stupid. Tiamat, like Gaea, manages to be both beneficent and malevolent. She first opposes her husband's destructive designs, but when Apsu is killed, she herself becomes the destructive monster.

Later, in a repetition of the succession motif, Tiamat is destroyed by her descendant Marduk, who becomes ruler of the world. Marduk is a local Babylonian city-god, but in the myth simply a substitution for Enlil, the ancient Mesopotamian storm-god. The Hittite *Kingship in Heaven* is similarly based on the succession motif. First Alalush was king, then Anush, then Kumarbi, then the storm god Teshub.

In both the *Enuma elish* and Hesiod's *Theogony* the first generation of gods is made up of primal pairs: Apsu, the male freshwaters, and Tiamat, the female saltwaters; Uranus and Gaea. The fathers Apsu and Uranus hate the first children, who are begotten within the mother. In an initial round of conflict the clever sons Ea and Cronus overthrow their fathers. In a second round of conflict, gods of the third generation—Marduk and the storm-god Zeus—revolt against an earlier divine generation. Terrible monsters are overcome: Tiamat and her army in *Enuma elish*; the Titans, Typhoeus, and the Giants, all children of Gaea, in the Greek story. The storm-god is then made king. Mesopotamian and Greek myths alike report a cosmic history that begins with mighty powers of nature and ends in the organization of the universe as a monarchic, patriarchal state. Both mythical traditions make use of the motifs of succession and dragon-combat.

Similarities between the Hittite and Greek myths are equally striking (Chart 4.4). According to *Kingship in Heaven*, first a primordial god (Alalush) was ruler, then the sky-god (Anush) ruled, then another god (Kumarbi), and then, probably, the storm-god (Teshub). The same sequence of generations appears in Hesiod: First came Chaos (= Alalush?), then Uranus/Sky (= Anush), then Cronus (= Kumarbi), then the storm-god Zeus (= Teshub). Both Anu ("sky") and Uranus

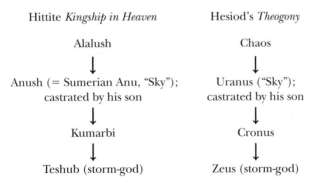

CHART 4.4 Hittite and Greek Theogonies Compared

PERSPECTIVE 4.2

THE BIBLICAL CREATION STORY

For many Westerners, the best-known story of creation is that reported in the biblical book of Genesis (1.1–2). The story is so familiar that many people find it hard to hear the words in their original meanings, but a close examination of the Hebrew text's opening lines reveals striking parallels with the creation myths of ancient Mesopotamia:

> In the beginning, when Elohim° created the heaven and the earth, the earth was a formless and unbounded mass, with darkness covering its fluid chaos and with a wind° from Elohim sweeping over it. Elohim said, "Let there be light!" and there was light.° Elohim saw the goodness of the light and separated it from the darkness. The light he called° "day" and the darkness "night." Thus evening and morning came into being, a complete day. Then Elohim said, "Let there be a partition° in the middle of the watery chaos, spreading out to separate the waters." So it came about, and the partition divided the waters below it from those above. Elohim called the partition "sky." The evening came and the morning, making up the second day.

> *Genesis* 1.1–8

Elohim: "The gods," but taken as a singular. *wind*: The word in Hebrew is *ruach*, which, like Greek *pneuma* and Latin *spiritus*, may mean air in motion, breath, psychological power. *light*: Light is what makes it possible for you to distinguish things. *called*: To name is to create. *partition*: Literally, "something solid."

The Hebrew text of Genesis, which did not reach its final form until perhaps 400 BC, is an edited account based on several earlier sources, some of which used different names for God. From these different sources Hebrew scholars created a text suitable to the doctrinal needs of a monotheistic religion. The Hebrew account differs from the Mesopotamian in its notion of a single transcendent God, with no rivals, who stands before and beyond the creation, but is similar to the Mesopotamian myth in its picture of a universe beginning in a watery mass that is split into an above and a below, Heaven and Earth (An and Ki). In the Mesopotamian and Hittite accounts, the great elements of nature are deified, whereas in the Hebrew account the powers that made the world are stripped of personal names and attributes. So An/Anu/Anush becomes simply "sky"; Enlil/Teshub/Marduk, god of storm, becomes the "wind" that moves across the water; Ki is the dry land; and Enki/Ea is the waters from which the dry land is separated, the earthly waters as opposed to those that existed before the creation. For centuries Christian theologians have debated whether creation took place *ex nihilo*, "out of nothing," or out of something formless, but the Hebrew text, like its Mesopotamian forebears, envisions creation as a process of separation.

In the *Enuma elish* the primordial waters are personified as the great dragon Tiamat, whom the creator of the cosmos must overcome. Although not a part of the biblical creation story, this myth is dimly reflected in other biblical passages: "In that day Yahweh with his hard and great and strong sword will punish Leviathan ["twister," "coiler"], the fleeing serpent, Leviathan the twisting serpent, and he will slay the dragon that is in the sea" (Isaiah 27.1).

("sky") were castrated by their sons, and gods were born from the severed organs. As long as heaven and earth are locked in sexual embrace, forming a solid whole, there is no space within which the created world can appear. Castration was a real practice imposed on enemies taken in war, but in the logic of the myth castration is separation, and separation is creation. Both Kumarbi and Cronus have children within themselves. The children of each, Teshub and Zeus, both storm-gods, overcome their fathers to win victory in heaven.

There are differences in detail and profound differences in tone between the Eastern and the Greek stories. The writing systems of the Mesopotamians and Hittites, unlike the Greek alphabet, were unable to record the suppleness and color of spoken language. Nonetheless, striking similarities prove that the myth is Eastern in origin. The Greek cosmogonic traditions are old and have been passed across linguistic, cultural, and racial lines. Greek cosmogonic myth partly reflects the Greeks' own attitudes, but its basic structure, and many of its cultural assumptions, come from non-Greek peoples. In trying to understand Greek myth, we are also trying to understand our much older precursors, to whom the Greeks owed so much.

KEY NAMES AND TERMS

cosmogony, 82
theogony, 82
Chaos, 82
Gaea, 82
Uranus, 82
Eros, 84
Titans, 84
Cyclopes, 84
Hecatonchires, 84
Cronus, 84
Oceanus, 85
Rhea, 86
Helius, 87
Eos, 87
Phaëthon, 87
Tithonus, 87

Erinyes, 89
Giants, 89
Sphinx, 91
Cerberus, 92
Chimera, 92
Thetis, 94
Titanomachy, 95
Atlas, 98
Typhoeus, 98
Typhonomachy, 100
succession myth, 100
Gigantomachy, 101
Tiamat, 105
Anu, 105
Ea, 105
Marduk, 106

SOME ADDITIONAL ANCIENT SOURCES

Ovid also tells of the Gigantomachy (*Metamorphoses* 1.151–62) and gives the story of the Egyptian gods changing into animals (*Metamorphoses* 5.325–41). Pindar's *Pythian* 1.15–28 tells of Typhoeus' imprisonment under Aetna, as does Aeschylus, *Prometheus Bound* 351–72 and Ovid's *Metamorphoses* 5.346–78.

FURTHER READING CHAPTER 4

Athanassakis, Apostolos, *Hesiod: Theogony, Works and Days* (Baltimore, MD, 1983). Good translation with valuable notes.

Brown, Norman O., *Theogony. Hesiod* (New York, 1953). A lucid prose translation prefaced by one of the best essays on the *Theogony* in English.

Hoffner, Harry A., and Gary M. Beckman, eds., *Hittite Myths* (New York, 1998). Up-to-date treatment.

Lamberton, Robert, *Hesiod* (New Haven, CT, 1988). A compact survey of the poet, his times, and his work.

Sasson, J. M., ed., *Civilization of the Ancient Near East*, 4 vols. (New York, 1995). Covers all aspects of the ancient Near East, with good essays on myth by M. L. West and W. Moran.

West, M. L., *Theogony* (Oxford, UK, 1966) and *Works and Days* (Oxford, UK, 1978). These scholarly editions of the Greek text contain introductory essays and commentary on all aspects of the poems and their mythical background.

CHAPTER 5

MYTHS OF CREATION

THE ORIGINS OF MORTALS

What does ravaging time not ruin?
The age of our fathers, worse than the one before,
brought forth ourselves, worse men than our fathers,
who will beget offspring more vicious still.

HORACE, *Odes* 3.6.45–48

WHERE DO HUMAN BEINGS come from? What sets them apart from other creatures? Why is it their fate to labor, suffer, and die? The myths of the ancient Greeks and Romans offered answers to these questions. Certain elements of these stories, too, are strikingly similar to stories from ancient Mesopotamia and the Bible. Still, the tales presented by Hesiod, Aeschylus, and Ovid reflect distinctive characteristics of the Greek (and Roman) experience of human life.

PROMETHEUS, MAKER OF MORTALS

The Greek tradition shows curiously little interest in the ultimate origins of mortals. Hesiod offers no explanation at all, although he does discuss other matters pertaining to the early life of human beings, as we see later in this chapter. Scattered references in later authors often are contradictory. Sometimes Zeus himself is identified as the creator of mortals, sometimes various gods are described as working together. But most often the maker of human beings is said to be **Prometheus** (prō-**mē**-thūs), the Titan who took Zeus's side in the battle against his cousin Titans.

Like Cronus, and like Zeus himself, Prometheus was known especially for being clever, the inventor of many things, including the race of mortals. The Roman poet Ovid, writing during the lifetime of Jesus, gives the fullest surviving version of the story. After describing the emergence of the world from Chaos, an account based on Hesiod, Ovid tells us that Prometheus made the human race by mixing primeval earth and water. Because the earth contained divine seed, the human was a superior being:

[76]   An animal blessed with a higher soul was still needed,
         one abler to reason more deeply, one able to govern the others.
         So man was born. Perhaps the maker of all things° produced him
         of heavenly seed, in hopes of creating a yet better world.
80   Or perhaps the newborn world, freshly set off from the aether,°
         still retained a few seeds of the heaven from which it had come.
         The son of Iapetus° fashioned earth and water commingled
         into the image of gods, who are rulers of all things created.
         The other beasts, four-footed, gaze at the earth, looking downward;
85   but man was given a posture which forces his eyes to the heavens,
         walking erect and lifting his sight to the stars in their courses.

OVID, *Metamorphoses* 1.76–86

78. *maker of all things:* Jupiter. 80. *aether:* Upper nonearthly realm. 82. *son of Iapetus:* Prometheus.

We have already seen (Chapter 4) how in the *Enuma elish* human beings were made from the blood of Kingu to be servants of the gods, which is why humans are disposed to wickedness and why they must work constantly. A related Eastern story also told how humans were made from mud or clay. Hence our bodies turn to dust when we die, a version that entered the biblical narrative of how "the Lord God formed man of dust from the ground and breathed into his nostrils the breath of life, and man became a living being" (Genesis 2.4). But the story is far older than the Bible.

PROMETHEUS, PROTECTOR OF MORTALS

Prometheus had much in common with his Eastern predecessor, the clever Enki/Ea, and in the classical tradition he was also the protector of mortals, an important figure to modern European culture. His lineage was as lofty as that of Zeus, for his father Iapetus was a first-generation Titan, brother of Cronus. Prometheus' essential quality is encoded in his name, which according to a popular etymology means "forelearner," like a character from folklore. His name *appears* to be related to Metis, "cleverness," Zeus's first consort, and points to his inventive intelligence (really the name probably means "thief," to judge from its Indo-European root). Prometheus is the folktale trickster who delights in outwitting those who appear more powerful.

In a contrast typical of folklore, Prometheus "forelearner" naturally has a brother Epimetheus "afterlearner," or "dummy."

In Chapter 4, we examined Hesiod's story of Zeus's rise to power. Through violence and deceit, Zeus overcame the older generation of gods and became the ruler of the universe. He remained on guard, however, against anyone who might usurp his power, and he was particularly jealous and fearful of Prometheus, as we see in the following tale told by Hesiod about an incident at Meconê (me-**kō**-nē), another name for the town of Sicyon in the northern Peloponnesus, on the Corinthian Gulf. We can see why Zeus was so nervous about this mortal-loving, dangerous being:

[535] For once, when gods and mortals were gathered to feast at Meconê,
 Prometheus, trying to hoodwink great Zeus's wits and attention,
 had cheerfully butchered and served up the succulent flesh of an ox.
 To the others, gods and men, he handed the meat in due portions,
 and sweetbreads, dripping with suet, wrapped in the outermost layer
540 of the ox's stomach, a haggis. But the white bones he slyly concealed
 in shining fat, and to Zeus he presented the neatly wrapped bundle.
 Pausing a moment, the father of mortals and gods asked politely,
  "Son of Iapetus, you are surely the cleverest man now alive,
 but haven't you split the portions as unequally as can be?"
545 So spoke the inscrutable Zeus. To him Prometheus answered,
 assuming a treacherous smile, "O Zeus, the noblest and greatest
 of all the eternal gods, pick whichever your heart may desire."
  This was only deceit. But Zeus, unchanging of purpose,
 saw through the trick at once, and planned in his vengeful spirit
550 a terrible future for mortal men, one they could never evade.
 He took the white suet in his hands, but within him his heart raged with anger
 as he saw that the tempting outside held the ox's white bones beneath.
 And ever since then, men of every race on the face of the earth
 burn the white bones on the altar in sacrifice to the immortals.

HESIOD, Theogony 535–557

The pile of glistening fat was more appetizing than the repulsive stomach, and Zeus accepted the fat and the bones hidden beneath. For this reason, at a sacrifice the Greeks ate the meat but burned the bones to the gods. "Prometheus at Meconê" is an etiological myth to explain a conspicuous detail of Greek sacrifice. Hesiod excuses Zeus's stupidity by explaining that he had really seen through the trick all along and made the wrong choice only to justify the pain he was planning to inflict on humans. In an earlier version, however, we cannot doubt that Zeus was the stupid ogre, as gullible as his father Cronus, who outwitted Uranus but could not distinguish a stone wrapped in swaddling clothes from a live baby.

Zeus was so angered by what happened at Meconê that, to punish Prometheus' favorites, he removed fire from the trees where it had lurked before, available to mortals when lightning struck or when branches, rubbing against one another, burst into flame. Mortals who had learned to sustain themselves by eating cooked meat now must starve. But Prometheus pitied his beloved mortals and stole fire from heaven by hiding it in a fennel stalk, a thick plant stem common in the Mediterranean with a soft inflammable pith and a hard fire-resistant coat, used in early times to transport live coals. Ever since Prometheus' theft, human beings have enjoyed the permanent possession of fire, although only constant labor at gathering fuel can maintain it. After the incident at Meconê, human life was one of unremitting labor.

Zeus now turned on the Titan himself, who twice had deceived him, who even threatened his rule. Zeus ordered Strength (*Kratos*) and Violence (*Bia*), children of the underworld river Styx, to bind Prometheus to a pillar in the Caucasus Mountains at the eastern end of the Black Sea (Figure 5.1):

[521]   He bound Prometheus the schemer in inescapable fetters,
       a torment to bear, and through them he drove a mighty stone pylon,
       and sent a long-winged eagle to gnaw his incorruptible liver.
       By day the bird fed upon it, but each night as much was replenished
525   as was lost on the day before.

HESIOD, *Theogony* 521–525

FIGURE 5.1 The punishment of the Titans Atlas and Prometheus on a Spartan black-figured cup from the sixth century BC. On the left, Atlas holds up the sky on his shoulders; the snake probably represents a serpent named Ladon, thought to protect the tree of life that grew in the magical Garden of the Hesperides at the end of the world. Prometheus, in a position like that in which real prisoners were bound, hangs from a pillar while an eagle tears his liver.   (Vatican Museums; Scala / Art Resource, New York)

PERSPECTIVE 5.1

KRATOS: GOD OF WAR

The compelling myth of the Greek hero has inspired several video games. *God of War* was released in 2005, the first installment in a *God of War* series, which sold eight million copies. Loosely based on Greek myth, its focus is on Kratos (Greek "strength"), one of the beings who bound Prometheus to the rock according to Aeschylus' account. In the game he is at first not a god, but a mortal. Kratos must stop the God of War, Ares, from destroying Athens by finding Pandora's Box.

The player typically has to navigate Kratos through a series of tests and mazes to reach intermediate goals. The hero's principal weapons are the magic Blades of Chaos and the Blade of Artemis. He can acquire, too, the magic power of Poseidon's Rage, Medusa's Gaze, Zeus's Fury, and the Army of Hades. Poseidon's Trident allows Kratos to breathe underwater. He can acquire a special ability called Rage of the Gods that provides a temporary invulnerability. Killing enemies recharges this ability.

In his adventures Kratos can find Health and Magic upgrades, called Gorgon Eyes and Phoenix Feathers, hidden in chests. Other chests contain colored orbs that allow Kratos to upgrade his magic and his weapons. An encounter with two maids on Kratos' ship permits a quick-time sex mini-game.

Kratos is in the service of the gods of Olympus. A series of flashbacks reveals that once he was an officer in the Spartan army who led his army to victory, until they meet a horde of invading barbarians (see Perspective 2). The Spartans are overwhelmed. The barbarian king is about to kill Kratos when Kratos cries out to Ares, the God of War, and pledges his life in servitude if Ares will only spare him and give him the power to destroy his enemies.

Ares hears the prayer and gives Kratos the Blades of Chaos—a pair of blades attached to chains forged in Tartarus. Kratos quickly cuts off the head of the barbarian king. The victorious Kratos then wages war against his fellow Greeks, leading an attack on a village in which Ares has secretly placed Kratos' wife and child. Kratos accidentally kills them.

Ares intends by this act to make Kratos the perfect warrior, indifferent to everything but destruction, but Kratos instead renounces his servitude to Ares. The oracle of the destroyed village curses Kratos, and the ashes of his murdered family stick to his skin, turning it ash-white so that now he is called the Ghost of Sparta. Bad dreams plague Kratos. In repentance he commits to ten years of servitude to the other gods of Olympus.

But Kratos tires of his servitude and summons Athena to see how he can get out of it. She says that if Kratos murders the treacherous Ares, he will be forgiven for murdering his family.

Athena guides Kratos to Athens, under siege by Ares' followers. Kratos battles his way to Athens' oracle and learns that the only way to defeat Ares is to find Pandora's Box, which contains the power to kill a god. Kratos traverses the Desert of Lost Souls. He summons the Titan Cronos. Cronos has the Temple of Pandora, which contains Pandora's box, chained to his back, a punishment from Zeus for Cronos' role in the Titanomachy. Kratos climbs the steps of the temple for three days before reaching the entrance. When he enters, he must overcome an array of traps and an army of monsters.

Kratos finds Pandora's Box, but as he leaves the temple Ares springs on him and kills him. Harpies take Pandora's Box to Ares and Kratos falls into the underworld. With the aid of a mysterious grave digger that he met outside Athens, he escapes and returns to Athens.

Kratos recovers Pandora's Box from Ares, opens it, and uses the power within to become like a god. Ares tries his best to strip Kratos of the Blades of Chaos, but Kratos survives and kills him. Athens is saved.

Although according to Athena Kratos' sins are forgiven, the gods cannot rid him of his nightmares. Kratos attempts suicide by casting himself into the Aegean Sea, but Athena brings him to Olympus. As a reward for his service, Athena grants him Athena's Blades. Kratos becomes the new God of War!

The game won many awards and has led to additional games. Whereas the game's creators have made up a "myth" using elements and traditional figures from Greek myth, the myth is very un-Greek in its story of a mortal who overcomes and replaces an Olympian god. As a Spartan, Kratos recalls Leonidas who stood against the barbarian at Thermopylae. In Homer Athena does oppose Ares and in one scene stands behind his wounding, but of course there can be no question of replacing him. Ares' secret hiding of the wife and child in the plundered village is something Hermes would do, not the one-dimensional Ares. Kratos' descent to the underworld does recall Heracles' journey there, yet Pandora's Box is not the source of evil, as it is in the Greek story: It is a magic box that holds the secret of victory. The Blades of Chaos and the Blade of Artemis and similar magic tools bear names that evoke the ancient past, but have little to do with it.

In real life vicious criminals were taken to the boundaries of a territory, stripped naked, nailed to a post, and allowed to die miserably, when eaters of carrion consumed their flesh. (Jesus, too, was crucified "outside the city.") But Prometheus, being immortal, can never die; his liver grows back each day, an image of everlasting intolerable torment. He did it for us. In Aeschylus' strange play *Prometheus Bound* (c. 430 BC), the Titan, hanging in his unbreakable bonds, describes the many benefits he conferred on mortals, for which he now suffered:

[442]   Now listen while I tell of mortals' pain,
how primitive they were till I fired their wits.
I tell you, not from disgust at men, but showing
445   how much they owe me. Before then, they had eyes

that blankly gazed, ears hearing empty sound.
Shapes in a dream, they blundered through long years.
They built no house of brick to catch the sun,
or even of wood, but antlike dwelt in ditches,
450   crowding in lightless crannies, with no sign
to show when winter would come or flowery spring,
or summer with its crops. Their work was mindless
till I explained the courses of the stars.
I taught them mathematics, wisdom's lore,
455   and words in letters, of all things remembrancer,
mother and servant of arts. I was the first
to harness beasts with saddle, yoke, and chain,
thus making them inherit mortals' sweat.
I set the horse, exulting in his reins,
460   to draw the car, image of wealthy pride.
Who before me, pray, made canvas wings
for sea-battered ships? I was the one
who found all this for men—but for myself,
no way to freedom from these pressing toils.

AESCHYLUS, *Prometheus Bound* 442–471

Ancient myth usually depicts early human beings as having lived in a paradise
that now is lost, a biblical Eden. The Greeks (and Mesopotamians) also told stories
of a better time in the remote past, as we shall see, but as Aeschylus tells it, nothing of the kind was true. Early humans were rude, witless, savage, and lacking self-
consciousness. Prometheus taught them brickmaking, woodworking, the calendar,
numbers, writing, animal husbandry, and seafaring. Prometheus boasts of his other
contributions:

[476]   Now hear the rest, and, hearing, wonder more
at the devices that I planned for men.
Until my time, whenever men fell ill
there was no help in diet, potion, ointment,
480   or draft; men simply shriveled up and died
for lack of drugs. I showed them gentle compounds,
remedies saving men from all disease.
I ferreted out dark ways of prophecy
and was the first to teach the lore of dreams,
485   what men would face when they awoke from sleep.
I taught them to divine from random sounds,
chance meetings in the road, the swoop of birds.
Some signs are good by nature, some are not.
I showed men which is which. The ways they live,
490   their loves and hates, with whom they flock—these too.
I showed the art of entrails: were they smooth?
what color should they have to please the god?
The liver too, its lobes of checkered beauty.
By burning joints and haunch, well wrapped in fat,
495   and showing them the unknown signs in flame,
I set them on the way to prophetic art.

So much for that. Who before me dared claim
to show men metals hidden deep in the earth—
copper and iron, silver, even gold?
500   No one. So, to put it in a word,
all human arts came from Prometheus.

Aeschylus, Prometheus Bound 476–506

The highest human skills, then, are the gifts of Prometheus: medicine, metallurgy, and prophecy from dreams, the shape of intestines, and astronomical phenomena. Prometheus is the great culture-bearer. He made human life what it is.

At last the hero Heracles killed the devouring eagle and freed the Titan. Zeus did not object, for Prometheus had by then done Zeus a great favor. When an oracle declared that a child greater than its father would be born to a certain woman, only Prometheus knew that the oracle referred to the Nereid Thetis, whom Zeus admired. While bound in chains, Prometheus the forelearner revealed the prophecy. Zeus backed off and compelled Thetis to marry a mortal—Peleus, father of Achilles, a son far greater than his father. **(For a complete version of *Prometheus Bound*, go to http://bacchicstage .wordpress.com/aeschylus-2/prometheus-bound/)**

PANDORA

Zeus punished Prometheus for stealing fire, but he also punished man by imposing what Hesiod regarded as the greatest affliction of all: woman! Hesiod tells the story, rich with sexual antagonism, in both the *Theogony* and the *Works and Days*. Here is the version from *Works and Days*:

[42]   The gods control our livelihood, holding it back from us mortals.
        You ought to be able to earn enough by a single day's labor
        as now you could in a year—and that in a leisurely fashion.
45   At the end of that day you could hang your rudder to dry in the smoke.
        The ox's toil would be finished, and that of long-suffering mules.
        But Zeus in his irritation holds back that sort of existence,
        because Prometheus fooled him, devising a treacherous scheme.
        Ever since then Zeus has plotted terrible pain for us mortals.
50   Zeus had deprived us of fire. But the noble son of Iapetus,
        to counter the schemes of Zeus, then stole it back for humankind.
        Stealthily hidden, it smoldered away in a dry stalk of fennel [Figure 5.2].
        The raging Compeller of Clouds upbraided defiant Prometheus:
        "Son of Iapetus, you surely are the slyest schemer of all.
55   You really delighted in swindling me by stealing the fire,
        but soon you will find it a curse to yourself and to men yet to be.
        I shall give them a present to compensate for the fire.
        May they all be merry at heart, forever embracing this horror!"
        With a nasty smile, the father of men and gods
60   told famous Hephaestus to hurry, to knead the water and clay,
        to add human speech and strength, to give it a goddess's form

FIGURE 5.2 Prometheus and satyrs, on a wine-bowl, c. 420 BC. Holding the fennel stalk that conceals the fire stolen from heaven, Prometheus (center figure) fences with satyrs who oppose the theft, probably an illustration of Aeschylus' lost satyr play *Prometheus the Fire-bearer*. (Ashmolean Museum, Oxford, UK)

and the lovely face of a maiden. Next he ordered Athena
to teach her womanly skill, to weave on a well-built loom.
Aphrodite the golden he told to crown her head with desire,
65   but with heartbreak as well, and all the aching sorrow of love.
Last of all he had Hermes the herald, the killer of Argus,°
to give her thievish morals, and to add the soul of a bitch.
Thus he decreed. The immortals obeyed Lord Zeus, son of Cronus.
The famous lame craftsman° molded a lump of clay to an image,
70   the form of a modest girl, as the son of Cronus designed it.
The gray-eyed goddess Athena saw to her clothing and hair.
The Graces and Lady Persuasion decked her with golden jewelry,
to accent the bloom of her flesh, and the fair-haired Seasons together
crowned her with flowers of spring.
75   Then the killer of Argus, the guide, the herald of gods,
filled her with lies, with swindles, all sorts of thievish behavior,
and named the woman Pandora,° since all who dwell on Olympus
gave her their gifts—a curse to men who must live by bread.
When the father at last had completed this inescapable trap,
80   he sent the famous killer of Argus, swift messenger of the gods,
to bring her to Epimetheus. But he in his folly ignored
Prometheus' warning, to accept no gift from Zeus of Olympus,
but to send it right back, lest it bring eternal trouble to men.
Epimetheus gladly received her, remembering too late the injunction.

66. *Argus:* A monster killed by Hermes, hence his epithet *Argeïphontes,* "Argus-killer."   69. *craftsman:* Hephaestus.   77. *Pandora:* "All-gifted."

85   Till then men had lived on the face of the earth
     far from all ills, without torment, pain, or dreadful disease,
     that bring men down to their graves. But now the hands of the woman
     lifted the jar's° heavy lid and allowed them all to escape,
     planning the bitterest sorrows for men. Hope only remained
90   in a prison she could not escape, under the lip of the jar.
     She could not fly out, for the woman replaced the great heavy lid.
     But the other numberless miseries were spread over all humankind.
     The earth is crowded with anguish, equally so the sea.
     Some pestilence strikes men by day; some comes on as it will
95   in night's quiet dark, its voice being silenced by Zeus's command.

HESIOD, Works and Days 42–104

88. *jar's:* Hesiod does not tell where she got the jar, but introduces it suddenly. Presumably it contained the gifts of the gods mentioned in line 78. Medieval tradition falsely reported it to be a box, hence our expression "to open Pandora's box" for "to let loose a host of troubles."

The folktale of **Pandora**, like the biblical story of Adam and Eve, is etiological to explain the origin of woman, marriage, and suffering in the world: They are all mixed together. Prometheus offered Zeus something that looked good on the outside, covered in glistening fat. Within were only bones. Zeus now offered a similar deception to man. It looked good on the outside, but within was filled with "lies, with swindles, all sorts of thievish behavior." Fortunately, we still have Hope (this seems to be his meaning, but how this can be, when Hope is inside the jar, Hesiod does not explain).

In Aeschylus, Prometheus presents an evolutionary vision of primitive human conditions, which Prometheus himself alleviated by introducing the arts of civilized life. In Hesiod's woman-hating story, life once was good—he is not bothered by the problem of reproduction in a unisexual world—before Pandora opened the jar. Now life is labor, misery, and disease, with death at the end. Oddly, Hesiod does not tell us that Pandora was forbidden to open the jar, perhaps because that was obvious. However, Epimetheus was explicitly told not to accept gifts from the gods, yet he disobeyed (Figure 5.3). As in the biblical folktale, which also depends on a violated prohibition ("Don't eat from the Tree of the Knowledge of Good and Evil"), the woman is responsible for suffering in the world.

Pandora's descendants, the "race" (*genos*) of women, are a species apart who contribute nothing to the production of food yet consume vast quantities of it:

[591]   From her descends the ruinous race and tribe of women,
     who live as a curse and cause of sorrow to mortal men,
     no partners in grim poverty, but only useless excesses.
     As bees in their dome-shaped hive faithfully tend to the drones,
595   who take no part in hard work while the workers toil through the day;
     till sunset they keep on loading their honey in the white comb,
     while the drones sit lazily peering out from the arching hive,

FIGURE 5.3 Epimetheus seduced by Pandora on an Attic vase, c. 450 BC. Zeus, on the far left, leans on his staff of office, while at his command Hermes conveys Pandora to Epimetheus. The two gods, party to a deception, exchange conspiratorial glances. Pandora's negative qualities were partly the gift of Hermes, god of deception. In his left hand Hermes holds a flower, a sign that a gift is about to be exchanged. In his right hand he holds his special scepter, the caduceus. Epimetheus, oblivious to the danger, reaches out to Pandora as she rises from the earth, wearing the adornments that Hesiod describes: a lovely garment, veil, and crown. Their eyes lock together, the gaze of sexual attraction symbolized by the small winged Eros above Pandora, who mocks the modesty expected of the bride by throwing wide her arms. The hammer in the hand of Epimetheus usually is associated with Hephaestus and is a puzzle: Perhaps the scene illustrates a lost play by Sophocles (c. 460 BC) called *Pandora, or The Hammerers.*   (Ashmolean Museum, Oxford, UK)

> sweeping the fruit of this labor into their own slow bellies°—
> just so Zeus, who thunders on high, saw to it that women,
> 600   curse of us mortal men, should invent work utterly useless.

HESIOD, *Theogony* 591–602

598. *bellies:* Hesiod did not know that drone bees are males and workers sterile females.

PERSPECTIVE 5.2

PROMETHEUS AND THE ROMANTICS

In the eighteenth century, the established political order of Europe seemed entirely corrupt, and the figure of Prometheus inspired many romantic rebels, especially during and after the French Revolution. The Romantic Movement in literature, which these rebels generated, usually is dated from the publication of the *Lyrical Ballads* (1798) of Coleridge and Wordsworth, two of the intellectual heirs of the American and French revolutions. Inspired by their call for a new world-order, Englishman Percy Bysshe Shelley (1792–1822), a well-to-do but wild-eyed political and moral radical, wrote a verse drama, *Prometheus Unbound* (1820), a sort of sequel to the *Prometheus Bound* of Aeschylus. Shelley's Titan is a heroic rebel for the sake of humankind; his opponent, Jupiter, is all cruelty and evil. Prometheus is finally relieved from his torments, Jupiter is driven from the throne, and a new era of love begins.

At about the same time that Shelley wrote *Prometheus Unbound,* his wife, Mary Wollstonecraft Shelley (daughter of the early feminist author of *The Vindication of the Rights of Women,* 1792) wrote *Frankenstein, or, The Modern Prometheus.* The young student Frankenstein, amoral and irresponsible, creates out of human body parts taken from dissecting rooms and cemeteries a humanlike creature, a *tabula rasa* ("clean palette") ready to accept whatever he is taught by his environment (hence the novel's title, because Frankenstein, like Prometheus, makes a man) (Perspective Figure 5.1). First, the nameless monster learns love and morality from a family he secretly observes. Then he learns to be angry and cruel when, after seeking his maker, he is denied respect and love. He kills Frankenstein's brother and Frankenstein's bride and finally Frankenstein himself, then disappears.

Other Romantics worked in the same vein, such as Lord Byron (1788–1824), who died at age thirty-six of a fever while fighting to free Greece from the Turks. Byron's amazing life was a titillating series of scandals. His verse was enormously and deservedly popular, and he too celebrated the suffering rebel in his short poem, *Prometheus* (1816):

> Thy godlike crime was to be kind,
>   to render with thy precepts less
>   the sum of human wretchedness,
> and strengthen Man with his own mind.
>   But, baffled as thou wert from high,
>   still, in thy patient energy,
> in the endurance and repulse
>   of thine impenetrable spirit
> which Earth and Heaven could not convulse,
>   a mighty lesson we inherit.

PERSPECTIVE FIGURE 5.1 Dr. Frankenstein (Boris Karloff) and Fritz (Dwight Frye) prepare to bring the monster to life in a scene from the 1931 movie version of Mary Shelly's "Frankenstein." (Courtesy of the Everett Collection)

The spirit of the Romantic poets is still alive in icons of popular culture. Like Byron and Shelley, such rock musicians as Jimi Hendrix, Janis Joplin, Jim Morrison, and Kurt Cobain led unconventional lives, inspired millions, and died young. Like their many musical heirs, these modern romantics rebelled against the constraints of convention, finding life's meaning in feeling, not reason.

As Prometheus had covered the good part of the sacrifice with the unappetizing stomach, so is Pandora nothing but a useless stomach, a consumer of food and wealth. The male is the food producer, the female the unproductive consumer. Hesiod does not mention and has no respect for woman's tireless labor in the bearing of children, the production of cloth, and in the maintenance of the household. Still, there is no hope of altogether abandoning women, Pandora's descendants:

[603]   Whoever keeps clear of marriage and the trouble fomented by women,
        and is quite content to stay single, must expect a gloomy old age,
605   with no one at hand to attend him. He may have plenty of money,

but when he dies his relations, often far distant, divide it.°
Even if someone is married to a wise and compatible woman,
all through his life he will find that trouble is mixed with his joy.

HESIOD, *Theogony* 603610

606. *divide it:* In Hesiod's time the inheritance of a man's property seems to have been limited to his family, first to his son and then to his brothers and more distant relations.

Modern readers are struck by the virulence of Hesiod's depiction of women (there are other examples in early Greek literature), presented as an unavoidable evil and a punishment for bad relations with the gods. Even the Bible, whose story of Eve's betrayal bears a similar message, accords to woman a partnership in the propagation of the species, a role that Hesiod barely mentions. The roots of misogyny are varied and not easily understood. In early times women were kept separate from men from a magical fear of woman's menses, considered an extremely dangerous and polluting substance. Hence the biblical command, "When a woman has a discharge of blood . . . this uncleanness of her monthly period shall last for seven days . . . Anyone who touches her will be unclean until evening. Any bed she lies on in this state will be unclean" (Leviticus 15.19–20).

Among the Greeks, however, misogyny seems to be based not so much on primitive magical terror, or economic resentment as in Hesiod's surly complaint, as on a male resentment of the institution of monogamy itself. Greek myth is obsessed with hostile relations between the sexes, especially between married couples. In considering the meaning of such passages as those we have just examined we need to remember that, with minor exceptions, ancient literature, and myth, was composed by males for males in an environment utterly ruled by males (as was the Bible).

Hesiod explains Pandora's name as reflecting the fact that every god and goddess endowed her with a charm, "all-gifted," but the name probably means "all-giver," a name for a mother-goddess, like Gaea, the giver of all things, here transformed into a young girl with "thievish morals" and "the soul of a bitch." Poor dumb Epimetheus, violating a prohibition, fell victim to her beauty, Aphrodite's gift, and took her as a wife. In Pandora is mirrored in miniature the grand mythical ambiguity of Gaea/Rhea. Pretty outside in fine attire and jewels of gold, within she is the Earth within which the male must plant his seed if he hopes to sire an heir and in this small way defy mortality. (**For the complete text of Hesiod's *Works and Days*, see http://www.sacred-texts.com/cla/hesiod/works.htm**)

Observations: Women as Containers

Pandora has a jar, and in Greek society women daily carried water to the house in jars with big bellies called *hydriae,* "water jars." Such jars often have pictures on them revealing scenes from women's daily lives (Figure 5.4).

The word *amnion* is used both for the membrane that surrounds the fetus (hence our "amniotic fluid") and for a jar that holds the blood of sacrifice. In Greek religious

FIGURE 5.4 Women at the well. The woman at the left fills her jar from the fountain while the middle figure waits, balancing her still empty water jar on her head. The woman at the right fills her jar from a second fountain spigot. Black-figured water jar, c. 530–520 BC.   (Musée du Louvre, Paris; Erich Lessing / Art Resource, New York)

ritual, women and girls often carry baskets, including the basket that contains the sacrificial knife hidden in a heap of wheat or barley. The grain is life, the knife is death, which through the shedding of blood guarantees new life. The basket and its contents, like the woman, are a mystery. When the young virgin *Arrhephoroi*, "basket-carriers," in the myths of Athens (see Chapter 16) peer into a basket supposedly containing the young Athenian prince Erichthonius, they are driven mad and leap to their deaths from the Acropolis. Painted Greek pots again and again show women receiving vessels, boxes, baskets, and jars, always from other women, never from men. At her wedding, especially, a Greek woman is surrounded by boxes (Figure 5.5).

To graves women carried a special flat basket containing magical objects for the dead. On the Parthenon temple reliefs in Athens, Demeter and Persephonê, who guarantee fertility, are seated on baskets. In a curious ritual, widespread in the ancient world, dedicated to the hero Adonis who died young, women planted seeds in broken jars, then allowed the hot sun to destroy the young plants. Perhaps the ritual's meaning was to drive away danger to the human young by providing a substitute for hostile spirits, a ransom; even so will the woman's jar, her womb, stay unbroken and her seed will not wither, but live. The Greeks called a pregnant woman a "closed jar." The Danaïds (**dā**-na-idz), who refused proper marriage and pregnancy when they killed their husbands on their wedding night, were condemned forever to carry water in broken jugs. The jugs symbolize their own bodies.

FIGURE 5.5 Aphrodite sits on a chest viewing herself in a mirror, while the winged Eros stands before her holding a sash, on an Apulian vase from southern Italy, c. 360 BC. Presumably the mirror, and other rich things, would be kept in the chest on which she sits, an object often associated with women. Behind the goddess a stele is inscribed APHRODITE.   (© The Cleveland Museum of Art, 2002)

Earth is the great container of seed (and of the dead), and a phrase in the Greek wedding ceremony urged the husband to "plow his wife for the begetting of new children." She too is the concealing, mysterious earth, holding treasure. The male enters into the dark recesses of the virgin's body, itself a treasure, and spills his milky fluid to mix with the woman's clay to form a new treasure, the future's hope.

As females bring males into the world from the jars within their bodies, so does woman, who is earth that holds dead bodies, make the dangerous preparations for burial. Only women dared touch the bodies of the dead to clean them and rub them with scented oils, and only women touched the bloody, soiled newborn to clean it and make it shine.

As earth and jars contain, so do they consume. Hesiod is depressed by the economic hardship imposed by female mouths. In myth (as in the story of Perseus) babies are placed into jars or chests from which they emerge born again, but into jars also go the bones of the dead. A euphemism for exposing one's newborn to die was "to put it in a pot."

In the myth of Pandora, the jar is the emblem of woman herself, the first woman. From her came all evils, out of the womb, so like a tomb, into the world. Hope, still within the jar, is like the child in the womb: unfulfilled, a possibility for good or ill. From the womb come children who in Greek myth will kill or curse their parents or go to bed with them or make them proud. Still, Hope remains in the jar, and there is no other way.

THE FIVE RACES

In the *Works and Days* Hesiod relates another story about the early days, describing the decline of humankind from a blessed past to a wretched present, the myth of the Five Races (*genea*, the same word Hesiod uses to describe the "race," *genos*, of women):

[106]   If you wish, I will use my skill to sketch you another story
    of how both men and immortals arose at the start of things.
    I promise you all my skill, so plant this account in your memory.
      The first race of men the gods who live on Olympus created,
110   in the days when Cronus was ruler in heaven, was fashioned of *gold*.
    They lived like gods, with hearts all unacquainted with trouble,
    removed far away from labor and sorrow. Old age and depression
    had not yet appeared, but vigorous of hand and foot, ever youthful,
    they passed their days in feasting, unaging, youthful of body,
115   and when they died at last, they vanished away like a dream.
    All good things were theirs. The land yielded grain in abundance,
    in harvests demanding no toil. They lived, contented and quiet,
    surrounded by blessings, with each man looking after his duties.
    But at last Earth covered this race, and now, by Zeus's design,
120   they walk the earth, kindly spirits, guards and defenders of mortals . . .
      The gods who live on Olympus made a second, inferior race,
    of *silver*, unlike the golden in form, and duller in reason.
    At the side of its lady mother, nursing and playing at home,
    a child spent a hundred years, no better, indeed, than a baby.
125   When finally he grew up and reached the measure of manhood,
    he lived for a few years more, in trouble through his own folly.
    They could not hold back their hands from violence aimed at each other,
    and refused to honor the gods with sacrifice at the high altars,
    an old universal tradition. So Zeus, the son of great Cronus,
130   angrily buried them out of his sight for their stiff-necked refusal
    to honor the blessed gods, the dwellers on lofty Olympus.
    But even though earth has hidden this race deep under the ground,
    mortals still call them blessed, though subterranean, spirits—
    second in rank, no doubt, but yet entitled to honor.
135   Zeus the Father then made yet another, a third race of mortals,
    this one fashioned of *bronze*, a terrible race and warlike,
    sprung from ash-trees, concerned with the bloody labor of Ares.
    They ate no bread from the earth, for their spirits were bent upon plunder.
    No one dared to approach them, so mighty and strong were the hands
140   that grew from invincible arms beneath their muscular shoulders.
    This race's weapons were bronze, and bronze as well were its houses;
    all its works were of bronze, for it had not discovered black iron.
    They fell by each other's hands, and nameless they all descended
    to the mildewy house of cold Hades, in spite of their terrible power;
145   when black Death seized them, they fled from the glorious light of the sun.
      Now when the grave had covered this generation as well,
    Zeus, son of Cronus, created a fourth on the life-giving earth,
    braver and juster by far, the godlike race of the *heroes*.
    Indeed, they are called half-gods, this race preceding our era,

150 over the whole wide earth. Dread warfare and terrible slaughter
carried some of them off at Thebes, in the land of old Cadmus,°
fighting each other for plunder, to loot King Oedipus'° cattle.
Warfare took others in ships over the sea's surging billows,
to fight for the sake of Helen, the woman with beautiful hair.

155 For most of them, death was the end which hid them away from our vision,
but on some, father Zeus, son of Cronus, bestowed a new way of living,
far from the haunts of men, at the very end of the world.
 There they remain, untroubled at heart and free from disturbance,
in the far-away Isles of the Blessed, by the swirling waters of Ocean,

160 prosperous heroes, to whom three harvests a year are accorded.
Cronus rules as their king, for the father of men and immortals
set him free from his chains and granted him power and honor.
But after them, broad-fronted Zeus made no such glorious race
to dwell on the face of the earth, the fertile mother of all.

165 O, that I did not live with men of the fifth generation!
that I had perished before it, or else had been born hereafter.
For now as things are, our race is of *iron.*
 Will the day never come for ceasing unending labor and warfare,
or a night to stop the destruction? Or will the immortals forever

170 keep piling fresh bitter causes of quarrels and hatred upon us?
Yet for a while some good will still be mixed with the evil,
till Zeus destroys this race like the others, when finally comes the time
when children are born with the cynical grizzled hair of old age;
when father shares no more with his son or son with his father;

175 when guest and host are at odds, oldest friend with his comrade;
when your brother no more is your truest friend, as he used to be.
When people abuse their parents as these grow older and weaker,
sarcastic and proud they will mock the certain revenge of the gods,
refusing any return for the cost and pain of their rearing.

180 Trusting in force, they will raid and plunder each other's dominions.
The faithful will win no regard, nor even the just or the honest.
Only the cynical doer of evil will win the world's admiration,
he who thinks his might makes right, whose heart is empty of scruple.
Knaves will cheat honest men, backing their falsehoods with oaths.

185 Mischievous envy, sour in face and tongue, will lay ambush,
entrapping all who are poor, entrapping all who are honest.
 When all this comes to pass, Shame and Indignation,
shrouding their honest faces from human sight with white veils,
will abandon mortals and hurry far from the wide-wayed earth,

190 fleeing back to Olympus and its gods, leaving only the prospect
to mortals of sorrow and pain, with no defenses against them.

       HESIOD, *Works and Days* 106–201

---

151. *Cadmus:* Founder of the city of Thebes. 152. *Oedipus:* A legendary king of Thebes.

  All later talk of a golden age depends ultimately on this passage in Hesiod and his description of the race of *gold*, who lived in the days of Cronus. They were happy and blessed and at death became spirits on the earth, watching over and protecting mortals. The time of the Golden Race was similar to life before Zeus sent down

Pandora, but Hesiod does not explicitly associate the myth of Pandora with the myth of the Five Races.

The next race, of *silver*, was far worse than the first. A child would stay young for a hundred years, then grow up suddenly, age, and die. The Silver Race acted with violence and did not respect the gods. Still, when they died, they became spirits who live under the ground.

The third race, made of *bronze*, was worse than the silver. Born from ash trees, from which the shafts of spears were made, they were terrible, strong, and violent. Their weapons and houses were of bronze; they did not understand ironworking. Unlike the preceding two races, at death they descended into the realm of Hades, where they dwell in darkness.

The fourth race, that of *heroes*, was in some ways better than the bronze. This race fought at seven-gated Thebes and on the windy plain of Troy to take back lovely Helen. Some heroes never died at all but were transported to the Isles of the Blessed at the end of the world, under the rule of Cronus, whom Zeus has liberated (from Tartarus). They live there still, never knowing sorrow.

The fifth race, of *iron*, is Hesiod's own.

Hesiod has inherited from the East a classification of the phases of human existence into gold, silver, bronze, and iron, a picture of ever-worsening conditions. A similar myth built around a metallic metaphor was told in ancient Persia, where many think Hesiod's myth originated. We might also compare the great idol in Nebuchadnezzar's dream in the biblical Book of Daniel (2.31–33), which refers to a sequence of kingdoms: "You looked, O king, and there before you stood a large statue—an enormous, dazzling statue, awesome in appearance. The head of the statue was made of pure gold, its chest and arms of silver, its belly and thighs of bronze, its legs of iron, its feet partly of iron and partly of baked clay" (hence our expression "feet of clay"). But under the influence of the Greek oral tradition, which told of wars against Thebes and Troy, Hesiod has inserted a fifth race, the race of heroes, between the race of bronze and his own iron world of crime and sorrow.

Hesiod's poems reflect the disturbances of a time of radical social and economic change in Greece. Land was moving from group to private ownership. The poor, forced to mortgage and finally lose their plots, sank into slavery or were forced to emigrate to the cities or to colonies far away in Sicily, Italy, and elsewhere. International trade in oil and wine was growing, coinage was beginning, and traditional social hierarchies were shaken to their foundations. The invention of the Greek alphabet around 800 BC was like an atom bomb, blowing to smithereens the earlier world that lacked texts of any kind, changing not only Greek but human life forever. Cities of artisans and sailors increased in size, and political and legal systems did not keep pace.

Later commentators interpreted Hesiod's account as a chronological one and attempted, with little success, to slot in such unrelated mythical events as the universal flood and the career of Prometheus. A basic contradiction always remained because the Golden Race lived under Cronus, who according to Hesiod's other account was tyrannous and evil. In *Works and Days*, Cronus returned to rule the Isles of the Blessed and the select survivors from the race of heroes. We can guess how Hesiod came to his contradiction: Cronus was an early king, the Golden Race was the first race, so Cronus ruled in the era of the Golden Race. He also ruled over the Isles of the Blessed, a kind of paradise like the world when the Golden Race was alive.

Hesiod's description of his own era, apparently the eighth century BC, reflects the same pessimism that characterized Mesopotamian myth, although his wish "that I had perished before it, or else had been born hereafter" suggests that conditions may improve in the future, even return to those of the race of gold. Hesiod does not so much picture a world in constant decline (although his mythical models certainly did) as he contrasts the Silver, Bronze, Heroic, and Iron races with that of Gold, when humans lived in Paradise. The races that followed were all degenerate, although in different ways. Vergil, a Roman poet influenced by Hesiod, writing around the time of Christ after a hundred years of bitter, brutal, and unprecedented civil war, reinterpreted Hesiod's myth as a historical but circular chronology—a sequence of events in time bound to be repeated. A new cycle had now begun, he and others declared. The Golden Age (not a race of gold) had returned to earth under the enlightened rule of the emperor Augustus (Chapters 23, 24), who vanquished Antony and Cleopatra and brought back the glories of earlier times. And many believed him.

THE UNIVERSAL FLOOD

In the biblical flood story, "Yahweh saw that the wickedness of humans was great in the earth and that every imagination of the thoughts of their heart was evil continually. And Yahweh was sorry that he had made humans on the earth, and it grieved him to his heart. So Yahweh said, 'I will blot out humans, whom I have created from the face of the ground, humans and beasts and creeping things and birds of the air, for I am sorry that I have made them'" (Genesis 6.7–8). Only Noah, because of his goodness, was saved from the flood that Yahweh sent. When the waters receded, Noah sent out a dove, which first returned because it found no place to rest. He released it again; this time it came back with an olive twig. He let it go a third time, but by now it had no need of the ark and disappeared for good. The waters receded, and Noah built an altar and sacrificed to Yahweh.

This story is far older than the Bible, although the biblical account has made it perhaps the most widely known story on Earth. Let us first consider the origin of the flood story in Mesopotamia, then the classical version, which Greece's dry and riverless terrain at once proves to be a foreign importation.

Ziusudra, Atrahasis, and Noah

In Chapter 3 we described how in 1872 the young Assyriologist George Smith shocked the world when he revealed his discovery of a prebiblical account of the deluge. Smith read this account on a cuneiform tablet from the library of the Assyrian king Assurbanipal, destroyed in 612 BC. Scholars have since discovered several other Mesopotamian prebiblical descriptions of the flood, including one from Sumer dating to the third millennium BC, badly preserved, but the oldest existing account.

The Sumerian story begins with the creation of humans, the animals, and the foundation of five important cities. The next part of the tablet is broken. When it resumes, the gods have decreed the destruction of humankind by means of a universal flood. Some gods were opposed to their plan, and the clever Enki, god of the freshwater, intervened to save Ziusudra (ze-u-**sūd**-ra), "long life," a pious man. Enki advised Ziusudra to build a large boat:

> All the winds, amazingly strong and powerful, attacked,
> and the deluge rampaged over the earth.
> For seven days and nights
> the deluge rampaged in the land.
> The huge boat was slung about on the vast waters.
> Then Utu° came forth, he who sheds light on heaven and earth.
> Ziusudra drew open a window of the huge boat,
> Ziusudra the king threw himself down on the ground before Utu.
> He killed an ox, slaughtered a sheep.

Utu: The sun god.

Most of the rest of the tablet is lost. We learn only that Ziusudra was made to be like a god and transported to Dilmun, a mysterious land in the East, like the Isles of the Blessed, where there is no pain or suffering, the Sumerian paradise.

The later myth of Atrahasis (a-tra-**hās**-is), c. 1700 BC, preserved in the Semitic Akkadian language, adds many other details to the story. The hero there is called Atrahasis ("exceeding wise," another name for Ziusudra). Twelve hundred years after humans were made from mud to serve the gods, the world was so filled with the shouting masses of humankind that the storm-god Enlil could not get any sleep (like Apsu in the *Enuma elish*). To reduce the population, Enlil, with the other gods' approval, sent first a plague, then a drought, then a famine, but each time the population rebounded. Enlil devised the final solution: a great flood to exterminate all humankind. Although bound by oath not to reveal Enlil's plan, Ea (= Enki) advised Atrahasis, whom he favored because of his goodness, to build a huge boat and lock inside it all kinds of animals and his family:

> The great flood roared like a bull,
> the winds howled like the screaming of a wild ass,
> darkness was all, the sun blotted out.

The gods were horrified at the violence of the flood. Everyone but Atrahasis and his family perished (the folktale motif of "all but one") so that no offerings came to sustain the gods, who began to starve. The storm raged for seven days and nights before the rain stopped and the ship ran aground. Atrahasis prepared a sacrifice around which the hungry gods gathered like flies to a carcass of meat—all except the storm-god Enlil, furious that a mortal had escaped. But he too was appeased when the gods devised various means to control the population. Some women would henceforth be barren, some would remain chaste for ritual reasons, and a demon would appear to kill some babies at birth. These new measures would prevent the world from again being overrun by humans.

Archaeological evidence proves that devastating floods did sometimes take place in Mesopotamia when the rampaging Euphrates burst its banks and spilled across the flatland toward the lower Tigris channel. The story may go back to an actual flood, although no cultural break ever involved all Mesopotamia. Still, many variants of the story circulated in that region and spread to Palestine, Anatolia, and Greece. Although the basic themes are constant, details reflect different environments and national interests.

The Mesopotamian story of Ziusudra/Atrahasis, in which divine powers send destruction to correct overpopulation, reflects human insecurity before the capricious powers of the gods; it also explains the origin of barren women and stillbirths. The Hebrew account, on the other hand, presents Yahweh as destroying humans because of their wickedness, their moral failure. Omnipotent though he is, after the flood Yahweh voluntarily limits his power by striking a covenant with Noah and Noah's descendants. Yahweh promises never again to destroy the human race with water, but he commands that humans not eat animal blood and that they execute those humans who murder other humans (Genesis 9.4–6). The biblical story also is etiological, explaining the origin of Hebrew customs concerning abstinence from eating blood and homicide. The story of Noah attempts to explain the origin of the special relationship between Yahweh and the Hebrews.

The myth of the flood must also be understood in the context of Mesopotamian cosmogonic myth. The universal flood is a return to the watery conditions before the creation, when Tiamat, the saltwater, was mixed with Apsu, the sweet, reminiscent of the biblical "darkness upon the face of the deep" and perhaps reflected in the biblical description of the flood: "All the fountains of the great deep burst forth, and the windows of the heavens were opened" (Genesis 7.11). The Hebrew word *tehom*, translated "fluid chaos" in the first chapter of Genesis, is related to the Akkadian name *Tiamat*, which in turn may be related to Greek *Tethys*, one of the twelve original Titans and the female counterpart to watery Oceanus.

Lycaon, Deucalion, and Pyrrha

We do not find full accounts of the flood myth in the classical tradition until very late, in the Roman Period in Ovid and Apollodorus, but such accounts are certainly based on lost earlier Greek examples. Hearing that all men were vicious and corrupt, Zeus descended among them disguised as an ordinary man. Human wickedness was exemplified by Lycaon (li-kā-on), king of Arcadia in the central Peloponnesus, who practiced human sacrifice and cannibalism. In Ovid's telling of the story, Zeus/Jupiter is reporting to the other gods what happened:

[211] "Stories had come to my ears of the wickedness of the age.
       Hoping to find them false, I came down from the top of Olympus,
       and, god though I am, I examined the earth in the guise of a human.
       Merely to list the crimes I discovered all over the world
215   would be a tedious task, and the rumors fell short of the truth.
       Crossing the Maenala region, alive with the lairs of wild creatures,

and the pinewoods of cold Lycaeus, along the hills of Cyllenê,°
as darkness drew on to night, I came to a grim-fronted palace,
the home of the tyrant king of Arcadia. I gave him a signal
220 to show that a god was present, and his people started to worship.
At first Lycaon just laughed at the pious prayers they murmured,
then boasted, "I soon shall discover if this is a god or a mortal,
by a sure and certain test; no shadow of doubt will remain."
     This was his test. At night, when I was buried in slumber,
225 he planned to put me to death, in a way no man could expect.
That was Lycaon's idea of a rigorous test of the truth!
But even this was too little. He cut the throat of a hostage
(one of a group of Molossians°), cut up his half-dead remains,
stewed some parts in hot water, while broiling some on the fire,
230 and set the meal on the table . . .
                         With a crash of my vengeful lightning,
I split the house on the heads of its lord and his lickspittle gods,
who ran off in fright to the fields, to win some refuge in silence.
Safe, as he thought, he attempted to speak, but an animal's howling
was all that came out. His face was wet with the froth of his madness,
235 and his grisly craving for murder was turned against cattle and sheep.
His royal robe turned shaggy, his arms were an animal's forepaws.
Though now a wolf, he retains some trace of his human appearance.
His hair is still gray, his face displays its bloodthirsty features,
his eyes still gleam with the flashing of the same cruel animal glare.
240 This one household has fallen, as many households deserve,
for as far as the wide earth stretches, the savage Furies hold sway.
You would think all men had conspired; the sooner, then, let them pay
the penalty that they deserve! This is great Jupiter's° sentence."
     Some of the listening gods approved great Jupiter's decision,
245 and poured their oil on his fire; some gave assent by their silence.
Yet all were saddened to think of the unforeseen liquidation
of all the race of humankind. What will the world be like,
they asked, without population? Who will sacrifice at our altars?
Does Jupiter plan to abandon the earth to savage wild beasts?
250 Foreseeing new problems arising, they raised such questions as these.
The king of the heavens calmed them and told them they need not worry.
He promised to raise a new race, unlike the one that they knew,
born in a wonderful way. He was about to rain thunderbolts over the nations,
when a worrying thought gave him pause: Would the sacred aether on high
255 be ignited by this conflagration? Would the axis of Earth take fire?
His mind recalled the warning of Fate: "The day is approaching,
when the fabric of earth and sea and the lofty palace of heaven

---

217. *Cyllenê:* Maenala, Lycaeus, and Cyllenê are all mountains in Arcadia. The first was named after Maenalus, a son of Lycaon; on the peaks of Lycaeus, human sacrifice was offered to Zeus reportedly down to classical times; on Cyllenê, in northeast Arcadia, was born the god Hermes.   228. *Molossians:* A people who lived in Epirus, in northwestern Greece.   243. *Jupiter's:* Ovid, of course, uses Roman equivalents for the Greek gods (see reference chart just before the index at the back of the book).

will pass away in fire,° and the world's great mass will be shaken."
He hastily stored away the thunderbolts, forged by Cyclopes,
260   and conceived a different design, of opening dark heavy rain clouds
in every quarter of heaven, and drowning humankind in the waters.

OVID, *Metamorphoses* 1.211–261

258. *pass away in fire:* A reference to Stoic cosmology, which predicted just such an end to the world.

Ovid goes on to describe the destruction of the human race. Only Prometheus'
son **Deucalion** (dū-kā-li-on) (by an obscure Titaness) and Deucalion's wife, **Pyrrha**
(**pir**-a), a daughter of Pandora and Epimetheus, survived:

[317]   The rugged mountain Parnassus° stretches twin peaks to the heavens,
with tops rising over the clouds, where Deucalion, the only survivor
(the sea had covered all others), was carried with Pyrrha, his wife,
320   saved as they clung to a raft that drifted onto the mountain.
Together the pair paid homage to the local gods and the nymphs,
and to Themis, Destiny's mouthpiece, who then was the oracle's ruler.
    No better man ever existed, nor one more devoted to justice
than he; no woman showed greater respect for the gods than did Pyrrha.
325   When Jupiter saw that the world was awash with slow-moving water,
that of all its thousands of men one only remained alive,
that one woman only was left of all its thousands of women,
both of them guiltless of crime, for pious souls were they both,
he scattered the clouds and dispersed the rain with a northwest wind,
and made the land show its face to the sky and the sky to the earth.
330   The wrath of the sea was calmed by Neptune, ruler of ocean,
who, laying his trident aside, summoned the sea-green Triton,°
who rose from the deep, displaying his barnacle-crusted shoulders.
Neptune gave him an order to sound trumpet calls on his conch shell
335   to recall, as if by a signal, the rivers and waves to their places.
    He took up his hollow trumpet, a twisted shell whose mouth
comes spiraling off to one side. This horn of Triton, when sounded
even far out in the sea, fills the coastlines in either direction.
So now, as the sea-god raised it to his mouth and his dripping beard,
340   the waters, both fresh and salt, all heard it sound the retreat,
which forced the listening currents at once to obey its command.
Down sank the rivers, making mountains seem to be rising.
The sea was bounded by shores, the rivers contained by their channels,
the ground emerged once more as the waters ebbed. Landmarks appeared,
345   and woods, though naked of foliage, once more raised branches on high,
their tattered leaves still fluttering, brown and slimy with mud.
The circle of lands was completed. Deucalion viewed the bleak desert,
a desolate land, one plunged in silence, profound and unbroken.
Tears welled up in his eyes as he opened his heart to his Pyrrha:

317. *Parnassus:* Delphi, Apollo's oracle in classical times, is built on the south slope of this precipitous mountain, the Mount Ararat (where Noah's ark alighted, variously identified) of Greek myth.   331. *Triton:* A god of the sea, son of Poseidon/Neptune.

350   "My sister, my wife, the only woman alive on the earth,
joined as cousin and kin, as bride, and as partner in danger,
we are the whole population of the world, from the rise of the sun
to where it sets in the west. The ocean has swallowed all else.
And how can we be assured that our own lives will safely continue,
355 under these threatening clouds, which arouse such fear in my heart?
What hope, poor thing, would you have, if fate had left you alone?
How could you master your terror? Who would comfort you in distress?
If you too had drowned in the sea, I would follow, dearest of women,
and—truly I swear it—I too would have perished, drowned in the sea.
360 How I wish I had mastered the arts possessed by my father Prometheus
by which to repeople the earth, mixing life-giving spirit and clay!
The mortal race of humanity now is reduced to us two,
to serve as the pattern of men, for so the gods have decided."
    Both of them wept at his words, but asked help of the gods above.
365 Hand in hand they hurried away to the stream of Cephisus,°
which, murky still with silt, was at least contained in its channel.
They solemnly purified their clothing and heads with its water,
then turned their steps to the shrine of Themis,° reverend goddess,
whose roof was stained with moss, whose altars stood without fire.
370 Reaching the temple steps, they prostrated themselves on the earth,
and, trembling, each pressed a pious kiss on the cold lifeless stones.
    "O goddess," they murmured, "if ever divinity softens at prayers,
won by the faith of their givers, if angry gods can be swayed,
tell us, O goddess, we pray, how to ward off our race's destruction,
375 and grant your unfailing help to a world engulfed in disaster."
    The goddess, stirred by their plea, returned this cryptic reply:
"Veil your heads when you leave; undo the knots of your clothing;°
then toss the bones of your mighty mother over your shoulders."
    For a while they stared in surprise. Pyrrha first broke the silence,
380 by refusing the goddess's orders, and begging in tremulous accents
for pardon; she trembled to think of insulting the ghost of her mother
by tossing her bones about. But as they repeated the riddle
concealed in the cryptic words of the oracle's strange revelation,
Prometheus' son's quiet words calmed Epimetheus' daughter.
385   "Either my wits have gone wrong," said he, "or the oracle's message
is urging us on to no sin. The earth is our mighty mother,
rocks, no doubt, are her bones. It is they we are bidden to throw."
    The daughter of Titans respected her husband's plausible guess,
but neither trusted the outcome, both doubted the oracle's word.
390 Still, how could it hurt them to try? Down they went from the temple,
veiled their heads, unfastened the knotted belts of their tunics,
and threw the stones, as ordered, behind them into their footprints.
Who would believe what happened, had not tradition assured us?
The stones began to give up their rigid inflexible structure,

---

365. *Cephisus:* A river northeast of Delphi.   368. *Themis:* At Delphi, where the Titaness gave oracles before Apollo took over the shrine.   377. *knots of your clothing:* The knot would magically tie up the mysterious power Deucalion is about to exercise.

395 and presently started to soften, and, softened, acquired new form.
  Soon, as they reached full size, and their gentler nature developed,
  the human form could be seen in a doubtful, tentative fashion
  as we see it in statues the sculptor has just begun to rough out
  from a block of unfashioned stone, not ready yet for display.
400 The earthly part of their matter became their muscles and sinews;
  the solider part, which cannot be bent, turned into their bones.
  The part of marble called "veins" still keeps that name in our bodies.
  And soon by the will of the gods the stones from the hand of the man
  acquired the features of men, those thrown by the woman were women.
405 This, then, is the reason our race is tough and enduring in hardship,
  why each of us shows his proof of the source from which we descended.
  The earth on its own gave birth to the rest of the animal kingdom,
  each animal after its kind. As the waters warmed in the sunshine,
  and the spongy ooze of the marshes swelled with the growing warmth,
410 the fertile seeds of things grew fat in the quickening mud;
  as a fetus does in the womb, they grew and acquired new features.

OVID, Metamorphoses 1.313–421

Most important of the children of Deucalion and Pyrrha was their son **Hellên** (**hel**-ēn), who gave his name to the whole Greek race, the Hellenes (Chart 5). Hellên had three sons: Dorus, Aeolus, and Xuthus. Dorus and Aeolus were the founders of the Dorians and the Aeolians, peoples who spoke two of the principal Greek dialects. Xuthus, the brother of Dorus and Aeolus, was father to Ion, from whom descended the Ionians, the third principal group of Greeks, which

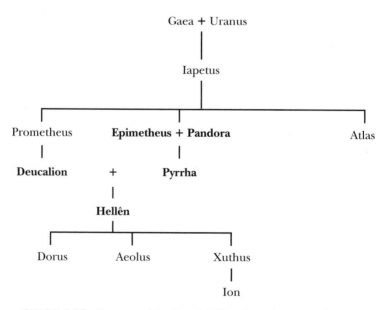

CHART 5 The Descent of the Greek Tribes from the Race of Titans

included the Athenians. These figures are eponymous ancestors of the Greeks as a whole (the Hellenes) and of the three principal ethnic divisions among the Greeks (Dorians, Ionians, Aeolians). *Eponymous* means "giving one's name to something," a place, people, city, or institution, and an **eponym** is the person whose name is so given. There are many eponyms in myth, but most are really named after the fact: First came a tribe called the Dorians, then came the legendary, and mythical, founder Dorus.

PROMINENT THEMES IN CLASSICAL STORIES OF HUMAN ORIGINS

The Greeks and Romans did not have a book of Genesis, an official account to decree what one should believe about the origin of humans and their early life long ago when mortals lived close to gods. Hesiod's account was by far the most popular, but there were other traditions. Although different in detail, most reports nonetheless agreed that humans came from the earth, a theme that first appears in Mesopotamian myth. Of course, the notion that Earth is a mother is logical and may appear independently in any culture.

Humans may simply emerge from the earth, growing like plants from seeds or semen placed within it. Deucalion threw stones over his shoulder like a man sowing a furrow, and up sprang men. In Greek versions, there is a play on words between the Greek *laos*, "people," and *laas*, "stone." The Giants, too, were born when the semen-blood from Uranus' severed genitals fell to the earth. In a variation on this theme, Hesiod's race of bronze sprang from ash trees. A second way for mortals to issue from the earth is at the hands of an artisan god. So Hephaestus made Pandora from clay. A tradition later than Hesiod says that Prometheus mixed clay with wind to make the first humans, as in the biblical story the creator made Adam by breathing on the dust of the earth. The image of humans growing from the earth is derived from agriculture; the tradition of the artisan-god derives from pottery making. The first image is more common. Many city-states had local traditions that told how its inhabitants, the first anywhere, had come from the earth.

A recurrent theme in these stories is that the human world did not arise all at once. There were delays and new beginnings. First came males, then females. First the gods made the Golden Race, then the Silver, Bronze, Heroic, and Iron. Zeus once destroyed all humanity in a flood. Only Deucalion and Pyrrha survived, who sowed the earth with stone seeds to provide a fresh start.

Human mortality separates humans utterly from the company of the gods. Because gods too emerged from Gaea/Earth, however, they and mortals share a common origin. Once upon a time human males dined on ambrosia and nectar in association with the gods, free from work, women, disease, poverty, and even death. The Golden Race did not so much die as become disembodied spirits. But some fault broke the intimacy between gods and humans. Now we live apart from the gods, eat cooked meat, labor for our keep, marry to reproduce, and die.

Hesiod's account of the incident at Meconê explains how this separation came about. Prometheus, by a trick, tried to give humans an advantage when the terms of sacrificial ritual were established. Zeus was angered, and humans attempted through sacrifice, whose unfair division had first offended Zeus, to restore good relations. Sacrifice was the central act of Greek religion and defined the human place in the world, midway between animals and gods. Animals, which eat food raw, are sacrificed; humans, who eat food cooked, sacrifice animals in honor of the gods, then eat the cooked flesh; gods, who eat neither raw food nor cooked food but dine on ambrosia and nectar, receive the smoke of the sacrifice performed in their honor.

The separation between human and divine became irrevocable when Zeus punished mortals for Prometheus' second offense, the theft of fire. He sent "a curse for humans," woman. She is beautiful, evil, costly, and insincere, a thorough calamity. Hesiod's word for "humans" before the making of Pandora is *anthropoi*, "human beings," not *andres*, "males" (hence *anthropology*, "study of humans," and *androgen*, the male hormone). After Pandora appears, he distinguishes between *andres*, "males," and *gynaikes*, "females," both of whom are *anthropoi*, "human beings." The story is a fantasy of male dominance, a Golden Age when there were no women.

How is woman to be integrated within humanity, *anthropoi*, when she is some-thing completely other than the male, a separate *genos?* In the Hebrew account, Eve is taken from Adam's body. Only after the woman has sinned by eating the forbidden fruit is she given a name: Eve, the mother of all the living (her name seems derived from a Hebrew root meaning "to live"). Pandora, by contrast, has a completely separate origin from the male. She is an artifact made by Hephaestus. Hesiod shows some confusion about Pandora's descendants, at one place saying that all women descend from her, but otherwise implying that from her womb all future humanity, male and female, will come forth. Thus Pandora/"all-giver" discharges for humanity the same function as Gaea/Earth did in the times of the world's for-mation. In any event, the social institution of the male's union with the female in human marriage grows directly from the final separation between humans and gods, when Zeus cursed man with woman.

There were many local traditions about the first men and women, and Deucalion and Pyrrha were ancestors of all the Greeks, but no Greek version tells the story of the origin of the whole human species as such. In thinking of themselves as alone descended from the first humans, the Greeks followed a common tradition. Most ancient peoples did not include within "humanity" those who lived beyond their own ethnic and linguistic boundaries. The sophisticated Roman Ovid's modern account and the biblical story of Adam, which explain the origin of the whole human race, are quite exceptional.

KEY NAMES AND TERMS

Prometheus, 116

Pandora, 124

Deucalion, 138

Pyrrha, 138

Hellên, 140

eponym, 141

SOME ADDITIONAL ANCIENT SOURCES

Prometheus: Hesiod, *Works and Days* 47–105; Apollodorus, 1.2.3, 1.3.6, 1.71–2, 2.5.4, 2.5.11, 3.13.5; Hyginus, *Fabulae* 54, 1444; Pausanias, 1.30.2, 2.19.5, 2.19.8.

FURTHER READING CHAPTER 5

Detienne, Marcel, and Jean-Pierre Vernant, *Cunning Intelligence in Greek Culture and Society,* trans. Janet Lloyd (Chicago, 1991). Traces the role of *mêtis,* "cunning," throughout Greek life and thought, including its role in the stories of Zeus's rise to kingship and his contest with Prometheus.

Dundes, Alan, ed., *The Flood Myth* (Berkeley, CA, 1988). A collection of essays offering a history of the discovery of a prebiblical story of the universal flood and a wide variety of interpretations.

Panofsky, Dora, and Erwin Panofsky, *Pandora's Box: The Changing Aspects of a Mythical Symbol* (New York, 1962; reprinted Princeton, NJ, 1991). The influence of this powerful myth from Hesiod to modern times.

Penglase, C., *Greek Myths and Mesopotamia* (New York, 1994). Parallels and influence in the *Homeric Hymns* and Hesiod.

Reeder, Ellen D., ed., *Pandora: Women in Classical Greece* (Princeton, NJ, 1995). Lavishly illustrated, with illuminating, sometimes penetrating essays.

Vernant, Jean-Pierre, *Myth and Society in Ancient Greece,* trans. Janet Lloyd (New York, 1980). Contains an important essay on the myth of Prometheus.

CHAPTER 6

MYTHS OF ZEUS, HIS WIFE HERA, AND HIS BROTHERS POSEIDON AND HADES

Homer and Hesiod have attributed to the gods all things that bring
rebuke and blame among men—stealing, adultery, deceit.

XENOPHANES OF COLOPHON,
Fragment 11 (DIELS-KRANZ)

WE HAVE SEEN THAT contradictory traditions are attached to the reign of
Cronus: that he was a cannibal tyrant who devoured his children and that he
presided over the world when the Golden Race lived, when want and disease and
hardship were unknown. In any event, his rule belonged to an era before his sons
and daughters by Rhea came to power. These six sons and daughters were Zeus,
Hera, Poseidon, Demeter, Hestia, and Hades. According to Hesiod, Aphrodite was
born of the foam that gathered around the severed genitals of Uranus. She is a primordial goddess, older than the children of Cronus. According to other accounts,
however, she is a daughter of Zeus. Except for Hades, ruler of the underworld, all
these deities, according to the poetic tradition, lived on Mount Olympus, the tallest
mountain in Greece, on the northern border of Thessaly. Zeus, Hera, Poseidon,
Demeter, Hestia, and Aphrodite, together with six of the children of Zeus and
Hera, were known collectively as the Olympians.

THE TWELVE OLYMPIANS

By the sixth century BC, the Greeks recognized a body of twelve Olympian gods and goddesses; at this time an altar to "The Twelve" was built in Athens, from which all distances in Attica were measured (Chart 6.1). The list was not fixed, however. Eventually, at least according to some sources, Zeus's divine son Dionysus (discussed in Chapter 11) replaced the colorless Hestia, goddess of the hearth.

Taken together, the twelve Olympians made up the divine family—brilliant, headstrong, quarreling, conspiring, feasting, loving and hating, immortal and immoral. Zeus stands at their head, "father of gods and men." Although he makes every final decision, he can give in to flattery, charm, bribery, and deception. Hera, his sister and wife, presides over the family, while his brother Poseidon rules the sea; his sister Hestia watches the fire, and his sister Demeter brings fertility to the earth. Hephaestus inspires the craftsmen, workers in metal, who made classical civilization possible. Ares is war. Hades is Zeus's brother, but because his house is beneath the earth, he is not an Olympian.

The children, too, have their spheres of influence. Athena, who knew no mother, presides over women's skills and practical knowledge of all kinds, including the art of war. Aphrodite, whether Zeus's daughter or not, is synonymous with the power of sexual attraction. Apollo, god of prophecy and healing, often called Phoebus (fē-us), perhaps meaning "shining," is one of the most important Greek gods. He is also the most complex and difficult to understand. In many stories he is inseparable from Artemis (the Roman Diana), goddess of wild animals and the hunt. In other myths, Artemis acts independently and achieves an identity of her own. Finally, the trickster Hermes, god of open spaces, travels from high to low and from near to far, even from this world to the next. As a traveler dependent on his wits, he is master of deception, lies, and (therefore!) commerce.

The Olympian gods were a projection onto cosmic canvas of the concerns and activities of the Greeks themselves. The organization of the Greek family and the tensions between the sexes are reflected in the family of the gods. The mighty Zeus rules his palace with an iron hand, but Hera, jealous and complaining, subverts

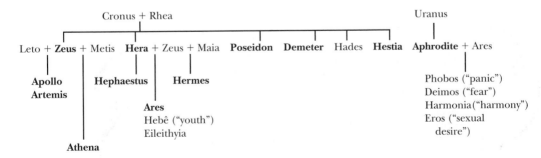

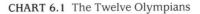

CHART 6.1 The Twelve Olympians

his authority constantly. While Zeus pursues women and boys, his vengeful wife insults and annoys him and takes revenge against women who foolishly submit to his caress, or even unwillingly suffer Zeus's attention.

Athena and Artemis were beings of great power, but they were celibate, without husband or child. In the human world, such female power was broken through marriage. Demeter sponsored fertility but seemed to have no husband; the fecundity of the female was an unfathomed mystery. Aphrodite was violent, like the sexual urges of young men, although men liked to tell stories of how frail women surrendered to typically immoral urges.

Although in Homer and Hesiod the familial relationships are well established, all these gods and goddesses have separate origins. In this chapter we examine the heads of the family, Zeus and Hera, and Zeus's powerful brothers Poseidon and Hades.

ZEUS, LORD OF THE SKY

Of all Greek gods, Zeus was greatest, at least in theory (Figure 6.1). The name Zeus is derived from an Indo-European root *di* meaning "shine" or "sky." Other Indo-European peoples, as we mentioned in Chapter 3, have gods with the same derivation. The Germanic god Tiu's name also means "sky" (hence Tuesday, "the day of Tiu"), and that of the Indic god Dyaus Pitar means "father sky." Likewise the name of the Roman god Jupiter, who was eventually identified with the Greek Zeus, also means "father sky." Presumably all these gods, including Zeus, are derived from an earlier Indo-European deity associated with the luminous heaven.

In Greek myth and religion, Zeus was identified with the sky in general, but more particularly with the weather. It was he who gathered the clouds and caused the rain. Homer calls him "the cloud-gatherer." His natural abode is on the tops of mountains, where the dark clouds gather before a storm. For this reason, no doubt, the Greek poets thought of his court as existing on Greece's highest mountain, Olympus, although Mount Ida near Troy was another special abode.

Zeus's outstanding attribute is his irresistible strength, which he used against the Titans, Typhoeus, and the Giants. In the *Iliad* he warns the other gods to remain aloof from the fighting at Troy. If they do not, they will:

[17]　"Learn how much stronger am I than all the rest of you gods!
　　　If you really want to know and to prove it to other immortals,
　　　let drop a golden cord from the heavens, and seize the end,
20　　O all you gods and goddesses! Pull it with all your might.
　　　Try as you will to drag me from heaven down to the earth—
　　　you cannot move me a bit! I am Zeus, the highest and wisest.
　　　But suppose I really wanted to pull you up to the heavens:
　　　Up you would come, and behind you would come both land and sea.
25　　The cord I would fasten securely to the highest peak of Olympus,
　　　leaving its burden to hang, twisting there in the wind.
　　　That is how far I surpass in power both gods and mortals!"

HOMER, *Iliad* 8.17–27

FIGURE 6.1 The great temple of Olympian Zeus at Athens, c. 550 BC–AD 130, with the ruins of the Parthenon in the background atop of the Acropolis. The largest temple in Greece, it was begun under the Athenian tyrant Pisistratus in the sixth century BC but not completed until the Roman emperor Hadrian. Its magnificent Corinthian columns were made of Pentelic marble, like those of the Parthenon. This photo was taken in the 1920s.   (University of Wisconsin–Madison Photo Archive)

The **aegis,** "goat skin," was an emblem of Zeus' power, a magical object that inspired terror in all who beheld it. Perhaps derived from a goatskin shield used in primitive times, it symbolized the storm cloud of the weather-god. In art it is shown as a shield with snake-headed tassels. Athena, to whom Zeus lent it, often wears it as a breastplate (see Figures 9.7 and 20.4). The thunderbolt is Zeus's weapon; he used it to overcome the Titans, the Giants, and the monster Typhoeus. Where lightning struck, the Greeks would erect a shrine to Zeus *kataibatês,* "Zeus who descends." In art the lightning bolt is shown as a two-pointed object (see Figures 4.6 and 4.7). The bull, because of its immense power and fecundity, was Zeus's special animal and was ritually sacrificed to him. The eagle, lord of the sky, was also associated with Zeus.

Zeus, God of Justice

As ruler of the world, Zeus presided over law and justice. But at least in the early stages of Greek history, law and justice were not abstract ideals. They referred simply to what had always been done and was therefore right—in other words, to custom. Zeus upheld the customary ways of Greek society. The Greek word for justice was *dikê* (**dē**-kā), a word whose root means "to point out" (as in *digit*, "finger"), namely the way things are done. *Dikê* is a critical term in the history of Greek and Western thought. Plato's famous dialogue *The Republic* is an elaborate effort to define what is meant by justice. Those who acted illegally or unjustly—that is, against *dikê*, against custom—also acted against Zeus.

Above all, Zeus protected the custom called ***xenia*** (ksen-ē-a), which we can roughly translate as "a formal institution of friendship" (*xenos* means "guest" or "stranger," as in English *xenophobia*, "fear of strangers"). *Xenia* enabled Greeks to travel safely to distant lands where other Greeks lived. A relationship was established when you received a wanderer into your household, entertained him, and gave him a gift. Should you one day visit the wanderer's home, you can expect a similar reception.

Obligations of reciprocal hospitality fell not only on the individuals originally involved, but also on their entire families and on their descendants. Obviously a host violated *xenia* if he killed or robbed his guest, as did a guest who stole from his host or seduced his host's wife. In legend, Paris seduced Helen, wife of his host Menelaüs, a violation of *xenia* that led to the Trojan War and ensured Zeus's approval of Troy's destruction, despite his love for the city. Similarly, Homer's *Odyssey* is a study in the observation and violation of the customs of *xenia*.

The Seduction of Zeus by Hera

In nature the god of storm, in society the protector of *xenia*, figuratively Zeus is "father of gods and men," overseer of all else that happens on earth and in heaven. In a more literal sense, he is father of numerous other gods and of many human heroes who founded Greek cities and peoples. He was also the father of Helen of Troy. As we might expect of a god who produced so many offspring, Zeus was celebrated for his numerous consorts or wives and his many dalliances with mortal women. Hellenistic commentators counted 115 of them!

The origin of these amorous tales, which distressed later moralizing commentators, is complex. While such stories often served simply to entertain, sexual generation is after all a form of divine providence, the way the world and all things within it were made. The sexual metaphor applied to the growth of crops supported such myth-making. The rain is male semen, and the receiving earth is the female womb. In certain Greek mystery-cults (see Chapter 10), a leader looked to heaven and cried, "Send rain!" then, looking down at the earth, cried, "Conceive!" (in Greek, the words rhyme).

THE LOVES OF ZEUS IN EUROPEAN ART

The many dalliances of the king of the gods offered to European artists rich opportunities for the representation of erotic themes and female nudes. The great regard in which classical authors were held, especially Ovid, offered protection against reproach from the church and other authorities. Apollodorus also was studied assiduously and seems to have been the basis for Titian's *Danaë* (Italian, c. 1488–1576, Perspective Figure 6.2a), of which he did five versions. Today, Titian is one of the most revered of the Old Masters, but he was also immensely successful in his lifetime, equally at home painting religious subjects, portraits, and scenes from myth, which he visualized as taking place in the natural world inhabited by humans like himself.

According to Book 2 of Apollodorus' *Library,* the daughter of Acrisius was imprisoned in a subterranean bronze chamber, but Titian shows her in a typical sixteenth-century boudoir among sumptuous bed hangings. She is the reclining nude, a beloved

PERSPECTIVE FIGURE 6.2a Titian (Tiziano Vecelli, Italian, c. 1488–1576), *Danaë* (1533–1534), oil on canvas. (Museo del Prado, Madrid, Spain, Erich Lessing/Art Resource, New York)

subject in sophisticated Venetian court circles during the Renaissance, especially when sanctioned by a mythical setting. Titian used live models. A hideous woman, not in Apollodorus' account, greedily attempts to snatch the golden coins that fall toward the virgin's legs, spread to receive them.

The well-known story of Leda and the swan does not appear in Homer or Hesiod but is found first in the prologue to Euripides' play *Helen.* The theme was a great favorite of Renaissance painters, just then recovering the antique past. Here (Perspective Figure 6.2b) Italian artist Antonio Allegri Correggio (1489–1534), influenced by Leonardo da Vinci and Michelangelo and sometimes admired as their equal, shows a narrative sequence in which Zeus as swan and Leda are represented three times. The swan arrives on the lower right as Leda, surprised and defensive, bathes in a pond. The swan has intercourse with her in the center, where Leda wears an expression of bemused pleasure. The swan departs in the upper right, watched by Leda and two

PERSPECTIVE FIGURE 6.2b Antonio Allegri Correggio (Italian, 1489–1534), *Leda and the Swan* (1534), oil on canvas.   (Staatliche Museen zu Berlin, Gemaldegalerie/Bildarchiv Preußischer Kulturbesitz, Berlin; photo by Jorg P. Anders)

female companions. Three cupid musicians lounge on the left, one playing the lyre, one blowing a horn, and one playing panpipes. A light from the upper right illuminates Correggio's softly modeled forms. The somber colors of the trees and earth highlight the flesh tones of the women and the whiteness of the swan.

Based on the description in Book 10 of Ovid's *Metamorphoses,* the painting *Jupiter Abducting Ganymede* (Perspective Figure 6.2c) by Charles-Joseph Natoire (French, 1700–1777) portrays the snatching-away with a mixture of passion and tenderness. Natoire had as patrons both the king and members of court, whose houses he decorated with mythical subjects, but he also accepted religious commissions and was director of the prestigious French Academy in Rome beginning in 1751. Here a dreamy Ganymede looks adoringly into the eagle's eye and with his left hand gently caresses the bird's head, while his right hand clenches a red fabric that wraps around both boy and bird. The massive claw wrapped around the boy's right leg leaves no doubt about Jupiter's intentions. Natoire made the painting for a private country house in a room entirely decorated by the loves of Jupiter, including also Leda, Europa, and Danaë.

PERSPECTIVE FIGURE 6.2c Charles-Joseph Natoire (French, 1700–1777), *Jupiter Abducting Ganymede* (c. 1731), oil on canvas. (Musée d'Art et d'Histoire de Troyes; Réunion des Musées Nationaux / Art Resource, New York)

In Perspective Figure 6.2d, Jean-Baptiste-Marie Pierre (French, 1713–1789) represents *The Rape of Europa* (1750), in which Jupiter appears twice, as an eagle in the dark cloud to the right of Europa and as the bull she rides upon. Closely following Ovid's story, Pierre shows the bull's muscular neck, small polished horns decked with garlands, and his friendly expression. Pierre captures the moment in the abduction when Europa's mood changes from gaiety to fear, as described by Ovid, but her anxious glance to shore is understated. There is no real sense of danger, but more of wonderment. Three cupids watch from the sky, carrying the flowers of love, while tritons (mermen) and sea nymphs swarm around her. One triton feeds the bull flowers as he rides on a sea monster whose enormous fishy eye peers out of the waves.

PERSPECTIVE FIGURE 6.2d Jean-Baptiste-Marie Pierre (French, 1713–1789), *The Rape of Europa* (1750), oil on canvas. (The Abduction of Europa, Jean Baptiste Marie Pierre, French, 1714–1789. Oil on canvas. Overall: 96 x 108 1/2 in. (2 m 43.84 cm x 2 m 75.59 cm) Dallas Museum of Art, Foundation for the Arts Collection, Mrs. John B. O'Hara Fund.)

FIGURE 6.2 The wedding of Zeus and Hera, a carving from a temple in Selinus on the southwest coast of Sicily, c. 550 BC. Hera unveils herself, preparing for sexual union with Zeus, while Zeus pulls her closer, seated on his throne and holding her by the arm in a gesture typical of Greek marriage. (Museo Archeologico Nazionale, Palermo; author's photo)

A humorous passage in the *Iliad* suggests the connection between Zeus's sexual exploits and the growth of plants. With the assistance of a magical embroidered belt lent by the sex-goddess Aphrodite, Zeus's wife Hera improbably seduces the king of the gods while he sits atop Mount Ida and watches the Trojan War (Figure 6.2). Hera intends to distract Zeus so that she may assist the Greeks without his knowledge. The magical belt makes her so lovely that, on glimpsing his usually cantankerous and unattractive wife, Zeus is overcome by desire, which he ridiculously compares with the desire he earlier felt for many other women:

[314]   "Come with me, my Hera. We two will lie down in love.
315   Desire for goddess or mortal has never so flooded my heart
        or made it thump in my chest as now my passion for you.
        Not when I fell in love with Ixion's lovely bride,°
        mother by me of the wise Pirithoüs,° wise as the gods;
        not in pursuit of Danaë, fair-ankled child of Acrisius,°
320   who bore me Perseus, my son, most honored of mortal men;
        not in abducting Europa,° daughter of glorious Phoenix,
        who bore me Minos the wise and the godlike Rhadamanthys;
        not in my loves for Semelê° or Alcmenê,° women of Thebes—
        the one bore Dionysus, the greatest joy of the world,
325   the second gave birth to my son Heracles, mighty of spirit—
        not in my love for Demeter,° lady with soft fair braids,
        nor that for glorious Leto°—nor my love, my darling, for you!
        None ever shook my heart with the passion that now I feel."

                                    HOMER, *Iliad* 14.314–328

317. *bride:* Dia, who otherwise plays no part in myth.   318. *Pirithoüs:* A friend of the Athenian hero Theseus.   319. *Acrisius:* Acrisius imprisoned Danaë in an underground chamber, but Zeus came to her in the form of a shower of gold that fell through the grating.   321. *Europa:* When Zeus appeared to her in the form of a bull, she climbed on his back; he swam to Crete and there possessed her.   323. *Semelê:* She saw Zeus "as he appeared to Hera" and was burned to a crisp.   323. *Alcmenê:* Zeus came to her in the guise of her own husband.   326. *Demeter:* The goddess of the harvest.   327. *Leto:* Mother of Apollo and Artemis.

Homer's male audience must have laughed heartily at a husband seducing his own wife by listing all the women by whom he had betrayed her! Yet behind the humor stands the fructifying religious union of Father Sky with Mother Earth that is central to ancient myth and religion. The cloud-gatherer Zeus takes his wife in his arms, assuring her that no one will see them, and as they embrace, flowers grow up around them:

[342]   "Hera, don't be afraid of a peeper, immortal or human.
        I'll bundle you up in a curtain of mist—opaque, yes, but golden,
        baffling even to Helius, keenest-eyed of immortals."
345   With that the son of great Cronus stretched out his arms like a bridegroom.
        Beneath from the radiant earth shot sweet young grasses of springtime,
        with lotuses, hyacinth, crocus, all flowers blushing and tender;
        all spring up to the light to curtain the amorous couple.
        So they embraced, reclined in a nimbus gleaming and golden,
350   their ardor cooled by glittering drops of the fresh-fallen dew.

                                    HOMER, *Iliad* 14.342–351

After intercourse, Zeus falls asleep, then wakes up later to discover that Hera has sneaked away to rouse the other gods against the Trojans. The male heavenly principle of fecundation becomes the enraged patriarch abused by a scheming wife:

[13]   Zeus, with a savage glare, poured his reproach on Hera:
        "I should have known! It was your dirty trick
15   that put lord Hector° out of the way and made his army panic!

15. *Hector:* Leader of the Trojan forces.

Maybe you'll learn a lesson if you yourself are the first,
lashed by a bolt of lightning, to suffer the consequence.
Don't you remember the time I strung you up by your wrists,
tied your arms with golden cords, hung an anvil on each leg,
20   and left you dangling up there in the winds and the clouds?
Of course the gods were sorry, all over mighty Olympus,
but dared not come to help. Whoever I caught I flung
headlong out of the door to land, more dead than alive,
down on the earth . . . So maybe you'll listen to me for once
25   and give up all your attempts to fool me, when once you have learned
that all the alluring wiggling of your hips from side to side
by which you used to get me into bed, away from the other gods,
will never work again as a sexy hoax to deceive me."

HOMER, Iliad 15.13–33

Zeus and Fate

Some stories of Zeus's sexual union with other goddesses (Chart 6.2) are perhaps mythical reflections of historical fact, the triumph of the invading Greeks'
male sky-god over the mother-goddesses of indigenous peoples. Other unions
have different meanings. Some are allegories illuminating the nature of Zeus
and the universe (for the large topic of allegory in myth, see Chapter 25). Zeus's
marriage with Metis, "cleverness," whom he swallowed while she was pregnant
with Athena, is such an allegory, meaning that the rule of Zeus combines
force with intelligence. His second consort was the Titaness Themis, "things-
established" (that is, "the unchangeable laws of the universe"), who personifies
the notion that the world is governed by rules. Zeus's union with her explains
allegorically that under Zeus's reign the universe is governed by law, not force
and whim. Their offspring are representations of visible order in the world. The
(usually) three Horae (hō-rē), "seasons," personify the regularly recurring divisions of the agricultural year but also embody good customs, orderly arrangement within human society. They are represented as women holding grass, grain,
and fruit.

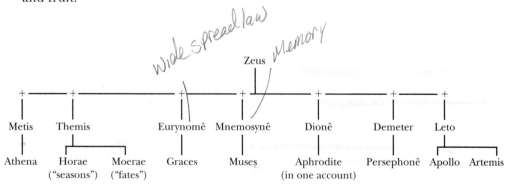

CHART 6.2 Zeus's Divine Consorts and Their Children

Hesiod's *Theogony* tells us first that the **Moerae** (**mē**-rē), "fates," were the children of Night, representing dark and implacable destiny, but later he says that they were children of Zeus and Themis, sisters of the Horae/Seasons. The Moerae establish the allotment that each mortal receives in life. The Romans called them *Parcae*, "bringers-forth." In Hellenistic times they are portrayed as three extremely old women, spinners of the threads of destiny: Clotho (**klō**-thō), "spinner," who makes the thread; Lachesis (**lak**-e-sis), "apportioner," who measures it; and Atropos (**a**-tro-pos), "she who cannot be turned aside," who cuts it off.

In Greek popular thought, one's fate, one's portion, can never be changed. Everyone is subject to unalterable fate, even mighty Zeus. In the *Iliad* Zeus wonders at one point whether he should act against fate and save his son Sarpedon from death, but Hera calls him up short:

[440]   "O mighty son of Cronus, what is this you suggest?
Do you want to exempt a mortal, long since destined to die,
from the gloomy decree of fate? Very well. Do as you please,
but realize that not all the immortals will clap their hands.
One thing I must point out for you to consider with care:
445   If you send Sarpedon back to his homeland, still alive,
why should some other god not also want to deliver
his own dear son from the deadly gamble of battle?
Many of those who fight for the mighty city of Priam°
are also sons of gods. Is exciting their rage what you want?"

HOMER, *Iliad* 16.440–449

448. *city of Priam:* Troy.

The passage implies that Zeus *could* act against fate, but that to do so would upset the scheme of things and violate his role in the cosmos as upholder of law. In fact, he never does act against fate. Paradoxically, he is subject to the dictates of his own daughters, the Moerae. Although in the Classical Period and later Zeus was exalted as the greatest god, the conception of Zeus as subordinate to fate prevented the Greeks from evolving a true monotheism in which a single God rules all things, familiar to the adherents of Judeo/Christian and Islamic religions.

Some Other Loves of Zeus

From Zeus's union with Eurynomê ("she with wide dominion," an Oceanid) were born the **Graces** (Greek *Charites*, Latin *Gratiae*), usually considered three in number, like the Seasons and the Fates. The Graces personify the feminine qualities that make young women attractive to men, and they are often portrayed in the company of the goddess Aphrodite.

Zeus then united with Mnemosynê (nē-**mos**-i-nē), "memory," to beget the Muses, who inspire poets and musicians. The story is an allegory for the fact that such oral poets as Homer and Hesiod generated their poetry from an enormous stock of themes and story patterns held within their memory, passed on by tradition.

PERSPECTIVE 6.1

THE THREE GRACES

In ancient representations the Graces are always shown as here (Perspective Figure 6.1a), from Pompeii, about AD 60, perhaps imitating an original sculptural group. The central figure turns her back, while the outside figures face the viewer. All figures are nude. Their hair is wreathed with crowns woven of leaves, and the outer figures hold a sprig. Shown like nymphs—virginal, small-breasted, and lovely—they stand in a country setting indicated by plants and rocks. Their eyes look demurely away, none seeing the other.

The iconography ("way of representing") of the Graces was rediscovered in the fifteenth century AD when a Hellenistic sculptural group was unearthed at Rome. The Renaissance artist Raphael (1483–1520) made a painting of them and thereafter "The Three Graces" type became so popular that brothels displayed it in Renaissance Italy!

In this example by Flemish painter Peter Paul Rubens (1577–1640) (Perspective Figure 6.1b), painted 1,600 years later than the painting from

PERSPECTIVE 6.1a The three Graces, from a wall painting in Pompeii, c. AD 60.   (University of Wisconsin–Madison Photo Archive)

Pompeii, the Graces adopt an ideal of feminine beauty unfashionable in our own day. Rubens' figures seem to move and breathe. They adopt roughly the traditional posture, but the left-hand goddess turns inward as her gaze meets that of the middle figure, and the third Grace on the right gazes at both. In the painting from Pompeii the Graces touch one another, but in Rubens' version they seem actually to feel one another's flesh. The middle goddess holds tightly the first goddess's biceps, perhaps encouraging her to smile, while her right arm is draped affectionately on the third goddess. Their faces are distinct as is the color and arrangement of their hair, for they are portraits of real women of Rubens' circle, according to a common practice in European art of the seventeenth century.

Unlike the formal setting of the painting from Pompeii, Rubens' scene has been cast in a partially realistic mode with deer and trees and flowers and a hut in the background. The goddesses have draped their clothes from the tree at the upper left. Evidently they have gone into the meadows, disrobed, and now prepare to dance. But symbols remain. The garland of roses over their heads stands for their loveliness, while the cherub holding a cornucopia in the upper right symbolizes their fecundity, the flushness and ripeness of burgeoning new life.

PERSPECTIVE 6.1b Peter Paul Rubens (1577–1640), The Three Graces, c. 1620, oil on canvas. (Museo del Prado, Madrid; University of Wisconsin–Madison Photo Archive)

Homer and Hesiod (as we have seen) begin their poems with a prayer to the Muses, setting a fashion in literature that remained vigorous until modern times.

Zeus's first four partners are allegorical figures, then. His fifth consort, by contrast, was Dionê (dī-ō-nē), a Titaness or Oceanid, whose name is linguistically a feminine form of Zeus's own name. Dionê may have been Zeus's earliest consort, before the Greeks migrated into the Balkan Peninsula, where Hera replaced her. At the oracular shrine of Dodona in northwest Greece, Dionê was still with Zeus well into Christian times. In the alternative tradition that Aphrodite was Zeus's daughter (and not born from the sea), Dionê was her mother.

We will leave Zeus's many affairs with mortal women to our discussion of Greek legend. In addition to his relations with women, human and divine, Zeus was also a lover of boys, as were Greek aristocrats. He fell in love with **Ganymede (gan-i-mēd)**, most beautiful of mortals, a prince of the Trojan royal house. One day while Ganymede shepherded his flocks on Mount Ida, Zeus seized him (Figure 6.3), or he

FIGURE 6.3 Zeus and Ganymede on an Attic cup, c. 455 BC. Zeus has dropped his thunderbolt and scepter, symbols of his power and his office, to seize the handsome boy. Although Zeus tries to catch the boy with his eye, Ganymede looks shyly to the ground. The rooster to the right is a common gift in pederastic relationships.   (Museo Archeologico Nazionale, Ferrara; Scala/Art Resource, New York)

sent an eagle to carry him to Olympus. There Ganymede remained as cupbearer to the gods, serving the same function as did handsome boys in the Greek symposium. (In Rome, Ganymede's name was corrupted to *catamitus,* the origin of our word *catamite,* a boy who submits to anal intercourse.)

HERA, QUEEN OF HEAVEN

Zeus's proper wife is **Hera** (identified with Juno by the Romans). The meaning of her name, probably of pre-Hellenic origin, is unclear, although some explain it as meaning "ruler" or "lady," the feminine of *hero.* Hera was chiefly a goddess of marriage and of women's fertility, but earlier she may have been a mother-goddess who sponsored the fertility of cattle and crops. The cow was her special animal; in Homer she is called "cow-eyed." Some of the earliest and most splendid temples in Greece were built to Hera: in Argos, on the island of Samos, and at Olympia, where her temple was older than Zeus's (Figure 6.4). Hera's association with Argos is reflected in her eager sponsorship of the Greeks in the Trojan War. Homer often

FIGURE 6.4 The temple of Hera at Olympia in the great sanctuary to Zeus, c. 600 BC. It is one of the earliest monumental temples in Greece, one hundred years older than the nearby great temple to Zeus, which held a famous statue by Phidias, one of the Seven Wonders of the Ancient World. Because of Hera's importance and precedence in Zeus's shrine, the sanctuary may have belonged to a mother-goddess in primordial times.   (University of Wisconsin–Madison Photo Archive)

calls the Greeks "Argives," that is, the men of Argos, near where stood the Heraeum, one of the oldest and holiest temples in Greece. Agamemnon, the leader of the Greek army, had his castle on the Argive plain very near the Heraeum.

Adultery is the great threat to monogamous marriage and the orderly inheritance of property and rank, and perhaps for this reason Hera vindictively persecutes Zeus's many mistresses and illegitimate children, especially the hero Heracles. Despite Hera's role in protecting the family, she is never addressed in religious cult as "Mother" or represented with children. In myth her own discordant marriage produced but three children: Ares, whom Zeus called "most hated of gods"; the divine midwife Eileithyia (ē-lē-**thī**-ya), whose name may mean the "coming" (that is, of the child) and who presided over the special function of childbirth (sometimes Hera herself was confused with Eileithyia); and Hebê (**hē**-bē), "youth," a colorless abstraction. None of these figures played a central role in Greek myth.

Although later traditions make Hephaestus a child of Zeus and Hera, Hesiod reports that Hera conceived him asexually, jealous because Zeus had given birth to Athena without the intervention of woman. Perhaps his lack of a father explains why Hephaestus was born a cripple, a fact that caused Hera some consternation. According to one passage in the *Iliad* (presented later in this chapter), Hephaestus complains that Zeus threw him from heaven, but according to a second version in the *Iliad,* Hera herself cast him out, disgusted by his deformity (the only time that the poet Homer gives two versions of a single myth). From incidental references we also learn that Hera joined with Poseidon and Athena in a palace conspiracy against Zeus. They actually succeeded in binding him, until Thetis summoned from Tartarus the Hundred-hander Briareus, who released Zeus from his bondage.

ZEUS AND HERA AT HOME ON OLYMPUS

King Zeus married Queen Hera in a formal ceremony on the islands of the Hesperides ("nymphs of the West"), far away in the western ocean. As a wedding gift, Gaea/Earth gave her granddaughter Hera golden apples that grew on a magical tree (Figure 6.5). Although married (and often henpecked), Zeus had a roving eye, as made clear in the catalog of mistresses quoted earlier. As in any unhappy marriage, tension ran high. Homer indelibly influenced the Greek tradition with his portrayal of these squabbling, all-too-human gods near the opening of the *Iliad.* The Nereid Thetis has come to Zeus to beg a favor for her son Achilles, but a prying, jealous Hera overhears their conversation:

[536]   When Hera saw him enter, she knew that he and Thetis,
        the Nereid nymph, had been putting their heads together,
        and she bitterly screamed at her husband Zeus, the son of Cronus.
        "Who's this who's plotting with you to set the divine agenda?
540   You never miss a chance of waiting till I'm out of sight
        to publish some scheme that you two have secretly plotted already,
        and you haven't got the guts to tell me what you have in mind!"

HOMER, *Iliad* 1.536–542

FIGURE 6.5 The serpent Ladon guards the tree of the Hesperides, a gift from Gaea to Hera, on an Attic water jug c. 460 BC. One of Heracles' labors was to steal golden apples from this tree, which gave eternal life to whoever ate them. Here to the left he flees with three of the apples while one nymph attempts to stop him, another raises her arms in dismay, and the third attempt to calm the serpent. (Nimatallah / Art Resource, New York)

The father of gods and men furiously rebukes his wife:

[561] "Woman, you're always suspicious. You never miss a thing.
A lot of good it will do if you make me angrier still—
if you go on with your nagging, it will be a cold day for you!
That's the way things are, because that's the way I want them.

565 So sit down and shut up, and listen to what I am going to say.
Not all the gods on Olympus will give you a bit of assistance
if I get sore and lay my irresistible hand upon you!"
At that the terrified Hera sat down and silently fumed,
and even in Zeus's house the heavenly gods were resentful.

570 But Hephaestus of skillful hands got up and spoke with a smile
in favor of Hera, his mother, the goddess of milky-white shoulders:
"Disgraceful indeed it will be, a state we cannot endure,
if you two start to squabble like this, and all because of a mortal,
wrangling among the gods! Our dinners will give us no pleasure,

575 if lesser matters distract from them our fullest attention.
I beg you, dearest mother, intelligent soul that you are,
to humor Zeus my father, lest he quarrel with you again,
ruining all the banquet and upsetting us all in addition.
For if the whim should seize the Olympian, hurler of thunder,

580   he could blast us out of our seats—he is mightier than we by far!
      So please! try to soften him down with gentle affectionate words.
      Then the Olympian again will show a benevolent face."
          So saying, he rose and put the two-handled cup
      into his dear mother's hands, and continued his sound advice:
585   "Courage, dear mother, be cheerful, however gloomy you feel.
      I don't want to stand by helpless while I watch him beating you up.
      For however great my anguish, I could not help you at all.
      The Olympian—this I can assure you—is a hard one to oppose.
      Do you remember the time, only a little while back,
590   when I was trying my best to stand up in your defense?
      He grabbed me by one ankle and flung me out through the door.
      For full twelve hours I fell. When the sun was about to set,
      I hit the ground in Lemnos,° rather more dead than alive,
      but the Sintians° promptly saved me by giving me first-aid."
595   His rueful-comical tale restored her former good humor
      to Hera the white-shouldered goddess. Smiling, she took the cup
      from the hand of her son, who moved in a clockwise direction,
      drew nectar out of the *krater*° and passed it on to the others.
      And endless laughter arose among the immortal gods
600   as they watched Hephaestus puffing around the banqueting hall.
          So they feasted all day, until the coming of evening,
      at the banquet where nothing was lacking, whatever the heart might desire—
      not the sound of the lyre so skillfully plucked by Apollo
      to accompany the notes of the Muses' clear-ringing treble.
605   The gleaming disk of the sun descended at last in the west.
      Returning to his own house, each Olympian lay down to slumber
      in the home that the lame Hephaestus had cleverly built for each one.
      To his own familiar bed, a comfort when weariness crushed him,
      went lightning-throwing Zeus, to embrace the golden-throned Hera.

                                    HOMER, *Iliad* 1.561–611

593. *Lemnos:* A large island in the northern Aegean.   594. *Sintians:* The native inhabitants of Lemnos.   598. krater: A large bowl used to mix wine with water before serving.

    In the *Iliad* Homer gives a picture of the gods' lives, politically monarchical and socially monogamous, an image of Greek life in the preliterate ages on which to some extent this mythical picture must be based. Hephaestus, god of smiths, is the dutiful cup-bearing son, himself a past victim of Zeus's overwhelming power, and sad to see his parents quarrel. Apollo, who presides over music, plays the same role on Olympus that such bards as Homer played in human society: to entertain at the banquet. Here he accompanies the singing of the Muses, inspirers of oral song.*

---

*The Muses were all concerned with communication: Clio, "making famous," ruled history; Euterpê, "delighter," flute-playing; Thalia, "flowering," comedy; Melpomenê, "singer," tragedy (compare Figure 3.9); Erato, "lovable," love lyric; Terpsichorê, "delighting in dance," dance; Polyhymnia, "with many songs," pantomime; Urania, "heavenly," astrology; and Calliopê, "pretty-voiced," epic poetry (compare Figure 3.9).

Homer's monogamous and sometimes misogynistic male audience will have enjoyed his tales of a disagreeable wife threatened with violence to keep her in her place.

POSEIDON, LORD OF THE DEEP

Having won their victory over the Titans, the three brothers Zeus, Poseidon, and Hades drew lots to apportion the world among themselves. **Poseidon** (the Roman Neptune), who ruled the sea, lacked Zeus's goodwill toward humans. In religion, he is master of the terrifying movement of the earth and the sea and the roaring thunder of horses' hooves beating over the plain. Homer calls him "shaker of earth."

The first part of the name *Poseidon* is Greek for "husband" or "lord" (*posis*), but the second part resists explanation. Some scholars take it to be the same as in *De*-meter, somehow meaning "wheat." Poseidon, then, would be the "wheat-husband," the male consort of the earth-mother and, like her, a god of fertility. This view finds some support in the myth that Poseidon pursued Demeter across the plains of Arcadia. To escape, she changed herself into a mare, but Poseidon became a stallion and possessed her anyway. The story is etiological, to explain a horse-headed statue of Demeter in the Peloponnesus, almost the only Greek example of a common Egyptian way of representing a deity. Their offspring was the mighty horse Arion (a-**rī**-on), who saved the Argive hero Adrastus in the war of the Seven against Thebes.

Poseidon's presence in Greece at an early date is proved by his name on Linear B tablets from Pylos in the southwestern Peloponnesus (c. 1200 BC). Some have theorized that Poseidon originally was an Indo-European fertility god associated with freshwater streams who became identified with the sea after the Greek migration into the Balkans. Wherever he struck his trident, a spring burst forth. Competing with Athena for the allegiance of Athens, he demonstrated his power by striking the Acropolis. From the rock sprang a well, although in this case one of seawater. It is not hard to see why the Athenians chose Athena as their patron, who gave them the domestic olive tree, basis of the Athenian economy. Poseidon was furious at the decision and flooded the Attic plain. In the Classical Period, what was supposed to be Athena's original olive tree still grew beside a temple on the Acropolis (called the Erechtheum), and an opening was left in the roof and porch to show where Poseidon had struck the earth (see Figure 16.1).

More often, and certainly by the time of Homer, Poseidon is in myth preeminently Lord of the Deep, of the great Mediterranean Sea, and married to Amphitritê (am-fi-**trī**-tē), a Nereid. Their child Triton (**trī**-ton) was shown in art as a merman, half-human, half-fish. When Triton blew his conch shell, the seas were calmed. As often with minor deities, we sometimes hear of tritons in the plural (compare Perspective Figure 6.2d).

Dangerous and unpredictable, Poseidon, who lived at the bottom of the sea, was responsible for the sorrows of seamen. He was father to the Cyclops Polyphemus, who cursed Odysseus, compelling him to wander for ten years before returning home. Homer well invokes the terror that Poseidon can arouse when in the *Odyssey* he describes the storm that broke up Odysseus' raft as he neared the last leg of his journey home:

[281]   But the glorious Earthshaker, coming back from the Ethiopians,°
        from far off in the mountains of the Solymi,° saw him
        as he sailed upon the sea. His heart swelled with anger
        and he shook his locks and spoke to his own heart:
285   "It seems that the gods have changed their minds
        about Odysseus while I stayed among the Ethiopians,
        and I see he's already near the land of the Phaeacians, where
        it is fated that he escape the bonds of misery.
        And yet I think that I can still do him some harm!"
290   So speaking, he rounded up the clouds and savaged the sea,
        brandishing his trident. And he raised up all the storm winds
        of every kind, and he darkened the earth
        and the sea with clouds, and night came from the sky.
        East Wind and South Wind smashed together,
295   and ill-blowing West Wind [Zephyr] and heaven-born
        North Wind [Boreas] rolled before him a giant wave.
        Then were the knees and heart of Odysseus loosened
        and with a groan he spoke to his own spirit:
        "I am wretched, what will happen to me now?
300   I fear that the goddess° spoke true words when
        she said that before I reached my native land,
        I would suffer trenchant pain. For her words are being fulfilled."

                                    HOMER, *Odyssey* 5.281–301

281. *Ethiopians:* They live in a vague region to the extreme south.   282. *Solymi:* Apparently in southern Asia Minor. Poseidon has traveled north from the Ethiopians and now turns west.   300. *goddess:* The witch Circê.

Mortals were doomed to ride in flimsy rafts and boats, but Poseidon traveled across the sea in a chariot drawn by horses or sea-monsters. Homer's description of him setting off to fight at Troy has colored our conception of him for all time:

[17]   Down from the mountain's rugged crags he thundered
        with flying steps. High hills and trees shook at the tread
        of his immortal feet as the lord Poseidon advanced.
20   Three mighty steps he took; the fourth one brought him home,
        to Aegae,° where his home arose in the depths of the gulf,
        gleaming and golden, a palace built to endure forever.
        He harnessed his pair of brazen-hoofed wind-swift horses,
        golden of mane, to his car. He buckled his golden armor
25   over his own strong limbs, took his strong and golden whip,
        mounted his chariot's box, and scudded over the surge.
        Beneath, great fish skipped up on every side from the deep,
        and the laughing waves gave way, acknowledging their lord.
        So the god and his team sped on, dry-axled, over the sea,

21. *Aegae* (ē-jē): A town in the northern Peloponnesus.

30   till the leaping horses reached the huddled Achaean vessels.
        A spacious cavern lies deep near the bottom of the strait
        that runs between rocky Imbros and Tenedos, the island off Troy.°
        Poseidon, shaker of earth, there halted his sweating team,
        unhitched them from his car, and gave them ambrosial fodder.
35   Around their fetlocks he set unbreakable golden hobbles,
        to keep them from wandering off before their lord returned.
        Then he himself set off to the Achaean encampment.

HOMER, *Iliad* 13.17–38

32. *island off Troy:* See Map IX, Chapter 20.

The Greeks did not like the sea. They knew too much about its dangers. Poseidon's role as god of earthquake was logical for a power that dwells in the depths. Greece and the Aegean are geologically unstable and subject to frequent and violent earthquakes. Such destruction was the doing of Poseidon. Poseidon's close association with horses may be connected to his role as god of earthquake, if the pounding of a herd of horses reminded early Greeks of earthquake. Or the association may go back to the horse-riding, landlocked Indo-Europeans, who knew more about horses than water. Horses were drowned in sacrifice to Poseidon. He impregnated the Gorgon Medusa. When Perseus beheaded her, from the neck sprang the warrior Chrysaör and the flying horse Pegasus (see Chart 4.3). Bellerophon rode Pegasus when he went out to slay the dread odd-shaped Chimera.

Poseidon has much in common with Zeus. He too admires women and from time to time imposes himself on them against their will. Both are represented in art as stern and lordly figures, not easily distinguished, except when Poseidon is shown carrying his characteristic trident (Figure 6.6).

HADES, KING OF THE DEAD

Together with Zeus and Poseidon, **Hades** (hā-dēz) shared the governance of the universe, though he did not live on Olympus. His name means "the invisible," appropriate as the embodiment of the unseen dead who are hidden beneath the ground, though they may be dimly glimpsed on earth as wandering and treacherous ghosts. Being dangerous to call by name, the death-god was often called Pluto, the "enricher," from the agricultural riches that spring from the earth and from the precious metals buried there. The Cyclopes gave him a magical helmet that made him invisible; other gods, and even mortal heroes, occasionally borrowed it. His childless marriage to Persephonê, daughter of Demeter, is described in the *Homeric Hymn to Demeter,* translated in Chapter 10. He commanded legions of demons. A pitiless master, he never willingly allowed any who came to him to return to the land of the living. We examine the geography and inhabitants of his realm in Chapter 12.

FIGURE 6.6 Poseidon or Zeus, c. 470–450 BC. One of the most celebrated sculptures to survive from the ancient world, this stunning over-life-sized bronze statue represents either Poseidon or Zeus majestically poised to strike with either trident or thunderbolt (the weapon has been lost). The statue was found in the sea north of the island of Euboea, evidently lost in a shipwreck. Few bronzes survive from the ancient world; most were later melted down to recover the valuable metal.   (National Archaeological Museum, Athens; University of Wisconsin–Madison Photo Archive)

Observations: Greek Anthropomorphism

Deeply influenced by the Mesopotamian tradition, the Greeks portrayed their gods as beings in the shape of men and women who act and think like human beings, honor kings, live in families, marry, procreate, have sexual liaisons, wrangle, intrigue, dine at banquets served by cupbearers, and are entertained by songs sung to the lyre. Such is Greek **anthropomorphism**. These gods have bodies and eat (although they do not excrete, which would be unseemly), and in their veins flows a divine fluid called *ichor* instead of blood. They can even be wounded, as

Ares is in Homer's description of the meeting of the war god with the Greek hero Diomedes (assisted by Athena) on the Trojan plain:

[855]   Once more Diomedes, screaming, struck with his brazen spear.
Athena added her weight. The point took Ares right in the belly,
a little above his belt, and gave him a terrible wound,
and the flesh was ripped when Diomedes yanked it back.
Ares let out a bellow like nine or ten thousand soldiers
860   when battle lines clash in war. Greeks and Trojans alike
shook in terror to hear the screaming of pitiless Ares.

HOMER, *Iliad* 5.855–863

Ares flees to heaven. Paean (**pē**-an), a name associated with Apollo as healing-god, cares for the wound:

[899]   With this Zeus ordered Paean to heal the wounded Ares,
900   which he did by sprinkling pain-killing drugs on the wound.
He healed the god only because a god is not fated to die.
If you drop the acid juice of a fig into liquid white milk,
it promptly curdles to solid; just so the torn flesh of Ares
was healed by the drug. Then Hebê° washed him and dressed him,
905   and once more he sat beside Zeus, proudly vaunting his glory.

HOMER, *Iliad* 5.899–906

904. *Hebê:* "Youth."

Anthropomorphism makes possible a large and diverse body of myths. Gods who are colorless abstractions, like the native Roman gods, or who take animal or other nonhuman form, like many of the gods of Egypt, make dull actors because it is hard to fit them into a plot—a story whose outcome is not predetermined. Homer's gods are like us, having similar powers although in far greater abundance. But life itself, which "the dying ones" (humans) one day will lose, is possessed forever by "the deathless ones" (the gods). The immortality of the Greek gods, exempt from the serious business of dying, makes them a fit subject for comedy, even burlesque. For death gives weight and meaning to human acts, a privilege the gods cannot share.

Shackled to immortality, Homer's gods live amid perpetual good times. Their world is a light-hearted wish-fulfillment of the humans who created it. Yet when Homer's poems were composed, and for a thousand years thereafter, the Greeks built expensive temples to these gods, made pious sacrifice to them, and were inspired by fear and awe in their presence. Thus we must distinguish between gods as actors in myth and gods as powers fit to receive sacrifice and to be adored in religious cult. Greek myths were in no sense "gospels" to be accepted by pious Greeks as trustworthy records of literal truth about the doings of the divine beings who govern our lives, or as revelatory of their inner natures.

In addition to the great gods who made the universe and who live on Olympus or beneath the earth, there were innumerable minor anthropomorphic deities in Greek myth, mostly personifications of natural powers. The broadest category is that of the **nymphs,** a word meaning "young women," referring in life to married women who have not yet given birth (Chapter 2), but in myth to lovely beings, often amorous, who inhabit wild places or who accompany the greater gods and goddesses. Although divine, the nymphs were not necessarily immortal. They were something like the fairies of European folklore. Nymphs were usually closely bound to a particular place and were favorite subjects of love poetry throughout antiquity. Many of the stories in Ovid's *Metamorphoses* describe their doings. Nereids and Oceanids were nymphs of the sea; the Nereid Thetis had considerable importance. We will meet various other categories of nymphs and spirits in this book.

KEY NAMES AND TERMS

Zeus, 145	Hera, 156
aegis, 147	Poseidon, 160
xenia, 148	Hades, 162
Moerae, 152	anthropomorphism, 163
Graces, 152	nymphs, 165
Ganymede, 155	

SOME ADDITIONAL ANCIENT SOURCES

References to Zeus are innumerable, but he receives his most characteristic portraits in Homer's *Iliad,* where he is father of gods and men, and in Hesiod's *Theogony,* where he is triumphant over his enemies. He never appears as a character in any extant classical play except for the comedy the *Amphitryon* of Plautus (second century BC), although he drives the plot of Aeschylus' *Prometheus Bound.* References to Hera, too, abound. She is vividly drawn in the *Iliad,* and she has a major role in the *Argonautica* of Apollonius of Rhodes. For Poseidon, see *Homeric Hymn* 22, to Poseidon; Ovid, *Metamorphoses* 4.531–542, 12.580–596; Pindar, *Olympian Odes* 1.25–88. Hades is dangerous to mention and is also rarely illustrated in art, but see Hesiod, *Theogony* 453–506.

FURTHER READING CHAPTER 6

Burkert, Walter, *Greek Religion,* trans. John Raffan (Cambridge, MA, 1985), section III.ii.1. Best modern synopsis.

Cook, A. B., *Zeus,* 3 parts (New York, 1964; orig. 1914–1940). An enormous classic study tracking the development of Zeus according to the cultural theories of Sir James G. Frazer, author of *The Golden Bough* (see Chapter 25).

Farnell, Lewis Richard, *Cults of the Greek States,* 5 vols. (Oxford, UK, 1896–1909). Still the standard reference.

CHAPTER 7

MYTHS OF THE GREAT GOD APOLLO

He whom the lord Apollo, who works from afar, makes a prophet,
    knows in advance what evil is lying in wait for a man.
The gods themselves give warning. But neither knowledge of omens
    nor sacrificial bribes can avert the sentence of Fate.

SOLON, FRAGMENT 1, 53–60 (DIEHL)

AS PROJECTIONS OF HUMAN concerns, the male gods specialized in typically male activities. Zeus ruled the family and all humankind because males did just that in human society. The underworld family was like a mirror image of the upper, so Hades was king of Death (in ancient Sumer, Death was a woman, Ereshkigal). Poseidon caused the devastating storms that afflicted Greek sailors, who were always male, but he was also the god of earthquake, which afflicted everyone. Higher knowledge was open only to males in ancient Greece, and Apollo guided them, although often through the mouth of a woman.

APOLLO THE FAR-DARTER, GOD OF PROPHECY

The historical origin of **Apollo** is unknown, as is the meaning of his name. Many think his cult must have come from Asia Minor because he is called Lycian—that is, from Lycia on the south coast of Asia Minor—and because in Asia Minor there were many sites of his cult. However, Lycian could just as well mean "wolflike," perhaps because

167

at an early stage he protected shepherds from wolves or had some other connection with wolves. Wherever Apollo's cult comes from, it has taken on associations with the far north: In winter, while Dionysus ruled at **Delphi**, Apollo dwelled among the Hyperboreans (hi-per-**bor**-ē-anz), "the men beyond the North Wind" (Figure 7.1). Apollo is not mentioned in the Linear B tablets, but by the time alphabetic literacy was established in Greece in the eighth century BC, he was already a great god.

With their Titaness mother, Leto, Apollo and Artemis formed a sort of divine family, although in origin they had nothing to do with one another. Leto is evidently an ancient mother-goddess and was worshiped as such in Lycia and perhaps on Crete, but in Greek myth she is simply the mother of the divine twins, who are ever ready to defend her honor. In the Classical Period, Apollo is sometimes called a sun-god—as Artemis was by then thought to represent the dark and the moon—but in origin he had no connection with the sun. Although represented as an archer-god, he is not a

FIGURE 7.1 Apollo and Dionysus at Delphi, Attic vase, fourth century BC. The ecstatic aspect of Apollo's oracle brought it into natural alliance with the religion of Dionysus, who ruled Delphi during the three winter months while Apollo was away among the Hyperboreans. Even the grave of Dionysus could be seen in Apollo's precinct. Apollo, shown as a beardless youth with a crown of laurel, bids goodbye to Dionysus, bearded and wearing tragic garb and carrying a special staff (the thyrsus). Beneath them is the Delphic omphalos or navel, said to be the stone that Cronus swallowed instead of Zeus, and behind them a palm tree, a symbol of Apollo. The other figures are maenads and satyrs, followers of Dionysus (for which see Chapter 10).   (© The State Hermitage Museum, St. Petersburg, Russia)

FIGURE 7.2 The temple to Apollo at Bassae, one of the best preserved of all Greek temples, c. 450 BC, in the wilderness of southwestern Arcadia, dedicated to Apollo in thanksgiving for release from a plague. Ictinus, architect of the Parthenon, designed it. This picture was taken about 1950. Today, the temple is covered by a huge ugly tent for protection. (University of Wisconsin–Madison Photo Archive)

god of hunters: His arrows are the shafts of disease, emerging from the spirit world, irresistible, unseen, striking down the luckless (Figure 7.2). This association is explicit in our oldest reference to him at the beginning of the *Iliad* (c. 800 BC) where Apollo is the dangerous god of plague, called Lord of Mice, the plague-bringers.

The Greeks have captured the daughter of Chryses (**krī-sēz**), a Trojan priest of Apollo, and given her as booty to King Agamemnon. Chryses comes to the Greek camp and begs for the return of his daughter. He offers a generous ransom. But Agamemnon, snarling and rude, refuses to give her up. Enraged, Chryses leaves the Greek camp, walks along the much-resounding sea, and raises his arms in prayer to Apollo, his patron and protector:

35 "Hear me, O god of the silver bow, the guardian of Chrysê,
the guardian of Cilla, who rules over Tenedos° with your power,
Lord of the Mice! If ever I roofed your glorious temple
or burned fat flesh of bulls or of goats on your altar,
grant that the Greeks may feel the piercing sting of your arrows,
40 and thus make reparation for their insults and all my tears."
So he spoke, and Phoebus Apollo heard his prayer.
Raging, down he came at a bound from the heights of Olympus,
his bow on his shoulder, its quiver firmly boxed at both ends.
The whining arrows sped out from the furious archer's shoulder.

36. *Chrysê . . . Tenedos:* Chrysê and Cilla seem to have been villages near Troy; the priest Chryses takes his name from the first of them. Tenedos is an island just off the coast of Troy.

45   Black he stood as night, aiming now this way, now that.
        First he knelt at a distance, far from the ships, aimed, and shot.
        Terribly, shrilly, resounded the twang of his silver bow.
        First he aimed at the mules, then at the keen-scented hounds,
        then at the huddled men. The death fires burned day and night.

HOMER, *Iliad* 1.35–52

The Birth of Apollo on Delos

One of the longest of the Homeric Hymns is dedicated to Apollo. It seems to be composed of two songs that once were separate. The first song, which scholars call "To the Delian Apollo," may have been composed in the seventh century BC and describes how the god was born, his parentage, and the greatness of his power. The second song, called "To the Delphian Apollo," evidently a later composition, tells about the founding of Apollo's oracle at Delphi.

The hymn tells how the Titaness Leto (daughter of Coeus and Phoebê) was a mistress of Zeus. Like many others in a similar position, she was persecuted by Hera. When pregnant Leto came to term, Hera maliciously decreed that no land that sees the light of day could receive her children. Bursting with pain, Leto wandered the earth seeking a place to give birth, but no place would accept her. At last, two tiny waterless islands in the center of the Cyclades agreed to receive the desperate goddess: **Delos** (dē-los, "clear, bright") and nearby Ortygia (or-**tij**-a, "quail island").

Delos and Ortygia were exempt from Hera's decree because they were floating islands, sometimes bobbing beneath the surface and hence not seeing "the light of day." Apollo was born on Delos, Artemis on Ortygia, although the Delian hymn mentions the birth of Artemis only in passing. Other versions of the story relate how Artemis was born first—and then with divine precocity assisted in the birth of her twin brother!

The hymn begins with a description of Apollo's honored place on Olympus:

1   Let me not forget to sing of Apollo who shoots from afar.
        In Zeus's house the immortals shake at Apollo's arrival,
        rising up from their seats as he tightens his wonderful bow.
        Leto alone keeps her place at the side of Zeus, lord of thunder.
5   It is she who looses his bowstring, she who closes his quiver.
        She lifts it off from his shoulders to hang on a peg of gold
        driven into a pillar supporting the house of his father.
        She leads her son to his seat, as his father offers Apollo
        a golden goblet of nectar. The others, taking their places,
10   rejoice that Leto has borne her mighty son, archer Apollo.
        Hail to you, blessed Leto, the mother of glorious children,
        the lordly Apollo and Artemis, she who delights in her arrows.
        Her she bore on Ortygia, him on the rocky island of Delos,
        bracing her back against the towering rock of Mount Cynthus,°

14. *Mount Cynthus:* Cynthus is the only peak (368 feet high) on Delos. From Cynthus comes our proper name *Cynthia,* "woman associated with Mount Cynthus," that is, Artemis (= the Roman Diana).

15   close to the palm tree that flourishes green, on the bank of Inopus.°
      How can I challenge the songs already sung to your glory?
      Everywhere, Phoebus, the strains of music resound in your honor,
      on the mainland, teeming with cattle, on islands girt by the sea.
      All crags and beetling ridges of mountains gladden your spirit,
20   rivers that flow to the sea, headlands awash with saltwater,
      and harbors locked from the sea.
          Shall I then sing the travail of Leto, the goddess who bore you,
      joy to mankind, who braced herself on the Cynthian mountain,
      on rocky Delos, the isle surrounded by sea? The dark surges
25   smashed in on either side, pressed by the whistling breezes.
      There you were born, there first you arose, the lord of humankind.

Homeric Hymn to Apollo 1–29

15. *Inopus:* A tiny stream.

The poem goes on to list thirty-two places that Leto visits in her search for somewhere to give birth. Fearing Hera's anger, none will admit her. When at last she came to poverty-stricken Delos, she proclaimed the advantages that would accrue to the place willing to allow the birth of the coming great god:

45   To all these places in turn came Leto, her labor upon her,
      seeking a place of refuge for the birth of far-shooting Apollo.
      But all of them, even the richest, trembled with cowardly fear,
      and none dared welcome the god, till Leto happened on Delos.
      There to the island she spoke in anguished and bitter words:
50   "O Delos, I wish you were willing to offer a home for Apollo,
      my son, and in it be willing to build him a well-endowed temple!
      For otherwise no one would dream of coming to you for a visit.
      I cannot see your island as rich in sheep, wines, or cattle,
      and you surely will never have trees. But if you erected a temple
55   to Apollo, who works from afar, men will come from all over the world
      with sacrificial cattle. The savory smoke of their offerings
      will rise up on high forever, and you could provide for your rulers
      the product of other men's hands—a blessing, for under the land
      you have no wealth of your own."
60   So she spoke, and Delos replied in delight to the goddess,
      "Leto, noble daughter of Coeus, I would be happy
      to win the glorious honor of bearing the far-shooting lord.
      I have a poor reputation, and doubtless you can improve it.
      But one thing, Leto, is scary. I must be frank, for they tell me
65   Apollo will be high and mighty, pushing himself to the fore,
      whenever immortals assemble, and among us mortals as well,
      here on the grain-giving earth. My personal feeling is this:
      From the very day he is born and looks to the light of the sun,
      he will scorn this poor little island, call it a desolate rock pile,
70   and stomp it into the sea. But the thing that really alarms me,
      like surf breaking over my head, is that some day, on a mere fancy,
      he will leave us to go somewhere else to build his wonderful temple,

surrounded by bushes and parks. After that, the octopus, doubtless,
and the sleek black seal can use me—if ever they run out of rocks—
75   as a place for making their homes. So, goddess, if you dare promise,
swear a great oath that here on Delos your son will first raise
his glorious temple, an oracle shrine for the whole of mankind—
then, once it is finished, he may build wherever he pleases."
    So Delos spoke, and Leto swore the great oath of the gods:
80   "Witness, O Earth, and you, the wide-spreading Heavens above,
and you, slow waters of Styx,° the greatest, most terrible oath
that binds the blessed gods: Here on this isle shall remain
forever the fragrant temple and altar of Phoebus Apollo,
and to you he will grant, O Delos, the highest honor of all."

Homeric Hymn to Apollo 45–84

81. *Styx:* "Hateful," one of the rivers of the underworld. An oath sworn by the gods and witnessed by this river could not be broken.

Even after nine days of labor Leto had not yet delivered. Although all the goddesses gathered to help (except, of course, Hera), Leto could not bring the god forth. Iris, "rainbow," the messenger-goddess, was sent to Hera to beg for her daughter Eileithyia, the divine midwife. Hera, although truculent, at last agreed, according to one account only after being bribed by a necklace of gold and amber thirty feet thick!

116   At once delivery started, and Leto labored in childbirth,
embracing the trunk of a palm, bracing her knees in the grass.
The earth smiled in joy, and the goddesses shouted for pleasure
as the god sprang into the light.

Homeric Hymn to Apollo 116–119

As soon as Artemis and Apollo were born, the hitherto floating islands of Delos and Ortygia suddenly were anchored in their present places. The sacred palm that Leto grasped was a landmark outside the elaborate temple complex that sprang up on Delos during the Classical Period (Figure 7.3). True to Leto's prediction, Delos, which has an area of two square miles, became one of the richest and most celebrated religious shrines in Greece (today the island is uninhabited). Another tradition reports that, only days after the twins' birth, Hera released the Giant Tityus from the earth to rape Leto, but Apollo and Artemis cut him down in a shower of arrows, and Zeus condemned him to eternal punishment in Hades (see Figure 12.2).

Apollo at Delphi

Apollo's role in prophecy was especially associated with the oracular shrine to him at Delphi, perched on a precipitous slope of Mount Parnassus near the Corinthian Gulf. The second part of the *Homeric Hymn to Apollo,* "To the Delphian Apollo," begins with a pretty account of how Apollo, after being born, joined the gods on Olympus:

FIGURE 7.3 The author stands before the palm tree (a modern replanting) on Delos; once this palm, to which Leto clung, stood within the sanctuary of Artemis. To the left, Mount Cynthus.   (Author's photo)

186	He passes, swift as thought, soaring up from this world to Olympus,
	to the palace of Zeus, where he joins with a crowd of the other immortals.
	There the thoughts of the gods are turned to dancing and song.
	The clear-voiced Muses together add their refrain to the hymn.
190	They chant the right of the gods to an endless and blissful existence,
	and the misery of men, whose lives drag, helpless and blinded,
	who have no cure for death, no defense against helpless old age.
	The fair-haired Graces dance in a ring, and the light-hearted Seasons,
	joining their hands in a chain, and with them Harmonia,° Hebê,
195	and Aphrodite, daughter of Zeus. No dancer is ugly or dwarfish,
	least of all Artemis, wondrously beauteous, stately, and tall,
	she who delights in her arrows, brought up with her brother Apollo.
	Joining the dance is Hermes, the far-seeing slayer of Argus.
	Apollo plays on his lyre, to lead the dance and the singing,
200	while glory shines all about from his robe and his dancing feet.
	Leto of golden hair and Zeus, designer of counsel,
	rejoice as they watch their dear son playing amid the immortals.

Homeric Hymn to Apollo 186–202

194. *Harmonia:* A daughter of Ares and Aphrodite (according to one account).

Again Apollo fulfills in the divine community the same function as the oral poet in the human, playing for choral dance and singing and entertaining at the banquet. As the oral poet was the bearer, through his song, of traditional male aristocratic Greek culture, including Greek myth, Apollo the singer became the god of the Greek elite *aristoi*, a projection of their own self-image. Many stories were told about Apollo's skill with the lyre, in art his common attribute (along with the bow and quiver of arrows). According to a story made famous by Ovid and beloved by European painters of the sixteenth to eighteenth centuries, the satyr Marsyas (**mar**-si-as), master of the double flute, challenged Apollo to a musical contest, the winner being allowed to do as he liked. Apollo won easily and flayed Marsyas alive.

After being presented on Olympus, Apollo wandered over the earth, searching for a place to establish his oracle. He headed south and came eventually to a spring in Boeotia called Telphusa (tel-**fūs**-a), after a prophetic nymph who lived there. Apollo told the nymph that he wanted to build an oracle, but Telphusa, fearing competition, persuaded Apollo to move on to the precipitous slopes of Parnassus (Figure 7.4):

FIGURE 7.4 The temple of Apollo at Delphi, on the precipitous slopes of Mount Parnassus, which rise behind it in the mist. These reconstructed columns stand near the entrance to the east. The adytum of the oracle was at the other end, to the left.   (V. Papaioannou; University of Wisconsin–Madison Photo Archive)

282   So forth you went, O archer, to Crisa,
a western foothill of snowy Parnassus, where crags of the mountain
hang over the place up above. Beneath is a rough rocky cavern.
285   "This is the place where I plan to build my glorious temple,
an oracular shrine, to which humankind may forever
bring me unblemished offerings from rich Peloponnesus,
from Europe, and from the wave-washed islands around in the sea.
Whatever they ask, I will offer them all unfailing advice,
290   telling them what is to be, from within my opulent temple."
      With this Phoebus Apollo laid out all the foundations,
their breadth and their great length. The sons of Erginus,°
dear to the deathless gods, Trophonius and Agamedes,
laid on these the footings of stone. Countless tribes of men
295   above them built a temple of carefully polished ashlars,
the theme of song forever. Nearby was a sweet-flowing spring,°
where the lord, son of Zeus, loosed his bow and slew a dread female
dragon°: a great fat savage beast, who used to do dreadful things,
not only to thin-legged sheep, but to their owners as well,
300   crimson plague that she was . . . If anyone stumbled upon her,
doomsday carried him off—till Apollo, who works from afar,
let fly a death-dealing arrow. Tortured by horrible pangs,
she lay there, twisting in pain and painfully gasping for breath.
Her racking screams reechoed as she squirmed about in the wood.
305   At last she gave up her life, coughing it out with her blood.
      Over her Phoebus Apollo proudly shouted his boast:
"Lie here now and rot unburied, here in the man-feeding ground!
No longer will you survive, you deadly plague to mankind.
They will eat the fruits of the earth, the supporter of many,
310   and hither they will bring me their offerings free of all blemish.
Typhoeus will be no help, nor evil-reputed Chimera,
against the pangs of your death. Dark earth and shining Hyperion
will bring it about that you, at least, will the sooner decay."
      So he boasted, and darkness covered the dragoness's eyes.
315   The holy power of the sun soon made her rot in corruption,
which is why, right down to this day, she bears the name of the Python,°
and men give Apollo the title "Pythian," because in the spot where
she perished the burning might of the sun rotted the monster away.

Homeric Hymn to Apollo 282–318

292. *Erginus:* An enemy of Heracles and king of Orchomenus in Boeotia. His sons, Agamedes and Trophonius, were famous builders.   296. *spring:* The Castalian Spring.   298. *dragon:* Python.
316. *Python:* Greek *pythô* means "to rot."

     Apollo's destruction of the serpent Python is a Greek form of the ancient Eastern story of the dragon-combat, like the fight of Marduk against Tiamat. The rest of the hymn reports Apollo's vengeance against Telphusa for sending him to a dragon-infested mountain in the first place. He buries her beneath a cliff and builds a small shrine for himself on top of it.

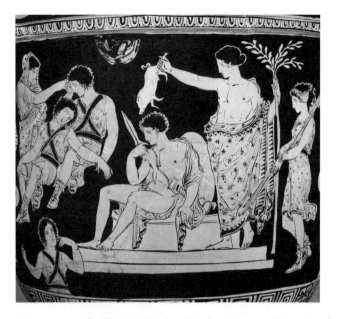

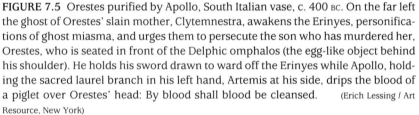

FIGURE 7.5 Orestes purified by Apollo, South Italian vase, c. 400 BC. On the far left the ghost of Orestes' slain mother, Clytemnestra, awakens the Erinyes, personifications of ghost miasma, and urges them to persecute the son who has murdered her, Orestes, who is seated in front of the Delphic omphalos (the egg-like object behind his shoulder). He holds his sword drawn to ward off the Erinyes while Apollo, holding the sacred laurel branch in his left hand, Artemis at his side, drips the blood of a piglet over Orestes' head: By blood shall blood be cleansed.   (Erich Lessing / Art Resource, New York)

While wondering how to entice priests for his new temple at Delphi, Apollo spied a Cretan ship at sea. Taking the form of a dolphin, he leapt on board, a terrifying portent. The sailors huddled together while Apollo guided the ship to Crisa, the coastal village near Delphi. There he revealed himself as a handsome man in his prime, with long locks drooping over his shoulders, and made them priests of his temple. (Evidently the poet derives Delphi from Greek *delphis*, "dolphin," the form in which the god appeared to the sailors.) When the Cretans saw Delphi perched on its precipitous slope, with no place for crops or herds, they fell into deep despair. But Apollo comforted them: They will have plenty to eat, he explains, from the rich offerings brought there. And so they did.

Other sources complete the tale. Having killed the dragon, Apollo had to be cleansed from *miasma*, "blood pollution." He therefore traveled to the Valley of Tempê in Thessaly at the foot of towering Mount Olympus, where he was ritually cleansed. Every eight years the Delphians celebrated the death of Python and the cleansing of Apollo. Because Apollo was himself cleansed of *miasma*, he could free others from it too, and many pilgrims journeyed to Delphi to submit to the appropriate ritual purification (Figure 7.5).

Observations: The Delphic Oracle

The second half of the *Homeric Hymn to Apollo* makes much of the god's eagerness to establish an oracular shrine so that he might enjoy its income and renown, but it tells us little about the history of the shrine and even less about the procedure followed there. Like the shrine at Delos, Delphi was a pan-Hellenic religious center to which all Greeks paid respect, regardless of their unending political differences. The oracle at Delphi functioned under Apollo for over a thousand years (c. 800 BC–AD 390). It was the most renowned oracle of the ancient world. The Greeks regarded Delphi as the center of the world, a location determined by Zeus when he sent out two eagles, one from each horizon, to see where they would cross. The conical *omphalos* marked the site as the world's navel (see Figures 7.1 and 7.5).

According to legend, there was an earlier oracle at Delphi, which functioned under Gaea or Themis, and some scholars interpret the slaying of Python, the earth monster, to stand for Apollo's displacement of the earlier earth oracle. The notion of the world-navel, in addition to the fact that at Delphi oracular responses were always given by a woman, encourages the view that the shrine did once belong to an earth-goddess, but archaeologists have found no evidence to confirm it.

The prophetess at Delphi was called the **Pythia** after the dragon Python. Originally she was a young virgin from the local village, but older women later served in this office. She seems to have had no special training. Most scholars understand her to have functioned as a medium or shaman, someone whose body serves as an instrument for communication with spirits, but the precise nature of her inspiration remains a mystery. Ancient traditions report that she inhaled vapors from a chasm in order to achieve a state of ecstasy. However, earlier archaeologists denied the existence of such a chasm, and recent suggestions that small fissures in the rock may have released an intoxicating gas are highly speculative. Other accounts state that she chewed hallucinogenic laurel leaves, but the laurel, sacred to Apollo, has no hallucinogenic power. The Greeks were as puzzled as we by how the Pythia functioned.

When preparing to answer questions, the Pythia took her seat on a bronze tripod in the inner sanctum or *adytum,* the section "not to be entered," of Apollo's temple, somewhat below ground level and off to one side (Figure 7.6). A male priest put questions to Pythia after the inquirer had made appropriate sacrifice (the priests received the hide and the meat). The Pythia, possessed by the god, made replies, which the priests recast in dactylic hexameters to give to the inquirer.

Archaeologists have found some inscribed lead tablets with real questions asked of the Pythia. Most questions were personal and could be answered by "yes" or "no," for example, should I marry so and so? should I move to Syracuse? am I the father of my wife's child? However, questions of communal interest were also asked. In the days of western colonization, during the eighth century BC and later, Apollo was consulted about where to settle, what gods to worship, and what form of government to adopt, and Delphi became a center for the exchange of information about all the Mediterranean world.

FIGURE 7.6 Aegeus before Themis in the shrine at Delphi, on an Attic drinking cup, c. 450 BC. Aegeus, earthly father of the Athenian hero Theseus, went to Delphi to learn whether he could beget a son. The Pythia (Themis) sits on the sacred tripod and gazes into a *phialē*, a kind of flat dish used to make drink offerings. In her other hand she holds a sprig of laurel. The column indicates that they are in an interior setting, the adytum of the temple at Delphi. The names of the figures are written above them.   (Staatliche Museen, Berlin; Bildarchiv Preußischer Kulturbesitz/Art Resource, New York)

The literary accounts of Delphic responses are quite different from those attested in archaeological finds, however, and were famous for their dark ambiguity. Herodotus tells us about Croesus, king of Lydia in Asia Minor in the sixth century BC, a rich and powerful ruler threatened by the Persians, who considered making a preemptive strike against them. Although not a Greek, he sent messengers with gifts to Delphi and asked what the outcome of the struggle would be. "If you make war on the Persians," he was informed, "you will destroy a mighty empire." Thus encouraged, he attacked, but was defeated and captured. The empire he destroyed was his own! In such literary accounts of oracular responses we must remember the prejudices and preferences of our written sources, whose principal purpose was to tell a good story.

In addition to its role in prophecy, the shrine at Delphi came to have a broadly ethical authority, encouraging the virtues of moderation and restraint and denying projects that were reckless or did not take sufficient account of the uncertainty of human fortune. Carved on the temple were the exhortations "Know yourself" and "Nothing too much," mottoes with a similar meaning: You are only human, so don't try more than you are able (or you will pay the price). A recurring theme in Greek myth is the man or woman who loses sight of human limitations and acts arrogantly and with violence, as if immortal—and pays a terrible price.

Apollo's Unhappy Loves

Apollo was father to many children and often was claimed as ancestor by families of prophets. However, many stories tell of his unsuccessful love affairs, which for some reason were numerous and beloved in late antiquity. Ovid makes much of them in his *Metamorphoses*.

Such stories sometimes refer to Apollo's power to make human beings prophets and the riddle and danger of this power. Priam, king of Troy, and his wife, Hecabê (**hek**-a-bē), had twins, Helenus (**hel**-e-nus) and **Cassandra** (ka-**san**-dra). Cassandra grew into a woman beautiful enough to rouse the lust of Apollo and shrewd enough to demand that he give her a prophet's powers in return for her sexual favors. Apollo agreed, but Cassandra nonetheless refused to sleep with him. Instead of taking back his gift, Apollo added a condition: Although Cassandra would always speak the truth, no one would ever believe her. Repeatedly she prophesied the ruin of Troy. No one listened. When Troy fell, Agamemnon carried off Cassandra as booty. Agamemnon's wife, Clytemnestra, butchered her along with Agamemnon (see Chapter 21). Today, we call someone whose truthful words are ignored a "Cassandra."

A similar story is told of Apollo's love for the first **Sibyl at Cumae**, to whom he gave as many years of life as the grains of sand that she could scoop up in her hands. The prophetic Sibyls, of whom there were many in the ancient world, seem to have been named after the Anatolian mother-goddess Cybelê (**sib**-e-lē). She accepted the gift, then she too refused to sleep with him. Apollo, still true to his word, failed to add one element to his gift—a lasting youth to accompany a very long life. The Sibyl grew older and older until she shriveled up like a cicada screeching in a cave. In the famous Roman novel called the *Satyricon* (first century AD) by Petronius, the "master of elegance" for the emperor Nero, an uncultured braggart and former slave in southern Italy boasts before his dinner guests: "Once with my own eyes I saw the Sibyl hanging in a bottle, and when those boys asked [he switches from Latin to Greek], 'What do you want?' she replied, 'I want to die.'" (T. S. Eliot quotes these words in Latin and Greek as an epigraph to his celebrated poem *The Waste Land,* 1922.)

One of Apollo's best-known affairs is his love for **Daphnê** (**daf**-nē), a nymph, daughter of the river-god Peneus in Thessaly. She rejected him, but he pursued her into the mountains (Figure 7.7; Perspective 7.1). To escape, she prayed to her father, who changed her into a laurel tree just as Apollo was about to possess her. The story is etiological to explain why the laurel is Apollo's sacred plant (Greek *daphnê* means "laurel"), given as a crown to victorious athletes in games at Delphi and emblematic of excellence in Apollo's arts (hence "poet laureates" and "Nobel laureates").

FIGURE 7.7 Apollo pursues Daphnê (probably), on an Attic water jug, c. 450 BC. The god is identified by his laurel wreath and the laurel branch he carries. To the left, Hermes departs in a winged chariot. Such pursuit scenes are common, for unclear reasons, on vases from the first half of the fifth century BC, sometimes of gods pursuing nymphs, sometimes of heroes or unidentified figures pursuing women. They also appear on a special kind of vase intended for the bride's bath (the *loutrophoros:* see Figure 2.10). The female figure, who may be Daphnê here, seems to spread her arms in alarm, but she turns back to Apollo and meets his gaze, as if willing to be caught.   (British Museum, London; © Trustees of the British Museum / Art Resource, New York)

Apollo, no less than Zeus, was attracted to young men. In another etiological tale, he loved Hyacinth (**hī**-a-sinth), a beautiful boy. One day they were practicing the discus (as good aristocrats do). A gust of wind caught the discus so that it swerved into Hyacinth's head and killed him. Apollo caused the hyacinth flower, white with splashes of red, to grow from his blood. Ever after, the dead youth was honored each year at his tomb near Sparta. Hyacinth's name is certainly pre-Greek. Perhaps originally he was a dying god of fertility (see Chapter 10).

Apollo, god of prophecy, is also god of healing, and one of his tragic love affairs was connected with the origin of the Greek god of medicine, **Asclepius** (as-**klēp**-i-us), whom he conceived on a mortal woman, **Coronis** (ko-**rōn**-is). While pregnant with Asclepius, foolish Coronis slept with a mortal named Ischys, a thoughtless deed witnessed by a crow, who reported it to Apollo. Ovid tells the story:

542   Coronis, a girl of Larissa, was the loveliest woman of all
   who lived in Haemonia's land.° Even you, O Delphic Apollo,
   found she was just to your liking, as long as she either was true,

543. *Haemonia's land:* Thessaly, in northeastern Greece.

PERSPECTIVE 7.1

BERNINI'S *APOLLO AND DAPHNÊ*

Between about 1550 and 1700, the predominant style in European art and architecture was the baroque, typified by dramatic, bold, curving forms and elaborate ornamentation. Gianlorenzo Bernini (1598–1680) was the greatest sculptor–architect of the period. Later in his career he designed the piazza in front of St. Peter's in Rome and, inside St. Peter's, the exuberant bronze canopy, supported by twisting columns, that protects the main altar under the soaring dome. In sculpture, the great innovation of the baroque was to create the illusion of a living scene, as if the scene before us were actually taking place, as on a stage.

His renowned *Apollo and Daphnê* (Perspective Figure 7.1) is a youthful work, full of tension and excitement. The figures are life-sized. Following Ovid's account closely, Bernini presents Daphnê just at the moment when the gods hear her pathetic pleas and change her into a laurel tree. She is nude, save for a strip of bark that strategically hides her genitals and buttocks. Behind her a youthful,

PERSPECTIVE FIGURE 7.1 Gianlorenzo Bernini (Italian, 1598–1680), Apollo and Daphnê, 1622–1625, marble, life-size.   (Villa Borghese, Rome; © Alinari/Art Resource, New York)

beardless Apollo reaches around with his left hand to touch her bare abdomen, realizing at the moment of victory that he has lost his prey.

The admixture of excitement, prettiness, sexual desire, and pathetic emotion perfectly mirrored the aesthetic taste of the aristocracy in seventeenth-century Europe, who loved Ovid and his stories for the Roman idle rich. They were the idle rich, too. Bernini magically worked the marble to catch the texture of the flowing drapery, floating hair, the bark, leaves, and branches—a dream of painting in exquisite marble, stone come to life.

545	or at least was not caught at her tricks. But Phoebus' pet, a white raven,
	nosed out her games, and, brimming with incorruptible virtue,
	ran off to tattle the story . . . how he had noticed Coronis,
	snuggling down together with a good-looking boy from Haemonia.
	As the tale unfolded, the laurels slipped from the brow of Apollo.
550	The color abandoned his features, the plectrum° fell from his hand.
	As his anger swelled and his heart was fueled with burning emotion,
	he reached for the bow, a weapon whose uses he knew so well.
	He pulled it back till the string came all the way to his shoulder.
	The arrow sped through the breast so often so close to his own.
555	With a groan the girl tore the dart away from her fair white flesh,
	which, as she watched, was crimsoned by blood that poured from her wound.
	Her dying words were these: "I deserve this punishment, Phoebus,
	but equally I deserve to have first given birth to our child.
	As it is, both he and I are destined to perish together."
560	At that she breathed her last, and her life ebbed out with her blood.
	As lover, Apollo repented—too late!—his terrible vengeance.
	He cursed his bow and his arrows, his hand that had brought them together.
	Stroking the lifeless corpse, with all the arts of the healer
	he attempted, too late and in vain, to annul grim Destiny's orders.
565	At last he knew he was helpless. He heard the sound of the servants
	building her funeral pyre to burn her remains in its flames.
	But Phoebus flatly refused to allow the child of his loins
	to crumble to ashes, cremated in the funeral pyre of its mother.
	Seizing the child from the womb, he bore it off to the cavern
570	where dwelt the double-formed Chiron, the Centaur. And as for the raven,
	who expected a great reward—after all, he had spoken the truth—
	Apollo erased him forever from the number of snowy-white birds.

OVID, *Metamorphoses* 2.542–547, 598–632

550. *plectrum:* the pick for playing the lyre.

The wise and virtuous centaur Chiron, to whom Apollo delivered the child, named Asclepius, was the tutor of other heroes and understood well the art of medicine (although we are not told where he learned it). He taught Asclepius all that he knew. Asclepius became the greatest doctor who ever lived. Like Jesus, he even raised the dead. Asclepius generally is pictured with a serpent wound about a staff, no doubt because the snake has the ability to restore its health and vigor by shedding its skin, and serpents were kept in his shrines (Figure 7.8). The name of Hygieia (hī-jē-a), "health" personified, said to be the wife or daughter of Asclepius, gives rise to our word *hygiene.*

FIGURE 7.8 Asclepius, marble, life-sized, c. 200 BC, from the great healing shrine of Asclepius at Epidaurus in the eastern Peloponnesus. The god is shown in heroic guise, with cloak loosely draped over one shoulder. He supports himself on a staff up which entwines the serpent of healing, the ultimate origin of the emblem of the American Medical Association (although they have confused the staff-with-serpent with the caduceus carried by Hermes, the staff-with-entwined-serpents-copulating).
(Epidaurus Museum)

Observations: Apollo, God of Shamans

In most preliterate societies appears a figure, usually male, who specializes in understanding the secret meaning behind ordinary appearance. Of the highest social standing, he receives the respect of all. He can read the inner meaning behind such signs and omens as the flight of birds, the appearance of entrails in sacrificed animals, and lightning or other heavenly phenomena. He can summon the spirits of the dead, and dreams reveal to him what will come to pass. Through his superior knowledge he controls the invisible and dangerous forces that interfere constantly in the lives of human beings, including the most dangerous and puzzling of all, disease. This is the medicine man of popular lore, so called from the French *médecin,* "doctor." The seer is also the healer.

One kind of medicine man, the shaman (Siberian for "he who knows"), can even leave his body behind in trance and travel through faraway realms to acquire knowledge of the future. He combats directly the hostile spirits that cause disease. He has friends in the spirit world, who may occupy his body and use his tongue to speak, although the voice is changed. Anthropological literature is filled with descriptions of such practices. In Greek religion, Apollo appears to embody the primitive shaman's role (although Orpheus too, as we will see in Chapter 12, has many shamanistic qualities).

Uniting inner and outer worlds, imparting knowledge, bringing healing, Apollo also commands the aristocratic privilege accorded to the shaman of preliterate societies. In Greek religion and myth, Apollo inspired both men and women, but in different ways. Apollo inspired male seers, who through heightened awareness saw hidden meaning behind appearance and healed the sick. But he also took possession of female mediums, who gave themselves up—even against their will—to the god, lost consciousness of themselves, and communicated the god's knowledge of past, present, and future.

In his functions as god of prophecy and healing and of the musical and poetic skills so valued by the Greek aristocracy, Apollo came to represent order against barbarism, reason against unreason, and what many have called "the Hellenic spirit." In the Classical Period, Apollo represented the Greek aristocratic ideal of young, vigorous manhood. On the pediment of the temple to Zeus at Olympia, whose cult statue was one of the Seven Wonders of the Ancient World, Apollo stands calm and beardless, arm outstretched against the savage Centaurs who (like the barbarian Persians) struggle to carry off Greek women (Figure 7.9).

In the Persian Wars, by supporting nonresistance to the invaders through many oracles, the Delphic Oracle lost much of its old respect, but in matters affecting individuals it remained influential. A friend of Socrates asked, "Who is the wisest of men?" The oracle replied, "Socrates." This reply puzzled the philosopher, until he realized that other men thought that they knew a lot, whereas he alone realized his own ignorance. About AD 100, Plutarch, himself a priest of Apollo, wrote a gloomy work on the growing decay of the oracles. The Christian Roman emperor Theodosius finally closed them down forever about AD 390.

FIGURE 7.9 Apollo, from the west pediment of the temple of Zeus at Olympia. The subject of the pediment was the Centaurs' rape of the Lapith women (from Thessaly). Apollo stands at the center of the melee, quietly reaching out his arm. Sculpted in the mid-fifth century BC, the mythical theme was a transparent allegory for the Greek victory over the Persians, understood as the triumph of reason and order over barbarian chaos.   (Olympia Museum; Alinari/Art Resource, New York)

KEY NAMES AND TERMS

Apollo, 167

Delphi, 168

Delos, 170

Pythia, 177

Cassandra, 179

Sibyl at Cumae, 179

Daphnê, 179

Asclepius, 180

Coronis, 180

SOME ADDITIONAL ANCIENT SOURCES

References to the **Apollo** are innumerable. Here are a few more detailed sources: Homer, *Odyssey* 15.243–253; Aeschylus, *Agamemnon* 1202–1212; Pindar, *Pythian Odes* 3.1–67; Ovid, *Metamorphoses* 5.204–266.

FURTHER READING CHAPTER 7

Calasso, Roberto, *The Marriage of Cadmus and Harmony* (New York, 1993). Good discussion of relationship between Apollo and Dionysus.

Fontenrose, J., *Python, A Study of Delphic Myth and Its Origins* (Berkeley, CA, 1959). An in-depth study of the dragon-slaying myth in the *Hymn to Apollo*, its origins in the Near East, and its meaning.

——, *The Delphic Oracle: Its Responses and Operations* (Berkeley, CA, 1978). A scholarly examination of the evidence for the nature of the oracle at Delphi, opposing many long-held views, especially that the Pythia was a medium and that the oracle was deliberately ambiguous.

Graf, F., *Apollo* (New York, 2008). Superior modern overview.

CHAPTER 8

MYTHS OF HERMES, PAN, HEPHAESTUS, AND ARES

I sing of Cyllenian Hermes, the slayer of Argus,
ruler of Cyllenê and Arcadia rich in flocks,
luck-bringing messenger of the gods, whom Maia bore,
the daughter of Atlas. Zus mixed with her in love,
though she was shy. She avoided the press of the gods
who never die, dwelling in her dusky cave.

Homeric Hymn to Hermes, no. 18, 1–6

Only males were smiths and warriors, and Hephaestus and Ares represented their interests, just as Hermes helped the traveling merchant, an exclusively male occupation. His son Pan was a minor god, but famous for his role as spirit of the wilds.

HERMES, GOD OF WAYFARERS

Except for Zeus, **Hermes** alone of the Olympians seems to have a name of transparent meaning: "he of the stone heap" (Greek *herma* = "stone heap"). Most interpreters explain his origin from the practice, still common today, of marking trails through remote areas by a heap of stones. Each traveler throws a stone on the pile for good luck. Thus Hermes is the spirit that lives in the stone pile, the protector of travelers and of those who wander on the edge of civilization. Like Artemis and

FIGURE 8.1 A herm from the island of Siphnos, c. 520 BC. (Vanni/Art Resource, New York)

the woodland spirit Pan, he was most at home in remote Arcadia in the central Peloponnesus, where he looked after shepherds and their flocks.

Later, the stone pile was stylized into a small pillar with a human head, usually bearded, and an erect phallus called a **herm** (Figure 8.1). Such stone pillars were used as boundary stones and as milestones and also placed in front of Athenian houses, to ward off intruders. The use of the phallus apotropaically, "to turn away evil," may be older than our species: Among higher primates aggressive males show their erect penis to warn off intruders (even as today some "flip the bird" to those who act abusively, to turn their aggression back on themselves). Just before the Athenians embarked on the disastrous expedition against Syracuse in 415 BC, vandals in one night mutilated most of the herms in the city. Suspicion immediately fell on the conservative faction, accused of conspiracy "to bring about a revolution and upset the democracy." The already divided command was so shaken by the charge that it did not act effectively and the expedition was a catastrophe.

Hermes' role in protecting travelers leads to additional functions. He protects thieves, for thieves travel in the night, taking what they want through intelligence and stealth. He protects merchants, who must travel to bring their goods to market. In the marketplace thieves also sell what they have taken. Our words *merchant* and *commerce* come from Latin *merx,* "merchandise," from which is derived *Mercury,* the Roman name for Hermes. He is the herald of the gods and protects human heralds, elect men who travel from one hostile community to another and who must not be harmed. As an emblem of their office they carry the god's wand, the **caduceus**, a staff intertwined with two snakes copulating. Hermes also protects orators, for orators persuade just as heralds and diplomats do. Finally, Hermes plays a role in the most momentous form of travel, from this world to the next. As **psychopompos**, "soul guide," he leads the dead into the House of Hades (see Figures 12.1 and 12.4).

One of Hermes' most famous deeds was to slay the hundred-eyed monster named Argus ("swifty"), whom Hera set up to watch over Io, a mistress of Zeus (see Figure 14.2). From this deed Hermes was ever after called **Argeïphontes** (ar-jē-i-**fon**-tēz), "slayer of Argus."

THE HOMERIC HYMN TO HERMES

The most amusing of all surviving oral poems recorded by dictation (and one of the latest) is the *Hymn to Hermes,* probably from the sixth century BC, which tells of the birth and extraordinary precocity of this trickster-god. When only several hours old, he invented the lyre, stole the cattle of his brother Apollo, then lied about it all to Apollo and Zeus. The poem is amusing in its celebration of rascality over pompous authority, but it may reflect deep social currents, coming from a time when the social classes favored by Hermes, the merchants, were gaining in influence over the old aristocracy, whose god was Apollo:

[1]   Sing, Muse, a song to Hermes, the son of **Maia**° and Zeus,
       lord of Arcadian **Cyllenê**,° land of sheep beyond number,
       the helper, the herald of gods. Maia, a fair-braided nymph,
       bore him to Zeus, as fruit of her bashful joining in dalliance.
5   She had shunned the noisy gathering of all the rest of the blest ones
       to hide in a shady cavern, but Zeus, soon hunting her out,
       embraced the fair-haired goddess in the darkest hour of nighttime,
       when sweetest sleep would hold the eyes of the white-armed Hera,
       when he might elude both gods immortal and men who must perish.
10   So he attained his desire. Ten months° were marked in the heavens.
       The child sprang into the light, to bring about wonderful things.
       Maia's infant was clever—a swindler, a robber, a liar,
       rustler of cattle, fast talker, burglar and cracker of safes,
       who promptly practiced his tricks on even the wisest immortals.
15   Born at the break of day, by noon he was twanging the lyre
       (this on the fourth of the month° when lady Maia had born him);
       before the evening had come he had stolen Phoebus' cattle.
       Once he had sprung from the deathless thighs of the lady his mother,
       he wasted no time in the winnowing fan° that served as his cradle,

1. *Maia:* A word meaning "venerable old woman" or "midwife." The daughter of Atlas and an Oceanid, she plays no part in myth except as the mother of Hermes.   2. *Cyllenê:* A mountain in the northeast corner of Arcadia in the Peloponnesus.   10. *ten months:* The ancients usually counted both ends in expressions of time; we would say nine months.   16. *fourth of the month:* Some days, like the fourth, were lucky, and both Aphrodite and Hermes were born on it; others were unlucky.   19. *fan:* The ancient Greeks used a kind of woven scoop to winnow the harvest (separate the grain from the hulls). The grain was first trampled by oxen, then tossed into the air, preferably in a breeze that would blow the chaff away. Hermes was put into a winnowing fan as a sort of bassinet (see Figure 8.2).

20 but jumped out and promptly departed to find the herds of Apollo.
Just as he crossed the threshold of the cavern, high, overarching,
he stumbled upon a tortoise, destined to make him a fortune,
for Hermes was first to construct a musical sweet-singing lyre.°
He met the beast in the courtyard, just in front of the doorway,
25 nibbling the soft sweet grass as it walked with its delicate feet.
The helper, the son of Zeus, watched it, giggled, and addressed it:
     "Good morning to you, my omen of luck° whom I must not disparage.
How fair your face! How nimble your feet! What fun at a party!
How happy I am to see you. Pray where did you get your fine costume?
30 that dappled shell that looks like a tortoise who lives in the hills?
Let me pick you up and take you inside, where I'm sure I can use you.
You'll be treated with all respect, since first you will benefit me.
You'd be safer inside the house, for the outdoors is always a danger.
While you live, you will be my defense against the perils of magic,
35 and, should you happen to die, you will warble the loveliest music."
So he addressed the tortoise, and, picking it up in his fingers,
he went back into the house, bearing his beautiful trophy.
With a gouge of sharp gray steel he scooped out the tortoise's entrails.
As fast as a passing thought traverses the breast of a thinker,
40 one whom repeated problems keep forcing to alter his plans;
as fast as the beams of vision flash from a viewer's eye,
so fast did glorious Hermes combine his thought with his action.
He carved a reed into slices of length that he carefully measured,
and fastened them tight in holes bored through the back of the shell.
45 Trusting his native wits, around it he mounted a drumhead.
Goat horns on either side were joined by a bridge up above,
whence seven harmonious strings of sheep gut stretched to the body.
When he had finished constructing his beautiful new invention,
he strummed each string with his hand, evoking melodious twanging.
50 Accompanied by the sound, the god improvised a sweet lyric,
just as young men at a feast compete with responding lampoons.
He sang the story of Zeus, son of Cronus, and fair-sandaled Maia,
their billing and cooing and whispered murmurs of love and affection,
and he sang of his own conception and birth, making much of his name.
55 He glorified the household, the splendid home of his mother:
the tripods and brazen cauldrons to be found all over the house.
But even while singing away, he was pondering various matters.
He bedded the hollow lyre in the holy winnowing fan,
for a whim had entered his mind that a juicy steak would be pleasant.
60 So he ran from the scented house to see what he might discover,
meanwhile plotting a scheme like those thieves make in the darkness.
     The sun, with chariot and horses, had set over dry land and sea,
when Hermes came to the shades of Pieria,° hill of the Muses,
where the herds of the blessed gods were safely shut in for the night,

---

23. *sweet-singing lyre:* Tortoise shells served as the sounding boxes for Greek lyres (see Figure 12.3).   27. *omen of luck:* Turtles were lucky and prevented harm from malicious magic.   63. *Pieria:* A mountain far north of Cyllenê in Macedonia, just north of Olympus, sacred to the Muses.

65   well fed by a long day's grazing in meadows fragrant and blooming.
        Of these the son of Maia, the far-sighted slayer of Argus,
        picked out and drove away fifty mooing head from the cow pens.
        By twisted byways he drove them, and wherever the roadway was sandy,
        turned them about back to front, reversing the hoof prints' direction
70   by driving them backward, while he himself proceeded on forward.°
        By the sandy shore of the sea he wove himself sandals of wicker,
        wonderful, hard to believe! of tamarisk twiglets and myrtle.
        A bundle of fresh green branches, verdant and heavy with foliage,
        he had plucked in his preparations for the rugged Pierian journey.
75   These light and flexible sandals, tied firmly under his insteps,
        saved him the labor of plodding the length of a long sandy road.
           An old man working a vineyard noticed the passing of Hermes
        as he went by Onchestus'° meadows, and then on down to the plain.
        Before he could ask a question, the son of Maia addressed him:
80   "Old man, bending your back as you dig away in the vineyard,
        you'll have a noble vintage, when all these vines bear their clusters.
        But listen, now, to my warning: if anyone asks you a question,
        tell him you've not seen a thing. Just mutter, forgetting the truth:
        Say you're deaf as a post, though your hearing is actually perfect.
85   Keep your mouth shut tight, if you know what's really your interest."
        That was enough. Famous Hermes prodded the cattle together,
        past many a hill, by many a meadow or flowering plain.
        Most of the misty darkness of night, his accomplice, had vanished,
        and beauteous Selenê had started to travel her rounds yet again
90   (Selenê was daughter of Pallas,° the son of the lord Megamedes),
        when the mighty son of Zeus drove the broad-browed cows of Apollo
        to the river Alpheus,° whose current they freely shambled across,
        and freely at last they arrived at the cattle enclosure of Hermes,
        to drink from troughs full of water at the edge of a beautiful meadow.
95   When he had given their fill of grass to the bellowing cattle,
        and driven them all in a herd back to their pens for the night,
        champing, as on they plodded, at lotus or dew-dripping cypress,
        he gathered a load of dry wood and invented the kindling of fire.
        Choosing a slab of laurel, he smoothed it down with a drawknife,
100   over it twirled a drill, and blew on the smoldering tinder.
        Thus Hermes discovered the way to kindle a fire by friction.
        To the fire-pit dug in the earth he carried a burden of faggots,
        unsplit, but as dry as tinder, and piled them over the fire.
        The flame blazed high and scattered its beams out into the darkness.
105   While the potent tool of Hephaestus, far-famed god of the craftsman,
        was still blazing up, he dragged two bellowing crumple-horned cattle
        out of their pen to the fire, displaying his muscular power,

---

70. . . . *proceeded on forward:* Greek cattle rustlers used this method of disguising their tracks down to the early twentieth century.   78. *Onchestus:* A town of Boeotia, northwest of Thebes.   90. *Pallas:* Hesiod tells us that Selenê (and Helius) were children of Hyperion and Theia; the Hymn apparently makes the Titan Pallas her father (*not* Athena—several mythical figures had the name Pallas). Megamedes is otherwise unknown.   92. *Alpheus:* The largest river (or stream) of the Peloponnesus, flowing from Arcadia west past Olympia and into the Ionian Sea. According to a common story, it ducked underground and emerged in the harbor of Syracuse in Sicily.

by wrestling the panting beasts, belly up, to lie on the ground.
He twisted and rolled them over, then cut their throats with a knife.

110 One task succeeded another. He sliced the rich fatty sirloins.
He speared the cuts to be roasted on skewers whittled of wood.
The rest he stuffed—yes, even the tenderloin, token of honor—
and the blackish blood, deep down in the gut, inventing the blutwurst.
All this he left by the fire, but the skins he dried on a layer

115 of rock, on which to this day those ancient hides have endured.°
    Then Hermes, merry of heart, slid the greasy fruit of his labor
onto a smooth stone slab, and carved it into twelve portions.
These he assigned by lot and topped each plate with a tidbit.°
Yet noble Hermes himself longed for the meat he had offered.

120 Immortal though he might be, he drooled at the wonderful fragrance,
but still his heart refrained from stuffing his gullet with goodies.
The fat and the meat he brought to the cavern, high, overarching,
storing it well out of sight, a sign of his skill as a rustler.
Fetching more wood, in the blaze of the fire he burned heads and feet.

125 This housework finished, he tossed his sandals into the river
Alpheus, swirling and deep. He quenched the fire and leveled
the ashes, working all night by the light of a silvery moon.
At dawn he ran back once again to the shining crest of Cyllenê,
and met not a soul all the way, no human, no blessed immortal;

130 no dog dared bark at Hermes, son of Zeus and bringer of fortune.
Squirming his way through the keyhole, he stole back into the cavern,
entering the house like a mist that comes in the chill of the autumn,
hurrying in on tiptoe and making no sound on the pavement.
The famous Hermes hastily jumped right into his cradle,

135 and, as any baby would do, rucked the blanket up round his shoulder.
He lay there, his fingers twisting the clothes on his fat little legs,
and cuddled the lovely tortoise, hugged in the crook of his elbow.
God though he was, his mother gave him a vigorous scolding:
    "You naughty shameless boy, where have you been, to get home

140 at such an hour of the night? Leto's son will certainly get you,
and take you away, tied so tightly that even you can't escape him.
Or else you'll turn into a bandit, prowling about in the mountains.
Whatever you stole, take it back! Your father created a nuisance
for mortals and gods alike, the night when you were begotten!"

145 With a crafty answer Hermes replied to the lady his mother:
    "Madam, why do you scold me as if I were only a baby,
whose heart has never been touched by blame or words of reproval?
Do you think I will timidly whimper because my mother is angry?
No. I shall pick whatever career may offer most promise,

150 with an eye to both of our welfares. Why should we two be contented,
we who are both divine, whose place is among the immortals,
without the honors of prayer and sacrifice, here in this hovel?
If that is what you are suggesting, I know a far better future:
Let us spend our days amusing ourselves among the immortals,

---

115. . . . *endured:* Evidently rock formations shown to pilgrims as the hides that Hermes had spread out. The hymn must have originated in the Peloponnesus, where such features were familiar.   118. *tidbit:* One for each of the Olympian gods; this is the earliest known reference to the Twelve Gods.

155   in a life of abundance and wealth, like lords of many an acre,
rather than twiddling our thumbs in this drafty echoing cavern.
And as for honor and rank, I too want the same as Apollo.
If my dear father won't grant it, I'll try—and I'm sure to succeed—
to earn the honor and riches that belong to the patron of thieves.
160   If the glorious son of Leto attempts to follow my traces,
I think he may run into something far bigger than he can expect.
I'll make my way to Delphi and tunnel into the temple,
where I'll find plenty of loot, like beautiful tripods and caldrons.
I'll make off with all the gold and the iron I may require,
165   not to mention the fabrics. You'll see, my mother, you'll see!"
      The pair exchanged such words, as they sat and chatted together,
the son of Zeus of the aegis, and lady Maia, his mother,
till early-born dawn appeared, bringing her light to us mortals,
rising from ocean's deep tides. Then Apollo came to Onchestus,
170   the lovely grove that is sacred to the rumbling shaker of earth.°
By the road he found the old peasant feeding his ugly old beast,
his trusty transport in the vineyard. The son of Leto addressed him:
      "Ancient grubber of thorns in the vineyards of grassy Onchestus,
hither I come from Pieria, hunting about for my cattle,
175   heifers all from my herd, with crumpled horns on their foreheads.
My black-skinned bull was grazing alone, left there by the others,
except four fierce-eyed dogs, who followed like trusty retainers.
The dogs and the bull alone remained, to my utter amazement,
for all the cattle returned last night, when the sun had descended,
180   back from their pleasant pasture, from the fragrant flowery meadow.
So tell me, you ancient man, have you seen a rustler of cattle,
passing along this road and driving the cows on before him?"
      The old man answered the question with subtle words of evasion:
"My friend, it's not at all easy, reporting all that you've noticed.
185   Moreover, a great many travelers choose this road as their highway,
some with nefarious schemes, some on their lawful occasions.
How can I tell which is which? I was digging away at my vineyard,
all through the livelong day, right down to the hour of sunset.
But, sir, I may have seen—I really can't tell you for certain—
190   what looked like a little moppet tending his spreading-horned heifers.
He carried a great long stick and skipped from one side to the other,
as he drove them along from behind, but he himself facing backwards."
      The old man finished. Apollo listened and hurried his footsteps.
Consulting a long-winged bird, he knew that the thief was none other
195   than the newborn boy who was fathered by mighty Zeus, son of Cronus.
The lord Apollo, himself Zeus's son, sped quickly to Pylos,°
down by the sandy shore, to hunt for his shambling cattle,
wrapping his brawny shoulders in a misty cloud for concealment.
There he who shoots from afar saw the tracks of cattle and shouted:
200   "What in the name of Heaven is this that startles my eyes!
It looks to me like the track of a herd of longhorned cattle,

---

170. *shaker of earth:* Poseidon, lord of earthquakes.   196. *Pylos:* Apparently not the famous Pylos on the
southwest coast of the Peloponnesus, but another one in Elis, about thirty-five miles north of the other.

but why are they turned the wrong way, to the meadow of asphodel?
And these—they can't be the tracks of mortal man or of woman,
nor yet of gray wolves or bears, or even of ravenous lions.
205   I can scarcely believe it's the track of a shaggy-necked Centaur,
yet something nasty has traveled this pathway on hurrying feet.
One set of tracks is horrendous, the other is simply appalling!"

So speaking, the lord Apollo, son of Zeus, continued his journey,
and presently came to Cyllenê, the mountain covered with forest,
210   to a shadowy cave in the rock, where dwelt the nymph, the immortal,
wherein she had given birth to the child of Zeus, son of Cronus.
A wonderful perfume distilled all over the mystical mountain,
where flocks of long-limbed sheep stood nibbling succulent pasture.
Apollo, who shoots from afar, rushed up, crossed over the threshold,
215   and entered in all his radiance into the gloom of the cave.

The son of Zeus and Maia knew him at once for Apollo,
the god who shoots from afar, enraged at the loss of his cattle,
and snuggled down the deeper in his sweet-smelling swaddling bands
    [Figure 8.2]
As coals burning deep in a log are hidden by layers of ashes,

FIGURE 8.2 Hermes and the cattle of Apollo, Attic vase, c. 490 BC. Hermes, back in Maia's cave, huddles down in his basket cradle after stealing Apollo's cattle. Wrapped in his swaddling clothes, he still wears his traveler's cap *(petasos)*. Maia, to his left, reproves him for the theft, while one cow licks the cradle.   (Photo Vatican Museums)

220 so Hermes huddled at sight of the god who works from afar,
contracting into small space his head and his hands and his feet.
He looked like a newborn baby, just washed and ready for slumber,
his tortoise tight in his arms. In fact, he was carefully watching.
The son of Leto and Zeus was not tricked for a moment. He knew
225 the beautiful nymph of the mountains and also her dear little boy,
a crook, always sticking his fingers in all sorts of knavish devices.
Apollo's eyes pried into the great house's every corner.
He drew out a gleaming key, and opened three locked storage cupboards,
only to find them full of nectar and fragrant ambrosia.
230 There was, indeed, ample store in the house of gold and of silver,
and dresses of crimson and silver, belonging to Maia, the nymph,
the sort of thing one expects in the homes of the blessed immortals.
At last the son of Leto, having snooped into every corner,
gave up the hunt and addressed his words to the noble Hermes:
235 "Look, kid, you who are lying so innocent there in your cradle,
tell me, where are the cows? If you won't talk, there'll be trouble.
I'll grab you and fling you down to the windy darkness of hell,
a miserable end, and one that you'll never succeed in escaping.
Neither your Mama nor Dada can bring you back to the light,
240 but you'll wander under the earth, with only moppets to boss."
Hermes replied to all this with words that were carefully chosen:
"Tell me, great son of Leto, just why are you talking so tough?
and why come into the house for beasts that live out of doors?
I never saw them, I never heard of them, nobody told me about them.
245 I couldn't tell you a thing or collect a fee as informer.
Do I look like a rustler of cattle, a brawny and muscular fellow?
That just isn't my style. I'm busy with other grave matters—
especially sleeping, and feeding on milk from the breast of my mother,
and blankets over my shoulders, and splashing in nice warm baths.
250 I hope that no one will ask you just how this argument started,
for even the gods would wonder, if you told them a newly born baby
walked right in the front door with a herd of wide-ranging cattle.
You claim what doesn't make sense! Only yesterday was I born,
my feet are still so tender and the ground beneath is so hard!
255 All right, if you insist I will take a terrible oath,
by the head of my father, and swear that I myself am not guilty,
nor have I seen any other who was driving your cattle away—
whatever 'cattle' may be, for I know of them only by hearsay."
So he spoke, but kept glancing from under half-closed lids
260 as he raised his eyebrows and watched his audience all around,
sometimes with a long low whistle, as if at a too tall story.
Apollo, who works from afar, laughed gently and spoke to him thus:
"Rascal, deceiver, and knave, how skillful you are at persuasion!
Of course, I know full well that you spent the nighttime in burgling
265 many a solid house, taking lots of poor men to the cleaner's,
noiselessly carrying off whatever you found in their households.
O, what a plague you will be to many a poor rustic shepherd,
out in the wilds of the mountain, when you feel a hunger for meat
and happen to smell out his pen of cattle and thick wooly sheep!

270   But now, unless you long for the longest and deepest of slumbers,
      GET OUT OF THAT CRADLE, QUICK! you partner of inkiest night!
      From now on all the immortals will give you the infamous function
      of championing all the bandits, whose ruler you will be titled."
      So speaking, Phoebus Apollo took up Hermes to carry him off.
275   But the mighty slayer of Argus was forming a different plan.
      The moment he felt himself lifted, he emitted a terrible portent,
      a hard-pressed slave of his belly, a messenger lacking good manners,
      then sneezed to cover it up.° Apollo heard with disgust,
      and dropped the glorious Hermes out of his hands to the ground.
280   He squatted down by the child, though eager to be on his way,
      and addressed to dear little Hermes the following menacing words:
      "All right, my diapered friend, the son of Zeus and of Maia,
      by these very omens of yours I shall presently sniff out my cattle,
      and you yourself will lead me and guide me where they are hidden."
285   At this Cyllenian Hermes sat up in great indignation.
      With both his hands he seized the blanket wrapping his shoulders
      and pushed it back from his ears, demanding this information:
          "Where are you taking me now, O you who work from afar,
      hottest tempered of gods? Has all this fuss over cattle
290   made you so cross that you feel you must take it out on poor me?
      I tell you, I wish the whole tribe of cattle would utterly perish.
      I didn't steal your cows, and I didn't see any rustler
      (whatever 'cows' may be; I know them only by hearsay).
      Let us take the matter to law and appeal to Zeus, son of Cronus."
295   The handsome sons of Zeus reached the fragrant peak of Olympus,
      the home of their father, Cronus' son. The balance of justice
      was set before the pair, the jury filled snowy Olympus,
      and the deathless gods assembled just after golden-throned dawn.
      At the knees of Zeus stood Hermes and Apollo with silvery bow.
300   Zeus who thunders on high thus addressed his glorious son:
          "Phoebus, whence comest thou hither, driving prodigious booty,
      this newly born child, who resembles ambassadors ancient and wise?
      A matter of weight, forsooth, is brought to the council of gods."
          To him replied Lord Phoebus, he who works from afar:
305   "Father, soon will you hear a matter of serious import.
      Do not reproach me as being the only one greedy for booty.
      This little child, who in fact is really a larcenous bandit,
      I found at the end of a tedious trip in the hills of Cyllenê,
      a cheat more plausible far than any I ever have seen,
310   god or human or swindler, who walks on the face of the earth.
      Stealing my cattle at evening from out the meadow, he drove them
      straight to Pylos, along the shore of the thunderous sea.
      They left two remarkable tracks, of a sort to leave one astonished,
      the work of a clownish goblin. The tracks of the cattle were clear,
315   preserved in the blackish dust, facing the asphodel meadows.
      But the animals' unknown driver crossed over the sandy ground

---

278. *cover it up:* That is, Hermes farted. A sneeze—when breath leaves the body—was considered to
be an omen demanding attention.

at the side of the path, lifted neither on feet nor on hands.
Some other miraculous scheme he employed to cover the journey,
as if he were walking on stilts he had fashioned of sapling oaks.
320 As long as he followed the cattle over the patches of sand,
all the footprints were clear and easy to see in the dust.
But once he had finished his weary journey over the prairie,
the marks of cows and master were lost on the iron-hard ground.
One poor mortal alone chanced to notice him hurrying onward,
325 straight down the road to Pylos, driving the broad-faced herd.
Hermes then shut in the cattle, scrambled the marks of his path,
made his way home to his cradle, and lay as still as the darkness,
in a dim and windy cave. Not even a sharp-sighted eagle
would have noticed the baby there. He kept on rubbing his eyes
330 with two chubby fists, and meanwhile planning a wily new scheme.
When I had come in, he looked me straight in the eye and declared:
'I never saw them. I never heard of them. Nobody told me about them.
I couldn't tell you a thing, or collect an informer's reward.'"
     Having thus finished his speech, Phoebus Apollo sat down.
335 Hermes arose in his turn and spoke these words in reply:
"O Zeus, my father, I promise to tell the truth, plain and simple.
for I am an innocent child, one quite untrained in deceit.
Early this morning, just as the sun was beginning his rising,
this fellow came to our house to hunt for his shambling cattle.
340 He brought not a single eye-witness, not one of the blessed gods,
but tried to make me own up by threatening horrible torments,
namely, that he would hurl me to the lowest levels of Hades.
Now he's in the vigorous flower of handsome and glorious youth,
but I—well, I'm sure he knows I was born only yesterday morning,
345 and don't even look like a rustler, a brawny muscular fellow.
So please believe my story, if your claim to paternity is true.
I didn't drive off his cattle—if I did, may I never be wealthy!
I never crossed our threshold, and all my story is truthful!
I have the highest regard for Helius and all the immortals,
350 and you, indeed, I love. But Apollo here fills me with terror.
You yourself know very well how perfectly harmless I am,
and I'm ready to take a great oath, corroborating my word—
not guilty! I swear by all these terribly costly surroundings.
And mark you, some day he'll pay for harassing me without mercy,
355 powerful as he is. But for now, be clement to me, a poor infant."
     So the Cyllenian slayer of Argus spoke, surreptitiously glancing
to left and right as he measured the persuasive effect of his words,
tightly holding his blanket over his infantile shoulders.
Zeus gave a cynical laugh at the sight of his plausible child,
360 how skillfully he rebutted the charge of rustling the cattle.
In the best paternal fashion he told them to be at one,
to go and hunt for the cows, with Hermes leading his brother,
and, laying aside his mischief, to show the secret enclosure
in which, so shortly before, he had hidden the cows he had stolen.
365 So the son of Cronus decreed, and glorious Hermes obeyed him,
for the will of Zeus, lord of the aegis, quickly won his assent.

The pair then hurried away, these handsome children of Zeus,
and came to sandy Pylos, by the ford of the river Alpheus.
At last they reached the pastures and high-roofed sheltering barn
370   in which the beasts were sheltered against the darkness of night.
Hermes went into the cave and was driving the cows to the light,
when out of the edge of his eye Apollo noticed two cowhides
up on the face of a rock. He demanded of glorious Hermes:
   "How were you able, you crook, to skin and dress these two oxen?
375   Right now you're only an infant, but I worry how strong you will be.
You don't need to grow very big, Cyllenian, offspring of Maia!"
At that, in his hands he braided a cord both pliant and tough,
eager to tie up Hermes with powerful willow-strip bonds,
but the willow strips did not hold. They fell to earth at a distance,
380   and right where they landed rooted themselves at once in the earth.
The willows entwined together and covered the wandering cattle,
by design of thieving Hermes, while Apollo watched in surprise.
Then the mighty slayer of Argus pretended to gaze at the ground,
but his eyes were twinkling with fire . . . trying to hide [? the shell].°
385   He easily softened the heart of the glorious son of Leto,
strong though he was, into doing exactly what Hermes desired.
With the lyre on his left elbow, he plucked each string with a pick,
so that it boomed and resounded. Apollo laughed with delight
as the wonderful sound of music stirred in the depths of his heart,
390   and longing possessed his soul as he listened. The great son of Maia,
plucking away on the lyre, took courage and stood to the left
of Phoebus Apollo. He presently lifted his voice in a song
with a sweet and melodious voice, of the start of created things,
of immortal gods and the earth, its face first covered with darkness,
395   how first they came into being and how each was given his share.°
First of the gods he honored Mnemosynê, mother of Muses,
who inspired the son of Maia. In their order of generation,
the glorious son of Zeus expounded the birth of each one,
honoring every immortal, and plucking the lyre in his arms.
400   Passionate longing attacked the heart in the breast of Apollo.
Opening his mouth, he addressed straightforward words to his brother:
   "Cow-killer, confidence-man, operator, a joy at a banquet,
this song of yours is worth far more than fifty fat cattle.
Moreover, I'm sure that our trifling quarrel is easily settled.
405   But tell me, son of Maia, you of so many great talents,
have you played like this from birth? or is this a gift of a god,
or even some mortal man? Either way, I can hardly believe it,
this wonderful gift of whoever taught you such heavenly song.
This beautiful music I hear, whose like has never been sounded
410   by any mortal man, or immortal who dwells on Olympus,
what sort of art is this? what charm for incurable sorrow?
what path presenting three choices, joy, sleep, or sweetness of love?
I too am the faithful servant of the Muses who dwell on Olympus,
whose greatest delight is the dance and the shining pathway of song,

384. *shell:* Something is wrong with the Greek text here.   395. *share:* The subject of his song is very like Hesiod's *Theogony.*

415   the intricate joy of rhythm, the passionate thunder of pipes.
But none of these arts of the feast have ever so shaken my heart.
And furthermore, son of Zeus, I'm astonished how sweetly you play.
After all, you are only a baby, prodigy though you may be,
so just sit still. Pay attention to the words of a wise older brother.

420   From now on you will be hailed as famous among the immortals,
you and your mother as well. This future, I tell you, is certain.
I swear by my cornel-wood staff, I will make you a glorious leader
among the immortal gods, and a fortunate leader as well.
I shall give you glorious gifts, and I promise not to deceive you."

425   Hermes responded to this with shrewd diplomatical phrasing:
"How tactfully, worker from far, you make your suggestion to me!
I haven't the slightest objection to your having a share in my music
and shall prove this very day how I long for friendly relations,
in fact, not only in words. As you sit with the gods, son of Zeus,

430   you can collect information to be quietly filed away.
You are powerful, strong, and rightly favored by plan-making Zeus,
who showers favors upon you. They tell me that right from his mouth
you learn, far-worker, the proper ritual owed to each god,
and all the pronouncements of Zeus, disclosed in oracular speech.

435   From sources like this, I imagine that you garner blackmail enormous,
because inside information is at hand whenever you need it.
But now, seeing your heart eager to master the lyre's sweet music,
take it from me as a gift. Go right ahead: play, sing, and frolic.
The merriment you will enjoy is quite sufficient reward."

440   Then side by side the pair of them drove the cattle back homeward,
to the holy meadow, then hurried away to snowy Olympus,
these good-looking sons of Zeus, delighters both in the lyre.
    Zeus, the giver of counsel, rejoiced to have made them such comrades,
and down to this day Apollo, son of Leto, and Hermes are friendly,

445   as is shown by the gift of the lyre that Hermes gave the far-darter,
which Apollo so skillfully strums, embracing it in his arms.
And as for himself, it was Hermes who invented a clever technique,
producing the sound of the pipe,° whose reedy notes echo far.

Homeric Hymn to Hermes 1–512

---

448. *pipe:* The panpipes, a group of reeds of different lengths bound together side by side.

Apollo and Hermes, according to the hymn, are social and political opposites. Apollo, with his fine herds of cows, is rich and established; Hermes is seemingly a helpless infant huddled in a cave. He has nothing and is nobody, a god's bastard. The mark of the aristocrat in the sixth century BC was the lyre with which he entertained his friends in the symposium, as Hermes describes to Apollo. Apollo, usually represented with a lyre, was the aristocrat's god. The aristocrat learned alphabetic writing in school and memorized poetry from written texts for performance to the accompaniment of the lyre. But who invented poetry in the first place? Who made the lyre that made the poetry possible?

    Hermes stands for those in Greek society who could actually do things, beginning with the oral poets who, without good birth, could make Greek song. The instrument in which the aristocrat most took pride came from the very social class that he despised, according to the hymn. As a people, the Greeks valued intelligence highly. Although the rustler threatens the basis of aristocratic wealth, his cleverness commands a grudging respect and even admiration.

Apollo, then, stands for the *aristoi,* the "best men," and Hermes for the *kakoi,* the "bad guys." The Athenian democracy, a radical departure from earlier forms of government, arose from a century of attempts to minimize such distinctions, the very period when this poem was composed. As gods opposite in interests but belonging to the same family were reconciled in the poem, so should the social classes of the *aristoi* and *kakoi* look past their differences to seek a common political interest, the poem seems to say. Making fire, which Hermes invented, may be dirty work, but it is nice to have cooked meat, which the rich man's wealth provides.

Until now in the poem, Hermes has claimed our sympathy as he struggles to win a place in the established order by his ingenuity against Apollo, but the rest of the hymn appears to have been composed by another singer, somebody with an aristocratic bias who wanted to reinstate the unquestioned position of Apollo. In this last and somewhat incongruous portion of the Hymn, Hermes promises, in return for Apollo's gift of the caduceus, never again to steal anything from Apollo. The major forms of divination will remain Apollo's, but Hermes keeps the minor power of divination from casting pebbles (perhaps a form of shooting craps). But the part we have given of this delightful tale sums up all of Hermes' qualities, not least his irreverence for established forms and law.

PAN, THE GOATHERD'S GOD

The two sides of Hermes—the guardian of flocks and herds and the master of theft, lies, and skullduggery—appear in his sons. One of these, Autolycus, the greatest liar and thief of his day, could make himself, and the things he stole, invisible. Odysseus the trickster was his grandson. That is one side of Hermes' nature. The other, his concern for pastures and fertility, is represented by **Pan,** one of the few deities in Greek myth whose form was sometimes only partly human, with the hoofs and legs of a goat, pointed ears or a goat's head, a little tail, and horns (Figure 8.3, but in Figure 11.3 he has human form; see also the lower central figure in Perspective Figure 11.1).

The god's name probably comes from an Indo-European root meaning "to feed"; from it comes English *pastor* and *pastures.* As "the feeder," Pan is the power that makes the shepherd's flocks get fat. His parents are usually given as Hermes and the nymph Dryopê ("oak tree"), but there are many other accounts. At birth Pan was so ugly that his mother ran off in terror. Pan was considered especially lustful, like a lecherous goat, and the nymph Syrinx, whom he desired, also ran from him, until she was changed into a reed. Pan slashed down the whole reed bed hunting for her, then made himself musical pipes by joining together reeds of unequal length (this version of the origin of the pan-pipe, or "syrinx," conflicts with that in the *Hymn to Hermes,* in which Pan's father, Hermes, is the inventor).

FIGURE 8.3 An ithyphallic ("with erect penis") Pan pursues a shepherd. Pan has the head and feet of a goat. Behind him the ithyphallic herm (with exaggerated penis) refers to Pan's parentage from Hermes, and also to the rural setting. The fleeing shepherd holds aloft a flail. Red-figured vase, c. 470 BC.   (Photograph © 2007 Museum of Fine Arts, Boston)

Pan did not live on Mount Olympus but wandered in the wild hills of Arcadia, the only region of Greece with no seacoast. There he lived in caves and danced across the mountains, leading choirs of nymphs. At noontime, when the Greeks believed a strange silence falls over the world, he slept. If a shepherd woke him, Pan gave a terrifying shout that inspired *pan*-ic, the feeling of irrational terror that can overcome one in remote and desolate country.

Pan also loved the nymph Echo, once an attendant of Hera. Echo entertained Hera with endless chatter while Zeus pursued other nymphs, until Hera punished her with a curious impediment: She could never begin a speech, but only repeat the words of others. Eventually she faded away to a mere voice, an "echo."

Latin writers identified Pan with Faunus and Silvanus, rustic deities who were among the last to succumb to the attacks of Christianity. These spirits were often spoken of in the plural, as pans, fauns, and *silvani*—really, they are interchangeable. From pictorial representations of such figures seems to come our horned, hoofed, pointy-eared, lustful devil.

PERSPECTIVE 8.1

PAN AND THE PASTORAL TRADITION

In the reign of the emperor Tiberius, about the time of the crucifixion of Jesus, a ship heading from Greece to Italy was startled to hear a great voice shouting to one of the crew, "Thamus, when you reach land, proclaim that 'Great Pan is dead!'" Thamus did so and was answered by a groan from all the mountains. Pan was the first Greek god said to have died in historical times.

But Pan was not dead. An author of the early fifth century AD incorrectly explained that Pan was in fact the totality (*pan* = Greek "all") of Nature, a notion appealing to a learned city-dweller of late antiquity. At roughly the same time a Christian bishop, exulting over the fall of the demons—that is, the pagan gods—complained that among the illiterate peasantry Pan's worship was still vigorous. *Pagan* comes from the Latin *paganus,* "rustic." Vergil had written that "he too is blessed who honors the farmer's gods, Silvanus ["he of the forest"], old Pan, and their bevy of nymphs," another reflection of the peasant's enduring feeling for the powers that ruled the countryside and the wilds.

Long after the end of antiquity, Pan and other rustic spirits continued to appear in the pastoral tradition of European literature and painting, which celebrated country life as an idealized antidote to the refined but corrupt ways of the city. John Milton (1608–1674), describing the Garden of Eden, evokes the mood in his epic poem on the fall of humankind, *Paradise Lost:*

> . . . In a shadier bower
> More sacred and sequester'd, though but feign'd,
> Pan or Sylvanus never slept, nor nymph
> Nor Faunus haunted.

John Keats (1795–1821) evokes the myth of Pan and the nymph Syrinx in his poem "I Stood Tip-toe upon a Little Hill," when he admires the poet

> . . . who pull'd the boughs aside,
> That we might look into a forest wide,
> To catch a glimpse of Fauns and Dryads ["oak-nymphs"]
> Coming with softest rustle through the trees . . .
> Telling us how fair trembling Syrinx fled
> Arcadian Pan, with such a fearful dread.
> Poor nymph—poor Pan—how did he weep to find,
> Nought but a lovely sighing of the wind
> Along the reedy stream; a half-heard strain,
> Full of sweet desolation—balmy pain.

French poet Stéphane Mallarmé (1842–1898), in *L'Après-midi d'un faune* ("The Afternoon of a Faun"), presented the monologue of a faun who meditates on his life, sleeping in the noonday sun, playing music, pursuing nymphs, and loving beauty. The poem inspired Claude Debussy's haunting musical composition *Prélude à l'après-midi d'un faune* ("Prelude to the Afternoon of a Faun," 1894), which Sergei Diaghilev later made into a renowned ballet (Paris, 1913).

HEPHAESTUS, GOD OF SMITHS

Hephaestus (he-fēs-tus, the Roman Vulcan) is non-Greek in origin and is probably native to the island of **Lemnos** in the Aegean Sea. We know that a non-Greek people, the Tyrsenoi, lived on Lemnos until the sixth century BC, with Hephaestias as their capital. Presumably Hephaestus was in origin a god of this people. A sense of Hephaestus' connection with Lemnos is preserved in the *Iliad* (1.597ff.). Hephaestus reports that he landed there after Zeus threw him from heaven for taking his mother Hera's side in a dispute.

Lemnos was once the site of an active volcano, and perhaps it was for this reason that Greek myths also associated Hephaestus with volcanoes and with the Cyclopes, who worked at their forges deep within them. He is sometimes simply the personification of fire, as Zeus is of rain: not the fire of the hearth, who is Hestia, or the celestial fire of Zeus's thunderbolt, but the fire of the metalworker's forge. He is the god of smiths, the patron of those who worked with their hands to form metals into useful or beautiful objects. As such he was one of the chief promoters of civilization and city life. His temple (today the best preserved in Greek lands) overlooks the Athenian agora, where manufactured goods were traded.

The ancient Greeks had ambiguous feelings toward such workers. On the one hand, the working of bronze and iron were technologies of central importance. The warriors in Homer are "bronze-clad," and many of the stunning achievements of Greek art, especially realistic sculpture, depended on smelting intractable copper ores (bronze is an alloy of copper and tin) (Figure 8.4).

On the other hand, filthy metalworking was repulsive to Greek aristocrats, who would not sully their hands with manual labor and who viewed the artisan class with contempt. Today we marvel at the elegance of Greek decorated pottery, but only twice in all Greek literature, in brief remarks of the comic poet Aristophanes and the lyric poet Pindar, can we find any mention of decorated pottery. The potter, like the smith, had no social standing (although some were literate and signed their works). Greek *aristoi* also despised lameness and physical ugliness, and the fact that in the real world slow-moving cripples sometimes became smiths inspired further scorn.

This ambiguous relationship was reflected in the Hephaestus of Greek myth. To him was attributed the working of all elegant and ingenious objects, as well as

FIGURE 8.4 A blacksmith's shop, from a drinking cup, c. 460 BC. In the center a bronze worker, wearing a cap often seen on Hephaestus, pokes at the coals in an upright furnace, while an apprentice, leaning on a hammer, looks on. To the right the bronze worker assembles a hollow bronze statue (compare Figure 6.6). Its head, waiting to be attached, is on the ground beneath his feet. From the wall hang other parts for statues and bronze-worker's tools.   (Staatliche Museen, Berlin; Bildarchiv Preußischer Kulturbesitz/Art Resource, New York)

weapons and other practical things. He fashioned Pandora from clay and made the manacles that bound Prometheus to the Caucasus. He was given a place among the Olympians, but he remained an upstart without proper parentage, an object of ridicule. His marriage to the sex-goddess Aphrodite was a laughable perversion, a union of beauty and the beast. No one need wonder why Aphrodite preferred the handsome, swashbuckling Ares as her lover.

According to a second version in the *Iliad* of the expulsion of Hephaestus (18.395ff.), Hera (not Zeus) threw Hephaestus from heaven. Although he was her own child, his lameness disgusted her. Hephaestus fell not to Lemnos, but into the sea, from which Thetis and her sister Nereids rescued him. They treated him kindly and kept him with them in a cavern for nine years. There he learned his metalworking skills.

Later stories report how, enraged by Hera's ill-treatment, Hephaestus manufactured a marvelous golden throne to which was attached a golden mesh so fine as to be invisible, which he sent to his mother on her birthday. As soon as she sat in it, the net bound her tightly. Only Hephaestus could free her, but he refused to return to Mount Olympus. At last Dionysus gained his confidence, plied him with wine, and led him to Olympus, drunk. Hephaestus then let Hera

FIGURE 8.5 The return of Hephaestus to Olympus, on an Attic vase, c. 430 BC. Hephaestus, drunk, crowned with ivy, is supported by a satyr, while Dionysus, to the far right, leads him to Olympus. Hephaestus carries the blacksmith's tools, a hammer in his left hand and tongs in his right.   (Museum Antiker Kleinkunst, Munich/ Hirmer Fotoarchiv, Munich, Germany)

go. The return of Hephaestus to Olympus was a common subject of Greek art, although curiously unattested in any literary account surviving from the Classical Period (Figure 8.5).

ARES, INCARNATION OF BLOOD LUST

Ares, the other son of Zeus and Hera, is often simply an embodiment of war and battle. Ares (the Roman Mars) personifies blood lust, the successful warrior's exaggerated desire to kill his fellow man. His name perhaps means "curser" and appears in the Linear B tablets. Under Ares' influence, the warrior is merciless, fearless, and indifferent to pain in the frenzy of combat. He seems to come from Thrace, north of the Greek lands.

Ares was little worshiped in Greek religion and has few myths. In art he is indistinguishable from any warrior. He was father to many, but had no regular wife, although he carried on an adulterous affair with Aphrodite long enough to father four children. Two of them, the allegorical Phobos, "panic," and Deimos, "fear," were fit offspring of the god of war. In modern times the two moons of the planet Mars are named after them. Another was Harmonia, "harmony," who married Cadmus of Thebes. The fourth child, according to some sources, was Eros (Cupid), reduced from Hesiod's cosmic principle of attraction to the companion (or irresponsible child) of Aphrodite and personification of sexual attraction.

Ares' adultery with Aphrodite is by far the best-known myth about him (Figure 8.6; compare Perspective Figure 9b). Because of its immoral content, this story, more than any other, inspired the Greeks of the Classical Period to question the veracity of their own myths. But Homer tells a humorous tale, placing it in the mouth of the oral poet Demodocus, who in the *Odyssey* sings the song on the athletic ground before a male, aristocratic audience with a taste for the salacious and irreverent. He intends to bring down the house, and does:

[266] Sounding his lyre, the singer began his beautiful song,
         a tale of the dalliance of Ares and fair-crowned Aphrodite,
         how they embraced in secret in the very house of Hephaestus.
         Loading the goddess with gifts, Ares sullied the nuptial bed
270   of the lord Hephaestus, to whom Helius° carried the story,
         that he himself had seen the couple embracing in passion.
         Hephaestus listened in silence to the news that broke his heart,
         then hurried into his workshop, contriving a fit retribution.
         Firm on a solid base he set a ponderous anvil and forged
275   a chain that could not be broken, escaped, or even unfastened.
         At last he finished his trap, and, seething in anger at Ares,
         carried it up to the chamber housing the couch of love.
         Around the bed-posts he draped his chain in voluptuous swirls,
         coiled directly over the bed, looping down from the rafters.
280   Yet it was fine as a cobweb, not to be noticed by watchers,
         even the blessed gods, such skill went into its making.
         Finally, when his trap was arranged all over the bedstead,
         he pretended important business in Lemnos, that well-managed city,
         "dearest by far," said he, "of all the cities of men."
285   Now Ares, golden-reined, had kept his eye on Hephaestus.
         Learning the god of craftsmen would be gone an indefinite period,
         he wasted no time, but ran at once to the home of Hephaestus,
         panting with lust to possess the beautiful-crowned Cytherea.°
         She had just said goodbye to her father, the mighty son of great Cronus,

270. *Helius:* As the sun-god, he sees all.   288. *Cytherea:* That is, Aphrodite.

FIGURE 8.6 The adultery of Aphrodite and Ares on a fresco from Pompeii from the first century AD. Ares (= Mars) reaches his hand inside Aphrodite's (= Venus') blouse while Eros (= Cupid) looks on.   (Museo Archeologico Nazionale, Naples; author's photo)

290 and was sitting there by herself. Ares scratched at the door,
squeezed her hand, and murmured tender endearments of love:
"Sweetheart, off we go, to snuggle down in the blankets.
Your husband? He's gone off. By now he must be in Lemnos,
amusing himself with the Sintian women,° with voices like crows."
295   Aphrodite agreed. Bed seemed to offer amusement.
Up the pair went to slumber together. Down came the chain,
tightly embracing the two, as wily Hephaestus had planned it.
Neither could move an inch and neither could lift up a finger.
They knew at once they had no possible way of escaping.

294. *Sintian women:* Native inhabitants of Lemnos.

300   The famous lame craftsman, meanwhile, had turned back to his house
       before he got to Lemnos, warned by Helius, his trusty informant.
       Savage with rage he approached, but checked himself in the doorway,
       then yelled at the top of his voice to summon all the immortals:
           "Come here, father Zeus and you other blessed immortal gods,
305   if you really want to guffaw at something shameful to see.
       Aphrodite, daughter of Zeus, is always mocking my lameness,
       billing and cooing with Ares, her muscular pretty-boy vandal.
       So I was born with a limp. Nobody can blame me for that.
       Charge the fault to my parents, who didn't have to beget me!
310   Just look here at the lovebirds, snuggled so sweetly together—
       and in my bed, if you please! You wonder why I resent it?
       Well, somehow I don't imagine they want to stay any longer.
       However fond they may be, they'd rather have separate beds.
       But this little gadget will chain them fast in loving embrace
315   till Daddy repays every penny I gave for the lecherous slut.
       Sure, his daughter is pretty, but empty of sense or of morals."
           At this the gods rushed up and clustered around his door—
       Poseidon, embracer of earth; Hermes the helper of mortals;
       and the lord Apollo, who hurls his flying darts from afar.
320   The feminine goddesses stayed at home for modesty's sake
       while the gods, the givers of blessings, gaped at the pair through the door.
       Unceasing bawdy laughter broke out from the blessed gods,
       eyeing the clever device contrived by inventive Hephaestus.
       Each slapped another's back as he flung him a salty jest:
325   "Crime never pays?" they asked. "The slow outrunning the swift?
       Why not, if limping Hephaestus can catch the swift-footed Ares,
       nimblest of all the gods who hold domain on Olympus?"
       "What if his legs are lame? His brain is certainly working."
           So they were joking together, and Apollo, son of Zeus,
330   questioned Lord Hermes thus: "O Hermes, giver of blessings,
       even if you were shackled with inescapable fetters,
       wouldn't you like to recline with Aphrodite the golden?"
       Hermes the guide, the slayer of Argus, promptly retorted:
       "O, what wouldn't I give for that, far-shooting Apollo!
335   I'd gladly be bound by thrice as many unbreakable chains,
       while all you gods looked on—yes, and the goddesses too—
       as long as I might lie there with Aphrodite the golden!"
           At this reply the immortals burst into hootings of laughter,
       but Poseidon, unamused, kept begging the famous inventor
340   to let poor Ares go. His words went straight to the point:
       "Loose him. I promise to pay you whatever you may demand,
       whatever is found satisfactory among the immortal gods."°
           The famous smith, who is crippled in both his legs, gave this answer:
       "Poseidon, embracer of earth, please don't ask this of me.

---

342. *among the immortal gods:* According to Greek laws surviving from Athens and Crete, the adulterer, when caught in the act, could be detained until appropriate compensation was paid. In Athens, he could lawfully be killed on the spot. Poseidon is volunteering to put up bail for Ares.

345   Promises made by the worthless are so much worthless wind.
           What can I claim from you before the immortals' assembly,
           if once this Ares escapes, eluding me and my bonds?"°
              Poseidon, shaker of earth, unhappily gave this reply:
           "Hephaestus, if Ares attempts to escape by jumping his bail,
350   I promise to make up his bond, repaying all that he owes."
              The crippled smith replied to Poseidon in these words:
           "I cannot refuse your offer, to do so would be impolite."
           So mighty Hephaestus unfastened the chain, and the lovers,
           once set free from its links, slender but terribly strong,
355   jumped up in silence and parted, Ares to warlike Thrace,°
           Aphrodite, lover of smiles, to her shrine in Paphos on Cyprus,
           with gardens around the temple and a fragrant altar within.
           The Graces washed and anointed her flesh with ambrosial oil
           of the sort laid up for immortals, and clothed the goddess
360   in robes of the loveliest sort, a wonder to see.

HOMER, Odyssey 8.266–366

347. *my bonds:* Hephaestus is at first reluctant to let Ares go, even on Poseidon's promise to guarantee Ares' payment of compensation. Ares will surely default, forcing Hephaestus to take action against Poseidon, which he does not want to do.   355. *Thrace:* Evidently Ares' homeland.

Although the story, embedded in the *Odyssey,* makes fun of the foibles of the gods in a parodic manner that goes back to Mesopotamia and Egypt, its theme of adultery and discovery parallels and mocks the story of Paris and Helen, whose adultery had led to the Trojan War. At the same time the story heightens the virtue of Penelopê who in the *Odyssey* remains superior to the crafts of Aphrodite: Although a goddess, Aphrodite (unlike Penelopê) could not resist the power of sexual attraction and fell into illicit sexual indulgence.

KEY NAMES AND TERMS

Hermes, 187	Cyllenê, 189
herm, 188	Pan, 200
caduceus, 188	Hephaestus, 203
psychopompos, 189	Lemnos, 203
Argeïphontes, 189	Ares, 205
Maia, 189	

SOME ADDITIONAL ANCIENT SOURCES

Hermes is common in ancient literature, but conspicuous in Homer, *Iliad* 24.334–469; *Odyssey* 5.28–148; (as Mercury) Ovid *Metamorphoses* 2.685–835, 8.618–724. Hephaestus: Aeschylus, *Prometheus Bound* 1–81, 365–369. Ares: Aeschylus, *Eumenides* 685–690.

FURTHER READING CHAPTER 8

Borgeaud, P., *The Cult of Pan in Ancient Greece* (Chicago, 1988). Discusses the evolution of this god through Greek history.

Brown, N. O., *Hermes the Thief* (New York, 1969; originally 1947). Argues that Hermes represents the emerging mercantile classes against the established aristocracy represented by Apollo.

CHAPTER 9

MYTHS OF THE FEMALE DEITIES APHRODITE, ARTEMIS, AND ATHENA

The race of gods and men is one, and from one mother
we both draw our breath. Yet all the difference in our powers
holds us apart, so that man is nothing,
but the brazen floor of heaven is eternally unshakable.

PINDAR, *Nemean 6* 1–4

T HE MALE OLYMPIANS HAVE spheres of operation that sometimes overlap or have outlines that are inexplicable (what is the nature of Poseidon's relationship with horses?). The female Olympians, by contrast, seem more to be aspects of a single religious concern with the fecund forces in life, both natural and human. Thus Demeter is the force that makes grain sprout from the seed. Hestia is the life of the house, where the fire burns and sustenance is prepared. Aphrodite is the horrific power of sexual attraction, indifferent to human happiness as it ensures the creation of a new generation. Artemis is the wealth of the wild, where game abounds. Only Athena has no clear relationship with fertility, but her province is skill in female crafts, especially weaving, in which Greek women spent their entire lives when they were not rearing their children. However, in studying male and female gods in Greek myth we must remember that all such portraits are the creations of Greek males, whose complex relationships with the other sex are a central theme of Greek myth. We know almost nothing about how Greek women themselves viewed any gods, male or female.

DEMETER, MISTRESS OF WHEAT

Whereas Gaea/Earth was the female power who presided over the birth of the world, Demeter (de-**mē**-ter) was the mother-goddess who oversaw the fruitfulness of agriculture, especially wheat. The -*meter* part of her name means "mother," but the *De-* has eluded convincing explanation. We wish it could mean "wheat" so that Demeter is the "wheat-mother," but the etymology seems impossible. Surely wherever wheat was grown, her religion was strong, especially at the town of Eleusis near Athens and in Sicily. Both in myth and in cult Demeter was closely linked to her daughter Persephonê; the two were called simply "the goddesses." We devote all of Chapter 10 to discussing the important myths of Demeter and Persephonê and related stories.

HESTIA, THE HEARTH

Hestia was the eldest child of Cronus and Rhea, the first swallowed and the last regurgitated. Her name means "hearth." She is the Roman Vesta and the most colorless of the Olympians, being nothing more than the fireplace in every house: There was her shrine and her presence, protectress of the home. She defined the internal space of the female world, for it was the duty of the women in the family to tend the domestic fire. By extension Hestia was also protectress of the city, the enlarged family, which sometimes kept a central hearth. In Athens, she was associated with a special building where the magistrates of the city dined together as members of the civic family. Few stories are told about her, and according to many accounts, Dionysus took her place among the twelve Olympians. She was always virgin and never left Olympus, as did the other gods. There she was the center of the divine household, even as the hearth was the center of the human family. Her Roman counterpart, Vesta, was treated as the chief symbol of the city of Rome. Vesta's shrine, tended by six virgins, contained an undying flame.

APHRODITE, GODDESS OF SEXUAL LOVE

Aphrodite (later identified with the Roman Venus) embodies the overwhelming power of human sexual attraction. Her constant companion, or child by Ares, is Eros, "sexual desire" (the Roman Cupid). In art he is a winged boy with bow and arrows or a flaming torch (a figure still familiar on Valentine's Day; see Figures 2.10, 5.5, and 8.6), a mischievous, irresponsible child, showering his arrows randomly and without regard for the harm born from the sexual passion he arouses.

Hesiod derives Aphrodite by a false folk etymology from *aphros,* "foam," but the goddess is certainly not Greek in origin, nor is her name. Most scholars think that the name must somehow be a distortion of that of the Eastern goddess of fertility variously known as Inanna, Ishtar, or Astartê (which themselves appear to be distortions of a single name). The goddess evidently came to Greece through Cyprus, a frequent point of transmission of Eastern culture to the West. At Paphos, in southwestern

PERSPECTIVE 9

VENUS: IMAGES OF BEAUTY IN EUROPEAN ART

The birth of Venus (the Roman name for Aphrodite) is the theme of one of the most famous paintings of the Italian Renaissance, by master artist Sandro Botticelli (1445–1510), on the walls of a rich patron's villa near the brilliant city of Florence (Perspective Figure 9a). At this time, artists rejected the earlier preference for flat, stylized religious art and grew enthusiastic about nature, naturalistic representation, and classical myth. Botticelli's presentation is especially striking because nude women were almost unknown in medieval art. However, such expressions of ancient myth were always understood in allegorical, Neoplatonic terms (see Chapter 25).

The goddess, in a pose derived from classical statues of Venus (see Figure 9.2), symbolizes the spiritual beauty to which every soul aspires, the airy floating object of the soul's contemplation. She stands on a scallop shell wafted over the sea by

PERSPECTIVE FIGURE 9a Sandro Botticelli (Italian, 1445–1510), the *Birth of Venus,* c. 1482, oil on canvas.   (Galleria degli Uffizi, Florence; Erich Lessing/Art Resource, New York)

the breath of the winds. Hesiod says nothing about a shell, a sea-creature from which a delectable meat emerges, in this case the human soul. Hesiod says nothing about the winds, here Zephyr ("West Wind") and Aura ("Breeze"), male and female, but the winds are the divine spirit (*spiritus* = "wind"), God's expressive will that drives every event. Rose petals, flowers of love, fall on the whitecaps stirred by the winds, because God's will is an expression of divine love. A Hora, Spring, spreads out a brocaded blanket to receive the goddess; even so does the body, obedient to the rhythm of life's seasons, symbolized by the grove of trees, enclose the soul. At birth unblemished and innocent, the soul is now encased in gross and vulgar matter, the robe cast by the nymph.

Born in Florence, Piero di Cosimo (1462–1521), a younger contemporary of Botticelli, is known for his imaginative, even bizarre, unorthodox, and poignant treatment of pagan and Christian subjects. Homer tells the humorous and salacious story of Aphrodite and Ares in the *Odyssey* (8.266–366; Chapter 8) but focuses on the chagrin felt by the captured lovers and the trick by which they were taken. Piero, by contrast, influenced by the landscape art and realism of Flemish artists, sees the story as an allegory expressing the true nature of love: It is stronger than strength (Perspective Figure 9b).

In the painting there is no hint of Hephaestus' trap. Simply, two lovers lie in the meadow after making love. Mars, on the right, is sound sleep, exhausted by love, whereas Aphrodite/Venus, who is Love, is wide awake, contemplating the fruit to come, the child in her arms and the fecund rabbit on her hip. The black and white doves on the ground between them must symbolize the same duality as Mars/Venus, yet both are doves, the birds of Venus. A butterfly, symbolic of new life, alights on Venus' knee. Winged cupids, the children of Love, play with the war-god's armor in the background, useless except as playthings in the conquering ambience of Love.

PERSPECTIVE FIGURE 9b Piero di Cosimo (Italian, 1462–1521), *Venus and Mars,* 1498, oil on panel. (Staatliche Museen, Berlin, Gemaldegalerie; Bildarchiv Preussischer Kulturbesitz / Art Resource, New York)

Ovid tells the story of the lovers Venus and Adonis in the *Metamorphoses* (see Chapter 10): When scratched accidentally by an arrow of her own son Cupid, Venus herself fell in love with the beautiful Adonis, born of an incestuous relationship. Happily they hunted the fields together. One afternoon, after hearing Venus' story of the huntress Atalanta, Adonis fell asleep on a couch of grass under a canopy of poplar. Venus flew to heaven, while Adonis' hounds awakened him to hunt the boar that will kill him. Veronese (1528–1588, really Paolo Caliari, called Veronese after his native Verona) was devoted to realistic presentation even of mythical scenes. Here he illustrates and expounds upon Ovid's story (Perspective Figure 9c). Venus, anticipating what must come, warns away the barking hound in the lower

PERSPECTIVE FIGURE 9c Veronese (Paolo Caliari, Italian, 1528–1588), *Venus and Adonis,* oil on canvas.   (Museo del Prado, Madrid; Scala/White Images / Art Resource, New York)

left, restrained by her son Cupid, the cause of her infatuation, while Adonis sleeps soundly. Although not an allegory, the painting nonetheless propounds the popular moral that Ovid intended: True love is ever fleeting.

The Toilet of Venus is the only surviving female nude by the most important Spanish painter of the sixteenth century and one of the great painters of all time, Velázquez (1599–1660). Mysteriously, it passed censure by the vigorous Spanish Inquisition. The commission for the painting must have come from the king himself or someone near him (Perspective Figure 9d). During the Napoleonic wars this painting belonged to the prime minister and effective ruler of Spain. It does not illustrate a myth, just the goddess of love in her naked glory, a tradition that began in the ancient world. Such a statue was Praxiteles' Aphrodite (see Figure 9.2). Venus is engrossed in beholding an image of her own beauty; the mirror was the ancient symbol for feminine self-love (compare Figure 5.5). Velázquez has made the image in the mirror larger than it should be, and a close look reveals that the image is beholding the spectator so that Venus is watching herself watching you. In Renaissance Italy similar paintings were prepared for the bedrooms of married couples to inspire lovemaking and the production of beautiful children. In 1911 a suffragist viciously slashed the painting as being a symbol of men's exploitation of women, but it has since been restored.

PERSPECTIVE FIGURE 9d Diego Velázquez (Spanish, 1599–1660), *The Toilet of Venus,* 1650, oil on canvas.   (© National Gallery, London; Art Resource, New York)

Cyprus, she was worshiped as early as the twelfth century BC in the form of a polished conical stone (which has survived, displayed today in the museum at Paphos on Cyprus). There the Greeks may first have learned about her. Her cult was also important on the island of Cythera, south of the Peloponnesus, where Phoenicians had a settlement. Other important temples were built to her in Sicily, where there were also Phoenician colonies, and in Corinth, a gathering place for seafarers of various nationalities. Greek myth preserves a clear sense of Aphrodite's connection with Cyprus and Cythera, both places said to be where the goddess first came to land after rising from the sea foam, and she was often referred to in literature as **Cypris** (**si**-pris) or **Cytherea** (si-ther-ē-a).

A striking feature of the worship of Aphrodite and Inanna/Ishtar/Astarte was temple prostitution. Women, often of good birth, voluntarily served in her temples, where they had intercourse with men who paid in the form of offerings to the goddess. Such service was a kind of ransom paid to the fecundating power of the goddess and ensured large families to the woman, once she married. Actual prehistoric maiden sacrifice may stand behind the practice: Rather than giving up her life, the girl surrendered her virginity "in honor of the goddess." The sometimes prudish Greeks had no taste for the practice, but temple prostitution did occur in temples to Aphrodite at Corinth and Cythera.

Sappho, who lived in the late seventh or early sixth century BC on the island of Lesbos and who was celebrated as "the tenth Muse," wrote one of the prettiest poems about Aphrodite. Nothing certain is known about Sappho's life or about the audience for her poetry. She is famous for her erotic celebration of women, but the social environment in which such poetry was performed has been the topic of controversy since ancient times. Not until after classical times was her poetry considered to be homoerotic (hence our word *lesbian*).

We have no information how or where her poetry was first performed, except we can be sure that it was in a public context. Some of her poetry must have been performed at weddings, the one occasion in which it was possible to celebrate publicly a young woman's erotic appeal. In her "Hymn to Aphrodite," she declares the love-goddess's power to sway the hearts even of the unwilling, while, ironically, leaving no doubt that the present situation has occurred many times before:

> Fancy-throned deathless Aphrodite,
> deceitful child of Zeus, I entreat you,
> do not overwhelm my heart with
> pains and anguish, O lady,
>
> come to me, if ever in the past
> you heard my voice
> and came acquiescing, leaving
> your father's golden house,
>
> yoking your car. Beautiful swift
> sparrows, with wings whirring
> brought you over the dark earth
> down from heaven, through

the middle air, and soon they arrived.
You, with a smile on your immortal
face asked what was it now
and why did I call,

and what, especially, in my mad heart
did I want to happen this time.
"Whom do I persuade to return
again to your love? Who, O Sappho,

brings you harm? If she runs
soon she will pursue. If she will
not take your gifts, soon she shall
give. If she does not love,

soon she shall love against her
will." Come to me, set me free
from anguish. Give me my desire.
Be yourself my companion in arms.

SAPPHO, FRAGMENT 1 (DIEHL)

Hermaphroditus and Priapus

In addition to her affair with Ares, Aphrodite had an affair with the messenger-god Hermes, by whom she gave birth to **Hermaphroditus** (her-ma-fro-**di**-tus), a boy of remarkable beauty. Ovid tells a famous story about him: One day a nymph, Salmacis (**sal**-ma-sis), noticed him wandering in the woods, fell hopelessly in love, and urged that they sleep together. Innocent Hermaphroditus ran away in confusion. Later, when Hermaphroditus dipped into a spring for a bath, Salmacis leaped in and clung to him tightly, praying that they never be separated. They were fused into one being with a woman's breasts but a man's genitals. The slightly titillating bisexual Hermaphroditus was a common subject of art in late antiquity.

Another child of Aphrodite, whose father was reputedly Dionysus or Hermes, was **Priapus** (prī-**ā**pus), an amusing Asiatic garden-deity and fertility fetish with an enormous erect phallus, who warded off the evil eye (as did the phallus on a herm). His name is not Greek, and he does not appear until late Hellenistic times. He was especially popular among the Romans, who suspended little tablets with clever, highly obscene poetry from the god's phallus, warning the most unpleasant sexual consequences to unwelcome intruders (Figure 9.1).

Pygmalion

Except for the affair between Aphrodite and Ares, all important stories about Aphrodite are set outside Greece, reflecting her Eastern origins. Her strong connections with Cyprus and with Eastern myth appear in traditions about the Cypriote

FIGURE 9.1 Priapus, the garden-god, weighs his phallus against a bag of gold (it seems an even contest!), c. AD 70. Priapus wears a Phrygian cap (Phrygia is home to fertility cults). His association with Dionysus is indicated by the wand (thyrsus) to his left, his power over gardens by the bowl of fruit at his feet. (Pompeii, House of the Vettii; Scala/Art Resource, New York)

royal house, best known through Ovid's story of **Pygmalion,** king of Cyprus, who had become disgusted with the profligate and immoral behavior of Cypriote women. In many respects, the story is a recasting of Hesiod's story of Pandora, set not in the early days of the world, but now in the age of heroes:

[243]   Pygmalion observed these women leading their shameful lives.
        Horrified by the vices of which nature has planted such plenty
245   in the mind of their sex, he started by living a celibate life,
        sharing his bed with no one. He presently carved himself a statue
        with delicate skill, of ivory, pure white, possessing a beauty
        greater than any mortal woman could ever hope to attain—
        and promptly conceived a passion for the product of his own hand.
250   The figure was that of a maiden so real you might think it alive [Figure 9.2].
        Perhaps she wanted to move, and only decorum restrained her;
        the skillful sculptor employed his skill in concealing his skill.
            Pygmalion gazed at his work, his heart inflamed with love
        for the counterfeit girl he had made. Again and again his hands
255   uncertainly fondled the work—is it ivory, or is it real flesh?
        At last he persuaded himself that the statue was ivory no longer.
        Pressing his kisses upon it, he was sure each kiss was returned.

FIGURE 9.2 The Capitoline Aphrodite, a Roman copy, c. 100 AD, that goes back to a celebrated statue by Praxiteles, fourth century BC, made as the cult statue of Aphrodite for her temple at Cnidus in southwest Asia Minor. Such statues stand behind Ovid's story. The earliest Greek sculpture, from the eighth century BC, represented males naked, but women were almost always represented clothed. About the original statue (known only from such Roman copies), Aphrodite was said to have asked, "When did Praxiteles see me nude?" The soft, languorous, sensuous style of Praxiteles, with the S-curve of the body, continued to influence sculptural styles for hundreds of years. The nudity of the goddess is explained by her having just arisen from a bath, taken in antiquity by pouring water over the body from a jug, here shown at her side, partially draped. The gesture of the left hand, covering the pelvis, is taken from ancient Eastern sculpture.   (Museo Capitolino, Rome; author's photo)

Whispering, he hugged closer—did his fingers sink in the flesh?
Has he been so rough that bruises appeared wherever he touched?
260   He kissed the hurt places. He gave her presents girls all adore—
sea shells and well-polished stones, little birds in their cages,
bouquets of a thousand colors, lilies, bright painted balls,
tears of the Heliad nymphs.° He clothed her in elegant dresses,
gems sparkled on her fingers, long looping chains on her neck.

263. *tears of the Heliad nymphs:* Amber. The Heliades were the sisters of Phaëthon, turned into poplar trees with tears of amber as they grieved for their dead brother.

265 From her ear lobes dangled light earrings, ribbons over her bosom.
 All in the best of taste, but without them she looked even nicer.
 He tenderly laid her down on a bed of Sidonian purple.°
 Murmuring "Share this, my couch!" he pillowed her drooping head
 on a cushion of softest down, as if it could feel what he wanted.

270 Venus' feast day arrived, beloved by the people of Cyprus.
 Victims with gilded horns bowed snowy necks and were slaughtered
 as incense fumed in each shrine. Pygmalion, his duties completed,
 bashfully stayed by the altar, and bashfully uttered his prayer:
  "Because you gods, as piety tells us, can grant any human request,

275 I beg that my wife may be—" (not daring "my ivory maiden,"
 he gulped and went on) "someone just like my ivory statue."
 Venus the Golden herself was there at her very own feast day.
 Knowing full well the intent of Pygmalion's stumbling prayer,
 she gave him a sign of good will: A flame leaped up on the altar,

280 not once, but three times.   Pygmalion returned to his workshop
 and hurried to seek the graven image of his true love.
 Throwing himself beside it, he smothered the statue with kisses.
 How's this? It seemed to get warm! His mouth returned to her lips,
 his hand to her breast. At his eager groping the ivory softened,

285 the chill of her flesh passed off, it gladly yielded to his touch
 and softened, as does the wax of the honey bees of Hymettus,°
 which, warmed by the sun and kneaded, is soft and easily shaped,
 better to handle, the more it is handled. Pygmalion, astonished,
 was unable to make up his mind. Rejoicing, he still hesitated

290 and kept his rejoicing in check, for fear it was all an illusion.
 Again he became the lover, with hands roving over the body—
 for body indeed it was! whose veins throbbed under his fingers.
 The grateful hero of Paphos poured out his praises of Venus,
 then pressed his lips to the lips no longer a statue's, but real.

295 As she felt his kisses, the maiden blushed and raised timid eyes.
 The love light and light of heaven together fell on her sight.°
 The goddess herself was a guest at the marriage she had arranged.
 Nine times the horns of the new moon rounded out to a circle,
 when the one-time statue gave birth to a daughter, named Paphos,

300 whose name the island preserves.

OVID, Metamorphoses 10.243–297

267. *Sidonian purple:* Sidon was a city of the Phoenicians, known for its purple dye. 286. *Hymettus:* A mountain near Athens, still famous for its honey. 296. *sight:* The Latin *lumen* may mean "light," "sight," or "eye."

The statue come to life was named Galatea, mother of the Paphos for whom Aphrodite's sacred city is named. Paphos in turn gave birth to **Cinyras** (**sin**-i-ras), whose wife boasted that their daughter **Myrrha** (or Smyrna) was more beautiful than Aphrodite. Aphrodite punished Myrrha's arrogant claim by causing Myrrha to fall in love with her own father, Cinyras. She lured him into a darkened chamber, where she slept with him for twelve nights. Cinyras, drunk, thought he had slept with a concubine while his wife was out of town. When he discovered the truth, Cinyras pursued his now pregnant daughter with a sword, but the gods transformed her into the myrrh tree. Her tears of sorrow became the precious resin myrrh, burned on the altar in Aphrodite's cult and other religious cults. Cinyras killed himself for shame over the incestuous union. After nine months, the myrrh tree split open, and the beautiful hero Adonis emerged (compare Perspective Figure 9c), whose story we consider in Chapter 10.

Aphrodite and Anchises

Another tale of Aphrodite's ominous love is found in the *Homeric Hymn to Aphrodite,* from the early seventh century BC. According to the common theme, Aphrodite became victim to her own power when, thanks to Zeus, she fell in love with a mortal, **Anchises** (an-**kī**-sēz), a prince related to the Trojan royal house. Although male gods regularly pursued mortal women, it was altogether shameful for a goddess to consort with a mortal man. The hymn nicely compares Aphrodite with the great goddesses Athena, Artemis, and Hestia, all of whom remained virgin:

[1]   Sing me, O Muse, the story of Aphrodite the golden,
    the Cyprian, she who arouses the sweetest desire in immortals,
    who conquers the races of mortals, even the birds on the wing,
    and all the numberless creatures supported by earth or by sea.
5   All that has life is concerned in the work of the fair Aphrodite.
    Three hearts alone Aphrodite can neither persuade nor deceive:
    Gray-eyed Athena is one, the daughter of Zeus of the aegis,
    who plays no part in the works of Aphrodite the golden;
    rather, her joy is in war and the savage workings of Ares,
10   battles and fights, though she cares for glorious craftsmen as well,
    for Athena first taught mortal workers the art of building a chariot
    with fittings of bronze. It is she, moreover, who teaches
    soft-skinned maidens the arts of the house, revealing her knowledge.
    And Artemis, mistress of arrows, sounding the cry of the huntress,
15   is immune to Aphrodite and her plots to ensnare men with love.
    Her delight is rather the bow, the killing of beasts in the hills;
    the lyre and dance as well, but chiefly the cry of the hunter,
    sounding in shadowy woodlands, by the cities of fair-minded men.
    Finally, Aphrodite and all her works are repugnant
20   to the lady Hestia, first-born of Cronus, who then, by Zeus's design,
    was born again as his last.° The lady was wooed by Poseidon,
    then wooed by Apollo as well, but both she firmly rejected
    and swore an unbreakable oath, her hand on the head of great Zeus,
    the father who holds the aegis, to remain forever a virgin,

---

21. *his last:* Hestia was the first born of the children of Cronus and Rhea, the first swallowed by her father, and the last to be vomited back to the light.

25 honored among the immortals. Instead of wedlock, Zeus granted
a noble reward to the goddess: She sits in the midst of his palace
by his side at the head of the table, picking the finest of morsels.
In all the temples of every god she is suitably honored,
and men owe due veneration to Hestia, first of immortals.

30 The hearts of these three Aphrodite can never trick or inveigle.
No other, blessed god or mortal, is able to flee her enticement.
She even beguiles the mind of Zeus, who delights in the thunder,
mightiest of all the gods, the holder of mightiest power.
Whenever the humor so moves her, she fools even his wily spirit,

35 and leads him to couple with women, evading the sharp eye of Hera,
his sister as well as wife, fairest of all the immortals.
Cronus the schemer begat great Hera, his comeliest daughter,
on Rhea, his consort; then Zeus, eternal in wisdom, received her,
and made her his modest wife, well-versed in arts of the household.

40 On Aphrodite herself Zeus cast a sweet spell of desire,
of lust for a mortal man: No more could she shyly dissemble
her knowledge of love of a mortal, experience in a man's bed.
Never again could she claim, when immortals were gathered together,
with a softly innocent smile, that she alone drove them to couple

45 with mortal women, who bore them sons who were destined to perish,
and deathless goddesses too she had driven to mate with mere humans.
Thus Zeus put into her heart a sweet desire for Anchises,
who, high on the slopes of Ida,° mountain of bubbling streams,
at that time was tending his cattle—a man with the form of a god.

50 No wonder that Aphrodite was smitten as soon as she saw him,
or that sweet pangs of desire seized on her heart and her spirit.
Off she hurried to Cyprus, to Paphos, her sweet-scented temple,
into its sacred precinct with its altar fuming with incense.
Behind her she closed the brazen doorway, gleaming and polished.

55 The Graces washed and anointed her flesh with ambrosial oil,
divine, sweet-smelling, that glows on the skin of bodies immortal.
Of this she treasured a store, of fragrance greater than earthly.
Then Aphrodite, lover of laughter, dressed in her finest array,
decked her body with gold, and, abandoning redolent Cyprus,

60 hurried her flight to Troy, through clouds and over the mountains.
At last she arrived at Ida, mountain of freshets, the mother
of animals wild and savage. Over the foothills she hastened,
to the hut of Anchises. Behind, there came a once man-eating bevy
of now-fawning dusky wolves, of lions still savagely glaring,

65 bears, and swift-footed leopards, insatiate killers of deer.
The goddess rejoiced at the sight. Into their hearts she injected
the spell of amorous desire. All of them, couple by couple,
lay down together to mate throughout all the shadowy forest.
The goddess soon drew near the shepherd's stoutly built cabin.

70 She found the hero Anchises, left all alone by himself.
His comrades had led out the cattle to graze in rich grassy meadows,
while he strolled about alone, strumming a tune on his lyre.

48. *Ida:* In northwestern Asia Minor, near Troy.

The daughter of Zeus, Aphrodite, stopped in front of the hero,
disguising her height and form, to resemble an unmarried maiden,
75   lest her godhead frighten Anchises as he opened his amorous eyes.
But the moment the Trojan saw her he viewed her form in amazement,
wondering at her stature, her beauty, her glorious garments.
She was wearing a long red dress, gleaming more brightly than fire,
lovely, embroidered in gold. And over her tender young bosom
80   it shone as fair as the moonlight, a wonder indeed to one's eyes.
Anchises, insane with desire, addressed these words to the goddess:
"I greet you, lady, whatever goddess you are, who have happened
to come to my cabin—Artemis? Leto perhaps? or the golden
Aphrodite? Thetis, lofty of birth? or even the gray-eyed Athena?
85   Could you be one of the Graces who accompany all the immortals,
immortal themselves, we are told? or maybe a nymph who has wandered
down from the pleasant woods where they dwell, or one who inhabits
the rising springs and the rivers, the grassy meadows and plains?
See, I shall build you an altar on a crag, to be seen from afar
90   and bring you rich offerings at every season of year.
This only I ask in return: With a kind and benevolent spirit,
grant that I grow in importance, a leader and prince of the Trojans.
Give me a fruitful posterity, keeping my name and my blood.
And last, for myself I pray that my life may be long and contented,
95   seeing the light of the sun, respected by all of my fellows,
and so live on till I come to the threshold of gloomy old age."
To him Aphrodite, daughter of Zeus, made this modest reply:
"Anchises, noblest of humans born on the face of the earth,
no goddess, of course, am I. Why liken me to the immortals?
100   I am no more than a woman. The mother who bore me was human.
You may have heard of my father, Otreus, that glorious hero,
ruler of all the dominion of Phrygia,° well-fortified region.
You notice that I speak your Trojan tongue, as I speak my own Phrygian.
A Trojan nurse took me over, when I was no more than an infant,
105   from my own dear mother's hands, and brought me up in the palace.
Thus I became as fluent in your language as in my own.
Just now golden-staffed Hermes, the famous slayer of Argus,
caught me up from the dancers of Artemis, gold-arrowed huntress.
Many of us together, both nymphs and girls fit for marriage,
110   were dancing, while all around a crowd uncountable watched us.
From such a throng gold-sceptered Hermes, the slayer of Argus,
bore me, past endless wheat lands worked by the labor of mortals,
by endless acres unworked, unclaimed, the haunt of wild creatures,
of savage man-eating beasts who roam about in the forests.
115   Nevermore, so it seemed, would my feet touch the life-giving earth.
But Hermes insisted that I was to share the bed of Anchises,
be named as his wedded wife, and bear you magnificent children.
All this the slayer of Argus narrated in every detail,
then made his way once again to the deathless gods on Olympus.

---

102. *Phrygia:* In the legend of the Trojan War, Otreus came to the aid of Priam, king of Troy, to fight
against the Amazons. Phrygia is a territory in the north-central plateau of Anatolia.

120 So I am come before you, as unswerving necessity orders.
In Zeus's name I implore you, and that of your glorious parents
(surely no common mortals could engender so splendid a son!),
take me, a maiden unwedded, and quite unpracticed in love.
Present me to your dear father, to your mother, wise and sagacious,
125 to brothers born to your house—no embarrassment will they find me,
but a daughter of high repute. Send a messenger quickly to Phrygia,
land of the speediest horses, to my grieving father and mother.
They will return you a treasure of gold and well-woven garments
for you to take as an ample—nay, a magnificent—dowry.
130 When all this business is done, set up a magnificent banquet
to celebrate our wedlock, honored by gods and by mortals."
        The goddess's words injected sweet longing into his heart.
Desire took hold of Anchises, and thus he spoke in reply:
"If you are indeed a human, if a mortal woman once bore you,
135 if Otreus, as you say, that famous man, is your father,
if you are here by the will of Hermes, the leader immortal,
and if you are willing forever to bear the title of wife—
then I tell you that nobody, nobody, be he immortal or human,
can hold me back in my passion, until we have bedded in love,
140 no, not if archer Apollo from his silver bow should let fly
his deadly unfailing arrows. Indeed, divinest of women,
I would gladly go down to Hades, if first I had entered your bed."
        At that he took hold of her hand. Aphrodite, the lover of laughter,
coyly averted her face, and, drooping her beautiful eyelids,
145 modestly feigning resistance, crept to the soft-covered bed.
This was warm and well covered with furs of beasts which the hero
had slain high up in the mountains, the pelts of lions and bears.
Once they lay down on the couch, solidly built and uncreaking,
the hero stripped from the goddess her pretty gewgaws and brooches,
150 her necklace and earrings as well. Anchises then loosened her girdle,
and everything else, and tossed them onto a chair made of silver.
So this mortal lay down by the side of a goddess immortal,
not by his own design, but by fate and divine intervention.
        At the hour shepherds return their flocks from flowery meadows,
155 driving their sturdy sheep and cattle back to the shelter,
Aphrodite arose, poured drowsy sleep on Anchises,
and dressed herself once again in all her beautiful raiment.
Then, fully clothed, the goddess stood by the couch in full glory,
her head as high as the roof tree. Beauty shone from her features,
160 beauty such as belongs to the golden-crowned goddess alone.
Then she awakened Anchises from slumber, addressing him thus:
        "Up, son of Dardanus! Tell me, why do you slumber so soundly?
Look at me now, and answer: Do I seem to resemble the woman
on whom you first cast your eyes no more than a few hours ago?"
165 So she teased him. Anchises awoke with a start and looked up.
As soon as he looked on the neck and the lovely face of the goddess,
in shame and terror he turned his eyes away from the vision,
lifting his shepherd's cloak and concealing his handsome young face.
In tones of humble entreaty he spoke these words from his heart:

170   As soon as my eyes beheld your comeliness, beautiful goddess,
          I recognized you as divine. It was you who then led me astray.
          I implore you in Zeus's great name, the father wielding the aegis,
          have pity, abandon me not, unmanned, among men. For the mortal
          who mates with a goddess undying can never again be a man."
175   To his reproach Aphrodite, the daughter of Zeus, gave her answer:
          "Pluck up your courage, Anchises, noblest of all mortal men.
          You need have no fear whatever of suffering harm at my hands—
          certainly not from mine, nor those of a godhead undying,
          for you are cherished indeed by all the blessed immortals.
180   You shall father a son, to be ruler over the Trojans,
          and generations from him shall be born, one succeeding another,
          Aeneas, after my terrible° guilt at bedding a human.
          Of all the races of men, the closest and dearest to gods
          in beauty and charm is that from which you and he are descended.
185   For example, Zeus the planner abducted the fair Ganymede
          for his beauty, and kept him to live with him among the immortals,
          pouring their drink in the house of Zeus, a wonder to see,
          honored by all the gods as he draws the deep ruddy nectar
          from a golden bowl. But aching grief held the heart of Tros,°
190   who knew not where the tempest of Zeus had carried his son.
          Day and night he lamented, until Zeus repented at last,
          giving him high-pacing horses, the sort that carry the gods,
          a gift in exchange for his son. And, moved by Zeus's commandment,
          the guide, the slayer of Argus, told Tros in every detail
195   how his son would never perish, but be ageless as an immortal.
          When Tros understood the promise of Zeus, he ended his grieving,
          but afterward traveled in joy, drawn by his storm-footed horses.

182. *terrible:* The Greek is *ainos,* punning on Aeneas.   189. *Tros:* Another early king of Troy, father of Ganymede.

Here Aphrodite tells the story of Eos' love for Tithonus as a second mythical parallel to her own passion for Anchises (see Chapter 4). She then continues:

[248]   "For my part, I cannot bear to have you face such a future,
          to be, like him,° immortal, but aging through days never-ending.
250   If you could live on forever, keeping the face and figure
          which now you enjoy, and if you bore the name of my husband,
          then my prophetic heart would not be darkened by sorrow.
          But well I know that grim old age will soon be upon you,
          pitiless, bringing the future which lies in wait for all humans,
255   a future deadly and grinding, one even the gods must abhor.
          And what of me? Shall I not suffer unending reproaches
          among the deathless gods, forever, on your account?
          Till now they always have dreaded my schemes and the wily devices
          by which I have driven them all to couple with mortal women.

249. *him:* Tithonus, who had eternal life but not eternal youth.

260 Immortal they might be, but my workings subverted them all.
Never again dare I mention such topics among the immortals,
for I have strayed in my folly, wretched and out of my mind,
bedding a mortal man and conceiving his child in my womb.
As soon as the boy is greeted by the light of the glorious sun,

265 deep-breasted mountain nymphs will undertake his upbringing,
they who inhabit the slopes of this great and sanctified mountain.
They live by neither the ways of gods nor those of humans.
For centuries they live on, eating the food of immortals,
treading along with immortals the steps of their lovely dance.

270 Sileni° and even the sharp-eyed slayer of Argus himself, Hermes,
mate with them, in recesses of a cool and convenient cavern.
When one of the nymphs is born, firs and lofty-crowned beeches
spring from the fertile earth, luxuriant, beautiful trees
high on the slopes of the mountains. Men say such places are holy,

275 sacred to the immortals, and touch them not with their axes.
But when the fatal day has come for a nymph of the mountain,
her tree first withers and sheds its foliage over the earth,
the shriveling bark peels off, the branches break from the trunk,
and tree and nymph together depart from the rays of the sun.

280 These nymphs will tend my son, watching over his childhood,
until he begins to display the first signs of developing manhood.
Then they will bring him here, to show him off to his father.
    Now let me explain the plan of the future I am designing:
Five years onward from now I shall come back with my son.

285 You will rejoice as your eyes first fall on him whom you fathered,
to see him so like a god. Then bring him to windy Ilium.°
If anyone there inquires, 'What mother bore this, your dear son,
carrying him under her girdle?' remember to tell him this story,
as I tell it now: 'This child was born of a flower-faced nymph,

290 who lives on a forest-clad hill.' But if, instead, in your folly
you boast of coupling in love with beautiful-crowned Cytherea,
Zeus in a rage will blast you with thunderbolts lurid and smoking.
Now I have told the whole story. Bury it deep in your heart.
Beware of speaking my name, or dread the wrath of the gods."

295   Ending with this injunction, she soared to the windy heaven.
Hail, O goddess who rules as queen of well-built Cyprus!
With you I began my song; now I turn to sing of another.

Hymn to Aphrodite 1–197; 248–297

---

270. *Sileni:* Woodland spirits.   286. *Ilium:* Another name for Troy.

Other sources tell how Anchises did reveal who was the mother of his child.
Zeus struck him in the thigh with a thunderbolt, as Aphrodite had threatened, and
ever after he was lame. So did Anchises suffer the fate he feared, to be unmanned
among men for having intercourse with a goddess.

Aeneas (ē-nē-as), son of Anchises and Aphrodite, is one of the few Trojan heroes to survive the conflagration of the city, escaping with his lame father and young son to the far West, where he founded the race of the Romans (Chapter 23).

ARTEMIS, MISTRESS OF ANIMALS

The name **Artemis** is not Greek, and her cult shows signs of reaching back into the Paleolithic Period, when hunting was a principal source of food. Homer calls her *Potnia Thêrôn*, "mistress of the animals," a title we associate with representations in art dating back to the Bronze Age showing a woman, sometimes winged, between a pair of wild animals (see Figure 3.3). As such, Artemis is closely associated with the Phrygian Cybelê, who is also shown in the presence of animals, usually lions.

In origin, then, Artemis was evidently a mother-goddess, protectress of the young, animal and human, making fecund the whole of nature. Her early role was never forgotten at Ephesus in Asia Minor, her most important cult center and the site of one of the largest temples that the Greeks ever built, one of the Seven Wonders of the Ancient World. There a cult image represented her with what seem to be dozens of breasts stacked like grapes on her chest (or they may represent bulls' testicles, hung on a primitive idol after sacrifice) (Figure 9.3). When St. Paul tried to speak in Ephesus, for two hours the shout of "Great is Artemis of the Ephesians!" drowned him out (Acts 19:28). That night, in fear of his life, he left town.

Despite her origins as a mother-goddess, in classical Greek religion Artemis paradoxically is the preeminent virgin-goddess. She is not mannish like Athena, who is really asexual, but dangerously alluring: Eternal virgin, she is eternally ready for impregnation. Her pure, remote, and untouched woodland can safely be entered only by those clean in body and spirit. Artemis is also a deadly huntress, wandering the wild, untamed places with her train of virgin nymphs, qualities emphasized in a *Homeric Hymn to Artemis* (probably sixth century BC):

> I sing the praises of Artemis, lady of golden-tipped arrows,
> her of the loud-ringing cry, virgin whom all men revere,
> slayer of stags, the goddess whose greatest joy is in hunting,
> sister of Phoebus Apollo, him of the golden sword.
>   Over the shadowy hills and wind-blown peaks of the mountains,
> she leads the hunt, delighting in drawing her bow, all of gold,
> and shooting her deadly shafts. The hilltops are shaken by terror,
> the dark of the woods resounds with the terrified screaming of beasts.
> The earth and the fish-laden ocean tremble in fear at her coming.
> She roves over all, fearless-hearted, slaying all races of creatures.
> But when the huntress, delighter in arrows, has sated her longing,
> rejoicing in heart, she loosens the string of her well-curved bow
> and returns to the mighty palace of Phoebus Apollo, her brother,
> in the fertile country of Delphi, to join with the Muses and Graces

FIGURE 9.3 Artemis of Ephesus, marble, second century AD. Portrayed in the likeness of the great statue of Artemis in her temple at Ephesus, she wears a zodiac around her neck. The bulls, griffins, and sphinxes that decorate her body and headdress stand for her rule over the animal kingdom, as do the two deer that stand beside her. Six thousand years earlier the goddess from Çatal Hüyük was represented in a similar way (Figure 3.1).   (Ephesus Museum; Vanni/Art Resource, New York)

in treading the maze of the dance. She hangs up curved bow and arrows
to lead off the chorus, decking her body with loveliest raiment.
With heavenly voices they carol, how Leto of beautiful ankles
bore her children, most famous by far for wisdom and action
of all who sit in the council on high, among the immortals.

Homeric Hymn to Artemis

At home a lover of music like her brother, abroad she is venomous and without mercy, a hunter of human prey who uses her bow and arrows to strike down women in childbirth or those who transgress against her terrible law. When a woman died suddenly without explanation, she was "struck by the arrows of Artemis," even as a man was "struck by the arrows of Apollo."

Homer tells a famous story about **Niobê** (**nī**-o-bē), wife of Amphion, the legendary cofounder of Thebes. Niobê boasted of her superiority to Leto: She had six sons and six daughters, whereas Leto had only two children. Artemis and Apollo took bloody revenge (Figure 9.4).

Homer places the story in the mouth of Achilles near the end of the *Iliad*, who offers it as an *exemplum*, a model for human behavior, a common use of myth in Greek society (as we saw in Chapter 1). Achilles has offered food to Priam, king of Troy, who, too broken by grief to eat, has come to beg for the body of his son Hector:

[600]   "At dawn, old sir, arise and take your son's body home.
         But now we need some refreshment, as fair-haired Niobê did,
         who had seen her children butchered before her, watching in horror,
         twelve of them, six fair maidens, and with them six handsome sons.
         The sons were shot by Apollo with shafts of the silver bow,
605   while Artemis, lover of arrows, brought down all Niobê's daughters,
         angered at Niobê's folly—comparing her children to Leto's.
         'She has born only two,' said she, 'but I have born a great many.'

FIGURE 9.4 Death of the Niobids, Attic vase, c. 450 BC. Apollo and Artemis shoot down the children of Niobê. A boy and girl lie dead among the rocks. To the right, a boy attempts to flee but is struck in the back. To the left, a boy attempts to pull an arrow from his stomach. The artist has abandoned the single ground-line usual in vase painting, probably imitating contemporary wall painting.   (Musée du Louvre, Paris; University of Wisconsin–Madison Photo Archive)

But those two, few as they were, annihilated her dozen.°
Nine days they lay in their gore. Nobody buried the corpses.
610   Cronus' son had turned the people to puppets of stone.
On the tenth day at last the gods from heaven entombed them.
Weary with hunger and sorrow, their mother swallowed a morsel.
Even now on a cliff of Sipylus,° haunted by eagles,
where they say the nymphs who race Acheloüs° dwell in their lair,
615   poor Niobê, turned into stone, broods over the miserable fate
assigned her by the immortals. So come now, noble sir,
let the two of us also remember our need of food and refreshment."

HOMER, *Iliad* 24.600–619

608. *dozen:* Traditions vary about how many children Niobê had, ranging from four to twenty.   613.
Sipylus: A mountain in Asia Minor, near Smyrna. A female image, said to be that of Niobê, was
carved on the rock cliff. When it rained, the water seeped through the porous limestone, making it
appear as if the figure wept. In fact, the image (still barely visible today) is of Cybelê, the Phrygian
mother-goddess of Asia Minor.   614. *Acheloüs:* A stream on Mount Sipylus. A far better-known river
of the same name flowed through northwestern Greece.

Orion and Actaeon

Most myths of Artemis are associated with hunting. One of the best known is the story
of the Giant **Orion** (ō-rī-on), a son of Poseidon, an inescapable hunter and a devotee
of Artemis. His father had given him the power to walk on water. Orion long courted
the daughter of Oenopion, "wine-face" (*oinology* is the study of wine-making), a king of
the island of Chios. Impatient at the king's reluctance to give up his daughter, at last he
raped her. For revenge, Oenopion put out Orion's eyes while he slept. Orion hoisted a
boy to his shoulders and set out toward the east. When he reached the eastern horizon,
the blazing sun cured his blindness. He tried to track down and kill Oenopion, but
could not find him. He therefore began an affair with Eos, the dawn-goddess.

Either because of his affair or because he had attempted to rape Artemis herself,
Artemis placed on his head a scorpion, which poisoned and killed him. As a reward for
its service, the scorpion was transformed into the constellation Scorpio. Orion became
the constellation that still bears his name, forever fleeing Scorpio (although placed
opposite in the heavens). Orion is the earliest named constellation (in the *Odyssey*).

The Theban **Actaeon** (ak-tē-on) also fell victim to the wrath of Artemis, and
again for a sexual transgression. Early versions of the story say that he wanted to
marry his aunt Semelê, the mother of Dionysus, but later explanations report that
while hunting on Mount Cithaeron near Thebes, Actaeon accidentally came on
Artemis/Diana bathing naked in a spring. Ovid tells the story, one of the best-
known Greek myths (Figure 9.5):

[138]   The cause of Cadmus'° sorrow, when all things were going so well,
was his grandson, upon whose forehead great antlers suddenly sprouted,
140   whose hounds were horribly sated on the flesh and blood of their master.
If you look at the matter closely, bad luck was really to blame.

138. *Cadmus:* Founder of Thebes.

FIGURE 9.5 Actaeon devoured by his own hounds, Attic vase, c. 470 BC. Although the stories ordinarily say that Actaeon was transformed into a stag, the vase painters usually represent him in human form, with the hounds attacking while Artemis draws her bow. (Photograph © 2011 Museum of Fine Arts, Boston)

No fault can be charged, for no blame can be placed on innocent error.
The hill of his hunt by this time was dyed with blood of his victims,
and the sun, halfway to his goal, had diminished the shadows of noon.
145   Actaeon called to his fellows, who accompanied him through the forest:
     "Our nets and knives are crimson with blood of beasts we have slain.
Enough of good luck for today. When Dawn in her yellow-wheeled chariot
brings back her light to the earth, then back to the hunting we love!
Half Phoebus'° journey is finished. His rays have heated the meadows,
150   so abandon our work for today and roll up our nets till tomorrow."
The young men did as he ordered and gladly relaxed from their labor.
    A nearby glade was hidden by thickets of pine trees and cypress,
Gargaphië, a sacred spot of Diana the huntress.
At its further end is a cave, in an open space in the forest,
155   made by no human hands, for nature herself was its maker.
She had carved it from living rock and arched it over with tufa.°
On its right there babbled a trickling fountain of cold limpid water,
its spreading basin encompassed by a soft green border of grass.
When Diana, goddess of woodlands, found herself wearied with hunting,
160   it was here she refreshed her maiden limbs in the cool of the waters.
To one of her nymphs she entrusted her javelin, quiver, and bow;

149. *Phoebus:* Ovid identifies Apollo with the sun.   156. *tufa:* A soft volcanic stone, easily worked for building.

another held out her arms for the mantle the goddess discarded.
Two more unfastened the bindings that laced the boots to her ankles.
Theban Crocalê skillfully braided her loose-flowing tresses
165 (more dexterous she than the others). Nephelê, Hyalê, Rhanis,
with Psecas and Phialê poured great basins of water above her.
But today, as the daughter of Titans was enjoying her usual bath,
the grandson of Cadmus appeared, postponing his usual hunting.
Alone and with innocent steps he joyfully strolled through the woodlands
170 until then unknown, for such was Destiny's order.
      The moment Actaeon entered the dewy cave of the fountain,
the nymphs filled the grove with screams and beat on their naked bosoms,
shielding Diana's body with their own from the young man's sight.
But Diana was taller and towered above them, full head and shoulders.
175 The color that tints the clouds across from the sun in the heavens,
or that of the purple dawn, arose to the face of the goddess,
embarrassed at being thus viewed without the protection of clothing.
Even though she was surrounded by so great a cohort of comrades,
she turned away to the side, but fixed her eyes on the stranger
180 as if she had arrows to aim. The best thing at hand was the water.
She scooped some up in her hands, and, throwing it over Actaeon,
she shouted this sentence prophetic of the destiny waiting to strike:
      "Now you can boast you have gazed on Diana naked of clothing.
Go right ahead—that is, if you still are able to boast."
185 So much for the menace of words. From his forehead antlers erupted,
the horns of a terrified stag, just where the water had spattered.
She forced his neck to grow long and crowned it with pointed ears.
She turned his hands into hooves and traded his forearms for forelegs.
His body she veiled to the view with a spotted velvety deerskin.
190 To crown it, she gave him the heart of a deer. Autonoë's son°
was astonished to find how nimble he was, how speedy of foot,
But O! what a horror to see his antlers reflected in water.
      "Can that be your face, Actaeon?" was what he attempted to utter.
Not a word would come out. He groaned. That was all he could manage.
195 Tears dropped down from a pair of eyes no longer his own.
Yet still the mind of a human was left. "What can I do?" he debated,
"Shall I flee to my father's house and the apparatus of power,
or hide in the forest?" but shame blocked one and terror the other.
Hesitant, thus he delayed, till his hounds were drawn to the scent.

190. *Autonoë's son:* Autonoë was sister to Semelê, mother of Dionysus.

The next twenty lines give the names of all Actaeon's hounds, thirty-five in number!

[225]   This pack, all eager to join in the kill, pursued its terrified master
over crags and hillsides, in places no human could follow,
wherever the track was rugged, where no track whatever existed.
He did his best to escape in places he often had hunted,
poor master, now fleeing his servants! He tried to call the pack:

230   "See, it is I, Actaeon. Have you forgotten your ruler?"
   but his mind no more ruled his words. He could not utter his plea.
     Now the whole heaven reechoed the triumphant baying of hounds.
   Blackhair was first, who sank his teeth in the back of his master,
   with Beastblaster right at his heels. Mountainbred buried his fangs
235   deep in his master's shoulder. These had been slow at the start,
   but had taken short cuts on the mountain to be first at the kill.
   The rest of the pack came together to rip with their slavering jaws.
   Soon not an inch remained unmangled, unlacerated.
   Actaeon gave a last groan, whose sound was not that of a human,
240   but was equally not a cry that a real stag ever had uttered,
   whose mournful complaint reechoed on the hillsides he knew so well.

OVID, Metamorphoses 3.138–199, 225–241

Other versions tell how Actaeon's hounds then wandered the mountains howling for their lost master. The myth may reflect primitive human sacrifice, the gift of a man to the goddess to ensure success in the hunt. In legends of the Trojan War, the Mycenaean king Agamemnon sacrificed his own daughter to Artemis because he (or his brother Menelaüs) had killed a stag in Artemis' sacred grove. In Roman gladiatorial combat, descended from Etruscan ritual human sacrifice, men dressed as wild animals were hunted down and killed.

ATHENA, MISTRESS OF THE CITY

Athena (whom the Romans called Minerva) seems to take her name from the city of Athens rather than the other way around. In origin she was not Greek, although she was established in Greece at an early date. Her name is mentioned in the Linear B tablets (c. 1200 BC). In Mycenaean times she may have been the protectress of the fortified Athenian hill known as the Acropolis and of the king's house built on it. Here, in classical times, the Athenians built the all-marble Parthenon, "house of the virgin," in honor of the virgin-goddess, one of the most beautiful and celebrated buildings in the world (Figure 9.6; compare Figure 2.1).

Athena's emblem is the owl, at home in palace rafters, and the domestic olive tree, which she gave to Athens. Thus Athenian coins have an owl and a sprig of olive stamped on them. Her common epithet is *glaukôpis*, which means either "owl-eyed" or "gray-eyed." She is sometimes shown with a snake, leading some commentators to identify her with a Minoan goddess who held snakes in her hands. In classical times she was the protectress of all cities (although she had her favorites) and of the crafts and arts that city life makes possible, and never more so than in Athens, the city named for her. She protects especially the woman's craft of weaving but also the male craft of carpentry: She directed the building of the ship *Argo* in the legend of Jason and was behind the building of the Trojan Horse.

Athena is always represented as wearing body armor and a helmet, often carrying a spear, usually holding a shield. As a breastplate she wears the aegis, given

FIGURE 9.6 The Parthenon, built all of marble, 447–433 BC, from the north-west. In the visible west pediment (the triangle between rooftop and roofline) was portrayed in sculpture the myth of the contest between Athena and Posei-don for rulership of Athens; the east pediment, on the other side of the building, portrayed the myth of the birth of Athena from the head of Zeus. The Parthenon was virtually intact, having been a Christian church then Turkish mosque, until 1687, when the Venetians were at war with the Turks, who used the Parthenon as an ammunition dump. The Venetians lobbed a shell through the roof, blowing out the roof and most of the south side. During the Napoleonic wars, Lord Elgin, the British ambassador to Turkey, removed most of the Parthenon's sculptures to London. The so-called Elgin Marbles are now in the British Museum, the best-known original works of art to survive from the high Classical Period. This photo is from the 1920s; today the temple is obscured by scaffolding.   (University of Wisconsin–Madison Photo Archive)

her by Zeus, or she drapes the aegis around her shoulders (Figure 9.7) or from her extended arm. Another story makes the aegis the skin of a Giant named Pallas, whom she flayed alive in the Gigantomachy. From the Giant she may have taken her epithet *Pallas*, a name of unclear etymology. If Greek, *Pallas* could mean "maiden" or "weapon-brandishing," but it may be pre-Greek.

Born from Zeus's head, not from woman's womb, Athena, always virgin, was a faithful servant of her father and a protectress of male heroes. She watched over Perseus, Heracles, Odysseus, and Jason. In the *Iliad* she encouraged the Greeks to glorious deeds, assisting them at critical moments in the fray. For example, the leaders marshaled their troops

[446]   and with them went Athena, she of the steel-gray eyes,
wearing the dreaded aegis, shield which is ageless, immortal.
From it a hundred tassels, all woven of gold, hang free,
each worth a hundred oxen. Sparkling, bright with its gleam,

FIGURE 9.7 Athena on a Panathenaic vase, c. 525 BC. Such vases, filled with olive oil, were given as prizes to winners in the Panathenaic festival and usually have the same scene: Athena with shield, snake-edged aegis, and spear, standing between two pillars surmounted by a cock, in front of one of which is written, "I am one of the prizes from Athens." The pillars may represent her temple, where the goddess dwells. A cuirass here decorates her shield because this is a prize for winning the armored footrace.　(Vatican Museums, Museo Gregoriano Etrusco' Alinari/ Art Resource, New York)

450　Athena marched down the ranks, arousing their will to attack.
In every heart she injected new courage to fight to the end,
and suddenly war seemed sweeter than sailing in hollow ships
and making a safe return to their own dear native land.

HOMER, *Iliad* 2.446–456

Athena represents reason's control over elemental force, as here she imposes order on an impending attack. In war Ares is unrestrained violence; Athena teaches strategy and disciplined tactics. Poseidon sired on Demeter the magic horse Arion, but Athena built the first chariot, which controls the horse. Poseidon rouses the waves, but Athena built the ship that rides on them. Hermes protects the flocks in distant mountains, but Athena taught how to spin the wool from which clothing is made. Vengeance has ruled from time immemorial; Athena established law. Not until the late Classical Period did she become the goddess of "wisdom" in the abstract sense. Her province is the practical knowledge that separates humans from beasts and protects them from the arbitrary or indifferent violence of the natural world. We may compare her interests with the achievements of Prometheus.

In Athens an annual festival to Athena, the Panathenaea, celebrated her birthday. The festival was of special grandeur every fourth year when a procession of high-born youths and maids carried sacred implements, led sacrificial animals, and rode in chariots to the Acropolis bearing a freshly woven robe for the statue of Athena. The procession was shown on the inner relief sculpture of the Parthenon.

Arachnê

In myth, Athena takes an interest in individual women when their interests as women are at stake. Woman's work (apart from childrearing) is preeminently the manufacture of textiles, and Ovid made famous the story of **Arachnê** (a-**rak**-nē), a young woman of Lydia in Asia Minor who boasted that her skill in weaving was equal to Athena/Minerva's. Although a typically Ovidian story of divine envy for human achievement, the story reflects Athena's sponsorship of excellence in the female craft of weaving:

[5] Minerva° called to mind the fate of Maeonian° Arachnê,
      who, she heard, had claimed to equal the goddess herself
      in the arts of the working of wool. Her rank and descent were the humblest,
      but in skill she held the first place. Colophonian° Idmon, her father,
      was a dyer of soft white fleeces with the juice of Ionian murex.°
10   Her mother, now dead, had been born of the same low rank as her husband.
      Although humble of rank and dwelling in a little town called Hypaepa,
      Arachnê had gained by her skill applause and a great reputation
      through all the land of Lydia, and in all its affluent cities.
      To see her incredible work, the nymphs would abandon the vineyards
15   on the slopes of Tmolus, the Naiads° would leave Pactolus' waters.°
      Not just the cloth that she made, but watching it made was a pleasure,
      and the grace she brought to her art—now rolling raw wool into balls,
      now twisting thread in her fingers, now drawing wool from the distaff
      and smoothing the knots of the fleece into yarn as soft as a cloud.
20   Sometimes her nimble fingers would be weaving the yarn into fabric,
      tossing a slender spindle with expert hand, or embroidering.
      Whatever she did, you would swear that Pallas Athena had taught her.
      Arachnê indignantly scoffed, "If she is so good she could teach me,
      maybe she'd dare compete. If I lose, I shall pay her a forfeit,
25   anything she might demand."
          Pallas heard this boast, and, disguised as a feeble old woman,
      with hair turned a straggly gray, with a cane for hobbling old footsteps,
      chided the girl in these words:
                              "Old age still has a few blessings—
30   experience comes with the years. So listen, my dear, to my counsel:
      Your greatest glory must come from human spinners and weavers.
      Yield to a goddess, rash girl, and humbly beg for her pardon.
      If you repent and confess, the goddess will surely forgive you."
          Arachnê glared at the goddess, laid down her half-finished task,
35   and was ready to slap Minerva. Her fury shone from her face
      as she hurled a reply to Pallas, not knowing to whom she was speaking:
          "You gaga old granny, your trouble is that you've been living too long!
      Get out and go talk to your daughters, or even your daughters-in-law,
      who might be silly enough to attend to your tedious sermons.

5. *Minerva:* Athena.   5. *Maeonian:* Homer calls Ionia "Maeonia."   8. *Colophonian:* Colophon was a Greek colony in Asia Minor.   9. *murex:* A shellfish of the eastern Mediterranean that produces a deep purple dye.   15. *Naiad:* Female spirit of the water.   15. *Pactolus' waters:* A stream, small but gold-laden, that ran down Mount Tmolus in Lydia, near Sardis.

40   I have the brains to look after myself. I don't need you to advise me,
     and I certainly won't change my ways. And as for that goddess of yours,
     why doesn't she come herself? perhaps she can't stand competition?"
         "She has come herself," shouted Pallas, casting off her disguise,
     no longer a feeble old woman, but revealed as a goddess.
45   The nymphs bowed down in worship, as did the Maeonian women.
     Arachnê alone was defiant, though she jumped to her feet in surprise.
     A blush stained her cheek for a moment, but as quickly vanished again.
     So the morning sky turns crimson as a sign that dawn is at hand,
     but after a few brief moments turns bright with the sun's new light.
50   Firmly she stood by her offer, and foolishly hurried to her fate,
     in hopes of the prize of the victor. For her part, Jupiter's daughter
     offered no further warning, nor tried to delay any longer. A pair of looms
     was set up, each facing away from the other,
     and the slender threads of the weft were interlaced with the warp.

OVID, Metamorphoses 6.5–54

Each wove a robe to demonstrate her skill by illustrating mythical scenes.
Minerva/Athena made a tapestry showing her contest with Neptune/Poseidon for
the overlordship of Attica and, appropriately, added pictures of the punishment
of mortals who challenged gods. Arachnê, too foolish to be frightened, brazenly
embroidered stories of the sexual scandals of the gods. When Arachnê had finished
her work:

[129]   Not Pallas, not Envy itself, could find a fault in the weaving.
130   The furious golden-haired goddess tore off the robe with its pictures
        of the escapades of the gods, and, seizing a shuttle of boxwood,
        again and again she slashed it across the face of Arachnê.
        The poor girl refused to be shamed, but hanged herself in a slipknot.
            When Pallas saw her suspended, she took some pity upon her.
135   "Well, poor sinner," said she, "you may live, but still you must hang
        with this condition, to keep you from feeling safe in the future:
        My order shall stay in force for all your descendants as well!"
        Then as she left she sprinkled the girl with one of Hecatê's poisons.°
        The instant she felt the venom, the hairs of her head disappeared,
140   and with them her nose and ears. Her head shrank down to a vestige
        of what it had formerly been, and the rest of her body grew tiny.
        Long skinny fingers stuck out as legs. All the rest became belly,
        from which she turns out the thread for her old occupation—a spider.

OVID, Metamorphoses 6.129–143

138. *Hecatê's poisons:* Hecatê, although tradition made her a Titan, becomes the evil counterpart of
Artemis—the dark of the moon, a deity of darkness, fear, and death. She was especially concerned
with witches and poisoners, who searched out her baneful herbs in the dark of the moon, cut them
with a bronze sickle, and used them for the most dreadful purposes.

From this story comes the modern scientific term *arachnid* to refer to spiders,
scorpions, mites, and ticks.

KEY NAMES AND TERMS

SOME ADDITIONAL ANCIENT SOURCES

Classical literature makes innumerable references to the great goddesses. Two *Homeric Hymns to* **Hestia** survive (24 and 33). Euripides presents an unpleasant portrait of **Aphrodite** in the prologue to his tragedy **Hippolytus.** Apollonius of Rhodes shows her mothering a rambunctious **Eros** in 2.25–155. Her weakness in war appears in Homer *Iliad* 4.311–430, 21.416–433. As Venus, she is important in Vergil's *Aeneid*. **Artemis** appears at the end of Euripides' *Hippolytus* to resolve the plot and in *Iphigenia at Aulis* Euripides describes a near human sacrifice to Artemis. **Athena** appears frequently in Attic tragedy, staged in the city she protects, in Aeschylus' *Eumenides*, Sophocles' *Ajax,* and in five plays of Euripides: *The Suppliants, Ion, Rhesus, Trojan Women,* and *Iphigenia among the Taurians.* She is important in the *Argonautica* of Apollonius of Rhodes.

FURTHER READING CHAPTER 9

Baring, Anne, and Jules Cashford, *The Myth of the Goddess: The Evolution of an Image* (New York, 1993). The female in religious imagery from the Paleolithic to modern times.

Delcourt, Marie, *Hermaphrodite: Myths and Rites of the Bisexual Figure in Classical Antiquity* (London, 1961). Explores the taste for this mythical form in the Hellenistic Period and later.

Neils, Jenifer, ed., *Worshipping Athena: Panathanaia and Parthenon* (Madison, WI, 1996). History and nature of the festival and the temple on which it focused.

Stehle, Eva, *Performance and Gender in Ancient Greece: Nondramatic Poetry in Its Setting* (Princeton, NJ, 1996). Includes good discussion of Sappho (and much more on early Greek poetry and society).

CHAPTER 10

MYTHS OF FERTILITY

DEMETER AND RELATED MYTHS

Three times blest are those mortals who behold those rites [at Eleusis]
before going down to the house of Hades.
They alone have true life there; to the rest, everything there is misery.

SOPHOCLES, FRAGMENT 837 (PEARSON-RADT)

ACCORDING TO THE GREEK myths of creation, as we saw in Chapter 4, female Gaea Mother Earth, came after sexless Chaos, and from Gaea sprang the world: first Sky, Sea, and Mountains and, ultimately, the Olympian gods and human beings. But it was not only the origin of the world that the Greeks traced back to a female source. Female power also drove the continual pattern of renewal seen in plant and animal life, the ever-recurring creation of new offspring. Thus the Greeks associated such diverse phenomena as the fertility of the soil, the reproductive capacities of wild animals, and sexual attraction between men and women with divine beings who were female. Despite the multitude of names, such goddesses have much in common, representing a religious figure whose cults and myths extended across racial and linguistic lines to exert enormous influence throughout much of the ancient world and to have influence today. To emphasize the unity of the type, modern scholars sometimes refer to this figure as the Great Mother, or the Great Goddess.

Greek myth never acknowledged a single great goddess, however, but divided the female functions rather sharply among a group of goddesses: Artemis controlled the fertility of wild animals, Aphrodite presided over human sexuality, and Hera protected marriage and the family. The Greek figure whose myths are most closely related to mother-goddesses found in other parts of the Mediterranean world is **Demeter** (de-**mē**-ter), goddess of the grain and the rich harvest. In this chapter we examine the myth of Demeter and her daughter **Persephonê** (per-**sef**-ō-nē), as told in one of the oldest of the *Homeric Hymns*, probably composed in the seventh century BC. Then we briefly examine several earlier stories that originated in the far older cultures of Mesopotamia and Egypt to which the story of Demeter is related. We find in all these stories a close association between the female, the underworld, the death of the male, and a focus on the cyclical processes of life forms, which die only to be born again.

DEMETER AND PERSEPHONÊ

Although the *-meter* of Demeter means "mother" (the *De-* is mysterious), the name of Persephonê has no clear etymology, and she is often simply called **Korê** (**kō**-rē), "daughter" or "girl"—she is a *parthenos*, an unmarried virgin. Many regard the goddesses as two aspects of a single figure, for they were often called the Two Demeters or the Two Goddesses: the permanently fertile earth and the seasonal giver of grain. The myth tells how Hades, lord of death, abducted Persephonê, daughter of Demeter and Zeus, and carried her away to be his bride. Demeter, enraged, refused to allow the grain to grow until a compromise was reached by which Persephonê spends a third of the year in Hades' house and two-thirds in the world above. The hymn is also etiological for the origin of the extremely important cult of Demeter at Eleusis, fourteen miles west of Athens.

1   I shall begin my song to the fair-haired holy Demeter
      and her daughter with lovely ankles, her whom Hades abducted,
      whom thundering all-seeing Zeus had given his brother to marry.
      The girl was playing one day, she and the daughters of Oceanus,
5   far from gold-sickled Demeter, ripener of bountiful harvests.
      In a soft grassy meadow she gathered roses, violets, crocus,
      hyacinths, iris, and, fairest of all, a glorious narcissus,
      which Earth had sent up as a favor to him who swallows whole armies,°
      in accord with the counsels of Zeus, a lure to the blossoming maiden.
10   Shining and wondrous to see, a marvel for gods and for mortals,
      up from its root there sprouted a hundred sweet-scented blossoms,
      at sight of which the high heavens all burst into laughs of delight
      and were joined by the earth beneath and the salty waves of the ocean.
      Astonished, the girl reached her hands to gather the lovely delight.
15   At once the wide-spreading earth split apart in the Nysian plain.°
      Out rode the swallower of hosts, drawn by his deathless horses—
      her uncle, Cronus' son, he who holds rule over many,
      he who is known by a myriad of names. He hustled her, screaming,
      into his car, and carried her off, disregarding the protests

---

8. *him who swallows whole armies*: Hades.   15. *Nysian plain*: Scholars have been unable to identify the Nysian plain, but presumably somewhere near Eleusis.

20   which she cried aloud to her father, Zeus, who is highest of gods.
But nobody, mortal or god, gave ear to her shouts for assistance,
not even the fair-fruited olive trees. Only the daughter of Perses,
Hecatê,° she of the shining tiara, thinking inexpressible thoughts,
from her cavern heard her appeal to her father, Zeus, son of Cronus.

25   Lord Helius too, mighty son of Hyperion, heard her lamenting.
But Zeus had delayed in his temple, thronged with pious believers,
to hear their requests and receive the reverent offerings of mortals,
far, far away from the gods.° Thus, then, by Zeus's decree,
Persephonê's father's full brother, receiver and ruler of many,

30   the many-named son of great Cronus, with his span of horses immortal,
carried her off to his kingdom. As long as she gazed on the earth,
the starry heavens above, and the rolling fish-laden ocean,
still in the light of the sun, she could hope that her reverend mother
and all the rest of the race of eternal gods might behold her.

35   For that short space of time she nourished her hope of salvation.
But once carried under the earth, she wailed aloud her despair.
The tops of the mountains, the depths of the ocean reechoed the cries
of her deathless voice. At last she captured her mother's attention.
Pain seized Demeter's heart. Her hands tore the dark purple veil

40   off her ambrosial hair, and she wrapped a dark garment of mourning
over her shoulders, then swooped like a bird over dry land and sea.
Nobody, mortal or god, was willing to say what had happened.
No bird would approach her, reporting reliable news of her daughter.
For nine whole days mighty Deo° wandered the face of the earth

45   holding in either hand a pair of bright-blazing torches,
refusing to taste of the nectar or ambrosia, sweet to the taste,
nor would she moisten her body with water, so great was her sorrow.
But when there broke in the sky the tenth day's light-bringing dawn,
Hecatê came out to meet her, with a shining torch in each hand,

50   and thus she addressed Demeter, to bring her news of her daughter:
"Lady Demeter, bringer of seasons, bestower of riches,
which of the gods immortal, or who of the race of mankind,
has carried Persephonê off and tormented your spirit with worry?
I heard her voice, yes, but I could not see for myself

55   just who it was. But this much, I faithfully promise, is true."
So Hecatê spoke, and the daughter of Rhea with beautiful tresses
did not even stop to reply, but taking her torches in hand,
leaped to her feet and set out with Hecatê leading the way.
Together they sought out Helius, watchman of gods and of mortals.

60   Standing before his chariot, the glorious goddess addressed him:
"Helius, pity my plight, for I too, like you, am a god.
Perhaps I have warmed your heart by what I have done or have spoken.
The daughter I bore, that sweet flower, charming and lovely to see—
I heard her heart-rending cry in the air, the voice of a victim

23. *Hecatê:* Perses (not Perseus!) was the son of Helius, brother of Circê, uncle of Medea, and father
(in this account) of Hecatê, at first a great goddess with power over the sky, earth, and sea, a giver of
riches, later a goddess of crossroads and witchcraft.   28. *away from the gods:* Zeus allowed Hades to
carry off Persephonê, but was careful to avoid the appearance of responsibility.   44. *Deo:* Another
name for Demeter, probably a diminutive.

65 abducted by violent power, though I could not see for myself.°
Now you and your piercing rays look down from the glorious heaven,
over all earth and sea. If you chance to have seen my dear daughter,
tell me, I beg you, the truth. Who dragged her far from her mother?
Who was it who seized her by force? Some human, or was he immortal?"

70 So she addressed the son of Hyperion. This was his answer:
"Lady Demeter, fair-braided Rhea's daughter, this you must know,
for the honor I bear you, as well as the pity I feel for your sorrow
as you weep for your fair-ankled daughter. Of all the immortal gods,
Zeus, the driver of clouds, alone must be held to account,

75 who gave the maid to his brother, Hades, as blooming young bride.
Hades is her abductor. He swept her into his chariot,
ignoring her protests, and carried her down to the wind-haunted darkness.
But, goddess, give up your anguish. Do not cherish profitless grief,
one which you can never avenge. What shame is it to a goddess,

80 to receive as son-in-law Hades, receiver of so many spirits?
He is, after all, your full brother, and he at the first allotment
received as his share the empire of those who surround him below."

Having thus spoken, the son of Hyperion turned to his horses,
who promptly drew up his chariot, faster than long-winged birds.

85 But deeper, more painful sorrow now settled over the goddess.
In rage at the dark-clouded son of Cronus, she left the immortals
who gather together in council on the broad expanse of Olympus,
and traveled down to the cities and farmland of men here below.
Hereafter her form was disguised, and nobody, low-waisted woman

90 or man, discerned at a glance the divinity hidden within her,
until at last she arrived at the palace of lofty-souled Celeus,
who in those years was the ruler and lord of fragrant Eleusis.
She rested, grieving at heart, by the road at the Well of the Maiden,
a spring which the village women frequented for fetching fresh water.
[Figure 10.1]

95 There she sat in the shade, beneath an olive tree's branches,
the very type of a grandmother, long past childbearing age,
long cut off from the gifts of garlanded Aphrodite,
the pattern of women who raise the children of law-giving rulers
or tend the household affairs of the busy echoing palace.

100 There she was seen by the daughters of Celeus, son of Eleusis,
who came bearing great bronze jars to carry freshly drawn water
back to their father's house. They were four, in the flower of youth,
like goddesses in their beauty: Callithoê, eldest among them,
Callidicê, lovely Demo, Clisidicê—four handsome sisters.

105 They had no idea that Demeter herself was seated before them,
for gods are not easily known against their will to mortals.
But as they approached, they spoke in words flying straight to the point:
"From what long-settled land do you come, O reverend lady,
avoiding our town, and refraining from entering into its houses?

110 There in the shadowy chambers are women of your generation,
and younger women as well, to respect you in speech and behavior."

65. *could not see for myself:* A few lines above it was Hecatê, not Demeter, who heard but did not see
Persephonê; such slips are typical of poetry composed orally.

FIGURE 10.1 The Well of the Maiden at Eleusis, where Demeter sat down to rest, situated near the elaborate classical entrance to the sacred enclosure. The fine polygonal masonry probably dates from the sixth century BC.   (Author's photo)

Thus they politely inquired, and the mighty goddess replied:
"Thank you, dear girls. Of course I shall gladly tell you my story
because you are so kind to ask, though I know not who you may be.
115   The name that my dear mother gave me is Doso, and I have come hither
against my will, from Crete, brought over the surge of the ocean
by pirate men, who by force carried me off from my homeland.
Their swift ship landed at Thoricus,° where they permitted us women
to walk in a group on the shore, as they themselves prepared supper
120   and busied themselves by the moorings. But I felt no longing for food,
not even the finest of meals, but quietly fled from my captors,
brutes that they were, who wanted to sell me and pocket my price,
refusing all hope of a ransom. I wandered along the dark seashore
and finally reached your village, without the slightest idea
125   what country this is I have come to, or who its people may be.
"Now I pray that the gods on Olympus may grant you vigorous husbands,
and a generation of children as fine as those all parents desire.
But, ladies, one more favor: Would you be so kind as to show me
whose house—be it man's or woman's—I first should approach for
employment,
130   the sort of work I do well, what is fit for old women like me.
I could dandle a newly born child in my arms to comfort its wailing;

118. *Thoricus*: A coastal village southeast of Athens, north of Cape Sunium.

tend the affairs of the household; spread the bed of my master
in an alcove off the great hall; and teach the women their duties."
Thus the goddess proposed. To her Callidicê answered,

135　Callidicê, maiden unmarried, the fairest daughter of Celeus:
"Whether we like it or not, old mother, humankind must put up
with whatever fate the immortals may give. They are stronger than we.
So let me tell you by name the men whose power and honor
are greatest here in our village, men of note with the people,

140　a crown of defense to the town, by counsel and virtuous judgment.
Such are Polyxenus, canny Triptolemus, Diocles also;
Dolichus, noble Eumolpus, but chiefly our own lordly father.
The wives of all these leaders rule the affairs of the households,
and none, after even a glance, could fail to see you as worthy

145　or refuse you a place in her home. No—they would give you a welcome,
for your features indeed are very like those that belong to a god.
"Now if you agree, wait here, while we find Metaneira, our mother,
and tell her your story. She surely will urge you into our household,
rather than hunting another. For here in our well-fitted palace

150　she nurses a late-born son, long prayed for, her joy and delight.
If you take care of his childhood till he reaches years of discretion,
no woman exists who could look upon you without feeling envy,
such boundless reward would he give as a recompense for his rearing."
So spoke the fair Callidicê, and the goddess nodded assent.

155　Delighted, the girls filled up their shining jars with the water
and with them quickly ran home to their father's glorious palace,
to relate to the lady their mother all they had heard and had seen.
Without hesitation she told them to return and invite the old woman
to take the place and to offer a bountiful wage for her service . . .

160　They found the venerable goddess still seated beside the road,
just where they last had left her, and led her back to their home,
the house of their father. She followed, though aching in spirit,
hiding her head with a veil, while her dark robe covered her ankles.
They presently came to the palace of Celeus, favored of Zeus,

165　and, passing on through the courtyard, they found Callidicê's mother
seated beside a pillar supporting the strongly framed rooftree,
her newborn child at her breast. The girls ran up to their mother,
but the goddess stopped by the door. Her head rose up to the lintel,
and her glory, divine and effulgent, blazed through the open doorway.

170　Awe overcame Metaneira, but pallid terror as well.
Yielding her throne to the goddess, she bade her sit down beside her.
But Demeter, bringer of seasons, bestower of wonderful gifts,
politely declined to be seated on the shining throne of the queen,
but quietly stood by the doorway, her lovely eyes fixed on the ground,

175　till Iambê tactfully brought her a stool and a silver-fleeced cover.
On it she sank, but held to her face the veil of her mourning.
For long she sat there in silence, her heart tormented with sorrow,
speaking no word to a soul, displaying no recognition,
unsmiling, tasting no crumb of bread and sipping no goblet,

180　wasting away in longing to regain her slim-waisted daughter.
But finally clever Iambê, with salt-flavored joking and satire,

won over the reverend lady to smile, to laugh, to be merry.
From that time on Demeter delighted in hearing her jesting.°
Metaneira filled for Demeter a beaker of wine that sweetens the heart,
185   but the goddess rejected the cup: It was impious, so she explained,
to drink the ruddy vintage, and she asked them for barley and water
to compound with fresh pennyroyal, to be drunk off as a potion.
The queen mixed up this *kykeon*° and handed it to the goddess,
who took the cup and drank, as ritual practice demanded.
190   Afterwards slim-waisted Metaneira spoke thus to the goddess:
"I greet you, my lady, assured that you are of no common descent,
but noble indeed, for grace and dignity shine in your features
such as we find in the faces of rulers, dispensers of justice.
We humans are forced to accept whatever heaven may offer,
195   however painful the gift, for this yoke weighs down on our shoulders.
Now since you have come to my country, you must share whatever I have.
Be nurse to this child of mine, born long after hope had departed,
a gift of the gods, whom they granted in answer to endless prayer . . ."
To this offer fair-crowned Demeter gave a straightforward reply:
200   "I heartily thank you, my lady. May the gods repay you with blessings.
I will happily take your child to bring up, just as you ask me.
Be sure no slackness of mine will allow him to suffer black magic,
for I know remedies stronger by far than the deadliest venom
and antidotes of great power against a sorcerer's malice."°
205   So saying, Demeter received the child in her fragrant bosom,
into her deathless arms, and his mother rejoiced in her heart.
In the palace she cared for the manly son of the wise-hearted Celeus,
Demophoön, whom the fair-girdled queen Metaneira had borne him.
The baby grew like a god, not eating, not nursed by his mother.
210   Demeter instead would anoint him as if he were child of a goddess,
with ambrosia, food of the gods, and breathed her sweetness upon him
while dandling him in her bosom. And every night she would plunge him
like a firebrand into the flames, all unknown to his own dear parents.
To them it came as a marvel how swiftly the baby was growing,
215   resembling the gods. Indeed, he would have been ageless and deathless,
had Metaneira his mother not secretly spied on the goddess
and left her own room in her folly, to see what was done to her child.
In terror she shouted aloud and slapped her thighs in distress,
anxious for her small son, but badly misled in her spirit.
220   Screaming for grief, she shouted words flying straight to the mark:
"O Demophoön, dearest child, this stranger woman has plunged you
deep in the flames and is causing me terrible sorrow and anguish."
Thus she cried in her grief. The glorious goddess Demeter,
she of the beautiful crown, enraged at the sound of her voice,
225   with her own immortal hands dragged the infant out of the fire,
the boy his mother had borne in the house when hope had departed,

---

183. *jesting:* Iambê is the eponym of Greek iambic poetry, characterized by insult and obscene abuse. Later authors report that Iambê made Demeter smile by pulling up her dress and exposing her private parts, a version too unrefined for the poetry of this hymn. 188. *kykeon:* The *kykeon,* literally "mixed drink," was drunk by initiates into the cult of Demeter at Eleusis, evidently a sort of beer mixed with spices. 204. *sorcerer's malice:* The inexplicable death of infants was often attributed to witchcraft.

and flung him down on the ground in a terrible passion of spirit.
Meanwhile her anger erupted on the head of well-girt Metaneira:
"O short-sighted mortals and stupid, you who can never foresee
230   the destiny, blessed or evil, advancing before your eyes!
What terrible hurt, Metaneira, your folly has brought on your head!
I swear the dread oath of the gods, by the terrible water of Styx,
that I would have made your son an immortal, honored forever.
But now that never can be. His death cannot be avoided.
235   True, he will always be honored; he has sat on the knees of a goddess
and fallen asleep in her arms. As his years advance in their courses,
the men of Eleusis will endlessly battle each other in warfare.°
Know that I am Demeter, everywhere honored, the greatest
comfort and joy to all, both mortal men and immortals.
240   Therefore let all the people erect in my honor a temple,
and beneath it build me an altar by the steepest wall of the city,
by the Well of the Dance° where I rested, on a high and projecting bluff.
I myself will establish your rites, so that forever thereafter
my blessing will rest upon you if you piously carry them out."
245   At this, the goddess transformed herself in size and appearance.
Vanished was wrinkled old age, and beauty breathed all around her.
Delicious aromas exhaled from the fragrant folds of her garments,
and a radiant halo surrounded the deathless flesh of the goddess.
The golden hair of her head floated down to cover her shoulders,
250   and flashes like lightning illuminated the firmly built palace.
       The goddess then disappeared. The knees of poor Metaneira
crumpled beneath her. For long she lay there speechless and fainting,
forgetting her newly born son, to pick him up from the ground.
His sisters heard the piteous wail of the child and came running,
255   leaving their warm soft beds. One picked up the boy, to cuddle
him safe in her arms, while another quickly rekindled the fire;
a third sped on hurrying feet to revive and comfort their mother,
lifting her up from the floor and helping her out of the chamber.
The girls all gathered around to bathe her and comfort her sorrow,
260   but the grieving heart of the child they were quite unable to solace,
for these new nurses of his by no means equaled the old.
       All the rest of the night they prayed to the glorious goddess,
still trembling with fear. But then, at the very first light of morning,
they told the whole story to Celeus, whose power spread near and far,
265   expounding Demeter's commands, as the fair-haired goddess had ordered.
Celeus called an assembly attended by numberless freemen
to bid them rear a rich temple for the goddess, fair-haired Demeter,
with an altar, high on a hillside. At once they heard and obeyed,
building the temple, thereafter to enjoy the goddess' favor.
270   At last the work was completed, the time to relax was at hand.
Each workman went to his rest. But as for fair-haired Demeter,
far from the rest of the blessed she stayed, though withering away

---

237. *warfare.* Nothing is known of the civil war here predicted. 242. *Well of the Dance.* Here called *Kallichoron,* "Well of the Beautiful Dance"; in lines 93–94 it is called *Parthenion,* "Well of the Maidens" (unless a different well is meant); see Figure 10.1.

with longing and grief for her daughter, girl of the slender waist.
She sent men a terrible year, a plague for the earth and its harvest.
275 The land did not foster the seed, for fair-crowned Demeter forbade it.
The oxen tugged the curving plows through the furrows, in vain,
and plentiful grains of white barley fell on the ground without fruit.
Demeter might well have destroyed the whole of humankind by a famine,
and robbed the gods on Olympus of the honor of proper offerings,
280 had Zeus not considered the matter and pondered it well in his heart.
First he sent golden-winged Iris° to summon the fair-haired Demeter.
Iris obeyed the order of cloud-driving Zeus, son of Cronus,
plunging on nimble feet down through the air of mid-heaven.
Reaching the fragrant town of Eleusis, she sought out Demeter,
285 and found her there in her temple, wearing a dark robe of mourning.
She spoke to the goddess in language that flew direct to the mark:
    "Demeter, Zeus the father, whose decision can never be altered,
has summoned you to attend with all the other immortals.
So hurry. Do not make any mission from Zeus be effort misspent."
290 So she politely requested, but resentful Demeter refused.
Once more the father made envoys of the blessed gods, the immortals.
In turn they approached, addressed her, and offered glorious gifts,
and honors which even a god might well be happy to welcome.
But none could make an impression on the mind and heart of Demeter.
295 Raging in spirit, she sternly rejected attempts at persuasion:
Never, she said, would she mount to the fragrant halls of Olympus;
never allow the wheat to rise from the bountiful furrows,
until with her own eyes she looked on her fair-faced daughter.
    When Zeus, who thunders aloud, whose eye encompasses all things,
300 heard their report, he ordered the golden-staffed slayer of Argus
down to the darkness of Hades to win him with words of persuasion,
to bring back holy Persephonê, back from the wind and the darkness,
into the land of light, the home of the other immortals,
all this in the hope that the mother, seeing the daughter once more,
305 might abandon her stubborn decision and no longer cling to her wrath.
Hermes obeyed him at once. He left his place on Olympus
and plunged down under the earth. Within he discovered the ruler,
seated in state on a throne, and beside him his reverend consort,
still resisting his suit and longing to see her dear mother,
310 while she, far away, was planning to outwit the other immortals.
    The mighty slayer of Argus stopped by the couple and spoke:
"Hades, with long dusky ringlets, the ruler over the dead,
Zeus, her father, has ordered that I bring back Persephonê,
the reverend lady, from Erebus° back to the place she deserves;
315 all this, that her mother, rejoicing to see her daughter returned,
may abandon her grudging resentment against the immortal gods.
For she plans a terrible scheme to wipe out the frail human races,
born and sustained by the earth, by hiding the seeds in the ground,
ending the offerings that men now make to the gods in the heavens.

---

281. *Iris*: Iris, or "rainbow," was a messenger of the gods, like Hermes. The blue, brown, green, or hazel ring around the pupil of the eye bears her name.   314. *Erebus*: "Darkness," that is, the underworld.

320 She is gripped by a terrible anger. She speaks no more to her fellows
but sulks, alone and far off, in the scented depths of her temple,
new-built for her, high on a rocky spur in the town of Eleusis."
To this, the lord of the dead smiled grimly, Hades the mighty,
arching his eyebrows, but did not reject the command of King Zeus.
325 Without hesitation, he spoke to Persephonê, woman of prudence.
"Depart now, Persephonê, to the side of your dark-robed mother
with kindly feelings toward me and better will in your heart.
Please, do not feel too resentful—no more than the others who come.
Even among the immortals you will find me a suitable husband.
330 Am I not the full brother of your own father, great Zeus?
Even from here below, you rule all that has motion and breath.
Together we two will be granted the highest of possible honors.
Our vengeance will fall forever on all the doers of evil,
those who fail to appease your pride with their ample offerings,
335 who neglect to give what is due us, a sacrifice proper and pious."
So he spoke, and the prudent Persephonê warmed at the message.
At once she leaped up for pleasure. But Hades, peering about
to be sure that no one was watching, casually gave her a seedlet
of a luscious and sweet pomegranate to eat,° thus making it certain
340 she could not remain forever by the side of dark-robed Demeter.
Hermes halted at last and brought the girl to her mother,
fair-crowned Demeter, in front of the well-scented temple. She looked,
then leaped as a maenad° leaps through the hills, through the forests.
Persephonê too, as she looked on the beautiful eyes of her mother,
345 jumped down from the chariot and horses and hurried up to embrace her,
flinging her arms round her neck. But even while hugging her daughter,
the heart of the goddess suspected a trick and trembled in worry.
Taking her arms from the girl, she asked the ominous question:
"Daughter, when down below, I hope that you tasted no morsel?
350 Tell me the truth that we both may know for sure what has happened,
that, freed from gloomy Hades, you may stay with me and your father,
Zeus, the son of great Cronus, by whom the rain-clouds are gathered,
honored by all the gods. But if you have tasted a morsel,
back you must go to the depths, to spend a third part of the year.
355 The rest you may stay here with me and with the other immortals.
For when earth blossoms again with fragrant flowers of springtime,
once more you will rise, a wonder to gods and the race of mankind.
Now tell me, how did the mighty receiver of many deceive you?"
Persephonê, beautiful maiden, at once replied to her mother:
360 "Mother, I promise to tell you all the details of my story.
Hermes the helper appeared, swift messenger of the immortals,
with word from my father, Cronus' son, and the dwellers in heaven,
to leave the darkness of Hades, that, seeing me with your own eyes,
you might abandon your grudging resentment against the immortals.
365 At this I leaped up for joy. But Hades stealthily forced me
to eat, though against my will, a honey-sweet pomegranate seed."

339. *eat*: Among almost all peoples, eating a meal—a slice of pizza on a date, a piece of cake at a
wedding, or the food and drink after a funeral—creates a bond between those who share it. The
pomegranate is also important in the myth of Cybelê and Attis (see below). 343. *maenad*: An
ecstatic follower of Dionysus.

PERSPECTIVE 10.1

ROSSETTI'S PROSERPINA HOLDING THE POMEGRANATE

The year 1848 saw the publication of Karl Marx's *Communist Manifesto* and the worst of the Irish potato famine: Millions died. In the same year in England, a group of artists organized the Pre-Raphaelite Brotherhood. Although they used techniques provided by realistic painting, they turned away from a disturbed and hungry Britain and the everyday subjects favored by contemporary realistic painters to find their inspiration in history, literature, and myth. They wanted to return to a time before, as they believed, art was corrupted by the technical skill of the Italian master Raphael (1483–1520), hence their appellation "Pre-Raphaelites." They were fascinated by death and the hereafter.

Dante Gabriel Rossetti (1828–1882) was a leader of the Brotherhood, son of an Italian immigrant to England. Educated at Oxford, Rossetti was fluent in French, Italian, and German and wrote poems in these languages, which he often illustrated by his paintings. Both his poems and paintings are noted for their gloom and sensuous beauty. When his wife, suffering from depression and tuberculosis, committed suicide, Rossetti in a fit of grief buried with her a manuscript of poems. Several years later he dug up the body to recover and publish them!

The dreary pessimism of his group, and the morbid state of Rossetti's mind worsened by addiction to alcohol and opiates, is reflected in his *Proserpina Holding the Pomegranate* (= Greek Persephonê) of 1874 (Perspective Figure 10.1). Proserpina, unlucky maiden and bride of death, appears as a beautiful but melancholy woman in dark, sensual robes, standing in a dark-walled room. Behind her is an open window through which comes a blaze of light, the land of the living. Her lips are pursed and moist in an expression of hopeless despair. She holds a pomegranate from which she has taken a bite, a sign of surrender to the mysterious lure of the underworld. The curling vine beside her face, like the lighted window beyond, suggests the life-force that balances death, as does the smoldering lamp on the table before her. Tacked on the wall is a small piece of paper bearing an Italian sonnet by Rossetti. Here is an English translation:

> How far away that light, shining above the wall!
> It scarcely flashes through. Then, in a moment,
> it will lead me from this gloom, to the gate above.
> How far away those flowers on Enna's hills°

Enna's hills: In central Sicily, where a variant tradition placed Persephonê's abduction.

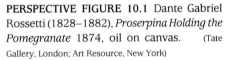

PERSPECTIVE FIGURE 10.1 Dante Gabriel Rossetti (1828–1882), *Proserpina Holding the Pomegranate* 1874, oil on canvas. (Tate Gallery, London; Art Resource, New York)

from this fruit of your gloomy shades, O Tartarus!
that brought me my bitter future. And O! how far
that open sky from this eternal gloom
that must cover me—forever.
And O! how far the nights
still to be passed, from days that once have been.
How far am I removed from my old self! In aimless search
I listen for the word one pitying heart
might breathe to another's soul. Its broken voice
will someday murmur condolence in my ear,
"O poor Proserpina, even we lament your fate."

The Pre-Raphaelite painters were more concerned with the Middle Ages than with antiquity, which usually appears in their work after filtered through Dante's *Divine Comedy* (fourteenth century). The group soon broke up, but their romantic interest in tales of long ago and far away remained important in British art down to World War I.

Here Persephonê retells how Hades carried her off. Then:

[399]   So the pair passed all the day, each one consoling the other,
400   soothing each other's sorrow, till at last their hearts were assuaged
         in giving and taking comfort for all their misery and torment.
         Presently Hecatê, lady of glittering veil, came to greet them,
         to embrace with delight the maiden daughter of holy Demeter,
         whose helper and friend she had been. And far-seeing thundering Zeus
405   sent fair-haired Rhea, his mother, to summon the dark-robed Demeter
         before the assembly of gods and to promise her choice among honors
         that she would receive in the presence of all the gathered immortals.
         Demeter consented to this: Her daughter thereafter would spend
         a third of each circling year below, in the wind-smitten darkness,
410   but the rest of the time with her mother and all the other immortals.
         Back Rhea came once more, down from the heights of Olympus,
         back to the Rarian plain,° before this the richest of plowlands,
         but now quite barren of life, its greenery withered and shriveled,
         its white barley hidden in earth by design of fair-ankled Demeter.
415   This was the day, at the very beginning of bountiful springtime,
         when fields should groan at the weight of swelling long-bearded ears,
         when the new-cut barley should load the plain's rich furrows with sheaves,
         when the reapers labored to bind the newly cut grain into bundles.
         There first Rhea alighted, flying down from unharvested skies.
420   The goddesses greeted each other, and each rejoiced in her heart.
         Rhea the silken-veiled addressed these words to Demeter:
              "Hear, O my child, what Zeus the far-sighted thunderer offers:
         You must return to the gods, but he has promised to grant you
         whatever honors you choose to possess among the immortals.
425   He decrees that your child must spend a third of the circling year
         down in the windy gloom, but the rest with you, her dear mother,
         and all the other immortals. Thus he decrees it shall be
         and has ratified his decision with the fateful nod of assent.
         Now take my advice, my daughter: Do not go too far in your anger
430   with Zeus, who rules the black clouds, but hurry to earth at once,
         to assure the crops will flourish, the source of life to humankind."
              Thus Rhea urged and fair-crowned Demeter gladly obeyed her.
         She sent the crops to the light from every deep-furrowed plowland
         and all the face of the earth burst out in leafage and flowers.
435   Demeter herself explained the rites of her cult to the kings,
         the givers of justice—Triptolemus, Diocles, lasher of horses,
         mighty Eumolpus as well, and Celeus, ruler of people.
         To them she revealed the observance and carrying-out of her rites,
         things which are reverend, holy, which no one must ever describe,
440   into which no one may inquire, which no one may ever reveal.
         Deep reverence for the divine restrains the tongues of the careless.
              Blessed the man who in life has viewed the mysteries' ritual.
         But the uninitiated many, who have no part in their teaching,
         will have no share in a future like his when they pass below,

─────────

412. *Rarian plain*: Around Eleusis. This was the first land to be sowed and harvested.

445   when they descend to the gloom and the moldering shadow of death.
            Now when the glorious goddesses explained all this to the kings,
        they made their way to Olympus to join the other immortals.
        There they dwell beside Zeus, beside him who rejoices in lightning,
        august, revered. How happy is he among earth-dwelling mortals
450   whom the goddesses bless and favor! They send as permanent comrade
        to live in his palace, Plutus,° bestower of riches on mortals.
            Hail, goddesses, ruling the folk of the fragrant town of Eleusis,
        of Paros,° girt by the sea, and the rockbound region of Antrum!°
        The ruler, the giver of gifts, season-restorer, Queen Deo!
455   And with her you too, her beautiful daughter, Persephonê.
        Benevolent ones, reward my hymn with heart-warming riches,
        and I in turn shall recall your deeds on another occasion.

Homeric Hymn to Demeter 1–381; 399–457

451. *Plutus:* "Wealth."   453. *Paros:* One of the Cycladic islands and site of an important cult to Demeter.   453. *Antrum:* A town in Thessaly, where was a cult to Demeter.

Observations: The Myth of Demeter and Persephonê

The myth of Demeter and Persephonê is one of the most perplexing of Greek myths. In ancient times the story was interpreted as an agricultural allegory, in which Hades was identified with earth and Persephonê (or Korê) with grain buried in the earth. Korê's return from the underworld was interpreted as the growth of the new wheat crop. However, this allegorical interpretation does not correspond with the facts of Greek agriculture.

In the hymn, Korê returns in the springtime (line 415: "This was the day, the very beginning of bountiful springtime"), whereas in Greece the wheat seed is placed in the ground in the autumn, sprouts soon after, and grows through the wet winter. It does not sprout in the spring at all. What must be meant, then, some argue, is that the seed, Korê, is placed in underground containers during the four hot, sterile summer months, until it is brought forth for the autumn planting. Although this interpretation accords with Korê spending one-third of the year in the house of Hades and two-thirds on earth, it disagrees explicitly with the hymn and with how the ancients themselves understood the story. Probably we should reject the allegorical approach and search for other ways to understand the myth.

Persephonê is a *parthenos* and, on one level, the hymn is a human story that exemplifies the experience of Greek *parthenoi* and their mothers. Persephonê's fate resembles that of Greek girls who, at age fourteen, were married to war-hardened men twice their age, whom they scarcely knew. Like the narcissus she could not resist, Persephonê is ripe to be plucked (so we say "deflower," to take a girl's virginity). The sudden loss of virginity is a death to childhood, an end to playing with friends in the sweetly scented meadow. Greek *parthenoi* dedicated their dolls to Artemis just before marriage.

Because she ate the pomegranate's seed, she can never return to her former state; Greek brides carried an apple or quince into their bridal chambers. A father had the right to give his daughter to whom he chose, even as Zeus gave Persephonê to her uncle, a common form of marital union in Greece to prevent the division of a family's property. Marriage was literal death for many Greek women, who died in childbirth.

Yet Persephonê's fate is different from that of real *parthenoi*, who at marriage permanently entered the sphere of their husband's house, where they bore children and became mothers in their own right. Persephonê, by contrast, lives in two worlds, belonging wholly to neither. She is forever Korê, forever childless, never fulfilled.

When a Greek girl died unmarried, she was said to be Hades' bride, and a wedding vase was placed over her grave as a memorial. The pomegranate seeds eaten by Persephonê are symbolic of her sexual union with King Death. The pomegranate is a fruit the size of an apple with a rough skin. Its interior is a mixture of a bright, bloodlike juice and seeds, an obvious sign of life in the present (blood) and life in the future (seeds). He offered her seeds, she took them within her body, but the seeds will never bear fruit. Never again can she return permanently to her mother's home. She is Death's proper mate, and with him she will rule the land of the dead (Figure 10.2).

Demeter's experience more closely exemplifies the real-life experience of Greek mothers, who must give up their daughters to a stranger's household. In many ways her grief is greater than her daughter's. In art Persephonê is shown consoling Demeter. Nor was the daughter entirely the innocent victim. She voluntarily reached for the flower, even as other women in myth are undone through curiosity about their sexuality. And she accepted the pomegranate. Persephonê's sexual curiosity brought division between herself and her mother.

Viewed more broadly, however, Demeter represents the loss that a mother feels for any child, as Greek mothers lost so many children to war and disease. Her loss causes her first to grieve and to rage, but eventually, as mothers must, she accepts that the world will go on, despite her irreparable sorrow. In popular Christianity, the Virgin Mary, whose cult derives from pagan cults of the mother-goddess, is also *Mater Dolorosa*, "the grieving mother," weeping over her dead child.

The myth of Demeter offers a mythical explanation, or etiology, for the presence of death in the world, explaining why the fertility of the earth cannot be separated from the inevitable presence of death. There can never be a world (except in the imagination of poets) in which there is only life and never death because life comes out of death, one feeding on the other. Life depends on death. The Two Goddesses are a mythic image of the intimacy between the two realms.

THE ELEUSINIAN MYSTERIES

The promise of regeneration through the power of Demeter was the premise of one of the most famous religious cults of the ancient world, the **Eleusinian Mysteries**, whose founding the Homeric Hymn celebrates. In the seventh century BC, when the *Homeric Hymn to Demeter* was written down, the city of Athens was growing rapidly. At about 600 BC Athens absorbed the nearby village of Eleusis, and ever after the mysteries were the property of Athens. Eventually they were visited by the whole Greek world, then by the Romans.

FIGURE 10.2 Persephonê, queen of the dead, enthroned beside her husband, Hades; clay plaque from the southern Italian colony of Locri, c. 480–450 BC. Persephonê holds in her left hand a stalk of wheat, appropriate to the daughter of the grain-goddess, and a cock in her right. Hades holds a branch of celery and a sacrificial bowl (*phialê*). A tiny cock is shown perched on top of the lamp in front of the figures, and a full-sized cock at the side of the throne: The cock was apparently sacrificed in rituals to Persephonê, whose cult was strong in southern Italy where this plaque was made. (Museo Archeologico Nazionale, Reggio Calabria; Scala/Art Resource, New York)

The word *mystery*, which entered our language from this Eleusinian cult to Demeter, comes from the Greek *mystês* (plural *mystai*), meaning "one who closes" the eyes and perhaps mouth in order to enter the temple, or closes them during the sacred rites. From the Latin translation of the word, *initiatus*, comes our word *initiate*, literally "one who has gone in," that is, into the temple of Demeter to participate in the secret ritual.

To divulge what happened within the temple, called the Telesterion ("hall of initiation"), was punishable by death, and all modern commentators on the Eleusinian Mysteries must begin by confessing that we do not know what happened there. Most of our information comes from unfriendly and unreliable sources, especially the founders of the Christian church. Yet archaeological investigation and careful examination of the surviving sources, including the *Homeric Hymn to Demeter*, have enabled us to form a rough picture of events.

In origin the Mysteries seem to have been an agrarian festival designed to promote the growth of the grain. They were certainly functioning by 1500 BC, in the Late Bronze Age. Two principal families were in charge: the Eumolpids, whose ancestor Eumolpus, according to the hymn, received them from Demeter herself, and the Kerykes, "heralds," descendants of Eumolpus' son Keryx ("herald"). The high priest, always a Eumolpid, was called the hierophant (**hī**-ro-fant), "he who reveals the *hiera* ('sacred things')." The family of the Kerykes provided the torchbearer and the herald. For their services, members of these families received a fee from the initiates. There was also a priestess of Demeter, who, like the hierophant, lived permanently in the sanctuary.

The principal ceremony of the mysteries was held annually in the fall. In classical times, a truce was called (and usually observed) for fifty-five days. Heralds went out to neighboring cities to invite participation. On the day before the festival, the *hiera* were removed from the Telesterion and carried to Athens in a majestic procession led by priests and priestesses. On the next day began the festival proper, which lasted for eight days. All who could speak Greek (except murderers) were eligible for initiation, including women and slaves.

On the fifth day, following various preliminary rites, the grand procession back to Eleusis took place, bearing the *hiera*. At night, carrying torches and chanting prayers and hymns, they reached Eleusis. The initiation proper took place on the next two days. The initiates had fasted, but now they drank the *kykeon*, the sacred drink offered to Demeter in the hymn. Although many have thought that a drug may have been taken, a barley drink mixed with pennyroyal has no drug-like effect.

The initiates entered the Telesterion, a building unique in Greek architecture. The ordinary Greek temple, elaborately decorated with sculpture, was meant to be viewed from the exterior, whereas the interior held the cult statue and the city's treasure. By contrast, the Telesterion was built to hold several thousand people under its great roof, supported by a forest of columns (Figure 10.3). Inside, off center, stood the Anaktoron ("palace," "place of the king"), a rectangular stone building with a single door at the end of one of its long sides, probably representing an ancient hut from the earliest days of the cult. Next to the door was a stone chair for the hierophant, who alone could enter the Anaktoron. A huge fire burned on top of the hut, its smoke passing through a hole in the roof.

Except for the flickering light from the fire and torches, the crowd was shrouded in darkness. Terrifying things were shown. A flash of light burst from

FIGURE 10.3 The Telesterion at Eleusis, constructed on the southeastern slope of a small hill overlooking the bay of Eleusis. The ancient town was on the top of the hill. During the Classical Period, steps at the northern end of the hall were carved into the living rock, visible in the picture. Remains of the columns that supported the roof are visible. The author stands at the site of the Anaktoron, the small room in the center of the building that only the hierophant could enter. From this room, according to one account, a bright light flashed at the culmination of the ceremony. (Author's photo)

the Anaktoron, and the hierophant "appeared from out of the Anaktoron in the radiant nights of the mysteries" (Plutarch, *On Advancing in Virtue* 81e). More than that we do not know, although some have thought that a dramatic reenactment of the myth took place. Evidently the *hiera* were shown and something was said, but what the *hiera* were or what was said we do not know. The myth speaks of the joy of reunion between mother and daughter, and the message of Eleusis, however communicated, must lie in the emotion excited by the return of the divine Korê. The initiates were blessed with hope not for immortality as such (never mentioned in connection with Eleusis), but for a pleasurable existence after death.

Barely mentioned in the hymn is **Triptolemus** (trip-**tol**-e-mus), one of the princes of Eleusis to whom Demeter taught her secret rites. After the fifth century BC his role grew in importance (Figure 10.4).

FIGURE 10.4 Demeter and Persephonê send forth Triptolemus to teach the growing of grain, on a marble relief from Eleusis, c. 440 BC. Demeter is on the left, in a restrained pose, wearing a matronly dress (called a Doric peplos), a staff of authority in her left hand. With her right hand she gives Triptolemus a grain of wheat (originally probably in gold, now lost). On the right Persephonê, wearing clothes appropriate to a *parthenos* (an Ionic chiton and a cloak), seems to place a grain of wheat (originally gold, now lost) on Triptolemus' head, while with her other hand she holds a torch. The Two Goddesses often are shown with torches, like those used in the nighttime procession from Athens to Eleusis to celebrate the mysteries, but also emblematic of resurrected life.   (National Archaeological Museum, Athens; author's photo)

Triptolemus was said to have mounted a chariot drawn by dragons and traveled over the whole world teaching the art of growing grain. The myth was a popular subject of Athenian art and gave support to Athens' claims to cultural supremacy.

The Eleusinian Mysteries advocated no doctrine. As a group experience, it fostered a feeling of community among Greeks. As a magical rite, it ensured the growth of the grain. As a personal experience, it promised a happy afterlife. A high moral tone surrounded the cult, which emphasized ritual purity, righteousness, gentleness, and the superiority of civilized life based on agriculture. The Eleusinian Mysteries were the most honored cult of Greek religion, giving hope and comfort to untold thousands from all over the Mediterranean world and commanding veneration until they were finally suppressed at the end of the fourth century AD. Some of the ideas associated with the cult, even before then, found their way into Christianity and are reflected in the words of St. Paul:

> But some one will ask, "How are the dead raised? With what kind of body do they come?" You foolish man! What you sow does not come to life unless it dies. And what you sow is not the body that is to be, but a bare kernel, perhaps of wheat or of some other grain . . . Lo! I tell you a mystery.

1 CORINTHIANS 15.35–37, 51

EASTERN FERTILITY MYTH

The Greek myth of Demeter and Persephonê follows a pattern found in the ancient Near East. In Mesopotamia, the widely honored goddess known as Inanna, Ishtar, or Astartê presided over fertility and sexuality. Similar powers were ascribed to the Phrygian goddess Cybelê (**sib-ī-lē**) and the Egyptian goddess Isis (**ī-sis**). In the Eastern myths, however, the fertility-goddess loses her consort, whereas in the myth of Demeter the goddess loses her daughter.

Inanna and Dumuzi

Of all Mesopotamian myths, the most influential on later religion and myth is that of Sumerian **Inanna**, "queen of heaven," goddess of love and war (Figure 10.5), and her lover, the shepherd-god **Dumuzi**. Here is a version from the third millennium BC.

One day Inanna decided to descend to the underworld. Either she wanted to become queen of the dead—she was already queen of the living—or she wanted to bring the dead back to life. She dressed in her best clothes and jewels and set off to

FIGURE 10.5 A female head from Uruk, c. 3500–3000 BC, of white marble, perhaps of the goddess Inanna. The head probably was set on a wooden statue, its eyes inlaid with lapis lazuli and shell and its eyebrows and hair of bitumen plated with gold. The head was stolen in the sack of the Baghdad Museum after the American invasion of 2003, but has been recovered. (Iraq Museum, Baghdad/Hirmer Fotoarchiv, Munich, Germany)

the "land of no return." Inanna entered the underworld and soon came to the temple of her sister, Ereshkigal (er-esh-**kē**-gal), made all of lapis lazuli:

> "Gatekeeper, let me in! Open your gate for me!
> Open your gate and let me in!
> If you don't open the gate and let me in,
> I will smash the gate and splinter the bolt!
> I will smash the doorjambs and knock down the doors.
> I will raise up the dead, who will devour the living.
> The dead will outnumber the living!"
> The gatekeeper demands: "Who are you?"
> "I am Inanna from the place of sunrise."°
> "If you are Inanna from the place of sunrise,
> why have you come to the land of no return?
> upon the road down which no traveler returns.
> How did your heart lead you?"

sunrise. She is the goddess of the morning star.

Inanna gave the doorkeeper a false explanation, but before admitting her, the gatekeeper consulted with Ereshkigal. Ereshkigal's face grew dark, she slapped her thighs, she bit her lips. Then she instructed the gatekeeper to lead Inanna inward through the seven gates of the underworld, but he was to follow "the ancient rites." At each gate, guards forced Inanna to remove a piece of her clothing or jewelry. At the first gate she gave up her crown:

> "O keeper of the gate, why have you taken my crown?"
> "Enter, my lady; these are the rites of the Mistress of Earth."
> At the second gate, she gave up her earrings:
> "O keeper of the gate, why have you taken my earrings?"
> "Enter, my lady; these are the rites of the Mistress of Earth."

At the third gate she gave up the beads around her neck; at the fourth, the brooches at her breast; at the fifth, the girdle of birthstones around her waist; at the sixth, the bangles on her wrists and ankles; at the seventh gate she took off her beautiful dress. When she came into the presence of Ereshkigal, she was stark naked. She complained bitterly, but was told:

> "Be quiet, Inanna! This is the way of the underworld.
> Do not question the rites of the underworld."

Undaunted, Inanna pulled Ereshkigal from the throne and sat down herself, but the Annunaki gods, the seven dread judges of the underworld, condemned her to death. She turned at once into a side of meat, green with decay, and was hung on a stake. Meanwhile, on earth, all sexual activity came to a halt:

> No bull mounted a cow, no jackass mounted a jenny,
> no young man had sex with a girl in the street.
> The young man slept by himself in his room,
> the girl slept with her friends.

When Inanna did not return, her minister went to various gods asking for help, as Inanna had instructed him. He finally came to the clever Enki, who agreed to help. From the dirt beneath his nails Enki fashioned two mysterious sexless beings, to which he gave the food and water of life and told them what to do when they came to Ereshkigal.

Buzzing over the gates of the underworld like flies, or slipping under the gates like lizards, the mysterious creatures came to Ereshkigal's chamber. They found the queen of the dead sick with grief for the children of the world who had died before their time. They joined her in lamentation. In gratitude for their sympathy, Ereshkigal offered them anything they wanted (the folktale motif of the hasty oath). Immediately they replied that they wanted the green piece of meat hanging in the corner. The goddess tried to dissuade them, offering instead the river in flood, or a field of grain, but they insisted. Ereshkigal had no choice. Casting over the meat the food of life and the water of life, which Enki had given them, the two creatures brought Inanna back to life.

Inanna was allowed to leave the underworld but only if she found someone to take her place (the folktale motif of the substitute sacrifice). Demons followed to make sure she complied. Her minister was first to meet them, but Inanna could not give him up, the man who had just saved her. In the first two cities they reached, the local inhabitants were draped in sackcloth, groveling in the dust—mourning for Inanna, who certainly could not give them over to the demons now!

At last they came to the country of Dumuzi, Inanna's husband. Instead of mourning her disappearance and wasting away from grief, he was dressed in finery and seated on a throne. Inanna looked at him a look of death. She shouted out a word of wrath to the demons who had followed her, "Take this one!"

In terror Dumuzi cried out for help to Utu, the sun-god, lord of justice, Inanna's brother and his own brother-in-law (see Figure 3.7). Despite the intercession of Utu, the demons at last trapped Dumuzi in his sheepfold. The first demon struck him on the cheek with a piercing nail. The second hit him with a shepherd's crook. As the other demons entered the sheepfold, the butter churn was overturned and the cup fell from its peg and was smashed. Dumuzi fell dead. His sheepfold was given to the wind. Dumuzi, the lover of Inanna's youth, will now dwell in the underworld. One day each year, however, he can return to this world, where rituals will be performed in his honor—apparently a reference to a rite of the month "Dumuzi" (June/July) when a statue of Dumuzi was washed, anointed, and allowed to lie in state in the city of Nineveh.

Observations: The Dying God and the Sacred Marriage

In Mesopotamian irrigation agriculture the impregnating water flows in channels across the receptive, life-giving earth. From the earth grow the life-sustaining crops that are cut down at harvest, but whose seeds later grow again. The cycle of life, death, and renewal of life is embodied in Inanna, who is both the fertile female, goddess of life, and the sister of Ereshkigal, goddess of death, whose realm Inanna covets. Tiamat, too, had both favored and opposed new generation

(Chapter 4). Inanna's descent to the underworld is her death and the end of fertility on earth. Her return to the upper world is her resurrection, the return of life on earth. But renewed life can be purchased only at the price of another's death, in this case of her consort Dumuzi. Herein lies the logic of ritual (even human) sacrifice.

The metaphor in which water is to earth as semen is to the womb, which appears repeatedly in Mesopotamian thought, underlies the myth. Water sinks into the earth, as semen into the womb, whence new life springs. The shepherd Dumuzi is connected with milk in many descriptions, and in this story his butter churns are overturned as he is killed. The milky white stuff is like semen, or like the water that makes the earth fruitful by flowing across it, impregnating it. When fertilization is complete, the fluid ebbs away beneath the earth, even as after human intercourse the penis wilts, the semen drains away, but the womb swells with new life. Inanna is the earth, now fruitful, now barren, now fruitful again. Dumuzi is like the necessary but expendable substance that fructifies it.

Of course the myth is a story, but the implied association between human sexuality and agricultural productivity was acted out in an important ritual of Mesopotamian religion. During the "sacred marriage" (Greek *hieros gamos*), the king took on the identity of Dumuzi. A priestess acted the role of Inanna. Within the temple on top of the ziggurat, the artificial mountain at the center of Mesopotamian shrines (Figure 3.6), "Dumuzi" really did have intercourse with "Inanna" so that their human intercourse might guarantee a rich natural harvest. (Magic based on the principle that like action produces like result is called *sympathetic magic.*) Similar rites are found all over the ancient world, including ancient Greece (perhaps in the Telesterion, as some have thought). The story of Zeus making love to Hera on Mount Ida (Chapter 6) may depend on the *hieros gamos.* Although religion and myth exist independently, the language of one easily crosses over to become the language of the other.

Isis and Osiris

The Egyptian myth of Isis and Osiris shares some features with the Mesopotamian tale of Inanna and Dumuzi, and they seem to be historically related. The Mesopotamian story, however, appears to have emerged from economic practice, whereas the Egyptian myth from early times supported the structure of the Egyptian monarchy and the powerful Egyptian religion of magical resurrection that underlay the monarchy (Figure 10.6).

At first this religion concerned pharaoh alone, but later it supported the aspirations of even common men and women. In Egyptian the name **Isis** means "throne" and her name was written with a throne-shaped hieroglyph. Some scholars think she was in origin the personified seat of the mythical king **Osiris** (ō-sī-ris), her husband and brother.

Isis gradually became the greatest goddess of Egypt, absorbing all other Egyptian goddesses (there were many). The Greeks said she was the same as

FIGURE 10.6 Isis and Osiris, from the temple to Osiris at Abydos, Egypt, built by Sethos I, Nineteenth Dynasty, 1304–1290 BC. Osiris on the right, wrapped in mummy clothes and wearing an elaborate headdress of feathers, cobras, and ram's horns, receives an offering from a priest. He carries the shepherd's staff in one hand and the crook and flail, emblems of royal power, in the other. Both hands grip the magical *was* ("strength") scepter. A table of offerings bearing flowers and beer stands before him. The priest casts beads of incense on a cup-brazier, from which smoke arises. Behind him stands Isis, who appears as the divine musician and accompanies the ritual by shaking the sistrum, a rattle used in her cult, and rattling the *menat,* a metal necklace-counterweight symbolic of female reproductive power. She wears the solar disc embraced by cow horns and a vulture headdress (sacred to the mother goddess). Both Isis and Osiris wear the uraeus serpent on their brows, sign of royal power. The inscription near the priest reads "burning incense for the King Men-Maat-Re ["the truth of Re endures," that is, the dead Sethos I, identified with Osiris] who is endowed with life." Near Isis: "Shaking the sistrum before your beautiful face, for ever and ever." Over the priest: "The incense is coming, god's perfume is coming, his incense is come to you, Lord of the Two Lands, Men-Maat-Re."   (Hirmer Fotoarchiv, Munich, Germany)

Demeter at least from the time of Herodotus, about 450 BC. Her religion was influential in Rome, and the cult remained vigorous in Egypt until the sixth century AD. The image of Isis suckling her baby Horus, which Osiris fathered after his death, was adapted by early Christians to represent the Virgin Mary and the baby Jesus and is still seen today in churches all over the world. The Virgin Mary's blue dress, crescent moon, and title *Stella Maris*, "star of the sea," were taken from the Roman form of the cult of Isis.

The Greek writer Plutarch, writing about AD 120, gives the fullest account of the myth of Isis and her brother Osiris (*Moralia, On Isis and Osiris*). The Egyptians never tell the dangerous story, although they often allude to it. In Plutarch's version, the goddess Rhea, pregnant by Cronus, gave birth to five children, including Osiris, Isis, and Typhoeus. (Plutarch uses Greek equivalents for the Egyptian gods: sky-goddess Nut = Rhea; the earth-god Geb = Cronus; Seth, god of storm and disorder = Typhoeus; Thoth, god of magic and writing = Hermes.) Osiris had united in love with his sister Isis while still in the womb, and in the fullness of time he married her and became king of Egypt. Together they led the Egyptians out of their crude and backward way of life. Osiris abolished cannibalism, established laws, and showed the people how to grow crops and revere the gods, while Isis taught women how to spin and persuaded the men of the advantages of married life. Osiris then set out to travel over the world, teaching the virtues of civilized life wherever he went, leaving the rule of Egypt to Isis.

When Osiris returned, the evil Typhoeus enlisted seventy-two collaborators in a plot to kill him. Typhoeus secretly measured the body of Osiris and made a beautiful box (that is, a mummy case) of exactly the same size. At a banquet Typhoeus promised the box to whoever could fit inside. Everyone tried, but only Osiris was the right size. As he lay in the box, the conspirators ran up, slammed down the lid, and threw the box into the Nile.

The coffin floated downriver into the sea and across it to Byblus in Phoenicia. There it washed up beside a tamarisk tree, which quickly grew around it. When the king of Phoenicia ordered the tree cut down for use as a pillar in his palace, the coffin was taken with it.

Isis, grieving and desperate, hunted everywhere for her brother and husband. At last she came to Byblus and, in disguise, sat by a well (as in the story of Demeter; this, and other details, Plutarch appears to take directly from the Greek story). Isis spoke to no one except the queen's maids, whom she delighted by braiding their hair and breathing a wonderful perfume on them.

Hearing of this, the queen brought Isis to the palace to care for her little boy. Isis suckled the child by putting her finger in his mouth. At night she placed him in the fire to burn away his mortal parts, while she herself turned into a swallow and fluttered around the pillar that contained Osiris' coffin, crying piteously.

One night the queen saw the child in the fire, screamed aloud, and so deprived the boy of immortality. The goddess revealed herself in her majesty and demanded the pillar that contained the coffin, which she brought back to Egypt and hid in the marshes. (Other sources report that on the return voyage, she opened the coffin and, in the form of a hawk, hovered over her husband's penis, inflaming it to life and taking its seed within her.) Typhoeus, hunting on a moonlit night, stumbled upon the coffin. He tore the corpse into fourteen pieces and scattered them over the country.

Isis set out in a papyrus boat to search for the pieces, and she built a temple to Osiris wherever she found one. She recovered all the pieces except for the penis, devoured by three different species of fish, which were forbidden food ever after. As a substitute, she made a phallus of wood, which was worshiped in many of the temples of Osiris.

Osiris presently arose from the underworld to prepare his son, the hawk-god Horus, born to Isis, to do battle with Typhoeus and avenge his murder. After many days of fighting, Typhoeus' allies deserted him, and Horus delivered Typhoeus in chains to Isis. Instead of killing Typhoeus, however, she inexplicably released him. In a fury Horus ripped off her royal crown, which the god Hermes replaced with a helmet shaped like a cow's head. That is why Isis is sometimes shown with a cow's head.

Although dead, Osiris appeared to Isis once more and begot another child on her, "Horus the child," a god represented as an infant sucking his own finger. The Egyptians were unclear whether Horus the hawk and Horus the child were the same; in a way they were, in a way they were not.

Such is the story that Plutarch tells. Much in the myth is etiological for features of Egyptian society and religion. It explains why there were so many temples to Osiris and why two gods with the same name—Horus—were represented differently. The myth also provided a context for the Egyptians' understanding of their pharaohs. Every reigning pharaoh was Horus, the hawk, son of Isis and Osiris; the dead father of every pharaoh was Osiris. As Horus avenged the cruel death of his father, Osiris, so does pharaoh, in life, guarantee that justice and equity prevail in the land of Egypt. As Osiris rose from the underworld to give birth to Horus, so does the dead pharaoh, who is Osiris, guarantee that the living pharaoh, Horus, will be potent and in death himself become Osiris. As Osiris was brother and husband to Isis, so could the pharaohs maintain political power within a single family through brother-sister marriages, especially common under the Macedonian-Greek Ptolemies (323–30 BC).

Beside its etiological function for these features of Egyptian society, the myth of Isis and Osiris incorporates elements found in non-Egyptian myths of the fertility goddess. Like Tiamat or Inanna/Ishtar/Astartê, Isis is curiously ambivalent. When Osiris dies, she mourns him, finds him, cares for him, reassembles him, makes a new phallus, and even conceives a child by him. She resurrects his power and ensures that the royal succession will pass to their son, Horus. Yet, she frees the evil Typhoeus after Horus has vanquished him in battle. Prominent is the theme of the death that ensures well-being. Osiris died, but around his coffin grew a wonderful tree. From the other world the dead Osiris watches over this world and, through his son, guarantees its prosperity.

In the myth Osiris lived, then died, then through his resurrected phallus lived again (Figure 10.7). In nature, the Egyptians identified Osiris with the Nile, which rose annually to fructify the black, cultivable land, then subsided, then a year later

FIGURE 10.7 The resurrection of Osiris, from a bas-relief carving in the temple of Sethos I at Abydos, Nineteenth Dynasty c. 1300 BC. His sister Isis, designated by the hieroglyph she wears as crown, holds her dead brother's head affectionately. Assisted by the god Sokar (another god of the dead, like Horus shown as a hawk), Osiris excites his phallus (badly damaged) with one hand while he raises the other in a gesture of awakening: He was dead, but now he lives. Beneath the couch Pharaoh offers unguent to the four "sons of Horus," spirits who protected the entrails of the mummy.   (Author's photo)

rose again. Isis was the cultivable land, impregnated by the semen of the river. Typhoeus was the hostile, waterless desert, where the corpses of the dead were buried, where no life was possible.

Cybelê and Attis

The Greeks were from an early time in direct contact with the Indo-European peoples who lived in the uplands of Anatolia not far from the Aegean coast, the Phrygians, who made a dramatic impression on Greek culture through the religion of their goddess **Cybelê** and her youthful lover, **Attis**. Cybelê was primarily a goddess of fertility, but she could also heal (and send) disease, give oracles, and give protection in war. She was the goddess of mountains and a mistress of wild nature. In art she was shown wearing a peculiar crown representing city walls (exemplifying her protective function) and attended by lions (reflecting her association with the wild) (Figure 10.8). By the fifth century BC the Greeks had identified her with Demeter or Rhea but often referred to her by her Phrygian name, which also gave rise to Greek

FIGURE 10.8 A bust of Cybelê, the Mother of the Gods, wearing a tower for a crown. Roman copy, c. second century AD, of an earlier Greek original.   (Museo Archeologico Nazionale, Naples; Art Resource, New York)

"Sybil" for a prophetess. In the third century BC, her cult was introduced to Rome on the advice of an oracle during a military and political crisis. Thereafter she was called *Magna Mater*, "Great Mother."

We have no direct knowledge of the original Phrygian myths associated with Cybelê. However, Arnobius, a Christian writer of the fourth century AD who wrote in Latin, preserves one important myth about her and her consort, Attis (*Adversus Nationes* 5.5–7). As a Christian writer, Arnobius was hostile to the pagan myth he told.

In his story, Cybelê was born from a great rock in Phrygia, the very one from which Deucalion and Pyrrha took the stones that became human beings. Zeus, seeing Cybelê asleep atop the rock, approached in a blaze of lust. She resisted him until he spilled his seed on the rock, which became pregnant. Presently the rock bore a son, **Agdestis**, whose strength and violence were so great that they could not be resisted. His bestial lust raged crazily toward both sexes. Fearing neither god nor man, he asserted that earth, sky, and stars held no one mightier than he.

Finally, Dionysus, god of wine and of the life force, undertook responsibility for the situation. He poured a powerful dose of wine into the fountain where Agdestis slaked his thirst after becoming heated by hunting. After Agdestis had drunk and fallen asleep, Dionysus made a noose of braided hair and slipped it over Agdestis' feet, at the same time making a vine grow over the monster's genitals. When Agdestis sobered up, he staggered to his feet, ripping the genitals from his body.

From the blood that spurted onto the earth grew a fruited pomegranate tree. Now Nana, daughter of Sangarius (either a river god or a king), astonished at the sight of the tree growing from the blood, plucked a pomegranate from it, slipped the fruit into her dress, and soon found herself pregnant. Her father, disgraced, locked her up to die of starvation, but Cybelê, the Great Mother, kept her alive with fruit and grain. Nana gave birth to a boy named Attis.

The Great Mother doted on Attis because of his lovely face, and the castrated Agdestis became the boy's guide in hunting. But King Midas (**mī**-das) of Phrygia arranged for Attis to marry his daughter (this is the same Midas as in the famous story of "Midas and the golden touch"; see Chapter 11). To keep ill-wishers away from the ceremony, he walled off the town.

Agdestis, furious that the boy had been taken from him and had transferred his affections to a woman, bewitched all the wedding guests and drove them mad. "Worship Attis, you Phrygians!" they shouted in their madness. A man named Gallus grew so crazed that he sliced off his genitals. The daughter of his mistress cut off her breasts. Attis seized Agdestis' flute and flung himself down at the foot of a pine tree. "Take this, Agdestis—" he cried, "this is what you wanted when you drove us crazy!" With these words he ripped off his genitals and with them poured out his blood and his life.

The Great Mother sadly took up the severed organs of Attis, washed them, and buried them under the pine tree. From his blood grew violets that wreathed the tree. The maiden who was to have been his bride covered the dead boy's breast with soft wool and, weeping, killed herself above his body. As she died, her blood was turned to violets too.

Cybelê buried them both in a common grave, from which grew an almond tree, to signify the bitterness of their fate. Cybelê joined her laments to those of Agdestis, who pleaded with Zeus to let Attis return to life. Their pleas were in vain: Zeus granted only that Attis' body should not decay, that his hair should continue to grow, and that his little finger should stay alive and in constant motion.

Observations: From Blood, Life

This bizarre tale, seemingly of great antiquity, is a mixture of traditional mythical elements with depictions of real rites in honor of Cybelê. Zeus's impregnation of the rock is a variation of the myth that human beings were made from earth. The rock is earth itself, the mother. Not only do Deucalion and Pyrrha take their stones from this rock, but Cybelê herself comes from it. Agdestis, like Typhoeus, is a monster who threatens the order of the world. But the means of the monster's undoing, his castration, is explained by the etiological function of the myth as a whole. The castration of Agdestis leads to the self-castration of Gallus and Attis, which in turn reflects actual practice by men called the *Galli*, real Phrygian followers of *Magna Mater* who castrated themselves in her honor, a kind of ultimate sacrifice. The Gallus of the story is the eponym for these followers, and his act provides a precedent and explanation for their practice.

Ritual self-castration strikes us as extraordinary, but we must remember that for many peoples sacrifice was necessary to appease the divine powers who rule and oppress the world. Human beings are in debt to the gods and to the angry ghosts, who must be bought off at any price. The value of sacrifice is gauged by the pain it causes. Many ancient cultures (perhaps including the preclassical Greek) practiced human sacrifice, where the sense of loss is greatest. One of the charges against the kings of Judah was that they "made their sons pass through the fire"—that is, killed them to the god Moloch (for example, Manasseh, in 2 Kings 21.6). Even Christianity, according to the formulation of St. Paul, accepted as a fundamental principle the sacrifice of God's son to atone for human sin. Animals eventually replaced human beings as ransom to the angry gods (except in times of crisis), as suggested in the biblical story of the ram substituted for Isaac, son of Abraham, and in numerous Greek stories. Castration was yet another form of substitution, and the myth of Cybelê and Attis explains its value.

From the blood of Agdestis, spilled like semen on the ground at his castration, comes new life: the pomegranate, ripe with bloody seeds, which in turn impregnates Nana with Attis. Blood is life: When the woman's periodic discharge stops, the child grows. Likewise, from the castrated Attis' genitals, planted by Cybelê, violets grew around the pine, a tree that, because of its seed-filled cones and erect straight growth, was an emblem for male sexuality, conspicuously in the Greek cult of Dionysus. Finally, from the bodies of Attis and his betrothed, Cybelê causes yet another tree to grow. Although dead, Attis is still alive in a way. His hair continues to grow and his little finger, like a phallus, continues to wiggle. His sacrifice placates the goddess and allows for life's renewal.

Aphrodite and Adonis

A similar mythic pattern appears in another Greek myth. We have already seen Aphrodite in the guise of Cybelê, the Phrygian mountain mother, in the *Homeric Hymn to Aphrodite* (see Chapter 9), where she seduces Anchises on Mount Ida in Phrygia. Wild animals, forgetting their wildness under the goddess's influence, follow in her train, as they follow the Phrygian Cybelê. In the story of Aphrodite and **Adonis** (a-**don**-is) again appear themes associating plant-life and blood and the death of the young male. The Eastern origins of this story are betrayed by the very name Adonis, Semitic for "lord" (in modern Judaism, *Adonai*, "my Lord," is still used as a word for God). Curiously, however, just this story is not told in any surviving Eastern literary source.

As we have seen (Chapter 9), Paphos, the son of Pygmalion and Galatea (the statue-turned-human), was father to Cinyras, whose daughter Myrrha, pregnant by her father, was turned into a myrrh tree. After nine months the tree split open and Adonis emerged. When Aphrodite saw him, she fell in love and spent all her time with Adonis, who cared only for the hunt (see Perspective Figure 9c). Aphrodite warned him against pursuing big game, but he ignored her advice, and one day a boar gouged him in the thigh. He bled to death from the terrible wound and from his blood sprouted the blood-red anemone. Ovid tells the story:

[708]   Venus thus solemnly warned him and made her way through the sky,
         drawn by her team of swans. But his courage rejected the warning.
710   Chance led his hounds to the recent scent of a savage wild boar.
         They roused the beast from his lair, and as it tried to evade them
         by flight through the woods, the son of Cinyras wounded its hide
         with a glancing blow of his lance. A sidelong twist of the snout
         knocked the weapon away, smeared with the blood of the victim,
715   a sight that enraged the boar. In fury it turned on the hunter,
         who tried to avoid its charge. In vain—the animal buried
         his tusks in Adonis' groin and tumbled the boy, as he perished,
         full length on the yellow sand.
                 Borne in her weightless car, propelled by the wings of her swans
720   through the mid-air of the heavens, Cytherea had not yet arrived
         in Cyprus, her goal, when she shuddered to hear the gasp of Adonis
         breathing his last. She wrenched her white birds back in their courses
         to the very place they had left, and soon, from high in the aether,
         she gazed on the newly dead body, still twitching in its own blood.
725   Down she jumped from her car. Tearing her hair and her bosom,
         she beat at her breast with hands unfit to perform such an action,
         and railed, "Not everything, Fate, will always succumb to your power!
         Forever, Adonis, this token of grief at your death will continue,
         this hint at the way that you died, this annual sign of my sorrow:
730   Your blood shall turn to a flower. Was not Persephonê granted
         the power of turning the flesh of a maiden to sweet-smelling mint?°
         Who out of envy refuses the same for Adonis, my hero?"
         With this she perfumed his blood with fragrant droplets of nectar.
         The mixture swelled like a bubble when rain falls down from the sky.
735   An hour had not fully passed, when a flower the color of blood
         rose from the blood-stained sand, like those the anemone bears,
         concealing its seeds beneath the pliant red outer rind.
         Even this protection soon passes. The light seeds soon fall away
         and are blown away by the breezes from which they receive their name.

                                   OVID, *Metamorphoses* 10.708–739

731. *mint*: Persephonê, queen of the dead, was allowed to turn her dead follower Mentha—a name cognate to our word *mint*—into the plant that bears her name.

In Hellenistic times the cult of Adonis spread from Asia into Greece and Rome. Thus women planted seeds in shallow earth, allowed them to die, then tore their hair and lamented the death of beautiful Adonis. The Bible refers to the practice: "He next took me to the entrance of the north gate of the Temple of God where women were sitting, weeping for Tammuz [= Dumuzi/Adonis]. He said, 'Son of man, do you see that? You will see even filthier things than that!'" (Ezekiel 8.14–15).

PERSPECTIVE 10.2

H. D.'S "ADONIS"

An important poet of the twentieth century, H. D., who identified herself with Sappho, received little attention until after her death in Switzerland in 1961. Born Hilda Doolittle in Bethlehem, Pennsylvania, in 1886, she went to Europe in 1911 for a short visit but stayed on. In London she joined the expatriate community of writers that included Ezra Pound and T. S. Eliot, a literary group composed of modernists who sought the spirit of the twentieth century in myth, psychoanalysis, and, in H. D.'s case, feminism.

Mostly adopting a modern voice, H. D. nonetheless often wrote poems on mythical subjects. One scholar lists eighty-nine of her poems with classical titles. Viewing the classical world through modern eyes, she used myth in a personal way to explore and reveal character. In particular, she was interested in Helen of Troy and wrote a monumental epic, *Helen in Egypt,* published in the year of her death. Another poem with mythical theme by H. D., "Adonis," appeared in 1916. In this remarkable poem the Adonis myth is taken to reflect recurring aspects of human experience.

1.*

Each of us like you
has died once,
each of us like you
has passed through drift of wood-leaves
cracked and bent
and tortured and unbent
in the winter-frost,
then burnt into gold points,
lighted afresh,
crisp amber, scales of gold-leaf,
gold turned and re-welded
in the sun-heat;

each of us like you
has died once,
each of us has crossed an old wood-path
and found the winter leaves
so golden in the sun-fire
that even the live wood-flowers
were dark.

*"Adonis" By H.D. (Hilda Doolittle), from COLLECTED POEMS, 1912–1944, copyright ©1925 by Hilda Doolittle. Reprinted by permission of New Directions Publishing Corp.

2.

> Not the gold on the temple-front
> where you stand
> is as gold as this,
> not the gold that fastens your sandals,
> nor the gold, reft
> through your chiseled locks,
> is as gold as this last year's leaf,
> not all the gold hammered and wrought
> and beaten
> on your lover's face,
> brow and bare breast
> is as golden as this:
>
> each of us like you
> has died once,
> each of us like you
> stands apart, like you
> fit to be worshipped.

The god is a symbol for each individual's winter and spring, death and rebirth. In the first stanza gold symbolizes the eternal: The leaf that dies is turned to gold, which never dies. In the second stanza, the dead leaves, turned gold, are more alive than the living flowers. In the third stanza, the dead leaf, a thing of nature, is more golden than the real gold on the god's temple, on his sandal, in his hair, and on classical sculptures of his lover Venus/Aphrodite. We, too, have a dying nature, but like Adonis have eternal, divine gold within, are even "fit to be worshipped," a startling conclusion.

CONCLUSIONS

Each of these stories shares common features, but has a different emphasis. In each story someone dies. The story of Persephonê and Demeter, although it is no simple allegory, nonetheless explains the cycle of vegetable growth (and by extension human life) as inevitable in the nature of things. The giving of Persephonê to Hades, her sacrifice, creates the seasonal pattern of the growth and harvest of the life-nurturing grain. Death is part of life itself so it is pointless to lament it.

The much older Sumerian story of Inanna and Dumuzi anticipates these themes in explaining the loss of fecundity as the disappearance of a force, the goddess, who has journeyed to the other world, that is, she has died. The only way to bring her back is through sacrifice, the death of the male who was her husband. The story explains the need for sacrifice to keep the earth fruitful.

In the Egyptian story of Isis and Osiris, Osiris is the god of the growing grain, a dying god like Dumuzi through whose death new life comes. But in the Egyptian royal funerary cult, pharaoh was the incarnation of Horus, the son of Isis and Osiris, and the dead pharaoh had become Osiris: That was official dogma. Hence the myth explains how the power of pharaoh is eternal and always regenerating itself out of itself.

The Phrygian myth of Cybelê and Attis is not nearly so refined. First semen falls on a rock, a monster arises whose blood soaks the earth, whence springs a tree with a bloody fruit that impregnates a girl who begets a youth who at his own wedding rips out his genitals! His dead body nourishes a plant. In this story, semen = blood = bloody seeds = a child = plant life. The blood is life and from its shedding comes new life, the theory and practice of blood sacrifice expressed in a forceful mythic pattern. The gory genitals of the Galli were pleasing to the Great Mother, who in return brought fertility to the land. The myth is in part an etiology for this exaggerated form of religious devotion. The story of Aphrodite and Adonis, too, explains the widespread religious practice of mourning the "lord" (= Adonis) in the form of seeds planted in a shallow dish.

In all these stories the earth-goddess represents the permanent fertility of the world. She is the same, always fruitful (unless she withdraws her favors). The male actors, by contrast, are temporary, disposable, but renewable through the power of the earth-goddess. Oddly, the male consorts do not beget children on the goddesses with whom they associate. Osiris must wait until dead before fructifying his sister/wife Isis. Everywhere are the symbols *blood* (the fluid of life, the male) and *plants* (growth from the fructified earth). Although the theme is muted in the story of Demeter and Persephonê, Persephonê devours a blood-red pomegranate seed, the same fruit that in the myth of Cybelê grows from the blood of Agdestis, whose seed will beget Attis.

The oddness of the Greek story stands out against the background of its Near Eastern antecedents and parallels. Where is the male counterpart to the mother-goddess, later resurrected in some form? Instead, it is mother and daughter, leading some commentators to suppose that the story comes from a time before the relationship between sexual intercourse and reproduction was clearly understood. But the theme of the mother's ability to beget without the male also appears in Hesiod's story of Gaea, from whom sprang Pontus/Sea and Uranus/Sky, and in stories that Hera gave birth to Hephaestus without help from Zeus. It is always the mother's prerogative to do this, if circumstances demand it.

KEY NAMES AND TERMS

Demeter, 237	*hieros gamos*, 258
Persephonê, 237	Isis, 258
Korê, 237	Osiris, 258
Eleusinian Mysteries, 250	Cybelê, 262
Triptolemus, 253	Attis, 262
Inanna, 255	Agdestis, 263
Dumuzi, 255	Adonis, 265

SOME ADDITIONAL ANCIENT SOURCES

Isis and Osiris: Plutarch, *On Isis and Osiris* 12–20. *Cybelê*: Apollodorus, 3.12.6; Apollonius of Rhodes, 1.1092–1152; Ovid, *Metamorphoses*, 10.102–105, 10.686–704, 14.535–555; *Homeric Hymn 14*, to the Mother of the Gods; Vergil, *Ciris*, 163–167; Hyginus, *Fabulae* 191. **Adonis**: Apollodorus 3.14.3–4; Ovid, *Metamorphosis*, 519–559; Hyginus, *Fabulae* 58, 248, 251, and *Poetica Astronomica*, 2.7. **Demeter and Persephonê**: Homer, *Odyssey* 5.125–128; Hesiod, *Theogony* 453–506, 912–914, 969–974; Ovid, *Metamorphoses*, 5.359–424, 5.642–661, 6.118–119, 8.738–878; Apollodorus, 1.15–1.2.1.

FURTHER READING CHAPTER 10

Clay, Jenny Strauss, *The Politics of Olympus: Form and Meaning in the Major Homeric Hymns* (Princeton, NJ, 1989). Contains good essays on the *Homeric Hymn to Demeter* and other Homeric Hymns.

Foley, H. P., ed., *The Homeric Hymn to Demeter: Translation, Commentary, and Interpretive Essays* (Princeton, NJ, 1993). Facing Greek/English text with excellent essays focused on gender.

Frankfort, Henri, *Kingship and the Gods, A Study of Ancient Near Eastern Religion as the Integration of Society and Nature* (Chicago, 1978; reprint of 1948 edition). Penetrating analysis of Egyptian and Near Eastern myth and society.

Mylonas, G. E., *Eleusis and the Eleusinian Mysteries* (Princeton, NJ, 1961). The best book on the topic, a thorough summary of the literary and archaeological evidence.

Richardson, N. J., ed., *The Homeric Hymn to Demeter* (Oxford, UK, 1974). The standard scholarly edition of the Greek text, with introductory essay in English and copious notes.

Roller, Lynn E., *In Search of God the Mother: The Cult of Anatolian Cybele* (Berkeley, CA, 1999). The widespread worship of Mata Kubileya in Phrygia, Cybelê in Greece, and *Magna Mater* in Rome.

CHAPTER 11

MYTHS OF FERTILITY

DIONYSUS

Wine sets free sad mortals from sorrow when
they are filled with the stream of the vine.
Wine gives them sleep and a forgetting of the troubles of the day,
nor is there any other cure for pain. He who is a god
is poured out in offerings to the gods,
so that by his means we may have good things.

EURIPIDES, *Bacchae* 280–286

DIONYSUS (dī-ō-nī-sus), god of wine, the life force, and the instinctive side of personality, stands somewhat apart from the other Olympians. He was admitted to Olympus later than the others and, according to some writers, displaced Hestia to become one of the twelve.

Few Greek myths have influenced the poetic and religious imagination of the West more than those of Dionysus (Figure 11.1). To the ancient Greeks, Dionysus (also known as Bacchus) was the god who taught the art of turning the juice of grapes into wine, their everyday drink. But this complex and multifaceted deity was much more than a god of wine. At the center of his mythic character was his identity as a male principle of fertility, complementary to the female principle embodied in Demeter (Chapter 10). As a god of fertility, Dionysus encouraged the burgeoning of everything alive: plants, animals, and human beings. Thick, luscious ivy was a sign of his presence. He wore a leopard skin, and panthers pulled his chariot.

FIGURE 11.1 Dionysus in ecstasy, Attic vase, c. 450 BC. The god, maddened by his own power, tears apart a live goat, his special animal, before eating its raw flesh. The leopard skin around his shoulders and the ivy that crowns his hair are emblems of the god.   (British Museum, London; © Trustees of the British Museum/Art Resource, New York)

The phallus and the horns of a bull were his emblems (Figure 11.2). Through his cult this fertility-god also came to stand for a distinctive form of human experience, a divinely inspired madness in which one's ordinary sense of self is lost, and with it the accepted norms of decent and rational conduct. Some features of the cult of Dionysus were later to find striking parallels in the new religion of Christianity.

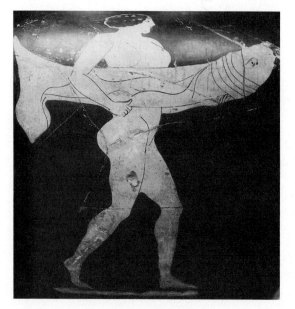

FIGURE 11.2 A *hetaira* (prostitute) carries a giant phallus, symbol of Dionysus' power, perhaps at the Athenian festival of the Haloa ("threshing"), dedicated to the fertility-gods Demeter and Dionysus, on a vase for mixing wine, c. 450 BC.   (Staatliche Museen, Berlin; Bildarchiv Preußischer Kulturbesitz/Art Resource, New York)

We must piece together the myths of Dionysus from many different sources. Homer has little to say about him. The aristocratic epic poet lacked sympathy for this god of drunkenness and sexual license. Two Homeric Hymns (eighth to sixth centuries BC) survive; one we give below, the other is only a fragment. Apollodorus has the most extended single account of his adventures, and Ovid tells some important myths. Our best-known source, however, is the *Bacchae* (**bak**-kē), a play by Euripides written about 406 BC, just before Athens fell to Sparta, beaten and demoralized in the long Peloponnesian War.

In this chapter we first consider the mythical biography of Dionysus, including his birth, his travels in the East, and his reception in Greece, specifically in Thebes. We then discuss the meaning of these magical and contradictory but deeply moving tales and examine the cult with which they were associated.

THE BIRTH AND EARLY YOUTH OF DIONYSUS

Zeus fell in love with **Semelê** (**sem**-e-lē), princess of the house of Thebes and daughter of the Phoenician immigrant King Cadmus (see Chart 18). Zeus came to her disguised as a mortal man, and Semelê was soon pregnant. Hera, Zeus's wife, inflamed with jealousy, disguised herself as an old woman and hurried to Semelê. Her hair was straggly and her skin furrowed with wrinkles. For a while the two women chatted. When Semelê revealed her affair with Zeus, the disguised Hera suggested that his claim to be king of the gods might be only a ploy. Perhaps he was an ordinary mortal who made up the ridiculous story only to bring Semelê to his bed!

The old woman departed, and Semelê began to have doubts. When Zeus next came, she asked for just one wish. Zeus swore by the underworld river Styx that he would give whatever she asked. "Appear to me as you appear to Hera, when you make love to her!" Semelê asked. Sorrowful, yet true to his word, Zeus appeared in all his glory. Semelê was burned to a crisp. Hermes saved the fetus within her, however, and carried it to Zeus, who promptly sewed it into his thigh. Three months later he removed the stitches. Dionysus was born again. Hence he was "the twice-born god."

Hermes then carried the child to **Ino** (ī-nō), queen of Orchomenus (or-**kom**-en-us), the Bronze Age capital of northern Boeotia, just as Thebes was capital of southern Boeotia. Ino was Semelê's sister and wife to King Athamas (**ath**-a-mas); she plays an important part in other Greek myths (see Chart 18). On Hermes' instruction, Ino disguised the divine child in girl's clothing, hoping to protect Dionysus from Hera.

Hera was not deceived. She drove Ino and Athamas insane. With a bow and arrow Athamas shot one of his two sons, mistaking him for a fawn. Ino seized the other, Melicertes, and boiled him alive in a pot. Completely insane, she ran with the pot in her hands down to the Gulf of Corinth and leaped into the sea. She and the dead child were transformed into sea-deities, saviors of distressed mariners (including Homer's legendary Odysseus). Ino's name was changed to Leucothea (lū-**koth**-e-a), the "white goddess."

FIGURE 11.3 The birth of Dionysus, on a South Italian vase, c. 380 BC. Dionysus' nurse, Ino, holding a thyrsus, reaches to receive him, while Hermes, with his caduceus, waits in the bottom right to carry the baby to the nymphs of Nysa, shown on the left lounging about with Pan (above Zeus, with panpipes) and satyrs (lower right). Apollo and Artemis (she is half off the photo) stand behind Zeus. (National Archeological Museum, Taranto, Italy)

To save Dionysus from further persecution, Zeus turned the child into a young goat, and in this form Hermes delivered him to the **nymphs of Nysa** (nī-sa), a mountain perhaps in Thrace, or India, or Ethiopia (Figure 11.3).

THE WANDERINGS OF DIONYSUS

In Nysa the young Dionysus discovered the vine and the art of making wine. Hera now struck the god with the same madness he was later to bring to others. In a delirium, Dionysus wandered to Egypt, Syria, and then Phrygia in west-central Asia Minor. Here he met the Phrygian goddess Cybelê, the Great Mother, whom the Greeks identified with Rhea. Cybelê, whose own followers danced to the wild music of tambourines and flutes and abandoned themselves to orgiastic rites, cured Dionysus of his madness, and she revealed to him her secret rites. From Cybelê Dionysus acquired his long robes, an effeminate style of dress that so offended Greek men.

From Phrygia Dionysus now headed east again, followed by his band of devotees. His female followers were called **Bacchae** ("women possessed by Bacchus"). The variant term Bacchantes (bak-**kan**-tēz) was applied to male and female followers alike. Sometimes the Bacchae were also called *thyiades* (**thē**-ya-dēz), "frenzied ones," or more often **maenads** (**mē**-nads, "the raging women"). They carried the **thyrsus**, usually a staff crowned with a pinecone or a bunch of ivy leaves (the thyrsi of Figure 11.3 are highly stylized). Male followers were **satyrs** (**sā**-ters), half-human creatures with erect phalli, sometimes of enormous size, and the tails and ears of horses (see Figure 11.5); later they acquired goatlike legs. **Silenus** (sī-**lē**-nus; plural, sileni, sī-**lē**-nī) is either a general term for any old satyr or the name of one satyr in particular: an ugly, drunken, extremely fat one, given to the telling of tall tales. He is shown in art with thick lips and pug nose, riding on an ass, so drunk he can barely maintain his balance.

Like Cybelê, Dionysus traveled in a chariot drawn by panthers. He and his band crossed the Euphrates river on a bridge made of grapevines and ivy. They swept east as far as India, to the sound of drums and cymbals, overcoming all who opposed them. Returning west, the god and his train paused again in Phrygia. There Dionysus rewarded the local king **Midas**, son of Gordias and Cybelê, for his generous hospitality by granting a single wish. The king asked that everything he touched be turned to gold. And so it was: even his food and drink!

In desperation, Midas begged Dionysus to take back his gift. The god told Midas to bathe in the headwaters of the Pactolus river, which flows near the citadel of Sardis, the capital of Lydia. The river carried away the cursed gift. The gold settled in the sands, and Lydia later became one of the richest kingdoms in the ancient world (the Lydians invented coins in the sixth century BC).

PERSPECTIVE 11.1

TITIAN'S *BACCHUS AND ARIADNÊ*

Many Western artists have depicted Dionysus and his wife, Ariadnê, including Titian (c. 1488–1576), a leading painter of the Italian Renaissance in Venice. In his *Bacchus and Ariadnê* (Perspective Figure 11.1), Titian follows closely the narratives of Catullus and Ovid, depicting the youthful god—soft, pudgy, and effeminate—naked except for a cloak loosely draped around him, as he leaps from his panther-drawn chariot. Ariadnê has been gazing out to sea at Theseus' receding ship, barely visible to the left of her shoulder. She turns, startled by Bacchus and his train of satyrs and maenads, who clash cymbals, brandish the thyrsus, and toss parts of animals. The pose of the satyr in the lower right, twisted with snakes, is modeled after the ancient statue of Laocoön, discovered in Rome during the Renaissance (see

PERSPECTIVE FIGURE 11.1 Titian (Tiziano Vecelli, c. 1488–1576), *Bacchus and Ariadnê,* c. 1520.   (© National Gallery, London / Art Resource, New York)

Figure 21.4). In the upper left shines the constellation of the crown that Dionysus gave to Ariadnê (Corona Borealis).

   In choosing a subject from classical myth, Titian was following the Italian Renaissance's powerful interest in pagan humanism. Whereas medieval art served primarily to exemplify the religious values of an age of faith, art in the Renaissance turned toward the natural and human worlds, focusing on the importance of the individual. At the same time, the revival of the Greco-Roman literary tradition brought with it a renewed interest in myth, especially as presented in Ovid's *Metamorphoses,* which offered to artists a whole new world of subjects. Here Titian focuses on the emotion and surprise of Ariadnê in the midst of a natural setting: Theseus has abandoned her, but the god-man Dionysus has found her again.

Dionysus married **Ariadnê** (ar-i-**ad**-nē), a daughter of King Minos. He found her on the island of Naxos in the midst of the Aegean sea where Theseus, hero of Athens, had abandoned her (see Chapter 17). While Ariadnê gazed across the sea to the distant sails of Theseus' receding ship, Dionysus came up behind her through the wilderness, accompanied by his crowd of maenads and satyrs, a scene described vividly by the Roman poet Catullus, a contemporary of Julius Caesar (c. 84–54 BC):

[254]   All around, on dancing feet the maddened Bacchantes thundered,
255   "Euhoi!" they shrieked, "Euhoi," tossing their heads.
          Here one waved a thyrsus, a vine stem tipped by a pine cone;
              there, bare-handed, they ripped apart a bellowing calf.
          Shouting delirious cries, they tossed its limbs to each other.
              Still others braided their hair with venomous snakes.
260   Here they gathered to hail the mystical basket of secrets,
              truths forever unknown to the uninitiate mass.
          These with delicate fingers beat rhythm from rumbling tom-toms;
              those drew a ringing clang from hollow cymbals of bronze.
          For many the horn blared out its brazen dissonant clamor,
265   or strident Phrygian flutes shouted their barbarous song.

CATULLUS, *Poem 64* 254–264

RESISTANCE TO THE GOD

Many of the myths about Dionysus tell of the resistance he met when he returned from his travels in the East, bringing his new religion. In the oldest surviving story we have about the god, from Homer's *Iliad*, Dionysus and his followers cross the Hellespont into Thrace, where one **Lycurgus** (lī-**kur**-gus), king of a tribe in Thrace, persecutes them:

[130]   Lycurgus, Dryas' son, dared fight with the gods of the heaven,
          but his life was not long. He tried to expel from holy Mount Nysa°
          the Bacchanal nurses who follow the maddening god Dionysus.
          Dropping the thyrsus behind, they scattered in abject terror,
          struck by the murderous blows of the ox-goad wielding Lycurgus.
135   In craven fear, Dionysus ran off, diving under the billows,
          where Thetis took him shivering in her arms to quiet his panic,
          while he trembled in cowardly terror at the man's tempestuous yelling.
          But the gods who live in bliss thereafter detested Lycurgus:
          Zeus struck him blind. Soon he died, despised by all the immortals.

HOMER, *Iliad* 6.130–140

131. *Nysa*: Here placed in Thrace.

Other authors report that Lycurgus went mad and attempted to rape his own mother. With a double-bitted ax he pruned off the legs of his son, thinking him an ivy plant, sacred to the god. These impious acts made the land sterile. An oracle announced that the king must die. The Thracians carried Lycurgus to nearby Mount Pangaeum ("all-bloody") and staked him to the ground. Wild horses ate him alive.

Dionysus headed south. In Orchomenus on the Boeotian plain, once the home of Ino and Athamas, celebrated for its wealth and power, Dionysus encountered further resistance. Although the city's inhabitants quickly accepted the god, the three daughters of King Minyas, the **Minyads** (**min**-yadz, "daughters of Minyas"), refused to join the new, ecstatic religion. Instead, like proper women, they sat in their chambers, dutifully worked their looms, and spoke critically of those who had gone to the mountains to rage as Bacchae. They told sentimental stories of nymphs in love. Dionysus himself appeared to them in the shape of a young girl, but the foolish Minyads refused his warning.

Enraged, Dionysus took on the form of a lion, a bull, and a panther. The room filled with the sound of drums and the trill of flutes, the clashing of cymbals and the scent of myrrh. The threads of the loom turned into vines. Nectar and milk dripped from the furniture as darkness filled the room. Suddenly hungering for human flesh, the Minyads cast lots for their own children. They tore one child into bits and ate him. Joyful, they danced from the palace into the mountains to join the other Bacchae. Dionysus later turned them into bats, which love the darkness and reject the light.

Crossing the Isthmus into the Peloponnesus, the god again met resistance from three daughters of a king, this time the daughters of King Proetus (**prē**-tus) of Argos, a great-uncle of the hero Perseus. Because the Proetids (**prē**-tids, "daughters of Proetus") refused to accept the rites of Dionysus, they were afflicted with a gruesome itching on their heads, a leprosy that soon covered their flesh. They went insane, thought they were cows, and wandered into the mountains of Arcadia. The disease spread to the other women, who left their houses, killed their children, and wandered in the wild. At last a seer named Melampus, famous for his knowledge of incantations and herbs, was able to cure them, in return for two-thirds of the kingdom of Argos.

DIONYSUS AND THE PIRATES

A story of Dionysus' encounter with a band of pirates is told in the *Homeric Hymn to Dionysus* from the seventh century BC. The god was standing on a promontory beside the sea, perhaps on the small island of Icaria near the coast of Asia Minor, when a ship of Etruscan pirates passed below him:

[1]   I call to mind Dionysus, Semelê's famous son,
        how he appeared one day by the shore of the barren sea,
        on a point reaching into the water, like a good-looking boy,
        maybe sixteen years old. His long dark hair hung loose,
5   and a dark blue jacket covered his muscular shoulders.
        From the benches of their ship, a speedy Tyrsenian° pirate,
        the crewmen disembarked, doomed to a terrible fate.
        They saw the boy, gave a signal, ran up, and dragged him away,
        and took their place in the ship, satisfied with their luck.

6. *Tyrsenian*: Etruscan.

10 Thinking him some lord's son, they tried to make him secure,
 but the ropes dropped useless away, off his hands and feet,
 while he sat grinning, and mockery shone from his dark eyes.
 The helmsman understood, and calling the others, he asked:
  "Messmates, what sort of god is the boy we have caught
15 and tried to secure? He's strong! Our ship is well built,
 but it can't carry this burden. He must be Zeus himself,
 the silver-bowed Apollo, or Poseidon. One thing is certain—
 he's like no mortal man, but a god who lives on Olympus.
 So come on, let's let him go, right away, here on the dark shore.
20 And don't lay a hand upon him, or he'll fly into a temper
 and raise up a terrible storm, a regular hurricane!"
  So he advised, but the skipper angrily cut him short:
 "Mind your own business! Just keep your eye on the wind
 and lend a hand when you're needed to heave away on a line.
25 Slave-drivers have to be tough! As for this fellow here—
 maybe he's headed for Egypt, or maybe the island of Cyprus,
 or maybe the ends of the earth and a hundred miles beyond.
 Sooner or later he'll tell us about his friends and family,
 the ransom they can pay. To us he's good luck from nowhere!"
30 At that he stepped the mast and set the sail on the ship.
 The strong wind bellied the sail as the crew hauled in on the sheets.
 But as she gathered way, all sorts of wonders appeared.
 The first was sparkling sweet-scented wine that gurgled
 deliciously through the ship, dark, with a heavy bouquet.
35 The terrified seamen gaped as a vine grew out of the topmast
 and snaked along the sail to the yardarms to port and to starboard,
 loaded with ripened clusters. Along with the vine, dark ivy,
 blooming with flowers and heavy with rich luxuriant berries,
 drooped down over the oars, crowning the groaning oarlocks.
40 The sailors panicked to see this and cried aloud to the helmsman
 to run at once for the shore. Dionysus then changed his form,
 turning into a lion that roared at them from the bows.
 Another portent: He raised a shaggy-necked bear amidships,
 rearing to growl at the men, while forward the lion glared.
45 In terror the sailors ran aft, crowding around the helmsman,
 the only sensible man. Then, with a sudden spring,
 the lion pounced on the master, while the horrified sailors looked on.
 To escape their fate they dived into the shining sea
 and at once were turned into dolphins. And as for the helmsman,
50 Dionysus kept him aboard, and calmed his heart with this word:
 "Courage, my friend, my spirit's greatest joy and delight.
 I am thundering Bacchus, born of Semelê, fathered by Zeus!"
  Farewell, O son of beautiful Semelê. He who forgets you
 never learns to compose sweet verse of harmonious measure.

Homeric Hymn to Dionysus

It is easy to see how this poem is appropriate to the symposium, a tribute to the god of wine. The Athenian master painter Exekias seems to have illustrated the

FIGURE 11.4 Dionysus and the pirates by Exekias, interior of Attic wine cup, c. 540 BC. The god lounges amidship surrounded by dolphins, perhaps once the crew. The yardarms have turned to ivy and vines from which hang bunches of grapes. When the wine in the cup was swirled, the dolphins would appear to swim. (Staatliche Antikensammlungen und Glyptothek, Munich; Erich Lessing/Art Resource, New York)

story on a black-figured vase, one of the most famous paintings from the ancient world (Figure 11.4; compare Figure 2.13, where sailors turn into dolphins).

DIONYSUS IN THEBES

The best-known resistance to Dionysus takes place in Thebes, the city of his birth. In Euripides' play the *Bacchae*, the god tells us that he returned to Thebes not just to spread his cult of ecstatic experience, but to take vengeance on his mother's sisters, Agavê (a-**gā**-vē), Autonoë (aw-**ton**-o-ē), and Ino (although Ino had been Dionysus' nurse; in this version, she is still alive). The sisters had denied Semelê's claim that she slept with Zeus, alleging that her lover was a mortal and that Semelê was destroyed for telling so outrageous a lie. To punish this slander against his mother, Dionysus cast a spell of madness over the sisters.

As the play opens, the sisters are roaming with their followers over Mount Cithaeron (si-**thē**-ron) behind Thebes. Only the stubborn king **Pentheus** (**pen**-thūs), championing reason against disorder, opposes the god, ensuring his own horrible end. There are two groups of Bacchae in Euripides' play: the maddened women of Thebes, punished for their slander, and the Asian Bacchae, loyal and sane followers of the god who make up the chorus. When the play opens, Dionysus gives a summary of his career and his travels and explains what he has already done to restore the slandered name of his mother:

[1]   *Dionysus*   I have come back to this, the land of the Thebans,
        I, Dionysus, whom Semelê, daughter of Cadmus,
        once bore to Zeus, with lightning flash as midwife.
        Changing my form, no more divine but human,
5   I show myself by Ismenus' spring and Dircê's.°
        See there, the place where Semelê's body lies,
        struck by the thunderbolt, down by the house
        whose ruins smolder with still-living fire,
        witness of Hera's violence to my mother.
10   Cadmus was right, who made this place taboo,
        his daughter's grave, which I have hidden deep
        in green and succulent tangles of my vines.
           I left the golden sands of Lydia
        and Phrygia, then Persia's high plateau,
15   scorched by the sun. Onward I marched,
        passing the walls of Bactria and traversing
        the grim and icy country of the Medes.°
        I reached the blessed land of Araby,
        then back the long road through Asia, to the salt sea,
20   lined by towered cities thronged with Greeks
        and men of other races, all together,
        teaching my dances, establishing my rites,
        to make these lands know my divinity.
        Thebes is the first of all the towns of Greece
25   to hear my followers' ecstatic cries.
        I flung the fawn skin on their eager shoulders;
        I thrust the thyrsus, ivy-twisted dart,
        into their hands. For here my mother's sisters
        spread the slanderous lie that Dionysus
30   was not—as Semelê claimed—the son of Zeus,
        but that she gave her maidenhead to some mere man,
        and laid the blame of fatherhood on Zeus.
        Her wedlock they called a lie made up by Cadmus,
        fiction to hide his daughter's fall from grace,
35   which Semelê spread abroad, to Zeus's fury,
        for which he killed her.
           For this I drove the sisters from their homes,
        forcing them, brainstruck, to wander on the hills
        and made them wear my Bacchic orgies' gear.

5. *Ismenus, Dircê:* The rivers of Thebes.   17. *Bactria . . . Medes:* Bactria, roughly northern Afghanistan, was part of the ancient Persian empire. The Medes are here equated with the Persians.

40   Then each last woman of the Cadmean race
        I drove in frenzy out from her quiet home.
        Now they are banded with old Cadmus' daughters,
        resting beneath green pines, by soaring cliffs.
            This city, uninitiate in my rites,
45   must learn, like it or not, that I am here
        to show my mother's glory, manifesting
        myself to men as the god she bore to Zeus.
        Cadmus himself abandons pride and power
        to Pentheus, child of one of these, his daughters.
50   Pentheus, a godless man, resists my ways;
        he drives me off from his solemnities;
        he skips all mention of me in his prayers.
        Well, for all this I soon shall make it clear
        to him and all the people of the Thebans
55   that I indeed was born divine.
            That well and truly done, my steps will turn
        to another land, another epiphany.
        And if the Theban city takes up arms
        and tries to drive the maenads from its hills,
60   I and my Bacchae will meet force with force [Figure 11.5].
        With this in mind, I have taken mortal shape,
        disguising myself beneath a human form.
        (Dionysus turns and calls offstage)

FIGURE 11.5 A maenad and a satyr, interior of Attic wine cup, c. 480 BC. The satyr, with erect phallus, attacks the maenad, who strikes his genitals with her thyrsus, a fennel stalk wrapped with ivy leaves. She wears the leopard skin around her shoulders and has ivy in her hair. The satyr has a pug nose and horse's tail. Although satyrs often attack maenads, they are never successful. Their sexual excitement is emblematic of their being filled with the god.   (Staatliche Antiken-sammlugen und Glypthek, Munich; Erich Lessing/ Art Resource, New York)

You women who left Tmolus,° Lydia's wall of defense,
band of my devotees, whom I brought from barbarian homelands
65   to follow my steps and travel along with me in my mission,
take up your pipes and your drums, your native Phrygian music,
inventions of me, Dionysus, and of Rhea, Great Mother of gods.
Come here—beat out your rhythms around the palace of Pentheus.
Let the whole city of Cadmus know well that my maenads have come.
70   I for my part will return to the shady woods of Cithaeron,
the haunt of my Bacchae, to join with them in ecstatical dancing.

63. *Tmolus*: A mountain in Lydia.

After an interlude in which the aged prophet Tiresias and the creaky old king
Cadmus, founder of Thebes, ludicrously make ready for the cult by decking themselves in fawnskins and ivy, the prurient scoffer Pentheus enters. He suspects that
the women have run away to indulge in uninhibited sex:

[208]   *Pentheus*   I happened to be absent from the country,
when word was brought that strange new-fangled cults
210   had seized the city: Women had left their homes
for bogus bacchanals, held in the dimlit hills,
in which they worshiped this new deity,
this so-called Dionysus, with indecent dances.
They tell me, right in the middle of their covens,
215   they keep the wine bowls constantly refilled.
First one, then another woman sneaks off to the woods,
to the nest she serves for some young lusty fellow.
All this beneath the mask of maenad priestesses—
of Aphrodite, rather more than Bacchus.
220   All that I catch are handcuffed and given over
to warders, who keep them in the city jail.
Of course, some get away. I'll catch them yet
when I turn my bloodhounds loose into the hills—
Ino and Actaeon's mother (you know, Autonoë)
225   even Agavê, Echion's wife, my mother.
I'll chain them up in good strong iron cages
and end their Bacchic nonsense once and for all.
They also say some wandering Lydian guru
has just appeared. He has curly yellow hair
230   that stinks of perfume. In his wine-dark eyes there glows
all Aphrodite's magic. Day and night
he always hangs around, proffering his cult
of ecstasy to all these silly girls.
Just let me catch him here inside the palace!
235   I'll end his pounding with his leaf-topped staff.
I'll stop that showoff tossing of his hair
by chopping his pretty head from off his body.

That fellow, they call him Dionysus?
That's the one Zeus once sewed up in his thigh?
240   the one who was vaporized by thunderbolts
along with his mother, self-styled "bride of Zeus"?
Whoever he is, he well deserves the gallows
for making such a blasphemous claim as that.

Tiresias and Cadmus attempt to persuade Pentheus to accept the new reli-gion, but he has no patience for their argument and orders that the stranger promulgating the new religion be arrested. As Pentheus goes into the palace, Tiresias and Cadmus go to the hills to join the Bacchae. A servant enters, lead-ing Dionysus in bonds. Pentheus, who does not recognize the prisoner as the god himself, comes back on the stage and questions the stranger in a debate. Critics call such exchanges the *agôn*, or contest, a regular feature in Athenian tragedy:

[451]   *Pentheus*   All right, untie his hands. He's caught in a net.
He may be nimble, but I don't think he'll escape.
You're quite good looking, stranger, to some women,
and they, of course, are why you've come to Thebes.
[455]   Your hair is nice and long, not like a wrestler's,
but curling sexily beside your chin.
Your skin—peaches and cream, untouched by sunburn,
but pale from hunting love in amorous shadows.
First question: just who are you? what's your family?
460   *Dionysus*   No need to shout. You want a simple answer.
No doubt you've heard of Tmolus' flowery hills?
Pentheus   Yes, it encloses the great city of Sardis.
Dionysus   That's where I come from. Lydia is my home.
Pentheus   And where did you get these rites you bring to Greece?
465   *Dionysus*   Dionysus, Zeus's son, passed through our land.
Pentheus   You have some sort of Zeus who breeds new gods?
Dionysus   No, the same one who wedded Semelê here.
Pentheus   Did he recruit in a dream or face to face?
Dionysus   We viewed each other when he gave his rites.
470   *Pentheus*   Tell me the form of these mysterious rites.
Dionysus   To uninitiates they may not be told.
Pentheus   What value do they have for worshipers?
Dionysus   Their worth is priceless—but you may not hear.
Pentheus   Hocus-pocus, to arouse my interest!
475   *Dionysus*   Your cynicism makes you mock our rites.
Pentheus   You saw the god so clearly—just how did he look?
Dionysus   However he pleased. I didn't make his choice.
Pentheus   You ducked that nicely, making no real reply.
Dionysus   Speak sense to a fool, he thinks it's only nonsense.
480   *Pentheus*   Is Thebes the first place where you brought this god?
Dionysus   All other lands already dance in his rites.
Pentheus   Their wits are feebler far than those of Greeks.

	Dionysus	In this, far stronger. All laws are not the same.
	Pentheus	Do you worship him by night, or in the day?
485	*Dionysus*	Mostly by night, for darkness fosters awe.
	Pentheus	But night seduces women into vice.
	Dionysus	If one should seek by day, she'd find it then.
	Pentheus	You deserve punishment for your clever speech.
	Dionysus	And you for your ignorant slander of the god.
490	*Pentheus*	This Bacchic priest speaks rash and slippery words.
	Dionysus	What dreadful torture, then, do you propose?
	Pentheus	First, to cut off your pretty curling hair.
	Dionysus	My locks are sacred; I tend them for the god.

(Pentheus cuts off the prisoner's hair.)

| | *Pentheus* | Hand over that thyrsus you've got in your hands. |
| 495 | *Dionysus* | You take it from me. It belongs to the god. |

(Pentheus snatches it.)

	Pentheus	We'll chain your body up in a cell, inside.
	Dionysus	The god himself will free me when I ask.
	Pentheus	Only when all your Bacchae join your prayer.
	Dionysus	No, he is close at hand and sees me suffer.
500	*Pentheus*	Really? Just where? My eyes don't see a thing.
	Dionysus	Right here with me. Your folly makes you blind.
	Pentheus	(*to jailer*) Take him away for mocking Thebes and me.
	Dionysus	I warn you triflers, trifle not with me!
	Pentheus	I warn you that I will, for I am the stronger.
505	*Dionysus*	What gives you power? What are you doing? Who are you?
	Pentheus	Pentheus, Agavê's son, fathered by Echion.
	Dionysus	A name of evil omen.° It fits you well.
	Pentheus	Take him away. Chain him up by the horse troughs.

Let him enjoy the black and murky darkness,
510 and dance his fill. Those women he brought with him,
accomplices in crime—perhaps we'll stamp them out,
perhaps we'll keep their hands from thumping drums,
by using them as slaves, bound to their looms.

507. *of evil omen*: Because Pentheus' name appears to mean "man of grief."

The guard takes away Dionysus, but a clap of thunder fills the sky, the earth quakes, the palace collapses. Dionysus reappears, freed of his bonds. Pentheus, in a towering rage, enters from the ruins of the palace and upbraids the stranger as a messenger arrives from Cithaeron, the mountains behind Thebes. The messenger describes what he witnessed there:

[678]	*Messenger*	Our herds of cattle were setting out to pasture,
		plodding their way to the hills, just when the sun
680		began to shed his rays to warm the land. And as I looked,
		three bands of dancing women met my eye: Autonoë led one,

your mother Agavê the second, Ino the third.
Exhausted in body, they lay there fast asleep,
some resting heads against a fir tree's trunk,
685   some pillowed in oak-leaves, sprawling anyhow—
but all was decent, not the way you think!
Not one of them, drunken with wine or song,
went chasing Aphrodite through the bush.
Hearing the lowing of our horned beasts,
690   your mother first jumped up and gave a cry
to rouse their sluggish bodies up from sleep.
They wiped refreshing slumber from their eyes
and jumped up, wide awake, in ordered ranks—
young women, grannies, maidens yet unwed.
695   First they let down their hair upon their shoulders,
then fixed disheveled fawnskins with fresh ties
of snakes, which licked their cheeks. And some of them,
whose newborn children had been left at home,
picked up a fawn, or cub of an untamed wolf,
700   offering white milk from a still flowing breast,
then crowned the cub with ivy, oak, and yew.
One seized her thyrsus and with it struck a rock:
out sprang the dewy water's limpid spring.
Another thumped her staff upon the ground:
705   For her the god sent up a spring of wine.
And those who felt an urge for whiter drink
scratched at the earth: A stream of milk gushed up!
Sweet honey drippings poured from ivied thyrsi.
Had you been there yourself and seen all this,
710   you would now reverence the god you scorned.
Shepherds and cowherds muttered to each other,
discussing, arguing the wondrous things
the women were performing. One of us,
a city boy, blessed with a slippery tongue,
715   made this suggestion: "Hey, you who spend your days
here in these dark mysterious mountain glades,
how about snatching Agavê, Pentheus' mother,
from out the revels, to do the king a favor?"
We all thought this a fine idea, and hid
720   ourselves in ambush, crouched in undergrowth.
   When the moment came, each woman waved her thyrsus,
in sign of revel, and all with one voice called
on Iacchus, on Bromius,° son of Zeus.
The hills returned their cry, the beasts responded,
725   nothing could stay unmoved by their wild rush.
Agavê led them, close by where I hid.
I jumped out from my cover to bear her off,

723. *Iacchus, Bromius:* Iacchus, "Lord of Cries," an epithet drawn from Eleusinian cult, where Iacchus personified the shouting of the procession from Athens to Eleusis; Bromius, "roarer," was an epithet of Dionysus.

but she let out a shout: "My hunting hounds,
a pack of men dares to pursue our band.
730 So follow me, follow, the thyrsus be your sword!"
We took to our heels, and so escaped the fate
of being torn to pieces by the Bacchae.
A herd of cattle was browsing in the wood.
The women seized them with unweaponed hands.
735 And then—you could have seen one woman brandish
in either hand limbs of a bellowing calf.
Others would rip apart a heifer as trophy.
Then you would see its ribs, its legs, its hoofs,
tossed through the air, and, dangling from a fir tree,
740 dripping its life-blood to the gore-smeared earth.
Arrogant bulls that charged with slashing horns
were tripped to the ground by countless women's hands,
and stripped, O king, of skin and flesh before
you could blink the eyelids on your royal eyes.
745 A few brave peasants, stung to a valiant rage,
charged out against the arms the Bacchae bore.
I shudder, lord, to tell what happened next.
Their pointed spears drew not a drop of blood,
but the Bacchae, tossing thyrsi at their foe,
750 disabled some and forced the rest to flee—
women subduing men, through some god's aid.
Then back they came to the place from which they started,
to springs of milk and honey sent by the god.
They washed themselves, while tongues of dappled snakes
755 licked from their cheeks the spatterings of blood.
    Whoever, lord, he is, this deity
you must receive in Thebes. While all his powers
are great indeed, greatest of all, they say,
is this: He gave the sorrow-drowning wine
760 for us poor men. Without it, love could not survive
nor any other pleasure for our race.

Still, Pentheus is not persuaded. He summons his troops for action against the Bacchae, but Dionysus, casting a spell over Pentheus, proposes an alternative course:

[810] *Dionysus* Wait! Would you like to watch their gathering in the hills?
    Pentheus I would indeed, though it cost an enormous sum.
    Dionysus What makes you feel so eager for the sight?
    Pentheus Disgust at seeing all these women drunk.
    Dionysus Would you really enjoy a thing that so disgusts you?
815 *Pentheus* Yes, if I hid, unnoticed, under a tree.
    Dionysus Even if you sneak up they'll track you out.
    Pentheus That's true, they will. Your point is taken well.
    Dionysus Shall we get started? Are you ready for the road?
    Pentheus Yes, yes. You lead. I'm impatient with this delay.

820	*Dionysus*	Well then, conceal yourself in this linen gown.
	Pentheus	How's that? Must I now turn woman, man no more?
	Dionysus	If you don't, they'll kill you, knowing you're a man.
	Pentheus	You're right again. You think of everything.
	Dionysus	Dionysus shows me everything I know.
825	*Pentheus*	How can we make this scheme of yours succeed?
	Dionysus	I'll go now, inside, to help you with your dress.
	Pentheus	Dress? In a woman's dress? I will die of shame!
	Dionysus	What, you no longer want to watch the maenads?
	Pentheus	All right. Then what concealment hides my face?
830	*Dionysus*	First you must wear a wig, long curling hair.
	Pentheus	Yes. What's the second part of my disguise?
	Dionysus	A skirt down to your ankles and a bonnet.
	Pentheus	What else would you suggest, besides all this?
	Dionysus	A thyrsus in your hand, and a spotted fawnskin.
835	*Pentheus*	But this is women's gear. I'd die of shame!
	Dionysus	When you meet the Bacchae, blood will surely flow.
	Pentheus	Good! Should we first spy out the terrain?
	Dionysus	Yes, trickery is less a crime than murder.
	Pentheus	How can I pass unnoticed through the city?
840	*Dionysus*	We'll go through empty streets. I'll lead the way.
	Pentheus	Anything, so these women do not mock me.
		So in we go. I'll work out what is best.
	Dionysus	Just as you please. You're safe, with me at hand.
	Pentheus	Forward. Maybe I'll take up arms . . .
845		or else I'll do exactly as you say.

Pentheus and Dionysus go into the palace, then return, a ludicrous Pentheus
wearing a long dress, fawnskin, and blond wig, waving a thyrsus:

[912]	*Dionysus*	You who are so desirous of forbidden sights,
		so eager for things you should never want to see—
		yes, Pentheus, I mean you—come here, before the house
915		and let us look you over, dressed as a woman,
		a maenad, yes, one of the crazed Bacchantes,
		to spy on your own mother and her attendants.
		My, you're as pretty as one of Cadmus' daughters!
	Pentheus	I see—do I really see it?—not one, but a double sun.
920		And look—a pair of Thebeses, the seven-gated town.
		And you—why, you're a bull who leads me forward!
		whose horns have sprouted out upon your head.
		—have you ever been a beast?—I'm sure that you're a bull.
	Dionysus	The god is here beside you, your onetime enemy,
925		now your good friend, who makes you see the truth.
	Pentheus	How do I look to you? Am I not just like Ino,
		or do I more resemble Agavê, my own dear mother?
	Dionysus	Looking at you, I think I'm looking right at them.
		But wait: this lock of hair has come astray,
930		not quite the way I tucked it in your scarf.
	Pentheus	Oh dear! I must have shaken it too hard,

when I tried out my dance's wilder steps.
Dionysus   There now, I'll put it back where it belongs,
like a good maid. Just hold your head up straight.
935 *Pentheus*   Yes, you fix it. Whatever you say, I'll do.
Dionysus   Your sash is loose, and makes your dress's folds
a bit uneven, down there at the hem.
Pentheus   Yes, so they are. But only on the right.
On the other side it falls just to the foot.
940 *Dionysus*   You'll understand how good is my advice,
when, in surprise, you see the modest Bacchae.
Pentheus   Should I hold the thyrsus up in my right hand,
or in the left, to make me look more like them?
Dionysus   The right. Be sure you raise it up in time
945 with your right foot. I'm glad you've changed your mind!
Pentheus   Won't I be strong enough to lift Cithaeron
with all its glades, and with the Bacchae too?
Dionysus   Of course, if you wanted. Your thought was all unsound,
till now, when you think exactly as you should.
950 *Pentheus*   Will we need crowbars? or are my hands enough
to rip off cliffs cracked by my arms and shoulders?
Dionysus   You surely won't destroy the home of the nymphs,
or the place where Pan relaxes with his pipes!
Pentheus   You're right. Mere courtesy demands restraint
955 in fighting women. I'll hide beneath a tree.
Dionysus   You're best concealed, in the most concealing way,
coming concealed as a spy upon these maenads.
Pentheus   That way, of course, I'll catch the little pigeons
billing and cooing, snuggled in their nests.
960 *Dionysus*   Exactly, you are sent to guard their morals.
You'll catch them at it—unless they catch you first.

After a choral song, a messenger enters and describes in gory detail the death of Pentheus. When the king and Dionysus, he reports, had gone out to view the maenads, Pentheus could not see them clearly. Dionysus magically made a pine tree bend low, and Pentheus climbed up on it. Dionysus let the tree snap upright, then disappeared:

[1078] *Messenger*   From heaven a voice resounded (Dionysus', I suppose)—
"Bacchae, I bring your enemy and mine,
1080 who mocks our sacred orgies. Avenge our wrongs."
So spoke the voice. A holy light flashed out
to paralyze for a time all heaven and earth.
The air fell silent, the forest leaves fell still,
the very beasts were quiet in the wood.
1085 The women heard the voice, but only faintly,
and stood erect, with darting, waiting eyes.
Again the summons of the god rang out.
This time Cadmus' daughters heard its call,
the voice of Bacchus. Swift as rocketing doves,

1090   they raced with drumming feet in hot pursuit . . .
      (Agavê directs the women to tear down the tree with their bare hands.)
      Crying in terror, down from his high perch,
      down to the earth poor Pentheus plunged,
      now fully conscious that his end was near.
      His mother first began this pious murder,
1095   flinging herself upon her fallen son.
      He tore away his headdress, in the hope
      that poor Agavê might restrain her hand.
      His hand reached out to touch his mother's cheek.
      "See, mother!" he implored, "I am your son,
1100   your Pentheus, whom you bore to Echion.
      Pity me, mother, do not slay your child,
      whatever, in your eyes, my guilt may be."
         She only rolled deluded bloodshot eyes,
      demented, stung by madness from the god.
1105   She caught his left arm, just below the shoulder,
      and bracing against his ribs, she ripped it out
      from the shoulder socket, with violence not her own,
      for the god had given power to her hand.
      Ino wrenched hard at Pentheus' other arm,
1110   and tore his flesh apart. The other Bacchae,
      led by Autonoë, rushed up for the kill.
         Then everything became one screaming clamor [Figure 11.6]:
      the poor man groaning while his breath remained,
      the women screaming in triumph. One waved an arm,
1115   one waved a foot, whose boot hung by one lace.
      His ribs were stripped of flesh by grasping claws.
      Each bloodied hand played a mad game of ball
      with Pentheus' flesh.
         His mangled body lay, scattered and torn,
1120   part on the jagged flints, part in the bushes,
      a gruesome task to gather up to bury.
      His wretched head fell to Agavê's hands.
      She waved it proudly, on her thyrsus' point,
      believing it a mountain lion's head.
1125   Leaving her sisters with the maenad crew,
      she marched, exulting, from Cithaeron's height,
      down to the city walls, hailing the Bacchic god
      as "fellow hunter," "comrade in the chase,"
      and "glorious in victory."

EURIPIDES, Bacchae (SELECTIONS)

     Agavê enters with the head of Pentheus stuck on her thyrsus. Cadmus and attendants carry the mangled body of Pentheus on a stretcher. Agavê boasts of her exploits and offers the head of Pentheus to her father, who gradually brings her back to her senses. With horror she realizes what she has done. Dionysus appears and sentences Cadmus and his daughters to exile, although

FIGURE 11.6 The dismemberment of Pentheus, a wall painting from Pompeii, AD 54–79. Agavê, on the left, seizes her son's hair and prepares to strike him with her thyrsus, which she holds poised in her right hand, while on the right Autonoë, Pentheus' aunt, seizes his arm to pull it from his shoulder. The other Theban women swarm in, carrying thyrsi and rocks to kill the intruder. (Pompeii VI; Museo Archeologico Nazionale, Naples; Scala/Art Resource, New York)

Cadmus and his wife eventually are admitted to a blessed life in Elysium (see Chapter 12).

Euripides' theme in the *Bacchae* was old. We know of several earlier treatments in plays now lost. In his play Euripides joined the wild irrationality of ancient Phrygian and Thracian religion with the theological skepticism of his own contemporary Athens. Posthumously produced, probably in 405 BC, the play won Euripides his last of only five first prizes, from a jury of men like those who, a few years later, would condemn Socrates to death for impiety and for corrupting the young. **(For the complete *Bacchae*, go to http://bacchicstage.wordpress.com/euripides/bacchae/).**

DIONYSUS' JOURNEY TO THE LAND OF THE DEAD

Several stories, less well known but no less important, describe the end of Dionysus' career on earth. Having introduced his cult to Greece and to the East as far as India, he prepared to ascend to Olympus to take his place with the other immortals. But he did not want to leave his mother, Semelê, in the house of Hades, and he decided to bring her back.

He himself did not know the way, but in Argos he encountered a shepherd who led him to the gloomy, bottomless Alcyonean lake near the swamp of Lerna. Plunging into its depths, the god presently emerged in the lower world and persuaded Hades to restore his mother. By the time they reached the upper world, the shepherd had died. Dionysus selected a branch of a fig tree and from it carved a phallus, the first of the many found all over the world, which he placed on the grave.

When they came to Olympus, Dionysus changed his mother's name to Thyonê, "she who receives the sacrifice." Although born a mortal, she became a god like her son, and they joined the other Olympians.

Observations: The Myths of Dionysus

Dionysus' name is perplexing. The *Dio-* part derives from the same Indo-European root as the name *Zeus*, but *-nysus* has not been explained. It might mean "son," so that Dionysus would be the "son of Zeus." It might also refer to the otherwise unknown place whence come the "nymphs of Nysa," so that Dionysus would be the "god from Nysa." Again, *Nysos* could simply be another name for Dionysus himself, which would explain why his followers sometimes were called *Nysai*, as the Bacchae were named from Bacchus. The "nymphs of Nysa," then, would mean simply "the followers of Dionysus."

In any event, many of the names and words associated with Dionysus are of Eastern origin. Some scholars have thought that Semelê's name, certainly non-Greek, is the same as *Zemelô*, a Phrygian name for the mother-goddess attested on inscriptions. If so, in the Greek myth an Eastern goddess has been downgraded into a mortal woman involved in an adulterous intrigue, a figure of religious importance recast in an all-too-human role. There are numerous parallels to such downgrading of gods into imperfect mortals in Greek myth. The word *thyrsus* may be related to Hittite *tuwarsa*, "vine." Even the name *Bacchus* itself may be derived from the Lydian name of the god: A Lydian inscription equates the name *bakivali* with Dionysus.

The myths of Dionysus also suggest Eastern origins. The god is usually said to have arrived in Greece from Thrace, the coastal area between Macedonia and the Hellespont, or from Phrygia and Lydia farther east, the hill country in Anatolia between the west coast of Asia Minor and the ancient centers of Hittite power in central Anatolia. This tradition accords nicely with the apparent Eastern origin of *Semelê, thyrsus,* and *Bacchus*. Certainly Dionysiac or similar religions were strong in Thrace and Phrygia in the Classical Period.

Scholars once thought that the tradition of Dionysus' Eastern origin reflected a historical fact, the late introduction of his cult into Greece from Asia Minor about 800 BC, at the beginning of the historical period. They pointed out that Dionysus had only a small role in Homer's epic poems, composed about 800 BC. However, the name Dionysus has now been found on fragmentary Linear B tablets from Late Bronze Age Pylos (thirteenth century BC), perhaps in association with wine. Important myths about him are localized in Orchomenus, in

Thebes, and on the Argive plain, all Bronze Age strongholds. And although it is true that Homer has little interest in Dionysus, several passing references prove that he was familiar with Dionysiac cult. For these reasons, scholars now consider Dionysus to be a god who was known and worshiped in Greece at an early date. His religion no doubt underwent revivals from time to time and was certainly influenced by foreign cults, but he was established in Greece long before the beginning of the historical period.

This conclusion leads to an important question of interpretation. The tales of his travels to Egypt and India might be etiological to explain the spread of vine-growing throughout the world, and stories of military conquest could serve as propaganda for the god, who claimed universal sway. But why is Dionysus portrayed as a strange and foreign god, if he was known in Greece at such an early date? Let us return to this question after first considering the general character of his myths and his role in Greek religion.

Many elements in the story are familiar from folktale. For example, "the short-sighted wish" appears in Semelê's request to see Zeus in his full glory and Midas' desire to have all that he touches turn to gold. Hera, who persecutes her stepson Dionysus, acts as "the vengeful stepmother." A folktale motif appears in the story of Proetus and Melampus: "a portion of the kingdom as reward," in Proetus' payment to Melampus for curing his daughters of madness. As in many other Greek myths, these folktale elements make the story entertaining.

To move to deeper levels of interpretation, we recall that in religion Dionysus was first a god of fertility, closely associated with certain plants and animals. Many of his epithets refer to power over fruitfulness in plant life and over the moisture that makes plant life possible. In some areas Dionysus was known as "he of the trees" (*dendritês*). The fig, from the lushness and sweetness of its rich, seed-filled fruit, was thought exemplary of the god. It was from a fig branch that Dionysus carved the phallus he implanted on the grave of the shepherd who guided him to the lake of the underworld. The pine, which remains green in winter and oozes a rich pitch used in the making of Greek wine, was also close to Dionysus. A pinecone, filled with seeds, was mounted on one kind of thyrsus.

From the juice of the grape comes wine, an "enspirited" drink that contains, through a mysterious transformation, something wonderful, unique, divine. Ivy is complementary to the vine as emblem of the god. On artistic representations, ivy entwines the god's hair, or he is worshiped as a staff entwined by ivy, surmounted by a mask (Figure 11.7). Like Dionysus, ivy is tenacious, strong, and luxuriant in growth, and remains green all winter.

In the animal kingdom, Dionysus loved creatures noted for their strength, ferocity, or sexual vitality. Zeus changes the child Dionysus into a goat, an animal whose male is renowned for its sexual power and whose female yields most of the necessities of life—milk and cheese, wool, hide, and meat. But more often he appears as a bull. The Thracian king Lycurgus pursued Dionysus into the sea with an ox-goad, appropriate if Dionysus is himself the bull. In Euripides' *Bacchae*, Pentheus falls into a trance and mistakes the god for a bull. The followers of Dionysus sometimes wore horns and were even called "bullherders."

FIGURE 11.7 The central figure, before which is an altar, is a wooden pillar draped with robes to the top of which is fastened a clay mask of Dionysus. Offerings to the god are pushed onto the vines behind the figure. The women dance to the sound of the double flute (really an oboe), said to inspire ecstasy. (Staatliche Museen, Berlin; Bildarchiv Preußischer Kulturbesitz/Art Resource, New York)

Finally, Dionysus was close to cats, especially the lion and the panther. Like the god, they are fecund, lithe, beautiful, and terrible. In art he is often shown in their company.

In his role as a fertility-god, we can compare Dionysus with Demeter. Demeter gives the grain, precious to human beings, but by nature is dry and passive. Dionysus represents a wet and active substance, the "juice" that gives life to things. Water is the natural element closest to Dionysus. Lycurgus drives him into the sea to the protective arms of the sea-goddess Thetis. Dionysus descends through the Alcyonean lake to bring back his mother from the underworld. His encounter with the Etruscan pirates takes place at sea, and Ino, his nurse and victim, becomes a sea-goddess. It is fitting that this watery god would also be associated with the wet components of living things: semen, sap, milk, and blood. The coincidence in color between wine and blood no doubt aided the identification, in Dionysus, of a single power that makes plants bloom and die and animals breathe, procreate, and kill.

Dionysus' associations with both the life force and with death give him the appearance of a dying god of the Dumuzi type (see Chapter 10). Like Attis and Osiris, he can be viewed as a companion to the fertility-goddess. He was the son of Semelê (compare the Phrygian *Zemelô*), an initiate of Cybelê, and husband to Ariadnê, whose name, "very holy one," suggests her own original divinity. Several stories tell of his death and rebirth. He is "killed" by the thunderbolt that destroys Semelê, then "born again" from Zeus's thigh. He descends to the underworld to find his mother, then returns with her to the realm of the living.

Departure and return, death and resurrection—these are recurring themes in Dionysiac myth.

But what makes Dionysus unique in Greek myth are the many stories of resistance to him and his cult and of the vengeance he takes on those who reject him. Lycurgus scattered the maenads and drove Dionysus himself into the sea, then went mad and pruned off the limbs of his child. The Minyads suffered horribly for their resistance and feasted on their own children. The Proetids experienced a similar fate. The Etruscan pirates, who failed at first to recognize the god's power, went insane and threw themselves into the sea. King Pentheus, who tried to arrest the god, grows delirious and marches eagerly to his own doom. Agavê, Ino, and Autonoë deny the god at first, then dismember Pentheus in a fit of Dionysiac madness. No one in these stories ever blames Dionysus for taking revenge on his opponents. The Greeks did not question Dionysus' right to destroy any more than they questioned the right of a thunder blast to level a building.

Those who resist Dionysus are not the only ones who suffer madness and destruction: Even those who welcome and assist him may come to a bad end. His mother, Semelê, was burned to ashes. Ino, his nurse, went insane and boiled her child alive. When Dionysus comes, disaster follows. He can bring death and madness to those who favor him as well as to those who resist.

Dionysus brings destruction, but paradoxically resurrection and life as well. After leaping into the sea, Ino becomes a beneficent sea-goddess. Semelê, although burned to a crisp, eventually joins Dionysus and the other gods on Mount Olympus. Called "the destroyer of men" and "he who eats raw flesh," he is also "the god of many joys," "the giver of riches," "the benefactor." Like living nature itself, this contradictory god is the master of both life and death, carrying his creatures to an inevitable destruction, then bringing new life. Madness is not merely punishment; it is the god's gift to those who follow him, offering the loss of the burdensome sense of self.

Not surprisingly, this god of madness and destruction was represented as "foreign" in the myths of the ancient Greeks. To the rational, conscious mind, which values order and balance above passion and spontaneity, Dionysus is the antithesis of all that is good and right. Reluctance to embrace this foreign being, unwillingness to acknowledge his power, is an understandable human response. To many ancient Greeks (who invented rationalism), he must have seemed by his very nature to be something especially strange, something new. Wherever Dionysus and his cult originated, the persistent portrayal of him as a new god, and likewise the many stories of the resistance he encountered, reflects the Greeks' aversion to the violent, irrational side of human existence, their reluctance, and ours, to accept the power and even legitimacy of unreason.

THE CULT OF DIONYSUS

Like the cult of Demeter, that of Dionysus is reflected in the myths told about him. The evidence we have makes clear that the Dionysian religion was quite different from those devoted to other ancient deities. A great gulf separated the original

Olympian gods from human beings, symbolized by the poetic conception of Zeus and his court ruling from the high peaks of Olympus. These gods were known through their works, helpful or harmful, but were rarely directly manifest to ordinary human beings. Dionysus was different. The Greeks believed they could feel his presence directly, and the cultivation of this experience was a central focus of his religion. Many features of the myths of Dionysus are best understood as reflections of his cult.

He was "the god who comes," and the myths tell of his sudden and violent arrival in Greek cities. The intense emotion felt by individual followers must have come in a similarly abrupt and decisive manner. The god's presence in his followers was called *enthousiasmos*, "being filled with the god" (the origin of our "enthusiasm"). His followers experienced *ekstasis*, "standing outside oneself" (hence our "ecstasy"). When Dionysus was present, his devotees lost their sense of personal identity and became one with the god.

So strong was this sense of oneness that the follower was called Bacchus too. With the loss of identity came a willingness to transcend ordinary standards of decent and rational conduct. Appropriately, Dionysus was *lysios*, "deliverer": Through their enthusiastic and ecstatic communion with the god, his devotees were temporarily released from the doldrums of everyday life and united with a divine, cosmic force.

The presence of a crowd of witnesses fostered the experience of Dionysian ecstasy, as suggested in myth by the band of followers who always surround the god, the maenads and satyrs. Continuous dancing to the beating of drums and the playing of flutes, and the consumption of wine, led devotees to direct experience of the god. So did the communal "tearing apart" (*sparagmos*) of an animal and the "eating of raw flesh" (*ômophagia*).

In prehistoric times this practice may have taken a cannibalistic form, with human beings as victims. The god's crazed followers tear Pentheus limb from limb (although do not actually eat him). Ino boils her son in a pot, and the Minyads eat their own children. The myths no doubt exaggerate the more sensational forms of the cult—cannibalism and human sacrifice were abhorrent by the Archaic and Classical periods. Still, we have inscriptional evidence that Dionysus' followers really did practice the "eating of raw flesh" as late as the Hellenistic Period.

The cult of Dionysus appealed especially to women, whose social responsibilities were to preserve the stability of the family. In myth Dionysus is surrounded by women: his nurse, Ino; the nymphs of Nysa; the maenads; and his wife, Ariadnê. The nymphs of Nysa in particular, as nourishers and followers of the god, were mythic models for the bands of female devotees. Although Euripides (who liked to defy his audience's expectations) describes the Bacchae's behavior as chaste, sexual profligacy was undoubtedly a feature of the real religion. It is not surprising that Hera, protectress of the family, would oppose the raging god who excited married women to madness and caused them to forget their duty to husband, family, and community.

Greek and Roman religions in general lacked creeds and claimed little moral authority, but they did develop local priesthoods, which eventually became integral parts of the institutions of the state. In this way the savage features of Dionysiac religion disappeared from the festivals of the Classical Period. Nevertheless, on several occasions the worship of Dionysus became a political threat. In Rome his cult grew to such proportions during the long and painful war with Carthage that in 186 BC an alarmed senate, after many executions, brought it under severe restrictions.

Early Christians viewed Dionysus as an evil demon. From his religion and the cult of Pan (Chapter 8) derive the goatish qualities of popular representations of the devil and the attribution to the devil of ritual indulgence in intoxicants and sex. Yet the Dionysian notion of the identification of god and worshiper ironically became central to Christian doctrine, sometimes expressed in terms similar to those in Dionysiac cults. For example, from the *Book of Common Prayer* of the Church of England (AD 1549, still used in churches of the Anglican Communion):

> Grant us therefore, gracious Lord, so to eat the flesh of thy dear Son Jesus Christ, and to drink his blood ... that we may evermore dwell in him and he in us.

Paradoxically, the pagan god of drunkenness and sexual license served as one model for the early Christians in their attempts to understand their own relationship to Jesus of Nazareth, who died and returned. Sarcophagi with scenes from the stories of Dionysus often were reused for Christian burials. In the eleventh or twelfth century AD an unknown Byzantine author, no doubt inspired by parallels between Pentheus' interrogation of Dionysus and Pontius Pilate's of Christ, put together a work called *Christus Patiens* (*The Suffering Christ*), the story of the crucifixion told as a Greek tragedy. *Christus Patiens* is made up entirely of lines taken from ancient drama, especially the *Bacchae*. Portions of the end of the *Bacchae*, lost from the manuscripts, have been recovered from this work.

DIONYSUS, GOD OF THE THEATER

Dionysus also played an important role in Greek culture through his association with the theater. Many of the best-known Greek myths are preserved as the plots of tragedies performed in his honor. Beginning in the sixth century BC, tragedies were performed at spring festivals of Dionysus in Athens, especially the City Dionysia, probably reorganized in the mid–sixth century BC by the popular tyrant Pisistratus. During the City Dionysia, held on consecutive days in the Theater of Dionysus on the south slopes of the Acropolis (Figure 11.8), each of three tragedians presented a group of three tragedies and one satyr play. The satyr play (a burlesque of a mythic theme) had a chorus of satyrs. On a fourth day, comedies were performed, a genre noted for ribaldry, obscenity, and verbal license. As a public service, a wealthy citizen paid for the costs of production. Some elements in Greek drama seem to be traceable to the cult of Dionysus, in whose honor the festivals were held, but more than a hundred years of intensive scholarship have been unable to clarify the precise relationship between the religious cult of Dionysus and the literary form of Athenian tragedy.

FIGURE 11.8 The Theater of Dionysus in Athens, built on the southern slope of the Acropolis. All extant Greek tragedies were performed in this theater. The horseshoe-shaped orchestra, constructed in the Roman Period, has replaced the original round "dancing place," or *orchêstra*. Foundation stones from the ancient stage building are visible behind the *orchêstra*.   (Author's photo)

PERSPECTIVE 11.2
NIETZSCHE'S *THE BIRTH OF TRAGEDY*

The figure of Dionysus played a prominent role in the writings of the influential German classicist and philosopher Friedrich Nietzsche (1844–1900), particularly in *The Birth of Tragedy out of the Spirit of Music,* an early work (1871) first published in German in which Nietzsche sharply criticized the prevailing view of Greek art and civilization. Before Nietzsche, Greek culture was understood as embodying the calm, rational values of balance and harmony. Greek art was worth studying and emulating, people thought, because it embodied "a noble simplicity and a quiet grandeur," as art historian Johann Winckelmann wrote in the eighteenth century. According to Winckelmann, Apollo was a perfect expression of these ideals. But Nietzsche's analysis of the origin of tragedy led him to a different view, that the creative spirit of the Greeks was Dionysus, who represented wild, exuberant emotion, the desire to break with convention, the longing to unite ecstatically with one's fellows and with nature itself.

Nietzsche used classical Greek tragedy to bolster his argument. Greek tragedy consists not only of dialogue between characters, but of commentary by the chorus. Nietzsche viewed dialogue as the Apollonian, intellectual part of the genre. Members of the historically earlier chorus, by contrast, were closely connected with the cult of Dionysus, he thought. According to Aristotle, the chorus was in origin dressed as half-goat, half-human satyrs, devotees of the god. Greek tragedy therefore reflects a tension between opposite forces, a synthesis of Apollonian and Dionysian principles and forces. If we overlook the Dionysian element and emphasize the Apollonian, Nietzsche argued, we reach a distorted understanding of Greek tragedy and of Greek culture itself.

Nietzsche considered his discovery of the Dionysian element in Greek culture to be important not only for classicists, but for everyone concerned with the rejuvenation of modern culture, dominated for too long by intellectuals who followed the rationalist Greek philosopher Socrates. What the modern world needed was a reawakening of the Dionysian spirit:

> Yes, my friends, believe with me in Dionysian life and the rebirth of tragedy. The age of the Socratic man is over. Put on wreaths of ivy, put the thyrsus into your hand, and do not be surprised when tigers and panthers lie down, fawning, at your feet. Only dare to be tragic men; for you are to be redeemed. You shall accompany the Dionysian pageant from India to Greece. Prepare yourselves for hard strife, but believe in the miracles of your god.

FRIEDRICH NIETZSCHE,

The Birth of Tragedy out of the Spirit of Music, SEC. 20

Nietzsche's later works developed the notion that modern Western culture, dominated by a "slave mentality" that Christianity fostered, was in a decadent condition and required radical reform. Proclaiming himself "the last disciple and initiate of the god Dionysus," Nietzsche, in *Beyond Good and Evil* (in German, 1886), called for the appearance of a new vitality, a new spirit embodied in a superior man who transcended the petty morality of bourgeois life, much as Dionysus crossed the boundaries of space and convention in Greek myth.

Nietzsche's life ended unhappily. He went insane after contracting syphilis and spent the last ten years of his life in the care of his family. In his deteriorated mental state, he identified more closely still with the Greek god who had inspired him. He sometimes signed his confused, incoherent letters with the name *Dionysus*.

FIGURE 11.9 A half-chorus of dancing youths, on an Attic vase for mixing wine, c. 500–480 BC, probably illustrating a lost play of Aeschylus, the *Youths,* older than any surviving Greek tragedy (our oldest is Aeschylus' *Persians,* 472 BC). Aeschylus' "youths" were followers of Dionysus and, in the story, may have had something to do with the punishment of Lycurgus. Their arms are outstretched as they dance barefoot toward a typically stepped altar, an important permanent prop in the theater of Dionysus (probably a stone outcrop in the orchestra). They wear light masks and embroidered outfits with a similar design. A suppliant sits on the altar.   (Antikenmuseum Basel und Sammlung Ludwig, Basel)

The origin of tragedy may depend more on literary invention and politics than religion. In discussing the origins of tragedy, Aristotle noted that a man named **Thespis** (late sixth century BC, none of whose works survive) added to a preexisting chorus, sung and danced by a group, "a prologue and a speech." We may interpret his remark as a remembrance that as a literary form tragedy was the invention of a single man, a new way to tell a story.

Before tragedy, characters in myth were described from the outside, in the third person, the way Homer tells a story. This was the natural form of storytelling at the aristocratic symposium. Thespis' innovation was to have an actor take on the role of a mythical character and speak in the first person as that character. The chorus, too, consisting of perhaps twelve dancers, always speaks as a character in a dramatic situation (Figure 11.9).

Aristotle also tells us that Thespis introduced "the first actor," by which he must mean someone speaking in the first person who presented a crisis in the career of a mythic figure, perhaps a moment of fateful decision. Thespis' innovations—and the use of masks—made possible the presentation on stage of visible, direct conflict between characters prominent in traditional tales. Later, says Aristotle, Aeschylus added a second actor and lessened the role of the chorus, and Sophocles added the third actor.

Thespis must have made his fateful invention some time in the reign of the Athenian tyrant Pisistratus, perhaps around 530 BC. To please the *dêmos*, the Athenian "people" from whom Pisistratus derived important political support, Pisistratus reformed an old festival of Dionysus and made of it something popular and well attended: Dionysus was a god of the *dêmos*. Pisistratus seems to have sponsored Thespis' new form of storytelling, one no longer confined to aristocratic symposia, but presented before all "the people" in the citywide drinking party that was the City Dionysia. In this way tragic drama was born, which Aristotle described as the "imitation of an action," the public presentation of personalities locked in conflict.

KEY NAMES AND TERMS

Dionysus, 271

Semelê, 273

Ino, 273

nymphs of Nysa, 274

Bacchae, 275

maenads, 275

thyrsus, 275

satyrs, 275

Silenus, 275

Midas, 275

Ariadnê, 277

Lycurgus, 277

Minyads, 278

Pentheus, 280

Thespis, 300

SOME ADDITIONAL ANCIENT SOURCES

Important accounts of the career of **Dionysus** are found in Apollodorus, 3.4.2–5.3 and Ovid, *Metamorphoses* 3.513–4.41, 4.389–419, 11.90–193. Various details—the destruction of **Pentheus**, the **Minyads**, pirates, **Midas**—are found in Hyginus, *Fabulae* 1–4, 7, 43, 129–134, 166–167, 169, 184, 191–192; Pausanias, 1.4.5. He is a comic figure in Aristophanes' *Frogs*. He is cited in innumerable places.

FURTHER READING CHAPTER 11
(SEE ALSO FURTHER READING TO CHAPTER 3)

Carpenter, Thomas H., and Christopher A. Faraone, eds., *Masks of Dionysus* (Ithaca, NY, 1993). The relationship of Dionysus to tragedy and his influence on the modern world; essays by leading scholars.

Dodds, E. R., introduction to *Euripides' Bacchae*, 2nd ed. (Oxford, UK, 1960). The best short discussion of the religion and myths of Dionysus.

———, *The Greeks and the Irrational* (Berkeley, CA, 1951; reprinted 1973). A classic investigation of the importance of unreason among the Greeks, the discoverers of reason.

Hart, Mary Louise, *The Art of Ancient Greek Theater* (exhibition catalog) (Malibu, CA, 2010). Considers the imprint that ancient Greek tragedy and comedy left on the visual

CHAPTER 12

MYTHS OF DEATH

ENCOUNTERS WITH THE UNDERWORLD

You will die and be silent. No memory will be left of you,
no regret when you are gone. You have never touched the Muses' flowers.
Shadowy forever in Death's realm,
you will be wafted on a ghost's fluttering wings,
one of the black dead.

SAPPHO, FRAGMENT 58 (DIEHL)

Τ HE GREATEST MYSTERY IN life is death, to which we are all subject. The Greeks, like all peoples, held complex attitudes toward death and the dead, and many stories reflect these attitudes. The myths of fertility we have just examined are concerned with the meaning of death and its place in the natural and human order. But death and the afterlife can be conceived in different ways. The Greeks' bleak conception of the afterlife (so different from that of the Egyptians, for example) contributed importantly to their conviction that happiness must be achieved in this world. Some mythical figures actually escaped death, either by becoming gods or by achieving immortality in a paradise somewhere at the edge of the world. A recurring theme in Greek myth is descent into and return from the world of the dead; we have already seen it in the myth of Demeter and Persephonê (Chapter 10). In this chapter we look at the principal ancient conceptions of death and the dead and examine mythical accounts of the underworld in Homer's *Odyssey* and Vergil's *Aeneid*.

THE GREEK VIEW OF DEATH

We think of death as a natural process, but the notion is modern. No doubt "natural death," as we conceive of it, was uncommon in the ancient world, and to the early Greeks and other early peoples death simply did not seem to come inevitably in the course of things. Death was caused by a hostile force from the natural world (a storm, an animal attack), from a human being (an enemy soldier), or from the invisible and inexplicable realm of gods, ghosts, magicians, and priests that we call disease. Unlike many modern peoples, the ancients attributed powers of choice and action to every-thing that exists and believed that human beings are the victims of these choices. Even when death is caused by such an obvious external event as a storm or a human or ani-mal attack, it could still be the result of a god's will or a malevolent spirit. In Homer's *Iliad* the gods stand beside their favorite heroes and guide their weapons or in other ways bring about the death of their opponents, and sometimes they themselves strike a blow directly. There were stories of men who never died, who had somehow escaped the dangerous forces that surround us and, for most, make death inevitable.

Any god could cause the death of a mortal, but one played a special role. **Hades** (**hā-dēz**), apparently "the unseen one," ruled over all the dead in the dark land he received when he and his brothers Zeus and Poseidon partitioned the world between them at the dawn of the present world-order. The dead, buried in the earth, are unseen, and that is where Hades rules. Thus he was also called **Pluto**, the "enricher," because from beneath the earth comes mineral and agricultural wealth. The Romans borrowed this latter Greek name, although they also called him Dis or Dives (**dī-vēz**), Latin for "rich." The Romans called the death god's realm Orcus, which probably means "the place that confines." Hades was often referred to by such epithets as *Polydegmôn*, "receiver of many," and *Polyxenos*, "host to many." Just as many people today avoid the words *die* and *death*, the Greeks often regarded Hades as a god too dangerous to call by his real name.

In spite of rationalist doubters, always important in Greece, most ancient Greeks believed that individual human beings continue to exist after death, although in an attenuated form. The buried body might decay or the cremated body turn to ash, but the soul survived as a sort of "image" (*eidolon*) dwelling thereafter in a separate realm ordinarily unseen by the living. Traditionally, the soul was associated with the breath, the invisible, barely tangible natural element that animates the living body. The con-nection can be seen in the derivation of the Greek and Latin words for "soul": The Greek *psychê* originally meant "breath," and the Latin *anima* is related to the Greek word *anemos*, "wind." From *psychê* comes psychology = "study of the soul" and psycho-analysis = "a breaking down of the soul." Similarly, the Latin word *spiritus*, "spirit," means "breath." In Sanskrit and Hebrew, too, the word for "wind" or "breath" (*atma* and *ruach*) is the same as that which designates the immaterial part of a human being.

No doubt the Greeks and Romans, like many other early peoples, observed that breathing is what distinguishes the living from the dead. We breathe continually for as long as we live—even in sleep, when we appear to be doing nothing else. The ancients logically inferred that breath is the basis for all the other activities of a living human being, such as sensing, thinking, and moving. The body performs these functions only as long as the breath or soul is present within it. The body is thus only the material part of a human being; the soul is the warm, invisible force that animates the body for the duration of the person's life. Such observations, when refined by Plato and Christian theologians, were to form the basis for deep philosophical speculations about the relationship of the human to the divine that remain of keen interest today.

Most peoples agree that the soul retains its airlike nature even after it has departed the body. The dead exist as ghosts, as bodiless breath-souls that are invisible, intangible, elusive, and ordinarily known only through their effects. We may dismiss the fear of ghosts as superstition (although some beware the cemetery at night!), but the existence of ghosts is a logical inference from the comparison of live with dead bodies. They are superficially the same, but one breathes, the other does not. Obviously the breath, the ghost, has escaped from the dead body and is abroad in the world, invisible, probably unhappy, no doubt vengeful for what has happened to it, and therefore very dangerous.

In the living body the ghost is present not only in the breath, but in the blood as well. (Consider the biblical injunction against eating blood: "For the life of the flesh is in the blood of it"; Leviticus 17.14.) That is why the shedding of blood brings death. Disembodied spirits usually lead a dark, shadowy existence in the underworld realm of Hades. Occasionally, however, they emerge to haunt the world of the living, especially when not properly "laid" through appropriate ritual. They appear in vivid dreams to family, friends, and allies, altogether a common experience today when someone close has died. In this way the ghosts assert their interest in the living and their power over them.

The need to remove the restless ghost from this world is nicely dramatized toward the end of Homer's *Iliad* when the ghost of Achilles' dead friend Patroclus appears to Achilles in a dream:

[61]   When lovely sleep came upon him, and his cares were gone,
        shed in sweetness all around him, weary in his fine limbs
        from running after Hector up to wind-swept Troy,
        then came to him the ghost of luckless Patroclus,
65   looking like himself in height and in eyes and in voice
        and dressed in the same clothes. He stood above Achilles' head
        and said, "You're sleeping? Have you forgotten me?
        When I was alive you remembered me, but dead you do not!
        Bury me swiftly, so that I pass within the gates of Hades.
70   For the ghosts keep me away, the phantoms of men done with their sufferings,
        and they will not allow me to join them on the other side of the river,
        and useless I wander through the wide-gated house of Hades."

                              HOMER, *Iliad* 23.61–74

Achilles does as Patroclus asks, burning him on a splendid pyre.

Ghosts are not always hostile, especially if you can get them on your side, when they work to protect human interests. Hesiod tells us that when the men of the Gold and Silver races died, they became beneficent spirits. More often, however, the ghosts of the dead aim to bring misfortune to human beings. They long to regain their former life above the ground and are envious of the living, whose bodies are intact and who still know the pleasures of food, sex, and wealth. Some are bent on revenge, as were the Greek **Erinyes** (e-**rin**-i-ēz), or Furies, mythical portrayals of the ghosts of slain members of one's own family. Precautions had to be taken to ensure the safety of the living without infringing on the rights of the often malevolent dead.

Many customs of ancient peoples originated as ways of warding off the angry, threatening ghosts. Some were designed to persuade the spirit that the survivors had not benefited from a person's death. Thus the person's most valued possessions, weapons and jewelry, were buried with the corpse or burned on the pyre. Dark and gloomy clothes showed the survivors' sadness, and the loosening of the hair and the scratching of the face and breasts by mourning women showed how they too suffered. To further mollify the envious and vindictive spirit, a special house might be built for the dead (the tomb), sometimes imitating the houses of the living. The Etruscans built elaborate houses underground for their dead, then buried the ashes in house-shaped urns. There the ghost might be happy, living on as a hero or honored family ancestor. Sometimes such ghosts would appear to well-wishers as a friendly snake (called *agathos daimon,* "good spirit"), eat honey cakes set out for it, then slither back into the tomb. Respect might also be given to the dead through mourning songs and eulogies and, at least in myth, even sexual companionship provided by the sacrifice of female slaves over the tombs of the mighty. Thus the Greeks cut the throat of the Trojan princess Polyxena over the tomb of Achilles (see Figure 21.5).

The famous pyramids of the ancient Egyptians were an exaggerated expression of ghost-cult, symbolic buildings in which dwelt the powerful ghost of the departed pharaoh. Because the breath-soul required a body to function properly, the Egyptians mummified the corpse (unlike Homer's Greeks, who ensured complete separation of soul from body by cremation). In case the corpse was nonetheless destroyed, the Egyptians made lifelike stone statues as substitute bodies, the origin of large-scale sculpture to imitate the human form. The early Greeks, copying Egyptian usage but not understanding it, put statues on graves.

One may banish the ghost by cutting the corpse to pieces, burning it on a pyre, or imprisoning it beneath a large stone (one origin of the tombstone). The feet of the baby Oedipus, exposed on the mountain to die, were pinned together to prevent the royal infant's ghost from walking. Because ghosts were considered stupid and readily confused, they might easily lose their way to the other world and thereafter bring misfortune to the living, who wish to be rid of them. Fortunately, Hermes was prepared to lead the dead to Hades' house and relieve this world of the burden of their presence. In this capacity, as we have seen, Hermes is called *psychopompos* (sik-o-**pom**-pus), "soul-guide" (see Figures 12.1 and 12.4).

A loud noise will frighten a ghost. The wails of mourners not only were flattering, but drove the ghosts away, as do noisemakers at weddings, where ghosts flock, attracted by the spectacle of human happiness and sexual pleasure that death has cruelly taken from them. Yet another strategy to appease the ghosts was to allow them one or two nights a year when they could mingle freely with the living. Thus ghosts were invited to the Athenian spring festival of the Anthesteria, "the festival of the sending up [of vegetation]," but on the last day expelled with the cry, "Out the door you go, you souls of the dead! The Anthesteria is finished!" A similar manner of thinking gives rise to our own Halloween ("All Hallows' Eve," the night before All Saints' Day, November 1), when the ghosts are allowed to come forth from their tombs and beg for food. If refused, they will do harm ("Trick or treat!").

PERSPECTIVE 12.1

VAMPIRES

In the popular imagination, the ghost's lust for blood, and the seemingly ineradicable human fear of ghosts, combines in the vampire, who is really dead but temporarily (or eternally) invigorated by drinking blood. The popularity and appeal of this mythical creature is proven by the recent success of Anne Rice's *Vampire Chronicles* (1976–2003), and especially by Stephenie Meyer's *Twilight* series, written for teenage girls. *Twilight* became an instant bestseller when published in 2005, quickly reaching the "New York Times" Bestseller list and remaining there for ninety-one weeks. In 2008, translated into thirty-seven languages, it sold more than seventeen million copies, the biggest seller of the year. The story concerns seventeen-year-old "Bella" Swan who moves to Forks, Washington, to find her life in danger when she falls in love with a vampire.

The English "vampire" derives from the Serbian word *vampir*, but what *vampir* means is not clear. After 1718, when Austria occupied northern Serbia, much Serbian folklore entered German literature, including stories about vampires. In most cases, vampires are the walking dead, often suicides, or they can be created by a malevolent spirit possessing a corpse, or by being bitten by a vampire. This undead creature is vengeful and jealous toward the living and needs the blood of the living to sustain its body's existence.

Vampires were usually said to be bloated and ruddy, purplish, or dark in color, attributed to their drinking of blood. Blood often seeped from the mouth and nose when the vampire was exposed in its coffin, its left eye open. Its teeth, hair, and nails may have grown since death. Over time, some attributes now regarded as essential were acquired. Fangs and vulnerability to sunlight appeared in the nineteenth century. The cloak was first used in stage productions of the 1920s.

Many practices were designed to prevent a recently dead loved one from turning into an undead revenant. Burying a corpse upside down was effective, or placing a wax cross on the corpse and a piece of pottery inscribed "Jesus Christ conquers." Other methods include severing the tendons at the knees or placing sand around the gravesite so that the vampire will be occupied all night counting the grains. Evidence that a vampire was active included the death of cattle, sheep, relatives, or neighbors.

Garlic was thought to be obnoxious to vampires, as well as a crucifix, rosary, or holy water. Vampires cannot walk on consecrated ground or cross running water. Vampires do not have a reflection and sometimes do not cast a shadow. A mirror placed outside will keep them away.

There are various ways to kill a vampire, but a stake through the heart usually works. Sometimes the head is buried between the feet, behind the buttocks, or away from the body, which will drive the soul away. In a recently opened burial from the sixteenth century, near Venice, archaeologists found a brick forced into the mouth of a female corpse, evidently from a vampire-slaying ritual. For stubborn cases the body can be dismembered, the pieces burned, mixed with water, and given to the family to drink.

Tales of supernatural beings devouring the blood of the living are found in every culture, although the word *vampire* is comparatively recent. In Greek myth, Empusa was the daughter of Hecatê, a demonic, bronze-footed creature who changed herself into a young woman, seduced men, then drank their blood as they slept. The similar Greek Lamia preyed on young children in their beds at night, sucking their blood.

During the early eighteenth century there was a frenzy of vampire sightings in Eastern Europe with frequent stakings and graves exhumed to kill the revenants. Executions of people believed to be vampires took place. The vampire hysteria raged for a generation, made worse by epidemics of vampire attacks. Tuberculosis, or "consumption," was believed to be caused by vampire visitations. By no means is vampire hysteria a thing of the past: In Malawi (in southeast Africa) allegations of vampire attacks swept the country during 2002. Mobs stoned one person to death and attacked four others, including the governor, who were believed to be colluding with vampires.

A whole genre of vampire literature arose, more popular than ever today. Johann Wolfgang Goethe wrote *Die Braut von Corinth* ("The Bride of Corinth") in 1797; Samuel Taylor Coleridge published his vampire poem *Christabel* in 1797–1800; and Lord Byron wrote *The Giaour* (Turkish word for "infidel") in 1813, an amazingly successful poem about vampires, read everywhere. *The Vampyre* (1819) by the physician of Lord Byron, John Polidori, established the charismatic and sophisticated vampire. Polidori's novella was adapted from a tale by Lord Byron himself and became the most influential vampire work of the early nineteenth century.

Bram Stoker's novel *Dracula,* published in 1897, provided the basis for modern vampire fiction. The suave, elegant villain can turn into a bat, as also in the classic film *Dracula* of 1931 starring Bela Lugosi. The novel portrayed vampirism as a contagious disease of demonic possession, with undertones of sex, blood, and death, and struck a chord in Victorian Europe where the highly communicable tuberculosis and syphilis were common. Stoker incorporated into his novel the story of the real Vlad III the Impaler, whose Romanian last name was *Drakulya* ("son of the dragon," reigned 1456–1462). Vlad Dracula was famous for his imaginative cruelties imposed on the Ottoman Turks and on domestic enemies. He preferred impalement as a form of execution, when the victim would sometimes take days to die.

The vampire has been a rich subject for the film and gaming industries (Perspective Figure 12.1). Dracula is a major character in more movies than any other except Sherlock Holmes, and many early films were based on the novel *Dracula,* or closely derived from it. Universal's *Dracula* (1931) was the first talking film to portray Dracula, and *Bram Stoker's Dracula* (1992) became the highest grossing vampire film ever, now surpassed by *Twilight,* which grossed more than $513 million worldwide!

PERSPECTIVE FIGURE 12.1 Poster for the 1958 French version of *The Horror of Dracula*. This classic is close to the Bram Stoker novel. The infamous count journeys from his native Transylvania to England, where he plunges into London nightlife and racks up victim after victim. Dracula (Christopher Lee) runs into his arch-nemesis, Van Helsing (Peter Cushing) in a battle of wills. Heavily censored in Britain when released, with the goriest scenes removed, the movie was restored around 1995.   (Poster advertising the French version of the film, 'The Horror of Dracula' (colour litho), French School, (20th century) / Private Collection; Roger Perrin / The Bridgeman Art Library International)

Intellectuals eventually questioned the common view of the breath-soul, which originated through fear of the dead and an effort to explain suffering. The invention of alphabetic writing made it possible to record traditional beliefs and analyze them in new ways. Many Greek philosophers came to doubt that the soul survived after death as a ghostly shadow in Hades' realm. The philosopher Epicurus (341–270 BC) claimed that death was the soul's end as well as the body's, a view widely held by modern philosophers. Still, the traditional view persisted among most ancient Greeks and Romans, and on this view were based several of the best-known classical myths.

ODYSSEUS' JOURNEY TO DEATH'S REALM

The earliest elaborate testimony to popular Greek belief about the dead comes from Homer's *Odyssey*. The Greek hero Odysseus tells the strange story of his experience with the ghosts of the dead, and his journey to the other world, at a banquet given by the king of the island of Phaeacia, where he was shipwrecked on his way home to Ithaca. He tells how he was lost on the high seas after sacking Troy. The witch Circê, whose island he visited, instructed him, before returning home, to seek advice from the ghost of **Tiresias** (ti-rē-si-as), the most famous seer in Greek myth and an important character in Euripides' *Bacchae* (Chapter 11).

Tiresias was descended from one of the Sparti ("sown-men"), the five founders of the ruling families of Thebes, who sprang from the teeth of a dragon that Cadmus killed (Chart 18). According to post-Homeric accounts, when still a young man, Tiresias saw a pair of serpents coupling and killed the female. As a punishment, he was turned into a woman. After seven years he (or she) again saw a pair of serpents coupling. This time he was careful to kill the male and was turned back into a man. (Shamans sometimes dress themselves in clothes of the opposite sex and imitate their behavior, perhaps the origin of this story.)

The Greeks spun a typical joke around the transformation of Tiresias. Zeus and Hera were battling furiously over who knew the greater pleasure in sexual intercourse, males or females. Because Tiresias was the only person who had both experiences, they put the question to him. Tiresias replied without hesitation that of ten parts in the enjoyment of sex, females receive nine, and males but one. In a rage at this impertinent reply, Hera blinded Tiresias. Zeus compensated him with the gift of prophecy and a lifetime extending through seven generations of men. In Greek myth one god cannot reverse the act of another god, but may award a compensation, as in this story.

To inquire of the prophet, now dead, Odysseus set sail for the shores of Ocean, the mythical river that surrounds the world:

[9]   We carefully checked the gear in every part of the vessel,
10   then all of us took our places. Wind and helmsman sped her along,
      and all day long her bellying sail drew the ship on her voyage.
      The sun set at last, and darkness had fallen all over the world,

when we finally reached the edge of the deep-tided current of Ocean,
to the land and city where dwell the Cimmerians, shrouded in mist,

15   sunken in endless dark clouds. The sun never looks down upon them,
with his radiant beam—not when he climbs to the stars in the heaven,
not when he turns once more to the earth, and the perils of darkness
once more enfold wretched men.
     We beached the vessel, and from it unloaded its cargo of sheep,

20   then out we set on foot along the shore of the Ocean,
until we arrived at the place described in Circê's directions.
Two of my men, Perimedes and Eurylochus, tethered the victims,
while I drew my sharp-edged sword from my side and dug out a pit
a foot and a half each way, into which I poured our offering

25   of drink for the dead to consume: first honey mingled with milk,
then sweet wine, and last of all water thickened with barley.
I promised the strengthless ghosts that, safely landed in Ithaca,
I would offer there in my palace a heifer that never had calved,
my best, and would load an altar with good things for them alone.

30   I also promised a ram, the best of the rams in my flock,
for Tiresias all by himself. So I promised the crowds of the dead,
then slit the throats of the sheep so the blood ran into the hollow.
     Up from Erebus° sallied the bodiless souls of the dead—
brides and unmarried young men; feeble rheumatic old gaffers;

35   maidens once happy but now broken-hearted; men killed by the spear;
young soldiers, still in their armor—all crowded around the pit,
with indescribable screaming, till cold fear seized on my heart.
     I hastily ordered my comrades to flay the sacrificed sheep,
dead by my sword, and to burn the bodies with prayer to the gods,

40   to mighty Hades and awesome Persephonê. Meanwhile I waited,
drawing my keen-edged sword, a menace to frail nerveless spirits,
keeping them off from the blood till I could question Tiresias.
     The first to approach was the ghost of my good comrade Elpenor,
whose body was not yet buried under the broad-stretching earth.

45   We had left it, unmourned and unburied, back in the palace of Circê,
for other labors were calling. My eyes filled with tears as I watched
and spoke these words of pity, words which flew straight to the mark:
     "Elpenor, how did you come down here to the echoing darkness,
traveling faster on foot than I in our dark-sided vessel?"

50   Such were my words. With a groan my comrade Elpenor responded:
     "Noble son of Laërtes, Odysseus the wise and resourceful,
an evil fate sent from heaven, and too much wine and too potent,
fuddled my wits and brought on my death in the palace of Circê.
From my bed on the roof I stumbled to find the long downward ladder,

55   but plunged headlong to the ground and broke the bones of my neck.
My soul fluttered down to Hades. Now hear my last supplication:
I beg you, by those you have left behind in the land of the living,
by your wife, by the father who raised you, tiny child that you were,
by Telemachus, your only son, whom you left at home in the palace—

---

33. *Erebus:* "Darkness," that is, the realm of the dead.

60   because I know that you will go back once more from the house of Hades,
     to Circê's isle of Aeaea in your speedy and well-built vessel—
     when you arrive there, my lord, remember my final entreaty.
     When again you set out for home, do not leave me unwept and unburied,
     abandoned, hateful to gods. But lay me to rest with my weapons,
65   with everything that is mine, in a grave on the coast of the sea,
     the tomb of a poor hapless man, a reminder to those who come after.
     Grant me that favor, and this: Mount on my tomb the same oar
     that I swung in the land of the living, seated alongside my fellows."
         So Elpenor requested, and at once I gave him my answer:
70   "Of course I shall do what you ask, poor fellow, in every detail."
         Thus then the two of us sat, discussing a matter so gloomy,
     I on one side of the blood-filled pit, with my vigilant weapon,
     the ghost of my friend on the other, showing what he wanted done.
         Presently up there came the ghost of my long-dead mother,
75   Anticlea, the daughter of Autolycus,° mighty of spirit.
     Her I had left, still alive, on my way to Troy's holy city.
     My tears welled up when I saw her, and pity filled all my heart;
     but, grieved though I was, I dared not let her come up to the blood,
     until I should learn the future from Tiresias, wisest of prophets.
80   The ghost of Tiresias the Theban, golden staff in his hand,
     was next to appear; he recognized me, and thus he addressed me:
         "Son of Laërtes, descendant of Zeus, pray tell me, poor fellow
     why have you left the light of the sun and come down to the dead
     in their grim and joyless land? Step back, I pray, from the pit.
85   Hold your weapon aside, so that I may drink your oblation,
     and afterward tell you the truth."

HOMER, Odyssey 11.9–96

75. *Autolycus:* A famous trickster and thief, a son of Hermes, from whom Odysseus doubtless inherited his wily intelligence.

After drinking the blood, Tiresias warns Odysseus about the dangers that lie ahead, the suitors who besiege his home, and the nature of the death that one day must come.

The Cimmerians (si-**mer**-i-anz) seem to have been a real people who in Homer's day lived north of the Black Sea—seemingly, to the Greeks, at the very end of the world. Homer mythologizes the Cimmerians and places them in the extreme west beside the river Ocean, which bounds the earth and separates the living from the dead. This region where the sun never shines is not presented as the land of the dead as such, though it symbolizes the world beyond, but as a place where you can approach the dead. The honey, milk, wine, water, barley, and blood that Odysseus pours into the pit are to feed the strengthless shades and allow them to speak. In the story, Odysseus plays the role of a necromancer, a magician who summons spirits of the dead to question them and gain knowledge from them. His ordinary sword functions as a magical weapon, restraining the thirsty, disembodied ghosts from the life-restoring vapors of the fresh blood.

FIGURE 12.1 Odysseus and the ghost of Elpenor, Attic vase, c. 460–430 BC. On the left Elpenor rises from the ground, attracted by the pit of blood. The skins of the sacrificed rams are heaped at his feet. Odysseus holds his sword in his left hand and thoughtfully supports his chin with the other. Hermes *psychopompos* is at the right, wearing a winged helmet and boots and carrying the caduceus.   (Photograph © 2011 Museum of Fine Arts, Boston)

Elpenor (el-**pē**-nor), ghost of one of Odysseus' own companions (Figure 12.1), is first to appear at the pit of blood. He is able to speak without drinking because his ghost is still abroad in the land of the living. Elpenor begs for proper burial, but the need to lay the ghost is, in origin, in the interests of the living.

After hearing Tiresias' prophecy about his own fortunes, Odysseus asks him how he might be able to speak with his mother's ghost, Anticlea (an-ti-**klē**-a):

[141]   "Tiresias, yonder I see the ghost of my dear dead mother,
waiting in silence beside the blood, not daring to face me,
her son though I am, nor address me in words. Now tell me, my lord:
How can she know it is I, how recognize me as her son?"
145   Thus I questioned the seer, who promptly replied to my question:
     "The answer to that is easy. Store my reply in your heart.
Whichever of these dead folk you allow to draw up to the blood,
will tell you the truth, but those you refuse must retire within."

With that Tiresias' ghost sank back again to the dwelling
150   of Hades, once he had finished revealing what destiny ordered.
But I stood waiting in silence, while my mother, approaching the pit,
drank of the dark-clouded blood and recognized me as I waited.
She heaved a sigh from her heart and asked the natural question:
"My son, how is it you come, still alive, to this echoing gloom?
155   No easy task for the living to find what is here in the darkness!
Great rivers and horrible torrents swirl between in the journey,
and chiefly the Ocean itself, which no one can ever pass over
on foot, but must make his voyage on the deck of a well-built ship."

HOMER, *Odyssey* 11.141–159

Anticlea tells of her death from grief over Odysseus' long absence. Odysseus, wanting to embrace her, three times reaches out his arms; three times she flutters away like a dream or a shadow (a scene later echoed by Vergil and Dante). Her reply suggests that cremation is the ordinary treatment of the dead (inhumation was usual in the Bronze Age):

[210]   "Dear mother, why do you shrink away and avoid my embrace?
Even in Hades, can we not put our arms round each other
and give full play to our grief? Has Persephonê sent an illusion
to deceive me and make me sorrow the more in my aching grief?"
To my plea the lady my mother replied, "Alas, my poor son,
215   miserable, more than all men, this is no deceit of the goddess
Persephonê, daughter of Zeus, but the fate of all who have perished.
No more do the sinews hold their flesh and bones in their places,
but the burning heat of the pyre overwhelms and crumbles our flesh.
Once the soul has abandoned the body, the poor homeless spirit
220   must flutter about like a dream, then vanish forever. So hurry!
Fight your way back to the light, to tell your wife your adventures."

HOMER, *Odyssey* 11.210–222

Persephonê, queen of the dead, sends other spirits up to drink the blood—first the women of olden times, then the heroes who died at Troy. Agamemnon, king of Mycenae—murdered by his wife, Clytemnestra, when he came back from Troy—appears and complains bitterly. He warns Odysseus to trust no woman, not even his faithful wife, Penelopê. Achilles, greatest of all the Achaeans, is next to come to the pit and address Odysseus:

[473]   "Noble son of Laërtes, Odysseus, the wise and resourceful,
man with a heart of steel, what harder task can you dream of?
475   How did you summon the courage to descend to the palace of Hades,
down to the half-conscious dead, the shades of men who have perished?"
So Achilles inquired, and I gave him an honest reply:
"Achilles, Peleus' son, by far the bravest Achaean,
I have come down to inquire of wise far-sighted Tiresias,

480   if he could direct me home to Ithaca, rugged and stony.
        For never have I drawn near to the coast of the land of Achaea,
        nor landed in my dear homeland, but am always dogged by misfortune.
           "No one, Achilles, of all men past or yet to be born
        has been more blessed than you. We Argives gave you honor
485   equal to that of a god, and, now you have migrated hither,
        you govern the dead. Don't mutter complaining of death, Achilles!"
           I scolded him in these words, but Achilles quickly retorted,
        "Don't attempt to teach me about death, O learned Odysseus!
        Better to serve as a hireling to another, a man who is
490   landless and hungry himself, than here to be ruler
        of all the shriveled-up dead."

HOMER, *Odyssey* 11.473–491

Achilles' famous reply nicely sums up Greek pessimism about the afterlife. Next to come up to the blood is Ajax, who from shame committed suicide when Odysseus, rather than he, received the armor of the dead Achilles. Even in death he bears his grudge: Too angry to speak, his silent ghost floats away among the crowd of spirits (Vergil and Dante imitate this scene, too).

At this point Homer forgets that Odysseus is on the shore of Ocean. Without explanation he shifts the hero into the underworld itself:

[568]   Next I beheld King Minos, the glorious son of great Zeus,
        seated, with scepter of gold, as arbiter over the spirits.
570   They crowded, seated or standing, before the wide portals of Hades,
        pleading their cause before Minos, who served them as ruler and judge.
           Behind him I noticed the form of mighty Orion, the giant,
        beating the bushes for game all through the asphodel° meadows.
        Some he slew with his bludgeon, off in the desolate mountains,
575   his club of unbreakable bronze, which he swung in his powerful hands.

HOMER, *Odyssey* 11.568–575

573. *asphodel:* A pale weed growing wild in Greece and southern Italy, associated with the dead and to this day often planted on graves.

Homer describes Minos (**mī**-nos) as a judge; a better English word would be arbitrator. He decides quarrels in accordance with existing custom, but they are fresh quarrels, not ones carried over from the litigants' life on earth. His sentences are not punishments of moral shortcomings, but decrees designed to maintain the existing order of society in the other world. Minos acts like other kings in Homeric society. The Cretans were famous lawgivers, and in later accounts we find as additional judges among the dead Minos' brother Rhadamanthys (rad-a-**man**-this) and Aeacus (**ē**-a-kus), once king of the island of Aegina in the Saronic Gulf near Athens. Orion, son of Poseidon, a famous hunter in life (see Chapter 9), continues to hunt after death. In Homer, life below the earth is much like life above the earth, at least for those of high social standing.

A few notorious offenders against the dignity of the gods suffer endless torment in the underworld, according to Odysseus' description:

[582]   Tantalus also I saw, who was suffering terrible torments.
           He stood in a swampy lake, whose water reached up to his chin.
           Strain as he might in his thirst, he never could drink of the water,
585   which soaked down into the mud that gurgled between his feet,
           sent by some demon. From trees that arched up over his head
           drooped fruit of the richest and ripest: clusters of juicy fat pears,
           pomegranates, sweet-fruited quinces, ripe olives, delectable figs.
           But whenever he tried to reach them, to pull them down with his hands,
590   a gust of wind would blow them away to the shadowing clouds.
               Sisyphus too I observed, down there in his terrible torment,
           pushing his boulder before him, straining with every limb
           to shoulder it over the crest of the hill. But just as it tottered,
           mocking gravity pushed it back, back again to the plain.
595   Once more he strained; once more the sweat poured down from his limbs,
           and clouds of dust arose from around his head as he struggled.

HOMER, *Odyssey* 11.582–600

Tantalus (**tan**-ta-lus) and **Sisyphus** (**sis**-i-fus) were guilty of violence against the gods, although Homer is more interested in their punishments than in their crimes (Figure 12.2). Tantalus, once a friend to the gods, tested their omniscience (like Lycaon) by serving them his own son Pelops (**pē**-lops) at a banquet. Of course instantly they knew the truth, except for Demeter, who was in mourning for Persephonê. Absent-mindedly, she ate Pelops' shoulder. The gods reassembled the unfortunate Pelops and made him a new shoulder of ivory. From Tantalus' punishment comes our word *tantalize.* Sisyphus was famed for his cleverness: He seduced Anticlea, Odysseus' mother, on her wedding night and, according to this tradition, was the true father of Odysseus. Sisyphus also tricked Death himself, at one time imprisoning him, on another time escaping to the upper world to live out a second life. Going a second time to the underworld, Sisyphus received his terrible punishment.

The tortures of the damned really are tortures of the living, transposed to the other world. Tantalus can never satisfy his gluttonous desires for food and drink; Sisyphus labors endlessly without result. The offenses of the damned are always against the honor of the gods, but it remains a fixed list. The average human need fear no such punishment, because he or she will have scarcely more reality than a bat gibbering in a cave.

Now Odysseus spies Heracles, but it is only an *eidolon,* an "image," of him, as the ghost is an *eidolon* of the living man. The real Heracles, when he died, was raised to heaven as a god. There he married Hebê, "youth," as everyone knew (see Chapter 15). Odysseus might have seen still more heroes, but

[632]   before I was given a chance
           an endless cloud of specters ran up with a scarce-human mutter.
           Cold fear clutched at my heart, that haughty Persephonê
635   might send from the House of Hades some Gorgon-headed destroyer.
           I hurriedly ran to the ship and ordered my trusty companions
           to embark and cast off the cables which moored the prow to the beach.

FIGURE 12.2 The tortures of the damned, from a fresco representing scenes from the *Odyssey* on the wall of a Roman house, copied from a Greek original, c. 40 BC. In the center of the picture a great rock looms over Tityus, as if about to fall upon him. He lies spread-eagle and tied down while two vultures pick at his liver (he attempted to rape Leto, pregnant with Apollo and Artemis). In the foreground the Danaïds (dā-na-idz), not mentioned by Homer, attempt to fill a trough with vases that have no bottoms (they murdered their husbands on the wedding night). In the upper left, Orion hunts through eternity, while Sisyphus pushes the rock that ever rolls backward. (Photo Vatican Museums)

Quickly they jumped on board and seated themselves in their places.
The surge of the current bore us down the waters of Ocean;
640   then first we tugged at the oars, till a stern wind freshened behind us.

HOMER, *Odyssey* 1.632–640

A blessed few are not subject at death to the standard treatment and may end up in a special afterworld called **Elysium** (e-**liz**-i-um), or the Elysian Fields. In Book 4 of the *Odyssey*, the Greek hero Menelaüs, stranded on a desert island while returning from Troy, asks the sea-god Proteus about his fate. Proteus replies:

[561]   "It is not your destiny, Menelaüs, friend of the gods,
           to die in horse-raising Argos and meet man's usual fate.
           No, the immortals will send you off to the Field of Elysium,
           to the very ends of the earth, where rules fair-haired Rhadamanthys.
565   There at the last you will find the most blessed fate for a mortal.
           Snow never falls, nor destructive storms or violent cloudbursts,
           for the ocean constantly sends the whistling breezes of Zephyr,°
           to brace and refresh the spirits, however fevered, of mortals.
           This is your lot as Zeus's son-in-law, husband of Helen."
570   At this the old man of the sea plunged into the depths of the Ocean.

                                         HOMER, *Odyssey* 4.561–570

567. *Zephyr:* The west wind.

No ordinary man or woman in Homer's time could hope to see the Elysian Fields as a reward for virtue, any more than fear the torment of Tartarus for one's sins. Menelaüs married Helen, daughter of Zeus and Leda, and for this reason he will go to Elysium: Family connections count even after death. Those destined for Elysium do not descend to the underworld, but continue a blessed life in a remote part of the earth. The word *Elysium* may be of pre-Greek Cretan origin and perhaps reflects a Minoan notion of a happy other world, like that of their trading partners, the optimistic Egyptians.

ORPHEUS AND EURYDICÊ

Another figure who journeyed alive to the land of the dead is **Orpheus (or-**fūs), the son of a Thracian named Oeagrus and a Muse. Orpheus was famous for his sweet singing to the lyre, an instrument some say he (not Hermes) invented. His music enchanted wild animals, stopped birds in flight, and uprooted trees and rocks, drawing them all into the magic circle of his song. He was one of the Argonauts (Chapter 19), but his most important myth described the tragic love for his beloved **Eurydicê** (yū-**rid**-i-sē).

On the wedding day of Orpheus and Eurydicê, a beekeeper named Aristaeus (a-ris-**tē**-us) pursued the bride across a field, intending to rape her. As she fled, a snake bit her on the heel and she died. Overwhelmed by grief, Orpheus was determined to bring Eurydicê back from the dead. He entered the other world through a cave in the southern Peloponnesus. Sweetly singing, he entranced the ghosts as he descended. He came to the palace of Hades and Persephonê and softened their icy hearts with the beauty of his song. They agreed to release Eurydicê on a single condition: While climbing the paths that lead to the upper world, Orpheus must not look back.

All went well until they neared the entrance, when an agonizing doubt seized Orpheus. Was she really there? He looked around, just in time to see Eurydicê recede into the shadows. He tried again to enter the underworld, but now Cerberus blocked his path. Orpheus wandered inconsolable over the world, playing his lyre and singing (Figure 12.3).

Wanting nothing to do with any other woman, he invented male homosexuality. He met his end in his wild homeland of Thrace, where Bacchae tore him to bits,

FIGURE 12.3 Orpheus in Thrace, Attic vase, c. 440 BC. Orpheus, sitting on a rock, sings and plucks the lyre, while Thracian warriors in Thracian dress listen, entranced. (bpk, Berlin/Antikensammlung, Staatliche Museen/Johannes Laurentius/Art Resource, New York)

either because he promulgated homosexuality, or because he neglected Dionysus, or because he excluded women from his sacred mysteries. The Bacchae threw the pieces of his corpse into the River Hebrus, the principal river in Thrace (now the boundary between Greece and Turkey), and they were washed down to the sea. The head continued to sing and prophesy even after it was washed ashore on the island of Lesbos. At last Apollo, envious of its powers, commanded the head to be silent.

The story of Orpheus and Eurydicê was popular in the Hellenistic and Roman periods. One of the best-known versions is that of Vergil in the *Georgics* ("poems about farming"). Aristaeus, who attacked Eurydicê, was punished by the loss of all his bees. He sought out the prophetic sea-god Proteus, who in explaining the consequences of Aristaeus' act gives a famous version of the story of Orpheus:

[457]   "Running from you in terror and splashing her way through a stream,
the poor girl, fated to perish, failed to see that a monstrous viper
lurked in the long thick grass on the bank just over the river.
460   Only his hollow lyre gave Orpheus some consolation:
'O dear lost bride!' he murmured, pacing the shore all alone.
Her name was his theme at daybreak, his theme as the sun sank down.

At last in despair he entered Taenarum's° grisly approaches,
the deepest portal of Dis° and the grove of black shadows and fear.
465 Passing the legions of ghosts, he sought the implacable ruler,
whose pitiless heart never learned to be softened by human entreaty.
His song fetched even the phantoms from the lowest circles of hell,
and the wraiths of unhappy spirits deprived of the blessing of light.
They flocked, as many in number as the migrant birds of the autumn,
470 driven together by darkness or the whistling storms of the winter.
Mothers of children, grown men, soldiers fallen in battle,
small boys, maidens unmarried, young men laid on the pyre
under the grieving eyes of anguished father and mother.
Black mud closes them in, and the rotting sedge of Cocytus,°
475 with its sluggish disgusting fens, through which the Stygian water
meanders in ninefold looping, cutting off any escape.
Yet even the lowest hell, the deepest circle of Hades,
even the Furies with livid vipers entwined in their hair,
gaped in surprise, even Cerberus silenced his triple-jawed barking,
480 and Ixion's wheel° stood still as the wind that drove it fell silent.
    When at last his prayer was granted, Orpheus, shunning ill luck,
was preceding his newly recovered Eurydicê up to the light.
Eurydicê followed behind him, for thus Proserpina ordered.
But just as she came in reach of the fresh sweet wind of the heaven,
485 madness seized the incautious lover—forgivable, yes,
but only if death knew how to forgive. He halted his step,
forgetful, besotted by love, and turned around in his folly,
back to his bride, just before Eurydicê entered the daylight.
    A second too soon! for now all his labor was fruitlessly wasted.
490 He had broken the stern condition of the iron ruler's decree.
As witness, three crashes of thunder resounded all through Avernus.°
'What folly' the girl sobbed out, 'has sentenced poor wretched me,
and you, my Orpheus, as well? A cruel fate now recalls me.
Farewell, farewell! My eyelids are drowned by my final slumber,
495 the darkness enfolds and abducts me. In vain do I stretch out my arms,
which now will never embrace you.' No more. From out of his sight
she vanished, as smoke disperses when touched by a whisper of wind.
He eagerly clutched at the darkness, longing to bid her goodbye,
but she no longer was there to see his frantic endeavor.
500 He tried to follow her down, but the grim-faced porter refused him
another passage across the marshes, now wider than ever.
    What could the poor man do? Where hunt for a twice-vanished wife?
What plea could avail with the spirits, what piteous cry to the gods?
Eurydicê's stiffening body already was crossing the Styx.
505   They tell us that Orpheus lamented Eurydicê seven long months,
under a windy crag of the lonely bank of the Strymon,°

---

463. *Taenarum:* A peninsula near Sparta, the southernmost tip of Europe (except for Gibraltar), where certain caves were thought to lead to the underworld.   464. *Dis:* Roman for Hades.   474. *Cocytus* (kō-**sī**-tus): "Moaning," another river of the underworld.   480. *Ixion's wheel:* Ixion was another of the eternally damned (see below).   491. *Avernus:* Roman for the underworld.   506. *Strymon:* A river of Thrace.

chanting his story aloud to the icy caves of the northland,
breaking the savage hearts of even the man-eating tigers,
moving the rooted oak trees to follow and hark to his song.
510 As a nightingale mourns its young, whom a callous peasant has stolen,
unfledged as yet, from the nest, she perches high in the branches
and all night long pours out the voice of her sorrow: So Orpheus
wept for his loss. No new love, no marriage offered him solace.
Alone he gazed at the ice of the Arctic, at snow-drenched Tanaïs,
515 at endless Scythian plains,° whose snow lasts all through the summer,
mourning Eurydicê's loss and the empty concession of Pluto.
    The women of Thrace were enraged, who, worshiping wild Dionysus,
rent Orpheus limb from limb in ecstatic orgies, and scattered
his flesh through the plains of their Thrace. Only his death-pale head
520 they tore from his neck, to hurl in Oeagrian Hebrus'° current.
Yet even as Hebrus carried the head out into the sea,
the ice-cold stiffening tongue gasped Orpheus' last invocation,
'Alas! my lost Eurydicê!' it cried with his final breath.
'Eurydicê!' back came the echo from Hebrus' sorrowing shores."

VERGIL, *Georgics* 4.457–527

515. *Scythian plains:* Tanaïs is the modern river Don, flowing through the Ukraine into the Black Sea. Scythia lies to the east of the Don.   520. *Oeagrian Hebrus':* Oeagrus was Orpheus' father; the Hebrus is the largest river in Thrace.

ORPHISM

In the sixth century BC, religious teachers began to claim the mythical Orpheus as the promulgator of special teachings about the nature and destiny of human beings. Like the Eleusinian Mysteries, these "teachings of Orpheus" evidently offered ordinary Greeks hope for salvation, a means of ensuring a more comfortable life after death. Unlike other Greek religious teachings, however, the Orphic doctrines were recorded and to some extent transmitted in written form. Only small fragments of Orphic writings survive from the Archaic and Classical periods, but from references in Plato and other authors, and from literature from the Roman Period, we can reconstruct Orphic teaching in a hazy way. They used elements from traditional myth for speculative purposes and to inculcate their doctrine. They justified their doctrine as based on knowledge that Orpheus gained in the world below and later taught while he wandered through Thrace. Making use especially of Hesiod's *Theogony,* the Orphics offered a specialized cosmogony, "origin of the world," and an anthropogony, "origin of humans."

    In the beginning was Chronos, "time," perhaps meaning "time without end." From Time sprang Aether, "radiance," probably the upper atmosphere, Chaos, and Erebus, "darkness." Chronos now forms an egg inside the Aether, from which sprang Phanes (**fan-ēz**), "he who appears," the bisexual creator of all that exists, a radiant being with the heads of various animals and golden wings. Phanes gives birth to Nyx, "night," then on Nyx begets Gaea and Uranus. Then follows the Hesiodic myth of the struggle between Cronus and Zeus. To reconcile

Hesiod's account with the Orphic version, Zeus is said to swallow Phanes and make the world anew, the world we live in. On Demeter Zeus begets Persephonê, and on Persephonê Zeus begets Dionysus, now called **Zagreus**, a name of unknown meaning.

Comments by an unfriendly Christian writer from about AD 200, Clement of Alexandria, who ridicules pagan beliefs that he finds absurd and offensive, provide us with information about the fate of Dionysus Zagreus according to the Orphic anthropogony:

> The mysteries of Dionysus are utterly savage. While he was an infant,
> the Curetes danced around him in full armor, but the Titans sneaked in,
> distracted the baby's attention with toys, and tore him limb from limb.
> The poet of initiation, Orpheus, tells the story:°
>
> > Tops and hoops and dollies,
> > with moving feet and hands;
> > pretty golden apples,
> > from singing western lands.
>
> To make you laugh, let me list the silly symbols of that rite of yours:
> knuckle-bones, ball, top, apples, wheel, mirror, fleece.
> Well, Athena stole the heart of Dionysus and, because it was still
> palpitating, she received the name of Pallas.° Meanwhile, the Titans
> who had torn Dionysus to pieces set a pot on a tripod. They tossed in
> his limbs, which they first boiled up, then put them on spits and held
> them over the fire. Afterward Zeus appeared (if he was really a god, he
> had doubtless caught a whiff of roasting meat, which those gods of yours
> claim as their due!). He blasted the Titans with a thunderbolt and gave
> the remains of Dionysus to his son Apollo to bury. Apollo would not
> dream of disobeying Zeus, so he took the mangled corpse to Parnassus°
> and buried it there.
>
> CLEMENT OF ALEXANDRIA, *Protrepticus* 2.15

story: Here Clement quotes from an Orphic hymn.   *Pallas:* On the assumption that Pallas means "beating" (a possible but improbable interpretation).   *Parnassus:* That is, Delphi.

The story appears to reflect an initiation rite common in preliterate societies. A young man (Dionysus Zagreus) is approached by older men (the Titans), symbolically "killed," and then brought back to new life in the adult world. Some accounts tell how the Titans smeared their faces with gypsum, an actual practice in some initiation rites when older men take on the role of the ghosts of tribal ancestors. But the purpose of the story within the context of Orphic teaching is to reveal a secret about human nature. As the story goes on to say, Zeus created human beings from the ashes of the blasted Titans. For this reason human nature has an evil, Titanic aspect, obvious to all. Because, however, the flesh of Dionysus, whom the Titans devoured, was mingled with the Titans' ashes, human beings also contain a divine

Dionysian spark encased in a gross Titanic body. Outside we are Titanic, but within we are divine. The goal of human striving should therefore be to free the immortal soul from its bodily prison, a view succinctly expressed in the Orphic slogan "The body is a tomb" (*sôma sêma*).

The Orphics also taught metempsychosis, or the reincarnation of the soul. According to this unusual doctrine, which strikingly also appears in northwest India at just this time, the souls of the dead do not remain forever in the realm of Hades, but return repeatedly to earth for new lives in different bodies (Plato will accept this view, and Vergil after him). It is only with great effort, austerity, and with the help of knowledge gained from the Orphic revelation that the soul can be purified and the cycle of rebirth broken. The soul's escape from its entanglement with matter requires a life of ascetic purity, including abstention from such animal products as meat and woolen cloth, from beans (for unknown reasons), and from sexual intercourse. Magical formulas can also be useful in the world below. Some inscribed gold plates from the Archaic Period, often thought to reflect Orphic teaching, are found in tombs in southern Italy and on Crete on which the dead person claims to be a child of Earth and Heaven, perhaps the Dionysian spark within.

In this context, the myth of Orpheus becomes more than a simple folktale, the story of a man who went to the other world and returned. Orpheus returned from the underworld in order to teach the truth about human nature and destiny. Although the origin and exact nature of the Orphic teachings are, like Hades' realm, shrouded in mist, they seem to be connected with the equally obscure doctrines of **Pythagoras** (sixth century BC). Pythagoras is best known for the philosophical claim that the essence of reality resides in mystical relations among numbers, proportions, and measures. Pythagoras also taught metempsychosis, and he taught his followers to lead ascetic lives based on principles much like those of Orphism. Plato's dualistic conception of human nature—the soul as a divine spark entombed in an earthly body—parallels Orphic teaching and probably depends on it, as do his views on metempsychosis and the virtues of an ascetic life. Through Plato, Orphic doctrines influenced the fathers of the Christian church, especially in Christian teachings about the soul and its relation to the body. Much of what we think of as Christianity is Platonic philosophy, some of it Orphic in origin. The early Christians themselves recognized the affinity, and paintings in catacombs show Christ as Orpheus.

Although Dionysus and Orpheus are closely related in these stories, and both Orpheus and Dionysus journeyed to Hades, an inherent hostility emerged between them. The Orphics changed the central rite of Dionysiac religion, the eating of raw flesh, into the Titan's primal murder of Zagreus, and in other details of Orpheus' myth we can see the master singer drawing close to Apollo, the shamanistic god and god of musical harmony, purification, righteousness, and prophecy. The followers of Orpheus pursue lives of self-denial, not orgiastic ecstasy. Sometimes Orpheus was called the son of Apollo. Orpheus met his end at the hands of maenads, followers of Dionysus—according to some accounts, while paying tribute at dawn to Apollo, equated with the rising sun.

PLATO'S "MYTH OF ER"

The religion of the Orphics was one part of a great spiritual ferment that appeared in many places on this planet in the sixth century BC, the age of the mystical philosopher Pythagoras, many of the Hebrew prophets including the great Second Isaiah, Zoroaster in Persia, Gautama the Buddha in India, and Confucius in China, although it is scarcely possible to trace a direct connection between these still influential teachers and their schools of thought. In the Mediterranean world this was the age of increased concern with the morality of the individual, and the effect of right action on a future life was the subject of close attention. Morality implies choice between what one knows to be good and what one knows to be wrong. Although the wicked may flourish for a while, an effective moral system requires that wrongdoers be punished later in this life or in a life to come, or that one's descendants suffer, that the sins of the fathers be visited on the children. The Orphics had advanced just such a moral system of reward and punishment, and in the fourth century BC, the philosopher Plato (428?–347 BC) offered a great refinement on it.

No one more than Plato is responsible for our modern notion of a myth as a fictitious, untrue story or version of events. So hostile was he to traditional tales that he banned poets from his ideal city. However, Plato did not object to making up his own myths to promulgate his views, as in his "myth of Atlantis," a description of a once powerful world sunk beneath the waves (Perspective 1.1).

In Plato's dialogue the *Republic,* Socrates attempts to arrive at a definition of justice. Opposing popular views claiming that injustice is rewarded, Socrates maintains that it is punished not only in this world, but in the next. To prove his point, Socrates describes the experience of a man named **Er** ("springtime," the season of rebirth) who came from the land of Pamphylia (a real place in southern Anatolia, but meaning "land of all races" or "everyman's land"). Er was killed in battle, but ten days afterward, when the bodies were placed on a funeral pyre, he was found still alive and able to tell his story.

He and all the other dead found themselves, he said, in a place where openings on either side led up to heaven or down into the earth. The souls were judged and sent under the earth, or into the heaven, to be punished or rewarded tenfold for the evil or good they had done. For a thousand years they suffered torment or enjoyed bliss. After this they returned to the place of judgment and were offered a choice of new lives to live when they returned to earth. A herald took a number of lots (prepared by Clotho, "spinner," one of the Moerae or Fates), from the knees of Lachesis ("apportioner," another of the Fates) and proclaimed: "Souls of a day, here you begin a new period of life. Nobody will choose for you. You must make your own decision. Do not blame the god for it. The responsibility will be your own." The souls then picked what they wanted. The famous singer Orpheus chose to be a swan; an ugly warrior who fought at Troy, Thersites, chose to be a monkey; Agamemnon, king of the Greek forces at Troy, chose to be an eagle; Odysseus, whose former life had taught him the folly of ambition, hunted for a long time before he found what he wanted: a quiet, obscure life, one that everyone before had rejected.

The destiny that each soul chose was confirmed by the third of the Fates, Atropos ("she who cannot be turned aside"). Then they all journeyed to the Plain of Lethê, "forgetfulness," through a burning, choking, stifling heat, for the plain was barren of trees and plants. There they camped at eventide by the River of Unheeding, whose waters no vessel can hold. Each one, as he or she drank from the river, forgot everything and went to sleep. It was the middle of the night. There was thunder and a quaking of the earth. Suddenly, the souls were carried away to their new birth, like shooting stars. Er himself was not allowed to drink the water, yet how he returned to his body he did not know. Suddenly recovering his sight, he saw himself at dawn, lying on the funeral pyre. Socrates concludes:

> "And so, Glaucon, his story has been preserved, and it would save us if we believed it. We shall safely cross the river of Lethê and keep our souls undefiled. But if we are persuaded by me, we shall believe that the soul is immortal and able to endure every extreme of good and evil. Thus shall we hold always to the upward path and always pursue justice with wisdom, so that we may be friends to ourselves and to the gods both during our time here and afterward, like victors in the games who go to collect their prizes. Thus both here and in that journey of a thousand years, which I have described, we will fare well."

PLATO, *The Republic* 621a–d

The "myth of Er" is not a traditional tale but a philosophical and intellectual recasting of ancient traditional accounts of life after death and of the underworld to teach that the soul is immortal and that a moral law governs the world. Plato follows Orphic practice in using traditional mythic elements for speculative purposes and in his acceptance of a moral law. Plato's principal contribution was to allow for a purification of the soul before it returned to another human life—for the presence, in more modern terms, of a Purgatory ("place of purification") as well as an Inferno and a Paradise. Although not a myth, Plato's vision of Er, which owed much to Orphic teaching, influenced other mythmakers, especially the Roman poet Vergil in his vivid account of the descent of Aeneas in the sixth book of the *Aeneid*.

So slippery does the category "myth" become!

AENEAS' DESCENT TO THE UNDERWORLD

Many popular conceptions about the other world still current today lead back directly to Vergil's description, which incorporates Greek and Roman myth, religion, and philosophy.

Aeneas, who has escaped from the burning wreckage of Troy, travels to the far West to found a new race, the Romans. Before his purpose is complete, he must descend to the underworld through an opening near sulphurous Lake Avernus, north of the Bay of Naples, to speak with his dead father, Anchises. (For Anchises' union with Aphrodite, who bore Aeneas, see Chapter 9.) The Romans thought the etymology of Avernus to be "birdless" because the foul vapors kill even birds that fly over it.

First he needed to find Apollo's onetime love, the Sibyl at Cumae, an early Greek colony near Avernus. The goddess Hecatê had revealed to her how to enter the nether realms. Now an old woman, the Sibyl will be his guide. Aeneas plucks a magical golden bough from a sacred wood, a sign that he is chosen by fate, then in the Sibyl's company descends into the realm of Dis. Vergil's report, which we summarize as follows, repeats much of that in the *Odyssey*, but includes many minor changes and some major ones.

After sacrificing to the gods beneath the earth, Aeneas and the Sibyl set forth at the earliest rays of the rising sun. At the entrance to the underworld hovers a crowd of personified abstractions, a tree filled with deceptive dreams, and beyond it a crowd of monsters. Hesiod has a few allegorical creatures like these, but their use was far more common among the Romans. Their journey soon brings them to the river **Acheron** (ak-er-on, "sorrowful"), the boundary proper of Dis's realm. If the dead have the fare, they are soon taken aboard the boat of the grim ferryman **Charon** (kā-ron; Figure 12.4); if not, they must wait a hundred years to cross:

[295]   From there the downward way led them to Acheron's waters,
        whose black and sluggish current eddied in whirlpools of mud.
        A filthy old guardian boatman kept watch on the banks and the river,
        Charon, whose red flaming eyes peered over a greasy gray beard,
        dressed in a dirty old scarf looped around and over his shoulder.
300   Scorning the help of a crew, he alone handles punt pole and sail,
        and loads the dead to the gunwales of his rusty, leaky old hull—
        an old man now, but old age in a god is green and resilient.
        Great crowds of the dead swarmed out and rushed on down,
        to the slimy banks of the water in an endless torrent of humans—

FIGURE 12.4 Charon and Hermes *psychopompos,* Attic vase, c. 380 BC. Charon, the figure on the left, wearing a rough cloak and cap, punts the boat of the dead, while in the middle Hermes *psychopompos,* wearing his winged cap and carrying the caduceus, leads the ghost of a woman recently dead. Such *lekythoi* (oil vases) were made expressly to bury with the dead.   (Staatliche Antikensammlungen und Glyptothek, Munich)

305   mothers of children, their husbands, great-hearted heroes,
    schoolboys, unmarried maidens, young men scarcely mature,
    but laid on the funeral pyre before the eyes of their parents.
    A crowd like swirling leaves that fall from the branches in autumn,
    when nipped by the first cold blast, or like the flocking of petrels,
310   when icy winter drives them in flight from the open sea
    in search of a warmer climate. Just so the dead, passing number,
    came stretching their hands in longing to cross to the opposite shore.

VERGIL, *Aeneid* 6.295–314

PERSPECTIVE 12.2

MICHELANGELO'S *THE SIBYL OF CUMAE*

A belief that the truest mouthpiece for prophecy is an inspired, often aged woman is very ancient. She appeared to the Greeks as the Pythia, Apollo's voice at Delphi; in the Bible as the Witch of Endor, who summoned the ghost of Samuel to foretell the grim future facing King Saul; and in Vergil's *Aeneid* as the Sibyl of Cumae, Aeneas' guide to the world below, said to be still alive in the early Roman empire. But there were other Sibyls in the ancient world, as many as ten.

Michelangelo Buonarroti (1475–1564), a poet as well as an architect, sculptor, painter, and engineer, lived at the end of a century and a half of extraordinary artistic and intellectual ferment in Italy. His most famous painting is in the Sistine Chapel in the Vatican, where in four years (1508–1512) he decorated in wet plaster the enormous ceiling and upper third of the side walls. Taking the creation, fall, and redemption of humankind as his topic, Michelangelo covered the ceiling with more than three hundred figures in a sweeping drama of human existence. On the side panels he represented prophets of Christ's coming. Here, curiously, he includes the old and muscular Sibyl of Cumae (labeled *CUMAEA;* Perspective Figure 12.2), who looks into one of her prophetic books while two nude youths look on.

Such an absorption of pagan motifs into Christianity was a logical outgrowth of the allegorical interpretations placed on classical myth by Renaissance intellectuals. Thus, according to Neoplatonic philosophical principles (compare Perspective 9), the Sibyl represents the physical body, the first youth behind her stands for the intellectual faculty by which humans contemplate divine truth, and the second youth is the immortal soul itself. In this way the three figures correspond to Plato's division of the soul into three parts: appetite, intellect, and spirit. A contemporary of Michelangelo understood Michelangelo's Sibyl in just this fashion. She is a true prophet whose books foretell Christ's coming. Within this intellectual ambience it was easy for artists to incorporate pagan images and themes, even in the private chapel of the pope.

PERSPECTIVE FIGURE 12.2 Michelangelo Buonarroti (1475–1564), *The Sibyl of Cumae* in the Sistine Chapel, c. 1510, fresco.   (Vatican Museums; Scala/Art Resource, New York)

Among those who hold out their hands in longing for the further bank is Palinurus, the helmsman of a ship of Aeneas. Palinurus, overcome by sleep, had fallen overboard and drowned, and like Elpenor in Homer's *Odyssey* (on whom he is modeled), he begs for a proper burial. (But Homer has no Charon and no underworld river to be crossed.) Aeneas and the Sibyl embark in Charon's skiff. Having human bodies, they very nearly swamp it (Dante will imitate this scene):

[384] Having completed this part of the journey, Aeneas and Sibyl
385   drew near the bank of the stream. The pilot, from out in the river,
       noticed them making their way through the silent gloom of the forest
       and hurrying down to the shore. He raised a threatening clamor:
          "Whoever you are, approaching in arms the bank of my river,
       stop right there where you are! Speak up! Say why you have ventured
390   to a place belonging alone to dreams, to night, and to shadows.
       I may not carry the living across in my Stygian ferry . . . "

. . . To this the Sibyl replied,
"Although you remain unimpressed by this man's feelings of duty"°
(drawing the golden bough from her cloak, she showed it to Charon),
395   "even so you will recognize this."
    Anger died in his swelling heart as he looked down in silence
at the awesome gift of the Sibyl. At last he slowly directed
his gloomy prow to the shore, drove out the rows of the spirits,
and cleared a way for the pair. When mighty Aeneas was boarding,
400   the rickety vessel creaked and groaned at the weight of the hero
and was nearly swamped by the water that lapped in over its gunwales.
But Charon finally landed the prophet and hero in safety,
to splash their way through the mud and drifted weeds of the river.
    From his triple throat the snarls of Cerberus rang to the sky
405   as he crouched, immense, by his cave, straddled across their pathway.
The Sibyl glanced at his neck, already bristling with vipers,
and threw him a morsel of honey and dough made narcotic with drugs.
Stretching three ravenous jaws, he snapped at the bait in the air.
At once his taut-muscled back went slack on the ground where he lay,
410   filling with his huge bulk the entire width of the cavern.
As the beast lay snoring, Aeneas hastily ran for the portal
and hurriedly ran on beyond the stream no mortal recrosses.

VERGIL, Aeneid 6.384–425

393. *duty:* The Latin word is *pietas,* duty to family, country, and gods. Aeneas was its great exemplar: At the command of Jupiter he has come down to the underworld to ask his father about the destiny of Rome.

The Sibyl and Aeneas next come to the region of the great mass of the dead, who are divided into various groups. The first is those who died too soon: infants, those wrongly convicted of crime, suicides, and those who have died for love. These last include the Phoenician queen of Carthage, Dido, whom Aeneas had abandoned. Next to these are soldiers who fell in battle, especially the dead of the Trojan War.

Now they come to a fork in the road. The way to the left leads to Tartarus, place of eternal torment and the great sinners, including Tantalus and Sisyphus. The Titans are there too, sent to Tartarus by the thunderbolts of Zeus according to Hesiod's *Theogony.* Another famous sufferer is **Ixion** (ik-**sī**-on), a king of the tribe of the Lapiths in Thessaly, who lusted after Hera. Zeus, not believing that anyone could really desire his wife, for sport made an image of Hera out of cloud. Ixion pounced on it and his seed tumbled through the cloud to the earth. Up sprang Centaurus, father of the Centaurs. Zeus bound Ixion to a wheel of fire that turns slowly through the eternal mists (Figure 12.5).

Sinners not mentioned by Vergil (or Homer) but common in later accounts are the Danaïds, the "daughters of Danaüs," who killed their husbands on their wedding night. Their punishment was to fill a vat by carrying water in jugs that had no bottoms (see Figure 12.2).

The crime of Vergil's great sinners, like Homer's, is impiety against the gods, but unlike Homer, Vergil universalizes the moral vision of crime punished and virtue rewarded to include the fates of ordinary humans. As in Plato's story about Er, to which

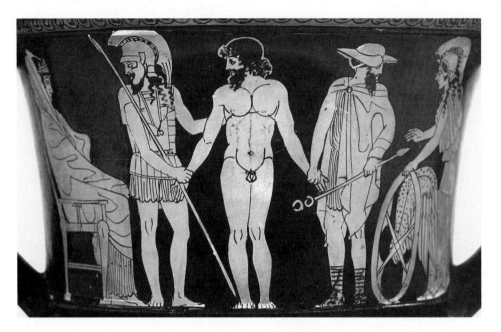

FIGURE 12.5 Ares and Hermes, holding Ixion fast, present the criminal before Hera, the goddess he thought he was ravishing, while Athena prepares the wheel to which he will be bound, on a red-figured Attic vase, c. 450 BC.   (British Museum, London; © Trustees of the British Museum / Art Resource, New York)

Vergil's account owes a good deal, we do not actually behold the torment of Vergil's sinners. Even the Sibyl is not allowed to see, but has learned about them from Hecatê:

[608]   Here are those who in life detested and envied their brothers;
          those who attacked their fathers, who cheated and swindled dependents,
610   who refused to offer to others a part of their chance-given riches,°
          but in avarice hoarded it all; of the greedy the number is legion.
          Here were the men who were slain in the very act of adultery.
          And faithless breakers of oaths° who fought for a criminal cause—
          all these, loaded with chains, lie dreading the penalty waiting . . .
615   Sadly they cry a warning in a voice that rings through the shadow,
          "Be warned by my words. Learn justice. Do not belittle the gods."
          Here is the traitor who peddled his country and set up a tyrant,
          who for a bribe would establish bad laws and abolish the good;
          here the incestuous man who corrupted the bed of his daughter—
620   darers of horrible crimes, who enjoyed the fruit of their daring.
          If I had a hundred mouths, I could not exhaust their offenses,
          nor could I even begin to expound the torments they suffer.

                                        VERGIL, *Aeneid* 6.608–627

610. *chance-given riches:* Magnanimity or liberality ranked high as a virtue in the ancient world and miserly greed as a great vice.   613. *breakers of oaths:* That is, the opponents of Augustus in the civil wars with Marc Antony.

PERSPECTIVE 12.3

DANTE'S *INFERNO*

Dante Alighieri (1265–1321) was a citizen of the powerful and independent state of Florence. In 1301 he was convicted, on political grounds, of corruption and spent the rest of his life in exile, writing poetry in his native Tuscan dialect instead of the traditional Latin. He was one of the first modern poets. So influential were his works that they are regarded as founding the modern Italian language. Until Dante's time it appeared that the Provençal dialect of southern France would become the speech of northern Italy.

Dante's great work was the *Divina Commedia,* comprising the *Inferno,* the *Purgatorio,* and the *Paradiso.* An allegory of the soul's progress from sin to redemption, the poem is a highly complex and learned exploration of morals, politics, theology, cosmology, and philosophy. From the time of its publication it has gripped the imagination by its vivid images, narrative power, and beauty of language, and in spite of its difficulty has always been a popular work.

The *Inferno* is deeply indebted to classical myth as transmitted by the Roman poets (Greek texts were not available, and Dante did not know Greek). Vergil, especially, was his literary model, and in the poem guides Dante through the underworld, an enormous inverted cone divided into nine layers. To each layer is assigned the punishment of some category of sin. From the underworld they enter Purgatory on the opposite side of the world, and from there Dante (but not Vergil) ascends into Paradise. Many of Dante's underworld scenes are modeled on those in Vergil, just as Vergil modeled his scenes on the *Odyssey* and on Plato. At the very bottom of the inverted cone, in the depths of Hell, stands Lucifer, with three heads and three mouths, chewing eternally on those who sinned against their masters: Brutus and Cassius, who killed Julius Caesar, and Judas, who betrayed Christ.

A persistent mythical image is the river one must cross to reach the world of the dead. For Odysseus, this water is the river Ocean, which encircles the world and which Odysseus himself navigated. For Vergil, it is the river Acheron, over which the boatman Charon ferries the souls of the dead. Although a "Christian" Hell, Dante's underworld is bounded by Acheron too, and, as in Vergil's *Aeneid,* Charon fears to transport a living man across it. In the following passage Dante describes the moment when Charon sees Dante and Vergil, his ghostly guide, at the river's edge, surrounded by the souls of the damned, who await transport to the other side:

[82]   And there I saw, poling his punt toward us,
          an ancient boatman, his hair grown white with years.
          "You're out of luck, you wicked souls," he screamed,

85   "who have no hope of ever seeing heaven.
 I'm here to ship you to the other side,
 to burning, freezing, to eternal darkness—
but you" (he looked at me), "you're still alive!
 Get out. You don't belong. All these are dead!"
90   When he looked again and saw I had not moved,
"Go, take another path, another vessel,"
 he cried to me. "To reach the other shore
 you'll need a nimbler boat than this of mine."
My leader told him, "Charon, don't get excited.
95   This was decreed where will translates to power.
 Accept it, then, and question it no more."
The pilot through that death-hued leaden swamp
 clamped shut his bearded jaws and angry tongue,
 though red flame still glared from his savage eyes.
100   Then all those poor exhausted naked souls
 turned pale and shook with trembling chattering teeth,
 hearing the bitter words that told their fate.
They cursed their god, their parents who begat them,
 their race, the time and place of their conception;
105   they cursed the day on which they saw the light.
And now together, crowded in one mass,
 they drew with screams of pain to the cursed shore
 that waits for every man who fears not God.
The demon Charon, glaring with hot red eyes,
110   drives them ashore and herds them in together,
 belaboring the stragglers with his oar.
Just as, in autumn, the leaves drop one by one,
 at last the naked branch looks sadly down
 to see the rustling pile upon the ground:
115   So from the bank there plunged the cursed seed
 of Adam, one by one, as falcons drop,
 when the huntsman gives the whistle to return.

DANTE, Inferno 3.82–117

Dante, overcome by the spectacle of the herds of the damned crowding into Charon's boat, faints and does not revive until he is on the other side.

Dante's description is a clear example how ancient stories and images are recast to acquire utterly new meanings. Michelangelo did the same with the Sibyl in the Sistine Chapel (Perspective Figure 12.2).

For Homer the other world is a dark, dismal, dull realm, across the great river or beneath the ground—a vision built on primitive fears of ghosts and our own sure end. For Vergil the other world can be happy because it holds an Elysium, where dwell the spirits who will be Romans, who will fulfill Rome's mission in history. For Dante Hell is the vicious unending pain of those who have chosen deliberately to reject God's love when they might have chosen to accept it. Homer is spooky and nostalgic, Vergil political, and Dante moral.

Aeneas leaves the golden bough as an offering to Proserpina (Persephonê) in front of the gate to Pluto's palace, and he and the Sibyl hurry on to Elysium, where dwell the ghosts of heroes who died in battle—many more than we find in Homer—and of many other sages and poets. Of course for Homer Elysium was some place in the upper world, while Vergil makes it a section of his underworld. Vergil's description owes much to Plato's vision of the mythical dead gathered for reincarnation:

[638] They passed to the happy region of green and flowering glades,
        the groves where the favored dwell, the blessed haunt of the heroes.
640   A purer aether enfolds them and clothes them in larger soft light.
        A sun of their own shines above, their own stars call them to slumber.
        Some find delight in wrestling in rings made soft by the grass;
        some exercise well-trained muscles in arenas of golden sand.
        Others delight in the steps of the dance or the singing of verses.
645   Orpheus, dressed as a bard, fits musical notes to the epic,
        sweeping the lyre with his fingers, or plucking with ivory plectrum.
        Here dwell the noble descendants of Teucer,° a glorious lineage,
        great-hearted heroes, the men of an earlier, happier age—
        Ilus, Assaracus, back to Dardanus, founder of Ilium.
650   Aeneas gazed at their ghostly weapons, their hurrying chariots,
        no longer loaded with fighters; at spears, just stuck in the ground;
        at their horses, now grazing in peace. Yet the joy of their owners
        in chariots, horses, and weapons, which once they enjoyed while alive,
        remained with these fortunate spirits, whose bodies lay in the earth.
655   And others Aeneas observed, relaxing at ease in the meadows,
        picnicking, singing, or dancing, or raising a paean in chorus,
        all through the perfumed thickets of laurel, watered by brooklets
        bickering down through the woods, from great Eridanus on earth.°
        Here were those who alive had shed their blood for their country,
660   and those who all through their days were pure and reverend prophets,
        wise men, uttering oracles worthy of Phoebus himself.
        Here were those whose talents have rendered life more attractive,
        and all who deserve our remembrance as generations roll onward.

VERGIL, *Aeneid* 6.638–663

647. *Teucer:* The first king of Troy. Ilus, Assaracus, and Dardanus were among his successors (see Chart 20.3). Aeneas himself belonged to this house and from his son Iulus sprang the Roman Julii (by a bad etymology), including by adoption Augustus, Vergil's patron.   658. *Eridanus on earth:* The Po. Because the lower world is a sort of copy of that above, its rivers presumably have the same source.

At the end of Book 6, Aeneas at last meets the spirit of his father. Just as Odysseus reached out to his mother three times, but his arms passed through her, so does Aeneas reach out to his father, with the same result. Anchises then shows to his son the procession of great souls awaiting their return to earth, naming those who are to be the mighty heroes of Rome.

Anchises prefaces this account with a cosmology (a theory of the universe) that accepts the cyclical nature of things: Everything that is happening now has repeatedly happened in the past and will happen again and again in the future. The Latin motto printed on the American dollar bill since 1935, *novus ordo seclorum*, "a new cycle of the ages," is a paraphrase of another line of Vergil (*Eclogue 4.6*), referring to his cyclical conception of history and time. When the souls of the good, corrupted by a life in the flesh, descend to the underworld, they are purified so that (as in Plato), after a thousand years, they might return to a new life in a new body. This is philosophy, not myth, but it is philosophy aided by images drawn from older traditional myth.

At the end of Book 6, we are told that there are two gates of dreams: one of horn, through which true dreams emerge, the other of ivory, through which false ones pass. Anchises directs Aeneas, and with him the Sibyl, to depart back to the upper world through the gate of ivory. No one has ever explained why.

KEY NAMES AND TERMS

Hades, 304

Pluto, 304

Erinyes, 306

Psychopompos, 306

Tiresias, 310

Tantalus, 316

Sisyphus, 316

Elysium, 317

Orpheus, 318

Eurydicê, 318

Zagreus, 322

Pythagoras, 323

Er, 324

Acheron, 326

Charon, 326

Ixion, 329

SOME ADDITIONAL ANCIENT SOURCES

Orpheus and Eurydicê: Apollodorus, 1.3.2; Apollonius of Rhodes *Argonautica;* Ovid, *Metamorphoses* 10.1–85, 11.1–84; Hyginus, *Poetica Astronomica* 2.7.

FURTHER READING CHAPTER 12

Burkert, Walter, *Ancient Mystery Cults* (Cambridge, MA, 1987). Lectures on the promise of salvation offered by various pagan cults, especially in the Hellenistic Period.

Garland, R., *The Greek Way of Death* (Ithaca, NY, 1985). Covers burial customs, attitudes about the dead, and hero cults.

Guthrie, W. K. C., *Orpheus and Greek Religion: A Study of the Orphic Movement* (New York, 1966). Scholarly study of the whole problem.

Johnston, Sarah Iles, *Restless Dead: Encounters between the Living and the Dead in Ancient Greece* (Berkeley, CA, 1999). Superior in-depth analysis of the Greeks' complex relationship with the world of ghosts.

Rohde, E., *Psyche, the Cult of Souls and Belief in Immortality among Ancient Greeks,* 8th ed., trans. W. B. Hillis (Chicago, 1987; first published in German, 1925). Pathbreaking study of ancient Greek conceptions of death and the soul.

Vermeule, Emily, *Aspects of Death in Early Greek Art and Poetry* (Berkeley, CA, 1979). A stimulating review of how the Greeks looked at death, including burial and mourning rites, visions of the underworld, conception of the soul, and historical connections with the Bronze Age and other Mediterranean cultures.

West, M. L., *The Orphic Poems* (Oxford, UK, 1983). The most modern review of our evidence for "Orphic" religion and literature. Although written for scholars, the general reader can follow most of the argument.

CHAPTER 13

GILGAMESH

INTRODUCTION TO HEROIC MYTH

Butch Cassidy Y'know, when I was a kid, I always figured on being a hero
  when I grew up.
The Sundance Kid Too late now.

FROM THE SCREENPLAY TO *Butch Cassidy and the Sundance Kid*,
BY WILLIAM GOLDMAN (1969)

IN DIVINE MYTHS THE principal characters are gods and goddesses, but in legends—the second major category of myth examined in this book—the protagonists are human characters. Gods and goddesses often play a role, but legends are chiefly stories about heroes, stories that purport to narrate events from the human past.

We commonly use the word **hero** very broadly to refer to the principal character in a play or film, to celebrate a neighbor who saves a cat in a tree, or to express admiration, as in the phrase "my hero." In modern journalism, soldiers in war, fighting on your side, are all "heroes," especially if they are wounded in some horrible way. For us, a hero is someone who stands out from others, someone distinguished by prominence, bravery, or merit.

For the ancient Greeks, however, the term *hero* had a much more specific meaning. Homer used it to mean any "noble" or "well-born" male, always alive, but later the term was applied to noble figures from the distant past, all dead. This shift in meaning, from Homeric warrior to subject of myth and religious cult, seems to have taken place when the *heroes* of epic came to be worshiped as powers dwelling beneath the earth.

THE TOMBS OF HEROES

Cult places for worship of heroes were called *heroa* (singular = *heroön*), and most heroes whose legends are told in the following chapters had them. Tombs normally had the shape of enormous earthen mounds heaped up to protect and monumentalize the grave of the hero (Figure 13.1). There are *heroa* attributed to Pelops at Olympia, to Achilles at Troy, and to Aeneas at Lavinium near Rome. Such mounds were deliberately built in conspicuous locations, within sanctuaries and along principal roads or maritime routes, to afford the deceased everlasting renown.

Religious cult and other activity performed at these tombs during the Classical Period reinforced belief in an earlier age of heroes for those who visited and maintained the shrines. In the early fifth century BC, the Athenian politician Cimon brought "home to Athens" from the island of Scyros the protective bones of a giant skeleton he took to be the Athenian hero Theseus. He established a cult in the Athenian agora to excite patriotic feeling. After his first victory over the Persians, at the Battle of the Granicus River near the Hellespont in 334 BC, Alexander the Great made a pilgrimage to Troy and ran naked three times around the tomb of Achilles. On a later visit to Troy, the half-mad Roman emperor Caracalla arranged for the sudden death of his own close friend Festus, so that he could reenact the hero Achilles' mourning for his dead friend Patroclus. He celebrated the funeral of Festus in Homeric style, complete with copious animal sacrifice, a magnificent funeral pyre, and a new earthen mound near Troy to imitate the tumulus of Achilles.

FIGURE 13.1 The tomb of the non-Greek Lydian king Alyattes, father of Croesus (595–c. 547 BC), one of the largest tumuli in Asia Minor (900 feet diameter, 220 feet high), in the royal cemetery near Sardis, sixth century BC (see Map XIII, inside back cover). There are about one hundred tumuli in this cemetery. Herodotus (1.93), who c. 450 BC saw five markers on the summit of this tumulus with inscriptions recording the labor required to build it, describes this tomb as the greatest work of human hands in the world, apart from those of the Egyptians and Babylonians. Greek heroic tumuli were never so grand, but constructed for similar reasons.   (Photo by William Aylward)

The religious cult celebrated at some preexisting Greek tumuli—sacrifice and offerings—seems to have begun in Greece in the late Iron Age around 800 BC. Many would connect such innovative religious behavior around ancient tombs to the popularization of Greek legends at this time, encouraged by the spread of alphabetic texts of heroic poems, now widely memorized and reperformed. Heroic cult was similar to that celebrated in cults to the gods, except that the souls of the dead were the objects of worship.

"THE EPIC OF GILGAMESH"

Few ancient cultures produced heroic myths. There are no heroes at all (in the Greek sense of the word) in the myths of ancient Egypt and almost none in the Bible (only Samson and perhaps David, who killed Goliath). Even the ancient Romans seem to have had no true heroes of their own devising. The ancient Mesopotamians, by contrast, did tell stories about a hero, the great king **Gilgamesh**, one of the oldest cycle of stories in the world.

The so-called epic of Gilgamesh that has come down to us was never an oral poem, like Homer's poems and Hesiod's, taken down in dictation from the mouth of an illiterate poet. The poem was rather a scribal exercise created in writing, meant to be read and studied by other scribes and those learning to be scribes. Still, the Gilgamesh stories have many elements in common with the legends of Greece. The Greek stories must depend in some way on Mesopotamian oral tradition both for style and content.

The parallels between stories about Gilgamesh and those found in Greece are more than mere coincidence. Many elements of Greek legend are not Greek in origin. Somehow such stories passed from East to West, not through written media, of course, but apparently through bilingual singers. We have good evidence that Greeks and Semitic seafarers intermarried during the early Archaic Period, which could explain such bilingualism and the transmission of Eastern stories to Greece. Before turning to the Greek legends themselves, therefore, we must first examine the ancient Mesopotamian tales of Gilgamesh, which precede in time and inventiveness Greek heroic tales, and which may very well serve as a model for what we expect to find in the myth of a "hero."

Gilgamesh was a real man who once ruled the Sumerian city of Uruk (**ur-ūk**, biblical "Erech"). According to king lists inscribed in cuneiform writing on clay tablets, he lived for 126 years sometime about 2600 BC. His example is strong evidence that legendary characters did live at one time, as is likely for most Greek heroes. He was best remembered for building the city walls of Uruk. Fragments telling of his life and deeds survive recorded in Sumerian, Akkadian, Hittite, and other languages and scripts. On twelve tablets from the library of Assurbanipal in Nineveh, destroyed in 612 BC, survives something close to a connected tale, a version of the story that may go back a thousand years earlier. The story had many separate episodes that a scribe named Sin-leqe-unnini—he signed his name—pieced together to form a coherent narrative.

Gilgamesh and Enkidu

The poem begins with a summary of Gilgamesh's career:

> The man who saw everything to the ends of the earth,
> who experienced everything, considered all!
> He saw what was hidden, he disclosed the undisclosed.
> He brought back a story of times before the flood.
> He went on a long journey. He was wearied; he rested.
> Everything he did he engraved on a monument made of stone.

The first lines of the Greek *Odyssey* seem to echo this opening of Gilgamesh, reflecting the continuity of traditions from East to West:

[1]
> Sing to me, O Muse, of the wily man,
> who wandered far after he had sacked the holy city of Troy.
> Many were the men whose cities he saw and he learned their mind
> and many the hurts he felt in his heart upon the sea,
> 5   trying to win his own life and the return of his comrades.

HOMER, Odyssey 1–5

Described as two-thirds divine and one-third mortal (just how that is possible is not clear), Gilgamesh was destined to die. He was king of Uruk but proud and mighty. He abused his royal power. He overcame every challenger. He slept with every virgin before her wedding night (the common royal male's right to be first to have sex with any woman). At last the people of Uruk could bear no more of Gilgamesh's arrogance and begged the gods for relief.

Aruru, mother of the gods, pinched off a piece of clay and fashioned a rival to Gilgamesh, someone who could temper his spirit. Her creation was **Enkidu** (**en**-ki-dū), a primitive man who wore his locks long like a woman. His body was matted with hair, and he lived in the wild, ran with gazelles, ate grass, and drank at the water holes.

One day a trapper saw Enkidu. Terrified, the trapper reported to Gilgamesh that he had seen a wild man on the steppe, who destroyed his traps and released his game. Meanwhile, Gilgamesh learned in a dream about the coming of one who would be his best friend:

> Gilgamesh says to him, the trapper:
> "Go, my trapper, and take a whore with you.
> When he [Enkidu] comes with his beasts to the water hole,
> she will pull off her clothing and lay bare her ripeness.
> When he sees her, he will approach her.
> Then will his beasts, raised on the plains, reject him!"

For two days the trapper and the whore waited beside the water hole. On the third day Enkidu came. The woman bared her nakedness. For six days and seven nights Enkidu made love to her until, satisfied at last, he arose and went back to the wild. But he was sadly changed:

Enkidu was lessened, he could not run so fast.
Yet he had acquired discernment, was wiser.
He returned, sat at the feet of the whore.

The woman explained to Enkidu that now he was like a god and that he should follow her. From the shepherds he learned how to eat bread, drink wine, and wear clothes. A report came from the city that on that night Gilgamesh would deflower a virgin about to be married. Enkidu leaped up and declared that he would challenge the tyrant.

Enkidu entered the city. Crowds gathered around him, admired his strength, and compared him with Gilgamesh. As Gilgamesh came down the alley, Enkidu threw up a challenge. The two mighty men wrestled. Walls shook, doors broke. At last Gilgamesh threw Enkidu to the ground. The rivals got up and, filled with mutual admiration, embraced one another warmly and began a lifelong friendship.

The motif of the true male companion is a significant component of Greek hero stories too, as we will see.

Gilgamesh and Humbaba

Gilgamesh proposed that he and Enkidu go together to the Land of the Living, also called the Land of the Cedars, ruled over by the sun-god Shamash (**sha**-mash = Sumerian Utu). Enkidu hesitated; he had already been there and feared **Humbaba** (hum-**bab**-a), the guardian of the forest. Gilgamesh dismissed his friend's fears: Even if they perished, their names would live on.

The heroes made careful preparations. They took with them mighty swords, axes, and bows. After crossing seven mountains, they came to the edge of the cedar forest, which extended one thousand miles in every direction:

They stood, they admired the forest,
stared and stared at the high cedars,
stared and stared at the entrance to the cedars,
where Humbaba left tracks as he paced on his rounds.
The paths were worn, the road was good.
They admired the Cedar Mountain, dwelling of gods.
The cedars gleamed on the side of the mountain.
Their shade was delicious, bringing happiness.
The undergrowth was thick, blanketing the forest.

But when Enkidu touched the gate of the forest, his hand was at once paralyzed. Gilgamesh helped him to overcome his fear. They entered the forest and traveled far. At night they had ominous dreams, for Humbaba knew of their presence.

Then Gilgamesh took up his ax and chopped at the forest.
When Humbaba heard the noise,
he was angered. "Who has come,
who has injured the trees
that grow in my mountains?
Who has felled the cedar?"

The sun-god Shamash urged Gilgamesh to attack Humbaba, but suddenly Gilgamesh was overcome with sleep and fell down on the ground as if dead. Enkidu could not stir him. Then Gilgamesh came to himself, stood up, and put on his armor. Overcome, with tears in his eyes, Humbaba begged for his life, even taking Gilgamesh by the hand like a friend. Gilgamesh struck Humbaba on the neck with his sword. Enkidu struck him too. Down fell Humbaba, dead. They offered his head to Enlil, the storm-god, but Enlil was furious that they had killed the guardian of the forest.

We will see how the motif of the broken taboo and divine retribution plays out repeatedly in Greek heroic myth.

Gilgamesh and Ishtar

When they arrived back in Uruk, Gilgamesh put away his dirty clothes and combed out his long hair. Ishtar (= the Sumerian goddess Inanna) saw how handsome he was and promised that, if he would only pour his seed into her, she would give him rich rewards. Gilgamesh sneered at the great goddess and abused her as follows, one of the best-known passages in Mesopotamian literature:

"You are a charcoal grill which goes out in the cold!
You are a back door that lets in the squall and the storm,
a fortress that smashes down the brave,
pitch that fouls its bearers,
a siege engine that wrecks the enemy's land,
a shoe that pinches its owner's foot!
Which lover did you love forever?
Which of your shepherds pleases you for all time?
Listen, I will name your lovers:
To Tammuz [= Sumerian Dumuzi], lover of your youth,
you have given moaning year in, year out.
You loved the spotted shepherd-bird,
then struck him, breaking his wing.
Now he sits in the woods crying, "Oh, my wing!"
You loved a lion, the perfection of power;
twice seven pits you dug for him.
Then you loved a stallion, a charger in war.
What is his lot? the whip, the spur, and the lash."

Gilgamesh gives other examples of those who suffered after yielding to the goddess of love, including her father's own gardener: When he brought her baskets of dates, she turned him into a frog! The male hostility toward the treacherous sexually aggressive female stands out strongly in this story, a powerful and recurring theme in Greek heroic legend.

Ishtar bursts into a fury and storms off to her father, Anu, king of heaven. She demands that Anu send down the Bull of Heaven to destroy Gilgamesh for his insolence. (In the *Iliad* 5.320–425, too, the love-goddess, injured by a mortal, begs her powerful sky-god father to intervene.) If Anu refuses, she threatens to crack open the gates of the underworld and release the legions of the dead (Inanna makes the same threat in the story of Inanna and Dumuzi, Chapter 10). The sky-god Anu agrees, and Ishtar enters Uruk, city of Gilgamesh, leading the mighty destroying Bull of Heaven.

The bull snorts, a chasm opens, and a hundred young men of Uruk fall in, then two hundred, then three hundred. The bull snorts again and a second chasm opens. In fall a hundred young men, then two hundred, then three hundred:

> When the bull snorted a third time a chasm opened,
> and Enkidu fell in,
> but leaped out and seized the Bull of Heaven by the horns.
> The Bull of Heaven shook spittle into his face
> and with its fat tail threw dung all around.

Enkidu, blinded with dung, called out to Gilgamesh, who plunged his sword into the monster's neck (Figure 13.2). The heroes cut out its heart for the sun-god Shamash. Ishtar, enraged, appeared on the towers of the city. Enkidu cut off the bull's genitals and threw them in her face! If he had the chance, he would lash the bull's guts to her body!

The two friends held a great celebration, but Enkidu's behavior had deeply offended the gods. One of the pair would have to die. Enkidu had terrible dreams. He knew that he would die. He dreamed that he had gone down to a place very like the Greek House of Hades:

> To the house which is never left, once entered,
> on the trail of no return,
> to the house where the dwellers live in darkness,

FIGURE 13.2 Gilgamesh kills the Bull of Heaven, terracotta votive relief, 2250–1900 BC. Such votives were placed in temples as offerings or carried in camels' saddlebags to gain the gods' protection. (Musées Royaux d'Art et d'Histoire, Brussels)

where dust and clay is food.
They are clothed like birds, have wings for garments,
and never see the light, dwelling in darkness.

Enkidu fell sick and for twelve days lay in bed. Then he died. Gilgamesh mourned, hovering over the body, waiting for it to revive. On the seventh day a maggot crawled from Enkidu's nose. Gilgamesh realized that, for Enkidu, the end had come.

The motif of the hero mourning for a companion whose death he in part caused is best known in Greek legend from the *Iliad*, in the story of Achilles and Patroclus.

The Quest for Eternal Life

Gilgamesh roamed the open country, terrified of the death that would one day be his lot as well. He decided to search for **Utnapishtim** (ūt-na-**pish**-tim, "he saw life" = Sumerian Ziusudra; Akkadian Atrahasis; and Hebrew Noah). Utnapishtim and his wife were the only mortals to have survived the flood, for the gods had transported them across the sea to a place where they enjoyed everlasting life. Gilgamesh set out to question Utnapishtim about the living and the dead.

On his long journey Gilgamesh (like Samson and Heracles) killed ferocious lions lurking in the passes, then came to the high mountains of Mashu, where the sun rises. At the gate of the mountain, Scorpion Men, whose glance was death, stood guard. Somehow (the tablet is broken here) he persuaded them to let him pass. He entered a tunnel of darkness, where no one could see ahead or behind. For twelve leagues of darkness Gilgamesh traveled on the path of the sun. At last he saw light and emerged into the garden of the gods at the edge of the sea (perhaps the Phoenician coast of the Mediterranean). Gorgeous plants made of precious stones grew there.

In the garden lived Siduri (si-**dur**-ē), the divine beer maid. Siduri advised Gilgamesh to give up his search, accept his mortality, eat good food and drink strong liquor, wear fine clothes, and love his family. No one, except Shamash, had ever crossed the lethal waters of the sea. But she could not persuade him and Gilgamesh set off, punting across the waters of death with special poles (we are not sure how to translate the text here). On the other side, Utnapishtim came up, complained about Gilgamesh's uncouth appearance, then delivered a speech about death:

No one sees Death,
No one sees the face of Death.
No one hears the voice of Death.
Brutal Death just cuts you down.
We may build a house, we may build a nest:
Our brothers divide it when we die.
There may be hostility in the land,
but then the river rises in flood.°

rises in flood: That is, death settles all disputes.

Dragonflies drift upon the water,
they turn their gaze upon the sun.
From the beginning there has been no permanence.
The sleeping and the dead are the same.
There is no picture of Death.

How did Utnapishtim escape the lot of other mortals? Utnapishtim answered this question by relating the story of the flood, in which he plays the part of Noah. He and his wife had escaped death because of Enlil, but who will intercede for Gilgamesh?

To prove Gilgamesh's innate mortality, Utnapishtim suggests a trial. Let Gilgamesh stay awake for six days and seven nights, the length of time of the flood. If he cannot conquer Sleep, the brother of Death, how can he conquer Death himself? Gilgamesh thought the trial easy, but promptly fell asleep and awoke seven nights later. Although he denied that he had slept, Utnapishtim pointed to seven loaves in progressive stages of decay that his wife had baked and placed, one each day, at the hero's side.

There was still a chance that Gilgamesh might escape at least the ravages of old age. Utnapishtim told him of a prickly herb that grew deep in the sea. Its flower, which looked like a rose, would restore youth to an old man. Gilgamesh tied stones to his feet and dropped down deep into the water, found the plant, and plucked it, although its thorns tore his hands. He cut the ropes that held the stones, bobbed to the surface, and came ashore. Gilgamesh set out for home. On the way he stopped to bathe in a cool well. A serpent that lived in the well emerged and ate the plant. That is why serpents can renew their youth.

Gilgamesh realized that immortality could never be his. He sat down and wept. He returned to Uruk and admired its great city walls, his true achievement. He engraved his tale on a stone (note the reference to writing), grew old, and died. He was given a splendid burial. **(For the complete text of the Gilgamesh epic, see http://www.ancienttexts.org/library/mesopotamian/gilgamesh)**

The Hero Caught Between Nature and Culture

The deep concerns and speculations that underlie this story developed specifically in Mesopotamia, a dangerous land with mysterious and unknown beginnings. Egyptians did not fear death and so did not seek a way to escape it; they had already found that way. Here for the first time appears the story of the journey in search of truth. We ourselves receive this story directly from the immensely influential Greek *Odyssey*, from which the West has taken its self-image as restless and inquiring, spinning inquisitively on across the prairies, to foreign lands, even into space, in search of the meaning of things. But this story is not Western in origin at all.

The Gilgamesh epic is the longest and most ambitious literary epic recorded in the complex, almost hopelessly arcane cuneiform writing. A central theme is the contrast and hostility between the natural world and the cultural world of humans. Enkidu is the "natural man"—his hair is long and he eats grass with the beasts of the field. After intercourse with a woman, he becomes "wise" and is separated from the natural world, the lot of all humankind.

Similarly, Adam and Eve, after eating from the Tree of Knowledge, see that they are naked (that is, discover their sexuality) and must leave the Garden of Eden (the natural world). When Enkidu is dying, he bitterly blames the world of culture for his undoing. He blames the trapper who found him and the woman who tamed him. Sympathizing with Enkidu's resentment, Gilgamesh puts on animal skins and wanders through the wild on a quest to the ends of the earth. When the quest fails, he returns from nature to the world of culture, dons clean clothes, and rejoices in the city walls, the symbolic divide between the human and natural worlds.

Although gods occasionally die, their ordinary lot is to live forever. Only a mortal like Gilgamesh can suffer anguish from speculating on the meaning of action and of life and on his hopeless future in a stale, dank afterlife where clay is food and good people and bad, kings and ordinary mortals, are treated just alike: The Mesopotamian underworld was similar to the Greeks'. This very torment is an essential part of his nature as a hero and explains our interest in him: We, too, live between nature and culture, and we, too, are destined to die.

FOLKTALE MOTIFS IN HEROIC MYTHS

Like other ancient legends, the story of Gilgamesh does have some connection with historical fact. We noted earlier that Gilgamesh really was a king of the Mesopotamian city of Uruk, a real place where his name has been found on clay tablets. We know nothing about him or his reign, but we can imagine that the real king Gilgamesh was a great ruler who accomplished much in his lifetime. It is easy to believe that he or his followers were eager to see his reputation enhanced and his memory preserved for posterity (just as the story tells of Gilgamesh's longing to be remembered in words graven on stone). The Mesopotamian legend of Gilgamesh, like many ancient Greek legends, probably began in such a wish to preserve a memory of the words and deeds of a real man whose life was exceptional.

In the fluidity of oral tradition, however, such stories about men of the past easily mix with other elements having no connection to any particular historical figure. The hero's name is preserved, but the stories told about him come to incorporate patterns drawn from other stories, many of them motifs known from folklore. By comparing the career of Gilgamesh, the oldest heroic legend in the world, with heroic stories from Greece, we can formulate a pattern of motifs that characterizes the "hero myth" and will help us to understand such stories:

- One of the hero's parents may be divine (Gilgamesh was partly divine).
- The hero's birth is miraculous or unusual, but of his childhood we know little (this motif is missing from the Gilgamesh story).
- The hero has great strength and is a menace to his compatriots as well as to others (Gilgamesh abused the people of Uruk).
- The hero's truest companion is another male (Enkidu).
- The hero falls under an enemy's power and is compelled to perform impossible labors (Gilgamesh destroys Humbaba).

- The hero breaks a taboo, and a terrible price is demanded (Enlil was angry that Gilgamesh and Enkidu killed Humbaba, lord of the forest).

- The hero resists the temptations of an enticing but dangerous woman (Ishtar).

- The hero is responsible for the death of a companion (Enkidu dies after he and Gilgamesh kill the Bull of Heaven).

- The hero goes on a quest, even to the underworld (Gilgamesh travels across the waters at the edge of the world to visit deathless Utnapishtim).

- He may have help from gods, spirits, or magical objects (Gilgamesh uses special poles to punt to the land of Utnapishtim).

- The hero returns home, atones for his crimes, and accepts his limitations (Gilgamesh returns to rule Uruk).

- The hero is rewarded with something of great value (the people of Uruk honor Gilgamesh).

- At his death, the hero receives a magnificent funeral and may become a god (Gilgamesh receives a fine funeral and his memory will never die).

PERSPECTIVE 13

J. R. R. TOLKIEN'S MODERN HERO IN *THE LORD OF THE RINGS*

The Oxford *Beowulf* scholar J. R. R. Tolkien (1892–1973) gives us a modern vision of a hero, Frodo Baggins, in his trilogy *The Lord of the Rings,* which shares many features with ancient myth. *The Lord of the Rings* trilogy, published in England in the mid-1950s and in the United States in 1965, became a cult classic and was widely read during the late 1960s, when many thought the world was changing in a fundamental way (and so it did). The trilogy has remained a favorite of fantasy literature aficionados. Starting in 2001 it was released in three successive years as three movies, winning for director Peter Jackson eleven Academy Awards in 2004 (for *Return of the King*) and bringing the epic to life for new generations.

The tale is set in Middle-earth, made up from elements of Anglo-Saxon England infused with heroic epic. Frodo, an invented character, is a modern, vulnerable, self-conscious hero. He completely lacks the bigger-than-life dimension of heroes of ancient legend, as well as their customary swagger. Frodo is an unwilling hero who accepts the burden of the quest to destroy in Mount Doom the "one Ring to rule them all," left to him by his adopted father Bilbo Baggins. The Lord of Mordor threatens to use the Ring to conquer all of Middle-earth.

A more obvious hero in Tolkien's tale might have been the ranger and future king, Aragorn, whose career is very like that of a classical hero. But Tolkien prefers to focus on the humble Frodo, a Hobbit with no aspirations other than to enjoy a happy life in the Shire among his friends, smoking his pipe by the fire. Aragorn or Galadriel or others would have been tempted to use the power of the Ring to achieve their own ideals, just what the fallen Saruman did, once wise, now corrupted utterly.

Frodo is like a classical hero, however, in several ways:

- He has a helper: his true companion and servant Samwise Gamgee, although he also receives help from the Fellowship of the Ring, including the mighty wizard Gandalf the Grey.

- He falls under the power of an enemy: the Ring, which seeks its maker and master, Sauron.

- He goes on a quest to the land of death: Mordor, at the edge of the world.

- He has the aid of magical objects: the Ring to make him invisible; an elven-made cloak, wonderfully light and warm; an elven crystal phial to provide light in dark places; Lembas, the compact high-energy food given him by the elves; and Bilbo's sword Sting, made by ancient elves.

- He returns home after completing his quest: Frodo returns to his beloved Shire, but he no longer takes pleasure from mortals and on each anniversary of his failure to destroy the Ring he feels the sickness of his wound. At last he joins Bilbo, Gandalf, and the elves leaving Middle-earth for the Blessed Realms (Menelaüs and Helen, too, now live in the Blessed Isles).

We might summarize his nonclassical features as follows:

- Frodo is humble, filled with self-doubt about his ability to perform the task set for him.

- Frodo does not seek a quest for glory. He is surprised to find himself volunteering in a small unheroic voice, "I will take the Ring, though I do not know the way."

- Frodo is a Hobbit (called by men a Halfling) without the clear physical strength of a Heracles or Theseus or Perseus, and unlike them he avoids violence when he can.

- At the moment when he should complete his task, after a strenuous journey to the edge of the world, he fails. Unable to throw the Ring into the Crack of Doom, he puts it on and claims it for himself, saying, "I will not do this deed." Only because the sneaking Gollum fell into the Crack, struggling to take the Ring, was it destroyed.

Some see in Frodo an essentially Christian hero—meek, carrying his cross, guided by pity and mercy toward his adversary Gollum. Tolkien was a devout Catholic. While writing from 1936 to 1949, Tolkien met regularly with a group of writers who called themselves the Inklings, including novelist and scholar C. S. Lewis, author of *The Chronicles of Narnia,* who converted to Christianity during this period because of his talks with Tolkien. At this very time raged over England the demonic spectacle of World War II, when fires filled the skies and the crash of bombs filled the air.

Many of the same elements recur in the legends of the ancient Greeks, as we will see in the following chapters. The story of the hero surely appeals to deep levels of human concern, but we must remember that this pattern of motifs belongs to the realm of folklore in which the principal objective is to tell a riveting, sometimes moralizing, tale, not to preserve the truth about the past or about human nature.

Observations: Heroic Nudity

In looking at representations of heroes in ancient Greek art (there are many examples in this book), we often have the impression of being in a world without clothing. During the Archaic and Classical periods, male nudity in art was pervasive, although never female nudity. In art of the Greek Bronze Age, by contrast, men were clothed and female nudity was common. Such Bronze Age naked female "idols" had magical functions to perform, unrelated to the commemorative sculpture of the Archaic and Classical periods.

Art historians call the striking male nudity in Greek art "**heroic nudity**," although Homer's heroes are never described as fighting naked and the nudity of a dead warrior stripped of his armor is the pinnacle of shame. Odysseus, exposed and ashamed, covers himself with sticks when discovered by Nausicaä (see Figure 22.4).

We wonder what could have been the origin and purpose of this "heroic nudity," then, but do not have clear answers. Many attribute this convention to the influence of Greek athletics, practiced in the nude since the sixth century BC. Of course, athletic nudity itself served a similar taste for the splendor of the well-muscled male body. In art male nudity quickly distinguishes the "heroic" Greeks from non-Greeks, and especially from Persians, who were always depicted in elaborate dress (see Figure 16.10).

Some of the best-known Greek nude males exist in the tradition of monumental stone statuary called *kouroi* ("young men"; singular, *kouros*). The same word appears in the *Curetes*, "youths," who beat their shields to drown the cries of the infant Zeus (Chapter 4). Statues of this type were carved primarily in the sixth century BC, usually as dedications in sanctuaries or as markers for graves (Figure 13.3). Large-scale (sometimes gigantic) freestanding *kouroi* were inspired by similar monuments in Egypt, but public statues in Egypt were always clothed.

Female nudity in public Greek art does not appear until late in the Classical Period. The first public representation probably belonged to the sculptor Praxiteles (c. 400–330 BC), who created a cult statue of Aphrodite for the town of Cnidus at the southwestern tip of Asia Minor in the fourth century BC (Figure 9.2; Figure 2.6 of the earlier nude *hetaira*, by contrast, belongs to the realm of private art). *Korai*, "girls," the female counterpart to *kouroi* in the Archaic Period of Greece, wear elaborately carved and painted garments (Figure 2.9). On the Parthenon sculptures of the mid-fifth century BC, gods and men are shown in heroic nudity, but drapery covers the goddesses and Greek women.

Because of its association with male Olympians and heroes in Greek art, mortals claiming divinity adopted heroic nudity for their portraits, including Alexander the Great and the emperors of Rome (Figure 13.4), who a thousand years after the Greek *kouroi* continued through manly undress to advertise close relations to the gods and to the great men of early times.

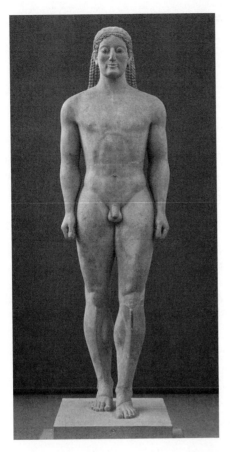

FIGURE 13.3 A *kouros* from Anavysos, near Athens, set up as a grave marker for Kroisos, a warrior who died in battle, here memorialized in heroic nudity. *Kouroi* like this one were also set up as dedications in sanctuaries, especially to Apollo. Marble, six feet high, c. 550–525 BC. (National Archaeological Museum, Athens; Scala/Art Resource, New York)

FIGURE 13.4 The Roman emperor Antoninus Pius (AD 86–161). He wears the cloak of a general as a symbol of military prowess, but is otherwise nude. Nudity, and especially bare feet, in Roman imperial portraiture was a sign of the ruler's divinity and legitimate claim to heroic ancestry. Marble, six feet high, second century AD. (The Art Archive / Museo Nazionale Palazzo Altemps. Rome; Gianni Dagli Orti)

KEY NAMES AND TERMS

FURTHER READING CHAPTER 13

Bottéro, J., *Mesopotamia: Writing, Reasoning, and the Gods,* trans. A. Bahrani and M. Van de Mieroop (Chicago, 1992). Essays on aspects of the culture, by a leading scholar.

Dalley, Stephanie, *Myths from Mesopotamia: Creation, the Flood, Gilgamesh, and Others* (Oxford, UK, 1989). Superior translations, with commentary, of the Mesopotamian myths of Atrahasis, Gilgamesh, the descent of Ishtar, and other important myths (see also Further Reading for Chapter 3).

Sandars, N. K., *The Epic of Gilgamesh* (Baltimore, MD, 1972). Readable, inexpensive compilation, with a good introduction, of the many fragments (written in several languages) that make up the epic.

West, M. L., *The East Face of Helicon: West Asiatic Elements in Greek Poetry and Myth* (Oxford, UK, 1997). Powerful argument that Greek literature is really Near Eastern literature.

CHAPTER 14

PERSEUS AND MYTHS
OF THE ARGIVE PLAIN

[607] The son of Abas remained, Acrisius, cousin of Bacchus,
    whom Acrisius churlishly drove away from the well-walled city of Argos.°
    Acrisius warred with the god, denying that Zeus was his father.
610 Perseus too he disclaimed, the child of the shower of gold
    that quickened Danaë's womb. Yet mark you the power of truth:
    Acrisius was forced to repent of both these arrogant gestures,
    violence toward the god and disowning the child of his daughter.

OVID, *Metamorphoses* 4.607–614

608. *Argos*: Still another myth of resistance to Dionysus.

N O DOUBT BECAUSE LEGENDS are attached to the names of men and women who really lived, their stories tend to be local, focused on a specific place or territory, as Gilgamesh was the king of Uruk, some of whose walls still stand today. In Greece no territory is richer in its physical remains from the Greek Bronze Age than the **Argive plain** (**ar**-jīv), or richer in its wealth of myths (Map IV, The Argive Plain). Even today the ruins of MYCENAE are some of the most impressive in Greece. Almost the only large sculpture to survive from the Bronze Age, two lions rampant on either side of a Minoan column, loom over the great entranceway to Mycenae, framed by enormous stones (Figure 14.1).

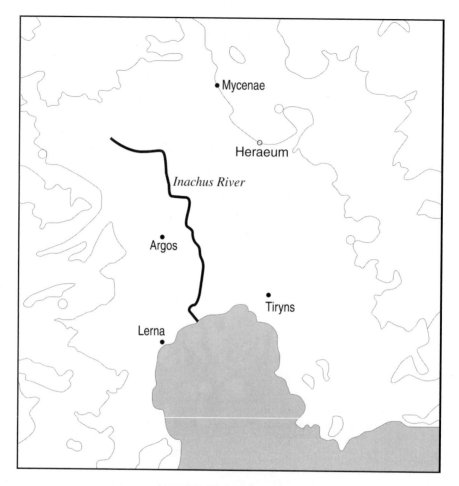

MAP IV The Argive Plain

Around the citadel are nine beehive tombs, domes constructed underground to house the remains of Mycenaean kings. The so-called Treasury of Atreus has the largest dome ever constructed until the Romans built the Pantheon fifteen hundred years later. Graves excavated in the nineteenth century contained an enormous quantity of golden objects of extraordinary quality. In the Bronze Age, Mycenae was a populous center of wealth and power. In myth, it was founded by **Perseus** (**per**-sūs, or **per**-sē-us) and later ruled by Atreus and then his son Agamemnon, who led the Greek forces against Troy (Chapters 20 and 21).

Ten miles south stands **TIRYNS** (**tir**-inz), smaller than Mycenae, a fortress surrounded by amazing walls of immense stones carefully fitted together. Tiryns is near the sea and may have been the port town that served Mycenae, although relations between Mycenae and Tiryns are confused in myth, as they may have been in reality. Perseus was king of Tiryns when he founded Mycenae, and Perseus' grand-

FIGURE 14.1 Victorian visitors at the Lion Gate at Mycenae. Nearly the only surviving large sculpture from the Greek Bronze Age stands in the "relieving triangle," a device that reduces structural weight, over the lintel of the main gate. The central pillar in the sculpture, beside which two lions stand heraldically, is carved in the same style as pillars found in Crete; perhaps it symbolizes the Tree of Life. Through the gate one can see the lower retaining wall of the citadel, which rises to the top of the hill.   (Deutsches Archaologisches Institut, Athens)

son Heracles lived in Tiryns for much of his career. Argos itself, between Mycenae and Tiryns but somewhat to the west and across the stream called Inachus, was the principal settlement of the Argive plain in the Classical Period. Argos was not important in the Bronze Age but in the mythical tradition was often confused with Mycenae.

In this chapter we consider stories of the founding of settlements on the Argive plain and the famous hero Perseus, whose stories are closer to folktale than those of any other Greek hero, a measure of these myths' great age. But the story of Perseus began generations before his birth.

IO AND HER DESCENDANTS

The Wanderings of Io

Melia, nymph of an ash tree, was an Oceanid, daughter of Oceanus and Tethys (Chart 14). She united with Inachus (īn-a-kus), god of the river that flows through the Argive plain, and bore two sons and a daughter, **Io** (ī-ō), ancestor of three great dynasties: the houses of Argos, Thebes, and Crete.

In the best-known version, Io, after whom Zeus lusted, was a priestess of Hera in the HERAEUM, the holiest classical temple to Hera in mainland Greece, built near Mycenae on a Bronze Age site on the northern edge of the Argive plain. Zeus surrounded her in a mist and within it had his way with her. Hera, seeing a mysterious cloud on an otherwise bright and sunny day, came to investigate. Zeus barely had time to disguise his philandering by changing Io into a cow. Hera was not deceived—she admired the handsome animal and asked for it as a gift. Zeus reluctantly turned his transformed lover over to his angry wife. Hera

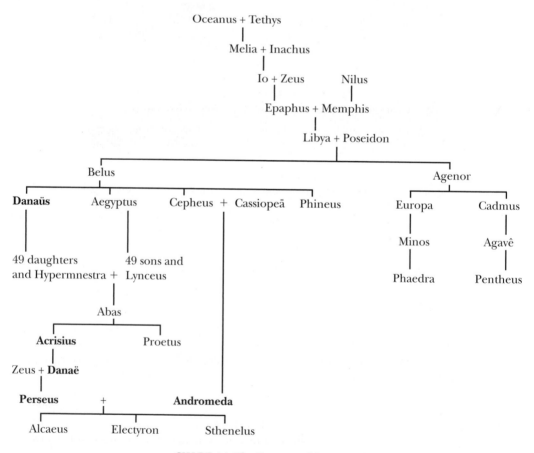

CHART 14 The Descent of Perseus

tethered the cow to an olive tree in a grove near Mycenae. To keep her away from Zeus, she sent the monster Argus, a child of Gaea who had a hundred eyes and never slept.

To free Io from his wife's malice, Zeus sent Hermes, god of stealth and thieves, but even Hermes could not at first get past Argus' ever-vigilant watch. While some of the monster's eyes slept, the rest were awake. Then Hermes, disguised as a shepherd, sang a lullaby, and one by one Argus' eyes grew heavy. When all were closed, the god moved in and cut off Argus' head. For this reason Hermes is called Argeïphontes (ar-jē-i-**fon**-tēz), "Argus-killer" (Figure 14.2). Hera placed Argus' eyes in the tail of the peacock, her favorite bird.

Io now was free, but Hera sent a gadfly to torment her. Stung constantly, she wandered through Greece to the northwest—the Ionian Sea around Ithaca was named after Io—then across the Pindus range to MACEDONIA, and through THRACE to the straits that divide Europe from Asia, site of the later Greek colony of BYZ-ANTIUM (see Map XIII, inside back cover). Renamed Constantinople after the first Christian emperor, who ruled AD 307–337, it is now the Turkish city of Istanbul. Ever since, these straits have been called the Bosporus, "cow-crossing."

After wandering through SCYTHIA north of the Black Sea in what is today south-ern Ukraine, she ended up in the CAUCASUS MOUNTAINS at the eastern end of the BLACK SEA (see Map I, inside front cover). There she found Prometheus, pinioned

FIGURE 14.2 Hermes slays Argus, hence his name Argeïphontes, "Argus-killer," Attic pot, c. 490 BC. Hermes, with his characteristic traveler's cap (*petasos*) and cape thrown back, prepares to stab the monster Argus, shown as a naked bearded man with eyes all over his body. Io, shown as a steer, watches; over her is written the word for "beautiful woman" (not visible in photo).   (Museum für Kunst und Gewerbe, Hamburg)

by Zeus to a mountain crag because he refused to divulge the name of the female whose offspring would be greater than his father (see Chapter 5).

The principal surviving account of the myth of Io appears in Aeschylus' play *Prometheus Bound* (c. 430 BC). Io tells Prometheus the story of her seduction and persecution, but leaves out Hera's discovery of the couple caught in the act:

[645]   Night after night foul dreams surged over my virginal bed,
    seducing me with their whispers: "You lucky, fortunate girl!
    Why are you still a virgin, when the greatest suitor of all
    is eager to enter your bed? Zeus burns and itches with lust—
    his heart is asking for you. Why, then, must you be so coy?
650   Come, girl, show some sense, and don't be so scornful
    of lustful philandering Zeus. Steal down to the meadows of Lerna,°
    down past the sheepfolds, past the pens where your father keeps cattle.
    There you can bring satisfaction to the lecherous craving of Zeus."
    Every night I was bothered, poor girl, by such endless phantoms,
655   until I gathered my courage and told my father the nightmares.
    He sent long strings of inquirers to Delphi, and even Dodona,°
    to ask what words or actions the gods would find to their liking.
    All they reported were mere conundrums, riddles, enigmas.
    Finally Inachus heard a command that was, at least, clear in its menace,
660   bidding him drive me out of the bounds of my home and my country,
    an exile destined to wander to the very ends of the earth.
    If he refused, a thunderbolt, blazing with fire from heaven,
    would fall on the land and annihilate all the race of humankind.
    Reluctantly he obeyed the command of prophetic Apollo,
665   driving me out forever, homeless, abandoned, reluctant,
    forced as he was to yield to great Zeus's imperious orders.
    At once my outward form and the soul within me were altered.
    Horns, as you see, grew out. Stung by a fire-mouthed deerfly,
    in maddened torment I plunged in the cooling stream of Cerchnia,
670   the fountain of Lerna. But Argus, the shepherd, the child of the Earth,
    malignantly followed my steps with his baleful hundred eyes,
    till a fate he never expected deprived him of life and of breath.
    Plagued by his ghost in the form of a deerfly, the vengeance of Hera,
    I wander from land to land, all over the face of the earth.

AESCHYLUS, *Prometheus Bound* 645–686

651. *Lerna:* A swampy plain near Argos.   656. *Dodona:* In northwest Greece; Zeus had an oracle there.

Prometheus predicts to Io what wanderings still lie ahead, a magical journey through a geography whose hopeless confusion reflects Greek ignorance and fancy about distant places, even in the fifth century BC. The prospect of these endless wanderings horrifies Io, but Prometheus gives her comfort: In Egypt she will regain her human form after Zeus touches her with his hands. She will then be pregnant with Epaphus (**ep**-a-fus), "he who has been touched," future king of Egypt. And her descendant in the thirteenth generation (Heracles) will set him, Prometheus, free.

The story of Io has the same general structure as that of the daughters of Proetus (Chapter 11), the brother of Perseus' grandfather Acrisius: A god causes Io to change into a cow, who wanders the world, persecuted; the Proetids, driven insane by a god, think they are cows, and wander the hills. In some versions Hera, not Dionysus, transformed the Proetids into cows. In origin Io may somehow be Hera herself, many have thought, whose animal was the cow and whom Homer regularly calls *boôpis*, "cow-eyed." The Greeks identified Io with the Egyptian goddess Isis, sister of Osiris. Not only did *I*sis seem to have the same word root as *I*o, but the Egyptians often represented Isis as a cow or with the head or horns of a cow (see Figure 10.6). **(For full text of** *Prometheus Bound***, see http://bacchicstage .com/Prometheus.htm)**

The Crimes of the Danaïds

Epaphus became king of Egypt and married Memphis, eponym of the Egyptian capital of the Old Kingdom at the juncture of the delta and the river, roughly the site of modern Cairo. (President Andrew Jackson named Memphis, Tennessee, after the Egyptian city because it, too, stands at the juncture of two waterways, the Wolf and Mississippi rivers.) Memphis was the daughter of Nilus, eponym of the river. Epaphus and Memphis had a daughter Libya, eponym of the country west of the Nile. On Libya Poseidon fathered two sons, Agenor, father of Europa, and Belus (= Semitic "lord"). Belus became king of a vast territory on either side of the Nile, married another daughter of Nilus, and by her had the twin sons Aegyptus (ē-**jip**-tus) and **Danaüs** (**dān**-a-us; see Chart 14).

Belus set up Aegyptus as king of Arabia (meaning Africa east of the Nile) and Danaüs as king of Libya (Africa west of the Nile). Aegyptus named the kingdom after himself. By numerous wives Aegyptus had fifty sons and Danaüs had fifty daughters, the **Danaïds** (**dān**-a-idz). When Aegyptus suggested to his brother Danaüs that the fifty girls marry his fifty boys, Danaüs suspected that Aegyptus' true motive was to gain power over Libya, birthright of the Danaïds. With Athena's help, therefore, he built one of the earliest ships and fled with his daughters across the sea to Argos in the Peloponnesus, the home of his ancestress Io. There in Argos, Danaüs, an eponym of the Danaä ns (**dān**-a-anz), became king.

The fifty sons of Aegyptus soon arrived across the sea in hot pursuit and demanded that Danaüs give his daughters to them. The story is the subject of a surviving play by Aeschylus, the *Suppliants* (unfortunately, the second and third plays of the trilogy are lost). Eventually Danaüs agreed to his brother's demands, but he gave each of his daughters a dagger and instructed them to murder their husbands on the wedding night. On the next morning forty-nine of the daughters presented their father with the heads of their husbands. Only Hypermnestra spared her husband, Lynceus (**lin**-ke-us), because Lynceus had spared her virginity—the folktale motif of "all but one." The heads were buried in the swamp of Lerna and the bodies given a funeral outside the city. For defying his orders, Danaüs imprisoned Hypermnestra, but later released her to remain with Lynceus. From Lynceus and Hypermnestra descend the later House of Argos.

Understandably, after the incident of the wedding-night Danaüs had difficulty finding suitable husbands for his daughters. At last he held a footrace and gave them away as prizes, offering fancy shields as an added inducement!

Observations: Springs and the Dangers of Woman

The myth of the Danaïds appears to be a conflation of different traditions. One explanation suggests that in an early form the burial of the heads of the sons of Aegyptus was etiological to explain the origin of the great swamps in LERNA at the southern edge of the Argive plain, "which have fifty heads." There are fifty Nereids, too, spirits of the water. The Danaïds' close association with freshwater springs emerges from another story. When the Danaïds arrived in Argos, the land was waterless, cursed by Poseidon because the local inhabitants chose Hera as presiding divinity rather than him (the Athenians also preferred a female god, Athena, over Poseidon). One of the Danaïds, Amymonê (a-**mu**-mo-nē), went in search of a spring. She encountered a satyr, who tried to rape her. Poseidon appeared, chased away the satyr with a cast of his trident, then raped Amymonê himself (Figure 14.3)! When he pulled the trident from the rock, out sprang the springs of Lerna.

FIGURE 14.3 Poseidon and Amymonê, on an Attic oil jar, c. 480 BC. Such scenes of pursuit were common in Attic art of the early fifth century and seem to have been a metaphor for courtship. Here Poseidon raises his trident, a tool used to spear tuna fish in the Mediterranean from the earliest times (other vase painters show the trident actually penetrating her thigh). Although Amymonê is running away, her gestures indicate the bride's submission: Her gaze meets Poseidon just as the bride first meets the gaze of her husband on the wedding night. Her left hand, raising her garment in the traditional bridal "unveiling," indicates the moment of highest sexual tension, as Amymonê prepares to submit. Such vases were given as gifts to young brides.   (The Metropolitan Museum of Art, New York; Image © The Metropolitan Museum of Art/Art Resource, New York)

The story of the Danaïds carrying water in the underworld in leaky vessels to fill a trough (Chapter 12, Figure 12.2), first attested in the Hellenistic Period, further associates them with freshwater springs, although the story is a late invention apparently inspired by Orphic teachings about the miseries of the underworld. Whatever their original association with springs and water, the myth of the Danaïds has taken on the undisguised theme of the resentment of the female at submitting to the male in lawful marriage. In early versions of the myth, the Danaïds were not punished for their crime, no doubt because they had saved their people from the wicked sons of Aegyptus, the Egyptians.

The association between Egypt and the Danaä ns who lived on the Argive plain may suggest a historical thread as well to the tradition, going back to the end of the Bronze Age, about 1200 BC. Egyptian texts from this time inscribed on temple walls report that dangerous seaborne invaders called the Danuna, one of the Peoples of the Sea, attacked Egypt, bringing with them their families and possessions. But the Egyptians destroyed them. Remnants settled in Palestine in Gaza, where they are remembered as the biblical tribe of Dan (who were therefore not at first Semitic speakers). In myth the Danaäns come from Egypt, but in history *Danaän* seems to have been the name of an early Greek tribe, some of whom invaded Egypt. By Homer's day the name was used interchangeably with *Argives* and *Achaeans* for the Greek forces at Troy, whose commander, Agamemnon, ruled Mycenae on the Argive plain. In Homer's time, the later name *Hellenes* referred only to the people of a small district in Thessaly.

THE LEGEND OF PERSEUS

Danaë and the Shower of Gold

Lynceus ruled Argos after Danaüs died. His son, Abas, had twin sons, **Acrisius** (a-**kris**-i-us) and Proetus, who hated each other so much that, like Jacob and Esau in the Bible (Genesis 25:22), they quarreled even in the womb (so Isis and Osiris hated their brother Seth even in the womb). After a long struggle for power, Acrisius took Argos and Proetus took Tiryns. Proetus fathered the Proetids (for their madness and fate, see Chapter 11), and Acrisius fathered **Danaë** (**dān**-a-ē).

However, Acrisius wanted a male heir. He consulted the oracle and was told that he would have one in the son of Danaë, but that this grandson would also kill him. Attempting to forestall fate, Acrisius constructed an underground chamber of bronze and imprisoned Danaë in it. Zeus fell in love with Danaë and came to her as a shower of gold that fell from the roof of the chamber into her womb (Figure 14.4). In this way was Perseus ("destroyer"?) conceived. Heroes are conceived in special ways and are often partly divine.

When Perseus was several years old, Acrisius heard a child's shout from inside the chamber and knew the truth. He refused to believe that Zeus was the father, however. Afraid to kill his daughter and grandson outright, he ordered

FIGURE 14.4 Danaë and the shower of gold. Danaë bares her body to the shower of gold. A mirror and two pots hang from the wall (compare Perspective Figure 6.1a). Red-figured bell crater from Boeotia, c. 430 BC.   (Réunion des Musées Nationaux/Art Resource, New York)

a wooden box built (Figure 14.5), placed them both within it, and cast the box into the sea.

Simonides, a lyric poet of the sixth and fifth centuries BC, wrote a charming choral poem (a poem sung by dancers) describing Danaë's anxiety for her young son as they drift over the high seas. A fragment survives:

She huddled down in the stout-walled box,
which the wind drove on, and the surges tossed.
Terror whitened her tear-stained cheek,
but she clung to Perseus with guardian arms.
     "Heaven save us both in this hour of peril," she murmured,
"and you, dear innocent, warm and well-fed, sleep on,
locked in our wooden prison with nails of bronze,
shrouded in darkness visible, blue-black night.
The crash of the breakers over your head,
     the driving waves and the hurrying wind,
mean nothing to you.
So snuggle down
in your warm dark blanket, upon my breast.
My heart would break if you knew that this storm
was a threat to you, if your baby ears
     might understand my terrified words.

FIGURE 14.5 Danaë and Perseus about to be locked in a box, Attic vase, c. 490 BC. Acrisius, the balding man to the left, oversees a carpenter who is drilling a hole in the box with a bow drill. Danaë stands behind the box, which will soon imprison her, with an imploring gesture. The nurse to the right holds the infant Perseus. Two breathing holes are drilled in the side of the box.   (Photograph © 2011 Museum of Fine Arts, Boston)

So sleep, my baby, and sleep, you winds,
and sleep, you trouble that knows no end.
O Father Zeus, send a blessed relief!
With humble and righteous heart I implore you!"

SIMONIDES, FRAGMENT 38

Instead of drowning, mother and child are unexpectedly saved when a fisherman named Dictys (**dik**-tis), "netman," catches the box in his net off the island of Seriphos (ser-**if**-os), one of the Cyclades, a poor and miserable place, little more than a cliff jutting up from the sea. Danaë and Perseus lived with Dictys, and the boy grew to manhood. Then Dictys' brother, **Polydectes** (pol-i-**dek**-tēz, "much-receiver," a common epithet of Death), the king of the island, desired Danaë as his mistress. Danaë was unwilling and Perseus defended her refusal.

Polydectes therefore pretended that he wanted to marry Hippodamia (the daughter of Oenomaüs in the myth of Pelops; see Chapter 20). He demanded a wedding gift of a fine horse from every young man on the island.

Perseus had no horses but boasted that he would instead bring anything else Polydectes wanted—even a Gorgon's head! "Fine, get that," Polydectes agreed, seeing an easy way to get rid of the young man who opposed his sexual designs on the young man's mother. The hero has found his adversary, the monster that he must overcome.

The Gorgon-Slayer

No one had ever returned alive from an encounter with the three death-dealing **Gorgons**: Stheno (**sthē**-nō, "strength"), Euryalê (yū-**rī**-a-lē, "far-leaper"), and **Medusa** (me-**dūs**-a, probably shortened from Eurymedousa, "wide-ruling"). In classical art, the Gorgons have enormous tusks and wide, staring eyes that turn anyone who sees them into stone; bronze hands; snakes for hair; and golden wings. One must approach them on foot because they live at the edge of the world. Only Medusa was mortal, but even if Perseus killed her, escape from her swift-winged sisters would be impossible.

Athena appeared to Perseus and gave him exact instructions. He must learn the whereabouts of certain helpful nymphs from the **Graeae** (**grē**-ē, "gray-haired women"), sisters to the Gorgons themselves (see Chart 4.3). The Graeae, two or three in number, were hideous hags (although they had beautiful cheeks) and lived near the place where Atlas supported the world. They had only one tooth and one eye between them, which they passed to whoever wanted to see or to eat.

With Athena's help, Perseus traveled almost to the edge of the world and found the Graeae in a cave. He grabbed the eye as it was being passed and demanded that the Graeae reveal to him where he could find the nymphs. Then he gave them back the eye (or, just to be mean, threw it into nearby Lake Tritonis).

Perseus received from the nymphs several objects essential to his success: the cap of Hades, which made the wearer invisible; winged sandals, which enabled him to fly through the air; and a special leather pouch in which he could conceal the Gorgon's head. Hermes also gave him a distinctive steel sword, a kind of scimitar, and a polished bronze shield. Finally, the nymphs instructed him how to find the Gorgons: Heroes need assistance to overcome the monster.

Perseus flew to the river Ocean (where Odysseus summoned the ghosts of the dead). There the Gorgons lay, sound asleep, surrounded by the twisted, petrified forms of those who had come too near (it is like the land of the dead). Because looking directly at them meant death, he crept past Stheno and Euryalê, using his polished bronze shield as a mirror, and slashed off Medusa's head (Figure 14.6). Medusa was pregnant by Poseidon. As the head came free, out sprang the winged horse Pegasus (from Greek *pêgai* = "springs" of water, because a spring burst forth where he struck the ground with his hoof). The hero Bellerophon will ride Pegasus when he slays the dread Chimera, and later Pegasus will become a constellation. Out from Medusa's severed neck sprang also a giant named Chrysaör (kri-**sā**-or), "he of the golden sword," who plays little role in Greek myth. Perseus quickly pushed the snaky head into the pouch and flew away on his winged sandals. Although Stheno

FIGURE 14.6 Perseus slays Medusa, from a relief-decorated amphora from Boeotia, early seventh century BC. He turns his face aside to avoid being turned to stone. Over his shoulder he carries the scabbard for his sword and the leather pouch. He wears the cap of Hades and the magical sandals. Medusa does not yet have the form typical later of a woman with a Gorgon's head, but is represented as a skull-faced woman with a mare's body attached at the waist. Mysterious plants frame the scene. No one has explained the salamander near Medusa's back.   (Musée du Louvre, Paris; © Giraudon/Art Resource, New York)

and Euryalê awoke and pursued him, they could see nothing, thanks to the cap of Hades (Figure 14.7).

Meanwhile, Polydectes, sure that Perseus would never return, pressed his wooing of Danaë with violence. When Perseus arrived back at Seriphos, he found his mother and Dictys cowering at the altar of the gods for protection from Polydectes. Perseus walked into the palace where Polydectes was partying with his friends and announced that he had returned with the Gorgon's head. Of course, no one believed him. He turned his eyes aside as he pulled the head from the pouch. Polydectes and his friends at once turned to stone. Perseus established Dictys as king of the island, gave his magical implements to Hermes to return to the nymphs, and delivered the Gorgon's head to Athena. Ever after she wore it on her breastplate or shield.

PERSEUS AND ANDROMEDA

In a later addition to the myth, Perseus did not return directly to Seriphos but flew first over Ethiopia, or Joppa on the Palestinian coast near modern Tel Aviv. The land was ruled by Cepheus (**sē-fūs**), who like Aegyptus and Danaüs was a son of Belus and hence a distant relative of Perseus himself. Looking down, Perseus saw Cepheus' daughter **Andromeda** (an-**drom**-e-da) chained to a rock and about to be devoured by the

FIGURE 14.7 A Gorgon pursues Perseus, Attic vase, c. 490 BC. Winged, with snakes in her hair, she has a fearsome face and huge mouth from which protrude boar's teeth and a thick, lolling tongue. Perseus, shown on the other side of the vase, wears winged sandals and magic hat and carries a scimitar and pouch over his shoulder. The Gorgon's head alone, often represented in ancient art, is called a *gorgoneion.* (Staatliche Antikensammlungen und Glyptothek, Munich; Hirmer Fotoarchiv, Munich)

sea-monster Ceto (but something is wrong with the genealogy, because as daughter of Cepheus, Andromeda should have lived four generations before Perseus; see Chart 14).

The situation had come about because Andromeda's vain mother, Cassiopeä (ka-si-o-**pē**-a), boasted that she was more beautiful than the Nereids. The infuriated sea-nymphs complained to Poseidon, who sent a flood and a sea-monster against the land. An oracle revealed that only the sacrifice of the king's daughter would prevent destruction. As he flew over, Perseus immediately fell in love with the lovely girl. Ovid tells the story in the *Metamorphoses*, explaining, on the way, the origin of reptiles in the Sahara Desert and coral in the sea:

[615] Bearing the glorious trophy, the head with a garland of serpents,
      he sped through the yielding air, borne on his murmuring pinions.
      But while the victor was hovering over the deserts of Libya,
      drops of venom rained down from the bleeding head of the Gorgon.
      Quickened by these, the earth gave birth to poisonous reptiles,
620   making the region a desert of noxious vipers and asps . . .

His winged sandals swept through the gentle wind of the heavens.
Below and behind he left the countless nations of mortals,
till off in the distance there lay Ethiopia, kingdom of Cepheus.
Ammon, strict god, had ordered that Cepheus' innocent daughter,
625   Andromeda, there must pay for the haughty tongue of her mother.°
The descendant of Abas gazed on her charms, secured to the rocks.
Only her hair, tossed gently by the wind that blew from the sea,
and her piteous streaming tears, as she wept for her imminent fate,
persuaded the hero that this was no marble statue, but a warm, live woman.
630   He checked his flight as the fire of love blazed up in his heart.
So taken was he by her beauty, his wings for a moment were still . . .

625. . . . *her mother:* According to Ovid's version, Cepheus had consulted the oracle of Ammon, a powerful Egyptian god, about the flood and sea monster, and Ammon had ordered Andromeda to be offered to the monster.

PERSPECTIVE 14.1

VASARI'S *PERSEUS AND ANDROMEDA*

Architect, painter, and writer Giorgio Vasari (1511–1574) is best known today for his history of Italian art, *Lives of the Best Italian Architects, Painters, and Sculptors.* Written in 1550 in the late Renaissance, the book is invaluable not only for the attributions of works to artists and anecdotes about them, but for its account of how people thought about art in Italy at this time. A close friend of Michelangelo and Titian, Vasari traveled throughout Italy to interview other artists and study their works for his book.

But Vasari was an accomplished painter in his own right. His well-known painting based on Ovid's account (Perspective Figure 14.1) shows Perseus freeing a stylishly naked Andromeda chained to a rock. Perseus wears the cap of Hades, which makes him invisible, and the winged sandals, which enable him to fly. At his feet is the polished bronze shield that he used as a mirror to avoid looking at Medusa. In the lower left is Pegasus, who sprang forth when Medusa's head was cut off. At the lower center is Medusa's head, whose terrifying power petrifies the leaves beneath it. Sea-nymphs on the right examine the new substance of coral. In the middle ground to the left of Perseus is the dying sea-monster Ceto. The people moving from the left to the gates of the fine Renaissance city in the upper right probably are the followers of Phineus, Andromeda's uncle to whom she was engaged.

Vasari painted *Perseus and Andromeda* in 1570 as part of the larger project of adapting the immense Palazzo Vecchio ("old palace") in Florence as living quarters for the family of Cosimo de' Medici, who ruled the city. Vasari himself decorated the Studiolo, a small, secret room in the Palazzo surrounded by cupboards where the prince kept his collection of minerals. On the ceiling was Prometheus surrounded by the elements. Along one wall, to represent the element of

PERSPECTIVE FIGURE 14.1 Giorgio Vasari (1511–1574), *Perseus and Andromeda,* 1570.   (Palazzo Vecchio, Florence; Scala/Art Resource, New York)

water, were paintings of aquatic activities with appropriate mythical subjects, including this Perseus and Andromeda. Vasari justified the mythical theme in his notebook, explaining, "Although they are false gods, it is lawful in this to imitate the ancients, who under these names hid allegorically the concepts of philosophy," that is, in this case, the division of the world into four elements.

Completely unheard of in the Middle Ages, the morally dangerous practice of drawing from live naked models, as Vasari did for his Andromeda, began in the early fifteenth century. By the second half of the century it was standard training. Our first Western treatise on the art of painting, written in 1435 by Leon Battista Alberti, already assumes the basis of academic training in art to be a scientific study of the nude. Alberti advises artists to "begin with the bones, then add the muscles, and then cover the body with flesh." Vasari noted that Antonio Pollaiuolo, who painted the *Labors of Heracles* for the Medici palace in 1460, was modern in his treatment of the nude because "he dissected many bodies to examine their anatomy." For moral reasons, dissection, like nudity in art, had been impossible in the European Middle Ages.

Perseus swooped down to Andromeda's weeping parents, who expected the monster to appear any moment. He offered to save the girl if he could marry her. They hastily agreed and promised him the kingdom as dowry. Then the sea-serpent appeared:

[632]   As Perseus' shadow fell on the waters, the monster rose to the bait.
        Like Zeus's eagle whose eye has lit on a glittering serpent
        sunning itself in a meadow, he plunges down from behind it,
635   and before the snake can reverse his poisonous fangs to attack,
        the eager talons impale the scale-covered nape of the viper.
        So the Inachean hero° plunged headlong down from the aether
        and sank his curving blade in the writhing neck of the monster.
        Struck by that deadly wound, it arched its back to the heavens,
640   then dived beneath the waters, as a wounded but still savage boar
        twists and turns to hear the barking of hounds who entrap him.
        Perseus evaded its snapping jaws with a twist of his pinions.
        Wherever he saw an opening, he darted a thrust of his saber,
        now at the back, encrusted with ancient barnacle remnants,
645   now at the sensitive ribs, now where ribs turned into a fishtail.
        The monster vomited up a clot of its life-blood mingled with water,
        and Perseus' feathery wings grew heavy and damp with the spray.
        No longer dared he entrust his life to the feathers thus sodden,
        but made for a reef whose crest was dry if the waters were quiet,
650   submerged if the winds arose. His left hand clung like a limpet,
        but again and again his saber drove at the monster's entrails.
        The cheers of the watchers resounded along the seacoast beyond him,
        and echoed all through the homes of the gods on Olympus above.
        Cassiopeä and Cepheus, Andromeda's mother and father,
655   hailed him in joy as son, as helper, as stay of the household.
        Andromeda, cause of the struggle, prize of the victor as well,
        free of her chains now approached as the victor drew himself water
        to wash his victorious hands. To keep from abrading the head,
        crowned with poisonous vipers, with the grating sand of the ocean,
660   he gathered a leafy blanket of seaweed that floats in the depths
        and on it he gently laid the head of the daughter of Phorcys.°
        The succulent fresh-cut foliage, still alive and absorbent,
        drank up the monster's venom, but hardened to rock at its touch,
        gaining a stony hardness spreading through leaf and through stem.
665   The nymphs of the sea kept testing this new and remarkable substance;
        in all the weed, they discovered, the wondrous change kept recurring.
        The mutant seeds were dispersed by the tossing waves of the sea,
        and down to this very day the coral in this is peculiar:
        Its stiffness comes from the air; the plant in water is supple,
670   but hardens into a stone when torn from the sea of its birth.

OVID, *Metamorphoses* 4.615–620, 667–677, 712–752

637. *Inachean hero:* Perseus is so called after the river Inachus (Io's father) near Argos.   661. *daughter of Phorcys:* Usually called a sibling, here Ceto is child of Phorcys, himself an offspring of Pontus and Gaea.

Unfortunately, when Cepheus agreed to Perseus' proposal, he neglected to mention that Andromeda was already engaged to Phineus, Cepheus' brother (it must have seemed unimportant when a monster was about to consume her). Cepheus held a splendid banquet. Phineus burst into the hall with an army behind him, but Perseus pulled out the Gorgon's head and turned Phineus and his men to stone. According to this version, Perseus remained in Ethiopia or Joppa for a year, where Andromeda bore a son, Perses, ancestor of the Persians. Only then did he return to Seriphos to free his mother.

The Death of Acrisius

Wanting to meet his grandfather Acrisius, king of Argos, Perseus now traveled there with his wife, Andromeda, and his mother, Danaë. Acrisius remembered the oracle that his grandson would kill him and fled north to Thessaly. One day, unrecognized, Perseus entered an athletic contest in Thessaly. He threw the discus, but the wind blew it astray so that it struck Acrisius in the foot as he stood in the sidelines and (oddly) killed him. Thus the oracle was fulfilled: Heroes can be a threat to civil society, even without meaning harm.

A mournful Perseus buried his grandfather with full honors, then returned to Argos. Ashamed to inherit Argos from the man he killed, his own grandfather, he traded Argos for Tiryns with a son of Proetus (named Megapenthes) who was then king of Tiryns. At this time Perseus also founded the nearby city of Mycenae and surrounded it with magnificent walls. He and Andromeda lived in Mycenae for many years. She bore him a daughter and several sons. At their deaths, Athena placed Perseus and Andromeda among the stars along with Cepheus, Cassiopeä, and the sea-monster Ceto. Like many heroes, Perseus returned after his dangerous quest to rule over his people, beget a dynasty, and be remembered forever.

Observations: Perseus and Folktale

Some motifs in the story of Perseus were anticipated in the story of Gilgamesh (Chapter 13), but the tone of the two stories is utterly different. Gilgamesh is a harsh, tragic tale of the defeat of our deep human aspirations. The stories of Perseus, by contrast, are like children's stories, with hideous monsters, ugly hags, magic implements, and beautiful distressed maidens. And they all lived happily ever after. One of our earliest representations of Perseus and Medusa is on a large pot (at Eleusis) that contained the body of a child, as if he might enjoy the story even after death.

Of all Greek legendary cycles, that of Danaë and Perseus is closest to folktale. The early part of the story is not about Perseus but about his mother, and it follows a folktale pattern sometimes called the **girl's tragedy**, which contains these elements:

- Prohibition
- Seclusion
- Violation of the prohibition
- Threat of punishment or death
- Liberation

Because of an oracle, Danaë is forbidden to marry (*prohibition*). She is locked in a chamber to keep her from men (*seclusion*), but nonetheless becomes pregnant (*violation*). A wicked relative, her father Acrisius, places her and the child in the box (*threat of death*), but she is saved by Dictys (*liberation*).

Perseus' own story follows a pattern similar to elements in the story of Gilgamesh, but the element of the quest is much emphasized. Partly divine (his father is Zeus), Perseus is conceived in an extraordinary way (from a rain of gold). His strength will one day accidentally kill his own grandfather Acrisius. Although he has no close male buddy and he violates no taboo, he performs impossible labors thanks to magical aids and the favor of the gods, then returns home where he is rewarded with a wife, a kingdom, and a glorious lineage.

Obviously folktale, a system of patterns and motifs, can have a lot in common with heroic myth, a story about a great man, just as stories about famous women can follow a folktale pattern too. When we investigate folktale, we are interested in recurring patterns, ways of telling a story; when we investigate heroic myth, we are interested in the meaning attached to a hero's deeds. In the stories of Perseus, the hero himself has little or no personality. He is just someone who does special things. We might say that there is no internal conflict. Conspicuously absent is the hero's conflict with woman or the divine female, so important to the fate of Gilgamesh and other heroes. That is an adult theme, and Perseus is a children's story. The story was never told as an epic poem, as far as we know, but epic poems are for adults. The monster-killing story must have circulated orally as a genuine folktale. Unfortunately, we have no direct evidence.

Medusa's Head

The beheading of Medusa, one of the most discussed incidents in all Greek myth, has attracted many psychological interpretations, although in ancient accounts the event is passed over briefly. Sigmund Freud, the creator of psychoanalysis, offered a bizarre explanation of the Gorgon's head as representing the female genitals, in particular those of the mother. Freud supposed that the young boy's glimpse of his mother's genitals inspired him with the fear of castration. He could become like her, without a penis. However, the phallic snakes reassure the boy about his own penis, as does "being turned to stone," which Freud thought refers to the boy's erection.

Later psychoanalytic commentators have developed Freud's thesis, arguing that the myth grows out of a social system in which mothers control the lives of young boys, as they did in ancient Greece. To behead the Gorgon is to overthrow the negative power of the mother, as the Greek boy did when he left his mother's care at puberty and joined the society of men. The positive, nurturing aspect of the mother, by contrast, is represented by the figure of Danaë (for more about psychological interpretations of myth, see Chapter 25).

However, the Gorgon may not have been an original element at all in the myth of Perseus. Our earliest information about the Gorgon is in Homer, who on several

PERSPECTIVE 14.2

CLASSICAL MYTH AND THE STARS

A surprising number of figures from the myth of Perseus became constellations—Perseus, Andromeda, Cassiopeä, Cepheus, and Ceto—no doubt because he is the only Greek hero to fly through the heavens (Perspective Figure 14.2). On this sixteenth-century woodcut by the great German artist Albrecht Dürer (1471–1528) you can make out these constellations in the upper central portion: Ceto (unnamed) is to the immediate right of the constellation Aries ("ram") and threatens Andromeda, chained and naked in a horizontal position beneath him. Perseus is to the left of the soles of Andromeda's feet, holding a scimitar in one hand and the head of Medusa in the other. Below Perseus and Andromeda is Cassiopeä on a throne, and beneath her, near the center of the diagram, Cepheus, prancing, naked, and crowned.

Far more than we, ancient peoples needed to use the heavens as indicators of times and seasons, and especially the heavens by night, when the stars and planets are visible. This need led to the organization of the night sky into various configurations or bodies, many of which received mythical names. Looking at the heavenly realms, one sees a chaos of disorganized points of light, but myths provided an intellectual framework for combining stars into groupings so they could be examined systematically. We still use these groupings today.

To an observer on the earth, most of the stars appear to be fixed in their relative positions. Ancient astronomers theorized that they were fastened to the inside of a great sphere that revolved around the earth. We can only see one end of the axis of the heavens, the star Polaris, which never moves. But they noted that not all stars are fixed in their places. The seven *planets* (Greek "wanderers") known to the ancients seem to follow a different path and to move at different speeds relative to each other. These seven—including Sun and Moon as well as Mercury, Venus, Mars, Jupiter, and Saturn—pass along a group of twelve constellations, the zodiac (Greek "animal show") in an apparently irrational way.

Dürer has placed the constellations around the circumference of his map. From Hellenistic times the Greek gods have been associated with the planets (for example, the Sun = Apollo, the Moon = Artemis), capable of purpose and action. Astrology, which arose in Mesopotamia in the eighth century BC, not in Greece, is based on the assumption that careful study can reveal profound laws about the influence of the planets, who are gods. *Astrology* is the "science" of the stars, their true and essential nature (at least in theory), as opposed to *astronomy,* the study of their arrangement.

The names we use for individual stars include many of Arabic as well as Greek and Latin origin. Dürer's map is based on Arabic celestial maps, but he has translated

PERSPECTIVE FIGURE 14.2 Albrecht Dürer (1471–1528), Map of the Northern Hemisphere, 1503, woodcut. The map has a Latin title that means "Figures of the northern sky with the twelve signs of the Zodiac." Note Hercules, beneath and to the right of center, wielding a club. In the corners are famous astronomers: Aratus of Cilicia (third century BC, upper left), Ptolemy of Egypt (second century BC, upper right), Asophi the Arab (that is, Al Sufi, really Abdul Rahman, tenth century AD, lower right), and Marcus Manilius the Roman (first century AD, lower left).   (Image © The Metropolitan Museum of Art/Art Resource, New York)

the figures into their Greco-Roman mythical forms. Sometimes the connection is far-fetched: The zodiac includes Aries, said to be the ram that saved Phrixus and Hellê in the story of Jason and the Argonauts, whose skin became the Golden Fleece; Taurus is the bull that carried off Europa; Gemini are the twins Castor and Pollux; Cancer is the crab that kept snapping at Heracles as he fought the Hydra; Leo is the Nemean lion of Heracles' first labor.

The other names of signs are obscure or improbable: Virgo is Astraea ("justice"), the last of the gods to leave the earth in the wicked Iron Age; Scorpio was produced by Earth to kill the hunter Orion, who had boasted that there was nothing he could not kill; Sagittarius ("arrow-man") is the very obscure Centaur named Crotus, devotee of the Muses with a fondness for hunting; Capricorn ("goat-horned"), is Amalthea, the goat who nursed the infant Zeus and was raised to the heavens as reward; Aquarius is the same as Ganymede, cupbearer to the gods. For Pisces ("fishes") the ancient astrologers had recourse to a non-Greek myth about a Syrian goddess, Derceto, equated with Aphrodite. Libra ("balance," "scales") also had no good mythical model, but in the Roman empire was claimed to be the spirit of Julius Caesar, famous for his fairness and clemency.

The slow change of the planets' position against the zodiac (the sun moves through the whole circle in about 26,000 years) gave rise to the notion of "ages" governed by the constellation on the eastern horizon at sunrise. About the time of the birth of Christ, the sun moved from Aries into Pisces, which is one reason the fish became a special Christian symbol. In the nearly worldwide youth movement of the late 1960s, at the dawn of the computer age, a hoped-for new era was greeted as the "Age of Aquarius."

---

occasions refers to "Gorgo" as a fearsome demon with staring eyes, unconnected to the myth of Perseus. According to Homer, Gorgo is represented on the shield of Agamemnon, leader of the Greek host, together with allegorical figures:

[33]   Round about it ten circles of bronze, and on it twenty bosses of tin,
        shining and white, surrounding a boss of metallic dark blue.
35   As a crown was the face of Gorgo, fearful for man to behold,
        glaring terribly; with her, as companions, Terror and Panic.

HOMER, *Iliad* 11.33–37

Gorgo also appears in the *Odyssey*, when Odysseus is describing his visit to the underworld:

[633]   Cold terror seized me
        lest noble Persephonê rise to me from the mansion of Hades
635   displaying the head of Gorgo, that dreadful monster.

HOMER, *Odyssey* 11.633–635

Gorgo, then, is a bogey with staring eyes, a terrifying demon with a life of her own outside the myth of Perseus. The origin of the Gorgon in Greek art as a head with large staring eyes, boar's teeth, and snakes for hair (see Figure 14.7) is obscure. Some associate this iconography with Eastern monsters, or an Egyptian good-luck god (Bes), and others trace it back to the Bronze Age and the Minoan cult of the snake-goddess (see Chapter 17). In any event, in religious behavior the Gorgon's head is often used as an *apotropaic* ("turning away") device, a magical means to deflect the evil eye, according to the magical principle that like is effective against like.

Belief in the evil eye, the notion that an unfriendly look can harm, is universal, and apotropaic eyes are found in many cultures to deal with this fear. Until the seventeenth century the English word "fascinate" meant "to fix with the evil eye." Gorgons often appear on the interior of Athenian wine cups, evidently because intoxication makes one vulnerable to magical harm. The outsides of these cups sometimes have two large eyes so that as the drinker raises the cup, the eyes reflect back any unfriendly stare (a few examples have an erect phallus for a base, allowing the drinker to "give the finger" to his companions as he drinks!). Apotropaic Gorgons also appear on early Greek temples, as gargoyles do on medieval cathedrals.

Evidently a folktale told how Perseus slew one of three wicked sisters, a monster named Medusa, "ruler," but her appearance was not well defined (see Figure 14.6). Only later did Greek artists borrow the iconography of Gorgo, an apotropaic bogey that turns away the evil eye, and attribute it to Medusa. The presence of a horse (Pegasus) and a small man (Chrysaör) together with Gorgo in temple sculpture from the seventh century BC show that Gorgo had by then been drawn into the myth.

KEY NAMES AND TERMS

Argive plain, 351

Perseus, 352

Tiryns, 353

Io, 354

Danaüs, 357

Danaïds, 357

Acrisius, 359

Danaë, 359

Polydectes, 361

Gorgons, 362

Medusa, 362

Graeae, 362

Andromeda, 363

girl's tragedy, 368

SOME ADDITIONAL ANCIENT SOURCES

Danaüs: Apollodorus 2.14–2.21; Pausanias 2.19. *Perseus:* Apollodorus 2.4; Ovid, *Metamorphoses* 4, 5; Hyginus, *Fabulae* 63, 64, 244.

FURTHER READING CHAPTER 14

Lloyd-Jones, Hugh, *Myths of the Zodiac* (London, 1978). Interesting, sometimes obscure myths associated with the zodiacal signs.

Marinatos, Nanno, *The Goddess and the Warrior: The Naked Goddess and Mistress of Animals in Early Greek Religion* (New York, 2000). Contains three chapters on Medusa "as adversary and patroness of men."

Vernant, J.-P., *Mortals and Immortals: Collected Essays by Jean-Pierre Vernant*, ed. F. I. Zeitlin (Princeton, NJ, 1991). Contains two excellent essays on Medusa.

Woodward, Jocelyn M., *Perseus: A Study in Greek Art and Legend* (Cambridge, UK, 1937; reprinted New York, 1976). Gathers together the most important Greek representations of the Perseus myth, with commentary.

CHAPTER 15

HERACLES

Tarantara! Lord Heracles, all hail, handsome in your victories!
  Yourself and Iolaüs, a pair of invincible spearsmen!
Lord Heracles, all hail, glorious in your victories! Tarantara!

ARCHILOCHUS, FRAGMENT 119

HERACLES, CALLED HERCULES by the Romans, was the greatest of Greek heroes. His image and career are strikingly similar to those of Gilgamesh, and his stories certainly owe much to importation from the East. Like Gilgamesh, Heracles is strong and willful. He lusts for adventure and experience. He understands loyalty and friendship. The contrast and hostility between the natural world and the cultural world of humans, a central theme in the story of Gilgamesh, is also strong in stories about Heracles. He shows his sympathy with the natural world by toting a primitive club, by shooting with bow and arrow (when shield and spear were "modern" weapons) and in his unruly behavior. Yet he rid the civilized world of dangerous animals and men.

After a life of suffering, victory, and defeat, Heracles traveled to Olympus, where he became a god, a fate that Gilgamesh only longed for and that Perseus never imagined. No town claimed his grave. He is among the earliest mythical figures in Greek art, perhaps as early as the eighth century BC. His Twelve Labors were the theme of the sculptural art on the temple of Zeus at Olympia, where the cult statue of Zeus by Phidias was one of the Seven Wonders of the Ancient World. His story inspired epic poetry (although only one poem survives), lyric, and tragedy. We

375

have no continuous literary account of his career, but mentions of Heracles and his deeds are so many that we can construct a complete biography. We must remember, however, that in this form the myth of Heracles is a modern reconstruction assembled from many pieces.

THE BIRTH OF HERACLES

About Heracles' special birth, appropriate to a great hero, we hear a complex tale. Perseus' son Electryon married his own niece, and they had a daughter, **Alcmena** (alk-**mēn**-a), and nine sons (Chart 15.1).

Of Electryon's other brothers, Sthenelus had a son, **Eurystheus** (yū-**ris**-thūs), and Alcaeus had a son, **Amphitryon** (am-**fit**-ri-on). Electryon became king of MYCENAE (see Map V, in this chapter) but soon pirates attacked him, killing all but one of Electryon's sons. Bent on revenge, Electryon prepared to leave on campaign, entrusting the kingship and care of his daughter Alcmena to his nephew Amphitryon, understanding that Amphitryon would respect her chastity. But before Electryon could leave, his trusted nephew Amphitryon killed him in a quarrel. Amphitryon was banished from Mycenae.

Taking Alcmena, Amphitryon fled north to THEBES, where Creon, king of Thebes, purified him of blood-pollution for killing his uncle. Amphitryon now married Alcmena, but she would not sleep with him until he avenged the death of her brothers, as her father, Electryon, had planned to do before Amphitryon killed him. Amphitryon gathered allies, including Creon himself, and set out against the pirates. Soon victorious, he headed for home, eagerly anticipating sexual relations with Alcmena.

However, Zeus also admired Alcmena's beauty, and before Amphitryon arrived, Zeus took on Amphitryon's likeness and appeared at Alcmena's door. He displayed booty, proof of victory over the pirates, and demanded the sexual favors he had obviously earned. After enjoying her body, the disguised Zeus took his leave, just

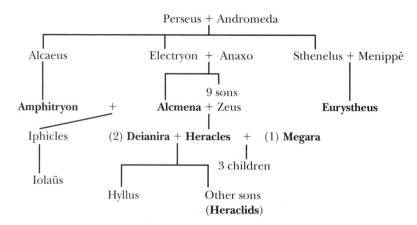

CHART 15.1 The Descent of Heracles

before the real Amphitryon appeared. To Alcmena's considerable confusion, the real Amphitryon proudly displayed to her his booty, proof of victory, and demanded the long-awaited sexual favors. Once again Alcmena retired to the wedding bed.

In this fashion she received two kinds of seed, divine and mortal, during a single night. From Zeus's seed came Heracles, the greatest Greek hero, and from Amphitryon's seed came Iphicles (**if**-i-klēz), a man of humbler stature. The humorous myth is told in an epic poem called the *Shield of Heracles,* attributed in antiquity to Hesiod but probably composed considerably later in the sixth century BC by an unknown oral poet:

[1] Or like Alcmena, the daughter of Electryon, shield of his people.
  Leaving her country behind, with Amphitryon, valiant in battle,
  she journeyed to Thebes. The fairest was she of all generations
  of women who suckle children, in beauty of face and of figure.
5 Of all the mortal women who have slept in the beds of immortals
  and borne them a race of children, there was none to rival Alcmena
  in wisdom and prudence of mind. From her brows and lustrous eyes
  an aura of charm breathed out as from Aphrodite the golden.
  Yet all her devotion was given to her wedded husband alone,
10 such an affection as never another woman has offered.
   Now Amphitryon had quarreled, alas, with his excellent father-in-law,
  over a herd of cattle, and slain him in violent anger.
  He therefore left his country and came as a suppliant exile
  to Thebes, where he made a home with the Cadmeans,° bearers of shields.
15 But he and his modest wife forswore the sweetness of passion.
  He might not enter the bed of Electryon's slim-ankled daughter,
  till he avenged the death of his great-hearted brothers-in-law
  by burning the towns of the heroes, the Taphians and Teleboans.°
  This he had promised to do and called the gods as his witness.
20 Dreading their wrath, he labored at the task commanded by Zeus.
  His allies obeyed his call to warfare and terrible conflict—
  horse-spurring men of Boeotia, shield-bearers, panting with rage.
  Locrians, hand-to-hand fighters, and valorous Phocians followed;°
  all these obeyed the orders of the mighty son of Alcaeus.
25 But the father of men and gods contrived quite another contrivance:
  to beget a son to defend both gods and bread-eating mortals
  from all the evil that threatens the common safety and comfort.
  From Olympus he came one night, deep in profound meditation.
  burning, as well, with lustful desire for the beautiful woman.
30 Zeus, most skillful of planners, descended at Typhaonium.°
  On the Hill of the Sphinx he rested, plotting wonderful things.
  Disguised as her husband, that night he enjoyed the bed of Alcmena.
   But on that self-same night came Amphitryon, guard of the people.
  His task accomplished, he hurried in such an amorous frenzy

---

14. *Cadmeans:* The Thebans. 18. *Taphians and Teleboans:* The pirates, who also claimed to be descended from Perseus. 23. . . . *Phocians followed:* Locris and Phocis are territories bordering on Boeotia. 30. *Typhaonium:* On the outskirts of Thebes, named after Typhoeus, the father of the Sphinx. The "Hill of the Sphinx" was the place where the Sphinx propounded her riddle and from which she hurled herself when Oedipus solved it (see Chapter 18).

35   to enter the bed of Alcmena that he greeted no mortal whatever,
      not even the rustic herdsmen and peasants who worked on the land.
      As a wanderer thanks his star for escape from terrible danger,
      from fever and deadly disease or the anguish of lying in prison,
      Amphitryon, now delivered from all the pangs he had suffered,
40   returned again to his home, overflowing with love and delight.
      The rest of the night he lay in the arms of his reticent partner,
      delighting himself with the gifts of Aphrodite the golden.
          Alcmena, having submitted to a god and the best of mankind,
      in Thebes of the seven gates gave birth to a pair of twin brothers—
45   brothers, but by no means alike in thought or in vigor of spirit.
      The one was by far the weaker, the other a much better man,
      terrible, mighty in battle, Heracles, hero unconquered.
      Him she bore in submission to Cronus' cloud-ruling son,
      the other, by name Iphicles, to Amphitryon, powerful lancer.
50   Of different sires she conceived them: the one of a human father,
      the other of Zeus, son of Cronus, the ruler of all the gods.

PSEUDO-HESIOD, Shield of Heracles 1–56

Although destined to become a god, Heracles was not to be king of Mycenae or
TIRYNS, but became the slave of his abject cousin Eurystheus. For when Alcmena was
about to give birth, Zeus swore that on that very day a descendant of his own seed would
be born who would rule over all surrounding lands. Hera, jealous once more because
of Zeus's infidelities, delayed the birth of Heracles while hastening that of Eurystheus,
the child of Menippê and Sthenelus, also a son of Perseus, hence Zeus's grandson. The
story is told in the *Iliad*, in the context of a warning against foolish action:

[91]   We are all victims of Blindness,° the oldest daughter of Zeus,
      who leads us on to our ruin. Her soft feet never make contact
      with stones and dust of the earth. She does her damage to humans
      by flying over their heads, now humbling one, now another.
95   She once, indeed, snared Zeus, strongest of gods or of humans,
      when Hera (a female, of course!) entrapped him in subtle deception.
      This happened upon the day that Alcmena hoped to deliver
      Heracles, mightiest of men, in the fair-crowned city of Thebes.
          Then Zeus arose and boasted in the midst of all the immortals:
100   "Listen to these my words, all gods and goddesses present,
      while I tell you the news my heart and my spirit bid me declare.
      Eileithyia, ruler of childbirth, today will bring to the light
      a man who will rule these regions°—a mortal, but born of my flesh."
          Hera, just like a woman, dissembled and gave him this answer:
105   "O yes, but you will see to it that this does not come about.
      Do you dare, Olympian, to swear me a great and terrible promise,
      that the child, descending today between the knees of his mother,
      human, but your own blood, is destined to rule the regions?"

91. *Blindness:* The Greek *atê* means roughly "failure to see the consequences of your actions." It is
sometimes rendered as "folly" or "madness."   103. *these regions:* He seems to mean around Mycenae,
although Alcmena is in Thebes.

110　Such was her challenge. But Zeus overlooked her secret deception
and swore a mighty oath, which would bring him sorrow thereafter.
Hera sprang from her place and sped from the peaks of Olympus,
down to the land of Achaea, to the famous city of Argos,
where she knew that the buxom wife of Sthenelus, Perseus' child,
had conceived a son, and by now was fully seven months pregnant.
115　This child Hera brought to birth, prematurely and well before normal,
but checked Alcmena's delivery, delaying the birth of her child.
　　She then reported the news in these words to Zeus, son of Cronus:
"Zeus, thou wielder of thunder, let me drop a word in your hearing.
A splendid man-child is born, who must rule the people of Argos—
120　Eurystheus, Perseus' grandson, and therefore your very own offspring!
Who has a better right, pray tell me, to rule the Achaeans?"
　　Thus lady Hera gloated, but anguish struck Zeus to the heart.
Blindness he took by the hair that circled her shining forehead
and hurled her forth in his rage, swearing a powerful oath
125　that never again should Blindness return to lofty Olympus,
or view the starry heavens—Blindness, deceiver of all.
Screaming these words, he whirled her around with his mighty arm
and flung her down from the heavens, down to the works of men.
Ever since he has groaned at the terrible deeds of Blindness,
130　seeing his dear son labor at the shameful command of Eurystheus.

HOMER, *Iliad* 19.91–133

Ovid adds an amusing detail to the story. Alcmena had been in the birthing room for seven days and was nearly dead from exhaustion. She cried out to the birth goddess Lucina (lu-**sī**-na, Greek Eileithyia) to help her. Lucina came, but at Hera's instructions sat outside in the antechamber with her legs crossed tightly together and her fingers intertwined. By magical sympathy she thus prevented the birth of the child, and she muttered dark spells under her breath.

Alcmena's terrible screams brought all the serving girls to her side, including the clever and loyal Galanthis (ga-**lan**-this). Noticing the strange old woman sitting outside the birthing room in an odd posture, the suspicious Galanthis realized what was happening and suddenly proclaimed, "Hooray! Alcmena's prayers are answered! A child is born!" "What!" shouted Lucina and jumped up, breaking the spell. In this way Heracles and Iphicles were born. Galanthis laughed, but the angry Lucina turned her into a weasel (*galanthis* = Latin "weasel").

Observations: Twins and Divine Birth

Many peoples viewed twins (about one birth in eighty) with superstitious awe and either killed them or regarded them with wonder. One logical explanation for fraternal twins is two fathers: one mortal, the woman's human consort, and one divine, an invisible being present at the moment of conception. Twins in Greek myth tend to be either very close friends or bitter enemies. There are four such sets in the legend of Perseus and his relations, two of deadly enemies (Danaüs and Aegyptus;

Acrisius and Proetus) and two of the closest friends (Heracles and Iphicles; Castor and Polydeuces, whom the Romans called Pollux).

The notion of simultaneous intercourse of man and god with a queen is old and was developed prominently in the Egyptian religious fiction that pharaoh, king of Egypt, was born not to a mortal, but to the god Amun, who came to the queen in the guise of her husband (just as Zeus, later equated with Amun, took on the shape of Amphitryon). Some would trace the story of Heracles' strange birth to the Egyptian tradition, portrayed in reliefs showing sexual union between god and queen in Egyptian temples. A charming poem inscribed on the funerary monument of Queen Hatshepsut (1490–1468 BC) accompanies such a relief, telling of Amun's appearance to Ahmes, wife of Tuthmosis I, to beget the divine child, and female pharaoh, Hatshepsut. Thoth, god of writing and magic, leads Amun to the queen's chamber:

[1]   The glorious god came,
      Amun himself, the lord of the two lands,
      in the guise of her husband.
      They° found her resting in the beautiful palace.
5   She awoke when she breathed the perfume of the god,
      and she laughed at the sight of his majesty.
      Inflamed with desire, he hastened toward her.
      He had lost his heart to the queen.
      When he came near to her,
10   she saw his form as a very god.
      She rejoiced in the splendor of his beauty.
      His love went inside all her limbs.
      The god's sweet perfume
      suffused through the palace,
15   the perfume of Punt,° the land of incense.
      The greatness of this god
      did to the woman what he pleased.
      She kissed him
      and delighted him with her body.

Egyptian Hymn on the Birth of Hatshepsut, c. 1460 BC

4. *They:* Amun and Thoth.   15. *Punt:* Probably Somalia.

If the story of Zeus and Amphitryon does descend from the Egyptian, it is a good example of the "downgrading" of a story that in an earlier culture had important political and religious meaning to a Greek heroic vignette, rich in comic potential. A comedy, the *Amphitruo* of the Roman playwright Plautus (second century BC), exploits this potential. Jupiter (Zeus) appears in the guise of Amphitryon, with Mercury (Hermes) disguised as his slave. He makes the night last three times its ordinary length, so great is the god's pleasure with Alcmena! All the while that Jupiter has his way with her, the clownish real Amphitryon stands outside the house, prevented by high jinks from getting inside and having intercourse with his wife. Just before World War II French playwright Jean Giraudoux wrote on the theme and named his play *Amphitryon 38* for the number of previous dramatic versions of one of the most popular of all ancient myths.

HERACLES' YOUTHFUL DEEDS

Amphitryon knew that he was father to one of the twins, and Zeus father to the other, but he was not sure which was which. Only when Hera sent serpents to destroy the infant son of Zeus did Amphitryon learn the truth: One of the infants seized the snakes and crushed them in his mighty hands, while the other lay helpless nearby (Figure 15.1).

Many of the stories told of Heracles were humorous, or are raw jokes in the spirit of "Hey, did you hear about the time that . . ." For example, a story told how Zeus ensured Heracles' greatness by placing the infant at Hera's breast so that he could imbibe the divine milk. Heracles bit down sharply, and Hera screamed

FIGURE 15.1 The infant Heracles strangles the serpents, fresco from Pompeii, c. AD 65. In the Roman representation, the baby Heracles strangles the serpents sent by Hera, while Alcmena, to the right, flees and Amphitryon, holding a staff, watches pensively. To the left, a nurse raises her hand in horror while an eagle, the bird of Zeus—Heracles' real father—looks on.   (Museo Archeologico Nazionale, Naples; University of Wisconsin–Madison Photo Archive)

bloody murder and dashed the child from her: The spurting milk became the Milky Way!

Another example concerns Heracles' fine and aristocratic education as he grew up tall and strong, his torso rippling with muscles. Heracles received instruction in wrestling, archery, fighting in heavy armor, and playing the lyre. He quickly mastered the martial arts, but as his big, clumsy fingers broke the lyre's strings, he could not get the notes right. His teacher complained so often that one day Heracles picked up the lyre and bashed in his music teacher's head. Tried for murder, he was acquitted on a claim of self-defense!

Another humorous story is just as easy to place within the all-male Greek aristocratic clubs. After the death of the music teacher, Amphitryon decided to remove his boisterous son from town until things cooled down. He sent Heracles to the country to tend cattle on the slopes of Mount Cithaeron (in southwestern Boeotia). There Heracles grew until he was eight feet tall. He defeated the local boys in throwing the javelin, shooting the bow, and similar activities.

When eighteen years old, he hunted an enormous lion that ravaged the flocks of Thespius (**thes**-pi-us), king of the nearby town THESPIAE (**thes**-pi-ē). For fifty days he hunted the beast. Each night, exhausted from stalking, he stayed in Thespius' house. Seeing how tall, strong, and handsome was Amphitryon's son, Thespius determined to have grandchildren by him. Each night he sent one of his fifty daughters to Heracles' bed. Heracles thought it was the same woman each night, and so begot his first fifty sons. Another tradition reports that Thespius got Heracles drunk and sent in all fifty daughters in a single night, one after the other. The drunken Heracles thought it was one woman and impregnated them all!

Eventually Heracles killed the lion.

MARRIAGE, MADNESS, AND MURDER

Heracles is often a buffoon or a sexual genius, but he soon goes too far. In a crisis the hero's greatness is useful, set against savage lion, invading horde, or dragon of chaos, but in peacetime he can be a danger to others (as was Gilgamesh) and to himself.

Amphitryon was killed in a war against Erginus, king of the Minyans. The new king of Thebes, Creon (**krē**-on), gave Heracles his daughter **Megara** (**meg**-a-ra) in marriage (Chart 15.2). Heracles settled down and fathered three children, but one

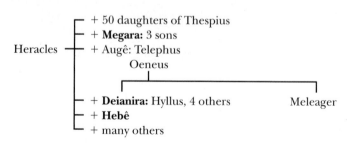

CHART 15.2 Heracles' Wives and Offspring

day he simply went mad—Hera was behind it—and without warning murdered his wife and children. The myth is the subject of a play by Euripides, *Heracles Insane* (414? BC). In the following excerpt a messenger describes the terrible crime. After destroying a pretender to the Theban throne, Heracles is about to perform a sacrifice, but suddenly he imagines he is traveling to Mycenae to kill the cowardly Eurystheus, who compelled him to undergo the Twelve Labors, which in Euripides' version took place before this incident:

[925]   The fair-faced group of children took their place;
     his father too, and Megara. The sacred basket
     was passed around the altar° as we watched
     in reverent silence. Waiting to take the torch
     in his right hand, to quench it in the font,°
930   Alcmena's son jerked to a sudden halt
     and stood without a word, without a step.
     At this delay the children turned their gaze
     to see their father change before their eyes.
      His bloodshot eyes rolled wildly in their sockets.
935   Foam trickled down his heavy-bearded chin,
     and thus he screamed, convulsed with manic laughter:
     "Father,° why light the purifying flame,
     doubling my work, before I slay Eurystheus?
     A single blow will set the matter right.
940   I'll fetch his skull, include it along with these
     of men already dead—then purify my hands.
     Pour out the holy water, toss the basket away!
     Here, someone, get my bow! somebody else, my sword!
     I'm off to smash Mycenae. All I need is a pick,
945   perhaps a crowbar. I'll turn those walls to rubble,
     walls the Cyclopes framed° by square and chisel.
     One twist of an iron bar, and down they go!"
     Then out he charged to a nonexistent chariot,
     climbed its imagined rails, and with his hand
950   stabbed out, to goad the horses that weren't there.
      What should we servants do—chuckle or shiver?
     Each glanced at the other with a muttered question,
     "Is this the master's joke? or has he gone crazy?"
     Heracles meanwhile prowled upstairs and down.
955   Charging into the quarters of the men,
     he shouted, "Here I am, in Nisus' town!"°

926–927. *basket . . . altar:* In sacrificial ritual a basket was circulated containing barley and the sacrificial knife. 929. *font:* Onlookers were purified by water sprinkled from a basin in which the sacrificer had quenched a torch. 937. *Father:* Amphitryon. in Euripides' version, Amphitryon is still alive. 946. *Cyclopes framed:* The classical Greeks called the visible Bronze Age walls of Mycenae, made of huge stones carefully fitted, "Cyclopean," as if only the giant Cyclopes could have built them. 956. *town:* Megara, between Thebes and Mycenae. Because Heracles is about to kill his wife, whose name is Megara, Euripides avoids introducing the confusing name of the city, although his audience would recognize it.

From there he went on in, not changing clothes,
squatted by the door, and had them pack a lunch.
After a little wait, he next announced
960 his passage through the Isthmus' wooded vales.°
Presently, stripping off his buckled cloak,
he wrestled furiously with himself alone,
demanded silence, crowned himself the victor.
He next imagined himself back in Mycenae,
965 bursting with rage against Eurystheus.
  Touching his mighty hand, his father pleaded:
"My boy, whatever has gone wrong with you?
On what mad journey have you now embarked?
I pray the blood of these, your recent victims,
970 has not destroyed your wits." But crazy Heracles
took him to be the father of Eurystheus,
a trembling suppliant clutching at his hand.
He shook him off, plucked arrows from his quiver
to aim at his own sons, blindly supposing
975 that he was slaying the family of Eurystheus.
  The frightened children rushed, now here, now there.
One sought his terror-stricken mother's skirts,
one hugged a pillar's all too slender shade,
one fledgling trembled at the altar's side.
980 Megara screamed, "To these you once gave life.
Will you, their father, be their cause of death?"
The old man and the slaves joined in her cries.
  But Heracles, unheeding, stalked the boy
who hid behind the pillar's treacherous bulk.
985 Cornered, the boy turned round to face him,
and Heracles stabbed. The child fell back,
his life-blood spurting out upon the walls.
The madman screamed a boast of victory:
  "One of your brood, Eurystheus, lies here dying,
990 part payment of the debt his father owes."
An arrow he aimed at the second, crouched by the altar,
hoping, in vain, to hide there unobserved.
Before the arrow could fly, the poor boy reached for a hug,
but fell, and vainly tried to clutch at his father's knees.
995   "O dearest Daddy," he cried, "Daddy, please don't hit me!
I'm not Eurystheus' son, I'm your own little boy!"
Heracles only rolled his wild and Gorgon eyes.
The child was too close as a mark for his deadly bow.
Like a blacksmith at his anvil, Heracles whirled his club
1000 down on the boy's fair hair and shattered the bones beneath.
  The second child dispatched, he stalked the third,
to make him a fellow-victim to join the others.
But Megara saw his plan: She snatched the child,
and bolted the doors behind. As though storming Cyclopean walls,

---

960. *wooded vales:* The narrow strip of land connecting the Peloponnesus with the mainland, where
athletic games were held similar to those at Olympia.

1005 Heracles pried at the doors, ripped their framing apart,
  and with a single arrow slew both his wife and child.
   This done, he savagely charged to Amphitryon's murder.
  But a ghostly form appeared before our horrified eyes—
  Pallas herself, with crested helmet and brandished spear,
1010 hurled a great stone which struck right on Heracles' chest,
  to end his murderous madness and put him into a coma.

     EURIPIDES, *Heracles Insane* 925–1008

Such descriptions of irrational behavior held great appeal for Euripides, a counterweight in popular entertainment to the glorification of reason heard in the streets of Athens. At the height of happiness Heracles suddenly lost control and committed a terrible crime; such is the uncertainty and terror of human life. In 416 BC the island of Melos revolted and tried to leave the Athenian empire. The Athenians crushed the uprising, killed every adult male in Melos, and enslaved the women and children. Euripides' play—if it was staged after 416 BC, as many think—may refashion an old myth to dramatize the horror of this contemporary event. **(For the complete *Heracles Insane*, see http://classics.mit.edu/Euripides/heracles.html)**

THE TWELVE LABORS

After murdering his wife and children, Heracles (according to the usual sequence of events) went to Delphi to learn what he must do to atone for the crime. The oracle replied that he must leave Thebes and travel to the Argive plain, his parents' homeland. There he would serve as bondsman to his cousin Eurystheus, king of Mycenae, and perform for him Twelve Labors. The Greek word is *athloi,* which really means "contests" (hence our *athletics*), for which the victor wins a prize. Heracles' prize would be immortality, the oracle said, and several of his contests were to be waged against Death himself.

In fact, Heracles completed far more than twelve tasks (or ten, according to some accounts). Ancient commentators divided his deeds into two categories: the Twelve Labors (*athloi*), accomplished mostly at Eurystheus' command, and the Deeds (*praxeis*), various other exploits, sometimes military. Later a third category was added: the Side-Deeds (*parerga*), subsidiary adventures that took place in the course of the Twelve Labors. In this account, we discuss the Labors and Side-Deeds together, then some of the better-known Deeds.

1. The Nemean Lion

The first task Eurystheus demanded was to kill a savage **lion** ravaging the country around **Nemea**, northwest of Mycenae (see Map V). Heracles fired at the lion with bow and arrow, and then realized, when his arrows bounced off, that the beast's skin was impenetrable. Heracles chased the lion into its lair, seized the

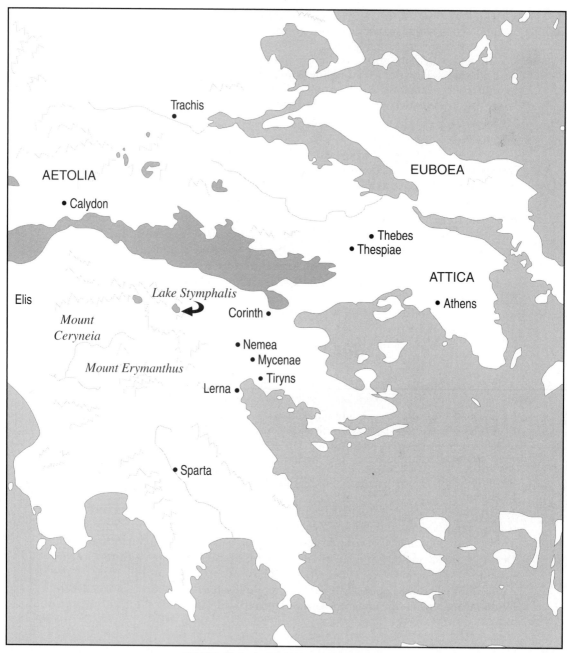

MAP V Heracles' Adventures in Greece

FIGURE 15.2 Heracles fights the Nemean lion, black-figured Attic water jar, c. 520 BC, the single most common theme in all Greek art; more than 500 examples survive represented on pottery alone. The hero has hung his cloak and quiver on a nearby vine. One of the lion's claws wraps around the hero's shoulder. Heracles is shown as the ideal naked Greek athlete.   (Erich Lessing / Art Resource, New York)

beast in a wrestler's grip, and through brute strength snapped its powerful neck (Figure 15.2). When he tried to skin the lion, his weapons could not break the immortal skin. Sometimes as clever as he was strong, Heracles took one of the lion's own claws and with this unbreakable tool cut the uncuttable pelt. Ever after, he wore the skin around his shoulders, its gaping jaws embracing his head like a helmet (see Figures 15.3 and 15.7), and he always carried the club he had cut at Nemea.

Heracles brought the dead lion back to Eurystheus, but in the comic vein of many tales about Heracles, the yellow-bellied king skulked in a corner of the palace, bellowing out orders that Heracles never again be allowed into the city. Henceforth he would announce his results to a herald named Copreus, "dung-man," who would in turn report to Eurystheus. To be on the safe side, Eurystheus also had an enormous bronze jar set into the ground in which he could take refuge when Heracles was anywhere near (Figure 15.3).

2. The Lernaean Hydra

Heracles' second labor was to destroy an enormous serpent, the **Hydra** ("water serpent") with many heads, which lived near the swamps of **Lerna** southeast of

FIGURE 15.3 Heracles and the Erymanthian boar, Attic water jug, c. 510 BC. Heracles, wearing the skin of the Nemean lion, poises his left foot on the edge of Eurystheus' underground bronze bowl and threatens to drop the boar on top of him. Eurystheus makes a deprecating gesture, and even Athena turns away in fear. On the right, Hermes, holding the caduceus, raises a hand in surprise.   (Musée du Louvre, Paris; Reunion des Musées Nationaux/Art Resource, New York)

Mycenae, where it ravaged the fields and livestock. Even its breath was death. Iolaüs (ī-ō-lā-us), Heracles' nephew (Chart 15.1), accompanied him to the springs. He is the hero's companion, like Enkidu (but the motif is much suppressed in stories about Heracles). Heracles soon drove the monster from its lair by shooting burning arrows. He moved in close with a sword. The Hydra wrapped its coils around one of his feet while a giant crab attacked the other. Every time Heracles cut off one head of the Hydra, two others grew, and the central head was immortal.

Although he smashed the crab, the outcome was uncertain. Iolaüs brought firebrands to cauterize the stump of each head, which stopped them from reproducing. Heracles cut off the immortal head and buried it beneath a rock (where it is today), then ripped open the fiend's body, spilling a filth of deadly bile. He dipped his arrows in the black liquor, so poisonous that a trace would kill the strongest man. Little did Heracles know that in so doing he prepared his own death. The crab became the constellation Cancer ("crab"; see Perspective Figure 14.2).

3. The Ceryneian Deer

His next task was to bring in the **Ceryneian deer**. Ceryneia (se-ri-**nē**-a) is a remote mountain in the northern Peloponnesus. This magical animal, although female, had golden antlers and brazen hoofs and belonged to Artemis. He tracked her for a full year until in Arcadia he wounded her with an arrow, threw the deer over his shoulder, and headed for Mycenae. On the way he met Artemis and Apollo. Apollo reproached Heracles for capturing his sister's sacred animal. The hero apologized, saying that he was under orders. Artemis allowed him to show the deer to Copreus, after which Heracles let it go.

4. The Erymanthian Boar

The **Erymanthian boar** lived on Mount Erymanthus in Arcadia in the central Peloponnesus, and Heracles was to capture it.

Side-Deed: The Friendly Centaur Pholus

While trying to pick up the boar's trail, Heracles stopped to visit a Centaur, named Pholus, in a remote cave. Wanting to be hospitable, Pholus offered Heracles cooked meat (he himself only ate raw). When Heracles asked for wine, pointing to a cask in the cave, Pholus explained that the wine belonged to all the Centaurs and he ought not to open it. Heracles assured him there would be no problem, but when the scent from the liquor wafted across the mountaintops, the neighboring Centaurs gathered, carrying stones and ash trees as weapons.

Alarmed at their aggressive manner, Heracles threw torches and fired arrows. They fled for refuge to the one wise Centaur, **Chiron** (**kī**-ron), who had migrated from northern Greece. Unlike the other Centaurs, Chiron was immortal, but in the melee one of Heracles' poisoned arrows wounded him. The venom that always kills now coursed through the veins of a being that cannot die, the sort of paradox in which the Greeks delighted.

Prometheus, chained on the Caucasus, eventually traded his mortality for Chiron's agonizing immortality, allowing Chiron to die (although Chiron is somehow still alive a generation later to tutor Achilles). We usually think of Prometheus as already immortal, but evidently he was not so originally, or the story is impossibly confused. The other Centaurs, including one named Nessus (**nes**-us), later the cause of Heracles' death, scattered to the four winds.

After the battle, the friendly Centaur Pholus picked up a stray arrow, astonished that such a puny thing could bring down a large, powerful Centaur like himself. Accidentally he let the arrow slip. It struck his hoof, and he, too, fell dead.

Heracles at last drove the boar from the bush, ran it down in a snow bank, and carried it to Eurystheus, who beheld it in terror from the bottom of his bronze jar (see Figure 15.3).

5. The Augean Stables

Augeas (aw-jē-as), a son of Helius, was king of the district of ELIS in the northwestern Peloponnesus. His father had given him many herds, but Augeas never cleaned his stables. After years of neglect, they were several feet deep in dung. Eurystheus, wanting to humiliate Heracles, ordered him to clean the stables. Without revealing that he was under orders, Heracles bargained with Augeas, who agreed that if he cleaned the stables in a day—an obvious impossibility—he would receive one-tenth of Augeas' cattle.

Heracles easily accomplished the task by diverting a nearby river through the stables. But when Augeas learned of Heracles' prior obligation to Eurystheus, he refused to pay. Later, as one of the Deeds, Heracles returned to Elis, killed Augeas and his sons, and instituted the Olympic Games.

PERSPECTIVE 15.1

DAUMIER'S *HERCULES IN THE AUGEAN STABLES*

Honoré Daumier (1808–1879) drew a series of parodies of Greek myth and Roman history called *Histoire ancienne*. Such traditions of satire go back to the ancient world. For example, in the *Iliad* Hera takes the arrows of Artemis and, like a comic-book buffoon, slaps Artemis around the ears with them. In antiquity Heracles was often shown in comic plays and on pots as a greedy, drunken bully. One pot shows him as a drunken satyr dancing around the tree of the Hesperides, from which hang golden wine goblets (he is a drunkard) instead of apples! In Daumier's lithograph of Hercules in the Augean Stables (Perspective Figure 15.1), from *Histoire ancienne*, the great hero is shown as a lumpy and disgruntled peasant, naked except for his deep boots and a tawdry lion skin, in the midst of the dung, shovel over his shoulder and mop in hand. The horse behind him is even now contributing to his task.

Daumier was a caricaturist, painter, and sculptor considered by many to be the greatest social satirist of his day. He was an early master of the technique of lithography (drawing directly on stone, from which multiple copies of an image can be printed). He contributed cartoons regularly to the weekly *La Caricature*. In 1832 his parody of Louis Philippe (king of France, 1830–1848) as Gargantua, a character in a famous satire by Rabelais (1483–1553), earned him a six-month term in prison. From 1835 on, the journal *Charivari* published as many as four thousand satiric lithographs, whose subjects were mostly contemporary urban industrial life.

PERSPECTIVE FIGURE 15.1 Honoré Daumier (French, 1808–1879), *Hercules in the Augean Stables,* c. 1848.   (Drawing from *Histoire Ancienne;* University of Wisconsin–Madison Photo Archives)

6. The Stymphalian Birds

In Arcadia around a lake called STYMPHALIS swarmed mighty flocks of the death-dealing **Stymphalian birds** with arrow-firing wings and armor-piercing beaks. Heracles drove them from their cover in the thick forest around the lake by clanging bronze castanets. As they flew into the sky, he shot them down with his arrows (Figure 15.4).

7. The Cretan Bull

So far the hero's tasks have been confined to the Peloponnesus, but now Eurystheus ordered Heracles to capture the **Cretan bull**, a magnificent animal summoned from the sea by Minos (see Chapter 16; Map VI). Heracles sailed to CRETE, seized the bull by the horns, tossed it in the sea, and rode it like a cowboy back to the Peloponnesus. After the herald inspected it, the bull got away and wandered north across the Isthmus to the plain of Marathon, where the Athenian hero Theseus killed it (Chapter 16).

FIGURE 15.4 Heracles and the Stymphalian birds, Attic water jug, c. 530 BC. In this version he hunts the birds with a slingshot. Some fly, some are shot, and others go about their business.   (British Museum, London; © Trustees of the British Museum / Art Resource, New York)

8. The Horses of Diomedes

Next Hercules was to capture the **horses of Diomedes**, a son of Ares and king of a savage tribe up north in THRACE. These horses, which were not ordinary animals, dined on human flesh.

Side-Deed: Alcestis

As we saw in Chapter 7, Apollo's son Asclepius was the greatest physician who ever lived. He even brought back to life Hippolytus, son of Theseus, after he was dragged to death (for his death, see Chapter 16). In anger at Asclepius' presumption in restoring Hippolytus (who was changed to a minor Italian god), Zeus killed Asclepius. In revenge, Apollo now killed the Cyclopes, who made Zeus's thunderbolts. Zeus struck back by forcing Apollo to serve for a year under **Admetus** (ad-**mēt**-us, "indomitable"), king over a town in THESSALY. Admetus treated the god so well that Apollo gave him this boon: Admetus need not die if he could find someone else to die in his place. Several, including his father, refused the honor. Only his dutiful wife **Alcestis** was willing to die for him (see Figure 2.11).

While traveling north toward Thrace, Heracles stopped in the court of Admetus. His visit is the subject of one of Euripides' best-known plays, the *Alcestis* (438 BC). Heracles notices that the house is in mourning but is not told why, except that a "neighbor" has died. Seeing no reason that the death of an unknown person should affect his amusement, Heracles demands wine, gets drunk, bawls out a song, and lectures a servant for going around with a long face. He should seize the day, Heracles advises, and enjoy its pleasures, a point of view natural to the rambunctious son of

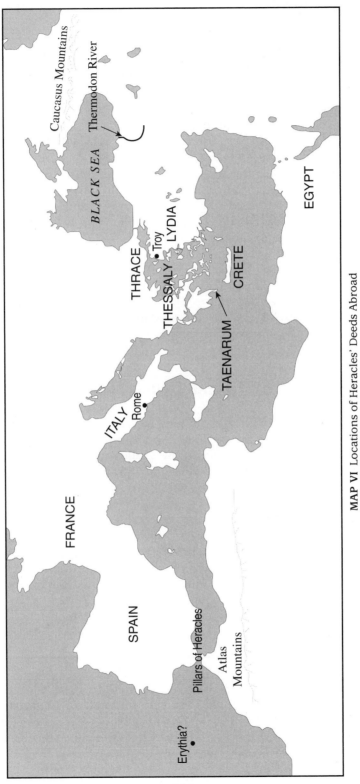

MAP VI Locations of Heracles' Deeds Abroad

Zeus. When Heracles learns that the house is in fact mourning for the queen, he regrets his thoughtless behavior and takes a characteristically bold course: If she must die, he will bring her back from the dead. He goes to the place (off-stage) where the body awaits its funeral, meets Death (*Thanatos*), wrestles him down, and takes back Alcestis.

The story is a combination of folktale motifs: the mate who dies for a spouse (with a substitution allowed); various substitutes rejected; the dying spouse reprieved. Even so Sumerian Inanna could return from the lower world only if a substitute were found. She rejected several, then fixed on the unwilling Dumuzi. Euripides never explains why Alcestis decides to die for Admetus, and he puts Admetus in the odd position of complaining bitterly throughout the entire play about his fate—poor man, he is losing a wife he loves so much! Everything bad happens to him! The force of the story-pattern appears to override the motivations of the actors in Euripides' odd, perhaps humorous play.

When Heracles reached Thrace, he promptly captured the horses of Diomedes. Because they enjoyed human flesh, he fed their master, Diomedes, to them. After the herald saw the man-eating horses, they ran away north to Mount Olympus, where they were themselves eaten by wolves. (**For the complete *Alcestis*, see http:// ebooks.adelaide.edu.au/e/euripides/alcestis/)**

9. The Girdle of Hippolyta

Theseus, Dionysus, and Achilles fought the Amazons; so did Heracles. Eurystheus ordered him to bring back the **girdle of Hippolyta** (hip-**pol**-i-ta, "horse-tamer"), the Amazon queen, for his daughter. The girdle was a belt that women wore above their hips: To loosen it was to offer oneself sexually, to take it forcibly was rape. This labor is a sexual one, directed against the queen of the man-hating Amazons.

Heracles gathered some companions and set out on the long journey to the river THERMODON on the southern shore of the Black Sea. When he arrived, Hippolyta gladly offered him the belt, so great were Heracles' charms. Seeing this, an angry Hera disguised herself as an Amazon and ran through the city proclaiming that Heracles had abducted their queen. The Amazons attacked, and Heracles, fearing treachery, strangled Hippolyta, removed her girdle, and sailed away. He gave the girdle to Eurystheus.

10. The Cattle of Geryon

For his tenth labor Heracles needed to capture the **cattle of Geryon** (**jer**-i-on), a monster who had three bodies joined at the waist and lived on the island of ERYTHIA (e-ri-**thi**-a), "red land" (perhaps named from the colors of the sunset), somewhere in the far west near the river Ocean. Geryon possessed a wonderful herd of red cattle, watched over by Eurytion and his demonic two-headed dog, Orthus.

Heracles trudged through the sands of northern Africa, finally reaching the narrows where the Mediterranean Sea opens into the Atlantic Ocean. He set up pillars on either side, known today as the Rock of Ceuta in Tangiers and the British-controlled Rock of Gibraltar. To the ancients they were the PILLARS OF HERACLES, the geographical boundary between the human world and the unknown vastness of outer space.

As Heracles traveled the African sands, it got so hot that, in exasperation, he fired an arrow at Helius, the sun. Helius admired his boldness and lent him the cup by which he traveled every night from the western to the eastern horizon, perhaps on the river Ocean (Figure 15.5). The image is taken from Egyptian religion, where the sun-god Re makes his daily journey in the boat of the sun. With this cup, Heracles crosses the waters to Erythia.

Heracles landed, bashed in Orthus' brains, and killed the herdsman Eurytion. He rustled the cattle and was driving them across a river when Geryon himself attacked. Heracles felled him with arrows, herded the cattle into the cup, and bobbed back to the known world. He landed on the Atlantic coast of Spain, then returned the cup to the sun-god.

Heracles drove the cattle across what is now Spain, then southern France, then for some reason turned south into Italy.

FIGURE 15.5 Heracles in the cup of Helius, interior of an Attic wine cup, c. 480 BC. Only his torso with lion skin shows. He grips his club and bow and stares across the great unknown. Fish and octopi play in the waves. (Photo Vatican Museums)

Side-Deed: Cacus

Near the future site of Rome, **Cacus** (kā-kus, Greek "evil man"), a three-headed fire-breathing monster, stole some of the cattle and hid them in a cave on the Palatine, one of the seven original hills of Rome. Heracles heard their lowing, climbed the hill, tore away the rocks at the top of the cave, leaped down inside, and demolished Cacus with his club. Vergil (70–19 BC), who is nostalgic about early Rome, tells the story in his epic poem the *Aeneid*. The speaker is Evander, an early Greek settler on the future site of Rome, explaining to Aeneas the origin of an important ritual:

[190]   First look up at this crag overhanging the fallen debris,
        how falling rocks of the mountain have left its caverns exposed,
        how the tumbled face of the cliff was left as a great pile of rubble.
        This used to be the cave in whose dark and sinister recess,
        never touched by the sun, dwelt the bestial half-human Cacus.
195   The ground used to stink with blood, and over its arrogant portal
        were nailed the bloodless heads of his victims, green with decay.
        This creature was sired by Vulcan;° Vulcan's fire would blaze
        from his maw as he wandered, deadly, threatening, enormous.
            But finally came the day of deliverance, answering our prayers,
200   the presence and help of a god, the greatest of all avengers.
        Alcides,° proudly driving his booty of great-muscled cattle,
        the spoil of his glorious conquest of Geryon, triple of body,
        approached to encamp with his loot here in our valleys and hills.
        Cacus' mind was enraged that a deed either cruel or treacherous
205   should remain undared, unattempted. He stole to the pastures,
        and stealthily drove away four of the mightiest bulls
        and an equal number of heifers, the finest of all the herd.
        To keep from leaving tracks, he dragged them away by the tail,
        and thus reversing the hoofprints,° hid them down in his inky den.
210   Time passed. Amphitryon's son was ready to move with his booty.
        Rested and bored in the pens, impatient to start on the journey,
        the cattle began to complain and to fill the forests and hillsides
        with bovine lugubrious bellows, although leaving so pleasant a spot.
            A heifer from the depths of the cavern promptly responded.
215   With the sound of a mournful "Moo!" she wrecked the ambition of Cacus.
        The blackest bile blazed up in the liver of raging Alcides.
        With his mighty fists he reached for his knobby ponderous bludgeon,
        and swift as the wind he thundered up to the mountain's peak.
        That was the first time our peasants saw Cacus' arrogant eyes
220   rolling in fear, as he hastened, faster than winds of the east,
        to seek the seclusion a cavern grants. Fear hurried his feet.
        The instant he got inside, he broke the chains and let tumble
        the massive boulder which hung on hooks put there by his father
        and propped it against the doorway, to block the angry intruder.

197. *Vulcan:* = Greek Hephaestus.   201. *Alcides:* "[Grand]son of Alcaeus," another name for Heracles. Alcaeus was the father of Amphitryon, Heracles' (human) father, and Anaxo, Heracles' maternal grandmother (see Chart 15.1).   209. *hoofprints:* Compare Hermes' trick with the cattle of Apollo (Chapter 8).

225 Raging, gnashing his teeth, the baffled Tirynthian hero°
rolled his eyes at the doorway, trying to find a way in.
Three times, boiling with rage, he studied the Aventine mountain;
three times he tried to smash the gateway's threshold of granite;
three times he had to retreat, exhausted, into the valley.
230 From the ridge above the cavern there arose a pillar of flint,
conspicuous, sheer on all sides, fit nest for fowl of ill omen.
The pinnacle, leaning a bit, overhung the left bank of the river,
so Heracles pushed to the right. Ripping it up by the roots,
he hurled it down with a blow like that of a bolt of thunder.
235 The banks of the river parted, its terrified water surged back.
The cave of Cacus lay naked, as big as the vault of a palace,
and the dark recesses behind it were opened up to the light.
   Imagine the crust of the earth has been peeled by some mighty power,
baring the region beneath, pale realms abhorred by the gods.
240 Down below in the pit you would see the terrified phantoms,
shrinking away in terror at the sudden influx of light.
Like them Cacus was trapped by the sudden glare and retreated
deep in his hollow of rock, with screams like none heard before.
   Alcides pressed his advantage: He shouted for all his weapons,
245 and even grabbed broken branches and millstones, mighty and massive.
Cacus, all hope being gone of ever escaping his peril,
belched (believe it or not) from his jaws a cloud of black smoke.
The cavern at once was shrouded in the inky blackness of night,
which stripped the eyes of their sight, and under the rocky roof
250 mixed choking sinister darkness with lurid flashes of fire.
But Alcides did not submit. One jump, he was over the flame,
into the cave, where the smoke was pouring its murkiest billows.
In vain did Cacus belch out his flames to lighten the darkness.
The hero, catching his neck, squeezed till his eyes started out,
255 till blood no longer was pulsing in the arteries of his throat.
   The black den's gates lay open, the stolen cattle restored,
the theft and the trick to conceal it now lay exposed to the day,
and the monster's ugly cadaver was dragged away by the heels.

VERGIL, *Aeneid* 8.190–269

225. *Tirynthian hero:* Heracles, who after completing his labors ruled in Tiryns.

After other adventures, Heracles brought most of the cattle to Mycenae, where Eurystheus sacrificed them to Hera.

11. The Apples of the Hesperides

Heracles' next task was to bring back the **Apples of the Hesperides** (hes-**per**-i-dēz, "the nymphs of the West"). These apples grew on a magical tree with golden bark and golden leaves. Zeus gave the tree to Hera as a wedding present, and Hera planted it in a garden at the foot of Mount Atlas (hence the name Atlantic Ocean, near Mount Atlas). Although the Titan Atlas was said to have become a mountain when Perseus showed him the Gorgon's head, he was still alive generations later in the days of Heracles. Because the Hesperides liked to pilfer from the tree, Hera set a ferocious hundred-headed serpent named Ladon as guard over it (see Figure 6.5).

Heracles did not know where to find the Garden of the Hesperides (just as Perseus did not know where to find the Gorgons). He had first to find and seize the sea-god Nereus, who changed into every kind of shape, until at last he gave Heracles the directions.

Side-Deed: Busiris

Although the Hesperides were in the far west, Heracles seems to have become confused and headed east. At least his next side-deed takes place in EGYPT, against **Busiris** (bu-**sīr**-is), a son of Poseidon and one of Epaphus' daughters (hence a cousin of Perseus). Some years before, when Egypt was barren, a seer told the king that to restore abundance he must sacrifice a foreigner. The king began with the seer himself! Ever thereafter he sacrificed every foreigner he could. Heracles allowed himself to be bound and led to the altar. Then, impatient with the tiny, effete Egyptians and their foolish airs, he burst his bonds, seized Busiris and his sons, and killed them all (Figure 15.6).

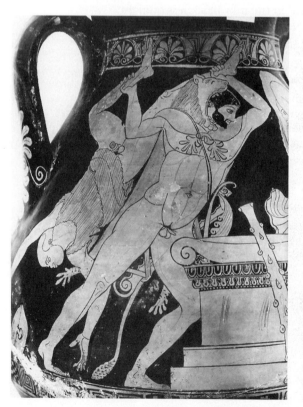

FIGURE 15.6 Heracles kills Busiris, on an Attic water jug, c. 470 BC. Heracles swings a shaven-headed Egyptian priest by both legs, as if he were a club by which he will kill other priests cowering on the other side of the altar. His ordinary club leans against the altar. (Deutsches Archaologisches Institut, Athens; Photograph: Hermann Wagner)

Busiris is a Greek corruption of the Egyptian *Bu-Osiris,* meaning "the place of Osiris," the name of a temple dedicated to the Egyptian god of the dead. Heracles' sacrifice of Busiris, then, is Death overcome.

Side-Deed: Prometheus

Trying to find the Hesperides, Heracles came to Prometheus, still nailed to a rock in the Caucasus, his liver devoured every day by an eagle. Heracles killed the eagle and set Prometheus free, as Hesiod reports in his *Theogony:*

[525] Heracles at last, mighty son
of fair-ankled Alcmena, slew the eagle and saved the child
of Iapetus° from his torment. Zeus, of course, consented,
he who governs the world from high on Olympus,
that the glory of Thebes-born Heracles might be greater
530 than ever before through all the abundant earth.
Considering all this, he honored his son and his fame.
Furious though he was, he gave up his long-held anger
that Prometheus had dared contest the plans of mighty Zeus.

HESIOD, *Theogony* 525–534

526–527. *child of Iapetus:* Prometheus.

At last Heracles came to the western edge of the world, where Atlas held up the heavens on his shoulders (see Figure 5.1). On the advice of Prometheus, Heracles persuaded Atlas to fetch the apples from the magic tree, a mission too dangerous even for Heracles. While Atlas was away in the Garden of the Hesperides, Heracles himself held up the sky. The Titan returned but, exultant with his freedom, declared he would himself take the apples to Eurystheus. Heracles could go on holding up the world. Heracles agreed, asking only that Atlas take the sky back for a moment so that he might place a pad on his head to cushion the immense weight. Stupid Atlas put down the apples and hoisted the sky. Heracles grabbed the fruit and hurried away (Figure 15.7; compare Figure 15.12). He gave the apples to Eurystheus, but because they were too dangerous to keep, Eurystheus returned them to Heracles, who gave them to Athena, who restored them to the Hesperides.

12. Cerberus

As his twelfth labor Heracles was ordered to descend to the underworld and bring back its many-headed guard-dog, **Cerberus.** He traveled to the entrance to Hades at TAENARUM, a system of caves at the southernmost tip of the Peloponnesus, about eighty miles south of Sparta (Orpheus descended here). As he came down from the upper world, the ghosts fled before him. He appeared before the king and queen of the dead and requested permission to take Cerberus.

FIGURE 15.7 The Roman emperor Commodus (ruled AD 180–192) as Hercules. Alexander the Great had shown himself as Heracles, and the tradition lasted among rulers until the end of antiquity. Here Commodus, son of the emperor-philosopher Marcus Aurelius, shows himself absurdly wrapped in the skin of the Nemean lion, with foppish hair and petulant smile. He carries the club over his shoulder and holds in his palm the Apples of the Hesperides. At his midriff, a shield with double Roman eagles and gorgoneion is flanked by crossed cornucopias atop a globe and goddesses (one lost) to either side. Toward the end of his reign Commodus, like Heracles, seems to have gone insane. He murdered many, performed as a gladiator in the ring, called himself the Roman Hercules, and was strangled shortly after this portrait was done. (Commodus was the historical inspiration for the emperor-tyrant in the film *Gladiator,* released in 2000.)   (Museo Capitolino, Rome; Scala/Art Resource, New York)

Hades agreed, so long as Heracles did not use any weapons. Protected by his lion's skin, he seized the hell-hound by the throat, although Cerberus' snake-tail lashed and bit him. Heracles passed a chain around the beast and dragged it, foaming and snarling, to Eurystheus (see Figure 4.4), then released it to the world below.

Observations: Heracles' Labors

Gilgamesh overcame a great bull, as did Heracles, and he destroyed the mysterious Humbaba. Heracles began his heroic career as an animal-slayer, then took on new adversaries. As Gilgamesh crossed faraway waters to consult with Utnapishtim, the man who never died, and Perseus went to the edge of the world to defeat a demon whose glance was death, so did Heracles go to Erythia in the far west (land of the dead), to the western land of the Hesperides, and to the underworld itself to bring back its guardian.

Scholars have wondered when and how originally separate and disorganized tales were placed into a group of twelve. Our earliest accounts show no trace of a standard list or number. In a genealogical passage explaining the parentage of important mythical monsters, Hesiod refers only to Geryon, the Hydra, Cerberus (although not explicitly connected with Heracles), and the Nemean lion (see Chart 4.3):

[287]   Chrysaör° bedded Callirhoë, daughter of far-famed Ocean,
       on whom he fathered Geryon, three human bodies conjoined.
       Geryon was herding his slow-moving cattle in rich Erythia
290   when mighty Heracles slew him, plundered the herds as his booty,
       and drove them across the ocean to the holy city of Tiryns,
       first stilling Orthus the hound and Eurytion, Geryon's cowherd
       in the windy pastures beside the coast of the far-famed Ocean.
       Callirhoë bore to Chrysaör another, like neither men nor immortals,
295   Echidna, divine, strong-minded, born in a hollow cave.
       Down to the waist a soft-cheeked maiden, glancing demurely;
       below, a speckled serpent, terrible, monstrous in size,
       feeding on human flesh in the sacred depths of the earth . . .
       They say that Typhoeus, the creature of cruelty, terror, unreason,
300   bedded this soft-eyed maiden, who bore him terrible children.
       First came Orthus the hound, Geryon's servant and watchdog.
       Cerberus next she conceived, an unspeakable flesh-eating horror,
       the bronze-voiced watchdog of Hades, fifty-headed and ruthless.
       The third of her spawn was the Hydra of Lerna, plotter of evil,
305   whom white-shouldered Hera brought up in her anger at Heracles.
       Yet Zeus's son slew the beast with the edge of his pitiless sword,
       Heracles, son of Amphitryon, and his warlike friend Iolaüs,
       all in accord with the plans of Athena who gathers the booty.
       And Echidna bore the Chimera, breathing unquenchable fire . . .
310   who, yielding to rape by Orthus, conceived a bane to the Thebans,
       the terrible Sphinx, and her brother, destruction to mortals,
       the savage Nemean lion, whom Hera, consort of Zeus
       raised from a cub and settled among the vales of Nemea,
       as tyrant over Nemea, Tretos, and Apesas.°
315   But he too fell to the valor and power of Heracles.

HESIOD, *Theogony* 287–332

287. *Chrysaör:* "He of golden sword," sprung from the severed neck of Medusa, along with Pegasus.   314. *Apesas:* Tretos and Apesas are mountains near Nemea in the northern Peloponnesus.

The earliest evidence for the canonical cycle of Twelve Labors is found not in literature but on the twelve stone panels, called **metopes** (**met-ō-pēz**), mounted above the front and rear porch columns of Zeus's temple at Olympia, built about 470 BC (compare Figure 15.9). The cleaning of the Augean stables was included on the temple in the twelfth position, evidently to honor Pisa, the site of the temple, in the territory of the legendary Augeas. This labor differs from the others that pit Heracles against dangerous enemies; it cannot belong to an earlier list. Twelve is a magical number and suitable for a collection—twelve Olympians, twelve Titans, and twelve months in the year—but in this case the number may be an accident: The sculptor had twelve spaces to fill because of the architecture of the temple, and the fame of these sculptures made the selection canonical (but in some accounts he only performed ten deeds).

By Hellenistic times the same twelve adventures always appear in roughly the same order. There is a logic to their organization. The early adventures are set in the Peloponnesus in an ever-widening circle around Mycenae. Of the first seven, six are simple combat between man and animal (once again, the cleaning of the Augean stables does not fit). Later adventures carry Heracles south to Crete (Cretan bull), north to Thrace (horses of Diomedes), east to the land of the Amazons (girdle of Hippolyta), and west to Erythia (cattle of Geryon), and the last labors are set in paradise (Garden of the Hesperides) and hell (Cerberus). So deliberate an arrangement must reflect a lost poem, although we do not know whether the poem came before or after the designer of the metopes at Olympia, or who composed it, or where.

Heracles' geographical exploration ever further afield made him a natural model for the many Greeks living overseas, especially those in the distant and dangerous west, in Sicily and Italy. Ninety percent of surviving illustrated Greek pots (such as those printed in this book) come from graves in Italy, and the abundance of scenes illustrating the adventures of Heracles no doubt reflects the western Greeks' reverence for him.

Heracles had traveled into the Atlantic Ocean and faced Death himself, and he easily overcame every foreign people. Heracles was the colonists' favorite hero, and even became a god. Alexander the Great also claimed descent from Heracles. The image of Alexander wearing the skin of the Nemean lion on his coins evokes the image of Heracles seeking to impose his will on all foreigners who might stand against him.

VARIOUS DEEDS

Released from servitude to Eurystheus, Heracles settled in Tiryns. He wished to marry again. He heard that Eurytus, king of Oechalia (a town of unknown location somewhere in EUBOEA), who had been Heracles' own archery instructor, was offering his beautiful daughter **Iolê** (ī-o-lē) as a prize in an archery contest. Heracles traveled to Oechalia and easily won the contest. But Eurytus would not give up Iolê, fearing, he said, that she and her children might share Megara's fate.

Heracles stormed off. Shortly afterward, Eurytus discovered that twelve fine mares were missing. Eurytus thought that Heracles must have taken them, but Eurytus' son Iphitus (**if**-i-tus), who admired Heracles, insisted that so great a man could never stoop so low. Iphitus said he would go to Tiryns and place the matter before the hero.

In fact the mares were in Heracles' herd, either because Heracles took them or because he had gotten them from someone else. Heracles welcomed Iphitus to Tiryns and invited him to the top of the stone ramparts, then for his nosiness pushed him over. For a second time Heracles had violated a sacred social code, this time that of *xenia,* "guest-friendship," whereby a host never for any reason harms his guest.

Heracles went to the Delphic Oracle to learn how to atone for his most recent crime. The Pythia refused even to answer, disgusted with a man twice accursed and blood-polluted. Heracles broke into the temple, seized the Pythia's holy tripod, and ran down the road, shouting that he would therefore set up his own oracle (Figure 15.8)! Apollo came down from Olympus and seized a leg of the tripod. Back and forth they tugged, until Zeus separated them with a thunderbolt.

Apollo agreed to purify Heracles on these conditions: He must serve a woman for three years as her slave, and he must give everything he earned to Eurytus,

FIGURE 15.8 Heracles struggles with Apollo over the Delphic tripod, on a red-figured water jar, c. 480 BC Athena stands to the left, wearing the aegis with gorgoneion, holding her helmet in her hand. Heracles wears his lion skin and carries his club while slinging the tripod over his shoulder. Apollo clings to the tripod, wearing a wreath of laurel and carrying his bow. Artemis stands to the right, with her deer between Apollo and Heracles.   (Musée du Louvre, Paris; Réunion des Musées Nationaux/Art Resource, New York)

king of Oechalia and father of Iphitus, as blood-money. Hermes led the hero to the slave market, a rope around his neck. **Omphalê** (**om**-fa-lē), queen of LYDIA, liked the hero's physique and bought him on the spot, thinking he would make a fine lover.

Omphalê and Heracles spent the next three years in such idle and debased pleasures as wearing each other's clothes. Omphalê lugged Heracles' club, smothered in his lion skin, while Heracles pranced in her negligee before settling down at her feet to spin thread.

One day they went to the wild for a little fun. When night fell, they entered a cave. Pan, goat-god of shepherds and flocks, saw them and in the night sneaked into the cave, bent on having his way with Omphalê. Feeling a negligee drooping from the bed, he leaped on his prey. Heracles (for they had exchanged clothes) awoke with a roar and smashed Pan against the stony walls. Never since has Pan worn clothing!

During his Lydian period Heracles captured the **Cercopes** (ser-**kōp**-ēz), two ruffians who robbed passersby and treated them cruelly. One day they saw Heracles sleeping beside the road and sneaked up, hoping to rob him, but instantly Heracles seized them in his massive hands, suspended them from the ends of a pole, and went down the road with the pole on his shoulders (Figure 15.9). But the ruffians, although hanging upside down, continued to crack jokes. Seeing Heracles' buttocks burned black from his journeys across deserts and through foreign lands, one shouted, "O, beware the great black buttocks! Beware the great black buttocks!" And the other giggled, "That must be what Mama meant!" Years before, their mother had warned them: Only "Black Buttocks" could defeat them. Heracles was amused by their carryings-on (as we are meant to be) and let them go. Zeus later turned the Cercopes into monkeys.

After his three years of servitude were complete, Heracles left Lydia, gathered an army, and set out to settle a few scores. He started with Troy, where he was badly treated on an earlier adventure. Heracles killed the king, Laomedon, and all his sons except for one, named Podarces: Before giving the king's daughter away as war-booty, he permitted her to save one prisoner. Podarces thereafter was called Priam (**prī**-am), which means "the ransomed one." Priam was king of Troy during the Trojan War.

THE DEATH OF HERACLES

Gilgamesh died peacefully in Uruk, and of Perseus' death nothing is known. Heracles, by contrast, died horribly at the hands of a woman scorned in love. Even so an angry Ishtar destroyed Gilgamesh's beloved friend Enkidu when Gilgamesh rejected her.

Heracles first heard of **Deianira** (dē-ya-**nī**-ra, "man-killer") when he was in the underworld. The ghost of her brother Meleager (mel-ē-**ā**-jer), hero of the Calydonian Boar Hunt (see Chapter 19), suggested to Heracles that he marry Deianira, should he ever escape from Death's realm. Now he set off to CALYDON, capital of AETOLIA where she lived, in the southwestern corner of the mainland.

FIGURE 15.9 The Cercopes, on a metope from Selinus in Sicily, c. 530 BC. The hero is seemingly naked except for a belt around his waist and the lion skin visible behind his left arm. The Cercopes, portrayed like naked dwarves, are bound around their ankles, knees, and wrists. The figures' faces turned to the front are unusual in art of this period. This evidently trivial tale is for unknown reasons the subject of artistic representations from Corinth, Sparta, Attica, south Italy, and Sicily over a span of two hundred years, between the sixth and fourth centuries BC. (Museo Archeologico Regionale, Palermo; University of Wisconsin–Madison Photo Archive)

The river-god **Acheloüs** (ak-e-lō-us), usually represented as a bull but sometimes taking on other forms (Figure 15.10), also wanted Deianira. Heracles wrestled Acheloüs and broke off one of his horns. In Sophocles' play *Women of Trachis* (**trā**-kis; c. 430? BC), whose subject is the downfall and death of Heracles, the chorus gives a good description of the fight:

[503] Tell me, who were the real heroes
          who advanced to fight for this girl as bride,
505   in contests with no holds barred, no times-out?
       One of them had the strength of a rushing river,
       resembling a long-horned, solid-set bull—
          that was Acheloüs of Calydon.

FIGURE 15.10 Heracles wrestles with Acheloüs, Attic vase, c. 520–510 BC. Here the river-god has the shape of a Triton, a sea-spirit with the pug nose and pointed ears of a satyr. Acheloüs' fish-body suggests the stormy water of the untamed stream. Heracles is about to break off his horn.   (British Museum, London; © Trustees of the British Museum / Art Resource, New York)

The other came from Thebes, the town of Bacchus,
510   brandishing bow and spear and bludgeon,
    the son of Zeus himself. The two together
    entered the ring, both eager for the girl.
The referee? Aphrodite the coupler
was there to see to fair play.
515   First came the thud of fists, then the twang of bows,
    then a noise like the combat of bulls in rut.
    They twisted and grappled, with the sound of butting heads,
and the angry screams of them both.
But the fair-faced kindly girl for whom they fought
520   sat quietly apart, on a distant bank—
I tell you this, as if I myself were her mother—
waiting to learn whose bride she was to be.
    A piteous sight!

SOPHOCLES, *Women of Trachis* 503–529

Taking his bride, Heracles headed for TRACHIS, a city built in a gorge above a plain northwest of Thermopylae, whose king had offered him hospitality. On the way he had to cross the river Evenus, where the Centaur **Nessus** ferried travelers for a small fee. Nessus had lived in the Peloponnesus until Heracles drove him out in his squabble with the drunken Centaurs, long ago. Deianira got on the Centaur's back while Heracles easily swam to the other side, but in the middle of the river Nessus assaulted the young woman. When Heracles saw what was happening, he shot the Centaur with a poisoned arrow (Figure 15.11). Nessus staggered ashore and with his dying words instructed Deianira to collect his blood and semen, a powerful love potion, should she ever need it.

Heracles and his new bride stayed at Trachis. Still resenting his treatment at the hands of Eurytus of Oechalia, however, who had cheated him of Iolê, Heracles organized a military campaign. He sacked the town, killed Eurytus, took the girl, and retired to a cape on the long island of Euboea to prepare a sacrifice to his father Zeus, in thanks for his victory. He sent a messenger, Lichas, across the strait to Trachis to fetch a clean cloak for the sacrifice. Deianira, learning about Iolê, now remembered the love potion:

FIGURE 15.11 Heracles and Nessus on a large Attic vase, c. 610 BC, used to mark a grave. Avenging the attack on his wife, Heracles here seizes the Centaur's hair, presses his left foot into his back, and prepares to bury his sword in the monster's chest, unimpressed by the Centaur's appeal for mercy by touching Heracles' chin. Heracles' name is written above him (from right to left), and Nessus' name (spelled NETOS) before his chest. Heracles wears a simple cloak crossed with a telamon ("strap") to support his sword scabbard under his left arm. He does not wear the lion skin, nor carry bow or club. Note his neatly trimmed mustache against the shaggy, unkempt beard of the Centaur. The belly of the amphora (not shown) preserves one of the earliest representations of Perseus slaying Medusa.   (National Archaeological Museum, Athens; Foto Marburg/Art Resource, New York)

[555]   Preserved in a bronze container for many a year,
      I keep an old gift of the ancient Centaur,
      which, still a maid, I took from the shaggy Nessus
      as he lay dying, weltering in his blood.
      He used to carry people in his arms
560   for a trifling fee, across Evenus' river,
      in his arms, not bothering with oars or sails.
      He carried me too, held up against his shoulder,
      when first I followed Heracles as wife,
      so ordered by my father. Out in midstream
565   he fondled me with his lubricious hands.
      I screamed aloud, the son of Zeus spun round
      and from his hands let fly a feathered arrow,
      which whistled into his lungs. The dying Centaur
      gasped out a few last words: "Child of old Oeneus,°
570   you are the last I shall ever bring across.
      So listen carefully, and profit from my labors.
      Take in your hands a blood-clot from my punctured lungs,
      black with Hydra's bile, which Heracles
      smeared on his arrows. This charm will never fail
575   to bind his heart: He will never look again
      at another woman, to love her more than you."
          With this in mind, my friends, since Nessus died
      I have kept the venom, safely locked away.
      Now I have brought it out, to stain this shirt.
580   All is made ready, as the living Centaur directed.

Sophocles, *Women of Trachis* 555–581

569. *Oeneus:* Deianira's father, Oeneus ("wine-man"), was king of Calydon.

(For a translation of the complete *Women of Trachis* by Sophocles, see http:// bacchicstage.wordpress.com/sophocles/women-of-trachis-aka-trachiniae/)
      She gives the shirt to the messenger, Lichas. In Sophocles' play, Hyllus (**hī**-lus), oldest son of Heracles and Deianira, tells his mother what happened next:

[749]   Because you insist, I'll tell the whole sad story.
750   When Heracles had sacked the town of Eurytus,
      away he marched, with trophies and great loot.
      There is a Cape Ceneium, washed by the waves,
      at the very tip of Euboea, where he dedicated
      an altar and grove to his ancestral Zeus.
755   After my separation, I was overjoyed
      to find him there, about to offer up
      a splendid sacrifice. But just as all was ready,
      his faithful herald Lichas came from home,
      bringing your deadly gift, the envenomed shirt.
760   He put it on, according to your command,
      then offered up a dozen perfect bulls,
      the best of all the booty, and made ready,

a hundred victims of every sex and age.
At first, poor man, his heart rejoiced at the show,
765   and he prayed with fervor, wearing your recent gift.
    But then, as the blood-fed fires of the sacred rite
blazed up and joined the resinous firewood's heat,
and his whole body broke into a sweat,
your shirt, as tight as any builder's mortise,
770   clung to his ribs, and then to every limb.
On every bone came cramping, torturing, fire,
as the serpentine and deadly venom gnawed.
He screamed in pain to bring him hapless Lichas,
who had no share at all in his distress.
775   "What scheming made you bring this deadly garment?"
Poor man, what did he know? He kept repeating
the gift was yours alone, he just the bearer.
As Heracles was listening to his words,
a wrenching torment tore apart his lungs.
780   He seized poor Lichas by one ankle joint
and dashed him down against a wave-washed reef.
The white stuff of his brain, marbled with blood,
burst from his shattered skull and soaked his hair.
No bystander but gasped and groaned in horror,
785   at Heracles' torment, Lichas' death,
yet not a soul dared to approach the hero,
now squirming in anguish, groveling on the earth,
now starting up in sharp spasmodic pain.
The cries of Heracles reechoed from the rocks
790   on every side—Locrian cliffs and headlands of Euboea.
    At last, exhausted, he collapsed to the ground,
cursing and groaning at the bitter wedlock
with you, the marriage bargained from old Oeneus,
which poisoned his life. At last he raised his eyes
795   uncertainly from the thick and clinging smoke,
and saw me weeping in the stricken crowd.
    "Come near, my son," he called, "don't run away,
though it may mean you join me in my death.
Lift me, carry me out, where none can see my pain.
800   If you have any pity, take me across the water
far from this place, and let me not die here."
    At this command, we laid him in a ship
and painfully rowed him here in his distress,
screaming in torment. When you see him next
805   he may still be alive; more likely not.

SOPHOCLES, *Women of Trachis* 749–806

Years before, Zeus warned Heracles that no living man could kill him, but that
he would die by the hands of the dead: The bile from the dead Hydra, coursing in
the veins of the wounded Nessus, killed him (folklorists call this "the dead-hand
motif"). Seeing what she had done, Deianira stabbed herself. Writhing in death's

agony, Heracles commanded Hyllus to marry Iolê, dragged himself to the top of Mount Oeta behind Trachis, made an enormous pyre, and lay down on it. No one dared to light the pyre, remembering the fate of Lichas, until a passing shepherd named Philoctetes (fil-ok-**tēt**-ēz) dared to do it. In gratitude, as his last human act, Heracles gave Philoctetes his bow, later important in the Trojan War.

A cloud gathered around the pyre, thunder cracked, and Heracles was raised into heaven—his *apotheosis* ("the process of being made a god"). When the ashes cooled, only his armor was found, no trace of bone. His spirit was led in high procession to the halls of Zeus on Olympus, where he became a god and married Hebê (**hē**-bē), "youth." Although Odysseus saw him in the underworld, that was not the real Heracles, but only a shade, a phantom:

[601] My eyes fell next, after him, on Heracles' apparition,
      a mighty form but a ghost, for he himself sits in the midst
      of the banquet of deathless gods, with Hebê, fair-ankled maiden,
      daughter of glorious Zeus and Hera of golden sandals.

605 From around him rose the terrified din of the gibbering phantoms,
      who fluttered away as he came, an image of blackest night.
      He carried his bow at the ready, with an arrow upon its string.
      His eye glanced fiercely around, always preparing to shoot.
      He wore an enormous game-bag strapped to his mighty chest

610 and a golden sword-belt as well, that pictured wonderful actions:
      hunts of savage bears, wild boars, and fierce glaring lions;
      hand-to-hand fighting, battles, murder, and sudden death.
      Skilled as he was, this maker of Heracles' wallet and sword-belt
      could never hope to design another such wonderful work.

615 Heracles knew me at once, as soon as his eyes fell upon me.
      Sadly shaking his head, he spoke words flying right to the mark:
        "Son of Laërtes, descendant of Zeus, inventive Odysseus,
      are you too forced to endure some destiny loaded with trouble,
      like that which I had to bear, alive in the light of the sun?

620 Although a child of Cronian Zeus, I carried limitless burdens
      for a man far worse than myself, who exacted impossible tasks.
      At last he ordered me here, to return with the hound of Hades—
      no labor, or so he thought, would be harder for me to accomplish.
      Yet I carried Cerberus up and away from Hades' domain,

625 with Hermes to show me the way, and gray-eyed Athena to help me.

HOMER, *Odyssey* 11.601–626

THE RETURN OF THE HERACLIDS

When Heracles died, Eurystheus was determined to kill the many sons, fathered on many women, whom Heracles had left behind, called the **Heraclids** (**her**-a-klidz). They fled to Athens, where the Athenians bravely refused to surrender the refugees, took up arms, and killed Eurystheus and five of his sons. Hyllus cut off Eurystheus' head and brought it to Alcmena, who, laughing, poked out its eyes with large bronze pins.

The Heraclids now entered the Peloponnesus and conquered it, but soon a plague struck the land. At the command of an oracle, they withdrew back across the Isthmus of CORINTH to ATTICA. Another oracle declared that they could return to the Peloponnesus after "the third harvest," which Hyllus took to mean "in three years." After waiting three years, Hyllus attacked again, but to his surprise was defeated by the new king of Mycenae, Tisamenus (tis-**am**-en-us, son of Orestes, son of Agamemnon). The oracle explained that "third harvest" did not refer to the fruit of the earth, but to the generations of men. True enough, under a certain Temenus, Hyllus' great-grandson and the great-great-grandson of Heracles, the Heraclids were victorious in the Peloponnesus.

The classical Greeks identified the legendary "return of the Heraclids" with the Dorian invasion that caused the collapse of the Mycenaean world about 1200 BC. Archaeologists have not been able to confirm this tradition. The Dorians of the Peloponnesus (especially the Spartans) always claimed to be direct descendants of Heracles and made him their special hero. But Heracles was never a local or tribal hero: At all times he belonged to all the Greeks.

Observations: Heracles *Kallinikos,* "Handsome in Victory"

Heracles' name, which seems to mean "the renown of Hera," or "he who gives renown to Hera," appears puzzling, because Hera persecutes Heracles relentlessly. In the Greek Bronze Age, however, when parts of this myth may have taken form, Heracles was perhaps a common name, like John or Paul, applied to the common folktale hero who suffered greatly, then was rewarded at the end.

The origins of Heracles remain obscure, and we do not know where his legends first appeared in Greece. The Argive plain, where he served Eurystheus, and Thebes, where he was born and first married, have equally strong claims. His character is complex and hard to summarize. Although often called the archetypal Greek hero, to the Greeks of Homer's day he was already old-fashioned, evoking a bygone age when violence could solve every problem. The historical period that begins with Homer was a tamer time (although still murderous) in which the stories of Heracles served as examples of the dangers of excess, though often with a humorous twist.

Heracles does everything too much. He commits terrible crimes, followed by humiliating expiation. He violates the most sacred human obligations, killing his wife, children, and his guest-friend Iphitus, after which he must live in degrading bondage first to the cowardly Eurystheus, then to a woman as her sexual plaything and slave; he wears women's clothing. A passing reference in Homer speaks of the time when Heracles shot Hera in the breast with an arrow. Another passing reference in Homer mentions that he even shot Hades "at the Gate, among the dead." Here is the hero's essence: reckless, fearless, sometimes tricky, getting away with things others cannot, violating every convention, attacking the very gods. He embodied the Greeks' naive eagerness to try anything without fear of the result, which too often proved disastrous. He destroyed evil, sinned greatly, loved unwisely, fathered a whole race, and died shamefully at a woman's hand. Yet he received his triumphant reward.

Of course, other heroes challenge Death—Gilgamesh inquires of Utnapishtim who never died, Perseus slays the death-dealing Gorgon, Odysseus and Aeneas descend to the underworld—but none so often or explicitly as Heracles, and no other is rewarded at the end with immortality, Heracles' reward for completing the Twelve Labors. After death, Heracles married Hebê, "youth," on Mount Olympus, that is, he never got old. In life he journeyed to the underworld and brought back Cerberus. The triple-bodied Geryon lives across water (where death's realm lies) in the far west (where the sun dies daily), and from there Heracles returned. The souls of the dead often are pictured as birds: Heracles slays the death-dealing species that hovers around Stymphalus. Busiris is the Egyptian lord of the dead, but Heracles kills him. He wrestles Thanatos, "Death," to the ground and frees Alcestis. The apples from the Hesperides' garden grow on the tree of eternal life; they fall, although temporarily, into Heracles' hands. In one version, his pursuit of the apparently harmless Ceryneian deer also takes him to this garden, for the deer is the magical but dangerous animal that appears in folktales, leading the hunter from the everyday world to the other side of the mirror, the land of dreams and of the dead.

As the best loved of all Greek heroes, Heracles was *alexikakos,* "the averter of evils," summoned as a god to turn away disease, human and animal attack, and every kind of harm. The most common oath in Greek was "By Heracles!"—just as we might say, "By God!" He was the paradigm of heroic tragic existence, but in many humorous tales, and on the comic stage, his reputation for womanizing and gluttony made him a figure of fun (Figure 15.12). Heracles is not a hero who fights other heroes, like the warriors before the walls of Troy and Thebes. Like

FIGURE 15.12 The Hercules of Farnese, marble Roman copy of Greek original by Lysippus, fourth century BC. The once elegant, aristocratic hero has become a muscle-bound brute as he leans wearily against his club covered by the lion skin. This is the gross, overmuscled Heracles parodied by the comedians. From the backside you can see that he holds the apples of the Hesperides in his hand. (Museo Archeologico Nazionale, Naples; © Erich Lessing/Art Resource, New York)

Gilgamesh, or the biblical Samson (who also killed a lion and was destroyed by a woman), he is the tough guy, the strongest man on earth, another folktale type, the animal-slayer who made the world safe by destroying dangerous beasts.

KEY NAMES AND TERMS

Heracles, 375

Alcmena, 376

Eurystheus, 376

Amphitryon, 376

Megara, 382

Nemean lion, 385

Hydra, 387

Lerna, 387

Ceryneian deer, 389

Erymanthian boar, 389

Chiron, 389

Augeas, 390

Stymphalian birds, 391

Cretan bull, 391

horses of Diomedes, 392

Admetus, 392

Alcestis, 392

girdle of Hippolyta, 394

cattle of Geryon, 394

Cacus, 396

Apples of the Hesperides, 397

Busiris, 398

Cerberus, 399

metopes, 402

Iolê, 402

Omphalê, 404

Cercopes, 404

Deianira, 404

Acheloüs, 405

Nessus, 407

Heraclids, 410

SOME ADDITIONAL ANCIENT SOURCES

Heracles is mentioned countless times in classical literature. Not only is his madness the subject of Euripides' *Heracles Insane,* and his death the subject of Sophocles' *Women of Trachis,* but he appears at the end of Sophocles' *Philoctetes* to resolve the plot. A full account of his career is found in Apollodorus 2.4.8–2.7.7, in Diodorus Siculus 4.9.1–4.39.4, with unsteady interpretations, and in Hyginus, *Fabulae* 29–36, which includes many odd details.

FURTHER READING CHAPTER 15

The *Herakles* entry in the *Lexicon Iconographicum Mythologiae Classicae,* spread over volumes 4 and 5 (Zürich and Munich, 1988 and 1990), is an invaluable review.

Brommer, Frank, *Heracles: The Twelve Labors of the Hero in Ancient Art and Literature,* trans. and enlarged by S. J. Schwarz (New Rochelle, NY, 1986). The best succinct review of Heracles in literature and art.

Dale, A. M., ed., *Euripides: Alcestis* (Oxford, UK, 1954). The introduction to the Greek text has a good analysis of the myth and how Euripides used it.

Galinsky, Karl, *The Heracles Theme* (New York, 1972). Surveys the development of the figure of Heracles from ancient through modern times.

CHAPTER 16

THESEUS AND THE MYTHS OF ATHENS

Our city is not ruled
by orders of a single ruler: No, it is free.
In yearly terms of office, men succeed
each other. The rich receive no more
consideration than the worthy poor.

THESEUS SPEAKING TO A THEBAN HERALD, FROM EURIPIDES,
Suppliant Women 405–408

IN THE CLASSICAL PERIOD, Athens was preeminent for achievements in literature, philosophy, and the arts, but the city's legendary history is unusually confused. Several characters bearing the same name turn up in different generations of the early kings, probably because later Greek mythographers ("writers about myth") tried to fill in gaps and fashion a coherent genealogy. In particular, many additions to the legends of Athens' greatest hero, **Theseus**, were made in the sixth and fifth centuries BC when Athens became an important military power and cultural center. Let us first examine the stories of the early kings of Athens, then Theseus' heroic career (except for his Cretan adventures, presented in the next chapter), and, finally, how Athenian politics shaped and used Athenian myth.

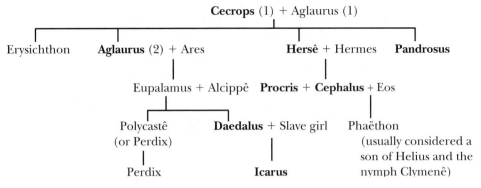

CHART 16.1 Cecrops and His Descendants

CECROPS, ERICHTHONIUS, AND THE DAUGHTERS OF CECROPS

The stories of the first kings of Athens are complicated and even self-contradictory. The Athenians made three claims about their origins: That they were descended from a mortal named **Cecrops** (sē-crops; Chart 16.1); that they were autochthonous (aw-**tok**-tho-nus), "sprung from the earth," like grasshoppers (certain high officials wore golden grasshopper pins in their hair in celebration of this claim); and that they were descended from Athena, after whom the city was named (even though Athena was a virgin goddess). The claims of autochthony and descent from Cecrops are brought together in the story that Cecrops simply sprang from the earth, with the form of a snake beneath the waist, a man above (compare Figure 16.2). The snake often symbolized origin from the earth. The Giants, also born from the earth, were represented in Greek art with the tails of snakes.

In a golden age Cecrops introduced the arts of civilization and monogamous marriage to the people. He taught them to worship Zeus, to abandon human sacrifice (although Erechtheus, a later king, sacrificed his own daughter), to build cities, and to bury the dead properly. In his reign Athena and Poseidon competed for recognition as patron of the city, Athena offering the olive and Poseidon a spring of saltwater on the Acropolis. The citizens' choice of Athena (Figure 16.1) reminds us that the land (producer of olives) was for a long time more important to the Athenians than the sea. The preference lasted down to the early fifth century, when Themistocles (the-**mis**-to-klēz, c. 524–460 BC) persuaded the people to spend the proceeds of newly discovered silver deposits on building a great fleet. This fleet defeated the Persians in 480 BC at the battle of Salamis near the harbor of Athens and made Athens the greatest sea power of the eastern Mediterranean, or of the whole world.

The theme of Athenian autochthony appears again in the story about **Erichthonius** (er-ik-**thōn**-i-us), another early king of Athens (Chart 16.2), who succeeded Cecrops. Erichthonius was born in this way: Athena had gone to Hephaestus' smithy for repair of her weapons. Missing his exwife Aphrodite, whom he had divorced for adultery, Hephaestus pursued the goddess lustfully across the Acropolis. Although lame, Hephaestus caught up with her and ejaculated semen onto her leg.

FIGURE 16.1 The Erechtheum, or House of Erechtheus, built about 420 BC during the Peloponnesian War (the Parthenon is visible on the far right). A door led into the shrine of Poseidon/Erechtheus through the porch on the left, as did a stairway down from the Porch of the Maidens (right of building). The sculptured maidens, used in place of columns, are called caryatids and may represent the *Arrhephoroi*, the girls who carried Athena's sacred basket. On the east behind the temple once stood the sanctuary to Athena, the predecessor of the Parthenon, where, many believe, stood the wooden statue of Athena supposedly fashioned by Erichthonius. In front of the temple grows the sacred olive (a modern planting), Athena's gift to the *polis;* a hole was left open in the ceiling and floor of the porch on the left to show where Poseidon had struck the rock with his trident.   (University of Wisconsin–Madison Photo Archive)

Athena wiped it off with disgust on a piece of wool, which she threw to the ground. Up sprang Erichthonius, whose name probably means "the man of wool and earth" (Figure 16.2).

Athena took the infant, whom she wanted to make immortal, placed him in a basket, and gave the basket to the daughters of Cecrops—Aglaurus (a-**glau**-rus), "shining" (the wife of Cecrops was also named Aglaurus); Hersê (**her**-sē), "dew"; and Pandrosus (**pan**-dro-sus), "all-dew." She warned the three daughters on no condition to look inside the basket. Pandrosus obeyed, but Aglaurus and Hersê could not resist. They saw something in the basket that drove them mad: a serpent, which sprang at them, or a child with serpent's tail instead of legs, or a child entwined by a serpent. In terror at the vision, Aglaurus and Hersê leaped from the Acropolis to their deaths, and Athena took back the child and raised him herself. When he grew up, Erichthonius became king of Athens. In honor of his "mother," Athena, he set up a wooden image of her on the Acropolis, where Pandrosus and Aglaurus also had shrines.

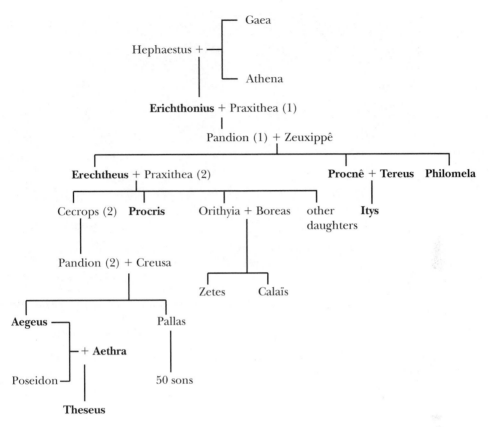

CHART 16.2 The House of Erichthonius

Observations: The Festival of the Dew Carriers

The story of the daughters of Cecrops is a good example of a myth that appears to reflect a ritual (see Chapter 25 for theories about myth and ritual), in this case one performed annually at year's end on the Acropolis at a festival called the Arrhephoria (ar-re-**for**-i-a, probably "festival of the dew carriers"). Two young girls, the *Arrhephoroi*, lived all year long in a special house on the Acropolis, weaving a robe offered each year to the statue of Athena. When the festival came, the priestess of Athena sent them at night into a grove of Aphrodite on the north edge of the Acropolis. There they took baskets on their heads, carried them down a secret stairway cut in the rock, and left them at the bottom. They then climbed back with a covered basket containing some mysterious thing (compare Figure 16.3).

The ritual and the myth associated with it are built on the motif of the maiden's sacrifice, with its prominent sexual overtones. Entrance into the grove of Aphrodite represents the virgins' loss of sexual innocence, as does their nocturnal descent underground, where Hades carried the virgin Persephonê to make her his bride. In the myth, Aglaurus and Hersê literally die; in the ritual the girls die symbolically, to end the virgin's life of sexual innocence.

FIGURE 16.2 The birth of Erichthonius, on an Attic wine cup, c. 435 BC. Cecrops, with a snake's body from the waist down, looks on while Gaea, with crown and scepter, rises from the earth to give the infant Erichthonius to Athena. Behind Athena stands Hephaestus, "father" of the child, and behind him Hersê rushes forward.   (Antikenmuseum, Berlin; Bildarchiv Preußischer Kulturbesitz/Art Resource, New York)

FIGURE 16.3 Athena and Erichthonius, on an Attic wine jug, c. 440 BC. Athena watches as Erichthonius waves, secure in his basket encircled by serpents.   (© Trustees of the British Museum / Art Resource, New York)

In the myth, two of the sisters die after looking at a terrifying thing in a basket, possibly a serpent. We can take the serpent as an emblem of the phallus, and thus the literal death of the maidens in the myth again reflects the death of sexual innocence—an experience, enacted at the Arrhephoria, which every *parthenos* must undergo to become a woman (*gynê*). The phallus engenders life, as the basket in the myth contains new life in the form of the infant Erichthonius. The loss of virginity, the death of the daughters, brings the promise of new life, and the daughters of Cecrops bear names related to the shining dew that appears on the ground in the morning after darkness, the moisture from the dark heaven that nourishes the coming day.

PROCRIS AND CEPHALUS

Ovid makes very different use of the story of the daughters of Cecrops and tells a sensational tale about the harm, to guilty and innocent alike, of uncontrolled sexual passion. In his version, all three daughters survived the viewing of the infant Erichthonius. Years later, Mercury (= Hermes) noticed Hersê in a procession and fell in love with her. When he searched for her on the Acropolis, Aglaurus offered to lead him to Hersê's bed in return for gold. Mercury gave her the bribe, but Athena, still angry that Aglaurus had looked inside the basket, inspired a ferocious jealousy in her. When in spite of the bribe Aglaurus tried to prevent Mercury from coming to Hersê, Mercury angrily turned Aglaurus to stone and went to Hersê anyway. Hersê became pregnant and bore **Cephalus** (**sef**-a-lus), who grew up and married **Procris**, daughter of Erechtheus (usually called the grandson of Erichthonius), in the desperately confused genealogy of the House of Athens. Before Cephalus' marriage, Aurora, the lustful goddess of dawn (= Greek Eos), carried Cephalus (his name means "head" for some reason) away to Syria, where she bore Phaëthon to him (although in another story Phaëthon is a child of the Sun; Chapter 4).

At first the marriage of Cephalus and Procris was happy. But Cephalus could not believe his good fortune and began to give way to irrational suspicion. To test Procris' love, he came to her in disguise, tempting her with ever-greater rewards to sleep with him. When he offered her a golden crown, she at last agreed. In a rage, he revealed who he was, and Procris, shamed and frightened, fled to the court of Minos in Crete.

There Procris attracted the amorous king's attention. Unfortunately, Minos could not consummate his passion, for his wife, Pasiphaë (pa-**sif**-a-ē), had placed a curse upon him: Instead of semen, he ejaculated spiders and scorpions that devoured the genitals of his mistresses! Procris cured him of the curse, and in return Minos gave her a magical hound named Laelaps (**lē**-laps) that always caught what it chased, and a magical spear that never missed its mark. Procris, fearing the anger of Pasiphaë, soon regretted her behavior and fled with the gifts back to Athens, disguised as a boy.

Although Cephalus still mourned his beautiful wife and the marriage he had so thoughtlessly ruined, he coveted the pretty "boy's" wonderful hound and unerring spear. The disguised Procris offered to give them up if Cephalus would only sleep with him/her. Cephalus resisted, then agreed, thereby convicting himself of the same weakness he had earlier discovered in his wife. The love-struck couple was reunited and for a while lived happily together again.

But Procris still feared that Cephalus was meeting Aurora (Eos), his former mistress, who had carried him away to Syria and conceived his child, especially because every morning he arose at dawn to hunt, a perfect chance to meet one's lover. One morning Procris followed him. Ovid tells this story twice, in the *Metamorphoses* and in the *Ars amatoria* ("The Art of Love"), from which the following selection is taken. The *Ars amatoria* is a kind of advice book in verse, tongue-in-cheek, for those wishing to seduce everyone in sight. Never listen to gossip, Ovid advises in the story. Ovid's poem (and some other unknown act of Ovid) so offended the emperor Augustus, who wanted to reform the sexual behavior of the Roman upper classes, that in AD 8 Augustus banished the famous poet to the cold and remote town of Tomis far away on the Black Sea. There the sad and lonely poet died in AD 17.

In Ovid's Latin version, *Aurora* is replaced by *Aura* = Latin "breeze." *Aura* is also a girl's name, here rendered by the feeble pun "Breeze":

[685] Don't you believe all you hear! The peril of trusting in gossip
      is clear from the sad example of Procris' wretched fate.
Close by the purple slopes of Hymettus'° flowering foothills
      there bubbles a sacred spring in a copse of soft green turf . . .
At the Zephyr's gentlest whisper, each life-giving sigh of the wind,
690   every grass tip trembles, every leaf springs to life.
To Cephalus quiet meant bliss. His hounds and huntsmen forgotten,
      he loved to relax his weary frame in that magical spot.
"Come, gentle breeze, who so often has cooled the heat of my bosom,"
      thus would Cephalus murmur to summon the whispering wind.
695 A gossipy friend heard the prayer and dutifully passed it along
      to the jealous ears of his wife, repeating it, word for word.
When Procris heard the name, she shivered with silent horror.
      Had Cephalus gone astray with a painted hussy named Breeze?
She paled, as a vine-leaf, clinging after the season of vintage,
700   turns a shivery white, touched by the wintry frost;
as ripening quinces pale, whose weight depresses their branches;
      as cornel-berries whiten while still not ready to eat.
When Procris revived from her faint, she tore open the delicate bodice
      covering her bosom. Her nails tore at her innocent cheeks.
705 No time to reflect. Like a crazy maenad stung by the thyrsus,
      her hair astream, she raced up the road that led to the hill.
What did you hope to accomplish by your mad attempt at an ambush,
      poor Procris? What hope had risen in your delirious heart?
Did you really think this "Breeze," whoever she was, would be waiting
710   for you to appear and denounce her sin with your furious tongue?
One moment you blushed for shame, hoping you wouldn't catch him,
      the next you were glad you knew. Love drove you opposite ways.

687. *Hymettus*: A mountain near Athens.

Whatever made you do this? the place, the name, the suggestion?
    These, and the human worry that what we fear must be so.
715 She noticed a place where grass had been crushed by a weary body.
    Her bosom quaked with horror that rose from her fevered heart.
Now as the sun of noon drew in to a sinister twilight,
    as the morning of hope descended in gloomy and hopeless night,
Cephalus, Mercury's son, returnê from the hunt in the forest
720   to splash his burning face from the icy depths of the spring.
Breathless, Procris, you waited. Nearby, her husband reclining,
    panted, "O wind, refresh me and you, O delectable breeze!"
The silly misunderstood pun flashed on the heart-broken woman,
    whose common sense returned, whose pallor turned to a blush.
725 Starting up to her feet, she eagerly parted the bushes,
    and, true wife that she was, ran to her husband's embrace.
But he in his childish error imagined a boar or a panther.
    He leaped erect and poised the spear in his swift right hand.
Stupid, what are you up to? No wild thing, that. Drop your weapon!
730   Alas, too late! for your spear flies out and pierces her breast.
"Alas!" she sobs, "my love has stabbed the heart of his lover,
    the heart so often wounded by the folly and haste of the head.°
Before the dawn I shall die, but not of being supplanted—
    this, at least, will make the earth lie light on my bones.°
735 My spirit departs with the breeze, which once I wrongly suspected
    for its name alone. Dear hands, now close my fainting eyes."
Close to his broken heart he lifted the form of his lady,
    washing with hot salt tears the gaping wound in her breast.
Slowly, her life ebbs away from her all too credulous bosom;
740   her final gasp is received on her husband's sorrowing lips [Figure 16.4].

OVID, *Ars amatoria* 3.685–746

732. *haste of the head*: Another pun: The name *Cephalus* = Greek "head."   734. *make the earth* . . . :
A common inscription on Roman graves was "may the earth lie light on your bones," usually abbreviated as S.T.T.L. (*sit tibi terra levis*).

The Athenians exiled Cephalus for life. He went to Thebes, at that time persecuted by a wild vixen fated never to be caught. Each month the desperate Thebans, to forestall worse disaster, exposed the son of a prominent citizen for the fox to devour. The hero Amphitryon (mortal father to Heracles), then resident at Thebes and under obligation to its king, Creon, offered Cephalus a great treasure for the loan of Laelaps, once a gift from Minos to Procris. Thus Laelaps, the hound that always caught its prey, chased the fox that could never be caught. Jupiter, impatient at the typically Greek contradiction, turned them both into stone.

PROCNÊ AND TEREUS

When Erichthonius died, his son Pandion (pan-**dī**-on) became king. Pandion had two daughters, **Procnê** (**prok**-nê) and **Philomela** (fil-ō-**mēl**-a), sisters to Erechtheus. In Ovid's account, when war broke out between Athens and neighboring Thebes,

FIGURE 16.4 The death of Procris, on an Attic wine-mixing bowl, c. 440 BC. Procris, dressed as a young man, her eyes half-closed in death, attempts to pull the spear from her side: Her soul (*psychê*) flies away as a human-headed bird from her head. Her father, Erechtheus, runs toward her from the right, while Cephalus, on the left, holding Laelaps by a leash, strikes his head in a tragic gesture.   (© Trustees of the British Museum / Art Resource, New York)

Pandion summoned to his assistance **Tereus** (te-rūs), king of the Thracians, a son of Mars (= Ares). Athens soon won the war. In gratitude for his help, Pandion gave Tereus his daughter Procnê for a wife. She soon bore Tereus a son, **Itys** (ī-tis). What happens next is told in one of Ovid's best-known stories of metamorphosis, another sensational tale about the familiar vice of uncontrolled sexual passion:

[424]   Tereus came to Pandion's aid and smashed the enemy armies,

425   thus winning a great renown for his glorious victory.
Pandion, impressed by his wealth, the number of his retainers,
and his glorious ancestry (which he traced back to Mars himself),
gave him Procnê as wife. But Juno, patron of wedlock,
avoided the feast, and Hymen.° No Graces attended their marriage.

430   Only the Furies were there, with torches snatched from a tomb.
Furies prepared their bed, and owls hooted high on the roof,
mocking the solemn rites. So Procnê and Tereus married,
shadowed by gloomy omens, and under these ominous portents
she soon bore a son. All Thrace, of course, was delighted.

435   Pouring out thanks to the gods, they consecrated the days
when Tereus married Procnê and Itys her son was born—
so far did their real advantage lie hidden from their eyes.
    Titan° had led the seasons five times from autumn to autumn,
when Procnê asked for a favor: "If indeed you think I deserve it,

429. *Hymen*: Mythical embodiment of the marriage song; the god of marriage.   438. *Titan*: That is, Hyperion, the sun.

440   either send me off to visit my sister or have her come here.
My father will surely consent, if you promise her speedy return.
For me the finest of presents would be seeing my sister again."
     Tereus agreed to invite Philomela, and summoned his galleys.
With oars and a following wind he sped to the harbor of Athens.

445   Cordially greeting each other, the kings began their discussion:
why Tereus was there, what Procnê had asked, and the promised return.
As they conversed, Philomela appeared, in luxurious garments,
but lovelier far for herself. Enchanted at sight of the maiden,
Tereus' heart caught fire, like dry straw touched by a spark.

450   Fair she was, it is true, but her beauty served only to kindle
the inborn lust of the man, the child of a lecherous race,
who burned with his people's vices, and added them to his own . . .
     He repeated Procnê's request.
Masking his own desire, he pleaded the longing of Procnê.

455   But love gave him eloquent words, and whenever his plea grew too eager,
"That," he exclaimed, "is exactly what Procnê so eagerly wishes."
He even would burst into tears, as if Procnê ordered that too.
Ye gods, what blackness of night confuses intelligent mortals!
All his duplicitous scheme won him praise as a dutiful husband,

460   the more so when Philomela implored the same favor as he.
Stroking Pandion's hands, she begged she might visit her sister,
not knowing the horror in store, thinking alone of the pleasure.
     Tereus watched, and squirmed with fantasy at the caresses
lavished upon her father—her kisses, arms round his neck—

465   all of them goading him on, torches and tinder to passion.
As she put her arms round her father, he wanted to be her father,
but not with a father's feelings toward his innocent child.
Pandion soon gave way to the fervent pleas of his daughter,
and gratitude blended with joy in poor Philomela's delusion,

470   gloating over a triumph concealing the ruin to come.
     No sooner had Philomela embarked in the bright-sided galley,
the oars driven into the waves, the shore out of sight astern,
than barbarous Tereus exulted, "Success! I have what I wanted!"
Gloating, not trying to hide the glee of his lecherous spirit,

475   an eagle loosing his talons from the terrified hare he has taken
up to his aerie on high, hopeless, contorted with fright,
the captor silently gloating at the pleasure soon to be his.
     The voyage at last is done. From wave-battered vessels they land.
The tyrant drags Philomela to a hunting lodge deep in the forest.

480   Trembling, weeping, she begged him, "Tell me, where is my sister?"
But snarling with bestial lust, he raped her, virgin, alone . . .
     Consciousness slowly returned. She tore her disheveled tresses,
beat at her breast with her fists and hurled a bitter reproach:
"Cruel uncivilized savage, what you are is shown by your deed!

485   Had my father's pleas no effect? or even his tears of farewell?
Did my sister matter so little? my innocence? even your marriage?
Go ahead, cut my throat, round out your wicked achievements!
I wish you had cut it before you dirtied my soul with your filth!
If heaven decides this matter, if the gods indeed possess power,

490 if all that I am or can do does not perish along with my breath,
some day—mark my words!—you will reap the reward of your crime.
Modesty thrown to the winds, I will trumpet your deed of shame,
through cities of men if I can; if not, through forest and hills.
Your crime I accuse to the sky, to whatever gods are in heaven!"

495 Tereus reddened with fury, from fear no less than from anger.
Goaded by both, he whipped the knife at his side from its sheath.
Seizing the girl by her hair, he twisted her arms behind her
and bound her immobile, secure. Offering her throat to the blade,
her heart conceived a new hope of a rapid and merciful death.

500 But no—as she vainly struggled to call the name of her father,
he seized her tongue with pincers and sliced it off at the root.
The stump convulsively twitched as the rest lay writhing about,
trying to add its protest to the dark and blood-stained ground.
Like half of an injured snake, it jerked in its mistress's track.

505 And then—the story goes on, scarcely possible to believe—
the sadist returned in his lust again, and again, to his victim.
After all this, the king in his insolence went in to Procnê.
Before she asked for her sister, he wept with fraudulent tears,
narrated a fictional death, winning Procnê's trust by his sorrow.

510 The queen ripped off her shoulders the veil with a wide gold hem
and put on the garments of sorrow. She erected an empty tomb,
made sacrificial offerings to the ghost of one still alive,
and mourned the death of a sister, not ready thus to be mourned.
A year passed by as the sun moved through the Zodiac's signs.

515 Philomela stayed locked in a cell of inescapable granite,
guarded on every hand. Her tongueless mouth could tell nothing.
What could the poor girl do? Great pain may mother invention
and cleverness come to the aid of those in profoundest distress.
She set up the threads of the warp, and with a barbarian shuttle

520 wove in its pure white threads and the purple strands of the weft
the tale of Tereus' crime. She gave it, complete, to a servant,
revealing by her gesture that she wanted it brought to the queen.
The slave girl in innocence took it and handed it over to Procnê.
The wife of the barbarous tyrant unfolded the damning indictment,

525 and on it deciphered the tale of woe Philomela had woven.
Procnê spoke not a word in her grief, too deep to be spoken.
No adequate words arose in her mind as she tried to express it.
Wasting no time on tears, she rushed to a mission of vengeance,
heedless of right or wrong, determined on punishing Tereus.

530 The season had come for the women to celebrate Dionysus
in their sacred biennial rites, observed under cover of darkness.
All night the slopes of Rhodopê° reecho with clanging of cymbals.
The queen goes out of her house, dressed for the Bacchic orgy.
She bears the signals of madness: a vine-leaf crown on her head,

535 a fawn skin hangs from a shoulder, a javelin rests on the other.
So Procnê with her mad crew run screaming over the woodland,
a terrible vision to see. Bacchus, she feigns, is her master;

---

532. *Rhodopê*: A mountain of Thrace, sacred to Dionysus.

in fact, it is you, O Furies of pain, who drive her along.
At last the Bacchanals come to the lodge hidden deep in the wood.
540   She shouts and crying the "Euhoi!" she smashes the doorway in.
She seizes her sister and on her drapes the insignia of Bacchus,
hides her features in ivy, and brings her, amazed, to the palace.
      Philomela soon understood she had come to the cursed household.
The poor girl bristled in fear, her face turned pallid in terror.
545   But Procnê, once they were safe, tore off the ivy of Bacchus,
unveiling the mortified face and wretched plight of her sister.
She tried to embrace her sister, whose eye clung fixed to the ground,
for shame at having been forced to defile the marriage of one so close.
Longing to swear to the truth, summoning gods to bear witness,
550   with hands replacing her voice she told of her rape and disgrace.
      Procnê blazed with anger and checked Philomela's lament:
"Weeping will do us no good. We must have recourse to the dagger,
or anything else you conceive more lethal to him than the steel.
I am fully ready to go to the furthest limits of vengeance—
555   to set the palace on fire over Tereus' criminal head,
to hack out tongue, eyes, whatever crushed your soul in disgrace.
Shall we watch his guilty life drain off through a thousand cuts?
No matter. Whatever we do, our revenge must make people tremble."
      As Procnê pondered her crime, little Itys came up to his mother.
560   His innocent face suggested the blackest vengeance of all.
Gazing with pitiless eyes, "How like you are to your father!"
she murmured. No further word, but seething in hot-blooded anger
Procnê prepared for her crime. And yet, and yet—
when her tiny son toddled up, little arms outstretched for a hug,
565   mixing his eager kisses with the lisping words of a child,
his mother's purpose was shaken, her murderous anger grew still,
her eyes overflowed with tears welling up from her aching heart.
At once she knew too great affection had weakened her purpose.
      Turning away from her child, once more she regarded her sister.
570   "How can I choose, when the one babbles his childish endearments,
the other, bereft of her tongue, can nevermore utter a word?
Philomela cannot call me sister, whom Itys addresses as mother.
Consider, O Pandion's daughter, the sort of man you have married.
Has the daughter fallen away from the spirit shown by her sires?
575   Crime toward a husband like Tereus is the truest virtue of all."
      Delaying no more, she seized little Itys and dragged him away,
like a tigress of India's dark jungle seizing a suckling fawn [Figure 16.5].
She hurried him off to a murky unfrequented part of the palace.
There Itys saw what was coming. Hugging his mother for comfort,
580   "Mommy, Mommy!" he wailed. She stabbed where flank meets breast,
fixing her eyes on her target. Although that one blow was enough,
Philomela again took the dagger and slashed it across his throat.
      Together they carved the flesh, still warm with traces of life.
Some flesh boiled in a big brass pot, some hissed and spat on a skewer.
585   The room grew slimy with blood. At last, when all was made ready,
Procnê invited her husband to join in a ritual dinner.
Alleging an ancient custom that no one, her husband excepted,

FIGURE 16.5 Philomela and Procnê prepare to kill Procnê's son, Itys, Attic wine cup, c. 490 BC, 500 years earlier than Ovid. On the left Philomela gestures, unable to speak because her tongue has been cut out. A sword, the murder weapon, hangs at her side. In the potter's version, Procnê, not yet convinced, seems to hang back, as if protecting her son. (Musée du Louvre, Paris; © Giraudon/Art Resource, New York)

might join the meal with a matron, she had the attendants depart.
Tereus sat there in state, high on the throne of his fathers,
590   greedily stuffing his belly with his own flesh and blood.
Blinded in soul, he shouted, "Let Itys be brought inside!"
No longer could Procnê conceal the cruel joy of her vengeance;
no longer need she delay announcing her murderous message.
     "It is Itys you want? But Itys is *already* inside—inside you!"
595   In puzzlement, Tereus repeated his wishes again and again,
Till Philomela sprang in, her hair bespattered with blood,
and flung the head of Itys straight in his father's face.
     "O, that I still had a tongue, to tell my delight at your fate"
(she thought), "in words you deserve!" Tereus shouted in horror,
600   kicked back the table, and called in pain on the Furies of Hades.
Gladly, could he have done so, would he have opened his entrails
and brought back into the light the grisly meal he had eaten.
All he could do was groan, "Wretched me, the tomb of my son!"
He draws his sword. He charges, pursuing Pandion's daughters.
605   But look! who would imagine that these, descendants of Cecrops,
could fly off, born as on feathers? Yet fly on feathers they did.
The one took off to the forest, the other nests among men—
yet still they bear on their bosoms the bloody tokens of murder.
Tereus, swiftened by grief that struggled with lust for revenge,
610   was transformed into a hoopoe, a bird with a feathery crown;
his beak resembles a sword, and he goes as if armored for battle.

OVID, *Metamorphoses* 6.424–674

Ovid is not clear about which woman becomes which bird, but most other sources agree that Procnê, the mother, became the nightingale with its haunting nocturnal song; tongueless Philomela became the songless swallow. Nonetheless, later poets, confused by the obscure line in Ovid and depending on a dubious etymology of Philomela = "song-lover," made Philomela the nightingale. Such is its meaning in classical English poetry.

Observations: Ovid's Literary Myth

A deeply human instinct is to feel kinship with the natural world, to think of animals and plants and even stones as inhabited by intelligence somehow like our own. Much religious cult is based on efforts to communicate, and negotiate, with the humanlike powers in nature. In theory we reject this interpretation of the natural world, but many who own pets treat them as equals (or superiors!), and the popularity of Babar, the Lion King, Bugs Bunny, and other cartoon characters shows how easy it is for us to accept that animals can behave and think as we do.

But Ovid does not tell stories about metamorphosis to appeal to an instinct within us to explain nature by humanizing it. Ovid is a highly urbane and literate poet, unlike Homer, Hesiod, and the singers of the *Homeric Hymns*. He created his poems in writing to be read aloud to upper-class Romans, women and men, who could themselves read and write both Greek and Latin and who were intimately familiar with Greek and Latin literature. He gave contemporary relevance to old stories, which contained primitive elements, by embellishing them with the rhetorical display familiar to the Romans from their education (as in the highly wrought speeches of Philomela and Procnê).

In the *Metamorphoses*, he usually does not focus on the metamorphosis itself so much as the events leading up to it, punctuated by elaborate descriptions of states of feeling. He concocts melodramatic situations and images (Philomela's tongue is compared to an injured snake twitching in the grass!). His stories have homespun morals. The story of Tereus, Procnê, and Philomela proves that one should not give in to irrational desire, as if we need to be told that. We are never sure when Ovid is mocking the reader's expectations and using simplistic morals to justify his touching or lurid descriptions.

Although Ovid's humans pay for their mistakes, we often have the sense that the god or goddess metes out an excessive punishment, that humans are the innocent victims of petty but divine emotion—did Actaeon really deserve to be torn apart by his own dogs? When Ovid does describe the psychology of metamorphosis, his focus is on the anguish of the human being trapped inside the beast, where its human mind continues to think and feel as it did before the transformation.

One type of Ovidian story tells of a deity having intercourse with a mortal woman, who is then turned into an animal (as Io became a cow) or of a human who inadvertently offends a god (as Actaeon turned into a stag after seeing Artemis naked). Procris and Cephalus and Procnê and Philomela are examples of another type of Ovidian story, in which the conflict is not between men and gods but within a human family. Still, Ovid concentrates on the rhetorical and moral aspects of the tale.

Procris and Cephalus is a tale of lovers who love too much until suspicion destroys them; lovers should trust one another. In Procnê and Philomela, the initial acts of impiety are horrendous, but the punishment is equally savage and the avengers as twisted as their attacker. Metamorphosis into birds is nearly an afterthought, a device allowing Ovid to attach the tale to his general scheme.

In such stories the gods do not figure in the action. Humans of their own will commit crimes against each other, making their lives a misery. When human passions are allowed to run unchecked, innocent and guilty alike are destroyed. In the elegant high society of Ovid's Rome, where men and women with equal legal rights to property mixed freely, where love affairs and sexual passion were a principal preoccupation of the great and the idle, such stories no doubt had a special appeal and poignancy, as they did in similar later epochs.

THESEUS

The Begetting of Theseus

When Pandion died, his son **Erechtheus** (e-**rek**-thūs), brother of Procnê and Philomela, became king. (But the name *Erechtheus* is probably a variation of *Erichthonius*.) Erechtheus married and had several children, including a second Cecrops, Procris (who married Cephalus), and Orithyia (or-i-**thī**-ya), whom Boreas, the winged north wind, loved and carried off (see Chart 16.2). Orithyia gave birth to Zetes (**zē**-tēz) and Calaïs (**cāl**-a-is), winged warriors who figure in the legend of Jason and the Golden Fleece (Chapter 19). During the reign of Erechtheus, Demeter came to Eleusis (Chapter 10).

Erechtheus soon died. The second Cecrops became king, then his son the second Pandion. Driven out of Athens, he became king of MEGARA. There the second Pandion married one Creusa (crē-**ū**-sa), who bore him four sons, including **Aegeus** (**ē**-jūs) and Pallas (**pal**-las). When the second Pandion died, his sons regained power in Athens. Aegeus had the upper hand over Pallas and his brothers, but his power was threatened because none of his several wives was able to bear him a son and heir. Pallas, who had fifty sons, despised the sterile Aegeus.

Aegeus went to the Delphic Oracle to learn how he could have an heir. "Do not open the swelling mouth of the wineskin until you come to the height of the Athenians," the oracle said. Aegeus could not understand the reply and went out of his way to TROEZEN (**trē**-zen) at the northeastern tip of the Peloponnesus, across the SARONIC GULF from ATHENS, to consult with Pittheus (**pit**-thūs), the local king, famous for his wisdom (Map VII). Pittheus understood the oracle immediately: Aegeus was destined to beget a child when next he had intercourse with a woman. Realizing that a child who joined the blood of Erechtheus with his own would be destined for glory, Pittheus plied Aegeus with much wine and sent in to him his daughter **Aethra** (**ē**-thra).

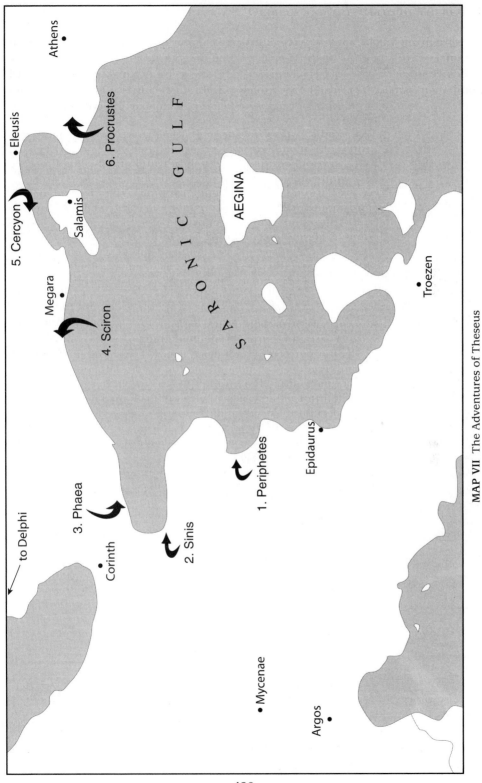

MAP VII The Adventures of Theseus

After intercourse with Aegeus, Aethra, instructed by a dream, rose and went to offer sacrifice on a nearby island, where Poseidon appeared from the sea and possessed her. Thus was Theseus conceived, at once the son of the mortal Aegeus and of the immortal Poseidon. The story of Heracles' divine birth (Chapter 15) probably was inspiration for the story: Alcmenê too slept with man and god on the same night (although Theseus has no twin).

The next morning Aegeus, suspecting that Aethra was pregnant, ordered her to raise their child in secret. He placed a sword and a pair of sandals under a large rock. When the child (Theseus) grew strong enough to lift it, he should take the objects beneath the rock and travel to him in Athens.

The Labors of Theseus

When Theseus grew to manhood, Aethra showed him the rock. Exerting his full strength, he lifted it and removed the sword and sandals, tokens that he was the true son of King Aegeus (Figure 16.6). With these he set off to Athens. Aethra and Pittheus, fearing the infamous bandits and killers along the route, begged him to go by sea, but Theseus insisted on the land route. In imitation of the Twelve Labors of his cousin Heracles, Theseus performed six famous deeds of strength on the coastal road (Figure 16.7; Map VII):

FIGURE 16.6 Theseus discovers the tokens of the sword and the sandals. Aethra stands behind her son, pointing. Roman relief in marble from the late first century AD.   (© Trustees of the British Museum / Art Resource, New York)

FIGURE 16.7 The labors of Theseus, on the interior of a red-figured Attic wine cup, c. 430 BC, found at Vulci in Italy. Center: Theseus drags the dead Minotaur from the Labyrinth, indicated by the vertical band of meanders. From top clockwise: Theseus wrestles Cercyon; with a double-bladed ax Theseus cuts Procrustes down to size; Theseus is about to strike Sciron with the foot-basin while the monstrous turtle waits at the bottom of the cliff; Theseus subdues the Marathonian bull; Theseus is about to release the pine tree to which Sinis clings; the old woman Phaea tries to protect the Crommyonian sow, while Theseus attacks with a sword. The painter omits the adventure with Periphetes but includes the Bull of Marathon instead.   (© Trustees of the British Museum / Art Resource, New York)

1. North of EPIDAURUS, he killed Periphetes (per-i-**fē**-tēz), nicknamed "club-ber." Periphetes, a son of Hephaestus, liked to bash passersby with his iron club. Theseus took the club, killed Periphetes with it, and thereafter carried it himself.

2. At the Isthmus of CORINTH, he slew Sinis (**sī**-nis), a giant and a son of Poseidon, nicknamed "pinebender" because he forced travelers to help him bend a pine tree to the ground. He then unexpectedly let go, catapulting the victim through the air. Or he would tie the victim to two bent trees pegged to the ground, then cut the ropes, to rip the victim apart. Theseus gave Sinis the same treatment.

3. North of Isthmus, at a place called Crommyon (**krom**-mi-on), he killed an enormous pig, the Crommyonian sow, bred by an old woman named Phaea (**fē**-a).

4. Near Megara, he turned the tables on Sciron (**sī**-ron), a rascal who made wayfarers bend over to wash his feet, then kicked them down the steep slope to the rocks below, where a giant turtle devoured them. Theseus forced Sciron to wash Theseus' feet, then kicked him down the precipitous slope.

5. On the way to Eleusis, he crushed to death Cercyon (**ser**-si-on), a powerful wrestler.

6. Finally, Theseus killed **Procrustes** (pro-**krus**-tēz), who had a house by the road with two beds, one large and one small. Procrustes offered travelers a place to sleep for the night, putting the big people in the little bed and the little people in the big bed. Because he enjoyed symmetry, Procrustes sawed off the protruding parts of the big people and stretched out the little ones. Theseus forced Procrustes to fit into one of his own beds (from him comes the English term *procrustean* to describe an arbitrary standard to which exact conformity is forced).

Arrival at Athens

Theseus entered Athens a conqueror, but Aegeus did not recognize him (but see Figure 16.8). The king had fallen under the influence of the sorceress Medea (me-**dē**-a; see Chapter 19), who had cured Aegeus' infertility by magic and drugs.

FIGURE 16.8 Aegeus greets Theseus, on an Attic drinking cup, c. 475 BC, as the hero enters Athens. Behind the hero a young woman reaches to crown him for his victories.   (Musée du Louvre, Paris; Réunion des Musées Nationaux/Art Resource, New York)

FIGURE 16.9 Theseus and the Marathonian bull, interior of a wine cup, c. 450 BC. On the outside of the cup, the hero kills the fifty sons of Pallas.   (Chazen Museum of Art, University of Wisconsin–Madison)

Recognizing Theseus and fearing him as a rival to the child she was herself carrying, she persuaded Aegeus to send the young stranger against a bull wreaking havoc on the plain of Marathon, the very bull that had begotten the Minotaur on Crete. Heracles had brought it to the mainland as one of his labors. Theseus attacked the bull, chained it up, and sacrificed it to Apollo (even as Gilgamesh and Heracles overcame dangerous bulls; Figure 16.9).

Medea, the vicious female antagonist in myths about Theseus, now planned to poison her rival. At a banquet in the stranger's honor, Theseus was raising the fatal goblet to his lips when Aegeus, who was in on the plot, recognized the sword hanging at his side. Leaping across the table, he knocked the cup to the ground. Medea fled in disgrace to her homeland in Asia. There she gave birth to Medus, ancestor of the Medes (that is, the Persians, Greece's greatest enemy). When the fifty sons of Pallas, Aegeus' brother, learned that Aegeus now had a proper successor, they laid an ambush to kill Theseus, but Theseus killed them all instead. At this time took place Theseus' famous adventure with the Cretan Minotaur told in the next chapter.

Theseus and Antiopê

When Theseus returned from Crete, he became king of Athens through a tragic lapse of memory. He had promised his father that if he were successful in overcoming the Minotaur, he would change his black sail to white before his ship approached Athens. If he perished, his companions would leave the black sail up so that Aegeus could know the truth before the ship docked. But in his excitement Theseus forgot to change the sail. When Aegeus saw the black sail in the distance, in despair he threw himself to his death into what became known as the Aegean Sea.

Upon becoming king, Theseus instituted many government reforms. He brought together the peoples in the outlying demes of Attica into a single federal system, called in Greek a *synoecism*, a "living-with," with Athens as capital of the new state. He instituted the Panathenaic festival, symbol of Attic unity, where in the Classical Period Homer's poems were recited before the *dêmos*, the "people." He founded the popular assembly, at which the people could debate and vote on decisions of state.

Longing for adventure, Theseus then sailed to the land of the Amazons to abduct their queen, Antiopê (an-**tī**-o-pē; sometimes called Hippolyta). To his surprise, the tribe of warrior women received him in a friendly way and offered many presents. When Queen Antiopê brought the presents to his ship, Theseus hoisted sail and carried her away, a captive, to Athens.

The abduction of Antiopê provoked the **Amazonomachy** (a-ma-zon-**o**-ma-kē), "battle with the Amazons." The Amazons invaded Attica, quickly overran the countryside, and set up camp on a hill northwest of the Acropolis where they sacrificed to their ancestor Ares. Ever since, the hill has been called the Areopagus, "hill of Ares," site of the oldest and most renowned law court in Athens. The name may really mean "hill of curses," because the Erinyes had a shrine there. After some initial setbacks, the Athenians utterly defeated the Amazons, whose graves were shown in classical times near the agora.

Observations: The Amazons

The Amazons are important and recurring figures in Greek myth. Many Greek heroes fought against them: Bellerophon, at the command of a Lycian king (in Asia Minor); Heracles, at the command of Eurystheus; Achilles at Troy; and even the god Dionysus. Their homeland was usually placed on the slopes of the Caucasus Mountains between the eastern end of the Black Sea and the Caspian Sea, or in Scythia, the southern steppe of what is today Ukraine, north of the Black Sea. They were descended from Ares and the nymph Harmonia. They hated men and would tolerate them only as slaves to perform the most menial tasks.

To preserve their race, the Amazons periodically came together with strangers and for a short time engaged in indiscriminate intercourse. Boy babies were killed or blinded and maimed. The Amazons were said to cut off the right breasts of young girls so that when they grew to maturity they might better draw the bowstring and handle the spear, a detail constructed on the false etymology of Amazon from *a-* (= no) + *mazos* (= breast). They followed Artemis and, according to some accounts, constructed the enormous temple of Artemis at Ephesus, one of the Seven Wonders of the Ancient World (compare Figure 9.3).

The Greeks themselves never questioned the historical reality of the Amazons. The historian Herodotus, for example, speaks of a tribe of female "mankillers" who roamed the Scythian steppe (although he does not call them Amazons), and modern archaeologists have found burial mounds there for women dressed as warriors. In fact, however, there never was a tribe of warrior-women. The Amazons are a good example of mythical inversion, in which a conspicuous feature of social behavior is turned upside down, in this case the values traditionally assigned to Greek, especially Athenian, women.

A good Athenian woman of the fifth century BC, as we have seen (Chapter 2), was expected to be submissive, sexually chaste, productive of male heirs, and zealous to preserve the stability of the family. The Amazons, by contrast, were brazen, licentious, and murderous to males and did not live in families. Amazons defied their destiny as women and lived like males, fighting, hunting on horseback, ruling themselves, and having sexual intercourse when they pleased. They lived in a perennial confusion between childhood and maturity, neither girls nor women, neither male nor female, at the edge of the world in a twilight zone between civilization and barbarism.

In myth they are a perversion of all that is proper and correct, a threat to the family, the basis of civilized society. The myth of the Amazons is a refinement of the traditional heroic motif of female hostility, but the threat is directed against all society. Thus they are always an army, and they do not tempt the hero with their sexuality (although this motif is submerged in Heracles' need to acquire the belt of the Amazon queen). Their incursion into the civilized world is the encroachment of darkness into light, and Greek heroes always overcome them as they defeat other denizens of the nightmare realm, ruthlessly and without mercy.

The Athenian myth of the Amazonomachy became especially vigorous after the astounding victory of Athenian hoplites over the Persian invaders in 490 BC at the battle of Marathon. After this time the Amazons were represented in Greek art as Persians, wearing long leather trousers and with Persian leather caps (Figure 16.10). Theseus' victory over the Amazons symbolized and justified Athens'

FIGURE 16.10 Theseus and a companion, perhaps Pirithoüs, defend themselves against an attacking Amazon, Attic wine-mixing bowl, c. 450 BC. The Amazon is mounted and dressed in Persian garb and wears a Persian leather cap.   (Museo Etrusco Gregoriano/Photo Vatican Museums)

moral and political superiority, not only over the Persians but over all peoples who would oppose its imperial democracy. The Amazonomachy was represented on a metope frieze of the Parthenon (begun in 460 BC), on the shield of Phidias' celebrated gold and ivory statue of Athena that stood in the Parthenon, and on the frieze in a temple to Hephaestus that still stands just off the Athenian agora.

Theseus and Hippolytus

The Amazon queen Antiopê, whom Theseus abducted, bore a son, **Hippolytus** (hip-**pol**-i-tus, perhaps "breaker of horses"), but Theseus later cast her off to take a new wife, **Phaedra** (fē-dra), daughter of Minos and sister of his former mistress Ariadnê (see Chart 17). Hippolytus was raised by his grandfather Pittheus, king of Troezen. When Hippolytus grew to manhood, he became a devotee of the virgin huntress Artemis, special goddess of the Amazons. As his mother had despised men, he despised women, denied his own sexual nature, and cared only for the hunt and the wilderness. Theseus' new wife, the Cretan Phaedra, like her sister Ariadnê and her mother Pasiphaë (next chapter), was unable to control her sexual desire. She fell in love with her own stepson!

The story is the subject of Euripides' play *Hippolytus*, performed in 428 BC. Aphrodite summarizes the plot in the play's prologue. Her statue stood on one side of the stage across from that of Artemis, on the other side of the stage. Theseus is living in temporary exile in Troezen (whence came his mother) across the gulf from Athens, because he killed his fifty cousins, the sons of Pallas, his father's brother. Aphrodite's speech is a vivid depiction of the relentless and calamitous power of sexual desire:

[1] All mortals know me, Cypris,° great in every land,
    a mighty goddess, great in heaven as well.
    From darkest Pontus° to the Atlantic shore
    they know my strength, all men who view the sun.
5   Those who respect me and my power I cherish;
    those who disdain me trip and are brought low.
    For the race of gods shares this with humankind:
    Honor from others feeds their self-esteem.
    I soon shall prove the truth this maxim holds.
10   The son of Theseus, born of an Amazon,
    is named Hippolytus, whom Pittheus reared.
    Alone of all the dwellers here in Troezen,
    he flouts me as the most corrupt of gods,
    scorns love's delights, disdains the marriage bed.
15   Apollo's sister Artemis, child of Zeus,
    he hails in honor, "Goddess of all most great!"
    He and his maiden huntress range the greenwood,
    trying, with their swift hounds, to wipe it clean
    of all its creatures. O, how he preens himself,

1. *Cypris*: Aphrodite. 3. *Pontus*: The Black Sea.

20 that he has found a more-than-mortal friend!
 Well, if he likes it, why should I object?
 But he has offended me in other ways
 for which today his punishment is due.
  My plans are laid, but little work is left.
25 Hippolytus once returned to Pandion's land,
 from Pittheus' house, to view the holy rites.°
 His father's well-bred bride, Phaedra of Crete,
 saw him. Her heart stood still—at my command!—
 trapped by forbidden love . . .
30 Later, when Theseus left the land of Cecrops,
 fleeing pollution for his murdered cousins,
 he brought his bride and settled in this country
 to spend a year abroad in expiation.
 Weeping and sick at heart with passion's sting,
35 she pines—in silence. None in the house knows why.
 But not of unspoken love will Phaedra die.
 Theseus will learn the truth, and all the world.
 Then will his father kill this priggish boy,
 who so disdains my ways. Poseidon, lord of the sea,
40 once promised Theseus that, ask what he would,
 three times his prayers would not go unfulfilled.
  By Theseus' curse Hippolytus will die.
 Phaedra? Her reputation will survive,
 but she herself must die. I cannot value
45 her misery higher than my own revenge
 on those who hate me. They must pay the price
 that shall to me seem best.
  Enough! for I see this son of Theseus
 has left the toil of hunting and drawn near.
50 I therefore must depart, for all around him
 a pack of yelping huntsmen dog his steps,
 barking their hymns to honor Artemis.
 That Hades throws wide its gates they do not know.
 This day which now is breaking will be his last.

EURIPIDES, Hippolytus 1–57

26. *the holy rites*: The Eleusinian Mysteries.

 Hippolytus comes on the stage and deposits a wreath before the statue of Artemis, a token of his devotion. He leaves and Phaedra is carried on stage, near death from lovesickness, contemplating suicide. Phaedra's old nurse twists the truth from her, that she has fallen in love with her stepson, and Phaedra rises from the couch to deplore the war between sexual passion and a woman's desire for respectability:

[373] Women of Troezen,° nearest to us of all
 who live in Pelops' land,° in years gone by
375 I used to lie awake through the long nights

373. *Women of Troezen*: The chorus. 374. *Pelops' land*: That is, the Peloponnesus.

wondering what most corroded human life.
Not from an inborn weakness of our reasoning
do we go wrong. Most of us know full well
how we should act. No, we must think of this:
380   With mind and soul we know just what is right,
but lack the character to make it real.°
Some of us act thus out of laziness;
some put some pleasure far ahead of duty,
and life holds many pleasures—that precious curse,
385   our hours of idle talk, being one of them . . .
      Now let me show you the line of my own reason.
I fell in love. I had to find a way
by which most honorably to bear the wound.
My first idea was this: keep my mouth shut,
390   suppress the whole affair. But who can trust the tongue?
How cleverly it admonishes human thoughts—
that is, the thoughts of others. But if it talks
about its owner, what damage it can bring!
      So next I tried to moderate my folly,
395   to conquer it by reasoning it away.
Of course, I could not thus control my passion.
Then what was left? to die. No one denies
that this was much the best course open.
For me, while my honor stands, all may applaud,
400   but if that falls, then let it fall unwitnessed.
Both act and inclination to the act bring disgrace
(I am a woman, this I know for sure)
in all men's eyes.
      Yes, cursed be she who first
405   defiled her husband's bed with other men.
Some woman, married within a noble house,
infected all her sex with this corruption,
for once such vice wins favor with the high-born,
it soon is modish in plebeian eyes.
410   How I detest those moral-sounding women,
who privately delight in viciousness!
How, Lady Cypris, mistress of the sea,
dare they to look into their husbands' faces?
Do they not shudder at the pandering darkness,
415   and dread indictment by the bedroom walls?
      O closest friends, this is what tortures me:
the shame my guilt would bring upon my husband,
upon the children whom I bore. May they live free
and confident, free men of glorious Athens,
420   rejoicing in their mother's fair renown.

EURIPIDES, *Hippolytus* 373–423

381. *make it real*: Medea in Ovid, trying to decide whether to obey her father or to run off with
Jason, has a similar line: "I see the better course, and I approve it—but I then pursue the worse."
See Chapter 19 for the story of Medea and Jason.

The nurse is at first horrified at Phaedra's secret and considers suicide herself. She soon has second thoughts (a recurring theme in this play). Speaking like an Athenian rhetorician in a court of law, the nurse turns black into white through ingenious speech, using examples from myth to prove her point that passion, being irresistible, should therefore not be resisted. Half-persuaded, Phaedra allows the nurse to approach Hippolytus on her behalf, but the virtuous sportsman is horrified, revolted at the offer of adulterous union with his own stepmother! He delivers a tirade against women, who bring to the male nothing but emotional and financial ruin. Like Hesiod, he wishes that Zeus had devised some other way to propagate the species:

[616] Why, why, O Zeus, did you ever bring to life
        and settle on mankind this false-faced breed of women?
        If all you wanted was to spawn our mortal race,
        there was no need for women. A man might have gone
620   into your temples, laid down the proper mass
        of bronze or gold or iron, and in exchange
        at a price to fit his station, bought himself a brood
        and lived in a quiet home thereafter, free of women.
        Why is it clear that women are a curse?
625   The man who fathered her, who brought her up,
        must pay still more to free himself from her,
        in dowry, from a purse already strained.
        The fool who bought her takes the creature home.
        He loves to pay outrageous bills for clothes
630   to deck his ugly idol. "No one's wife
        has nicer clothes than you!"—till he goes bankrupt.
        A pauper has no trouble of this sort,
        but a silly woman is a plague at best.
        And how I loathe the clever of that sex!
635   Never may a woman knowing more than woman ought
        infest my house. For Cypris stirs up mischief
        much more in clever women. The stupid doll
        is saved from folly by her witlessness.
        No woman needs a clever serving-maid.
640   Better a dumb and snarling animal
        with nothing to say, nothing she wants to hear.
        But as things are, women contrive their schemes
        within the house, and the servants bring them forth.
            Thus, you old bitch, you sidled up to me
645   with an unholy offer, to share my father's wife,
        whose person should be sacred in my eyes.
        Bring holy water! I'll pour it in my ears,
        to wash away your foul polluting bargain.
        What made you think that I could be so vile,
650   I, whose purity shrinks at the very thought?

EURIPIDES, *Hippolytus* 616–655

Phaedra overhears his speech. Terrified that Hippolytus will tell Theseus and desperate to preserve her honor, she hangs herself in the bedroom. She leaves behind a note pinned to her bosom, saying that she killed herself for shame after Hippolytus assaulted her.

Theseus, away consulting an oracle, now comes home. He places Phaedra's charges before Hippolytus, but the noble young man is unable to defend himself: He had sworn to the nurse, before she propositioned him, never to reveal her words. Disgusted, Theseus uses one of the three wishes given him by Poseidon (a folktale motif) to curse his own son. As Hippolytus races his chariot along the sea, an immense bull, sent by Poseidon, comes out of the sea and frightens the horses, who rear and throw him from the chariot. He is tangled in the reins and dragged to his death over the rocks. Too late, Theseus learns the truth from Artemis, how he has destroyed his own flesh on the false testimony of a lascivious woman.

Euripides' innovation in his *Hippolytus* is to cast the woman as a sympathetic character, Aphrodite's helpless victim caught in a divine plan to destroy Hippolytus. His audience expects to see the wicked woman vilified and the chaste youth exalted; that is the tradition. Instead, Euripides portrays his Phaedra as a highly moral woman struggling against the shame of her passion whereas Hippolytus is an intolerant prig.

Fond of overturning his audience's expectations, Euripides changes basic assumptions of an old story. His is a morality play: To think you can live without sex is a destructive illusion. Hippolytus, like the Amazons, his forebears, refuses his biological and social obligations to marry, have sexual relations, and engender a new generation. Like the Amazons, he follows the virgin Artemis. Although he foolishly hopes to dam the deluge of sexual desire, the waters of passion sweep everything away. **(For the complete Hippolytus by Euripides, see http://classics. mit.edu/Euripides/hippolytus.html)**

PERSPECTIVE 16

BOCCACCIO'S MISFORTUNES OF FAMOUS MEN

Giovanni Boccaccio (1313–1375), fired with Renaissance enthusiasm for the classics, is best known for his *Decameron,* a collection of stories that has had immense influence in the development of modern literature. He also liked to recount Greek myths, giving his mythical characters the thoughts and feelings of his own contemporaries. He sometimes attempted to explain the complex meanings he found in these stories.

In one work, *De casibus virorum illustrium,* "Concerning the misfortunes of famous men," Boccaccio gathers together stories about the disasters that befell famous men and women in myth, history, and the Bible. One of the stories he retells is that of Theseus, Phaedra, and Hippolytus. Finding a moral for everyone,

Boccaccio chastises Phaedra for slandering her stepson and Hippolytus for jumping to hasty conclusions. *De casibus,* translated into Italian, French, German, and English, was immensely popular all over Europe. Here (Perspective Figure 16.1) is an illustration from a French manuscript of *De casibus* from 1470, showing the suicide of Phaedra.

In Boccaccio's version, Phaedra first confesses her slander to Theseus (to the left, on his throne), then stabs herself in the belly. Members of the court stand in the background. Neither Boccaccio nor the illustrator could conceive of the appearance of ancient people and places in terms other than those suggested by their own experience, even as today many condemn the past for not holding ideals obvious to us. Little was known of real Greek costume, architecture, and daily life until the eighteenth century, and not until the twentieth century did we begin to see clearly who the ancients were and how they really lived.

PERSPECTIVE FIGURE 16.1 *Phaedra killing Herself,* from a manuscript of Boccaciao's *De casibus virorum illustrium,* 1470. (© British Library Board. All Rights Reserved. Harley 1766, f.39.)

Observations: The Folktale of "Potiphar's Wife"

The story of Phaedra and Hippolytus is one version of the common folktale story-type about family life called "Potiphar's Wife." Named after the biblical story of Joseph, the story is far older than the Bible, surviving in an Egyptian papyrus from about 1250 BC, which scholars call the "Story of the Two Brothers," the oldest recorded folktale in the world. In the story, the wife of Anubis (also a god's name) propositions her husband's handsome brother Bata, and when he refuses, she rubs herself with fat and grease to make it appear as if she has been beaten and sexually abused. She tells Anubis that Bata made advances to her and, when she refused, he beat her up.

Anubis hides behind the door of a shed, intending to kill Bata when he returns from the fields, but Bata sees him first and runs away. Here the story drops its realistic guise and becomes an exploration in symbolic form of the ever-renewed vitality of pharaoh, who embodied Egypt: Repeatedly Bata, who represents pharaoh, dies and is reborn. A woman's treachery repeatedly brings death, but pharaonic vitality again and again triumphs over death. The folktale is a political myth.

The later biblical tale, perhaps from the fifth century BC in the form preserved to us, reads like a historical account, moralizing how with Yahweh's help the Jewish Joseph survived the foreign devil:

> Joseph was taken down to Egypt, and Potiphar, an officer of pharaoh, the captain of the guard, an Egyptian, bought him from the Ishmaelite who had brought him there. Yahweh was with Joseph, and he became a successful man in the house of his master the Egyptian, and his master saw that Yahweh was with him . . . and left all that he had in Joseph's charge . . .
>
> Now Joseph was good-looking and attractive. After a time his master's wife cast her eyes on Joseph and said, "Lie with me." But he refused and said to his master's wife, "Lo, having me, my master has no concern about anything in the house, and he has put everything that he has in my hand . . . How then can I do this great wickedness, and sin against Yahweh?" And although she spoke to Joseph day after day, he would not listen to her, to lie with her or to be with her.
>
> But one day when he went into the house to do his work, and none of the men of the house was present, she caught him by his garment and begged him, "Lie with me." But he left his garment in her hand and fled and got out of the house. And when she saw that he had left his garment in her hand . . . she called to the men of her household and said to them, "See, he [Potiphar] has brought among us a Hebrew to insult us. He [Joseph] came in to me to lie with me and I cried out with a loud voice, and when he heard that I lifted up my voice and cried, he left his garment with me and fled and got out of the house . . ."
>
> Then she laid up his garment by her until his master came home, and she told him the same story . . . And Joseph's master seized him and put him into the prison.

GENESIS 39

Fortunately, Yahweh is with Joseph, whose ability to interpret pharaoh's dreams leads to his release. In the Bible the folktale becomes a religious myth, glorifying Yahweh's protection of his people.

The same folktale appears in Homer's *Iliad*, told about the Corinthian hero **Bellerophon** (bel-**ler**-o-phon). After Bellerophon rebuffed the lustful wife of King Proteus while residing at Corinth, she accused him of making advances. The king could not kill Bellerophon, his guest-friend, so he sent him across the sea to his father-in-law in Lycia (in southern Turkey), carrying sealed tablets with instructions, "kill the bearer" (the only reference to writing in Homer).

The king of Lycia sent Bellerophon on impossible tasks. First, he was to kill the dread Chimera (compare Figure 4.5), but Bellerophon mounted the winged horse Pegasus, which had sprung from the severed neck of Medusa, and killed the monster. He fought the Amazons and performed other tasks but was always successful. In the end he married the princess and received a portion of the kingdom. The folktale is now a heroic myth with the familiar ingredients of dangerous woman, treacherous king, conquest of a monster, victory, marriage, and kingship. Still, Bellerophon came to a bad end. Arrogantly flying to heaven on Pegasus, he fell to his death.

The story-type, given such different meaning by Egyptians, Jews, and Greeks, appeals to the same male fear of woman's vindictive power that underlies tales about the Mesopotamian Inanna/Ishtar/Astartê who, when she failed to seduce Gilgamesh, sent the Bull of Heaven, then killed his companion Enkidu.

The Exploits of Theseus and Pirithoüs

Pirithoüs (pī-**rith**-o-us), a son of Ixion (damned in the underworld), was king of the **Lapiths**, a Thessalian tribe. Having heard of Theseus' prowess, he decided to test him, so he came into Attica under cover of darkness and raided Theseus' flocks on the plain of Marathon. Theseus caught him red-handed. They were about to come to blows when Pirithoüs, admiring Theseus' physique, apologized and volunteered to become Theseus' slave. Theseus was equally impressed by Pirithoüs and suggested that, instead of killing one another, they swear eternal friendship (like Gilgamesh and Enkidu, or Heracles and Iolaüs).

Pirithoüs married a woman named Hippodamia (hip-po-da-**mī**-a; there were several in Greek myth) and invited the monstrous **Centaurs**, half men and half horse, to the wedding feast. The Centaurs were cousins of Pirithoüs because Centaurus, their forebear, had sprung from the seed of Pirithoüs' father, Ixion, when he ejaculated into a cloud that looked like Hera (Chapter 12). Being wild, uncivilized, and unaccustomed to wine, the Centaurs lost control of themselves after a few drinks, as in the story of Heracles and the friendly Centaur Pholus (Chapter 15). They attacked the bride on the altar and tried to rape her attendants, too.

Theseus joined the fight to rescue Hippodamia. Thus began the famous war between the Lapiths and the Centaurs. Like the Amazonomachy, the **Centauromachy** in Greek art came to symbolize the struggle between civilization and barbarism, between Greek and foreigner. Like the Amazonomachy, it was often represented on Greek temples, including the celebrated west pediment of the great temple to Zeus at Olympia (Figure 7.9).

After Phaedra and Hippodamia both had died, Theseus and Pirithoüs decided to look for new wives together. Because they were famous and of high birth, only a daughter of Zeus could satisfy them. Helen, a daughter of Zeus and Leda, although not yet of marriageable age, was said to be very attractive, and Theseus chose her. The two companions traveled to Sparta and snatched up Helen as she was performing a ritual dance to Artemis (just as Hades snatched Persephonê as she played in the meadow with her virgin friends). They escaped to the Isthmus, then drove hard to Athens. Because Helen was too young for intercourse, Theseus took her to an outlying village and left her with his mother, Aethra, for safe-keeping until she matured.

Pirithoüs now revealed that he wanted to marry another daughter of Zeus—Persephonê! Reluctantly, Theseus accompanied his friend to the underworld. Hades listened politely to their request, then invited them to sit down to a meal. They sat in stone chairs and immediately their flesh clung to the seats and their limbs were bound with serpents. Later, when Heracles came to the underworld to fetch Cerberus, Theseus cried out to him as the conqueror of Death. Heracles seized Theseus by the arm and wrenched him from the chair, leaving a good part of Theseus' backside attached. That is why the Athenians have such slender hips! (Figure 16.11). Heracles also tried to save Pirithoüs, but when the earth trembled, he backed away. Pirithoüs remains there still.

FIGURE 16.11 Heracles and Theseus in the House of Hades, on an oil jar, c. 475 BC. Heracles, carrying his club and wearing his lion skin, pulls Theseus from the stone seat where he is imprisoned, while Theseus, wearing a cloak and broad-brimmed traveler's hat, pushes down hard with his spear.   (Johannes Laurentius/ Bildarchiv Preußischer Kulturbesitz/Art Resource, New York)

The Death of Theseus

When Theseus returned to the upper world, he found Athens in turmoil. The Dioscuri (dī-os-**kur**-ī, "sons of Zeus"), Castor and Polydeuces (pol-i-**dus**-ēz), Helen's brothers and mighty heroes in their own right, had come in his absence and taken Helen back, along with Theseus' mother, Aethra. She appears in the *Iliad* as Helen's slave, who went with Helen to Troy. Menestheus, the first demagogue of Athens, had taken over the city, calling Theseus a tyrant. Menestheus would later lead the Athenian contingent to Troy.

Theseus fled to the island of Scyros (**sī**-ros), east of Euboea, hoping for hospitality, but the local king, envious of Theseus' greatness, led him to a cliff to see the view, then pushed him off. Theseus died not gloriously as a hero should, but shamefully and by treachery. His father, Aegeus, inadvertently betrayed by his careless son, had also plunged from high rocks to his death.

Observations: Myth and Propaganda

By the fifth century BC, the golden age of Greece, the days of Aeschylus, Sophocles, Euripides, Pericles, and the Parthenon, Theseus had become the official hero of Athens and its empire, celebrated in sculpture and song. It was not always so. Just a hundred years before, he was scarcely known, except for the adventure in the Labyrinth (see next chapter) and his participation in the Centauromachy; these are his oldest myths. No important family claimed him as its ancestor, no town or village was named in his honor. In the *Iliad* and the *Odyssey*, from the eighth century BC, he is mentioned only three times, always in passing, and Menestheus commands the Athenians at Troy. Only in the sixth century BC did Theseus rise to prominence when a festival was named after him, and he became prominent in Athenian art. Before the end of the sixth century, an unknown poet composed an epic, now lost, called the *Theseïs*, "Song of Theseus," which must have given form to the standard cycle of legends recounted here.

The popularization of the legends of Theseus, including the composition of the *Theseïs*, took place under the sponsorship of **Pisistratus** (pī-**sis**-tra-tus), the famous leader of Athens who first came to power in 561 BC and governed Athens off and on until his death in 527 BC, when his sons Hippias and Hipparchus succeeded him. The dynasty began to come apart in 514 BC after Hipparchus was assassinated in a homosexual intrigue. Like Theseus, Pisistratus unified Attica under the political and cultural rule of Athens and fought for Athens' interests overseas, in Ionia and on many islands. Parallels were constantly drawn between the accomplishments of Theseus and Pisistratus. Theseus often received credit for Pisistratus' important deeds, such as the unification of Athens, the so-called *synoecism*. Such parallels between myth and contemporary events strengthened Pisistratus' reputation as a benevolent and powerful leader.

By the fifth century BC, the Athenians claimed Theseus as the founder of their democracy, but it was Pisistratus who, in the sixth century BC, encouraged the individualism and cultural enlightenment that made the democracy possible. In myth,

Theseus founded the Panathenaic games, which celebrated the unity and glory of Attica; in reality, Pisistratus gave this old festival its special character, including a celebration of special magnificence every fourth year when portions of the *Iliad* and *Odyssey* were recited. Theseus defeated a wild bull on the plain of Marathon; Pisistratus returned from temporary exile in 546 BC on this same plain, from which he drew much of his support. Shortly afterward Athenian vase painters began to portray Theseus and the Bull of Marathon (see Figure 16.9).

In myth, Theseus invented coinage, one of the most important economic innovations of the sixth century BC, but Pisistratus probably was the first Athenian to strike coins in Athens; they bore a bull's head after the Marathonian bull. In myth Theseus stopped at the island of Delos after escaping from the Labyrinth; in history Pisistratus exerted powerful influence over this strategic island, site of an ancient cult of Apollo and Artemis. Theseus destroyed the bandits living on the edge of the gulf from Troezen to Athens; Hippias, Pisistratus' son, rid the Saronic Gulf of pirates. Scenes showing Sinis, the Crommyonian sow, Sciron, and Procrustes appear in sculpture and painting soon after Hippias' achievements.

After the murder of Hipparchus, his brother Hippias' rule became oppressive, and he was soon driven out. One might have expected the myths of Theseus, which glorified the Pisistratids, to decline in popularity, but the opposite occurred. Athenians remade old cults in Theseus' honor, and he appears ever more often in art. From the model for benevolent autocratic rule by the Pisistratids, Theseus became the hero of the Athenian democracy, which Clisthenes (**klīs**-then-ēz) founded in 508 BC. Attic drama celebrated Theseus' kindness to such suppliants as Oedipus, Adrastus, the sons of Heracles, and Orestes, all refugees from cities hostile to Athens in the fifth century BC. In myth Theseus renounced autocracy in favor of democracy, but there was no democracy in Greece before the reforms of Clisthenes. By modifying traditional tales, Athenians legitimized the new style of government, a drastic departure from traditional forms.

In 490 BC a badly outnumbered Athenian citizen army under the leadership of Miltiades (mil-**tī**-a-dēz) turned back a Persian host on the plain of Marathon. Eyewitnesses reported that the ghost of Theseus rushed up before the Athenian lines: On the plain of Marathon Theseus had captured the bull. Earlier myths telling of Theseus' rape of the Amazon queen (Heracles had performed a similar deed) shifted to emphasize the Amazons' invasion of Attica and Theseus' destruction of their army. From swashbuckling adventurer and lover-boy, Theseus became the magnanimous and stalwart defender of homeland and freedom, and Miltiades was his successor.

Cimon (**kī**-mon), the son of Miltiades, further politicized the myths of Theseus in the early fifth century BC. An aggressive general and politician like his father, Cimon led an alliance of Greek states formed after the Persian invasions to victory after victory, sponsored trade, captured slaves, and took booty that enormously enriched the city of Athens. He, too, made use of Theseus' story when, after an outbreak of piracy in the northern Aegean, he occupied the pirates' hideout on the island of Scyros, where Theseus died.

An oracle directed Cimon to find the bones of Theseus, a task proper for the son of one who, aided by the ghost of Theseus, had led the Athenians to victory at

Marathon. In a grave on Scyros, Cimon found an enormous skeleton, bronze spear and sword at its side (did Cimon find a Bronze Age tomb?). Obviously, these were Theseus' bones, and Cimon proudly brought them to Athens. A new Festival of Theseus was added to the calendar and a shrine built in the agora for the bones, decorated with scenes from the Amazonomachy and the Centauromachy. Cimon was the new Theseus, who brought fresh glory to a new Athens.

When the threat of Persia receded and Athens and its often unwilling allies began to square off against Sparta, the myths underwent further transformation. Theseus now stood for the Ionians under Athens' leadership, while the Dorian states under Sparta claimed Heracles as their hero. Parallels between the two cycles of myth were carefully drawn.

Such developments furnish a good example of the use of myth as propaganda. The legends of Theseus encapsulated, symbolized, and justified Athenian policies: ascendancy at sea, suppression of marauders, and determined resistance to the barbarian. It took only a century for Theseus to become the official hero of Athens because Pisistratus, Miltiades, and Cimon all consciously, for political gain, made Theseus their model. To accomplish this goal, they remade or reformed the traditional legends.

The Athenians pioneered use of myth for political ends, but today such practice can be found in every country (see Chapters 23 and 24 for political myth in Rome). In our own day stories of the exemplary lives of George Washington and Abraham Lincoln inculcate values useful to a modern democracy but bear small resemblance to the actual deeds and thoughts of these men. History and myth are a perennial tangle. Humans are mythmaking animals, retelling ancient stories to fulfill present needs.

KEY NAMES AND TERMS

SOME ADDITIONAL ANCIENT SOURCES

As spokesman for the Athenians' self-image, Theseus appears in numerous tragedies as the defender of justice and the oppressed. In Sophocles' *Oedipus at Colonus*, he protects the old, blind, exiled Oedipus and his daughters from Creon, who wants to carry them to Thebes.

In Euripides' *Suppliants* he compels Creon to give up the dead for burial after the failed campaign of the Seven against Thebes. In Euripides' *Heracles Insane*, he befriends Heracles after he has murdered his family. The hero's career is related at length in Plutarch's *Parallel Lives* and in Apollodorus 3.15–"Epitome" 1.

FURTHER READING CHAPTER 16

Hurwit, Jeffrey M., *The Athenian Acropolis: History, Mythology, and Archaeology from the Neolithic Era to the Present* (Cambridge, UK, 1999). Superb review of Athenian traditions, including myth, focused on Athens' most prominent landmark.

Knox, Bernard M. W., "The Hippolytus of Euripides," in *Oxford Readings in Greek Tragedy*, ed. E. Segal (Oxford, UK, 2001). Enlightening essay about the forces that drive the play, by a leading modern critic of ancient literature.

Mills, Sophie, *Theseus, Tragedy and the Athenian Empire* (Oxford, UK, 1997). Brings together the scattered evidence for his early myth and discusses in depth his treatment in four Greek tragedies.

Neils, Jennifer, *The Youthful Deeds of Theseus* (Rome, 1987). His early deeds in art and literature.

Tyrrell, William Blake, *Amazons: A Study in Athenian Mythmaking* (Baltimore, MD, 1984). Argues that Amazons take their character from an inversion of traditional Greek values.

CHAPTER 17

THE MYTHS OF CRETE

There is a land called Crete, in the midst of the wine-dark sea,
where a countless number of men inhabit a full ninety cities.

HOMER, *Odyssey* 19.172–174

THE STORIES OF THE House of Crete, closely related to those of Athens, are a complex of folktales about brave men, tricksters, lascivious or victimized women, and monstrous beasts. In contrast to the myths of Athens, which were told by Athenians as well as being about Athens, the myths we have about Crete were told by Greeks living on the mainland, most of them in Athens itself. Until about 1450 BC the Cretan upper classes were, of course, not Greeks (see Chapter 2), but archaeology has revealed that in the second millennium BC Crete was a great sea power and that bulls and goddesses, personifications of fertility, played important roles in their religion.

The powerful kings, served by a caste of scribes, oversaw and collected the agricultural produce of rich inland and coastal plains. They lived in enormous, complex palaces, which they decorated with remarkably realistic frescoes. The richness and power of seafaring Crete have survived in story, but the king has become a folktale figure: the evil persecutor finally overthrown by a wandering hero who wins the love of a princess. The elaborate buildings became in story a prison-maze constructed by a trickster-artist, and the bull of Cretan fertility religion has turned into a half-human monster, demanding human sacrifice. The myths of Crete appear to be a clear example of history becoming myth, but unfortunately we have only the myths. There is Cretan archaeology, but no early Cretan history.

Many myths about Crete took on a nearly official form in the works of Greek dramatists—both Euripides and Sophocles wrote tragedies about Europa and the bull—but their works have been lost. For most Cretan legends we rely on Roman writers who hark back to the Greek classics but prefer to emphasize the erotic, the rhetorical, and the bizarre.

EUROPA AND THE BULL

Agenor (a-**jēn**-or = Semitic "leader of men") was descended from Zeus and Io (Chart 17.1). While his brother Belus (**bē**-lus = Semitic "lord," biblical Baal) ruled Egypt, Agenor traveled to the coast of the eastern Mediterranean. There, in the land later called Phoenicia, he settled, married, and had a daughter, **Europa** (yu-**rōp**-a, perhaps Semitic for "dark"), and three sons: Cadmus, Cilix (**sī**-lix), and Phoenix. Zeus fell in love with the beautiful Europa and came to her in the form of a bull (Figure 17.1). The most famous account of the story is found in Ovid's *Metamorphoses*, in which the divine bull is a handsome seducer and Europa the innocent but not unwilling virgin (see Perspective Figure 6.2d). As in Roman love poetry, addressed to an upper-class

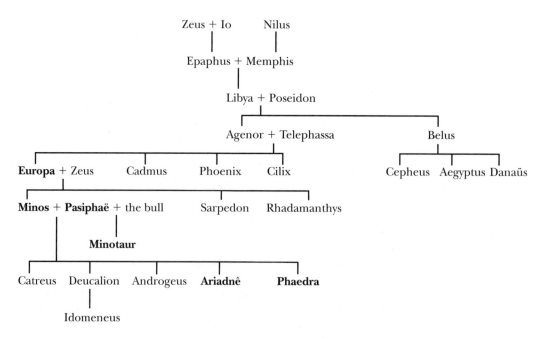

CHART 17.1 The House of Crete

FIGURE 17.1 Europa and the bull, Attic vase, c. 490 BC. Europa wears a himation (a kind of robe) over a sleeved chiton (a kind of shirt), bracelets, and diadem in her hair, while she touches the magnificent bull by the horn. (Museo Archeologico Nazionale, Tarquinia; Scala/Ministero per i Beni e le Attività culturali / Art Resource, New York)

urban audience familiar with sexual escapades, the seducer needs a helper to over-come obstacles to the satisfaction of his lust. The passage begins with Jupiter/Zeus summoning Mercury/Hermes, go-between of the gods, to help his wooing:

[834]   When the grandson of Atlas° heard this, he left behind the land
835   that takes its name from Pallas,° arising into the air
      on flying wings. His father beckoned, concealing the truth,
      that love demanded his help. "My son, my messenger trusty,
      fly down at once, the way you know so well, to the country
      left of the seven stars of your mother, the Pleiades,°
840   called by its natives Phoenicia. Seek out the herd of the king,
      and drive it down to the sea." Down from the hills flew Mercury.
      The cattle flocked to the shore, where the sovereign's daughter
      used to play with her Tyrian friends.° Now grandeur and love
      rarely go well together. Zeus—father and ruler of gods,
845   whose right hand is armed with triple fire, whose menacing scowl
      shakes the firm earth—put off his scepter and donning the mask
      of a bull calf, he joined the heifers. Beautiful in their eyes,
      he wandered softly mooing and chomping the tender grass.
      No anger wrinkled his brow, no fierceness glared from his eye.
850   His face just begged to be fondled. Agenor's daughter, entranced,
      cooed, "What a lovable creature! He wouldn't hurt even a fly!"
      (Yet for a while she stayed a little way off from the creature.)
      At last she dares to approach with flowers to that mild face.
      His heart leaps up, but for now he only licks at her fingers

834. *grandson of Atlas*: Mercury.   835. . . . *name from Pallas*: Athens.   839. *the Pleiades*: The mother of Mercury/Hermes was Maia, one of seven daughters of Atlas. Orion the hunter fell in love with them and pursued them for five years, until they were turned into doves (*Pleiades* = "doves"). Zeus raised them into the sky as the star-cluster in the constellation of Taurus, still called the Pleiades.   843. *Tyrian friends*: Tyre was one of the two principal cities of Phoenicia, the other being Sidon.

855   as he waits for pleasures to come. Now closer, closer they draw.
In sport, he writhes and squirms about in the succulent grass.
His snowy flanks lie churning the warm yellow sand of the shore.
Europa's fears shrink away as he offers his mighty dewlaps
to be stroked by her virginal hand, his horns for garlands of flowers.
860   Soon the innocent princess, not knowing what lay in her future,
dares climb up and sit on his shoulders. Slowly the god arises,
slowly moves down to the shore and dips his feet in its ripples.
Then—just a few steps further, and off he goes with his prize.
The girl begins to worry, looks back at the shore she has left.
865   Her right hand clutches a horn, the other clings to his back
while her thin and fluttering dress is blown by a gathering breeze.
    At last the god abandons his treacherous masquerade,
as they reach the coastline of Crete.

OVID, Metamorphoses 2.834–3.2

When Agenor discovered that his daughter was missing, he instructed his three sons, Cadmus, Phoenix, and Cilix, to search for Europa and not to return without her. They traveled over the wide world but, finding nothing and afraid to return home, settled in various lands: Phoenix near his first home in the land ever since called Phoenicia (roughly, modern Lebanon); Cilix in Cilicia (si-**lish**-a, in southeastern Turkey, northwest of Lebanon); and Cadmus in Thebes (in central Greece).

Zeus and Europa meanwhile had several children: **Minos**, Sarpedon (sar-**pēd**-on), and Rhadamanthys (rad-a-**man**-this). For protection, Zeus gave Laelaps to Europa, the wonderful dog that always caught its prey, later the possession of Cephalus; and Talus (**tā**-lus), a gigantic bronze robot that ran around the island three times each day and pelted with enormous boulders any ship that attempted to land (later important in the story of Jason, Chapter 19; Figure 19.6).

MINOS AND PASIPHAË

After Zeus tired of Europa and returned to Olympus, a local Cretan, Asterius, married her and looked after her three sons. When the sons grew up, they all fell in love with the same boy. They quarreled furiously until Minos drove out his two brothers. Sarpedon went to Lycia in southwest Anatolia, and Rhadamanthys went to Boeotia, the plain northwest of Attica. When Rhadamanthys died, he became a judge among the dead, as did Minos and Aeacus (a king of the island of Aegina and grandfather of the Trojan-fighter Ajax).

When Asterius died, Minos claimed the kingship for himself, boasting that the sea-god Poseidon had promised him the throne. He asked that a bull should rise from the sea as a sign of his election; this he would sacrifice to the god who sent it. A magnificent bull did rise from the sea, but one so splendid that Minos could not bear to give it up. Instead, he sent it to his herds and in its place sacrificed another. Thus Minos became the powerful king of Crete, oversaw the land, and promulgated laws. He married **Pasiphaë** (pa-**sif**-a-ē, "all-shining"), a daughter of Helius (the sun), who bore him many children, among them Ariadnê, Phaedra, and the prince Androgeüs (an-**drōj**-e-us).

Poseidon, angered that Minos had not sacrificed the bull, contrived a terrible punishment. He caused Pasiphaë, his wife, to fall hopelessly in love with the bull. Determined to satisfy her uncontrollable passion, Pasiphaë confided her problem to an Athenian then living on Crete, **Daedalus** (**dēd**-a-lus), the greatest craftsman of all time, a consummate architect and the inventor of statues. A descendant of Cecrops, Daedalus had been exiled from Athens for hurling his nephew and student Perdix from the Acropolis (but according to one version, Perdix was turned into a partridge, which in Greek = *perdix*). This he had done in a fit of jealousy because Perdix, not he, invented the saw, in imitation of a fish's backbone.

Daedalus constructed a hollow wooden cow for Pasiphaë and covered it with a cowhide. Little wheels mounted in the legs enabled him to roll it into a pasture where the bull from the sea liked to graze. Pasiphaë climbed inside. The bull, snorting with desire, mounted the wooden cow and impregnated the queen, who stood hunched over inside. The fruit of this union was the dread **Minotaur** ("the bull of Minos"), a man-eating monster with the head of a bull and the body of a man (Figure 17.2). Ovid describes Pasiphaë's obscene passion in his brilliantly amusing *Ars amatoria*, "The Art of Love," in which he advises the ambitious male

FIGURE 17.2 Pasiphaë with the baby Minotaur, on the interior of an Etruscan wine cup, c. 340 BC. An affectionate Pasiphaë is shown in her boudoir, indicated by the basket hanging from the wall and the pet goose at her feet. She gazes somewhat disheartened at the monster she has begotten. (Bibliothèque Nationale de France, Paris)

lover to keep his cool and let the woman make the first move, as Pasiphaë did in her approach to the bull:

[275]   Men and women alike delight in counterfeit coolness,
        but men soon blurt what they feel, girls pretend to be coy.
    If we males refused to show interest and let the girls make advances,
        be sure they would start an affair, setting the pace for the suit.
    Look at the beasts of the field: The cow moos her amorous passion,
280   the stallion is always entrapped by the whinnying voice of the mare.
    Humans alone can claim that their passion is kinder and gentler;
        the fire in a masculine breast is ruled by custom and law ...
    Once in the shadowy glades on the wooded slopes of Mount Ida,°
        as pride and joy of the herd, there sported a snowy white bull [Figure 17.3].
285   Except for a tiny black spot between the horns on his forehead,
        his coat was a milky white, faultless, unblemished, unmarked.
    Every cow in the kingdom of Cnossus° or western Cydonia°
        longed to tremble, half-crushed by his thrusting weight on her back.

283. *Mount Ida*: There are two mountains named Ida, one is near Troy; this is the Cretan Ida.   287. *Cnossus*: The main city of Crete, near modern Heraklion in the middle of the north coast.   287. *Cydonia*: The modern Chania, in the northwest of the island.

FIGURE 17.3 Mount Ida in central Crete, home of the Great Mother, above a Cretan village.   (De Agostini Editore/PhotoLibrary)

Pasiphaë shouted for joy when the animal made her his mistress,
290   but scowled with jealousy's pangs at a shapely heifer's approach.
All of you know the old tale. All Crete, with a full hundred cities,
      where every man is a liar,° must still acknowledge its truth.
The queen herself, so they say, with hands not used to such labor,
      plucked him the tenderest leaves, the softest grass of the field.
295 She follows the herd. No thought of her husband keeps her from going.
      Minos must now wear horns,° cuckolded now by a bull!
Pasiphaë, what is the use of your color-coordinate costumes?
      Your bull-friend isn't aware that richness is better than rags.
What use to you is a mirror, as you plod through mud to your pasture?
300   Why waste time on your hair, endlessly changing its braids?
Can't you believe your mirror's assurance that you're not a Holstein?
      How long will you ache for horns to bud and sprout from your brow!
If you are content with Minos, why seek an adulterous lover?
      If a manlier man you prefer, at least find a man you can love.
305 Slipping away from the palace, Pasiphaë runs to the woodland,
      like a Bacchanal driven along by the maddening Aonian god.°
Again and again she glares at a sweet and innocent heifer:
      "What on earth can my lover see in that ugly old cow?
Just look at the way she goes slinking before him, there in the meadow.
310   I suppose she's silly enough to believe she's prettier than I!"
So she would sneer, but at once would order her innocent rival
      to be dragged from the herd, to labor tugging the yoke and the plow.
Better yet, she would slay her as sacrificial offering,
      gleefully rubbing her hands in the entrails, steaming and hot.
315 So she appeased the immortals, and with each envy-born murder
      she muttered, "Go back to my lover. See what he thinks of you now!"
One moment she longs to become a Europa, another an Io;
      one of whom was a cow, the other seduced by a bull.
Well, the lord of the harem, deceived by a wooden plush-covered dummy,
320   got Pasiphaë pregnant. The child looked just like his dad.

OVID, *Ars amatoria* 1.275–282, 289–326

---

292. *liar*. The Cretans had a reputation as liars. The Cretan philosopher Epimenides is quoted by St. Paul (letter to Titus, Bishop of Crete, 1.12): "One of their own kind, one of their own prophets, said, 'the Cretans are always liars, evil beasts, dull bellies.'" But because a Cretan made this statement, can it be true? The paradox of the Cretan liar was a favorite plaything of ancient logicians.   296. *wear horns*. The cuckold, a man whose wife has been unfaithful, was for some reason thought to grow horns (in modern Italian a cuckold is *il cornuto*, "the horned one"). Hence the slang term *horny* for someone in need of sexual gratification.   306. *Aonian god*: Dionysus. Aonia was a district in Boeotia, whose capital was Thebes, where Dionysus was born.

Although shamed by his wife's behavior, Minos hesitated to kill the Minotaur, who, after all, was family. He ordered Daedalus, who built the cow, now to build a prison capable of holding the monster. So Daedalus designed a complex maze of windings and turnings, and in the center of this **Labyrinth** (**lab**-e-rinth) Minos imprisoned the Minotaur. No one who entered could find a way out, doomed to be eaten by the monster within.

MINOS AND SCYLLA

In another story that Ovid made famous, Minos' son Androgeüs, an athlete of exceptional prowess, traveled to Athens to participate in the Panathenaic games, held each year on Athena's birthday. Defeating every contender in every contest, he so annoyed Aegeus, king of Athens, that Aegeus ordered him to fight a wild bull that was ravaging the plain of Marathon, apparently the same bull that had impregnated Pasiphaë, which Heracles transported to the mainland as one of his labors. (Theseus will kill this bull.) The ferocious animal killed Androgeüs.

When Minos learned of his son's death, he immediately collected a fleet and set sail to attack Athens. On the way he besieged the coastal town of Megara, between Corinth and Athens, ruled over by Nisus (**nī**-sus), a brother of Aegeus. Nisus was invulnerable as long as a certain purple lock grew on his head. His daughter **Scylla** (**sil**-la), standing on the ramparts of the city, saw the handsome Minos in the distance and fell instantly in love with him. She sent a secret message to the invader saying that she would cut away her father's purple lock if, when Minos captured Megara, he married her. Minos agreed, but when the city fell, he spurned the treacherous daughter.

Scylla's love turned to hate as she watched the ships leave without her. She could neither stay at home in the city she had betrayed with the father she had ruined, nor join the man for whom she had committed these crimes. She dived into the sea and swam after the ship, overtook it, and clung to the stern. Nisus, turned to an osprey, swooped down on her with talons extended. She fell back into the waves and turned into a bird called in Greek "the shearer" (Ciris), because she had sheared her father's hair. In this form she escaped.

THESEUS AND AMPHITRITÊ

Having captured Megara, Minos turned to Athens, but could not take it even after a long siege. He prayed to Zeus for help. The god heard him and sent plague and famine on the city. The Athenians died in large numbers. An oracle instructed them to capitulate to Minos, who ordered as punishment for the death of Androgeüs that every nine years (or every year) the Athenians send seven boys and seven girls to be devoured by the Minotaur.

Several bands of youths had already met their gruesome deaths when Theseus, newly arrived in Athens from Troezen, volunteered to join the band of sacrificial youths. A curious poem by a choral poet (Bacchylides, fifth century BC) describes a sort of boasting contest during the fateful voyage to Crete. Minos, captain of the ship, attracted by the beauty of one of the Athenian *parthenoi*, made a pass at the girl. Theseus warned him off and bragged that his own ancestry was as glorious as that of Minos, a son of Zeus: He was himself a son of the sea-god Poseidon. Minos threw a ring into the sea and ordered Theseus to retrieve it. Theseus dove in and soon brought back a wreath from Amphitritê, wife of Poseidon, as proof of his own divine descent (Figure 17.4). For some reason, nothing further is heard of the ring. For Theseus the Athenian, anything was possible.

FIGURE 17.4 Theseus and Amphitritê, Attic wine cup, c. 500–490 BC. On the right, the boy Theseus, protected by Athena in the middle, reaches out to the sea-goddess Amphitritê on the left in her underwater realm, indicated by the three dolphins behind Theseus. A small, bearded Triton, with a serpent's body, supports Theseus in the water. (Because Poseidon is father to both Triton and Theseus, they are half-brothers.) Amphitritê holds her gift, a wreath, in her right hand (not visible in the photo).   (Musée du Louvre, Paris; Réunion des Musées Nationaux / Art Resource, New York)

PERSPECTIVE 17.1

RICK RIORDAN'S PERCY JACKSON

Rick Riordan (b. 1964) wrote *Percy Jackson and the Olympians,* set in the United States as a series of adventure and fantasy books based on Greek myth, directed toward a young adult audience. The books have sold over 1.2 million copies, been released in hardcover, paperback, and audio editions, and have been translated into many languages, a publishing sensation. *The Lightning Thief,* the first book, was made into a film in 2010 (*Percy Jackson and the Olympians: The Lightning Thief*).

The protagonist is Percy Jackson, whose name recalls Perseus. He is, however, the son of Poseidon, like Theseus. In the novels, the beings of Greek myth really exist, including monsters, Cyclopes, Titans, and the gods. Olympus is on a mythical 600th floor of the Empire State Building. Percy is frequently attacked by monsters because he is a child of one of the "Big Three" gods, that is, Zeus, Poseidon, and Hades.

In *The Lightning Thief* (2005) Percy Jackson is a dyslexic twelve-year-old with attention-deficit hyperactivity disorder (ADHD). After being attacked by his math teacher on a field trip—in fact a Fury in disguise—he discovers that he is the son of a Greek god. His best friend, a satyr named Grover Underwood, brings him to Camp Half-Blood off Long Island, reserved for children with a Greek god as a parent. He meets and befriends Annabeth Chase, daughter of Athena ("Annabeth" is an anagram of Athena with a couple of extra letters).

Soon Poseidon, lord of the sea, claims Percy as his son. Percy is accused of stealing Zeus's masterbolt, the model for other lightning bolts. He, Annabeth, and Grover must return the thunderbolt to Mount Olympus within ten days to stop a war between the gods and save his mother, held hostage in the underworld after capture by the Minotaur. They go on a quest across the United States and encounter many monsters (like Medusa) on the way. They discover that Luke, whom Percy met at camp, had stolen the bolt for Lord Kronos, who is attempting to rise from Tartarus.

In The *Sea of Monsters* (2006), *The Titan's Curse* (2007), and *The Battle of the Labyrinth* (2008) the hero continues his fantastic adventures. In *The Last Olympian* (2009) Percy Jackson and his friends fight a war much like the Titanomachy with the powerful Lord Kronos. The last Olympian standing is Hestia, to whom Percy gives Pandora's jar, telling her she is the most important Olympian "because hope survives best at the hearth." Eventually they overcome Lord Kronos and the gods recognize all their children.

The series continues with new publications. These are children's books but with a powerful narrative line that introduces a young generation to the language of Greek myth. Rick Riordan began the series to entertain his son when he was diagnosed with ADHD and dyslexia. His son had been studying Greek myth in second grade and wanted some bedtime stories based on Greek myth. The stories are like folktales that show the weak really to be great powers in disguise. They do not resemble Greek stories but use the elements of Greek myth in a kind of grab-bag style, beginning with the attractive notion that the Greek gods are real. Thus has always been the role of Greek myth—to be recreated according to the temper of the times.

THESEUS AND THE MINOTAUR

When Theseus arrived on Crete, Minos' daughter Ariadnê saw him and immediately fell in love, just as Scylla had fallen in love with Minos (and Ishtar with Gilgamesh). She promised to show Theseus how to subdue the Minotaur, if he would take her away and marry her. Following instructions that Daedalus gave to

FIGURE 17.5 Theseus kills the Minotaur, interior of an Attic, wine cup, c. 470 BC. Holding one of the bull's horns with one hand, with the other he decapitates the beast, his feet propped against the frame of the painting. The rocks indicate the labyrinth; a hat hangs from the wall indicating an interior setting.   (Museo Archeologico Nazionale, Florence; Deutsches Archäologisches Institut, Rome)

Ariadnê, Theseus tied the end of a ball of thread to the door of the labyrinth and unrolled it behind him as he penetrated the mysterious corridors (our word *clue* originally meant "a ball of thread"; its common metaphorical use is taken from this very story). Theseus found the Minotaur in the innermost recess of the Labyrinth and killed it with his sword (Figure 17.5), then followed the thread back to the entrance. That night he and Ariadnê fled in his ship, soon landing on the Cycladic island of Naxos.

Ovid liked the story of "Ariadnê on Naxos" so much that he told it three times (in the tenth letter of the *Heroïdes*, "famous women"; in *Ars amatoria* 1.527–564; and in *Metamorphoses* 8.174–192). Another famous literary description of these and earlier events of the legend is found in the Roman love-poet Catullus, who lived in the generation before Ovid (84–54 BC). In the poem that follows, Catullus' subject is actually the wedding of Peleus and Thetis, the parents of Achilles (see Chapter 20), but he devotes more than half the poem to the story of Theseus and Ariadnê embroidered into a coverlet spread on the wedding couch. This kind of story within a story (called an *epyllion*, "little epic") was a favorite device in Greek literature of the Hellenistic Period and its Roman imitators:

[76]　　　Long ago, says the legend, a plague forced the city of Cecrops
　　　　　　to atone at a terrible price for the murder of Cretan Androgeüs.
　　　　　　Each year the city must send, as meat for the Minotaur's banquet,
　　　　　　a chosen group of young men and the flower of unwedded maidens.
80　　　　The little town was groaning as the day of the tribute drew near,
　　　　　　when Theseus offered himself on behalf of his well-loved Athens:
　　　　　　Better that one should die° than a dozen fall prey to the monster.
　　　　　　So the light ships, driven by oars and a following breeze,
　　　　　　soon reached great-hearted Minos, in arrogance there on his throne.
85　　　　　Ariadnê, just out of childhood, gazed from the scented nursery
　　　　　　where she lived, till now secure in the sweet embrace of her mother . . .
　　　　　　She could not tear her eyes from their longing gaze on the hero,
　　　　　　till the flame that gaze enkindled was searing her inmost heart.
　　　　　　O Cupid—must I call you holy?—mixer of heaven and hell,
90　　　　and Venus, who rule over Golgi and wooded Idalia in Cyprus,°
　　　　　　what a tempest you two churned up in Ariadnê's emotions
　　　　　　of endless sighing for Theseus, the fair-haired wonderful stranger!
　　　　　　What fear tormented her soul, what pallor shone in her features,
　　　　　　when Theseus announced he was ready to battle the furious monster,
95　　　　be the outcome glorious death or life with a garland of glory!
　　　　　　Ariadnê's vows were not petty, and the prayer of her silent lips
　　　　　　rose up to heaven like incense, to win the assent of the gods.
　　　　　　　　The monster slashed with his horns at the unresisting breezes,
　　　　　　but Theseus' sword brought him low in a thunderous earth-shaking crash,
100　　　like an oak laid low by a storm on the rocky summit of Taurus.°
　　　　　　Led by the slender thread he had laid to guide his returning,
　　　　　　to keep him from losing his way in the labyrinthine turnings,
　　　　　　unharmed, the victor retraced his steps to safety and glory.
　　　　　　　　Must I leave my song's first theme for its tragic continuation?
105　　　Ariadnê fled the face of her father, the arms of her sister,
　　　　　　the anxious tears of her mother, who wept for the girl she was losing—
　　　　　　above all these she treasured the honeyed endearments of Theseus.

Catullus 64 76–120

82. . . . *one should die.* In Catullus' version Theseus goes as substitute for all the youths.　90. *Golgi* . . .
Idalia. Towns in Cyprus.　100. *Taurus.* The high mountain range in southern Anatolia, modern
Turkey. But there is also a pun: Latin *taurus* = "bull."

The eloping Theseus and Ariadnê sailed to the island of Naxos, sometimes
called Dia. Theseus, disgusted by Ariadnê's treachery to her father, abandoned her
and returned to Athens:

[52]　　　From Dia's wave-beaten shore Ariadnê looks out on the ocean,
　　　　　　watching the flight of Theseus with all his swift-running vessels.
　　　　　　Passion tortures her heart. She cannot believe what she sees,
55　　　　for only a moment ago she had shaken off treacherous slumber,
　　　　　　to find herself wretched, abandoned, alone on a desolate shore.
　　　　　　　　Theseus, his eye on the weather, urges his men at the oars,
　　　　　　forgetful of poor Ariadnê. Embarrassed, he tries to speed homeward,
　　　　　　leaving his empty promises blowing like scraps in a tempest.

60   Minos' daughter wades out till the seaweed swirls at her ankles,
         watching with horror-struck eyes, the form of a graven Bacchante.
     Waves of trouble, as savage as those of the sea, fall crashing upon her.
     The wind has blown the soft head-scarf free of her soft yellow hair.
     Lost is the silken blouse that covered her milk-white bosom.
65   No more did a thin-woven girdle encircle her swelling breasts.
     All her beautiful clothing was tumbled about by the waves,
     swirling around by her ankles. But she gave it never a thought.
     Stunned by her lot, to Theseus she directed heart, mind, and soul.

CATULLUS 64 52–70

Catullus gives a vivid portrait of the betrayed and love-stricken Ariadnê loudly
lamenting her fate. She ends by cursing Theseus in what she is sure is her last
breath. Catullus then narrates Theseus' tragic return to Athens and Ariadnê's unexpected rescue by Dionysus (see Perspective 11.1).

Many versions report that, before returning to Athens, Theseus stopped on the
island of Delos, which was, with Delphi, the greatest sanctuary of Apollo in classical
times. There in the temple he dedicated a statue of Aphrodite that Ariadnê had
given him. He and the youths and maidens he rescued danced a complicated dance
in a circle that mimicked the turns of the Labyrinth, called the crane dance, actually performed in classical times in festivals on the island.

DAEDALUS AND ICARUS

Minos was enraged when he learned of Theseus' escape and his daughter's treachery. In revenge, he imprisoned Daedalus and his son **Icarus** (**ik**-a-rus), born to a
Cretan slave girl, inside the Labyrinth that Daedalus had himself built. He sealed
off every escape. Daedalus had started the chain of disaster, first constructing the
wooden cow for Pasiphaë, then devising the trick of the clue. Ovid tells the story
of Daedalus' escape twice, once in the *Metamorphoses* and again in the *Ars amatoria*.
Here is the version from the *Ars amatoria*, which Ovid introduces in order to make
the point that as Daedalus was unrestrainable and made wings to fly, so is Cupid
unrestrainable too, the troublesome winged spirit of sexual desire:

[25]   "Mercy," Daedalus begged, "O Minos, justest of mortals!
           Grant that the land of my fathers receive my ashes as well!
       Envious Fate has forced me to live far off from my homeland.
           Back in my homeland, I pray, allow me to finish my days.
       At least let my boy return, though return is denied to his father.
30   Or pity the father's fate, though you grudge return to the son."
       Such was his prayer, and he might have added additional reasons.
           All would have been in vain. Minos denied his request.
       Daedalus had to agree, but thought, "Just what, pray, is lacking?
           All that I need I have, plus the wits to put it to use . . ."
35   Adversity sharpens the mind. Would anyone think that a human
           could follow the path of a bird, soaring on wings to the sky?

PERSPECTIVE 17.2

PICASSO'S *MINOTAUROMACHIA*

Pablo Picasso, a versatile explorer of many fields of art, was prolific and influential throughout his long life (1881–1973). Although Spanish-born, he lived mostly in France, leader of the so-called School of Paris. Picasso drew imaginatively on Greek art in his monumental nudes and monsters, and the Minotaur was a favorite mythical symbol for his own artistic fecundity, imagination, and brutal sexual vitality, and for these qualities in all of us. In a dreamlike print called *Minotauromachia* of 1935 (Perspective Figure 17.2), alluding to a series of prints of bullfights by his predecessor Goya called *Tauromachia*, Picasso lets free the symbol-making power of the unconscious mind to present a complex image of danger, fear, cruelty, hurt, hope, and opposition.

On the left a man in a loincloth climbs a ladder while looking over the scene. In a darkened room to his right are two women with doves, the bird of peace. They look down at a candle held by a small girl, who clutches a bouquet. Between the girl

PERSPECTIVE FIGURE 17.2 Pablo Picasso (Spanish, 1881–1973), *Minotauromachia,* 1935, etching.   (Réunion des Musées Nationaux / Art Resource, New York)

and the Minotaur leaps a mare, whose entrails, ripped out, spew onto the ground. Across the mare lies a female matador, evidently wounded. With his left hand the Minotaur touches her extended hand, which holds an executioner's sword. At first glance, the Minotaur appears to be holding the sword, or he is covering a wound in his shoulder; in fact, he hoists a large sack on his back. With his right arm he shields his eyes, as if in terror from the candle's light. In the distance, between the Minotaur's knee and the horse's tail, sails a ship on a peaceful sea.

The Minotaur is evil but may not see well, and he is frightened by the light in the hand of the innocent girl, who reminds us of Ariadnê in the Greek story; there she holds the life-saving clue of thread. Theseus killed the monster, but here the man on the ladder, shown like Christ taken down from the cross, with a Christ-like face, flees away. The women of peace, with their doves, look down, dispassionate and uninvolved, as spectators watch a bullfight, where horses really are gouged by the bull's horns. Everything in this scene is topsy-turvy and contradictory: The matador is a woman, the bull is half-man, the child is unafraid, the hero is in flight, the women of peace sit in darkness, the Minotaur has a burden to bear.

The symbols in Picasso's etching are like terrifying images in a dream, hinting at meaning but never revealing it. The artist owes a good deal to his Spanish background, evoking emotions that surround the bullfight. He owes still more to a revolutionary social, intellectual, and artistic movement important in the early twentieth century called surrealism, "beyond the real," which rejected the authority of the conscious mind and the science that served it. That was half the picture. The other half was the dark, dream-time world of raw desire and raw impulse, the source of all artistic inspiration and probably of life itself.

Picasso designed the first cover to a famous surrealist publication, called appropriately *Minotaure* (in French), showing a heroic Minotaur holding out a defiant dagger. He often painted bulls. The best-known example is in his painting *Guernica,* inspired by the German saturation bombing of the small Basque town of Guernica on April 26, 1937. The beast, Minotaur or bull, could be evil, but it was also the ocean of power and thrilling force that gives life meaning and makes art possible. The bull was Picasso himself, as the artist often claimed. Biographers of Picasso have identified real people behind the female characters in *Minotauromachia,* although even they, in the surrealist vision, have become symbols of unspeakable things we can acknowledge and draw pictures of, but never really understand.

> Daedalus picked out feathers, the weightless oars of the eagle,
>   and bound a delicate frame with slender fetters of thread.
> The lower stubs he anchored in wax, made soft by the fire,
> 40   and thus he finished his careful work on the new device.
> Icarus stroked the wax and the gleaming feathers it bonded,
>   not yet aware that the pinions were made for his slender arms.
> "This is our ship of hope, in which we shall fly to our country,"
>   Daedalus smiled at the boy, "by which we can baffle the king.
> 45 Minos has blocked all our ways, but he cannot cut off the heaven.
>   The wings my wits have invented will waft us wherever we will.

But remember this: Do not climb toward Helicê, maid of Tegea,°
  or Orion with flashing sword, Boötes'° trustworthy friend.
Soar on the wings I have given along the way that I lead you.
50 Your only task is to follow in safety your trustworthy guide.
Consider: Too close to the sun, too high in the fiery heaven,
  the wax on which we depend will droop and melt in the heat.
But if we direct our wings too low, down by the threatening waters,
  our dampened feathers will droop, heavy with salt-laden spray.
55 So fly on between the two, bewaring the squall and the tempest;
  wherever a gentle breeze directs you, that way in safety set sail."
So he instructs his son while fitting the wings to his shoulders,
  showing the boy their use, like a bird with a fledgling chick.
Next he adjusts the pinions on his own muscular torso,
60 carefully poising himself to embark on the perilous trip.
Lastly, before taking off, he presses a kiss on the stripling,
  unable to hold back the tears that dampen his trembling cheek.
A knoll arose from the plain (too small to consider a mountain);
  from it the father and son started their ill-fated flight.°
65 Daedalus plied his own wings, but kept his eyes on the boy,
  smoothly gliding along on the line of the course he had laid.
The courage of Icarus mounted with joy at the newly found motion.
  Higher, more rashly he flew, as he mastered the wonderful art.
A fisherman, down below, was casting his bait. He looked upward,
70 gaped at the soaring pair, and hurried off home with his tale.
Samos they saw to their left after passing Naxos and Paros,
  and Delos, island beloved by Apollo, the Clarian god.°
On the right was the island Lebynthos and shaded woody Calymna;
  Astypalaea as well, girded with fish-laden pools.°
75 Then Icarus, overly rash in his adolescent bravado,
  abandoned his father's side and soared up into the sky.
The bindings slacken, the wax gives way as the hot sun grows closer.
  Pull as he will, his wings no longer maintain their grip on the wind.
Shaken by terror, he stares from the upper vaults of the heaven
80 at the rolling sea below, and faints from his gathering fear.
The wax gives way. He thrashes his arms in profitless panic,
  knowing he has no check on his headlong precipitate fall.
"Daddy, Daddy, come help me!" he screams in vain as he tumbles,
  but the livid waves close in and stifle his cry as he falls.

OVID, *Ars amatoria* 2.25–34, 43–92

47. *maid of Tegea*: Helicê was a nymph of Tegea, a town in eastern Arcadia, in the central Peloponnesus. After death Zeus transformed her into the constellation Ursa Major, the Greater Bear, also known as the Big Dipper.   48. *Boötes*: The Wagon Driver, a constellation near Ursa Major but much lower in the heavens.   64. . . . *ill-fated flight*: In Ovid's version they do not seem to be in the labyrinth.   72. *the Clarian god*: Claros was a town in Ionia with a famous oracle of Apollo.   74. . . . *pools*: Samos, Naxos, Paros, Delos, Lebynthos, Calymna, and Astypalaea are islands of the Aegean Sea.

This is an unlikely route for anyone traveling from Crete to Athens, but the poet had to accommodate the story that the Icarian Sea (east and south of Samos) and the island of Icaria, where the body of Icarus was washed ashore, were named for the luckless boy.

The story of Icarus is a mythical illustration of the Greek maxim "Nothing too much," one of the proverbs inscribed over the temple of Apollo at Delphi. Doubtless because overdoing things was a common weakness of the Greeks, their sages enjoyed preaching the Golden Mean, the virtue of going neither too high, nor too low. Aristotle would define virtue as the mean between opposite extremes, so that courage is the middle way between cowardice and foolhardy rashness. Even so Icarus should have followed his father's advice and kept to the middle path.

THE DEATH OF MINOS

Daedalus seems to have given up his plans to land in Attica. He was flying east when Icarus drowned, but now flew west to Sicily, where he took refuge at the court of **Cocalus** (kok-a-lus), king of Camicus (later Agrigento) on the central southern coast of Sicily (Map I, inside front cover). Raging for revenge, Minos sought Daedalus everywhere. He carried a spiral conch shell with him and promised a grand reward to whoever could pass a thread through its windings. Minos well knew that only Daedalus was clever enough to accomplish the feat.

He presently came to the court of Cocalus. Pretending that he could solve the puzzle, Cocalus secretly took the shell to Daedalus. The master craftsman drilled a hole in one end, attached a thread to an ant by a drop of honey, and allowed the ant to draw the thread through the labyrinthine shell (much as Theseus had followed the clue through the windings of the Labyrinth).

When Cocalus presented the shell to Minos, the tyrant knew that he had found his man. He demanded that Cocalus surrender Daedalus. Cocalus agreed, but invited Minos first to join him for dinner. When Minos went to bathe before the feast, Cocalus' daughters filled the tub with boiling water (or pitch) and burned him to death. Of the further adventures and death of Daedalus, nothing is known.

Observations: Archaeology and Cretan Myth

The long island of Crete lay at the intersection of trading routes from all directions: Egypt to the southeast, Cyprus, Phoenicia, and all of Asia Minor to the east, Greece to the north, and Sicily and Italy to the west. Peoples from many different lands had settled in Crete during its long history, bringing their religions, myths, and legends with them. According to modern archaeological research, the principal population, whom we call Minoans, may have come from Anatolia as early as 7000 BC, with a second wave of immigration about 3100 BC.

In the Bronze Age Cretans used several scripts for recording information. The earliest (undeciphered) script was pictorial, found in short pieces on seals and tiny objects. Later these signs seem to have been schematized into the (still undeciphered) Linear A, found on clay tablets and some pottery. Its deciphered successor Linear B recorded Greek: Invading Mycenaean Greeks used it to keep tallies and inventories of commodities.

Minoan power evidently came to an abrupt end about 1450 BC, when palaces all over the island were destroyed by an unknown agency. From this catastrophic

PERSPECTIVE 17.3

BRUEGHEL'S *THE FALL OF ICARUS*

Flemish painter Pieter Brueghel (c. 1525–1569) was fond of combining scenes of daily activity with landscape. In *The Fall of Icarus* (Perspective Figure 17.3), he reduces Ovid's story to an inconspicuous pair of flailing legs (lower right, near the ship).

Most of the canvas is devoted to a fisherman (lower right), a plowman, and a shepherd (center). In Brueghel's ironic version of the story, no one notices the boy's death, as in the folk-saying, "No plow stops for the man who dies."

Modern Anglo-American poet W. H. Auden (1907–1973) was a stretcher-bearer for the Republican Army during the Spanish Civil War (1936–1939), during which took place the bombing of Guernica (see Perspective 17.2). Influenced by his experiences there, he wrote *Musée des Beaux Arts,* "Museum of Fine Arts" (Brussels, Belgium) where Brueghel's painting hangs, to which he refers. Auden speaks of the commonplace nature of suffering:

PERSPECTIVE FIGURE 17.3 Pieter Brueghel the Elder (c. 1525–1569), *Landscape with the Fall of Icarus,* c. 1554–1555, oil on panel.   (Musées Royaux des Beaux-Arts, Brussels; © Scala/Art Resource, New York)

*Musée des Beaux Arts**

About suffering they were never wrong,
The Old Masters: how well they understood
Its human position; how it takes place
While someone else is eating or opening a window or just walking dully along;
How, when the aged are reverently, passionately waiting
For the miraculous birth, there always must be
Children who did not specially want it to happen, skating
On a pond at the edge of the wood:
They never forgot
That even the dreadful martyrdom must run its course
Anyhow in a corner, some untidy spot
Where the dogs go on with their doggy life and the torturer's horse
Scratches its innocent behind on a tree.

In Brueghel's *Icarus,* for example: how everything turns away
Quite leisurely from the disaster: the ploughman may
Have heard the splash, the forsaken cry-,
But for him it was not an important failure; the sun shone
As it had to on the white legs disappearing into the green
Water; and the expensive delicate ship that must have seen
Something amazing, a boy falling out of the sky,
Had somewhere to get to and sailed calmly on.

*From *W. H. Auden: Collected Poems* by W. H. Auden, ed. by Edward Mendelson. Copyright 1940 and renewed 1968 by W. H. Auden. Reprinted by permission of Random House, Inc.

period comes archaeological evidence of ritual cannibalism of children and of human sacrifice, no doubt in an attempt to stave off the impending disaster. Some of the native Minoans escaped to high mountain retreats or fled the island. Scholars once thought that an enormous volcanic explosion on Thera caused the universal destruction (Perspective Figure 1.1), but evidence from tree-ring dating (if it can be trusted) now indicates that the explosion took place about 1630 BC, too early to be the immediate cause of the catastrophe of c. 1450 BC.

After 1450 BC only Cnossus was rebuilt, to be destroyed again by fire about 1400 BC. The third and final destruction occurred c. 1200 BC. The conflagrations that accompanied the second and third destructions accidentally preserved thousands of clay tablets inscribed in Greek in the Linear B writing. Mycenaean Greeks seem to have taken over Cnossus after the earlier destruction of 1450 BC, which they may have caused. We know no details. Nor do we know what caused the second and third destructions of Cnossus in 1400 and 1200 BC—insurrection, perhaps, or internecine struggles among the Mycenaeans themselves. The biblical Philistines, who settled in five cities on the coast of Palestine south of modern Tel Aviv in about 1200 BC, seem to have been Mycenaean Greeks from Crete, although by c. 600 BC they had adopted a Semitic language, as proven by recent inscriptional finds. Palestine takes its name from this Greek people.

In thinking about Cretan myths, and about Crete, we must remember that the Cretan elite before about 1450 BC were Minoans, racially, linguistically, and culturally distinct from the Cretan rulers after 1450 BC, who were Mycenaean Greeks, presumably invaders. Gradually Greek language and culture replaced the indigenous Minoan culture, and Greek is spoken on Crete today, but the influence of the complex older world was profound. We do not have any Minoan myths. We have Greek, especially Athenian, myths about Crete.

Even in the ancient world, intellectuals tried to distinguish historical truth from myth in stories about Crete, and scholars continue today. In the fifth century BC the Athenian writer Thucydides (thu-**sid**-i-dēz), in the introduction to his history of the Peloponnesian War (1.4), argued from mythic accounts that the kingdom of Minos was the first thalassocracy, a political order having "supremacy over the sea." Thucydides was a pioneer in efforts to distinguish myth from history:

> Minos was the first whom we know—granted, only by hearsay—to build a navy. He was able to take control of most of the Aegean Sea, to govern the islands we call the Cyclades, and to start colonies in many of them. First of all, he had to drive out the Carians.° He then set up his own sons as rulers, and, as far as he could, wiped out the pirates, no doubt in the hope that their income would thereafter flow into his own pockets.

Carians: A people of Asia Minor whom Thucydides assumed to have ruled these islands.

The archaeological record behind myths about Crete lay buried until 1899 when the Englishman Arthur Evans, inspired by the German Heinrich Schliemann's discoveries of Troy in Asia Minor and Mycenae on the mainland, purchased with his own funds part of the northern central plain of Crete. There a low mound showed promise of concealing ancient remains. He gradually uncovered the ruins of ancient Cnossus, an enormous palace complex dating from the earliest European civilization, which flourished from about 3100 to 1200 BC (Figure 17.6). It was Evans who applied the term *Minoan* (after the legendary Minos) to this culture and to the people who fashioned it. Since Evans's day, archaeologists have enlarged his excavations at Cnossus and explored many other palace sites on Crete.

From the evidence, the Minoans were a vigorous, pleasure-loving, seafaring people with a taste for vibrant, naturalistic art and elegant, sophisticated living. Their palaces rarely were fortified; they must have had no enemies. Frescoes discovered on the nearby island of Thera, a northern Minoan outpost, show grand flotillas of ships and armed warriors, supporting Thucydides' description of them as the first thalassocracy. In 1992, to the amazement of the scholarly world, Minoan frescoes from about 1600 BC were found in the Nile delta, further testimony to the far-reaching power of this extraordinary people.

The tales of Theseus and the Minotaur and the doings of Daedalus are connected intimately with Athens. Those who trust myth to preserve real history see in these stories a memory of hostilities between Athens and Crete at some time before 1450 BC, when the Cretan thalassocracy could have exerted direct influence on the mainland. We have never understood how the Greeks came to take possession of

FIGURE 17.6 The Bronze Age palace at Cnossus. Sir Arthur Evans reconstructed portions of the ancient labyrinthine palace at Cnossus. In this photo are visible the typical Minoan wooden columns, thicker at the top than at the bottom. The walls were of masonry cushioned by internal wooden beams, to lessen the shock of earthquakes. Behind the reconstructed portion was the central courtyard, where the bull games may have been celebrated.   (Author's photo)

the island, and perhaps the story does preserve a recollection from a time of actual hostilities. We can neither prove nor disprove the thesis.

Most features of the myth certainly belong to a later time. Athenian supremacy in artistic production after about 900 BC must have increased the popularity of stories about a great Athenian artist named Daedalus, and the exploits of Theseus are in large part Athenian propaganda generated in the late sixth and fifth centuries BC (see Chapter 16), when the sea power of Athens grew until it was unrivaled. The Athenians were glad to draw mythical parallels between their own sea empire and that of Minos, especially when such a parallel allowed them to show Theseus defeating the Minoan king in a contest requiring intelligence and bravery.

In addition to possible historical elements, we can occasionally identify Cretan religious practices in the Cretan stories, although interpretations of Cretan religion are difficult. Most scholars agree that the Cretans worshiped a mother-goddess represented as a bare-breasted woman holding serpents (Figure 17.7). Ariadnê, whose name means "the very holy one," may have been a name for this goddess, reduced

FIGURE 17.7 The snake-goddess from a deposit in a sanctuary in the palace at Cnossus, faience, c. 1600 BC. She may be a priestess, who wears a dress with breasts exposed, characteristic of Minoan women, but the odd feline (perhaps a leopard) on her head, the serpents in her hands, and her posture with extended arms suggest that she is the goddess herself.   (Heraklion Museum, Crete; © Giraudon/Art Resource, New York)

in legend to a folklore heroine. Her original function as mother-goddess would be reflected in a cult on Cyprus of Ariadnê Aphrodite, in which a young man would lie down and pretend to give birth. The bull was central to Cretan cult and figured in an acrobatic bull game often illustrated in Minoan art (Figure 17.8). The game was certainly dangerous and may underlie the legend of the man-devouring Minotaur, which means "the bull of Minos," as does, perhaps, the ritual cannibalism for which we have evidence during the period of Crete's collapse. The bull is an embodiment of divine power and in historical religion was the animal of Zeus, to whom the bull was sacrificed in bloody ritual.

FIGURE 17.8 The bull-vaulting fresco from Cnossus. To the right a woman (indicated by her white skin) holds out her arms to receive a man (dark skin) somersaulting over the back of a bull, while a second woman, to the left, takes hold of the horns of the charging bull. All four of the bull's feet are off the ground in a "flying gallop." The naturalistic representation of the animal is characteristic of Cretan art. This perilous game seems to have been celebrated in the large central courtyard of the palace at Cnossus, perhaps the origin of the myth of the Minotaur. (Heraklion Museum, Crete; Marie Manzy/Art Resource, New York)

Other scholars trace the myth of Athenian youths given to the Minotaur to the practice of child-sacrifice in accordance with widespread Near Eastern custom. The bull would represent the Semitic storm-god Baal (**ba**-el, "lord"), often represented as a bull, whose cult is closely related to that of Zeus. Certainly Semites were living on Crete in the Late Bronze Age and even had a port town on the southern coast of the island (at Kommos). Such child-sacrifice is mentioned in the Bible as dedicated to Moloch, probably not a god's name, but simply meaning "king," that is, "the lord."

Another Cretan religious emblem, often found in shrines, was the double ax, which many scholars take to represent the sacrificial tool by which the bull was felled in Cretan cult. A Greek grammarian tells us that the Cretan word for a double-edged ax was *labrys*, so that Labyrinth would mean "place of the double ax," the place of sacrifice, where in legend Athenian youths were fed to the bull-man.

Sexual surrender of a female victim as a substitute for her sacrifice is perhaps reflected in the story of Zeus's possession of Europa in the guise of a bull, and some such ritual may actually have been performed in Minoan Crete, wherein someone wearing a bull's mask had intercourse with a priestess in a ritual context. A similar pattern appears in the tale of Pasiphaë, who couples with the "bull from the sea" sent by Poseidon, in a sense Poseidon himself, lord of the sea, with whom the Minoans had a special relationship. Once, young women were sacrificed to gods; later, as a substitute for their lives, they surrendered their maidenhood in a "sacred marriage" (*hieros gamos*) to a priest or king.

If such a ritual gave rise to the stories of Europa and Pasiphaë, the religious background had long since dropped away by the Greek Classical Period, when the focus fell on Pasiphaë's unseemly lust. Unfortunately, no surviving Greek works from the Classical Period deal with the house of Crete, but we should suspect a humorous origin to principal features of the myth: Pasiphaë, a queen, inside a cow, waiting for the bull to possess her, can only be pornographic or ludicrous and conforms to a Greek stereotype of women as hopelessly lustful and unashamed.

Similar patterns of abhorrent or excessive sexuality characterize the house of Crete in general, also appearing in Ariadnê's willingness to betray family and country to satisfy her passion, in Minos' assault on the Athenian maiden en route to Crete, and in the incestuous love of Pasiphaë's daughter Phaedra for her stepson, Hippolytus (see Chapter 16). Scylla, princess of Megara, although not a member of the house of Crete, is inspired to commit her parallel treachery by lust for Minos. For the Athenians of the fifth century BC, the Cretans had become a type: the lustful, incestuous, violent, tyrannical cousins who live over the hill, who never tell the truth about anything.

The overall pattern of the story belongs to folktale: A wandering hero (Theseus) comes to a strange land (Crete) oppressed by a wicked king (Minos) in league with a man-eating monster demanding human sacrifice (the Minotaur). The daughter of the king (Ariadnê) falls in love with the hero. Assisted by her and a trickster-magician (Daedalus), the hero kills the monster. The wandering hero and princess flee, but the hero, abhorring her treachery, abandons the princess and returns to his home, where he becomes king (Gilgamesh rejected Ishtar, too, for her treacherous nature). The prominence of such standard traditional narrative elements forces us to be extremely cautious in searching for historical events behind the myth.

Some scholars have emphasized how elements in the story also resemble patterns of male initiation into adulthood. In the story:

- Theseus journeys to a far land.
- He overcomes death and a monster.
- He has an amorous adventure.
- He is elevated to the kingship.

In widespread patterns of ritual male initiation, these corresponding elements appear:

- The young initiate is driven from his native town.
- He undergoes mock death and encounters demons from the other world (often in the form of grotesquely masked men).
- He has some form of sexual experience.
- The initiate returns to society with the full privileges of an adult.

In Athens, Theseus was the protective spirit of male initiates. Called *ephebes* ("on the verge of adulthood"), between the ages of eighteen and twenty they underwent a time of stringent testing after which they invoked, in an oath, the model of Theseus' career and were admitted to full citizenship. Such parallels are interesting, but demonstrate the profound difference between myth and ritual: One is a story, with its own internal rules and demands; the other is a pattern of social behavior.

Important in Cretan legend is Daedalus, the trickster-inventor so common in folklore. He invented the tools of carpentry, built the wooden cow for Pasiphaë, designed the Labyrinth, and threaded the conch shell. He is the prototype of the passionate artist, so jealous of his powers that he murdered Perdix, his nephew and only rival, and risked his life to show off by threading the shell. Imprisoned within the maze of his own making, he is the emblem of the artist captivated by his own creation.

Although many explain his origin as a late personification from the common Greek adjective *daidalos*, which means "skillfully made," his name may appear on a Linear B tablet from Cnossus. He is mentioned already in the *Iliad*, where Homer describes the design on a wonderful shield that Hephaestus, Daedalus' divine counterpart, makes for Achilles:

> The god of the brawny arms, displaying the skill of the artist,
> modeled a dancing floor, as Daedalus once did in Cnossus,
> for Ariadnê, the maiden of lovely soft-flowing ringlets.
>
> HOMER, *Iliad* 18.590–592

Greek writers of the Roman Period attributed to Daedalus the invention of realistic sculpture and the construction of many famous buildings, including the Bronze Age conical towers on Sardinia and various temples in Egypt. Early Greek sculpture is still sometimes called "Daedalic."

KEY NAMES AND TERMS

Europa, 450	Labyrinth, 455
Minos, 452	Scylla, 456
Pasiphaë, 453	Icarus, 461
Daedalus, 453	Cocalus, 466
Minotaur, 453	

SOME ADDITIONAL ANCIENT SOURCES

Europa: Apollodorus 3.1.1–2; Homer, *Iliad* 14.321–322; Ovid, *Metamorphoses* 2.836–875; *Minos:* Apollodorus 3.1.1–4, 3.15.1, 3.15.7–8, "Epitome" 1.12–15; *Daedalus:* Apollodorus 3.1.4, 3.15.8, "Epitome" 1.8–15; Ovid, *Metamorphoses* 8.183–262; *Ariadnê:* Homer, *Odyssey* 11.321–325, *Iliad* 18.590–592.

FURTHER READING CHAPTER 17

Chadwick, J., *The Decipherment of Linear B*, 2nd ed. (Cambridge, UK, 1967). Riveting account of the decipherment.

Doumas, Christos G., *Thera, Pompeii of the Ancient Aegean* (London, 1983). Popular description of the volcanic eruption that destroyed Thera, once thought by many (and still thought by some) to have caused the destruction of Minoan civilization.

MacGillivray, Joseph Alexander, *Minotaur: Sir Arthur Evans and the Archaeology of the Minoan Myth* (New York, 2000). The life of Evans, a capsule history of Crete, and Evans's not always scientific reconstruction of the past.

Marinatos, Nanno, *Minoan Kingship and the Solar Goddess* (Chicago, 2011). Original, exciting interpretation of Minoan religious symbols.

Marinatos, S., and M. Hirmer, *Crete and Mycenae* (London, 1960). Lavish illustrations of the archaeological finds on Crete and the mainland, with an excellent text.

Morris, Sarah, *Daidalos and the Origins of Greek Art* (Princeton, NJ, 1992). Thorough study of the myths and origins of Daedalus, tracing him back to Near Eastern prototypes.

Nilsson, Martin P., *Minoan–Mycenaean Religion, and Its Survival in Greek Religion*, 2nd ed. (New York, 1950). Authoritative account by one of the greatest historians of Greek religion.

Pendlebury, J. D. S., *The Archaeology of Crete* (London, 1939; reprinted New York, 1965). A classic description by a distinguished archaeologist.

Robinson, A., *The Man Who Deciphered Linear B: The Story of Michael Ventris* (New York, 2002). Fascinating account of the decipherment and of Ventris' life.

CHAPTER 18

OEDIPUS AND THE MYTHS OF THEBES

> But do not worry about marriage with your mother.
> No end of males has dreamed of sleeping with theirs.
>
> SOPHOCLES, *Oedipus the King* 980–982

THEBES, THE PRINCIPAL CITY of the plain of **Boeotia** (bē-ō-sha), lay on a ridge that divides the plain near the chief land route from the northern Balkans south to Attica and the Peloponnesus (see Map II, Chapter 2). It was a center of power in both the Bronze Age and the Classical Period and a focus for a complex cycle of legends next in importance only to those of Mycenae. The site has been occupied continuously for more than five thousand years. Unfortunately for scholars, the modern town covers the ancient remains and inhibits archaeological exploration. In Thebes "mortal women were the mothers of gods [Dionysus and Heracles]," as Sophocles put it in a surviving fragment, and there men fought the greatest war in Greek legend, except for the Trojan War: the Seven against Thebes. Some of the best known Athenian tragedies describe the myths and legends of this city, taking many of their stories from an epic poem now lost, the *Thebaïs*, "Story of Thebes," attributed (perhaps rightly) to Homer.

THE FOUNDING OF THEBES: CADMUS AND THE DRAGON

The city of Thebes was unique in Greek legend because two separate stories were told of its foundation. One of them begins with the story of Europa, the Phoenician princess who disappeared over the sea on the back of a bull. Her father, Agenor, ordered his sons, including Cadmus, to search for their sister and not to return without her (Chapter 17). They had little hope of success, and the brothers Cilix and Phoenix soon gave up the search and settled permanent colonies to which they gave their own names: Cilicia (in southeast Anatolia) and Phoenicia (the coast of eastern Mediterranean).

Only Cadmus continued the search, but he too was unsuccessful. He went to Delphi, where the Pythia told him to give up—he would never find Europa. Instead, he should follow a cow with special markings and found a city where the cow became exhausted and lay down. Cadmus did as he was told, came to a hill in southern Boeotia, and on it built the city of Thebes.

Wishing to sacrifice the cow to Zeus (or Athena), Cadmus sent companions to a nearby spring, sacred to Ares, to get water for the sacrifice. When they did not return, he went himself and found that a huge serpent, a dragon, had killed his companions. Cadmus defeated the dragon in a great battle (Figure 18.1), then at Athena's suggestion knocked out the dragon's teeth, plowed the ground, and sowed half of the teeth into the furrow. (Athena gave the other half to Aeëtes, king of Colchis, who figures in the legend of Jason; see Chapter 19.)

FIGURE 18.1 Cadmus kills the serpent, Attic wine-mixing bowl, c. 450 BC. Beside the dragon sits Harmonia (probably), future wife of Cadmus. Her father, Ares, stands behind her. The plants behind the serpent indicate the spring. Cadmus holds the pitcher for the sacrificial water in his left hand, while with his other he prepares to stone the serpent. Athena stands beside him. (Image © The Metropolitan Museum of Art/Art Resource, New York)

Up sprang armed men. Cadmus threw stones among them. Thinking they were being attacked, the newborn warriors battled each other until only five remained, the **Sparti**, "sown men," ancestors of the principal aristocratic families of Thebes. (The Sparti had no connection with the famous city of Sparta.) Ovid has fun telling this story of dragon combat and miraculous birth:

[3] In panic over Europa, her father gave orders to Cadmus,
      her brother, to search her out and warned him not to return
5   until he had found the girl, lest he be banished forever—
      a virtuous order, indeed, but one of a criminal harshness.
      He hunted on land and sea, but in vain. What mortal can ever
      hope to detect the concealments and wiles of an amorous Zeus?
      Abandoning hope of return to the home and wrath of his father,
10   he wandered to Apollo's oracular shrine and humbly inquired
      where he might find a land to live in thereafter.
      "In the lonesome plains nearby," replied the prophet of Phoebus,
      "an ownerless heifer will meet you, one never yoked to a plow.
      Follow wherever she goes, and where she lies down in a meadow,
15   there you must build your walls and name the region Boeotia."°
      Hardly had Cadmus gone down from the lofty Castalian precinct°
      than he noticed an ambling heifer, bearing no scars of a yoke.
      Checking his eager advance, he followed her wandering footsteps,
      silently breathing his thanks to Phoebus, who showed him the way.
20   He passed the stream of Cephisus and left the Panopean plain.°
      The animal halted and, raising her face and beautiful horns
      to heaven above, gave tongue, filling the air with her bellows.
      Coyly turning her head to be sure that the comrades of Cadmus
      were following close behind, she yawned and stretched herself out
25   full length in the juicy grass. Cadmus gave thanks to the gods,
      kissing the new found land, saluting its mountains and plains.
      Then he made ready to bring to Zeus an ample offering.
      He ordered his servants forth, to hunt for a living fountain
      of water fit to employ in the rites which the god had demanded.°
30   An ancient grove lay nearby, untouched by hatchet or billhook.
      Within, half-hidden in bushes, there opened the mouth of a cavern,
      a shallow arch, supported by rough fitted pieces of stone.
      Plenty of water poured out—but within lurked a terrible serpent,
      sacred to Mars. Its head bore a crest resplendent and golden.
35   Fire shot from its eyes. Its body was puffy with venom.
      Triple its tongue, and triple the line of its snapping teeth.
      The Tyrian wanderers° entered the grove with ill-omened footsteps,
      but when they lowered a cauldron down in the babbling water,
      it uttered a brassy sound. From within the depths of the cavern,

15. *Boeotia:* "Cowland"; compare Io's crossing of the *Bos*porus, "cow-crossing." 16. *Castalian precinct:* At Delphi, near where the Pythia gave oracles, was a famous spring called Castalia. 20. *Panopean plain:* North of Delphi. It is watered by the river Cephisus, which rises on Mount Parnassus, flows north and east across the Panopean plain, and ends in a lake north of Thebes. There is another Cephisus in Attica. 29. *demanded:* Apollo, in his instructions to Cadmus. 37. *Tyrian wanderers:* From the major Phoenician settlement of Tyre.

40   the livid dragon protruded its head with terrible hissing.
The water-jars fell from their hands, their faces whitened in terror,
chattering fear seized upon them, they stood there, weakened and trembling.
The serpent twisted his coils in rolling knotted gyrations,
enormous, unpredictable, changing his way in a flash.

45   Raising full half his bulk to the sighing breezes of heaven
(as big, compared with the sky, as the space dividing the Bears°),
he glanced at the grove. A few of the men were scrambling for weapons,
more had elected to run, but, paralyzed, most could do neither.
Some he snapped up in his jaws, some in a crushing embrace.

50   The rest he slew with a murderous blast of his poisonous breath.
　　The sun, now high in his course, had shrunk the shadows of noonday,
when Cadmus began to wonder at the long delay of his comrades
and set out to follow their track. For defense he put on a hide
ripped from a lion's body; for offense, he carried a javelin

55   and lance with a bright steel head. But no such armor could equal
the hero's stoutness of heart as he entered the forest of death.
Before him on every side lay the grisly remains of his comrades;
behind them, the bloated victor, licking with bloodstained tongue
the mangled remains of his victims, Cadmus' own partners and friends.

60   　　"You fell giving proof of devotion, loyal right to the end.
I will either avenge your passing or be your partner in death."
So he swore. Then, poising a boulder as big as a millstone,
he let it fly with a force to shake the ramparts of heaven.
The serpent ignored the blow. His scales behaved as a breastplate

65   and his black adamantine hide brushed off the ponderous missile.
But toughness did him no good against the thrust of a javelin
piercing the joints of his spine and the tender entrails beneath.
The reptile twisted his anguished head to gaze at the torment,
to bite at the clinging spear (thus enlarging its sad laceration),

70   at last to wrench it away from entrails mangled and screaming,
but even then the point broke off and clung to his backbone.
　　This newly experienced pain only roused the furious creature.
The swollen veins of its throat poured pale and venomous foam
that drooled from its lethal jaws. The rattling noise of its scales

75   reechoed over the earth, and the Stygian° breath of its nostrils
(such as it still retained) polluted the breezes of heaven.
One moment it twisted its coils in vast and tangled contortions,
then suddenly stretched itself up, as straight as the mast of a ship.
Now it charged like a torrent swollen with rain in the springtime,

80   leveling acres of forest by its weight and momentum alone.
　　Slowly the son of Agenor retreated before the beast's fury,
checking its forward rush with his buckler, the skin of a lion,
and blocking its jaws with the outthrust iron tip of his javelin.
Baffled, the dragon's mouth came clamping down on the spearhead,

85   doing no harm at all, but the poisonous blood from its palate
went spattering over the soil, staining the grass with its venom.
The wound was only a trifle. The dragon recoiled for a moment,
drawing its head from danger, by yielding preventing more damage

46. *Bears:* The constellations Ursa Major and Minor.　75. *Stygian:* From Styx, a river in the underworld.

while keeping the son of Agenor from following up his advantage.
90   Now Cadmus took the offensive, driving the steel at its gullet.
Back, back he drove the monster, whose retreat was finally halted
by the trunk of an ancient oak, which blocked all hope of escaping.
Cadmus' javelin flew, transfixing the neck and the oak tree.
The tree bent under its weight and creaked as the tail of the dragon
95   thrashed at its trunk, while the monster vainly struggled with death.
       Amazed by his enemy's bulk, the victor regarded his victim,
till roused by the sound of a voice—whose or whence, he had no idea.
But hear it he certainly did. "What, son of Agenor, still viewing
the snake you have killed? Still alive, in the form of a serpent,
100   you too will become an object of the wondering gazes of men."°
       Shaken with fear and amazement, bereft of poise and of color,
his hair all abristle in terror, Cadmus stood fixed to the spot.
But see! A divine protectress came gliding down from the heavens,
no other than Pallas Athena. She told him to dig up a furrow
105   and bury the teeth of the dragon as seed for a new generation.
The hero did as she told him. As soon as a furrow was finished,
he scattered the teeth in the earth as seed of a new race of humans.
Faster than eyes could believe, the plowland began to crack open,
and the first keen tips of spears rose up from the soil of the furrow.
110   Then came the headgear of soldiers, nodding with colorful crests.
Shoulders and chests emerged and stout arms brandishing weapons.
At last a whole army had grown, of bellicose shield-bearing soldiers:
As when the curtain is lifted at the end of a play in the theater,°
the figures painted upon it at first show only their faces,
115   then, in their leisurely rising, the rest of the body emerges,
till firm-set feet appear at the lower edge of the curtain.
       Alarmed at the sudden appearance of the packed and menacing host,
Cadmus felt for a weapon. "Don't draw it!" cried one of the soldiers
newly born of the earth. "Don't meddle in other folk's quarrels!"
120   At that he thrust with his sword at a neighboring son of the earth,
then fell with a crash at the blow of a javelin thrown from afar—
whose owner did not survive the man he delivered to Hades,
but breathed out the last of his breath, drawn but a moment before.
So the whole regiment perished in crazy internecine struggle.
125   For a moment turned into brothers, each fell by his brother's stroke.
Strong young men that they were, they lived for only a moment.
Soaking their mother's breast in blood, they groaned, then they died.
Five of them only were left. At the warning of Pallas Athena,
Echion, one of their number, had thrown aside all his weapons,
130   giving and asking for peace, which the other four had accepted.
These were the only supporters to stand by Sidonian° Cadmus
in founding the city ordained by Phoebus Apollo's instructions.

OVID, *Metamorphoses* 3.3–130

---

100. . . . *gazes of men:* A prediction of Cadmus' ultimate fate, to be turned into a serpent.   113. *the-ater:* The Greek theater had no curtain. Ovid's Roman theater had one, often painted, which during the action lay rolled up at the front edge of the stage. At the end of a play it was raised to conceal the stage.   131. *Sidonian:* Sidon was another city of Phoenicia.

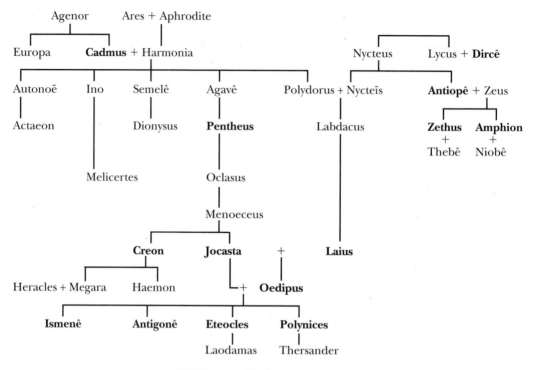

CHART 18.1 The House of Cadmus

Cadmus was forced to serve Ares for eight years in penance for the dragon he had killed. Once purified, he married Harmonia, daughter of the adulterous liaison between Ares and Aphrodite (Chart 18.1). Their wedding was one of the two most splendid in Greek myth, the other being that of Peleus and Thetis, the parents of Achilles. The gods attended, sat in golden chairs, and sang songs of praise. For a wedding gift, Aphrodite gave Harmonia a necklace made by Hephaestus himself and a robe that gave its owner royal dignity—objects of wondrous beauty, but a jinx to whoever owned them in later generations. The children of this union were to lead accursed lives: Ino killed her own children, then jumped off a cliff; a thunderbolt burned Semelê to a crisp; Agavê ripped her son Pentheus to bits; his own hounds devoured Autonoë's son, Actaeon.

Grown old and worn out with grief, Cadmus and Harmonia left Thebes. They wandered across the Pindus range to Illyria (modern Albania). There, too, Cadmus became king. Enfeebled by age, he and his wife were changed into serpents (as predicted) and sent by Zeus to live forever in the Elysian Fields.

The Twins Amphion and Zethus

After Cadmus abdicated, his grandson Pentheus ruled briefly until coming to his gruesome end (Chapter 11). The dynastic succession then becomes confused. A separate tradition reports that an otherwise unknown son of Cadmus, Polydorus, came to the throne, married a woman named Nycteïs ("daughter of Nycteus"), and then on his deathbed turned over the kingship to his wife's father, Nycteus. In the meanwhile, Zeus seduced Nycteus' other daughter, **Antiopê (an-tī-o-pē)**, who became pregnant. Shamed by her misdeed, Nycteus drove Antiopê from Thebes. Antiopê took refuge with a king of Sicyon in the Peloponnesus and married him.

Still stinging from shame because of his daughter's behavior, Nycteus commanded his brother, **Lycus (lī-kus)**, to avenge the family honor, then killed himself. Lycus followed Nycteus' command and mounted a campaign against Sicyon, killed the king, took Antiopê prisoner, and dragged her back to Thebes. On the way, Antiopê crawled into the bushes on Mount Cithaeron and gave birth to the twins she was carrying. Antiopê then returned to her Uncle Lycus, leaving the twins behind. A shepherd found and raised the twins, named **Amphion (am-fī-on) and Zethus (ze-thus)**.

When Lycus returned to Thebes, he handed Antiopê over to his wife, **Dircê (dir-sē)**, who conceived a particular hatred for the girl, locked her in a cell, and tortured her daily. Eventually Antiopê escaped her tormenter, fled to the mountains, and by chance took refuge in the hut of Amphion and Zethus! Somehow they recognized her and, eager for revenge, tracked down Dircê, a follower of Dionysus, while she was reveling in the mountains. They tied her to a wild bull, which dragged her to death. They threw Dircê's body into a spring, ever after called Dircê, and then killed Lycus (Figure 18.2).

While growing up, Amphion and Zethus showed themselves to be utterly opposite in nature. Zethus was a cattle breeder, a man of action and practical affairs. Naturally he scorned Amphion, who spent his time practicing the lyre. But the power of art proved itself when the two brothers set out to build the walls of Thebes, a story that describes, in effect, a second foundation: The first thing one does in founding a city is to build protective walls. Zethus struggled to carry mighty stones on his back, while Amphion merely strummed on his instrument; the stones rose miraculously from the ground and settled into place.

Despite their different dispositions, the brothers were friendly and ruled together in harmony. Zethus married Thebê, after whom Thebes was named. Amphion married Niobê, daughter of Tantalus, whose seven sons and seven daughters Apollo and Artemis killed (Chapter 9).

Observations: The Two Foundings of Thebes

Most Greek colonies had stories of their foundations and the reasons for them, but the old mainland cities lacked such traditions. Why, then, should Thebes alone have two foundation stories? No one has answered this question persuasively, but it is clear that separate traditions have come together in a clumsy way.

The founding by Cadmus is an adaptation of the ancient Near Eastern myth of creation as dragon combat, whose basic pattern we examined in the story of Marduk's victory over Tiamat (Chapter 4). Cadmus kills a terrible dragon that guards a spring, as Marduk kills the monster Tiamat who represents

FIGURE 18.2 Death of Lycus and Dircê, on a South Italian wine-mixing bowl, c. 380 BC.
A play of Euripides seems to have inspired the scene. To the left a bull tramples Dircê
to death. Within a cave, the entrance framed by two trees bent together, Amphion
and Zethus are killing Lycus, while Antiopê flees to the right. Hermes hovers in the
air outside the cave, prophesying that the twins will have a glorious future and that
Dircê will be changed into a spring. From above hangs a panther skin, a dedication
to Dionysus (Dircê was a Bacchante).   (Antikenmuseum, Staatliche Museen, Berlin; Bildarchiv
Preußischer Kulturbesitz/Art Resource, New York)

the primeval chaotic waters from which the world emerged. To judge from a
fifth-century BC vase (see Figure 18.1), the dragon-slayer's prize was a woman,
Harmonia, as often in the folktale pattern (unless the woman represents the
spirit of the spring). Cadmus' sowing of the dragon's teeth is a variation on
another Near Eastern motif whereby the first men grow from the earth like
plants. A tale that once described the origin of the world, then, has been "downgraded" to describe the origin of a city. Because the story is Eastern in origin, it
is plausible that immigrants from the East brought it to Greece. Many have wondered whether Phoenicians really did found a colony at Thebes in the Bronze
Age, perhaps bringing with them the ancient Mesopotamian myth of creation,
an explanation supported by Cadmus' name. Semitic in origin, it means "man
from the East."

In 1963 an astonishing hoard of forty-two Mesopotamian cylinder seals (compare Figure 3.7) was found in a basement in the modern town of Thebes on the

site of the ancient city, the largest collection of cylinder seals found anywhere. The hoard seemed to provide hard evidence of Eastern settlement. But the seals come from different Eastern lands and belong to different periods, the earliest from about 2500 BC and the latest from about 1300 BC. Apparently a precious collection, which may have been acquired as trade or booty, was kept in a single box when the Mycenaean palace was burned about 1250 BC. No other evidence for Eastern presence has been found in Thebes.

According to a strong tradition, Cadmus brought with him from the East something more precious than seals, called *phoinikeia grammata,* "Phoenician scratchings," or *kadmeia,* "Cadmeian things," early Greek terms for the alphabet. However, this story cannot be accurate because the Greek alphabet (which includes signs for the vowels) was invented on the basis of the Phoenician syllabic writing about 800 BC. Cadmus belongs sometime in the middle of the Bronze Age, perhaps about 1600 BC, according to mythical chronology based on counting generations. Mythographers knew that the model for the Greek alphabet came from Phoenicia, and they knew that Cadmus was a Phoenician; therefore, they reasoned, Cadmus must have introduced the alphabet.

The story of Cadmus and the dragon is a recasting of an ancient Eastern story, but that of Amphion and Zethus is a folktale of the tribulations and eventual triumph of magical twins. Foundlings lost in the world, the twins discover in the nick of time who they really are, just as the "wicked stepmother" Dircê is about to kill their mother. Deservedly, Dircê dies instead. Although on the best of terms, Amphion and Zethus are opposites in temperament, embodying a common contrast between the man of action (Zethus) and the man of intellect (Amphion), the man "good at doing" and the man "good at talking." Rome, too, had a tale about twins who founded the city, also opposites, but hating one another bitterly.

Why Thebes should have attracted two stories to explain its origins, one a creation myth and the other a folktale, we cannot say, but the Thebans reconciled the stories by saying that Cadmus had founded the higher city on the Acropolis, called the *Cadmeia* (cad-**mē**-a), whereas Amphion and Zethus had walled the lower city, named after Thebê, the wife of Zethus. The mighty walls of Thebes had seven gates, about which many tales were told.

OEDIPUS THE KING

Later mythographers tried to tie the story of Amphion and Zethus to the House of Cadmus by reporting that Polydorus and Nycteïs had a son named Labdacus (**lab-da-kus**), whose son **Laius** (**lā-**yus) fled from the confusion in Thebes to take refuge in the court of Pelops in the province of Elis in the northwestern Peloponnesus. There Laius fell in love with Chrysippus, son of Pelops, lured him out of town, and raped him. For this outrage, and violation of *xenia,* Pelops cursed Laius. Laius fled back to Thebes, where Amphion and Zethus by now had died, leaving the throne unoccupied. The Thebans acclaimed him as king, and he married **Jocasta** (jō-**kas**-ta), a descendant of the Sparti. Learning from an oracle that he would die at the hands of his own son, Laius avoided intercourse with his wife, until one night he got drunk and slept with her anyway.

When Jocasta bore a son, Laius ordered that the child be exposed to die. He pinned together the child's feet with an iron pin (to keep the ghost from walking) and delivered the baby to a shepherd, with orders to leave him on the slopes of Mount Cithaeron near Thebes. However, the shepherd took pity on the child and gave it to a friend, a visitor from Corinth, who delivered the child to Polybus, king of Corinth. His childless wife, Meropê, took the child as her own, calling him Oedipus (ē-di-pus, e-di-pus), "swollen foot."

When Oedipus was grown, some of his envious age mates taunted him about his birth, saying he was adopted. Because neither Polybus nor Meropê would tell him anything about this, Oedipus went to Delphi to discover the truth. Instead of answering his question, the Pythia told him that he was going to kill his father and marry his mother. Thinking that the oracle referred to Polybus and Meropê, the horrified Oedipus vowed never to return to Corinth and instead headed east toward Thebes. At a fork in the road, a man in a chariot came from the other direction and drove him off it. A wheel of the chariot grazed his foot, and the man in the car struck him with his goad. In a rage, Oedipus leaped onto the chariot and killed the driver, his passenger, and all his retainers, except for one who got away.

Before long, Oedipus came to Thebes, a city in turmoil. The Sphinx, a daughter of Typhoeus, had perched on a nearby hill and was devouring the Thebans one by one. Before killing her victims, the monster posed a riddle. There are many versions, but the best known is: "What goes on four legs in the morning, two at midday, and three in the evening?" Only when the riddle was answered would the Thebans be delivered from the Sphinx.

Laius, the king, had gone to Delphi to find out what to do about the situation. When his brother-in-law Creon, who ruled in his absence, heard that bandits had killed Laius, he decreed that whoever solved the riddle and freed the city could marry the queen and become the next king. There seems to have been a rule in dynastic succession at the time of the formation of these stories that the surviving female member of the royal line could not rule, but determined through marriage who did. (In Homer's *Odyssey*, the suitor who marries Penelopê will take the place of Odysseus as king; see Chapter 22.)

Quick-witted Oedipus quickly saw that the answer to the riddle was "a human" (= Greek *anthrôpos*). Infants crawl on all fours in the morning of their lives, walk on two legs in their maturity, and in the evening of their lives, old and doddering, they walk with the aid of a cane. The Sphinx was so chagrined at the successful answer that she threw herself from the cliff and was dashed on the rocks below (Figure 18.3).

Thus Oedipus married the queen and became the king. They had two sons, **Polynices** (pol-i-nīs-ēz) and **Eteocles** (e-tē-o-klēz), and two daughters, **Antigonê** (an-**tig**-o-nē) and **Ismenê** (is-**mēn**-ê). Our earliest literary source for the story of Oedipus is the *Odyssey*, in which Odysseus, reviewing the ghosts of famous dead women, sees the mother of Oedipus, whom Homer calls Epicastê:

FIGURE 18.3 Oedipus and the Sphinx, interior of an Attic drinking cup, c. 490 BC. Oedipus is shown as a mature man, fully bearded, wearing a traveler's broad-brimmed hat, his left hand poised pensively beneath his chin, his traveler's staff between his legs. He ponders the riddle of the Sphinx, a winged lion with a woman's head perched on an Ionic column. Similar actual monuments survive as grave markers. (Museo Etrusco Gregoriano, Vatican Museums; Scala/Art Resource, New York)

[1271]   Oedipus' mother I saw, Epicastê, famous in story.
She, all unknowing, committed a great and terrible crime,
marriage to her own son. Unknowing, he murdered his father,
then married Epicastê. The gods set the pair as a warning.
[1275]   In lovely Thebê he reigned, over all the people of Cadmus,
but suffered terrible things: She suspended a noose from a rafter
and sank through the iron gate of the house of implacable Hades.
Clutched by remorse, she bequeathed a legacy grim and undying,
vengeance his mother's Furies relentlessly wreaked on her son.

HOMER, *Odyssey* 11.1271–1280

Sophocles' *Oedipus the King* (c. 430 BC), the most famous play from the ancient world, treats this shocking story in clinical detail and seems to have added certain important elements. When the play opens, a plague has fallen on the city. Oedipus, decisive in action and attentive to the needs of his people, learns from an oracle that *miasma*, blood-pollution, has caused the plague. In the confusion surrounding the Sphinx, no one had taken time to find the murderer of King Laius. The ghost of King Laius was angry and vengeful. Anxious to find the murderer and lift the plague, Oedipus declares before the Theban people:

[224]   To all Cadmeans do I now proclaim: *picks of his body*

225   If any of you knows by whom your king,
       Laius the son of Labdacus, was slain,
       I order him to tell me all he knows.
       But if he fear that punishment may fall
       upon himself, let him remain assured
230   of amnesty: He shall remove the charge
       by going into exile, nothing more.
       Or, if he knows some wandering stranger guilty
       of murder, let him speak the truth, to win
       a great reward, and public thanks as well.
235   But if you still keep silent, fearing for yourself,
       or for some friend, hear what I next propose.
       I order that no dweller in the country
       of which I hold the power and the throne,
       shall shelter the killer, whoever he may be;
240   shall say a word to him; shall be his partner
       in prayer, in sacrifice, in purification.
       Rather, all men must thrust him from their homes,

PERSPECTIVE 18.1

GUSTAVE MOREAU'S *OEDIPUS AND THE SPHINX*

The Romantic painters of the late nineteenth century were interested in the myth of Oedipus, and here Gustave Moreau (1826–1898), sometimes called a symbolist, sets the scene in a melancholy and darkened wilderness (Perspective Figure 18.1). Whereas the Greek story celebrated the power of the intellect to unravel the mysteries of irrational nature, Moreau was interested in the struggle of male against female. He sets the scene in the mountains outside Thebes, the city faintly visible in the distance through the cleft. At the forefront of the picture are the decaying feet and hands of someone who succumbed to her power. To the right a serpent winds around a column on top of which is an antique pot with griffins' heads. With her rear claws she supports herself against Oedipus' inner thighs, emphasizing the sexual threat, while she keeps herself aloft with beating wings. Incongruously, she wears an enticing belt around her hips. Her lovely eyes look into his, but his determined lip and fierce counter-gaze show that he will be triumphant over her seduction. Moreau said that in this painting, his best-known work, he wanted to show moral idealism pitted against sensual desire.

Victory over mind & control over the body

PERSPECTIVE FIGURE 18.1 Gustave Moreau (1826–1898), *Oedipus and the Sphinx,* 1864, oil on canvas.   (Image © The Metropolitan Museum of Art/Art Resource, New York)

for he pollutes us all. That this is true
the Pythian oracle has just assured me.
245   Taking these measures, then, I prove myself
true ally of both murdered man and god.
I hereby call down curses on this killer—
be he alone, or helped in secret crime—
that horribly, as he is horrible,
250   he may drag out his wretched unblessed days.
This too I pray: Though he be of my house,

if I learn of it, and let him still remain,
may I receive the curse I have laid on others.
    All this I order, on my own behalf,
255   at the god's orders, for our country's sake,
which now lies helpless, blasted, cursed by the gods.

SOPHOCLES, *Oedipus the King* 224–254

Thus Oedipus curses himself, for the man he killed at the crossroads was his own father, and the woman he married was his mother, as the oracle foretold.

The rest of Sophocles' play is a masterful unfolding of how these terrible events have come to pass. On Creon's advice, Oedipus summons the blind seer Tiresias, who at first refuses to speak. When Oedipus accuses him of conspiring with Creon, Tiresias blurts out the fantastic truth. Oedipus dismisses it and turns against Creon, suspecting him of aiming at a tyranny. But he is shaken by the close correspondence between the death of Laius, as now for the first time described to him, and his own experience at the crossroads.

A messenger arrives to inform Oedipus that his "father," Polybus, has died, and that he may now succeed to the throne of Corinth. Although grieving for Polybus, Oedipus is relieved at seeming proof that oracles are fallible. He did not kill his father after all! Still, he will not return to Corinth for fear that he might somehow marry his mother. He need not worry on that account, the messenger points out, for he is, in fact, not the son of Polybus and Meropê. The messenger himself had given Oedipus, a foundling, to the king to raise, having received him from a shepherd on Mount Cithaeron. Whose son, then, is he?

Jocasta realizes the truth and leaves the stage. Oedipus summons an old shepherd, the only survivor of the massacre at the crossroads, who by an extraordinary coincidence was the very man to whom Laius once delivered his infant son. Out of pity, the shepherd admits, he gave the child to the Corinthian messenger (another surprising coincidence). Oedipus too sees the truth and rushes into the palace. A messenger reports the fate of the queen and what Oedipus did when he found her:

[1241]   Frenzied, Jocasta rushed inside the house
and flung herself upon her marriage bed,
tearing her hair with both her maddened hands.
She slammed and locked the door by which she entered
1245   and cried the name of Laius, long since dead,
joined with his son's, the man he once begat,
at whose hand he then died, leaving her to mother
sons by her son—a dreadful generation.
How then she died I cannot know or tell,
1250   for Oedipus burst in with cries of torment,
preventing us from gazing on her end—
for all our eyes were riveted on him,
as he stormed about and clamored for his sword.
    "Where will I find the wife who is no wife?"
1255   he cried, "the womb twice plowed, twice harvested,
of me at first, then later of my children?"
Some demon, doubtless, pointed out the way

to the frenzied king. It surely was none of us.
With madman's scream he charged the double doors,
1260   led by some guiding instinct, dragged the bolts
from out their pair of sockets, and ran inside.
   Hanged from the ceiling, there we saw his wife
choked by a twisted rope around her neck.
Oedipus saw her too. With a piteous groan
1265   he loosed the throttling noose around her throat.
Her huddled body lay there at his feet,
a piteous sight, but worse was still to come.
He ripped the golden pins from off her robe,
raised them on high, and plunged them in his eyes,
1270   choking out words of anguish, such as these:
   "Never again will these eyes ever watch
me doing or suffering what I have done or suffered!
Only in inner darkness of my soul
shall I hereafter see the faces of those
1275   I never should have seen,° and I shall fail
to see the missing forms, for which I longed."°
   Cursing himself, again, and yet again,
he slashed his eyes, and with each frenzied blow
the bleeding sockets dripped down on his beard,
1280   until at the last the drops became a storm.

SOPHOCLES, *Oedipus the King* 1241–1279

1275. *have seen:* That is, his mother as his wife and his children as his brothers and sisters.   1276. *for which I longed:* His father and mother as parents rather than as victims.

Gore streaming from his face, Oedipus returns to the stage and begs to be sent into exile. The actual blinding is not seen by the audience—this would be too horrible— but is only described. (**For a complete translation of** *Oedipus the King*, **go to http://bacchicstage.wordpress.com/sophocles/oedipus-rex/**)

Observations: Heroic Sufferer for Truth or Victim of Curiosity?

Oedipus usually is called a "hero," although he does not have divine parents, and we need not look far to uncover familiar elements: his unusual birth, his journey and mission to save the world from monsters, the deadly dangers of woman, and his mysterious death (see following). Yet the tenor of the story, focused on parricide and incest, and the difference between being and seeming, is very different from that of stories about Gilgamesh, Heracles, and Theseus. We saw long ago, in the stories Hesiod tells, how the organizers of the cosmos, Cronus and Zeus, overthrew their own fathers to establish the world, while Gaea, mother of the world, both favored and opposed its development (she begot Typhoeus). Here, in heroic legend, Oedipus kills his father but creates only chaos, whereas the ambiguity of the female receives a surprising twist by being represented within the context of the human family: As Jocasta gave birth to Oedipus, so does her protective love destroy him.

Homer knows the essential elements of the story, that Oedipus killed his father and married his mother, but says nothing about Oedipus' self-blinding. There are many variants to the story in other writers, but this detail may be Sophocles' own invention, appealing to the Athenian popular taste for horror and gore in drama. The shocking act also allows Oedipus to commit one truly free act of will. In Homer, Oedipus continues as king after the truth is discovered; in Sophocles' play, he becomes a homeless outcast.

Aristotle saw in Sophocles' *Oedipus the King* the perfect tragedy because in it the two essential elements in a good plot come together at the same moment: *anagnorisis*, "recognition," when the identity of someone previously unknown or in disguise is revealed, and *peripeteia*, "a turning around," when the leading actor's fortunes turn from good to bad. When Oedipus recognizes who the murderer really is— himself—his fortunes turn around. He ceases to be the wise king and savior of his people, revealed as a terrible criminal who violated the deepest taboos.

Earlier critics saw in Oedipus a victim of fate, a plaything of the gods. Whatever he did to escape the oracle's prediction only brought him closer to its fulfillment. But foreknowledge is not fate. Although Jesus predicted to Peter that "Before the cock crows, you will deny me three times," Peter might have chosen otherwise. Nor do the gods compel Oedipus to *know* what he has done. The power of the story lies in the spectacle of a man who freely chooses to pursue the truth, regardless of the consequences, even his own ruin.

Oedipus is a man of high intelligence who solved the riddle of the Sphinx and saved the city. He is a man of action who bravely defended himself at the crossroads and slew his vile attacker. To our minds, conditioned by two thousand years of Christian ethics, he may appear violent, hasty, and overconfident, but the Greeks would not have seen that. In their eyes Oedipus had no moral fault, He wants to obey the will of the gods, as conveyed through Apollo's instructions, and he wants to save his people. He applies his intelligence and courage to discover the truth for the benefit of the citizens he serves. He freely chooses a course leading to his own undeserved destruction.

Everything that seems true about Oedipus is false, the reverse of appearance. He is a study in the contrast between being and appearance. He thinks he is Corinthian, but he is Theban born. He deciphers riddles, but cannot solve, until too late, the riddle of his own life. In the city he is judge of right and wrong, but he is the worst of criminals. He is a seer who is blind. He is Thebes' savior and its destroyer. The greatest of men, comparable even to the gods, and an honored ruler, he is also the worst of men, worse than an animal, a despised outcast and object of horror. He who raised himself to the highest rank is reduced to the lowest.

Here is a riddle: What can walk on four legs, two legs, and three legs? The answer: "a human being." Here is another: How can someone be brother to his own children and husband to his mother? The answer: "Oedipus." Oedipus solves both riddles, first saving Thebes, then destroying himself. He is savior, who thwarted the Sphinx, and destroyer, who brought the plague. Both riddles have the same answer. Oedipus embodies the restless human intelligence, always prying and never letting go until every riddle is solved. That the truth should be horrible is typically Greek in its pessimism. When the riddle is solved, human happiness is shown to be based on illusion.

The power of Greek myth is never clearer than in the story of Oedipus. Writers who knew little about ancient culture have attempted to elucidate it (see Chapter 25). The old myth has generated new myths, as such interpretations have been called, stories sprung from the human imagination that themselves require interpretation. Yet Sophocles' play, a literary masterwork, remains as mysterious and disturbing as ever.

THE SEVEN AGAINST THEBES

Oedipus' sons, Eteocles and Polynices, agreed to share the power of the city equally, one ruling one year, the other the next. But after the first year, Eteocles, whose name means "true glory," refused to relinquish the power and drove his brother Polynices, "filled with contention," from the city. Polynices fled to Argos, taking with him the heirloom necklace and robe the gods gave to Harmonia at her wedding many generations before.

Adrastus, king of Argos, had learned from an oracle that he must "yoke his daughters to a boar and a lion." He did not understand the meaning of this saying, until one night he heard a clamor in the forecourt of the palace. He rushed out and discovered Polynices fighting with Tydeus (**tī-dūs**), son of Oeneus. Tydeus, half-brother to Deianira (see Chapter 15) and to Meleager (see Chapter 19), had been exiled for homicide from Calydon in Aetolia, north across the Corinthian Gulf in the southwestern mainland. When Adrastus saw that one man had a boar painted on his shield, the other a lion, he realized the meaning of the oracle, settled the quarrel, and married them to his daughters. Furthermore, he agreed to restore Polynices and Tydeus to their kingdoms. First they would attack Thebes, then Calydon.

Adrastus summoned his chieftains for a great campaign. Among the heroes came **Amphiaraüs** (am-fi-a-rā-us), a seer of the first rank. Amphiaraüs, realizing that all the leaders except Adrastus were going to die, argued vehemently against the war. His efforts were in vain for this reason: To patch up a bitter quarrel with Amphiaraüs, Adrastus had arranged for his sister **Eriphylê** (e-ri-**fīl**-ē) to marry Amphiaraüs, on condition that in any future quarrel between the two men, Eriphylê would decide the issue. Polynices, learning of the agreement, offered Eriphylê the necklace of Harmonia if she would decide the dispute about the coming war in Adrastus' (and his own) favor (Figure 18.4). Amphiaraüs could only accept the decision, but before leaving he told his son Alcmaeon to avenge his inevitable death.

The army set out. Seven heroes led the way: Adrastus, Amphiaraüs, Capaneus (**kap**-a-nūs), and Hippomedon, all from the leading houses of Argos; Polynices from Thebes; Tydeus from Calydon; and Parthenopeus from Arcadia.

Oedipus at Colonus

In his last play, produced in the year after his death in 406 BC, Sophocles describes the last days of Oedipus. The army of the Seven is marching toward Thebes when the blind old man, exiled from Thebes and accompanied only by his daughter

FIGURE 18.4 Polynices bribes Eriphylê with the necklace of Harmonia, on an Attic wine jug, c. 450 BC. Leaning on his staff, he has removed the necklace from a box and dangles it toward her extended hand. Shamelessly, Eriphylê meets his eyes. The iconography is the same as when a young man propositions a prostitute.   (Musée du Louvre, Paris; Réunion des Musées Nationaux / Art Resource, New York)

Antigonê, wanders into the Grove of the Furies at Colonus, a beautiful suburb of Athens. The chorus of inhabitants, learning who he is, warns the accursed Oedipus to leave the grove so that it will not be polluted, and they send for Theseus, king of Athens. Meanwhile, Ismenê, daughter of Oedipus and sister of Antigonê, arrives to tell about the quarrel of the brothers and to report that Delphi has declared that whichever city possesses the bones of Oedipus cannot be captured. For this reason, Creon (representing Eteocles) and Polynices both appear and try to abduct Oedipus, until Theseus orders them to leave. But first the furious Oedipus curses his own sons Polynices and his brother Eteocles and predicts their fate:

[1354]   And as for you [Polynices], you hypocrite, you who once
1355   held the same power that now your brother holds,
        you drove me out from Thebes—me, your own father!—
        and made me homeless, reducing me to tatters
        that now draw forth your tears, now that you too
        have met with misery as great as mine.
1360   I shall not weep for wrongs so long ago,
        whose burden I must bear until I die,
        never forgetting you, my parricide.
        You are the man who brought me down to this.
        You drove me out. By your doing I must wander,
1365   begging my daily bread from kindly strangers.
        These girls [Antigonê and Ismenê] I raised, but not to be my nurses.
        Except for them, I would by now be dead,
        for all you cared. They alone preserve me,
        they stand beside me, sharing all my troubles.
1370   They are true men, not women. As for you,
        the pair of you are bastards, not my sons.
            The gods are watching with unhurried gaze,
        not as they will if all those troops of yours
        march against Thebes. There is no way
1375   for you to take the city. Before that day appears
        you will lie weltering in your blood—your brother too.
        That curse I laid on the pair of you long ago,°
        that curse I now call back to my defense,
        that you two may learn that parents must be honored,
1380   blind though your father was, begetting such as you.
        Your sisters here committed no such sin.
        Not prayers, not royal state, will help you now
        against my curse, if ancient justice still
        sits in her place beside the laws of Zeus.
1385   Get out! I spit you out and I disown you!
        Get out, you slimy thing, bearing this added curse
        which I pronounce: Your spear will never
        win back your homeland, nor will you ever again
        see hill-girt Argos. By your own brother's hand
1390   your doom will come, his from you whom he banished.
        This is my curse. To bring it all to pass
        I invoke Hell's awful dark to call you home.
        I summon the Furies, worshiped in this spot,
        and with them Warfare, who stirred up your hate.
1395   Now you have heard me, go. Tell all the Thebans,
        tell all your loyal allies, "this is the legacy
        that Oedipus is leaving to his sons."

                    SOPHOCLES, *Oedipus at Colonus* 1354–1396

1377. *long ago:* Apparently Oedipus refers to the time when his sons failed to give him the best cut
of meat from a sacrifice, and he cursed them for it (reported in the lost epic the *Thebaïs*).

Peals of thunder warn Oedipus that his time has come. He withdraws into the grove, blesses his daughters, and in the presence of Theseus disappears, forever an invisible spirit in the grove of Colonus, protecting Athens from her enemies. **(For the complete *Oedipus at Colonus*, go to http://bacchicstage.wordpress.com/ sophocles/oedipus-at-colonos/)**

The Battle Before Thebes

The army arrived before seven-gated Thebes. There were seven heroes on either side, an Argive to attack each gate, a Theban to defend. Aeschylus in his play *Seven against Thebes* (467 BC) places in a messenger's mouth a description of the arrival of the Argive army and the Thebans' response:

[39]   Eteocles, most noble ruler of the Cadmeans,
40   fresh from the army I am here with news,
    myself an eyewitness of all that happened.
       Seven aggressive officers met together
    to cut a bull's throat over an iron shield.
    They dipped their hands into the blood he [Polynices] shed
45   and swore an oath, by Ares and his mother,°
    and by the bloodthirsty Panic of the Battle:
    "Either we level Thebes and plunder its ruins,
    or we die and soak this whole land in our blood."
       With their own hands they decked Adrastus' chariot
50   with tokens for their parents back at home,
    stained with their tears. None spoke a word of grief,
    for their iron spirits burned to show their fire,
    hot as the wrath of lions glaring for war.
    No hesitation makes this news grow cold.
55   I left them just as they were drawing lots,
    allowing chance to say against which gate
    each officer should lead his faithful band.
       Since things stand thus, select your bravest men
    and station them at the mouths of the city gates,
60   each with his own command, to guard the town.
    Hurry! for the well-trained Argive army
    is advancing fast. Its dust makes dark the air.
    The foam of its panting horses stains the ground.
    You, like a skilled sea-captain, have the duty
65   to batten down the city's hatches before
    the hurricane of war can roll her over.
    Just so this war on land screams down upon us.
    Let him whose mind is quickest now take charge.

AESCHYLUS, *Seven against Thebes* 39–65

45. *his mother.* Hera.

Tiresias informed the Thebans that they could win the war only if Creon's son, Menoeceus, was sacrificed to Ares. Overhearing this, Menoeceus willingly killed himself outside one of the gates. The Theban heroes drew lots for the gates they would defend. Eteocles found himself paired with his brother, Polynices.

When the battle began, the Thebans were soon driven back into the city. Capaneus threw a ladder against the walls and climbed to the top, exclaiming that not even Zeus could stop him: A thunderbolt from the clear sky cast him to his death. Soon the battle turned against the Argives. The Theban hero Melanippus dueled with Tydeus, and each was mortally wounded. Athena loved Tydeus and begged Zeus to give her a potion of immortality, but Amphiaraüs, who hated Tydeus for favoring the war, knew her intention. He quickly cut off Melanippus' head and brought it to the dying, vengeful Tydeus, who broke open his enemy's skull and scooped out the brains. He was eating them just when Athena arrived at his side. In disgust she dashed the life-giving potion to the ground. So brave Tydeus died (but see Figure 18.5). Amphiaraüs fled in his chariot, but as he was about to be speared in the back, Zeus (who loves seers) caused the ground to open and swallow him alive. In classical times the hero gave oracles from an underground shrine near where he disappeared.

FIGURE 18.5 Tydeus kills Ismenê caught in the act of intercourse, on a Corinthian water jar, c. 560 BC. The figures are labeled. We do not have classical literary versions for all myths represented in Greek art, but the story is mentioned by a certain Sallustius, a Neoplatonic writer of the fourth century AD. Tydeus, one of the Seven against Thebes, naked and with sword drawn, is about to kill Ismenê, who reclines half-naked on a couch. In the stories we have examined she is still alive much later. Periclymenus, one of the Theban heroes who fought the Seven, also naked, runs away, apparently caught in the act with Ismenê. On the far left is a mounted youth, labeled Clytus, otherwise unknown.   (Musée du Louvre, Paris; Réunion des Musées Nationaux / Art Resource, New York)

Eteocles and Polynices met in hand-to-hand combat and each killed the other, as their father predicted. A passage describing the duel comes from Euripides' *Phoenician Women* (about 411 BC), so called from the chorus of Phoenician women, uninvolved in the action, who have stopped in Thebes on their way to Delphi. The *Phoenician Women* is the longest extant Greek tragedy and recounts the entire Theban saga:

[1359]   Girding their bodies in shining brazen armor,
1360   the pair of sons of poor old Oedipus
marched out and halted in the no-man's land
between the armies, each ready to display
in single combat his prowess with the spear.
    Facing toward Argos, Polynices prayed,
1365   "My lady Hera—mine, since I wed the daughter
of King Adrastus, and dwell within your land—
grant me my wish, that I may kill my brother,
and soak my hand as victor in his blood."
A shameful gift he asked—his brother's murder.
1370   Many an eye shed tears at this mad jest of fate,
as furtive eye met furtive eye of neighbor.
    Turned to the house of golden-shielded Pallas,
Eteocles begged this: "O child of Zeus,
control my audacious spear, that it may fly
1375   straight from this hand into my brother's heart,
and waste the man who came to waste my city."
    The trumpet-blast of the Tyrrhenian horn°
burst on our ears, a blood-red call to battle.
They ran a dreadful race straight toward each other
1380   and clashed like savage boars whetting their teeth,
the white foam slavering down to soak their chins.
Each hurled his spear, then ducked behind his shield,
from which the other's harmless dart would glance.
Whenever either noticed the other's eye
1385   peeping above his shield's rim, he stabbed out,
hoping to get in first with his deadly point.
But both were skillful at dodging the other,
and thus their brandished spears did them no good.
Indeed, from fear their friends might suffer damage,
1390   the watchers sweated more than did the actors.
    A stone beneath Eteocles' foot
rolled as he stepped. He kicked it to the side,
and for a moment lost the shield's defense
for his bare shank. Polynices darted forward,
1395   glanced at the mark thus offered to his spear,
and drove the point clear through his brother's calf,
while all the Argive army jumped and cheered.
But Eteocles, though wounded, saw that his brother
in his eagerness had left a shoulder bare.

1377. *Tyrrhenian horn:* A horn of Etruscan manufacture.

1400   He hurled his lance clean through his brother's breast.
       The Cadmeans' hearts leaped up—but the point broke off.
       Now weaponless, he staggered back a pace,
       picked up a rock and threw it at Polynices,
       snapping his spear in half. On equal terms
1405   once more, but empty-handed, they faced each other.
            Each took his sword in hand and charged the other.
       Their shields collided with a brazen clang.
       Back, forth, they struggled, fighting hand to hand.
       Eteocles remembered a Thessalian gambit,
1410   something he learned while traveling in that land.
       He took one backward step onto his left foot,
       keeping his eye fixed on his brother's belly,
       then swung with his whole weight onto his right.
       The sword transfixed the side of Polynices
1415   and stuck between his lower vertebrae.
       The poor man fell, contorting ribs and belly,
       coughing his life out in spouts of crimson blood.
            Eteocles, convinced that he was winning—
       nay, that he had already won—the battle,
1420   dropping his sword to earth, began to strip
       his brother's armor. Intent on that alone
       he took no thought for guarding his own safety,
       an oversight that killed him. For Polynices,
       though gasping out his last tormented breath,
1425   still clutched his sword, and painfully, feebly
       (for he himself had been the first to fall),
       managed to thrust it through his brother's vitals.
            So side by side the brothers fell to earth,
       one by the other. Thus they shared the realm.

EURIPIDES, *Phoenician Women* 1359–1424

Only Adrastus escaped in his chariot drawn by the magical horse Arion (a-rī-on), begotten of the union of Poseidon and Demeter. **(For a translation of Aeschylus' *Seven Against Thebes*, go to http://bacchicstage.wordpress.com/aeschylus-2/ seven-against-thebes/; for a translation of Euripides' *The Suppliants*, go to http:// bacchicstage.wordpress.com/euripides/suppliant-women/)**

SOPHOCLES' *ANTIGONÊ*

What happened after the battle is the subject of Sophocles' *Antigonê,* his best-known play after *Oedipus the King.* In nineteenth-century Europe many critics considered this play to be the finest literary creation of all time. Creon, now the king, has cast out the corpses of the attackers, including Polynices, to rot on the Theban plain. No one is to give them proper burial. Death will be the punishment for anyone who defies the edict. Still, Antigonê is determined to bury Polynices. She declares her intention to Ismenê, who cannot believe that Antigonê plans to defy the king's decree. Certainly *she* will not break the law. Antigonê insists that her own first duty is to family and to ancient custom. Her duty to the state and its capricious decrees comes far behind.

When Creon, cast as a political strongman (a type all-too-familiar to Sophocles' democratic audience), learns that someone has cast a handful of dust on the corpse, he immediately suspects a political conspiracy. He is astonished when guards drag Antigonê before him as the culprit, a *parthenos* and member of his own family, engaged to marry his son Haemon (**hē**-mon). True to his vision of the *polis* and its rights that transcend the archaic emotional attachments of the family, he condemns her to death, as she fully deserves:

[441]   *Creon*   You there, with eyes fixed on the ground for shame,
          do you admit this, or deny your guilt?
          Antigonê   I admit it proudly; this I don't deny.
          Creon   Then tell me this, and keep your story short:
445   Did you know that my decree forbade the deed?
          Antigonê   Like everyone else, I knew. Just what did you expect?
          Creon   But still you dared to flout the city's law?
          Antigonê   I did indeed. That law was not prescribed by Zeus,
          nor are such rules laid down for us by Justice,
450   who works with even those dark gods below.
          I cannot think your law could have such force
          that you, mere man, could negate the unwritten
          inviolable statutes of the gods.
          They are not of today or yesterday,
455   but live forever. None knows when they were given.
          I do not so fear one man's selfish plans
          that I would pay the price the gods demand
          from those who break their laws. Of course I knew,
          even without your edict: I must die.
460   If I die before my time, so much the better.
          Whoever lives in endless pain, like me,
          must surely take death as the greatest prize.
          I am not worried at my own destruction,
          but—leave my brother's rotting corpse unburied?
465   That is a thing that really gives me pause.
          In your eyes I'm a fool, but—just perhaps—
          the fool is he who charges me with folly . . .
          Creon   Remember, to be too rigid risks collapse.
          Iron, if smelted in too hot a furnace,
470   may snap and shatter. I have seen fiery horses
          tamed by a tiny bit. Pride has no place
          in slaves obeying what their neighbors order.
          This woman knew quite well what she was doing
          then, when she broke the law's express command,
475   and now she glories in the things she's done!
          I am no man. That name belongs to her,
          if she can act thus, and get off unharmed.

SOPHOCLES, *Antigonê* 441–478

Haemon pleads that his father yield, but Creon will not and in anger threatens even Haemon with death, so overriding is the obligation of the leader of the *polis* to uphold the public interest and enforce the public law. Creon sends Antigonê to a cave to be buried alive. Like Persephonê, she will be the bride of Death.

Tiresias reports horrid omens in the city and warns Creon to retract his harsh decree. At last relenting, the king goes to the cave to release Antigonê. When he arrives, he finds Haemon clinging to Antigonê's corpse: She has hanged herself. Maddened with anger and grief, Haemon draws his sword and lunges at his father, misses, then buries the blade in his own chest. Creon hurries back to the palace. His wife, hearing of Haemon's suicide, has killed herself as well. "Lead me away. I've been hasty and foolish," Creon concludes, but softens his responsibility by adding, "Savage Fate has ruled my course." (**For the complete *Antigonê* of Sophocles, go to http://bacchicstage.wordpress.com/sophocles/antigone/**)

Observations: Revenge of the *Parthenos*

Sophocles' fine drama manages to express all the principal conflicts in the human condition: between women and men, old and young, state and family, the living and the dead, humans and gods. Such conflicts can never be resolved, but only dealt with, and the characters in this play deal with them very badly.

The story takes place at several levels. First, the political level: Viewers side with Antigonê, who touches the audience with her fire and righteous indignation, whereas Creon repels with his insistence on abstract law and the rights of society. Although head of the state, to the contemporary Athenian Creon is transparent as the sort of tyrant ("I am the law!") against which the Athenian democracy struggled. In history, such a man was Pisistratus and his sons of the sixth century BC, whose power violence overthrew. The danger was always great that one man would gain enough personal power to be a king, to end the power of the Athenian *dêmos*, the body of adult male warriors. Civil authority in Athens had almost within memory become transcendent over the family, yet the family remained the basis of society. Its obligations were entirely real. Antigonê's voice, which opposes Creon, is the "voice of the people," what everybody wants. A conservative, she advocates the old ways of family right against the modern authority of the state. The family's obligation was to bury its own dead or they would be the first to suffer from an offended ghost. No decree was going to change that.

But if the people's voice is heard, how can progress be made? And if the people's voice is drowned, where is freedom? Antigonê is ferocious in her knowledge that she is right and, like all vigilantes, she is proud to take the law into her own hands. Creon, by contrast, advocates civic law supported by a community united through common economic and political interests that transcend the ties of blood. A progressive, he scorns the primitive religious commandments that justify Antigonê's actions and also justify human sacrifice and cannibalism and other forms of bestial behavior. By forcing Creon to kill her, Antigonê, although weak, female, and a child, places in jeopardy all that Creon stands for. With his impulsive and artificial laws of the *polis,* Creon must gain his power from those he rules, and he has lost their confidence.

Second, there is a philosophical level to the play. Contemporary debate was heated over the conflict between the laws of custom (*nomos*), from which Creon derives his authority, and the laws of nature (*physis*), from which Antigonê derives hers. Although against the *nomos* that allows a state to preserve its own interests, it is *physis,* "natural," to bury one's brother, and Antigonê gains courage from the gods, who will justify her in the other world.

Third, the play is a study in the power of the untamed female. Creon constantly expresses conflict with Antigonê in these terms. She, the female, is determining the action, acting on the male, while he, the male, is being acted upon. Antigonê, still a *parthenos,* is untamed by the marriage prepared for her, and no power on earth can stop her destructive force—not law, family, persuasion, or threat. Alone and unaided she unravels the state. An indignant and emotional girl, more suicidal than unafraid of death, she ruins Creon, the man of tyrannical reason. Even today the state is almost helpless against fanatical individuals prepared to die for traditional views.

THE EPIGONI

While Oedipus' family destroyed itself at Thebes, Adrastus escaped to Athens and took refuge at the Altar of Mercy. Theseus took pity on him and his dead companions and led an expedition against the Thebans, who would not allow the Argives to bury their dead, an act celebrated again and again by Athenian politicians proud of their city's righteous mythical past. Evadnê, wife of Capaneus, threw herself on her husband's funeral pyre and was burned alive (there is no other example in Greek myth).

Ten years later the sons of the original seven, called the **Epigoni** (e-**pig**-o-nī), "descendants," organized a second expedition. Eriphylê was bribed again, now with the robe of Harmonia, which had fallen into the hands of Polynices' son, Thersander. She persuaded her son by Amphiaraüs, named Alcmeon, to go on the campaign, too. The ruler of Thebes was now Laodamas, son of Eteocles. On the advice of Tiresias, the Thebans fled by night. Tiresias himself died on the way (at last), but Laodamas survived to lead his people to Illyria (roughly, modern Albania). The Epigoni took the city and sacked it. Ten years earlier, Amphiaraüs had ordered his son by Eriphylê, Alcmeon, to kill his mother for sending him to his death with the Seven. Encouraged by the Delphic oracle, after the war Alcmeon now carried out his father's orders. Driven insane by the matricide and polluted by *miasma,* he was later ambushed and murdered.

KEY NAMES AND TERMS

Boeotia, 475

Sparti, 477

Antiopê, 481

Amphion, 481

Zethus, 481

Dircê, 481

Laius, 483

Jocasta, 483

Oedipus, 484

Polynices, 484

Eteocles, 484

Antigonê, 484

Ismenê, 484

Adrastus, 491

Amphiaraüs, 491

Eriphylê, 491

Epigoni, 500

SOME ADDITIONAL ANCIENT SOURCES

Cadmus: Apollodorus 3.4.1–2, 3.5.2, 3.5.4; Herodotus 2.49, 4.147; he is a character in Euripides' *Bacchae* and often mentioned in his *Phoenician Women*. *Amphion and Zethus:* Apollodorus 3.5.6–6; Ovid, *Metamorphoses* 6.146–312. *Oedipus:* The Roman Seneca wrote a play *Oedipus* that has survived, and he appears prominently at the end of Euripides' *Phoenician Women*; Apollodorus 3.5.7–9; Aeschylus, *Seven against Thebes* 742–1084. *Antigonê:* Important in the (possibly spurious) ending of Aeschylus' *Seven against Thebes*; almost unknown outside the Attic tragedies on the Oedipus theme and outside later writers, like the Roman Seneca, who imitated them. *Seven against Thebes:* The subject of a long poem by the Roman Statius (AD 45–96), the *Thebaid*.

FURTHER READING CHAPTER 18

Edmunds, Lowell, *Oedipus: The Ancient Legend and Its Later Analogues* (Baltimore, MD, 1985). Collects all the ancient variants of this myth and later examples of similar stories.

Edwards, Ruth B., *Kadmos the Phoenician: A Study in Greek Legends and the Mycenaean Age* (Amsterdam, 1979). Thorough review of the myth: its origins, relations with Eastern sources, and general conclusions about the value of Greek legend for the study of the Bronze Age.

Knox, Bernard, *The Heroic Temper: Studies in Sophoclean Tragedy* (Berkeley, CA, 1964). Good overall study, with emphasis on character.

Steiner, George, *Antigones* (New York, 1981). Reviews treatments of the story of Antigonê throughout European literature.

CHAPTER 19

JASON AND THE MYTHS OF IOLCUS AND CALYDON

No ship has ever come near these moving rocks and escaped them,
for waves of the sea and fiery blasts bring them all to destruction.
Their timbers swirl to and fro with the rotting bones of the sailors.
One vessel alone has sailed through, the *Argo,* famous in story,
sailing over the sea on her way to the land of Aeëtes.
And surely she would have foundered, striking these terrible rocks,
but Hera let her go safely for the sake of Jason, her favorite.

HOMER, *Odyssey* 12.66–72

THESSALY, THE WIDEST PLAIN in Greece, was the northernmost mainland outpost of the Hellenes before colonization in the Archaic Period carried them further north on the mainland and across foreign seas (Map XIII, inside back cover). In Homer's tale of the Trojan War Thessaly was best known as the birthplace of Achilles. Later it was backward socially but famed for its horses and horse-breeders. The Peneus (pe-nē-us) River flows through Thessaly, issuing as a torrent from the steep Pindus range, the backbone of Greece. The river later pours forth into the sea through a spectacular landscape famed in ancient poetry as the lovely sylvan Vale of Tempê (after which is named Tempe, Arizona). Beyond the low mountains at the south-eastern edge of the plain lies the Gulf of Pagasae (**pag**-a-sē), formed by the embracing arm of a scimitar-shaped, forested, and mountainous peninsula called Magnesia. The highest peak of Magnesia is Mount Pelion, original haunt of the centaur Chiron.

At Pelion's foot lay the Bronze Age city of **IOLCUS** (i-**ol**-kus), a name corrupted into that of the modern harbor town of Volos. Although the modern town covers most of the ancient ruins, traces of two Mycenaean palaces have been found there.

From Iolcus, Jason and the Argonauts set forth, a generation before the Trojan War. Homer's *Odyssey*, composed in the eighth century BC, refers to the voyage of the Argonauts as a tale already familiar (see quotation at beginning of chapter). But the most important literary version is the *Argonautica* of **Apollonius** (a-pol-**lōn**-i-us) **of Rhodes** (third century BC), whose account of the voyage we generally follow. Its Hellenistic taste for obscure adventures and refined developments do not always appeal to a modern taste, but reflect the intellectual mood of the international world that came after the conquests of Alexander the Great. Euripides' play *Medea*, from the Classical Period, gives the best-known story of Jason's later years.

PRELUDE TO THE ARGONAUTICA

Phrixus, Hellê, and the Golden Fleece

Jason belonged to the family of the Aeolids (ē-o-lids), descendants of Aeolus (ē-o-lus), eponym of the Aeolians, a tribe of northern and central Greece (Chart 19.1). Aeolus was king of Magnesia, in Thessaly, a son of Hellên and grandson of Deucalion (the Greek Noah) and Pyrrha. He had seven sons, including **Athamas** (**ath**-a-mas), one of the unluckiest men in Greek legend.

When Athamas came of age, he migrated south to Boeotia and became king of the town of Orchomenus on the western shore of the enormous Lake Copais, which

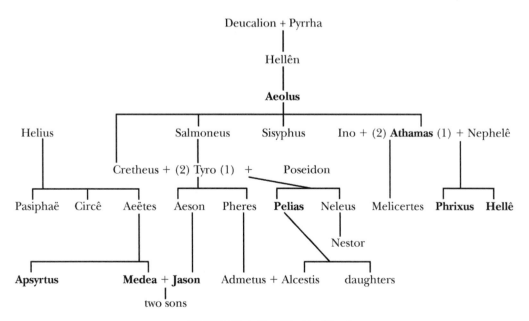

CHART 19.1 The House of Aeolus

dominated the geography of Boeotia until it was drained in the nineteenth century AD. Athamas' first wife, Nephelê (**nef**-e-lē), "cloud," bore him a boy, **Phrixus** (**frik**-sus), and a girl, **Hellê** (**hel**-lē), but eventually Athamas tired of Nephelê and took a second wife, Ino (**ī**-no), daughter of Cadmus of Thebes (she was nurse to Dionysus; Chapter 11).

Ino bore Athamas two sons and was insanely jealous of Phrixus because she feared that he, instead of one of her own children, might inherit the throne. She therefore contrived a plot to destroy her stepchild. She persuaded the local women to parch the seed grain. Of course, the crop failed and famine soon fell on the land, so Athamas—as Ino had foreseen—sent messengers to the oracle at Delphi to ask what to do. Ino intercepted the messengers and bribed them to report that Apollo had replied that, to restore fertility to the land, Athamas must sacrifice his firstborn child, Phrixus. It was all an elaborate plot to murder her stepson.

Athamas sorrowfully led Phrixus to the altar, knife in hand, but just as he was about to stab, a golden ram appeared beside the altar (like the ram in the Bible that appeared as a substitute for Isaac, Genesis 22.13). Athamas stood back while Phrixus and his sister, Hellê, climbed up on the back of the animal. The ram soared away to the east. No one in Greece ever saw the children again.

As the ram passed over the entrance to the straits between the northern Aegean and the Propontis (prō-**pon**-tis), Hellê lost her grip and tumbled to her death in the narrows below, still today called the **Hellespont**, "sea of Hellê." The Propontis is also called the Sea of Marmara (really it is the "lake" between the Aegean Sea and the Black Sea). The straits of the Hellespont are also called the Dardanelles, after the legendary Trojan king Dardanus. The ram flew on and at last alighted in the distant town of **Colchis** (**kol**-chis), in the land of Aea (**ē**-a, "earth") at the eastern end of the Black Sea, perhaps in modern Georgia. There the tyrant **Aeëtes** (ē-**ē**-tēz, "earthman"), ruled. Aeëtes was a son of Helius, the Sun, and brother to Circê (the witch who entertained Odysseus; Chapter 22) and to Pasiphaë, wife of King Minos of Crete.

Phrixus sacrificed the ram to Zeus in gratitude for his deliverance and gave the skin to Aeëtes, who hung it from an oak tree in a grove of Ares. Pelts of sacrificed animals often were hung from trees near the altar. A great dragon protected it, born from the blood of the monster Typhoeus. Aeëtes honored Phrixus by giving him one of his daughters to marry.

Pelias and Aeson

Salmoneus, brother of Athamas, had a daughter named Tyro (**tī**-ro), who became the grandmother of Jason. Odysseus encountered her shade at the pit of blood on the shore of the river Ocean:

[235]   The first of these that I saw was Tyro, daughter of princes,
          child of high-born Salmoneus, as she herself told her story,
          adding that she was the wife of Cretheus, Aeolus' son.
          She had fallen in love with Enipeus, the patron god of a river,
          the fairest of all the waters that run on the face of the earth,

240 and often would wander alone by Enipeus' beautiful current.
  Poseidon, the shaker of earth, disguised himself as the river
  and lay with Tyro in love at the mouth of the eddying stream.
  A mountainous sea-purple wave rose curving over the couple,
  hiding the deathless god who lay with his mortal bride.
245 Then, when the god had ended the bliss of amorous pleasure,
  squeezing her hand in farewell, he gave her a fond loving promise:
   "Dearest of women, goodbye! When the year has finished its cycle,
  you will bear me glorious sons. Gods do not love women in vain.
  Take them for now in your house and bring them up into manhood,
250 but refrain from naming their father—for I indeed am Poseidon,
  the shaker of earth." With that, he dived down into the billows.
  Pregnant indeed, she bore twin children, Pelias and Neleus,
  who both grew up into manhood as mighty henchmen of Zeus.
  Pelias dwelt in Iolcus, land of meadows and cattle,
255 Neleus in sandy Pylos. As for Tyro, queen among women,
  she bore other children to Cretheus, her dear wedded husband:
  Amythaon, lover of horses, and also Pheres and Aeson.

HOMER, Odyssey 11.235–259

  Pelias (**pel**-i-as), son of Tyro, grew up to be arrogant and intolerant. He aspired to supreme power over Thessaly and drove out his brother Neleus (**nē**-lūs), who migrated to Messenia in the southwestern Peloponnesus, there to found the royal dynasty of Pylos. Pelias kept his half-brother Aeson (**ē**-son) imprisoned in the palace of Iolcus, for some reason said to be the rightful heir. Pelias took a wife and fathered several daughters (including Alcestis, who married her cousin Admetus, the son of Pheres, whom Heracles brought back from the dead; Chapter 15).

  Aeson's wife bore a son, but, fearing for the child's life, they spread the rumor that he was stillborn. In fact, they sent him to the wise and civilized Centaur **Chiron** on the slopes of Mount Pelion. Chiron named the boy Jason, taught him the arts of civilized life, and raised him to manhood. In the meantime, Pelias learned from an oracle that a man with one sandal would one day bring about his downfall.

  When Jason grew to maturity, he headed toward Iolcus, determined to claim the throne as his own. He arrived during a festival to Poseidon (Pelias' father). Jason came to a rain-swollen stream by which an old woman sat crouched. Hurried though he was, Jason hoisted her to his shoulders and carried her across, but lost a sandal in the torrent. Having no time to look for it, Jason set down his burden and hastened to the city, not realizing that the old woman was Hera in disguise.

  Hera hated Pelias because he did not honor her, and she had decided to destroy him through the wiles of the beautiful sorceress Medea (me-**dē**-a), daughter of Aeëtes, king of Colchis. Jason's kind act proved to Hera's mind that Jason was a man capable of bringing Medea to Greece, thereby punishing the irreverent Pelias. It was all an exceedingly roundabout plot for the slighted Hera to exact vengeance!

  Pelias was busy at sacrifice when he learned that a one-sandaled man was standing in the marketplace. Straightaway he confronted the stranger: "What would you do if you knew someone was going to kill you, someone over whom you had power?" "Why, I'd send him to recover the Golden Fleece," Jason replied. "I shall do as you suggest," snarled Pelias. "Go!"

THE VOYAGE OF THE *ARGO*

Jason summoned Argus ("swift"; the son of Phrixus, according to some accounts), who constructed the largest ship ever made, which could hold fifty men. Athena inserted into its prow a magic, speaking beam, cut from Zeus's oracular oak at Dodona. The ship was christened *Argo* after its builder.

Jason sent out a call to the best fighting men of his day, who gathered from far and near (Figure 19.1). Among them were Heracles; Orpheus; the Dioscuri (dī-os-**kūr**-ī), Castor and Polydeuces, sons of Zeus and brothers of Helen of Troy; the **Boreads** (**bor**-e-adz), Zetes (**zē**-tēz) and Calaïs (**kāl**-a-is), sons of Boreas (the North Wind); Telamon, father of the Trojan war-hero Ajax, and his brother Peleus (**pē**-lūs), father of Achilles; Meleager, brother of Deianira and hero of the Calydonian Boar Hunt (see below); the brothers Idas and Lynceus; Admetus, who married Alcestis and whom Apollo served for a year as a slave; Augeas, whose stables Heracles cleaned; Tiphys (**tī**-fis), the helmsman; the seer Idmon; and Argus himself. At the last minute, as they were pulling out, Pelias' own son Acastus ran and leapt into the ship, either defying his father or just looking for adventure.

Before their departure, Idmon read the entrails of a sacrificed animal and saw that they would all return safely, except for himself. As the ship pulled out into the harbor, the speaking beam declared its impatience for adventure. Rowing all the harder, the Argonauts rounded Cape Magnesia, turned north along the coast, passed Mount Pelion to the west, then Mount Ossa, then Olympus, then headed due east across the Aegean toward the island of Lemnos (see Map VIII; Map XIII, inside back cover).

FIGURE 19.1 The gathering of the Argonauts (?), on an Athenian wine-mixing bowl, c. 575–550 BC, found in Etruria. Heracles is easily recognized in the middle with his club and lion skin. Athena stands on the left, and the man in between, touching the rim of his shield, is probably Jason. Other heroes lounge about or try out their armor. (Musée du Louvre, Paris; Réunion des Musées Nationaux / Art Resource, New York)

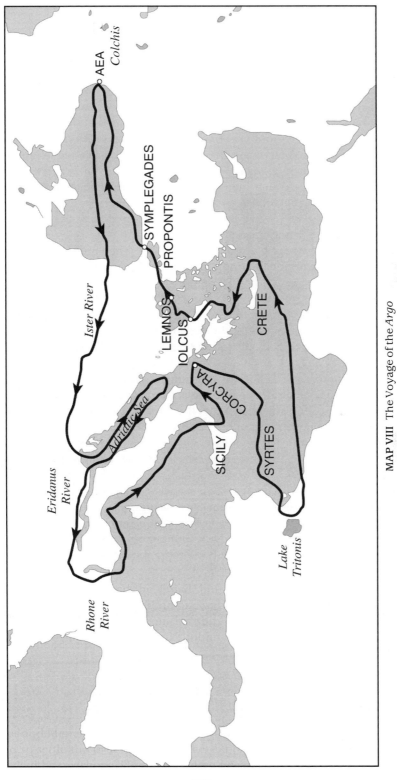

MAP VIII The Voyage of the Argo

Early Adventures

They landed on the man-less island of LEMNOS, populated by sex-starved women who had killed their husbands in a general disagreement the year before. After a year of eager intercourse, from which a new race of Lemnians sprang forth, the Argonauts remembered their purpose and set forth again, past the Trojan headland through the narrow Hellespont into the PROPONTIS, watery anteroom to the Black Sea. Coasting along the south coast, they came to a peninsula attached to the shore by a narrow strip. They put ashore. The local king of the Doliones (dol-i-ō-nēs), Cyzicus (**siz**-i-kus), was a young man of Jason's age, newly married. He welcomed them warmly, for an oracle told him to be kind to strangers.

After nights and days of entertainment, the crew bid good-bye to Cyzicus and put to sea, working their way around the peninsula. Near dusk, a strong headwind caught them, blowing them backward. As night fell, they pulled into the nearest harbor. Immediately the inhabitants attacked them. The fighting was hard. Dawn revealed dead Doliones everywhere: The Greeks had returned unknowingly to the harbor from which they set out! In the midst of the corpses lay Cyzicus, Jason's own spear piercing his throat. After a funeral and effusive apologies, the Argonauts continued east along the south coast of the Propontis.

Heracles, showing off his gigantic strength, pulled so hard on his oar that he snapped it in two. They put in at the coast of Mysia on the south shore of the Propontis for him to cut another. While Heracles looked for a good tree, his boyfriend Hylas, along for the ride, went inland to look for water. Lustful water-nymphs pulled him into a spring. Heracles heard the scream, but found nothing. The boy now lived with the nymphs deep in the pond.

The next morning the Argonauts put to sea, not noticing that Heracles and Hylas were missing. When they discovered their mistake, some wanted to turn back, but Zetes and Calaïs, the winged sons of Boreas, insisted that they go on (for which Heracles later killed them). The Argonauts sailed for a day and a night. They put in to a land ruled by the braggart Amycus (**am**-i-kus), an ugly, brutish man who challenged all passersby to box. He always won, but Polydeuces (brother of Helen and of Castor), although not so big or strong, dodged a killer blow, slipped in behind, and crushed the bones into the brain. The bully Amycus dropped dead (but see Figure 19.2).

Phineus and the Harpies

The Argonauts reached the eastern end of the Propontis. Sailing into the Bosporus, they put ashore where King **Phineus** (**fin**-e-us) was in a terrible plight. He had abused the gift of prophecy received from Apollo. According to some accounts, Phineus is a son of Phoenician Agenor, hence a brother to Cadmus, Phoenix, and Cilix. Apollonius of Rhodes describes the poor man's condition:

[179]   Phineus, son of Agenor, dwelt there on the coast of the sea,
180   tortured beyond all men by gnawing affliction and torment,
       for abuse of oracular gifts that the son of Leto had granted.

FIGURE 19.2 The binding of Amycus, from a South Italian water jug, c. 400 BC. Here the boxing bully has been tied to a rock, evidently after being defeated by Polydeuces, probably the youth to his left who sits on a pot and holds a strigil, a tool for cleansing the body after a sports event. The other youth is probably Castor. To the far right, a winged Nikê, goddess of victory; to the far left, a maenad and a satyr (for unclear reasons). (Bibliothèque Nationale de France, Paris)

Ignoring the reticence due to Zeus's sacred intention,
he fearlessly bared the future to the eager hearing of men.
Zeus therefore gave him the burden of long and painful old age,
185 but took from his eyes sweet light and also denied him enjoyment
of the bountiful food his people piously brought to their ruler,
offering gifts when they came to his house to ask of the future.
For down from the clouds would sweep a flock of venomous Harpies,
who snatched the food from his fingers, or even his open mouth,
190 and carried it off in their talons, now not leaving a morsel,
another time only a crumb, to keep him alive, but in torment.
Over it all they shed such a stench of putrid decay
that none dared even approach, let alone dispose of the remnants.
 Phineus, hearing the tramp of the Argonauts' marching feet,
195 arose to meet the heroes, aware that those who approached him
were restorers, promised by Zeus, of all his pleasure in feasting.
He staggered up from his bed, as weak as a bodiless phantom.

Limping on shriveled old feet, he hobbled in with his crutches,
leaning at times on the walls to rest his feeble old bones.
200   His skin, all filthy with scab, alone kept his body together.
On trembling shanks he limped down through the court to the threshold
and sank back into a chair. Black swirling darkness descended.
Silent, helpless, he lay, as the earth spun churning about him.
The bystanders gaped in surprise as Phineus, gasping in torment,
205   uttered from deep in his heart a dark and prophetical message.

APOLLONIUS OF RHODES, *Argonautica* 2.179–206

Phineus' wife, Cleopatra, a sister of Boreas' winged sons Zetes and Calaïs, and
the desperate Phineus agree to give Jason exact information about the future course
of the *Argo* if Zetes and Calaïs would only free him from the Harpies ("snatchers,"
probably in origin spirits of death; see Figures 4.3 and 19.3). The Argonauts baited
a trap, a table set with delicious food. When the Harpies appeared, Zetes and Calaïs
drew their swords and rose against them, pursuing them at lightning speed through
the air until they fell from the sky.

FIGURE 19.3 The blind Thracian king Phineus reaching out to a table set with food,
on a red-figure pot from the fifth century BC. Behind him is a young warrior with
poised javelin. To the right is the bearded and winged Boreas, the North Wind, father
to the winged Boreads, Zetes and Calaïs, and to Cleopatra, Phineus' wife.   (Réunion
des Musées Nationaux / Art Resource, New York)

The Symplegades

Phineus now revealed the Argonauts' future course in great detail. He warned them especially about the **SYMPLEGADES** (sim-**pleg**-a-dēz), the "Clashing Rocks," which until that time had barred access to the Black Sea. These massive rumbling rocks, which lay in an impenetrable mist, smashed together and destroyed anything between them. Before attempting to get past, the Argonauts should release a dove. If the dove made it through, so would they; if it were killed, they should forget about their adventure and go home.

When they got near the Clashing Rocks, they released a dove, which sailed through, losing only a tail feather when the rocks smashed together. Now the Argonauts took their chance. After rowing hard, nearly in desperation, they too got past the rocks. Just as the tail feather of the dove was caught by the rocks, so was the banner on the *Argo*'s stern snapped away.

Medea and the Golden Fleece

Unnerved, Jason and the crew made their way along the south coast of the Black Sea. After various adventures, they landed at the mouth of the river Phasis, which flows through the land of Colchis. On its bank was AEA ("earth"), city of King Aeëtes. Jason and several companions went up to the palace to make their request. First of the Colchians to see the hero was the sorceress **Medea**, the king's daughter, agent of Hera's complicated plan to destroy Pelias. Hera persuaded Aphrodite to send Eros to prick Medea with such love for Jason that she would help him against her cruel father Aeëtes, who despised foreigners and had no intention of giving up the fleece.

Because an oracle had warned Aeëtes that a foreigner would be his undoing, he greeted the foreigners brusquely. He hoped to make an example of Jason and his crew. Although Jason protested that he merely wanted the fleece and would then be on his way, Aeëtes announced that he would gladly let Jason take the fleece once he had yoked two fire-breathing, bronze-hoofed bulls, plowed up the ground, and sowed in the furrow the dragon's teeth left over from the monster that Cadmus killed at Thebes. He would also need to destroy the armed warriors who would spring from the teeth.

Jason fell into a deep depression. He could see no escape. Fortunately, Medea, driven by her passion for Jason, secretly met with Jason and gave him a magic ointment to spread on his sword, shield, and body. Jason gratefully said he would marry her if only he lived. On the next day:

[1278]   The men hauled in on the hawsers that drew the ship to the beach,
and Jason jumped from the stern, armored and ready for battle
[compare Figure 19.4].
1280   Along with his spear and shield he carried a glittering helmet,
brazen, filled with teeth, each one with the point of a needle.
His sword hung over his shoulder, like that of bellicose Ares,

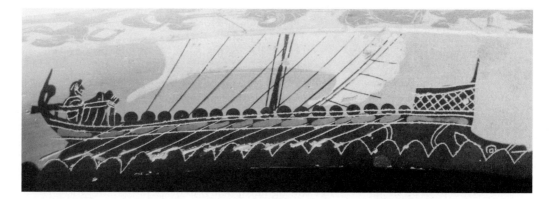

FIGURE 19.4 A Greek ship of the Classical Period, from the interior lip of an Attic wine-mixing bowl, c. 520 BC. When the bowl was filled with wine, the ship seemed to sail upon it. The ship has a single mast, which can be raised or lowered. There is no jib, so you cannot tack into the wind and much traveling is under oar. Thirteen banks of oars are shown, surmounted by shields. The rowers sit on benches in the undecked midship. At the rear, on a partial deck, sits the captain. The prow has an animal-shaped ram by which enemy ships could be sunk. (Cleveland Museum of Art, Cleveland, OH)

but he left his head uncovered, like golden-weaponed Apollo.
He glanced down into the meadow at the brazen yokes of the oxen
1285 and their plow with adamant share, constructed all in one piece.
Thither he went and fixed his spear in the earth by its side,
pushing the butt in the ground and leaning the helmet against it.
Holding his shield before him, he followed the trail of the oxen,
which led to a cave in the earth, half hidden in billows of smoke.
1290   The pair of oxen emerged, breathing out flashes of fire,
looking like bolts of lightning that leap from a sinister sky,
one gleaming after another from clouds overflowing with rain.
The heroes shook at the sight, but Jason stood firm and unshaken
and met the advancing beasts like a granite reef on the seashore,
1295 unmoved by thundering waves driven on by perpetual storm winds.
He kept his shield before him as the bellowing animals charged,
and even their slashing horns did not budge him, no, not an inch.
As bellows under a furnace make fire blaze up in a foundry,
but must stop to suck back the air, roaring and wheezing in turn,
1300 just so the oxen roared, blowing the flame from their gullets,
and after the roar came a flash like the blaze of a bolt of lightning.
Yet Jason went quite unharmed. The ointment afforded protection.
The horns of the right-hand ox he seized in a powerful grip
and twisted, to force the beast to bow its head in submission.
1305 The other he brought to earth by a sudden kick at its fetlock.
Tripping, it fell to its knees, downed in a single deft motion.
Jason now freed both arms by tossing his shield to the ground
and, darting to left and right, clutched at the kneeling oxen,
trusting the ointment's power to keep him safe from the fire

1310   while Aeëtes stared in amazement at the man's incredible power.
Obeying an old prophecy, the sons of Tyndareus° lifted
the yoke off the ground for Jason to lay on the animals' withers.
He set this over their necks, lifted the bronze-fitted drawbeam,
dropped it between the oxen, and jammed it down on its peg.

1315   Avoiding the flame, the brothers hurried back to the *Argo*
while Jason retrieved his shield and hung it over his shoulders.
He lifted the mighty helmet, filled with the teeth of the dragon,
and grasped his invincible spear with which to goad on the oxen,
as a peasant pokes his staff at the tender flanks of his cattle.

1320   With sure and certain hand he controlled the well-fitted handles.
       The oxen snorted and raged, pouring out billows of fire.
The noise arose like the sound of a hurricane, terror of seamen,
warning the crew to reef and ease the stress on the mainsail.
But presently, prodded along by Jason's spear, they moved onward,

1325   as the wiry turf of the meadow was plowed and broken behind them,
split by the oxen's might and the massive weight of the plow.
The sod torn out by the plow, in pieces a man could just carry,
fell with a ripping sound along the sides of the furrow.
Jason followed and pressed with all his weight on the plowshare

1330   and scattered the teeth behind him in the land already prepared,
repeatedly glancing back, to be sure that a crop as destructive
as this of earth-born men would not face him until he was ready.
       The oxen meanwhile plodded ahead on bronze-armored hooves
with only a third of the dying light of the day still remaining,

1335   when weary peasants are longing for the blessed hour's arrival
for oxen to be unharnessed and bedded down for the night.
At last the four-acre meadow was tilled by the tireless plowman.
Jason unfastened the terrified beasts, who fled to the lowlands,
while he himself turned back to revisit the furrows, still empty

1340   of men of the earth-born race . . .
       By now the earth-born soldiers had sprouted all over the meadow
and the field of man-killing Ares bristled with two-ended lances,
the brazen faces of shields, the gleaming crests of the helmets.
The glitter of arms flashed up from earth to the peak of Olympus.

1345   As when a blizzard of snow has folded the land in a blanket:
A west wind harries the clouds, and all the stars of the heavens
shine out again through the murky gloom and darkness of night—
so these men and their weapons broke out and shone from the soil.
       Jason recalled the advice of the shrewd and clever Medea.

1350   He picked up a rock from the ground (a discus fit for an Ares!).
No four men, heavy of sinew, could stir it up from its base.
He picked it up with a flourish and tossed it into their midst
while he himself sat in hiding, his shield concealing his body.
The Colchians shouted in glee, like a wave smashing into a headland,

1355   but silence fell on Aeëtes to see Jason tossing the boulder.
Each earth-man snarled at another, like dogs attacking a quarry,
then, prey to his neighbor's spear, fell to the earth, his mother,
as oaks and firs of a forest fall at the blast of a tempest.

    1311. *sons of Tyndareus:* Castor and Polydeuces.

As a fire-star falls from the heavens, leaving a luminous trail,
1360   a portent to humans observing its beam shining out in the darkness—
just so the great son of Aeson ran charging into the earth-men,
pulled out his naked sword, and dealt out wounds left and right.
Part of the victims, still buried up to the flank and the navel,
risen half way into the air, received his terrible slashes.
1365   Some were freeing their shoulders, others were standing upright,
and a few were even advancing with eager step to the battle.
You know how war may erupt in a hot dispute over boundaries:
how a farmer, in terror of raiders, takes up a new-whetted sickle
and runs to bring in his crop, though it still stands green and unripened,
1370   not daring to wait for the rays of the sun to ready the harvest.
Like that farmer, Jason cut down a crop of the sons of the earth.
The furrows brimmed with blood, as ditches draining a spring
run overflowing with water. Some men fell down on their faces,
biting the soil as they fell, some on their backs or their hands,
1375   some in a fetal position, as crooked as some sea-born monster.
Many died of their wounds before their feet were yet lifted
out of the ground. They crumpled to earth, a few minutes after
lifting themselves to the heavens. Now back to earth they tumbled
with the deadly sweat on their faces, as damp as Zeus's cold rain.
1380   Bitterest grief came down on the heart of the lordly Aeëtes.
Back he returned to the town, the mighty city of Colchis,
wondering how at one blow to checkmate the Argonauts' planning.
Thus, then, ended the day, and with it the labor of Jason.

APOLLONIUS OF RHODES, *Argonautica* 3.1278–1407

Although his plan failed, Aeëtes was not going to give up the fleece. He decided
to destroy the Greeks at once. Medea, realizing that she was about to be discovered, led Jason to the fleece and put the unsleeping protective dragon to sleep with
a magic potion. They snatched the fleece, ran to the *Argo,* and rowed downriver
toward the open sea (Figure 19.5).

Aeëtes gathered his fleet and gave pursuit. The *Argo* made for the mouth of
the ISTER (= Danube) at the other end of the Black Sea. According to the fantastic
geography of Apollonius, the Danube joined with another river that opened into
the Adriatic Sea somewhere near the modern border between Italy and Slovenia.
When he came near the Ister's mouth, Aeëtes split his fleet and sent half south
toward the Bosporus, to come at the Argonauts from the south, and half westward
upriver, commanded by Medea's brother **Apsyrtus** (ap-**sir**-tus).

The parties of Apsyrtus and Jason met in the ADRIATIC. Medea lured Apsyrtus
into a trap where Jason killed him, chopped off his fingers and toes, and three times
sucked up a mouthful of the blood and spat it out (to confuse the ghost). He then
buried the corpse, according to Apollonius of Rhodes. According to a better known
version, however, Apsyrtus was a little boy whom Medea kidnapped, cut into pieces,
and dropped piece by piece overboard to slow her pursuing father (the folktale
motif of the trail of objects dropped to delay a pursuer, given a bloody twist!).

The Argonauts' further course carried them, according to more impossible geography, up the ERIDANUS (= Po) RIVER (in northern Italy) to the RHONE (in southern

FIGURE 19.5 The serpent disgorges Jason, interior of Attic wine cup, c. 470 BC. The scene seems to preserve a version of the myth absent from the literary accounts. Apparently the dragon has swallowed Jason, who emerges again alive. A protective Athena stands in front of him, holding an owl in one hand, a spear in the other. Note the *gorgoneion* on her breastplate and the sphinx on her helmet. The Golden Fleece hangs from a tree in the background. (Photo Vatican Museums)

France), then again to the Mediterranean, down the west coast of Italy, past SICILY, around the boot of Italy and across the Ionian Sea to CORCYRA, land of the hospitable Phaeacians. When they arrived, the second Colchian flotilla, which had come through the Bosporus, intercepted them. The Colchians demanded that Alcinoüs, king of the Phaeacians, surrender Medea, but he would do so only if Jason and Medea had not yet had intercourse. Jason hastily arranged a wedding ceremony, led Medea to a cave, and slept with her. The defeated Colchians tired of the chase and settled on Corcyra.

Libya

The Argonauts set out once more, heading south. A storm drove them to the SYRTIS, a "dead sea" filled with seaweed off the coast of Libya. In one of the most fanciful twists in the voyage of the *Argo,* a huge wave threw the ship inland, dropping it amid the burning sands. The desperate sea-roving Argonauts picked up the ship on their shoulders and carried it for nine days until they reached the large, brackish inland LAKE TRITONIS.

Staggering under the weight and overcome by thirst, they set the *Argo* down in the sand and dragged themselves to a nearby grove, hoping to find water. They came instead upon the Garden of the Hesperides—not in the far western seas, but in the middle of the desert! Its nymphs wept inconsolably over the snake Ladon, which had long protected the golden apples, now killed by Heracles, the former Argonaut, who had arrived just before the Argonauts in his quest for the apples. (Other forms of the story do not mention that Heracles *killed* the snake; see Chapter 15.) The Argonauts sent out trackers who saw the great man tramping away, once a member of their crew, but they could not overtake him.

Bedraggled and hopeless, the Argonauts reembarked in the *Argo* and for a long time rowed aimlessly around Lake Tritonis. At last the water-god Triton guided them through treacherous waters back to the Mediterranean. They headed north to CRETE. As soon as they caught sight of land, huge boulders crashed around them, tossed by the bronze giant **Talus** (tā-lus), whom Zeus had given to Europa after he abducted her in the form of a bull. The giant had a single vein of ichor, the liquid that serves as blood for the gods, replenished through a hole in his ankle. Every day Talus ran around the island looking for strangers to attack. Medea fixed Talus with her evil eye so that he struck his ankle against a rock and dislodged the plug that held in the divine ichor. Fatally weakened, he stumbled and fell from a cliff into the sea (Figure 19.6). They rounded Crete, then continued north to the Gulf of Pagasae, from where they had begun their journey. At this point the sophisticated poem of Apollonius ends. (**For a complete version of the *Argonautica*, see http://classics.mit.edu/Apollonius/argon.html)**

Observations: Jason, the Deflated Hero

The notion of a sailing quest to the eastern end of the Black Sea to bring back treasure may echo real exploration in the Bronze Age (although no archaeological evidence for this has been found), but must depend principally on historically attested Greek experience in these cold and dangerous northern waters during the late Iron Age, beginning before 800 BC. After this time Greek colonization in the Black Sea became extensive, especially from the mother city of Miletus in Ionia. To this real history has been added the folktale of the quest that carries the hero, hidden at birth and brought up by a magical animal, to a magical land where he is compelled to accomplish impossible tasks. His reward is marriage with the local princess, but the kingship that came to Gilgamesh, Perseus, Theseus, Oedipus, and Bellerophon escaped the very unheroic Jason, as we shall see.

Apollonius of Rhodes, unlike the oral poets Hesiod and Homer, composed his poetry in writing, as we do today. He consciously imitated the "literary style" of Homer, never knowing that such distinctive features of Homer's poetry as the use of descriptive epithets like "swift-footed Achilles" and "Hector of the shining helm" depend on the original oral nature of Homer's verse. Such epithets were a device enabling poets to compose in the presence of a live audience, but

FIGURE 19.6   The death of Talus, Attic wine jug, c. 400 BC. In this version, the collapsing Talus (painted gold, to simulate bronze), is caught by the mounted Dioscuri, Castor, and Polydeuces.   (Museo Nazionale Jatta, Ruvo; Deutsches Archäologisches Institut, Rome)

Apollonius and other imitators (for example, Vergil, Ovid, and Milton) mistook them as merely stylistic contributions to epic grandeur. Homer and Hesiod composed orally for live audiences of illiterate warriors and farmers (some of their poems were recorded by dictation, according to the most likely explanation), whereas Apollonius composed his poem in writing for a socially elite audience that read Greek very well and could appreciate the ways in which he rang clever variations on ancient literary themes.

Apollonius' poem is curiously modern, then, presenting Jason as an amorous, indecisive, even incompetent figure. He falls into a deep depression when he is told what he must do. Medea stands behind his success in subduing the dragon and getting the fleece. She is by far the braver and stronger of the two. Apollonius consciously inverts, or perverts, expected patterns of heroic behavior inherited from the preliterate past. Homer would never show a woman wielding so much power directly.

No doubt the voyage of the Argonauts lacks the interest of the sea journey of Odysseus that the great genius Homer told. Apollonius is more concerned with vivid descriptions of technical seamanship and with Jason's erratic emotional life than in the gutsy heroic society that makes Homer's characters and stories so memorable. The learned and affected taste of Apollonius' day enjoyed descriptions and explorations of romantic individual emotions, and in the powerful romantic element lies Apollonius' originality and lasting contribution. He profoundly influenced the Roman poet Vergil, who modeled his Carthaginian heroine Dido on Medea (Chapter 23). Vergil's tragic love story, in turn, became the model and inspiration for countless later tales in European literature and, especially in modern film, is still felt today.

AFTER THE VOYAGE OF THE *ARGO*

The Death of Pelias

Meanwhile back in Iolcus, the rumor spread that the *Argo* had sunk with all hands aboard. Pelias congratulated himself on being the first human to escape the fate predicted by an oracle. He decided at last to finish off his hated half-brother Aeson, Jason's father. At a sacrifice he graciously permitted the old man to drink bull's blood (a deadly poison!). Aeson's wife, Jason's mother, ran screaming into the palace, cursed the king, and killed herself with a sword. She left a young son, but Pelias killed him too.

Jason's voyage had lasted four months. When he returned unexpectedly and presented the fleece to Pelias, the haughty king accepted it but showed no sign of relinquishing the throne. Medea decided to get rid of Pelias with the aid of his daughters. Through the power of her magic she could make Pelias young again, whose power only old age could challenge, Medea explained to the daughters. To show what she meant, she cut up an old ram, boiled the pieces in a pot for several hours, then removed the top (Figure 19.7). Out popped a feisty spring lamb. The daughters were persuaded. That night they sneaked into their father's chamber, chopped him in pieces, and brought the pieces to Medea. She cooked them for several hours, then removed the lid to reveal a thick, gluey stew. She apologized, admitting that she must have omitted an ingredient.

So Pelias met his end, as the oracle had foretold, and Hera's vengeance was fulfilled. However, the murder outraged the Iolcans. They celebrated splendid games in the dead king's honor, then drove Jason away from Iolcus forever, hero or not, and his foreign girlfriend too.

Jason and Medea in Corinth

The star-crossed couple traveled south to Corinth on the Isthmus and settled there. Jason dedicated his ship at a shrine of Poseidon. They lived happily for several years, and Medea bore two sons. But Jason grew dissatisfied with his irregular liaison with

FIGURE 19.7 Medea boiling the ram, from an Attic wine jug found in Vulci, Italy, c. 510 BC. Jason stokes the fire while Medea points out the old ram, boiling in the pot, to old king Pelias. One of his daughters stands to the far right. (© The Trustees of the British Museum/Art Resource, New York)

this strange woman from the Black Sea and arranged to marry Glaucê (**gla**-sē), the daughter of Creon, king of the city (no relation to the Theban Creon; Creon simply means "ruler"). He needed only to get rid of Medea, the subject of Euripides' celebrated play *Medea*, a seemingly modern tale of the bitter emotions that accompany the breakup of marriage in a monogamous society. The play was performed in 431 BC, the first year of the Peloponnesian War between Sparta (allied with Corinth) and Athens.

As the play opens, Medea has just learned of Jason's intention to take a new wife. She appears on the stage to complain about a woman's wretched lot, speaking to the chorus of Corinthian women:

[225]   *Medea*   An unexpected chance has struck me down
and blasted my heart. I only long to die,
forsaking all the charm that life once held.
There was a time, my friends, when in my heart
my husband stood as the type of all good things—
230   alas, that time is gone. He now turns out
to be the wickedest of mortal men.
    Of all the creatures who have heart and soul
we women are the most unfortunate.
All that we have we give to buy a husband

235 and, even worse, a tyrant of all we are.
A dreadful gamble, be he good or bad,
for no escape lies open to a woman,
save in dishonor. She cannot be free.
Blindly she enters a new estate, new ways.
240 Untaught at home, she now needs second sight
to learn to deal with him she sleeps beside.
If she succeeds, if her husband is content
to dwell without rebelling at his yoke,
then she is blessed. If not, far better dead.
245 Men bored by endless petty household chatter
can take an evening off from household cares
while we must always worry how he feels.
They tell us what untroubled lives we lead
while they must stand against the hostile spear.
250 What nonsense!
Better three times to face the foe in battle
than only once to bear the pangs of childbirth.
    But you and I face different situations.
This is your city, this your father's home,
255 here you are used to life, your friends are here.
But I am all alone. I have no home.
My husband scorns me as a worthless chattel
picked up as loot in some barbarian land.
I have no mother, brother, kin, whose aid
260 might shelter and protect me from disaster.
    Only one favor dare I ask from you:
If I can find a way to repay my husband
for all the misery he has laid on me—
along with the king, who bought him with his daughter,
265 and with the girl he miscalls his wedded wife—
if I do this, I beg you, hold your tongues.
Women, no doubt, in other ways are timid.
They dread a fight and shudder at cold steel.
But when their marriage beds appear dishonored,
270 no other creature has a deadlier heart.

EURIPIDES, *Medea* 225–266

Creon rightly fears this dangerous woman and banishes her from the city. She coaxes him into giving her just one more day to settle her affairs. Euripides' opportunistic Jason comes onto the stage to rail at Medea:

[446] *Jason* This is not new! How often have I seen
the raging anger of hysteria° that leaves
the witness helpless. You know very well
that if you had shrugged your shoulders and accepted

447. *hysteria:* = "Trouble with the womb," originally considered a specifically female disorder.

450   decisions of men stronger than yourself,
      you could have lived in quiet in this city
      and kept your house and children. But no,
      your stupid talk went on—and now you face
      immediate exile. Defame me as you please,
455   tell all the world how foul a cur is Jason.
      I am not bothered by your silly slander.
      But when your words reflect upon the rulers,
      think yourself lucky only to be exiled.
      I tried to soothe the ruler's rising anger.
460   I begged him to allow you to remain.
      But you still screamed aloud your silly charges
      against the king, until he lost his patience.
      No wonder you are exiled from the land!
           Still, madam, I admit my obligation.
465   I have come to see you well provided for,
      you and the children, not penniless or lacking
      what you may need as you go into exile,
      for exile brings discomfort in its train.
      And keep in mind that, however you may hate me,
470   never could I bear you the least resentment.
      Medea   Most evil of cowards—you deserve that name,
      the worst my tongue can give your spinelessness.
      Have you no sense of shame? You ruin me
      and then come back and justify yourself?
475   It is not just arrogance or self-esteem
      to wrong a friend, then look him in the eye,
      but plain remorselessness, the world's worst blight.
      Still, I am glad you came. It will ease my pain
      to publish your sin and make you blush to listen.
480   To start at the beginning, it was *I* who saved you
      (as all the Greeks of *Argo*'s crew know well)
      when you were sent to break the fire-breathing bulls
      under the yoke and sow their field of death.
      My sleepless labor saved you from the coils
485   of the dragon who enfolded the fleece of gold.
      I killed him and restored your hope of safety.
      My home, yes, my own father I betrayed
      and followed you to Pelian Iolcus,
      cold-blooded and efficient—but unintelligent.
490   Pelias I murdered by a most painful death
      at his daughters' hands and crushed his family's power.
      All this, ungrateful man, I did for you,
      yet you betrayed me, courting your new bride,
      although I had already borne your children.
495   Had you been childless still, you might be pardoned
      for so desiring this new marriage bed,
      but, as it is, trust in your oath has flown.
      Do you believe the ancient gods still reign?
      Or have they made new rules for men to obey?

500 How can I learn the answer? This alone is sure:
      Your guilty conscience knows you lied to me.
      My poor right hand! that you so often clasped.
      Poor knees! that often felt your false embrace,°
      a perjurer's, designed to cheat my hopes.
505   Well, should I talk with you as with a friend,
      should I expect a kindly act from you?
      These very questions make you seem the viler.
      Where would you have me turn? to my father's house,
      I, who for you betrayed my home and country?
510 Shall I flee, perhaps, to Pelias' poor daughters?
      They would gladly welcome home their father's killer.
      In short, this is my story: To my old friends at home
      I am become a deadly enemy, and those
      I least had cause to harm abhor me now
515 for all the ill I did because you asked.
          In exchange, of course, you've made me truly blessed
      in the eyes of many women here in Greece.
      What a splendid faithful husband in you have I,
      poor wretch, abandoned, exiled from the land,
520 bereft of friends, alone with lonely children.
      A fine reproach for a newly wedded bridegroom,
      that she who saved you, and the children whom she bore,
      now wander through the world as hungry beggars.
      O Zeus, who gave humankind sure ways of trial,
525 to see if gold be true or counterfeit,
      why did you set no stamp upon our features
      by which we might tell honest men from knaves?
      Chorus   Terrible rage, never totally cured,
      boils up when lovers turn to enemies.
530 *Jason*   I must display my modest skill at speaking,
      and, like a sailor of old and long-tried skill,
      close-reef my sail and run before this storm,
      the vitriolic blast of your angry tongue.
          Now, since you boast too much of your own share
535 in this my enterprise, it seems to me
      that Cypris, alone of gods or men, preserved me.
      Your mind, I know, is quick and very subtle,
      but envious Rumor mutters that it was Eros
      who forced you on, with his unerring arrows,
540 to save my life. This point I shall not stress,
      but rather dwell on benefits to you.
      For surely you received far more reward
      by saving me than was the price you paid.
          First, you now dwell in no barbarian land,
545 but here in Greece. You know what "justice" means,
      and how to live by law, not by compulsion.

---

503. *embrace:* Holding another's hand or clasping another's knees emphasized the sanctity of a promise, as when we raise our right hand when taking an oath of office.

All Greece has learned that you are wise and skillful,
and honors you for this. But if you lived hidden
in some unheard-of place at the world's end,
550 no word of you would hither penetrate.
What use a store of gold within a house,
what use a lovelier song than that of Orpheus,
unless one's fortune rings in all men's ears?
For my own exploit, such is my reply.
555 But you go too far, warring with words of spite
and carping at my marriage with the princess.
First I shall prove that I was wise and prudent,
next moderate and restrained, then finally
how great a friend to you and to my children—
560 no, no, control yourself and let me speak.
When I migrated here from the land of Iolcus,
with me I brought a desperate load of troubles.
What better way for me, a helpless exile,
to free myself, than marriage to this princess?
565 I did so not, as jealous envy prompts you,
from boredom at your bed or lust for a new woman,
nor yet from eagerness to father children—
two is enough, I find no fault in this—
but hoping—mark you well—to live in comfort,
570 wanting for nothing. I have learned the lesson well,
that each man tries to avoid his needy friend.
I could raise children as befits my house,
begetting brothers to the sons you have borne,
and, joining families, live happily together.
575 What need have you of children? But consider:
I can help the living through those yet unborn.
Have I planned so unwisely? You would agree,
but feel humiliated to lose your rank.
Things now have gone so far that you women think
580 that if your marriage prospers, you need no more.
But if some great disaster strikes your wedlock,
what once was beautiful you think a horror.
O that men might have sons some other way,
and that the female sex did not exist!
585 Without it, blest indeed would be mankind!

EURIPIDES, *Medea* 446–575

Medea concocts a magnificent revenge. She sends Jason's new wife, Glaucê, a beautiful wedding gift. Soon a messenger reports that the princess and Creon both are dead:

[1133] *Medea*   Now take your time, my friend,
to tell the story. Just how did they die?
1135 You would give me twice the pleasure, if you replied,
"They died in torment."

Messenger   When your two children entered with their father
into the bridal house, we slaves rejoiced,
we who before had grieved for all your troubles.
1140   The word went round that you and he had settled
your long-time quarrels. One servant kissed the hands,
one the fair hair of your two boys, then I myself
followed with joyful steps to the women's quarters.
Our lady, whom in your place we reverenced,
1145   kept her adoring eyes fixed upon Jason
until they fell upon your pair of boys.
At that she quickly turned away her gaze
and drew a veil over her fair white features,
as though embarrassed by the children's presence.
1150   Your husband tried to calm her angry temper,
and thus addressed her: "Please, don't be offended
at those who wish you well. Forget your anger
and turn again a smiling face upon them.
Consider friends those whom your husband loves.
1155   Accept their gifts and mollify your father.
For my sake, let him revoke the children's exile."
    Seeing the presents, she did not persist
and promised everything her husband asked.
But scarcely had your children and their father
1160   gone from the house, when she at once unwrapped
the splendid garment and quickly tried it on.
Upon her curls she set a golden tiara
and fixed her hair before a polished mirror,
smiling for joy at her own lifeless likeness.
1165   Then up she rose from her chair and paced the room,
gloating over her gifts, mincing on dainty feet,
gazing delighted at her slender ankles.
Then, all at once, a dreadful sight to see,
she turned dead white, she staggered to the side,
1170   trembling in every limb. Into a chair she crumpled,
barely escaping ruinous collapse.
An old handmaiden, doubtless imagining
a fit from Pan or another god had struck her,
screamed out a cry of terror, even before
1175   she saw the foam come boiling from her mouth,
the eyes protrude, the blood ooze from her flesh.
    Another cry at that the handmaid uttered,
this one a dismal moan of suffering.
One maid ran off to the bride's father's dwelling;
1180   another to her newly wedded husband,
to tell the bride's disaster. All the house
resounded with panic running to and fro.
In the time a sprinter runs a hundred yards
and reaches the finish, the poor girl came to,
1185   opened her eyes, and gave a shriek of pain.
A double torment was advancing to attack.

The gold tiara resting on her tresses
poured out an awful stream of gnawing flame,
while her clinging robe, your children's wedding gift,
1190 devoured the tortured woman's milky flesh.
She leaped, ablaze, up from her seat and fled,
desperately throwing her head this way and that,
trying to fling the crown from off her hair.
But the golden links clung firmly, and at each toss
1195 the flames blazed higher. To the floor she fell
writhing in torment, crushed by a dreadful fate,
unrecognizable to all, save to her father.
Her eyes dissolved into a shapeless chaos,
her face's native beauty shriveled away,
1200 a flux of blood came pouring from her scalp,
her flesh dropped peeling from her tortured bones,
scaled by the poison gnawing from within,
like pitch from a burning pine—a dreadful sight.
None of us dared to touch the poor girl's body,
1205 to offer help. Her fate gave us its warning.
　　Her father, who had no word of her disaster,
suddenly entered the hall. With a dreadful groan,
he flung himself headlong upon the body,
embraced it in his arms, and cried aloud,
1210 "O my poor daughter, say, what ruthless god
has thus destroyed you? Who made this poor old man,
bereft of you, into a living tomb?
Alas, alas, my child, would I might die with you!"
　　At last his tears of sorrow were exhausted.
1215 The old man longed to rise and hide himself,
but his body clung as tight to her fine clothing
as ivy does to branches of the laurel.
A grisly wrestling match arose between them:
the father trying to stagger to one knee,
1220 the daughter clinging fast to hold him down.
Each time he pulled, he ripped his ancient flesh
right off his bones. Exhausted, he gave up
the fight he could no longer hope to win,
and breathed his last. Together there they lie,
1225 father and child, asking your tears in death.

EURIPIDES, *Medea* 1133–1221

To put a fine touch on her revenge, Medea then puts her two sons to the knife,
throws them into a chariot drawn by dragons (a gift of her grandfather Helius), and
prepares to leave the city (Figure 19.8).

Jason runs in, aghast:

[1323] *Jason*　Woman most hated, most loathsome to the gods!
Loathsome to me, to all the race of men!
1325 You did not scruple to take up a sword,
to murder the children you yourself had borne,

FIGURE 19.8 Medea stabs her child, on a South Italian water jar, c. 330 BC. Without pity, she holds her son by the hair as she plunges a knife under his arm. Uselessly, he runs for asylum to the altar on the right, surmounted by a statue of Apollo.   (Musée du Louvre, Paris; © Reunion des Musées Nationaux/Art Resource, New York)

<blockquote>

leaving your husband desolate and childless.
Unholy crimes you dared. Dare you still gaze
up to the sun of heaven, down to the earth?
</blockquote>

<blockquote>

1330   My curse fall on you! My sense at last returns,
lost when I took you from your savage house,
your savage land, and brought you home to Greece,
horror that you are—betrayer of your father
and traitor to the fatherland that bore you.
</blockquote>

<blockquote>

1335   The gods have hurled on me the curse you earned
by murdering your own brother by his hearth,°
then daring to go aboard the sleek-prowed *Argo*.
So you began. And then you married me
and bore my children. Now you butcher them,
</blockquote>

1336. *hearth:* Euripides gives still another version of Apsyrtus' death.

PERSPECTIVE 19.1

SENECA'S *MEDEA*

The character of Medea has meant many things to many people. In his tragedy *Medea,* the Roman philosopher, statesman, and dramatist Seneca (c. 4 BC–AD
65) made her a bloodthirsty sorceress who rules the elements for her own ends
through magic and horrible incantation. Euripides' disillusioned heroine coldly
plans revenge on her betrayer; an apparition of the Furies and the ghost of her
brother Apsyrtus, dismembered by her own hands, drives Seneca's Medea mad.
Euripides has Medea kill her children off-stage; in Seneca she butchers them
in full view, slowly, gloatingly, one at a time. In the following passage Seneca's
Jason appeals to Medea to spare at least one child:

[1002]   *Jason*   By every god, by perils we have shared,
         by our marriage bed, its honor still unsmirched,
         I beg you, spare this child! Blame what you will,
1005   on me let your blame fall. Take me, O Death!
         Butcher this noxious, guilty soul of mine!
         Medea   Where most you shrink in pain will I drive the knife.
         Go, run away to your little sweet sixteen,
         and leave real life to women who know its pangs.
1010   *Jason*   Is one child not enough for your revenge?
         Medea   This hand would not have struck, had that been so.
         No, even two scarcely mollify my pain.
         Jason   Then grant me this: Either complete the deed,
         or else delay it, moved by my agony.
1015   *Medea*   Draw out his torment, my tormented heart.
         A long day lies before me. Make the most of the time.
         Jason   Kill me, you hag of hell, kill me!
         Medea   I, pity you?
         [Stabs child]
         There, that is all, my heart. I have no more revenge
1020   to soothe your pain. Well, Jason, aren't you pleased?
         Lift up your swollen eyes to know your wife
         for what she is.
         [A chariot drawn by two snakes appears behind her]
         This is the way I travel. The sky lies open.
         My team of dragons bows its scaly necks
1025   beneath the yoke.
         [Medea gets into the chariot]
         Here, daddy, take your sons

[Throws him the bodies]
>   while I fly down the winds in my winged car.
>   *Jason*   Depart, through highest reaches of the aether!
>   Wherever you go, proclaim, "the gods are dead."

SENECA, *Medea* 1002–1027

Seneca studied and wrote on science and philosophy. He tried to live by the dictates of Stoicism, living in self-imposed poverty, although he was one of the richest men in Rome. He enjoyed immense status as a chief advisor to Nero, but eventually fell from favor and was forced to commit suicide (he opened his veins while taking a hot bath, to keep his blood from clotting).

Seneca wrote eight other tragedies based on Greek myth. These plays, full of psychological improbabilities and gruesome horror, were not meant for theatrical presentation but probably were read aloud without action. However, they were acted in the Renaissance, especially in the universities, before the Greek tragedies became well known. Seneca's plays were widely imitated. Shakespeare's *Titus Andronicus,* for example, is a welter of incest, gore, and mutilation in which Seneca would have seen his own influence. Today we still call a blood-and-guts play based on motives of revenge *Senecan.* **(For a complete version of Seneca's *Medea*, see http://www.theoi.com/Text/SenecaMedea.html)**

1340   all for the sake of your lost marriage bed.
>   No women ever born of good Greek blood
>   has ever dared to dream of such a deed—
>   women whom I rejected, choosing you,
>   destructive, hostile, hateful foe of mine.

1345   As wife I chose a tigress, not a woman,
>   one with a fiercer heart than Tuscan Scylla.°
>   Why waste my time? Ten thousand condemnations
>   would leave no mark on your conceited heart.
>   Get out, perverted murderess of your children!

1350   All I can do henceforth is groan at fate,
>   I, who will have no fruit of my new bride,
>   to whom no child whom I begot and nourished
>   is left to say "good-bye" above my grave.
>   O lost! O lost!

1355   *Medea*   I could draw out an answer to your speech,
>   but Father Zeus already knows full well
>   what you received from me, and what you gave.
>   Was it your duty to degrade my marriage,
>   to live in pleasure while you mocked at me?

1346. *Scylla:* A monster perched on one side of the Straits of Messina between Italy and Sicily ("Tuscan" = Etruscan, Italian). She had once rejected the advances of some deity, who persuaded Circê (Medea's aunt) to change her to a monstrous form. Scylla lived by snatching sailors from passing ships (see Chapter 22).

1360   Did you suppose your princess or that Creon,
        who offered her in marriage, could drive me out
        and still escape my vengeance? Call me tigress,
        call me a Scylla in her Tuscan cave—
        I still have wrung your heart as it deserved.

EURIPIDES, Medea 1323–1360

Medea flies away to Athens in the chariot drawn by dragons, where Aegeus, father of Theseus, had earlier promised to receive her (see Chapter 16; illustration on cover). So ends the play.

Jason never recovered from the disaster. Depressed, ill, old, he sat down one day beneath the prow of his old friend *Argo*, where it lay decaying near the precinct of Poseidon. The rotten prow broke off, fell on Jason's head, and killed him—a fitting end to a hero who had too much of everyman in him.

The wonderful witch Medea never pays the price for her crimes. After escaping to Athens, she later returns to Colchis with her new son by Aegeus, Medus, who kills Aeëtes and takes the power. Medus spreads his realm to the east and becomes the ancestor of the Medes, another name for the Persians, Greece's deadly enemy during the Classical Period. There are no traditions about Medea's death. Perhaps she never died. According to one story, she married Achilles in the Elysian Fields. (**For a complete version of Euripides' *Medea*, see http://bacchicstage.wordpress.com/euripides/medea/**)

Observations: Medea, Sorceress and Wife

Circê, daughter of Helius (see Chapter 22), and Medea, granddaughter of Helius, are the best-known sorceresses in Greek myth. Unlike the witches of European folklore, however, they are not ugly hags, but beautiful and sexually alluring. Circê likes to change men into pigs, but Medea is a more realistic figure who uses potions to achieve her ends: protecting Jason from the fire-breathing dragon, putting to sleep the snake that guards the fleece, and, in Iolcus, resurrecting the aged ram (she might have resurrected Pelias too). She impregnates with terrible potions the cloth that kills Glaucê. Although a witch, she is close to the traditional practitioner of herbal remedies, and Euripides presents her as little more than a foreigner who understands exotic medicines. In deemphasizing her powers as magician, Euripides portrays her as almost an ordinary human, a victimized wife betrayed by a callous and philandering husband.

Of course, as a foreigner Medea can expect special hardships, but Athenian women also were strangers in their own homes, tied to their husbands' families only by the children they bore. Should these children die, a woman would ordinarily return to her father's house, a possibility not open to Medea. Because women were perpetual outsiders from the "men's club" that was democratic Athens, a man could never be sure of his wife's intentions, of the harm she might do to him and to the established order he represented, if she only got the chance.

Marriage was meant to tame the *parthenos*, but marriage was not always successful. The woman's tools were always the same: intrigue and sex. Euripides' *Medea* is the Athenian husband's worst nightmare, a ruthless woman who cannot control her violent emotions and her jealousy, who kills even her own children to settle a domestic dispute.

Still, we must not take dramatic presentations of women, written by men for men, as reflecting closely the realities of a woman's life in Athens. Although divorce was easy for a man, the wife was protected legally and financially and her dowry returned (if she was a member of the *polis*, which Medea was not). Through exaggeration of a wronged woman's plight, Euripides tweaks the audience's self-confidence in the righteousness and superiority of their civilized customs. Jason comforts Medea by reminding her that, although divorced and outcast, at least she is living in Greece where "justice" prevails. The audience could only smirk at such pretension.

PERSPECTIVE 19.2
DELACROIX'S *MÉDÉE*

The French poet Baudelaire observed that the Romantic painter Eugène Delacroix (1798–1863) brought to his works "the feeling which delights in the terrible." Although Delacroix usually chose his subjects from nonclassical or postclassical topics, including events of his own time, occasionally he drew from the classical world. Inspired by the Senecan *Médée* (1635) of French playwright Pierre Corneille (1606–1684), he painted Medea three times. In the illustration shown here (Perspective Figure 19.2), Delacroix's first version, Medea sits with her dagger, holding (not very firmly) her two sons. The breasts with which she suckled them are bared. The boys are wriggling to get away. Medea herself, wearing the diadem and earrings of a queen, gazes off fearfully through the opening of a cave at the man for whom she has done so much, who has brought her to this.

Corneille's version was written when stage technology was in its infancy, but by Delacroix's lifetime many improvements in scenery and lighting had been made, which allowed the full horror of the gruesome story to fill the stage. The proscenium arch and curtain made possible movable sets, which could be painted as realistically as a director wanted. Gas light came into use soon after 1800 and made possible unheard-of dramatic contrasts.

For example, mysterious and gigantic figures could be produced by stretching gauze at the back of the stage, behind which a backlighted actor walked, casting an immense shadow. Romantic caverns could be constructed with a dark background, dim lights by the entrance, and a brightly lit Medea (with interesting shadow effects) killing her sons in the center stage. Delacroix the painter evidently was inspired as much by anonymous stage designers and technicians as by the stories told by Euripides, Seneca, and Corneille.

PERSPECTIVE FIGURE 19.2
Eugène Delacroix (1798–1863),
Medea about to Kill Her Children,
1838, oil on canvas.   (Musée des
Beaux Arts, Lille; © Reunion des Musées Na-
tionaux/Art Resource, New York)

THE CALYDONIAN BOAR HUNT

A minor but famous local myth involving some of the heroes who sailed on the
Argo comes from **Aetolia** (e-tōl-i-a), the district north of the entrance to the Gulf
of Corinth, whose capital was **Calydon** (Map II, Chapter 2). The king in the days
of Heracles was Oeneus (ē-nūs), "wineman," a descendant of Aeolus and the first
man in Greece to grow grapes for wine. His wife, Althaea (al-**thē**-a), sister of Leda
(mother of Helen of Troy), bore him **Meleager** (mel-ē-**ā**-jer; Chart 19.2); a later wife
of Oeneus also gave birth to Tydeus, one of the Seven against Thebes (Chapter 18).

On the seventh day after Meleager was born, the three Fates appeared in the
room. Two of them promised that the child would be handsome and brave, but the
third pointed to a log burning in the fireplace. "When that log is consumed," she

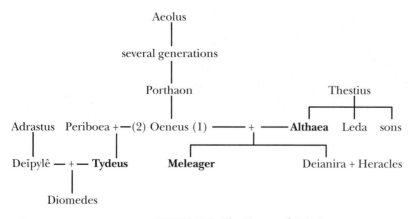

CHART 19.2 The House of Calydon

said, "the child will die." Althaea leapt from the bed, took the burning log from the fire, extinguished it, and placed it at the bottom of a chest, which she hid in a secret part of the palace.

Meleager grew to manhood. He was handsome and brave and joined the Argonauts. When he returned from Colchis, he married and fathered a child. Many years before, Oeneus had offended Artemis by forgetting to include her in the harvest sacrifice. She now took revenge by sending an enormous boar against the countryside around Calydon. The boar tore up crops, uprooted trees, and killed anyone who crossed his path.

As Jason had summoned heroes from far and wide, so did Oeneus. Many who had sailed on the *Argo* also joined the Calydonian Boar Hunt. Accounts differ, but most include the Dioscuri, Castor and Polydeuces, cousins of Meleager from Sparta; Theseus of Athens; Admetus from Pherae in Thessaly; Jason from Iolcus in Thessaly; Pirithoüs, king of the Lapiths, son of Ixion and good friend of Theseus, from Larissa in Thessaly; Peleus, the father of Achilles, from Phthia in Thessaly; Iphicles, twin brother of Heracles, from Thebes in Boeotia; and the seer Amphiaraüs of Argos, who would die in the war against Thebes. Meleager's uncles, his mother's brothers, also joined in the hunt, as well as the Calydonians' usually hostile neighbors, the Curetes (kū-**rēt**-ēz, unconnected with the Cretan protectors of the crying infant Zeus; "Curetes" means "young men").

The famous female athlete **Atalanta** (at-a-**lan**-ta), from Arcadia in the central Peloponnesus, also joined the hunt. Her father, wanting only boys, had exposed her at birth, but a she-bear found and suckled her and hunters raised her. Like her sponsor and model, Artemis, she cared only for hunting. Many objected to a woman coming on the Calydonian Boar Hunt (Jason had turned her away from the *Argo*, fearing a woman's presence), but Meleager was attracted to Atalanta and demanded that she be admitted.

The heroes closed in on the boar. Several went down before its flashing tusks. Others died when hit by their companions' spears gone astray. Atalanta got in close and fired an arrow in the pig's ugly red eye. The Argive prophet Amphiaraüs also wounded the creature, but Meleager made the kill (Figure 19.9). He skinned out

FIGURE 19.9 The Calydonian Boar Hunt, on an Attic wine-mixing bowl (the famous François Vase), c. 570 BC. Most figures have labels. Moving from left to right are an archer, then Melanion and Atalanta (with white flesh) with a dog named Methepon ("follower"). Peleus, father of Achilles, and Meleager stab into the boar's mouth while the hound Ormenos ("rusher") lies dead beneath the boar's hooves. A warrior lies dead beneath the boar, while Castor and Polydeuces stab it in the rump. Other hunters and dogs approach from the right.   (Museo Archeologico Nazionale, Florence)

the beast. He gave the pelt to Atalanta, ostensibly because she had drawn first blood, but also because he wanted to sleep with her. Meleager's maternal uncles loudly protested that a woman received the trophy and snatched it from her. Meleager tried to get it back and in the scuffle killed his uncles.

When Meleager's mother Althaea learned that her beloved brothers were dead, she broke down with grief. In her rage at the son who had killed them, she ran to the hidden trunk, took out the log, and threw it into the fire. So Meleager died.

The choral poet Bacchylides tells the story in a hymn from the Classical Period. Heracles, descending to the underworld to bring back Cerberus, suddenly sees Meleager's ghost. He thinks it is real and draws his bow, but instead of attacking, listens to Meleager's tale:

[56]   For once, they tell us, the smasher of gates,°
    invincible son of Zeus, lightning-bolted,
    went down to the halls of fair-ankled Persephonê,
    to drag to the light from Hades' domain
60   the jagged-toothed whelp of dreadful Echidna.°
    There he saw the ghosts of the grief-torn mortals
    who wander in woe on the banks of Cocytus,°
    shaken by sorrow, like leaves in the wind
    that swirls over Ida, pasture of sheep,
65   shaking its sun-whitened headlands.
      Among them most striking he saw the shade
    of Porthaon's son,° that hurler of spears.
    When the mighty hero, the son of Alcmenê,
    saw the gleam of his armor, he strung his bow

56. *smasher of gates*: Heracles, who had sacked several cities.   60. *whelp of dreadful Echidna*: Cerberus.   62. *Cocytus*: "Wailing," a river of the underworld.   67. *Porthaon's son*: That is, Meleager, son of Oeneus but grandson of Porthaon.

70   with a loud-twanging string, took the lid from his quiver,
        and pulled out an arrow, headed with bronze.
        Meleager's ghost, knowing well what he planned,
            floated up, face to face, and spoke to the hero:
                "Son of great Zeus, calm your fiery spirit;
75   do not rush to attack, nor let fly from your hands
        your deadly barbed arrow at the ghosts of the dead.
        It will do us no harm. You have nothing to fear."
        In amazement the hero, great son of Amphitryon,
        replied to his words, "What line of the gods,
80   what stock of mere mortals, engendered this man?
        In what land was he born? By whose hand was he slain?
        Perhaps well-girt Hera will send this man's killer
        to bring my head low. But fair-haired Athena
            will see to the matter of my defense."
85   With tears in his eyes, Meleager replied,
        "A difficult task for us mortals on earth
        it is to deflect the designs of a god!
        If this were not so, Oeneus my father,
        goader of horses, might have ended the wrath
90   of rose-crowned Artemis, white-armed, revered,
        by his humble prayers, by his sacrificing
        of numberless goats, of tawny-backed oxen.
        But no, she clung to implacable anger.
        The maiden goddess sent a wide-ranging boar,
95   berserk in his fury, to Calydon's meadows.
        Overflowing with rage, he savaged the vineyards,
        disemboweled the sheep, their owners as well,
            if those owners ventured to face him.
            For six days we fought the terrible fight,
100   we, bravest of Greeks, all valiant of spirit.
        At last the god gave the Aetolians mastery.
        We buried those fallen to the boar's savage rage:
        Agelaüs, Ancaeus, both dearest of brothers,
        born to Althaea in Oeneus' house.
105   And many more fell by a horrible fate,
        for the huntress Artemis, daughter of Leto,
        still clung to her anger and drove us to fight
        the aggressive Curetes, who claimed the trophy,
            the rough, tawny hide of the boar.
110   I slew many men, the noble Apharês
        and Iphiclus too, my mother's swift brothers,
        for hard-hearted Ares does not favor one's friends
        in the heat of the battle. The spear flies blind
        from the hand of the thrower to the heart of the foe,
115   bringing its death at the whim of some god.
            Forgetting all this, my star-crossed mother,
        the daughter of Thestius, fearless and clever,
        planned my destruction. From its well-carved chest
        she drew the stick which the Fates had marked

120 at the time of my birth for a sign of my death
  and threw it into the fire.
   By the towers of Pleuron, his city of refuge,
 I had just run down and was poised to kill
 Clymenus, noble son of Deïpylus,
125 handsome of body and valiant in battle,
 when all at once my dear soul shriveled,
 and I groaned at feeling my strength decay.
 With my dying breath I mourned for the brightness
  of the youth and joy I was leaving behind."
130 They say that this was the only time
 that the son of Amphitryon, fearless in battle,
 let tears of pity well from his eyelids,
 in his grief for Meleager's sad fate.
 "Man's happiest lot would be 'not to have lived,
135 not to have looked on the light of the sun.'
 Platitudes! useless as comfort to mourners,
 so let us consider practical matters.
 Tell me, does warlike Oeneus' house
 hold an unmarried daughter as handsome as you?
140 Such a one would I have as my glorious bride."
  Brave Meleager's ghost gave an answer:
 "Fair-necked Deianira I left in my house,
 a maid unacquainted with the man-charming arts
 of the golden witch Aphrodite."

BACCHYLIDES 5.56–164

At the end of the poem, Heracles arranges to marry Meleager's sister, Deianira, once he has returned to the upper world. We learn from other sources that the remorseful Althaea hanged herself after killing her son, and Meleager's wife followed suit.

There is more to tell of Atalanta. She returned to her father's house. He wanted her to marry some young man, but she was determined to remain a virgin. At last she agreed to marry whoever could overtake her in a footrace. When a suitor lost (as all did), Atalanta chopped off his head and hung it from a staff at the edge of the stadium. Her method was to give the suitor a head start, then come from behind and skewer him in the back with her spear. Soon skulls in varying stages of decay dangled from staffs around the stadium.

Then came Melanion (sometimes named Hippomenes). Aphrodite favored him and gave him three golden apples from the tree of the Hesperides. As usual, Atalanta allowed Melanion a good lead. She must have liked him better than the others, however, because she allowed him to distract her from her murderous habits: When she came near, Melanion let go an apple, which she would stop to pick up, allowing him to win the race. Unfortunately, the couple could not contain their lust, and in a nearby shrine of Zeus they enjoyed ecstatic intercourse (forbidden, of course, within sacred precincts). For this act Zeus changed them into lions, a fitting end: According to Greek folklore, lions can mate with leopards, but never with other lions.

Observations: Heroic Myths of the Hunt and the Hunter

Meleager's extraordinary birth is part of the heroic pattern. His quest is to hunt the boar, but there things go wrong. The hero is a hunter, and various features emerge in myths of the hunt: the similarity between hunting and sacrifice, the similarity between hunting and war, the dangers that hunters meet and that they themselves pose to society, and patterns of the dragon-combat or ritual initiation.

The ancient Greeks acquired meat to eat by sacrificing (usually) domesticated animals or by hunting wild animals. Strict prescriptions of behavior governed both activities, although sacrifice often took place in the city and hunting always in the wild. Whereas the purpose of sacrifice was to procure good relations with the gods, the purpose of the hunt was to obtain meat or destroy savage animals. In the dangerous wild where the hunt takes place, the hunter sometimes becomes the hunted, and his fate can resemble that of the sacrificial victim. Euripides makes much of the closeness between hunting and sacrifice in his story of Pentheus (Chapter 11), who sets out to hunt the Bacchae, then is himself hunted down and dismembered in a scene closely resembling ritual sacrifice.

Ancient hunting was always close to war and entailed similar dangers. In each activity a human group organized to kill an adversary. The social and technical skills useful in war—solidarity of the group, weaponry, athletic prowess, and bravery— also brought success in the hunt, and in Greek myth martial heroes are accomplished hunters, too. However, there are important differences, because in the hunt one does not negotiate with the adversary, and the quarry of the hunt is eaten, unlike the enemy in civilized warfare. (But Tydeus, half-brother of Meleager, split open the head of Melanippus to devour his brains; Chapter 18.)

Although the hunt is conducted for the benefit of society, the hunter can easily give in to the passion excited by the chase and become a danger to those he hoped to benefit. This danger haunts the hero always. Hippolytus is so devoted to the hunt that he denies his human sexuality, bringing destruction to himself and to his house (Chapter 16).

The wilderness obeys its own laws, but within the group of hunters social relations are determined strictly by convention. In the eyes of his family, Meleager disobeys the laws of his hunting group by giving the skin of the boar to the female Atalanta, a thoughtless act that changes the hunt into war and brings about the deaths of Meleager and his relatives. Although the hunter's victory over the animal marks him as a hero, he remains a threatening figure, living at the edge of society. Even in the midst of the city, Heracles wears his lion skin and drags around his club, an image of untamed violence.

Hunters who are too successful often come to a bad end, as did Orion and Actaeon, whom Artemis sent to their deaths, and Cephalus, who killed his beloved Procris. Success in the hunt seems to generate sexual excess or misbehavior. Hippolytus, lover of the hunt, tries to put sex out of his life, but his scorn for Aphrodite only excites her special attention. Orion rapes Oenopion's daughter and attempts to rape either Artemis herself or one of her nymphs. Actaeon sees Artemis naked. Meleager, although married, loves Atalanta. When Melanion defeats the huntress Atalanta, they immediately have sexual relations in a forbidden place, causing their transformation into hunting animals.

The legendary hunt of a single hero against a savage animal has the appearance of the myth of the dragon-combat. The hunter-hero is a culture bearer, and the animal is extraordinarily menacing, a threat even to human survival. The animal's defeat allows human life to return to normal. Gilgamesh's fight against Humbaba, or the bull of Heaven, Heracles' hunt for the Nemean lion, and Theseus' capture of the bull of Marathon are examples of such heroic encounters of one man, using his bare hands, against a prodigy of nature. Collective hunts, on the other hand, such as the Calydonian Boar Hunt, have the earmarks of male initiation, binding together human males as a group. Atalanta does not belong here, and her presence leads to disastrous family conflict. The king's son, Meleager, leads the band because it is a royal prerogative to free the land of monsters and to unite the young males of his realm through camaraderie in the hunt.

Hunting, the killing of animals in the wild, was an important activity in early Greece, as was sacrifice, the killing of animals in religious ritual. Both activities brought great benefits: a chance to consume meat and a neutralization of the hostile forces that surround human communities in the wilderness or come from the realm of the gods. Few myths are devoted entirely to the hunt, but few are free of some reference to this primordial activity and to the exemplary qualities or unmanageable feelings that the killing of animals can encourage.

KEY NAMES AND TERMS

Thessaly, 502
Iolcus, 503
Apollonius of Rhodes, 503
Jason, 503
Athamas, 503
Phrixus, 504
Hellê, 504
Hellespont, 504
Colchis, 504
Aeëtes, 504
Pelias, 505
Chiron, 505

Argo, 506
Boreads, 506
Phineus, 508
Symplegades, 511
Medea, 511
Apsyrtus, 514
Talus, 516
Aetolia, 531
Calydon, 531
Meleager, 531
Atalanta, 532

SOME ADDITIONAL ANCIENT SOURCES

Pindar's *Fourth Pythian Ode* has the oldest account of Jason's quarrel with Pelias. Apollodorus has a good summary: 1.9.16–28, 3.13.7. Ovid, *Metamorphoses* 7.1–397 goes into detail about Medea's support of Jason in Colchis and Iolcus. Hyginus, *Fabulae* 12–14, 24–25 tells much of Jason's story.

FURTHER READING CHAPTER 19

Bartel, Heike, and Anne Simon, eds., *Unbinding Medea: Interdisciplinary Approaches to a Classical Myth from Antiquity to the 21st Century* (London, 2010). The story of Medea through the ages, with excellent photographs.

Beye, Charles Rowan, *Epic and Romance in the* Argonautica *of Apollonius* (Carbondale, IL, 1982). Lively study of literary aspects.

Clauss, J., and Sara Iles Johnston, eds., *Medea: Essays on Medea in Myth, Literature, Philosophy and Art* (Princeton, NJ, 1997). Representative modern criticism.

Fontenrose, Joseph, *Orion: The Myth of the Hunter and the Huntress* (Berkeley, CA, 1981). Comparative study of Greek and Near Eastern hunting myths, including Orion, Actaeon, Callisto, Hippolytus, and Atalanta.

Fowler, B. H., *Hellenistic Poetry: An Anthology* (Madison, WI, 1990). Has the best translation of the complete *Argonautica*, plus representative selections from other Hellenistic poets.

———, *The Hellenistic Aesthetic* (Madison, WI, 1990). Companion volume to her anthology, this book describes attitudes toward love, nature, art, and myth in the Hellenistic Period.

Hunter, Richard, *The* Argonautica *of Apollonius* (Cambridge, UK, 1995). Scholarly study of the poem as literature.

CHAPTER 20

THE TROJAN WAR

So Paris, visitor in the Atreïds'° palace,
dishonored the laws that bind guest and host:
ate the king's bread, then eloped with his wife.
Behind her she left a vengeful clangor of shields,
of citizen spearmen, of seamen in arms.
Bringing as dowry destruction of Ilium,°
gaily she passed through the gate of the city,
daring a crime no human should dare.

AESCHYLUS, *Agamemnon* 399–408

Atreïds: The "sons of Atreus," Menelaüs and Agamemnon.   *Ilium*: Another name for Troy.

N○ CYCLE OF STORIES is better known than those surrounding the Trojan War, and many scholars believe that these stories began with a real historical event: the sack of a Bronze Age city near the Hellespont around 1200 BC (see Chapter 21). However, on present evidence we cannot definitely know the relationship between stories told by poets beginning around 800 BC and historical events hundreds of years before. The songs of Homer and later ancient poets are not about historical events, but about the difficult choices and sometimes tragic consequences that face all human beings as they attempt to answer the demands of society and their own desires. In this chapter we consider the events leading up to the war and the story that Homer tells in his *Iliad*; in the next two chapters we consider what happened when Troy fell and the heroes returned home.

THE HOUSE OF ATREUS

The kings who led the Greek expedition to Troy came from the House of Atreus (ā-trūs), which ruled the Argive plain from either Mycenae or Argos (see Map IV, Chapter 14). This dynasty is unrelated to that of the earlier Mycenaean king, Perseus, which became extinct after the death of Heracles' persecutor, Eurystheus. The new line went back to Tantalus of Lydia, the arrogant king who dined with the gods, stole their nectar and ambrosia, then to crown his folly tempted them to cannibalism (Chapter 12). The descendants of Tantalus committed crimes worthy of the founder of their line: hideous crimes of treachery, adultery, cannibalism, incest, rape, and murder. According to the myths that were told about this family, their misfortunes resulted from crimes committed in the early days of the dynasty and the curses that these crimes provoked from their enemies.

Pelops, Oenomaüs, and Hippodamia

Tantalus had invited the gods to a banquet, then chopped up his son **Pelops** (pē-lops; Chart 20.1) and served the pieces in a stew—to test their omniscience, so the story went. All the gods recognized the dish at once as human flesh and rejected it, except Demeter, preoccupied with the disappearance of her daughter Persephonê. She accidentally consumed Pelops' shoulder. Zeus ordered Hermes to put the pieces back into the pot and boil them some more. Out came a fresh child, minus his shoulder. Hephaestus made a prosthetic shoulder of ivory.

At this time, **Oenomaüs** (ē-nō-**mā**-us) ruled as king over Pisa, a village in the northwest Peloponnesus, in classical times the site of the Olympic Games (where an

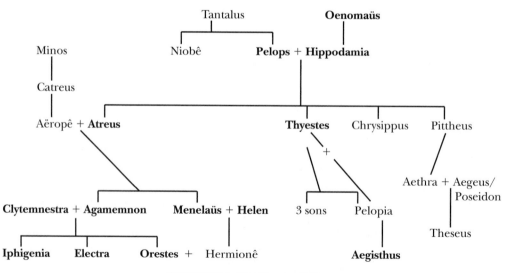

CHART 20.1 The House of Atreus

ancient tourist could see the ivory shoulder of Pelops, kept there as a relic). Oenomaüs was in love with his own beautiful daughter, **Hippodamia** (hip-po-da-**mī**-a; there were other legendary women with the same name). She refused sexual relations with him, but he prevented her from marrying anyone else by offering her as a prize in an unwinnable contest.

The suitor had to carry her away in a chariot, was given a head start, and sent racing toward Corinth. Oenomaüs, who had a team of horses sired by the wind, always caught up with the suitor, speared him from behind, cut off his head, and nailed it to the door of his palace (like Atalanta). Hippodamia was so beautiful that these gruesome conditions were no deterrent. Soon the door was covered with twelve decaying heads of unsuccessful suitors.

Pelops heard of Hippodamia's beauty and was determined to win the contest. He crossed the sea from Lydia bringing a golden-winged chariot drawn by horses that never tired, gifts from his divine lover, Poseidon. Just to be sure, Pelops also bribed **Myrtilus** (**mir**-ti-lus), the king's charioteer, promising him the first night in bed with Hippodamia if he helped him win the race. Myrtilus therefore removed the bronze cotter-pins at the end of the axle of Oenomaüs' chariot, which kept the wheels from falling off, and replaced them with wax. When Oenomaüs raced toward the Isthmus after Pelops (Figure 20.1), the heated axle melted the wax and the wheels flew off. Oenomaüs was tangled in the reins and dragged to his death.

Myrtilus, Hippodamia, and Pelops traveled on together. They stopped on a headland so that Pelops could get some water for his new and thirsty wife. When Pelops returned, he found Myrtilus clawing at Hippodamia, eager for his reward.

FIGURE 20.1 Pelops flees with Hippodamia, South Italian jug, c. 425 BC. He looks over his shoulder to see whether Oenomaüs pursues, while Hippodamia raises her right arm in alarm and looks ahead.   (Museo Archeologico Nazionale Firenze)

In a rage Pelops threw him from the towering crag into the sea. As Myrtilus fell, he screamed out a curse on Pelops and all his line: Curses on the lips of dying men are particularly effective!

The Banquet of Thyestes

Pelops, once purified of his murders of Oenomaüs and Myrtilus, returned to Pisa and became its king. He named the land *Peloponnesus*, "island of Pelops," and produced many sons, including Pittheus, father of Aethra, Theseus' mother; Chrysippus, whom Laius, father of Oedipus, raped (for this crime Pelops cursed Laius, which explains the many disasters that befell the House of Cadmus; Chapter 18); **Thyestes** (thī-**est**-ēz), father of **Aegisthus** (ē-**jis**-thus); and **Atreus**, father of **Menelaüs** (men-e-**lā**-us) and **Agamemnon**.

After the Heraclids had killed Eurystheus, persecutor of Heracles and last descendant of Perseus to sit on the throne of Mycenae, an oracle ordered the Mycenaeans to choose a child of Pelops as the new king. The Mycenaeans sent across the mountains to Pisa and asked for Atreus or Thyestes to come and rule them as king. But which of the two brothers would that be? Atreus, as the older, was the obvious choice, but Thyestes declared that a token was needed, a sign, and suggested that whoever could produce a fleece from a golden lamb should be king.

Years before, Atreus had vowed to Artemis to sacrifice his finest lamb to her, but when a lamb with golden fleece appeared in his flocks, he killed it and hid the skin in a trunk instead of burning the fleece on the altar as he should have. The only other person who knew about this was his wife, Aëropê (ā-**er**-o-pē), a granddaughter of the Cretan king Minos. Unknown to Atreus, she was carrying on a love affair with her brother-in-law Thyestes and had secretly given *him* the fleece. When Thyestes proposed that whoever could produce the skin from a golden lamb should be king, Atreus hastily agreed, only to see Thyestes produce the very fleece he thought safe in his own trunk!

Atreus was sure that Zeus, god of kings, nonetheless wanted him to be king, and to prove it, Atreus declared, Zeus would on the next day make the sun rise in the west. Thyestes thought this impossible and so agreed to the additional test, but when the sun did rise in the west, crossed the sky backward, and set in the east, Thyestes withdrew his claim to the throne. Atreus banished his brother from the land.

Atreus began to wonder how Thyestes had acquired the fleece and soon discovered his wife's infidelity. Burning for revenge, he invited Thyestes, now living abroad, to return to Mycenae; bygones would be bygones. While Thyestes was entertained in an outer room, Atreus murdered Thyestes' three little boys, cut off their extremities, and roasted their trunks in the kitchen, then served the parts to Thyestes at a banquet to celebrate their reconciliation. After a tasty meal, Atreus asked Thyestes whether he knew what he had eaten. He showed him the heads and limbs of his children.

Thyestes fled, cursing Atreus and all his line. Some attribute the sufferings of the House of Atreus to this curse rather than that of Myrtilus. Thyestes traveled to the Delphic Oracle to ask how he could even the score with his brother. He learned that he must beget a child by his own daughter, Pelopia (pe-lō-pī-a). Ignorant of his daughter's whereabouts, however, Thyestes left Delphi and at night came to a stream near Sicyon in the northern Peloponnesus. In the flickering light of a sacrificial fire, he saw a girl go to the water. He jumped from the bushes and raped her, but in the confusion left his sword behind. He did not know that the girl was his own daughter Pelopia, nor did she know her attacker.

In the meanwhile, Atreus was searching for the adulterous Thyestes, sorry that he had let him get off so lightly. He came to Sicyon and saw the pretty Pelopia, whom he thought was a daughter of the king. Atreus took her as his new wife, not knowing she was his niece, or that she was pregnant by Thyestes. When Pelopia bore a son, Atreus naturally thought it was his own and named him Aegisthus.

Years passed, but the vengeful Atreus continued to search for Thyestes. At last he sent his two older sons, Agamemnon and Menelaüs, to Delphi to ask Apollo where his brother was. Amazingly, Thyestes was at Delphi too. Unable to find his daughter (he thought), he sought new advice from Apollo on how to take revenge on Atreus. Agamemnon and Menelaüs seized Thyestes and dragged him back to Mycenae.

Atreus, delighted that he could finally settle scores with the brother who had seduced his wife, summoned his other "son," Aegisthus, now grown, and ordered him to go to the prison and finish off Thyestes. Aegisthus drew his sword and prepared to behead Thyestes. Suddenly, Thyestes called out, "Where did you get that sword?" "From my mother," Aegisthus replied. "But that's my sword!" cried Thyestes.

Pelopia was summoned in secret. She revealed how she had taken the weapon from a nocturnal rapist, Aegisthus' real father. Now recognizing her own father, and realizing that he was the rapist, in horror Pelopia seized the sword and plunged it into her heart. Aegisthus, recognizing his true paternity, drew out the bloody weapon from his mother's dead body and carried it to Atreus, seeming proof in its blood and gore that he had performed Atreus' murderous command to kill Thyestes. Relieved, Atreus sacrificed to the gods, then went to the river to wash his hands. Aegisthus came up from behind and knifed him in the back.

This complex, detailed, and extravagant myth is a distillation of typical plots of lost plays by Euripides, who must be responsible for the myth's general shape. With Atreus dead, Thyestes mounted the throne of Mycenae. Agamemnon and Menelaüs, the sons of Atreus, took refuge with **Tyndareüs** (tin-**dar**-e-us), king of Sparta. He was sympathetic to their cause and raised an army. Together they returned to Mycenae and drove Thyestes from the land. Agamemnon would now be king of Mycenae.

THE HOUSE OF TYNDAREÜS

Leda and the Swan; The Dioscuri

Tyndareüs had married **Leda** (lē-da), sister of Althaea, Meleager's mother (Chart 20.2). Leda's beauty was so great that even Zeus took notice. He appeared to her in the form of a swan, seized her by the nape of the neck (as swans do), and had his way with her (Figure 20.2). Tyndareüs also had intercourse with Leda on the same night. She gave birth to four children: **Polydeuces** (= Roman Pollux)

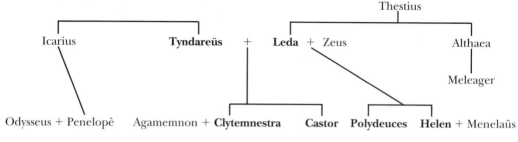

CHART 20.2 The House of Tyndareüs

FIGURE 20.2 Leda and the swan, from a South Italian wedding vase, c. 330 BC. An elaborately dressed Leda, her name written above her, clings to the swan's head with both hands as the swan stands on tiptoe and beats its wings for balance. She kisses it passionately. Her hair falls in long curls down her back. She wears an earring and a double coil bracelet on each arm. You can read the label "Sleep" (*YPNOS*) over the figure (not shown) behind Leda, extending a long white wand, imparting the sleep that comes after intercourse.   (The J. Paul Getty Museum, Malibu, CA)

and **Helen**, fathered by Zeus, were semidivine; **Castor** and **Clytemnestra**, fathered by Tyndareüs, were mortal. According to one version, Leda actually laid a pair of eggs—from one egg hatched Zeus's children, from the other those of Tyndareüs!

As we have seen, Leda's children Castor and Polydeuces are the inseparable Dioscuri, "the sons of Zeus," who traveled on the *Argo* and joined the Calydonian Boar Hunt. When Theseus carried away a youthful Helen, the Dioscuri went in hot pursuit and brought her back from Athens, together with Theseus' mother, Aethra (Chapter 16). When Castor was killed in a cattle raid, the grieving Polydeuces gave up half his immortality to Castor. On alternate days the brothers lived in Hades, then on Olympus. On the edges of more prominent mythical cycles, they have considerable importance in their own right. Some scholars trace their origins back to a very early Indo-European myth about divine horsemen twins (see Chapter 25). To the Romans, the Dioscuri were protectors of the Roman state, who appeared to them on horseback during a desperate battle of the early fifth century BC. But in Greek religion, the Dioscuri were preeminently the protectors of sailors in distress (perhaps because of their participation in the voyage of the *Argo*).

The Oath of Tyndareüs

Tyndareüs married Clytemnestra to Agamemnon but was worried about Helen, who had grown up to be the most beautiful woman in the world. The richest and best-born young men from all Greece gathered in Tyndareüs' halls to seek her hand. Among them were Odysseus, son of Laërtes; Diomedes, son of Tydeus who fought against Thebes (and ate the brains of Melanippus); Ajax (the common Latin form for the Greek Aias), son of Telamon, who would be the second best Greek warrior at Troy; Philoctetes (fi-lok-**tēt**-ēz), son of Poeas, who had dared to light the funeral pyre of Heracles; Patroclus (pa-**trok**-lus), son of Menoetius, who became Achilles' best friend (and perhaps his lover); Menelaüs, son of Atreus; and many others. Being young, headstrong, and dangerous, the rejected suitors were likely to turn on Tyndareüs once he had made a choice.

Odysseus understood Tyndareüs' position and realized that he himself was too poor to be chosen as Helen's husband, coming as he did from rocky Ithaca, an obscure island in the western seas. He therefore went to Tyndareüs and offered a solution to his dilemma, if only Tyndareüs would arrange Odysseus' marriage with Tyndareüs' niece, Penelopê (pe-**nel**-o-pē). Odysseus' solution is called the **Oath of Tyndareüs**, described by Hesiod in a fragment from a poem that cataloged the famous women of olden time:

[78]   Of all the suitors her father° demanded unbreakable pledges,
        making them swear an oath, with libations poured in the fire:
80   "The victor, be he who he may, can rely on my giving support
        in defense of his marriage with Helen, maiden of beautiful arms."
        He ordered the suitors, moreover, to assent to another condition:

78. *her father*: Helen's, that is, Tyndareüs.

If anyone carried her off, forgetting his own reputation,
and with it the vengeance to come, then all the suitors together
85   must join in pursuit and exact due punishment from the offender.
Most of the suitors assented, in empty hopes of the marriage,
but the son of Atreus was victor, Menelaüs, delighting in battle,
who offered a price for the bride greater by far than the others.
Now off in Pelion's forests Chiron was training Achilles,
90   nimble of foot, the bravest of men, though only a stripling.
Had nimble Achilles come home from the wooded valleys of Pelion
while Helen still was a maiden, not Menelaüs the warlike,
nor any man of the suitors would have met success in his wooing.
But long before then Menelaüs had won and had wedded fair Helen.

HESIOD, *Catalogue of Women* (MERKELBACH-WEST) 78–93

Helen bore Menelaüs a daughter, Hermionê (her-**mī**-o-ne). But trouble was brewing that had actually begun a long time before, at the wedding of Peleus (**pē**-lūs) and Thetis.

PERSPECTIVE 20.1
YEATS'S "LEDA AND THE SWAN"

William Butler Yeats (1865–1939) was born in Dublin and at age twenty-one dedicated himself to literature. In his life he worked successfully toward the establishment of a national Irish theater, which still exists, but he is best known for his lyric poetry, some of the finest in the modern English language. Yeats's work was much influenced by the Golden Dawn, a secret society dedicated to occultism and magic. His poetry also appealed to contemporary politics and took inspiration from history and, sometimes, classical myth, as in the following sonnet, published in 1924:

Leda and the Swan *

A sudden blow: the great wings beating still
Above the staggering girl, her thighs caressed
By the dark webs, her nape caught in his bill,
He holds her helpless breast upon his breast.
How can those terrified vague fingers push
The feathered glory from her loosening thighs?
And how can body, laid in that white rush,
But feel the strange heart beating where it lies?
A shudder in the loins engenders there

*Reprinted with permission of Simon and Schuster, *Collected Poems of W. B. Yeats*, revised second edition, edited by Richard J. Finneran (1996).

The broken wall, the burning roof and tower
And Agamemnon dead.
                              Being so caught up,
So mastered by the brute blood of the air,
Did she put on his knowledge with his power
Before the indifferent beak could let her drop?

In his book *A Vision* (1925) Yeats explains the union of Leda and the swan as symbolizing the opening of a new two-thousand-year age of the zodiac, that of Sagittarius, which ended with the birth of Christ, at which time began the cycle of Pisces ("fish"), now about to end. According to Yeats, the union of woman and god was "the annunciation that founded Greece . . . , remembering that they [the Greeks] showed in a Spartan temple, strung up to the roof as a holy relic, an unhatched egg of hers; and from one of her eggs came Love (Helen and Clytemnestra) and from the other War (Castor and Polydeuces)."

Yeats here refers to the tradition that Leda's four children did not come from her womb directly, but from two eggs that she laid, fecundated by her union with Zeus and Tyndareüs. Yeats saw history—especially that of antiquity—as a record of the endless struggle of Attraction and Repulsion, Love and Hate, both issuing from the same divine force. However, we might prefer to read his sonnet on Leda more simply: as a metaphor for mortal incomprehension of the divine.

THE WEDDING OF PELEUS AND THETIS

Peleus was born on the island of Aegina in the Saronic Gulf (Map II, Chapter 2). When his father, Aeacus, came to the island, it was uninhabited until Zeus changed the ants into people, afterward called Myrmidons, "ants." Peleus and his brother Telamon so envied their half-brother Phocus for his superior athletic ability that they murdered him. For this terrible crime Aeacus exiled them, on pain of death if they ever returned. Perhaps because of this stern judgment, Aeacus was believed, by the time of Plato, to be one of the judges of the dead, along with Rhadamanthys and Minos.

Telamon fled to the nearby island of Salamis, just off the harbor of Athens, and became king. There he fathered **Ajax**, a suitor of Helen and one of the greatest heroes in the Trojan War. Peleus traveled north to Phthia (**thī**-a) in southern Thessaly.

We saw in our study of Greek cosmogony how Zeus had lusted after Thetis and relented only when Prometheus revealed that Thetis' child would be greater than the father. To repay the Titan for warning him, Zeus allowed Heracles to shoot the eagle that daily devoured Prometheus' liver. At last the Titan was released from bondage. This story is now attached to that of Peleus, because Zeus arranged for Thetis to marry Peleus instead.

Peleus knew where Thetis danced with her nymphs on the seashore at night. He lay in wait, leaped out, and pinned her down. As he clung tightly, she changed into many shapes—fire, a tree, a lion, a bird—but returned at last to her womanly shape. Powerless, Thetis agreed to marry the son of Aeacus (Figure 20.3).

FIGURE 20.3 Peleus wrestles with Thetis, interior of Attic wine cup, c. 500 BC. Peleus, kneeling, holds Thetis around the waist. The lion and three snakes, which seem to attack Peleus, symbolize her many transformations. (Antikenmuseum, Staatliche Museen, Berlin; © Foto Marburg/Art Resource, New York)

Hera, evidently grateful to Thetis for not having slept with her husband, arranged for Thetis the most splendid wedding ever held, on the slopes of Mount Pelion. Euripides describes this famous wedding in a choral passage from one of his last plays, *Iphigenia in Aulis* (**aw**-lis), probably produced after the poet died in 406 BC:

[1036]   What wedding songs rang, what Libyan fluting,
    echoes by lyre-strings, apt for the dance,
    joining the reedy notes of the Pan-pipe
        sounding their strain,
1040   when on Pelion the fair-haired Pierian Muses°
    danced in the banquet given by gods,
    striking the earth with gold-sandaled feet,
        for the marriage of Peleus,
    and lifting their glorious voices for Thetis,
1045   singing her marriage to Aeacus' son
    all through the mountain haunted by Centaurs,
        and the forests of Pelion.
    The child of Dardanus, Zeus's beloved,
    darling delight and sharer of pleasure,
1050   Phrygian Ganymede, poured out the wine
        from craters of gold.
    Weaving their figures on silvery sands,
    fifty maidens, daughters of Nereus,
    linking hands and, singing for joy,
1055   danced for the wedding.
    Up through the pine trees, garlanded green,
    a herd of Centaurs, half man, half horse,

1040. *Pierian Muses*: Pieria, near Mount Olympus, was the birthplace of the Muses.

came to the feast the gods had provided,
   to the crater of Bacchus.
1060   They shouted for joy, "O daughter of Nereus:°
Chiron, versed in the arts of Apollo,
sends you the message, 'The son you will bear
   will be Thessaly's glory.
With his Myrmidons,° expert with shield and with spear,
1065   he will ravage the storied country of Priam,
clothed in the armor made by Hephaestus
   at Thetis' bidding.'"
Then the gods all sang at the blessed marriage
of the high-born eldest daughter of Nereus,
1070   and joined her name in the wedding hymn
   with the name of Peleus.

EURIPIDES, Iphigenia in Aulis 1036–1079

1060. *daughter of Nereus*: Thetis.   1064. *Myrmidons*: Although Achilles comes from Thessaly, the ethnic title *Myrmidons*, "ants," descends to his followers through his father, Peleus, who came from Aegina.

THE JUDGMENT OF PARIS

In the midst of the wedding of Peleus and Thetis, Eris, "strife," appeared at the door of the wedding tent, resentful because she had not received an invitation (who wants "strife" at a wedding?). Eris rolled an apple across the floor, crying, "May the most beautiful goddess take it." (In some versions, the apple had a tag, reading "to the fairest," a detail added after the invention of the Greek alphabet.) The vain Hera, Aphrodite, and Athena each claimed the apple for herself. They made such a ruckus in the middle of the party that Zeus ordered them to be quiet and to present themselves for impartial appraisal before Paris, a son of the Trojan king Priam (Chart 20.3), known to have an eye for the ladies.

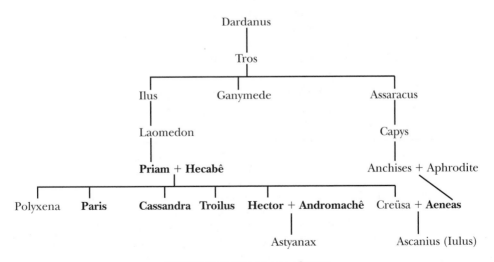

CHART 20.3 The House of Troy

In Homer's account, the Trojans are viewed as a foreign people whose allies, at least, speak foreign tongues. However, Trojans share the same gods and, although Priam has many wives, they otherwise behave much like the Greeks, whom Homer calls without distinction *Achaeans* (men from the territory of Achaea, here the Argive plain), *Argives* (men from Argos), or *Danaäns* (descendants of Danaüs). *Greeks* (Latin *Graeci*) was the name of one of the first Greek tribes the Romans knew in northwestern Greece. *Hellenes* as a term to describe all the Greeks does not appear until after Homer.

Priam was the sole surviving son of Laomedon, whose many other sons Heracles had killed (Chapter 15). Priam married **Hecabê** (**hek**-a-bē, Latin Hecuba), who bore many children, including Hector, destined to be the greatest fighter of the Trojans. When Hecabê became pregnant after Hector was born, she dreamed that she gave birth to a firebrand. A seer explained that the next child would cause the city's destruction. Priam therefore ordered the child exposed on Mount Ida behind Troy, but a shepherd found the child, called him Paris, and raised him as his own. Far more handsome and stronger than the rude hill folk, Paris single-handedly defeated a band of robbers, after which he was also called Alexander, "warder-off of men."

The Trojan Paris awoke from a nap to find before him the god Hermes, who presented the three feuding goddesses for inspection (Figure 20.4). One by one they undraped to show their naked bodies to the astonished shepherd. Each also

FIGURE 20.4 The judgment of Paris, Attic jug, c. 470 BC. Paris sits, holding a lyre, beside a ram from his flocks on Mount Ida. A buxom Aphrodite, holding the Apple of Discord, stands before him (but some think she is Hera, because of the scepter). Behind her are Athena, wearing the aegis and carrying a spear, and Hera, demurely clad in a concealing robe.

offered a bribe, if only Paris would call her fairest: Hera offered dominion over all the world; Athena offered a glorious military career; but Aphrodite offered the best prize, the most beautiful woman in the world. Paris declared Aphrodite fairest. As prize she gave him Helen, daughter of Zeus and Leda, who lived in Greece across the sea. Unfortunately, Helen was already married.

Paris came down from the hills, was recognized in Troy as a lost child of the royal family, and took a ship to Sparta to claim his reward. Menelaüs received Paris warmly, according to the conventions of *xenia,* "guest-friendship." When Menelaüs was called to Crete to attend a funeral, Paris and Helen, irresistibly attracted to each other, gathered up the treasure in the palace and eloped. Thus Helen left behind her lawful husband, her young daughter, Hermionê, and her good name—such is the power of Aphrodite.

THE TROJAN WAR

The Gathering at Aulis

When Menelaüs returned from Crete and found that Paris had violated the solemn bonds of *xenia,* he fell into a black rage. To restore the family name, he appealed to his brother Agamemnon in Mycenae. The brothers invoked the Oath of Tyndareüs, and soon from all over Greece Helen's former suitors assembled with their armies at the port of **Aulis** on the coast of Boeotia, opposite the long island of Euboea.

Odysseus, however, who had devised the Oath of Tyndareus, did not appear, and Menelaüs and several companions went to Ithaca to collect him. Recently his wife, Penelopê, had borne a boy, Telemachus (tel-**em**-a-kus, "far-fighter," more appropriate to the father than the son). Happy in his new domestic life, Odysseus had lost his taste for war.

When the embassy arrived, they were astonished to find him on the seashore, dressed like a madman and following a plow to which was hitched a bull and a jackass. **Palamedes** (pal-a-**mēd**-ēz), son of Nauplius, was not deceived. Famed, like Odysseus, for his cleverness, he had invented the alphabet, dice, numbers, and astronomy. Palamedes seized Telemachus from Penelopê's arms, raced to the beach, and cast the child into the sand in front of the blade of the plow: If Odysseus were mad, he would plow on, but if sane, he would spare his infant son.

Odysseus stopped the plow and joined the expeditionary force. Later, during the war, Odysseus took revenge on Palamedes. He planted a letter on a Trojan captive implying that Palamedes intended to betray the Greeks for gold. When the Greeks uncovered a sack of treasure in Palamedes' tent (which Odysseus placed there), they stoned Palamedes to death and left him to rot unburied, a traitor's death. (Palamedes may be a historical figure—the name of the very man who invented the Greek alphabet.)

While the Greek forces were still gathering at Aulis, **Calchas** (**kal**-kas), prophet of the expedition, declared that the Greeks would never take Troy without the help of Achilles, the son of Peleus and Thetis, who had been too young to be a suitor of Helen. When he was an infant, Thetis placed him on the hearth by night to burn away his mortal portions (as Demeter did to Demophoön; Chapter 10). One night Peleus discovered them. Thetis angrily removed the child, cast him to the ground, and left the world of mortals to return to her father, Nereus, in the depths of the sea.

A much later story, well known in modern times but not attested until a Roman poet of the first century AD, told how Thetis held Achilles by the heel and dipped him in the river Styx. He could never be wounded except in the heel where her hand kept off the water, the origin of our phrase "Achilles' heel" to describe a point of vulnerability. Late in the war, according to this version, Apollo guided an arrow shot by Paris that hit Achilles in the heel, bringing about his death.

Later, Achilles (like Jason) was entrusted to Chiron on Mount Pelion for his education (Figure 20.5). There he lived the outdoor life, hunting every day with his companion, Patroclus. When he grew to maturity, however, Thetis took him to the island of Scyros east of Euboea (where Theseus was murdered) and

FIGURE 20.5 Chiron with Achilles, Roman fresco painting from Herculaneum, c. AD 60. The wise Centaur instructs the young Achilles in the art of playing the lyre, hallmark of the Greek aristocrat.   (Museo Archeologico Nazionale, Naples; Scala/Art Resource, New York)

concealed him in the women's quarters, dressed like a girl. She hoped to prevent him from joining the upcoming war, where he surely would perish on the windy plain of Troy.

Calchas detected through his seercraft that Achilles was on Scyros, but he did not know just where. Odysseus devised a plan. He and Diomedes, pretending to be peddlers, appeared before the palace, hawking trinkets and gewgaws, dainty feminine things for the daughters of the king. The gifts were spread on a table, but a shield and a sword were placed nearby.

The girls were picking over the dainties when a trumpet blast sounded from the shore, as if to announce an attack by pirates. One "girl" seized the shield and sword and leapt to the top of the table, shouting "Let me at them!" "Surely you are Achilles," observed Odysseus, "and we need you for the war." Achilles agreed instantly. The plan to hide him among the women had been his mother's idea.

The Journey to Troy

Finally, all the warriors were gathered. Important figures, in addition to the suitors of Helen already named, were another Ajax (called the Lesser Ajax), son of Oileus (unrelated to Ajax, son of Telamon, called the Greater Ajax); Nestor, king of Pylos and a son of Neleus (Pelias' brother; see Chart 19.1); and Idomeneus (ī-**dom**-e-nūs), king of Crete. They set out across the Aegean, but no one knew where Troy was (any more than the Argonauts knew how to find Colchis). Eventually they came ashore south of the Troad, the area around Troy, in a land called Mysia (portions of Mysia also face the Propontis northeast of the Troad, where the Argonauts landed). The local king Telephus (**tel**-e-fus), a son of Heracles, tried to drive them off, and Achilles wounded him in a skirmish. Realizing they were not at Troy and not knowing what to do, the Greeks got back in their ships and returned to Aulis.

The wound of Telephus refused to heal. Following an oracle that "only that which harmed you can cure you," Telephus crossed the sea, searching for his enemy Achilles. He found him at Aulis and agreed to lead the expedition to Troy if Achilles would heal him. Achilles saw the meaning of the oracle, scraped off some corrosion from his spear ("that which harmed you"), and placed it in Telephus' wound. It healed at once.

Again the Greeks were ready to sail, but now the winds blew constantly in the wrong direction. They waited while the troops grew restless, food ran short, and disease threatened. At last Calchas revealed how Artemis was behind it all: Agamemnon (or Menelaüs) once boasted, while hurling his spear at a deer, that "even Artemis could not do so well." To save the expedition, Agamemnon would have to sacrifice to Artemis his own daughter **Iphigenia** (if-i-jen-ī-a).

Agamemnon sent a herald to bring Iphigenia to Aulis, pretending that Agamemnon wanted to marry her to Achilles. Decked out in saffron wedding clothes, Iphigenia was led to a wood, where Agamemnon slashed her throat on an altar. The chorus in Aeschylus' play *Agamemnon*, the first in a trilogy called the

Oresteia after Agamemnon's son Orestes, performed in 458 BC, tells of Agamemnon's initial hesitation, then commitment to the bloody deed:

[218]   But once he bowed his neck to Necessity's yoke,
         a sigh gave proof of his terrible change of heart,
220   unholy, faithless, obscene.
         Grim and unyielding he stood, unmoved by scruple.
         Wicked intention arouses a sort of courage,
         stubborn, deranged, begetter of endless sorrow.
         He nerved himself to be his daughter's butcher,
225   to prosecute a war fought over a woman,
             to make this payment on his navy's budget.
         Her youth, her pleas, her anxious cries of "Father!"
         affected not at all the grim old men
             whose plans demanded war.
230   Her father finished reciting ritual prayers,
         and gave the acolytes their orders:
         to see her properly dressed (though collapsed and fainting);
         to bring her, quickly and smoothly, and lift her on the altar,
         just as they would a sacrificial goat; to gag her pretty mouth,
235   to silence her words with calm but wordless force,
         to keep unseemly cries from polluting her family.
             She let her wedding dress drop to the ground.
         She shot a piteous glance at each of her killers,
         eager to speak, like a picture from happier times,
240   when she used to sing at feasts in her father's halls,
         when the cheerful wine cup had passed three times.
         With clear maiden voice she would add to the grace
             of the luck-bringing hymn of Apollo.
         I saw no more. I have no more to tell,
245   but Calchas' prophecies always come true.

                                  Aeschylus, *Agamemnon* 218–251

According to another tradition, similar to the story of Phrixus and Hellê (Chapter 19), at the last second Artemis sent down a doe as a substitute. The doe was killed while the goddess carried Iphigenia to the land of the Taurians in the remote northern regions of the Black Sea, the modern Crimea (Figure 20.6). There she became priestess to a foreign and even more savage Artemis, who demanded the human sacrifice of all strangers.

As predicted, the winds now blew fair. Again the fleet set sail, stopping at an island to take on water and to sacrifice to the gods. A snake beneath the altar bit **Philoctetes** (fi-lok-tēt-ēz) on the foot. As the Greeks sailed on, Philoctetes' wound festered, ran with pus, and smelled so foul that, in disgust, his companions abandoned him on the island of Lemnos. There he eked out a wretched existence lying at the mouth of a filthy cave, saved only by the bow that he received from Heracles as reward for lighting his pyre, with which he shot small game.

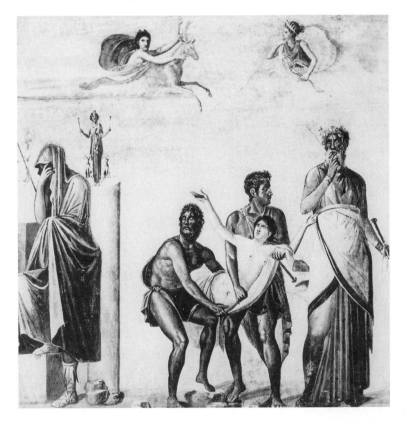

FIGURE 20.6 The sacrifice of Iphigenia, Roman fresco painting from Pompeii, c. AD 60. Two warriors, perhaps Odysseus and Diomedes, carry Iphigenia to the altar on the left, presided over by a statuette of Artemis accompanied by two hounds. Agamemnon stands waiting to perform the sacrifice, his head veiled in sorrow. To the right stands the prophet Calchas holding a prophetic wand(?). Above, Artemis watches as Iphigenia, riding on Artemis' deer, is carried away to the land of the Taurians.   (Museo Archeologico Nazionale, Naples; University of Wisconsin–Madison Photo Archive)

The Greeks approached the Troad, but an oracle had declared that the first to land would be first to die, and no one wanted to go ashore. Finally, Protesilaus (pro-te-si-lā-us) bravely leapt from his ship and ran up the beach. The Trojan warrior Hector came over a rise and cut him down, the first to die in the long war (Map IX).

Helen on the Wall

Odysseus and Menelaüs went to the city to ask for the return of Helen and the treasure and so settle the issue without further bloodshed. For their efforts, they were nearly killed by treachery. Thus the fighting began. Our most complete source for

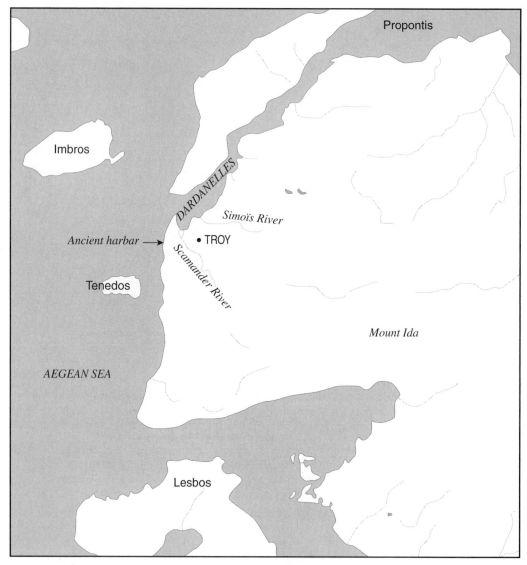

MAP IX The Troad

the events of the Trojan War is Homer's *Iliad*. Although it focuses on a single incident in the tenth year of the war, the quarrel between Agamemnon and Achilles, it contains many descriptions of earlier episodes, including one that properly belongs to the first years of the war, often called "Helen on the Wall." The Trojan elders have climbed to the top of the city walls to overlook the warriors on the plain below. One elder complains at risking so much for the sake of a woman, when Helen herself comes to join them:

[150]   By now they were old and no longer able to enter the battle,
but wise and skilled in counsel. As locusts perch in the foliage,
endlessly chirping away in their thin and tremulous voices,
so the old men of Troy conversed as they sat on the tower.
Their words flew swift as arrows into the heart of the matter:

155   "No one can blame the Trojans or yet the well-greaved Achaeans
for enduring so much and so long for such a beautiful woman.
To my eyes, indeed, she resembles the form of a goddess immortal.
Yet beautiful as she is, let her sail away to her country,
and not be left here in Troy, a scourge to us and our children."

160   So the old men chattered on, but Priam called out to Helen:
"Hither, my daughter, come sit beside me here on the rampart,
to watch your first husband, your brother-in-law, and your friends.
You bear no blame in my eyes. The gods themselves were the authors
of our war against the Achaeans and all the misery that followed.

165   Tell me, now, who is that man, a very giant in stature?
What is his name, that Argive, that man so strong and so noble?
Others, I grant you, stand taller than he by as much as a head,
but these eyes of mine have never fallen upon one so handsome,
nor with such an appearance of power. He must be a king indeed!"

170   Helen, loveliest of women, replied to him with these words:
"Certainly, father. You know the respect and honor I owe you,
but—would I had met bitter death when I eloped with your son!
when I followed him here to Troy, abandoning husband and kindred,
even the daughter I loved, at the age when children are dearest.

175   Well, it was not to be thus, and I wither in self-reproach.
So let me answer the question and tell you what you inquire.
That man is the son of Atreus, Agamemnon, ruler of empire,
combining the wisdom of kings with a soldier's courage and skill.
Brother-in-law to a slut—but so distant it seems like a dream."

180   At that, old Priam gazed at the hero in wonder and murmured,
"Ah, lucky son of Atreus, favored by gods and by fortune,
how mighty a host are your subjects, the valiant youth of Achaea!
I once served, long ago, in Phrygia, country of vineyards,
and saw the Phrygian troops, their horses flashing with bronze,

185   the people of Otreus° and Mygdon, kings very like the immortals,
advancing up the Sangarius° to make their way into battle.
I was a young cadet, who had gone along for my training,
that day when the Amazons came, women, but equals of men.
But even that numberless host was less than these clear-eyed Achaeans."

190   Next, observing Odysseus, old Priam inquired of Helen,
"Now tell me, daughter, I pray, who that man is, over yonder,
the one who is short by a head of Atreus' son Agamemnon,
but broader, at least to my eye, of shoulder and deeper of chest.
He has laid his weapons aside, nearby on the life-giving earth.

195   Like a ram with a dirty coat he prowls the ranks of his soldiers,
a ram with a flock of ewes, bearers of fleeces of silver."

---

185. *Otreus:* Aphrodite claims to be a daughter of Otreus in the *Hymn to Aphrodite,* Chapter 9.
186. *Sangarius:* A major river in Asia Minor that runs through Phrygia and into the Black Sea.

Helen, the daughter of Zeus, responded at once to his query.
"A different sort of man! For that is the crafty Odysseus,
son of Laërtes, brought up in rocky Ithaca's village,
200   skilled at all sorts of devices and clever deceitful maneuvers."
Then thoughtful Antenor° broke in and added this observation:
"My lady, what you remark is indeed nothing less than the truth.
Some time ago noble Odysseus, with Menelaüs the warrior,
came here to Troy to discuss the issues your presence had raised.
205   I entertained the two in my house as beloved companions,
and thus came to know their characteristics of body and spirit.
When they met the assembled Trojans and entered in the debating,
if they stood up, Menelaüs was taller and broader of shoulder,
but seated, Odysseus appeared to me of the two to be more impressive.
210   Again, when the time arrived for open (and secret) proposals,
Menelaüs, a man of few words, would bluntly offer suggestions,
brief ones, yes, but straightforward, the words of a younger man.
Then Odysseus would slowly arise. Hesitant, eyes on the floor,
he stood with never a gesture, holding the scepter in silence.
215   People would say he was tongue-tied, or maybe exceedingly stupid.
You would think him dull and slow, or even a half-witted idiot.
But—when out of his throat a thunderous voice came resounding,
and words poured out like snow, blown by a blizzard in winter—
then no man on this earth dared argue against such a speaker.
220   No one who gazed on his face could refrain from admiring Odysseus."
Thirdly, old Priam saw Ajax, and thus he inquired of Helen:
"And who is that other Achaean, so big, of such noble appearance,
taller than all the Argives by a head, and broader of shoulder?"
Helen, the glory of women, she of the long-skirted gown,
225   replied, "That is Ajax the mighty, wall of defense to the Greeks.
Beyond him is Idomeneus, like a god in the midst of his Cretans,
whose marshals are gathered around him. Ah, many and many a time
the warlike king, Menelaüs, showed welcome to him in our palace,
whenever he came there from Crete. And many fierce-eyed Achaeans
230   stand there in my sight, men I know and whose names I could list.
But two men I cannot see, both of them rulers of peoples,
Polydeuces, mightiest of boxers, and Castor, tamer of horses.
One mother bore the pair, who indeed are full brothers of mine.
Perhaps they did not follow the army from fair Lacedaemon,
235   or they may be coming soon, in ships that traverse the ocean.
Again, they may not be willing to join in the battle of heroes,
fearing disgraceful reproach may follow the shame of their sister."
So Helen answered Priam, but in fact the life-giving earth
of Lacedaemon, their own dear country, enshrouded the two.

HOMER, Iliad 3.150–244

201. Antenor. A Trojan nobleman. After the war he escaped to Italy, where he founded the city of Padua.

The *Iliad* does not seem to know the story about the Dioscuri sharing immortality between them, but it appears in the *Odyssey* (11.300–304).

The Anger of Achilles

The quarrel between Achilles and Agamemnon, which led to Achilles' unbridled anger and its fateful consequences, is the subject of Homer's *Iliad*. The poem begins in the tenth year of the war when Chryses (**krī-sēz**), a priest of Apollo, comes to the Greek camp to ransom his daughter **Chryseïs** (krī-**sē**-is, "daughter of Chryses"), whom Achilles had captured in a raid. In the distribution of the booty, Agamemnon received Chryeïs. Although the assembled Greeks urged that the girl be given back to Chryses, Agamemnon bluntly announced that it would be unworthy for him as supreme commander to lack a girl as booty: According to the heroic code, booty, or war-prize (*geras*), is the outward and visible sign of a man's honor (*timê*, literally "value"), which a Homeric warrior covets above all else. Agamemnon brusquely dismisses Chryses: If ever again he appears near the camp, Agamemnon will kill him.

PERSPECTIVE 20.2

THE BEAUTY OF HELEN

The image of Helen stands for supreme feminine beauty, the pleasures and dangers that the female can offer to the male, and the eternal feminine. Her figure has inspired countless poets, including English poet Christopher Marlowe (1564–1593), who may have written parts of several of Shakespeare's plays. He died at age thirty, stabbed in the eye in a tavern brawl (perhaps in connection with his work for the queen's spymaster) after a brilliant career in the theater. In his play *Dr. Faustus* he tells the story of a man who sells his soul to the Devil in exchange for earthly pleasure and power. The hero announces to Mephistopheles (the Devil) that he wants to sleep with Helen, the most beautiful woman who ever lived. His famous words to her, when a demon takes her form and appears to Faustus, show how well known were the events of the Trojan saga to a popular audience in the late sixteenth century AD:

> Was this the face that launched a thousand ships
> And burnt the topless towers of Ilium?
> Sweet Helen, make me immortal with a kiss.
>   [She kisses him.]
> Her lips suck forth my soul. See where it flies!
> Come Helen, come, give me my soul again.
> Here will I dwell, for heaven is in these lips,
> And all is dross that is not Helena.
> I will be Paris, and for love of thee
> Instead of Troy shall Wittenberg° be sacked;
> And I will combat with weak Menelaüs

Wittenberg: Faustus's home.

And wear thy colors on my plumèd crest.°
Yea, I will wound Achilles in the heel
And then return to Helen for a kiss.
O, thou art fairer than the evening's air,
Clad in the beauty of a thousand stars.
Brighter art thou than flaming Jupiter
When he appeared to hapless Semelê,
More lovely than the monarch of the sky
In wanton Arethusa's° azured arms,
And none but thou shalt be my paramour.

CHRISTOPHER MARLOWE, DR. FAUSTUS 99–118

. . . crest: A medieval knight would attach to his armor a piece of cloth given to him by his beloved.   *Arethusa*: Marlowe does a little myth-making of his own: Arethusa, a water nymph who governed a fountain on the island of Ortygia near Syracuse in Sicily, was never loved by Zeus in recorded Greek myth.

American poet Edgar Allan Poe (1809–1849), master of Gothic tales of horror and inventor of the mystery story, also called on the image of Helen in a famous poem, "To Helen," written for a woman he knew:

Helen, thy beauty is to me
Like those Nicaean° barks of yore,
That gently, o'er a perfumed sea,
   The weary wayworn wanderer bore
   To his own native shore.
On desperate seas long wont to roam,
   Thy hyacinth hair, thy classic face,
Thy Naiad° airs have brought me home
   To the glory that was Greece
And the grandeur that was Rome.°
Lo! in yon brilliant window-niche
   How statue-like I see thee stand!
The agate lamp within thy hand,
   Ah! Psyche,° from the regions which
   Are Holy Land!

Nicaean: Poe made up this adjective, which does, however, suggest the ancient port of Megara (named after Nisus, who had the single lock of purple hair).   *Naiad*: Female spirit of the water.   *To the glory . . . Rome*: The source of this famous phrase.   *Psyche*: The Greek word for "soul."

The priest Chryses walks away along the loud-resounding sea, then raises his arms to his special god, Apollo, lord of plague. Apollo hears his prayers for vengeance against the Greeks. He loosens his plague-arrows on the camp. The funeral pyres burn day and night. After nine years of exhausting war, the Greeks are no closer to victory than when they came, and now disease decimates their ranks.

Calchas announces that only by giving up the girl Chryseïs can they be saved. Agamemnon is backed into a corner. He agrees in a public assembly to give her back, but declares that he will then take another woman, for the sake of his own honor. Achilles reminds him that there are no unassigned girls stored away to give out, and that Agamemnon should wait until Troy is sacked, when he can have all the women he wants. If all the women are assigned, Agamemnon retorts, then he will take someone else's, even Achilles' own prize, **Briseïs** (brī-sē-is). After all, he is supreme commander and he can do what he wants, words that fire Achilles' wrath:

[148]   Achilles, speedy of foot, glared at Agamemnon and answered:
"See here, you good-for-nothing, greedy for ill-gotten profit,
150   why should an honest Achaean be ready to follow your orders,
to take to the field, to battle even to death with the Trojans?
I did not come here to fight their men in some personal quarrel.
These men have done me no wrong, rustling my cattle or horses,
or wasting the bountiful crops of the fertile meadows of Phthia.°
155   Between us stretches a waste of thundering sea and dim mountains.
No, it was you that we followed, scoundrel lacking in scruples,
to win great glory for Menelaüs and you, you scavenging jackal.
All this you ignore and pretend it is none of your business,
and now you haughtily threaten to steal the prize of my valor,
160   for which I labored and fought, and which the Achaeans awarded.
When we Achaeans have sacked a prosperous town of the Trojans,
my share of loot is never the equal of what is awarded to you.
Although my arms have always endured far more of the labor of battle,
when the time to distribute has come, you get the bigger award,
165   and I reel back to the ships, worn out, consoled by a pittance.
     Very well. I shall return to Phthia. It is certainly better
to sail in the sharp-prowed vessels back again to my homeland
than remain dishonored at Troy, amassing loot for your coffers."
     To this the lord Agamemnon, the leader of armies, retorted:
170   "Go ahead, if that's how you feel. I don't intend to implore you
to stay here just for my sake. I have plenty of other supporters
who treat me with proper esteem, and among them Zeus the Adviser.
But you are the man I most hate of all these god-favored rulers,
for discord, quarrel, and war are always your favorite pleasures.
175   You can fight, no credit to you. Some god has given that talent.
So go on home with your ships, and take your Myrmidons with you
to serve as your subjects. I don't care at all what you do,
and I'm not afraid of your anger. But let me give you a warning:
Phoebus Apollo demands the return of Chryseïs; so be it.
180   I shall send her in my own ship, with an escort of my companions.
But you can be certain of this: I shall go myself to your shelter
and personally carry away your booty, the fair-cheeked Briseïs.
Then, perhaps, you will learn how much your better I am,
and others will hesitate to think of themselves as my equals."
185   The challenge enraged Achilles. His angry spirit debated:
Should he draw his keen-edged sword, hanging down by his thigh,
thrust the others aside, and assassinate proud Agamemnon,
or should he swallow his anger, controlling his furious spirit?
He had barely started to draw his great sword out of its scabbard

154. *Phthia:* In southern Thessaly, Achilles' homeland.

190 when down from the heavens Athena came flying, urged on by Hera,
who cared for both men in her heart and did her best to protect them.
Standing behind him, she caught at the yellow hair of Achilles,
appearing to him alone, unseen by the rest of the council.
    Astounded, Achilles turned round and at once knew Pallas Athena,
195 for her eyes flashed a terrible gleam. The hero addressed her
in words that flew to the target: "O daughter of Zeus of the aegis,
why have you come? to gaze at the folly of vain Agamemnon?
I tell you straight out what is sure: that Agamemnon will perish,
gasping out life for the folly he showed in his treatment of me."
200   At once to Achilles retorted the goddess, gray-eyed Athena:
"I have come to quiet your fury, so show some sense and obey me.
Hera, white-shouldered goddess, has sent me racing from heaven,
Hera, who cares for you both, and does her best to protect you.
So quit—at once!—your anger. Stop fumbling about for your sword.
205 Stab him with words of scorn, show your irrevocable purpose.
For I can safely assert the consequence certain to follow:
He will be forced to concede gifts thrice the worth of Briseïs
to pay for this shameful behavior. Just listen to me and endure."
    Achilles, swiftest of runners, made this reply to Athena:
210 "A man must follow the orders of two such immortals as you,
however enraged he may be. Such a course is always the wiser,
for whoever obeys the gods will find that they listen to him."
    With that, he checked his hand on the silver hilt of his weapon
and thrust the mighty sword with a crash back into its scabbard,
215 obeying the words of Athena, who soared back up to Olympus,
to the house of Zeus of the aegis, amid the other immortals.
    Once more the son of Peleus poured out his bitter invective
on Agamemnon, not checking the flow of his blistering fury.
"You sot, with the face of a mastiff to cover the heart of a doe,
220 your courage was never enough to drive you to put on your armor
and charge along with the rest of us into the heat of the battle,
or even to join with the bravest Achaeans in laying an ambush,
something you think is the equal of choosing to go to your death.
How much more pleasant to go through all the host of Achaeans,
225 stealing the prizes of any who dare to protest your embezzling!
A king who devours his people rules a nation of cowards;
otherwise, son of Atreus, your insolence now would be ended.
One more thing I shall say, and swear a great oath to confirm it:
Look here, at this staff I hold. No more can branches and leaves
230 sprout from its stem, cut away so long ago in the mountains.
A bronze knife peeled bark and leaves. Its life has forever departed.
Yet still the Achaeans take it in hand while making decisions.
They draw inspiration from Zeus and make this scepter a token.
With it in my hand, I swear that soon desire for Achilles
235 will settle on all the Greeks. You too, Agamemnon, will share it,
but regret will do you no good when men fall dying by hundreds,
slain by the murderous hands of Hector. Your spirit will ache
and curse the way it dishonored the bravest of all the Achaeans."

HOMER, *Iliad* 1.148–244

Achilles withdraws to his tent and sulks. Agamemnon's men come and take away Briseïs. Weeping, Achilles begs his mother, Thetis, for revenge on Agamemnon, who has wronged him, and on the Greeks who allowed him to do it. She asks Zeus, who owes her a favor, to destroy the Greeks so that they might realize how wrong they were when they dishonored Achilles by taking away his prize. And Zeus agrees.

HECTOR AND ANDROMACHÊ

The fighting between Greeks and Trojans is in full fury when Hector returns briefly to the city, then, in one of the most famous passages in world literature, leaves his wife **Andromachê** (an-**drom**-a-kē) and his infant son **Astyanax** (as-**tī**-a-naks, "king of the city") in order to return to battle. In this short passage Homer sums up the roles of men, women, and children in a very cruel and very dangerous world, the world of the Greek hero:

[390]   Hector ran from the house, back again by the well-surfaced streets,
crossing the whole great city, and came to the Scaean gateway°
leading out of the town. There his wife came running to meet him,
Andromachê, rich in her dower, the daughter of noble Eëtion,
the king who once had dwelt by the wooded mountain of Placos,

395   above the city of Thebê, and had ruled the men of Cilicia.°
His daughter was married to Hector, hero with armor of bronze,
whom now she met by the gate. Beside her was walking a nursemaid,
bearing their good-humored baby, an infant still, on her bosom—
Hector's beloved small son, as bright as a star in his beauty.

400   "Scamandrius"° Hector had named him, "Astyanax"° everyone else,
for Hector, as everyone knew, was Troy's only hope of defense.
Hector stood there in silence, smiling down at the baby,
while Andromachê stood nearby, but could not hold back her tears.
She clasped his hand in her own and spoke her heartfelt entreaty:

405   "Hector," she pleaded, "your prowess is going to be your undoing.
Do you not pity at all this babe, or your poor troubled partner,
doomed to be called your widow, as soon as the gathered Achaeans,
making a charge, bring you low? Far better for me, if I lose you,
to pass at once to my grave. Thereafter no comfort, for sorrow

410   forever will follow my steps, once death has ended your days.
Pain alone will be left. My father, my mother, have perished.
My father was slain by the hands of the glorious hero Achilles,
when he plundered the populous city, high-gated Cilician Thebê
and slew its defender, Eëtion. Yet he did not strip him of armor.

415   His chivalry paid due respect, leaving his well-fashioned weapons
to cover the corpse on the funeral pyre he heaped for my father.
Nymphs of the mountain, daughters of Zeus who carries the aegis,
surrounded the spot by planting a beautiful thicket of elm trees.
Those seven brothers I had, brought up with me in the palace—

391. *Scaean* (**sē**-an) *gateway*: The "left" gate, the main gate of Troy.   395. *. . . of Cilicia*: In southern Anatolia; Thebê is unconnected with Boeotian Thebes.   400. *Scamandrius*: "He of the Scamander river."   400. *Astyanax*: "King of the city."

420   where are they now? In a single day they descended to Hades.
        Achilles, quick on his feet, dispatched them all in one battle,
        in a raid for slow-gaited cattle and sheep with silvery fleeces.
        My mother, one-time queen of the land under wood-covered Placos—
        Achilles carried her hither as part of the loot of his foray,
425   but gladly released her again in exchange for a bountiful ransom.
        Artemis, lady of archers, destroyed her,° at home in the palace.
            Thus, Hector, you have become to me both father and mother,
        you have become my brother—but above all, the husband I cherish.
        Now hear the prayer of my anguish: Stay safely here on the tower
430   so that your dear son might not be orphaned, and I left as your widow.
        Check the advance of the army before it passes the fig tree,
        where the city is hard to defend and the wall is easy of access.
        There three times the bravest Achaeans have probed our defenses,
        led by the pair of Aiantes° and Idomeneus,° glorious hero,
435   by the two sons of Atreus, and by Tydeus' powerful son.°
        Perhaps some seer has revealed a prophetic account of our ruin.
        Perhaps their own native courage is driving them on to attack."
            Hector, the shining-plumed hero, answered Andromachê thus:
        "Dear wife, I constantly worry over all the matters you mention,
440   but even more for my fame in the mouths of the people of Ilium,
        both men and long-skirted women, if they discovered me skulking
        like a coward here in the city, away from the tumult of battle.
        A longing to skulk has never kept me away from the fighting,
        since the day I learned the lesson of how to summon my courage
445   and always join the struggle amid the first ranks of the Trojans,
        defending the fame of my father, and my own reputation as well.
            But this too I know full well, down deep in my heart and my spirit:
        The day will certainly come when holy Ilium shall perish,
        and Priam of the stout ashwood spear, and all the people of Priam.
450   Yet not the misery coming hereafter to Troy and her people,
        not even the woe of Lord Priam and of Hecabê, mother who bore me,
        not yet the pains of my brothers, so many and so courageous,
        destined to fall in the dust at the hands of implacable foemen,
        affects me nearly as much as the thought of your terrible future,
455   when some bronze-armored Achaean shall ruthlessly drag you away,
        mourning the loss of your freedom. As drudge for some other woman,
        you will plod to and fro at the loom, perhaps in faraway Argos,
        or labor beneath urns of water drawn from a faraway spring,
        and bitter compulsion will force you to endure perpetual shame.
460   Perhaps somebody will notice your sorrow and tears and remark,
        'That woman is widow of Hector, bravest of horse-taming Trojans,
        he who protected the city, in the war they fought over Troy [see Perspective
            Figure 21.1d].
        So perhaps will he speak. Fresh grief will rise in your spirit
        at the loss of the one man able to fend off slavery's approach.

---

426. *Artemis . . . destroyed her*: Homer speaks of the sudden, nonviolent death of men as "dying by the arrows of Apollo," that of women as "dying by the arrows of Artemis."   434. *Aiantes*: Plural of Ajax (= Greek Aias): Ajax son of Telamon and Ajax son of Oileus.   434. *Idomeneus*: Leader of the Cretans.   435. *Tydeus' powerful son*: Diomedes.

465   Heaven grant that piled-up earth may long have covered my body
before I hark to your screams and the brutal cries of abduction."

So speaking, glorious Hector reached out for his little son,
but the baby whimpered and buried his head in his nurse's bosom,
scared at his father's array, the bronze and the horsehair crest,
470   as he saw it shaking and trembling above the peak of the helmet.
His father and lady mother together burst out into laughter,
but Hector at once took it off, set down the glittering helmet,
gave his small baby a kiss, and dandled the child in his arms,
offering up this entreaty to Zeus and the other immortals:
475   "O Zeus and the rest of you gods, grant that my son may develop
into a champion like me, a man of renown to the Trojans,
courageous and mighty in battle, a ruler of Troy by his might.
Some day people may say, as my son is returning from battle,
'Indeed, this man is much braver than even Hector, his father.'
480   May he bring blood-stained trophies, spoils of the enemy dead;
may his mother rejoice at heart, after all the woe she has suffered."

He silently put the baby in the loving arms of his wife,
who hugged it close in her fragrant bosom, smiling through tears.
Hector watched her in pity, caressed her, and spoke to her thus:
485   "Don't be too troubled at heart. No one will send me to Hades
until I am destined to fall. For no one, brave man or coward,
once he was born on the earth, has ever avoided that hour.
So go back to the palace, to all the tasks of the household,
back to the loom and shuttle, to keeping the maids at their work.
490   War is the task of all men born in Ilium—mine most of all."

Hector picked up his helmet, smoothing its horsehair crest,
while Andromachê slowly retreated, weeping, back to the palace.
She presently came to the well-built house of man-slaying Hector.
Within it she found a group of her women all huddled together,
495   all of whom burst into tears to see her returning alone.
Those women lamented for Hector, not knowing he still was alive,
and did not imagine he ever would come unscathed from the battle,
or escape alive from the furious hands of the warlike Achaeans.

HOMER, *Iliad* 6.390–502

The Embassy to Achilles

Zeus has granted Thetis' request that he give victory to the Trojans, and after much
fighting the battle turns against the Greeks. Fearing they will be destroyed and
regretting his own behavior, Agamemnon decides to offer Achilles an enormous
reward to persuade him to come back and fight. Here Agamemnon speaks to his
councilors, addressing Nestor, who has urged reconciliation with Achilles. The passage well exemplifies what was considered valuable in the eighth century BC:

[115]   "O wise old man, how truly do you catalogue all my offenses!
How blind I have been! And I cannot deny your impeachment.
When Zeus delights in a man, that man is worth a whole army.

So he has honored Achilles and is ravaging all the Achaeans.
Since I am clearly to blame for my terrible blindness of spirit,°
120   I will gladly make my amends with recompense knowing no limit,
and now in your ears will list the glorious gifts that I offer.
     Seven tripods, not marked by the fire. Ten talents of gold.
Twenty well-burnished kettles. A dozen solid-hoofed horses,
winners of prizes, swift-footed victors in many a contest.
125   Nobody owning such horses could be considered a pauper,
nor could he ever be lacking in gold, that bringer of honor,
if the horses win such prizes as those they have won for me.
Seven women from Lesbos, all highly skilled with the needle,
whom I received as my share when the city was sacked by Achilles,°
130   who in loveliness far outshine all other beautiful women.
These will I give, and with them will go Briseus' daughter,
she whom I dragged from Achilles. I shall also swear a great oath
I have never entered her bed, nor slept with her in the manner
which is common to all humankind, the joining of men and their women.
135   All this I promise at once. If the gods allow us to plunder
the mighty city of Priam, he may load a ship to the gunwales,
bronze and gold as he wishes, when we Greeks distribute the loot.
He may pick of the Trojan women whatever twenty he chooses,
of those who are next after Helen of Argos in womanly beauty.
140   If ever we make our way home to Argos, in fertile Achaea,
he may marry a daughter of mine and in honor equal Orestes,
my son, who is now being reared in a house of power and riches.
Three daughters I have in my palace, a house as firm as a rock:
Chrysothemis, Iphianassa,° Laodicê—his the decision,
145   which he shall take as his bride back to the household of Peleus,
paying no bride-price at all. I shall add by way of atonement
gifts like none ever offered to go with a daughter in marriage.
For he shall receive no less than seven populous cities:
Enopê, Cardamylê, Irê surrounded by meadows,
150   Pherae beloved by gods, the fertile fields of Anthia,
Aepia fair to the eyes, and Pedasus° rich in its vineyards.
All these lie near to the sea, on the borders of Pylos the sandy.°
Those who live in these towns are wealthy in sheep and in cattle
and will reverence him as a god, paying him homage and tribute,
155   and obeying his righteous decrees beneath his benevolent scepter.
     All this I will happily grant if he ceases his indignation.
Let him not be like Hades, most hateful of gods to us mortals,
implacable, not to be swayed. May he yield to me and my pleading,
who am senior to him by as much as my kingly rank is the higher."

HOMER, *Iliad* 9.115–161

119. *blindness of spirit*: The Greek word is *atê*, the same word Zeus uses of the Blindness that he casts from heaven after being tricked by Hera in the prophecy about the birth of a descendant of Zeus who will "rule the people of Argos."   129. *sacked by Achilles*: On one of his marauding expeditions, otherwise unknown.   144. *Iphianassa*: Evidently a variation of *Iphigenia*. Homer does not seem to know about the sacrifice at Aulis.   151. . . . *Pedasus*: Scholars have been unable to identify these places.   152. *Pylos the sandy*: In the southwestern Peloponnesus, the kingdom of Nestor.

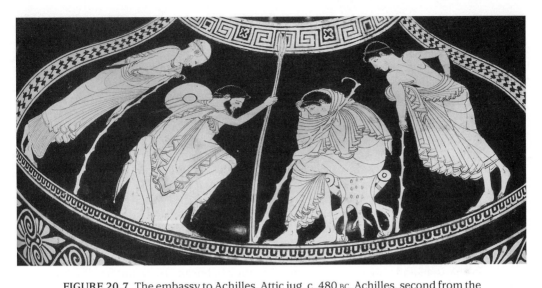

FIGURE 20.7 The embassy to Achilles, Attic jug, c. 480 BC. Achilles, second from the right, sits gloomily on his stool, cloak pulled over his head, while Odysseus, seated before him and wearing the *petasos,* or traveler's cap, attempts to persuade Achilles to return to battle. Behind Odysseus stands Phoenix, Achilles' tutor, and behind Achilles his good friend Patroclus.   (Staatliche Antikensammlungen und Glyptothek, Munich)

Odysseus, the great fighter Ajax, and Phoenix, Achilles' former tutor, who as an old man accompanied Achilles to Troy, walk along the sea to the tent of Achilles. They report Agamemnon's offer (Figure 20.7). To their astonishment Achilles turns them down:

[308]   "Kingly son of Laërtes, thoughtful and clever Odysseus,
          I must answer you frankly, declaring not only my feelings,
310   but my intention as well. I would not have you trying to talk me,
          one of you after the other, into consent with your offer.
          As much as I hate the gate of Hades do I hate a man who says one thing,
          secretly thinking another. I shall bluntly declare my decision.
          It does not seem likely to me that Atreus' son Agamemnon
315   nor any other Danaän can persuade me to alter my purpose.
          You see the thanks that I get for brutal and endless contention
          with fierce and determined foes. As well to stay out of the battle
          as enter and fight like a hero. The reward is exactly the same,
          for equal honor is given to coward and soldier of courage.
320   Doers of mighty deeds die as surely as those who do nothing.
          For year after worrisome year I risked survival in battle.
          What does it profit me now? A bird brings food to her nestlings,
          whatever morsel she catches, though she herself may go hungry.
          Like her I have lain and tossed all through the sleepless nights
325   and battled the bloodstained days against men defending their women.
          Twelve populous cities I sacked, attacking by sea in my ships;
          eleven more did I capture by land, in the fertile-soiled Troad.

From all these cities I plundered rare and uncountable riches,
which I used to bring back and deliver to Atreus' son Agamemnon.
330   He for his part would stay behind by the swift-running vessels,
receiving the loot and dealing it out in niggardly portions,
keeping the bulk for himself. What he doles out to the nobles,
that he allows them to keep. From me alone of the army
by force he reclaims what he gives. He has a wife, freely chosen.
335   Why can't he be contented to enjoy himself sleeping with her?
Why must the men of Argos embark to fight with the Trojans?
Why did the son of Atreus collect and bring the host hither?
Wasn't it all for the sake of a woman, the lovely-haired Helen?
He doubtless assumes that, of all the mortal race of mankind,
340   only the sons of Atreus have feelings of love toward their wives.
Someone should tell him that every decent intelligent husband
cherishes his—as I do, though she be but my captive and booty.
    Well, he has stolen my prize as well as cheating me roundly.
He'd best not try me again, I know him too well to believe him.
345   Perhaps he and you, Odysseus, and the other Achaean commanders
can work out a trick to save his ships from destruction by fire.
Just look at all the work he has done without my assistance.
Why, he has built him a wall, and a great wide moat to protect it,
and inside, a palisade of stakes bedded firm in the ground.
350   But even all this cannot hamper the fury of man-slaying Hector.
As long as I was in battle at the side of the other Achaeans,
Hector preferred not to sally forth from the walls of the city.
He would only advance as far as the Scaean gate and the oak tree,
where once he dared to engage me. He was lucky to get out alive.
355   But since I no longer desire to battle with glorious Hector,
tomorrow—first paying respect to Zeus and the other immortals—
I will drag my ships to the sea and load them up to the gunwales
(come and watch if you like, if you really have any interest).
At break of day you will see, as they travel the fish-laden waters
360   of the Hellespont, my ships and men, straining away at the oars.
Then, if the Shaker of Earth will grant me a quick happy voyage,
in three days I should arrive in the fertile region of Phthia.
There is the treasure I left—alas!—by voyaging hither.
There I shall pile up more, in gold and in ruddy bronze,
365   in women shapely of figure, in masses of tough gray iron—
all I acquired by lot. But the honor which he himself gave me,
imperious Agamemnon took back by force for himself.
    Give your report of my answer to Agamemnon in public
and give it in my own words, so that all the other Achaeans
370   will veto his next attempt to cheat some other Danaän.
For the man is devious and crooked, a shifty mongrel at heart,
and would never dare to confront me openly, face to face.
I certainly won't assist him, either by word or by deed.
He has lied to me and has cheated me shamelessly. Never again
375   will he swindle me with his tongue. Enough about Agamemnon.
He can go straight to hell! Zeus already has stolen his senses.
His gifts don't move me a bit. He himself is entirely worthless.

Suppose he gave me ten times, twenty times all that he owns,
as much as Orchomenus holds, or Thebes, that city of Egypt,°
380   where treasure packs the houses, whose wall has a hundred gates,
each broad enough for two-hundred men with chariots and horses.
Suppose he offered as many gifts as the sand of the seaside,
as specks of dust of the air—Agamemnon would make no impression
until he could make reparation for insults galling my spirit.

385   I shall not marry a daughter of Atreus' son Agamemnon,
though her beauty makes her a rival of Aphrodite the golden
and her skill is almost as great as that of gray-eyed Athena.
Very good. Let him marry her off to one of the other Achaeans,
to someone more pliant than I, to a personage higher in station.

390   If the gods are willing to bring me in safety back to my homeland,
Peleus himself will find me a wife and arrange for my marriage.
In Hellas° and Phthia are plenty of daughters of noble Achaeans,
rulers of towns. Whichever I want I will take as my wife.
In days gone by, in fact, my strongest feelings would urge me

395   to woo and marry a wife, a good and suitable woman,
and settle down to enjoy the wealth that Peleus had gathered.

I value my life far more than all the treasure of Ilium,
which they say that populous city possessed in the days gone by,
long ago in the times of peace, before the Achaeans descended.

400   I value it more than all that the marble temple encloses,
the temple of Phoebus Apollo the archer, in rock-bounded Pytho.°
Cattle and sheep can be rustled, tripods and fine horses bought,
but once his spirit departs and passes the gate of his teeth,
a man's life is gone beyond reach of any rustler or buyer.

405   Now silvery-footed Thetis, my goddess mother, informs me
that I must choose one or other manner of life and of death.
If I remain here, attacking the city and land of the Trojans,
all hope of returning is lost, but I win a glory undying.
If, however, I choose to return to the land of my fathers,

410   I must bid farewell to my glory, but survive to a quiet old age.
Death, the end of all men, will be slow and tardy to find me.

If you others want my advice, I urge you to sail back home.
You will never succeed in the capture of Ilium's towering walls,
for the hand of far-sighted Zeus protects the city from danger,

415   and a confident people has gained new will and courage in battle.
So go you back and report to the very highest Achaeans,
and—privilege granted the aged—tell them to work out a program,
better than that which they tried, to save the Achaean armada,
and the men of Achaea too, who camp by their deep-holded vessels,

420   for the ruse their leaders concocted has foundered on my refusal.

But Phoenix, I hope, will stay and sleep tonight in my quarters
and tomorrow will follow me back again to my own dear homeland—
that is, if he so desires, for I would not dream of compulsion."

HOMER, *Iliad* 9.308–429

379. . . . *Egypt*: Not the city in Boeotia but the Egyptian capital of the Late Bronze Age.   392. *Hellas*:
A territory in Thessaly near Phthia, not yet the name for all of Greece.   401. *rock-bounded Pytho*: Delphi.

The battle resumes, without Achilles. Things now go so badly for the Greeks that Patroclus, Achilles' best friend and tent-mate, comes to him in tears, begging that he relent in his wrath, which is killing so many of their former spear-mates. Or at least he should allow Patroclus to appear in battle wearing Achilles' armor, to give breathing space and save the ships, about to be set on fire under Hector's relentless assault. Achilles reluctantly agrees, but cautions Patroclus not to go near the walls of Troy, where Hector is strongest.

Patroclus storms into battle and kills many, including Sarpedon, a son of Zeus. Then, carried away by bloodlust, he forgets Achilles' words, comes up under the walls, and three times jumps onto the escarpment. Hector corners him, kills him, and strips off the armor—Achilles' own—and puts it on.

The Death of Hector

When Achilles hears that Patroclus is dead because of his own stubborn anger toward Agamemnon, he is maddened by grief. He thinks only of revenge. His mother, Thetis, brings him new armor made by Hephaestus to replace that taken by Hector. Like a demon he storms onto the plain, killing Trojans left and right. The river Scamander, which flows through the plain, is so choked with corpses that in self-defense it rears above the plain and attacks the hero, nearly drowning him! But Achilles escapes and continues to rout the Trojans, who pour into the city, except for Hector, who waits beside the Scaean gate. His mother, Hecabê, and his father, Priam, climb to the walls and call down, begging him to come inside.

FIGURE 20.8 The duel of Achilles and Hector, from an Attic wine-mixing bowl, c. 490 BC. Achilles has just dealt the fatal blow; blood gushes from Hector's wound, here in the chest, as he staggers backward. The figures are labeled. (© Trustees of the British Museum/Art Resource, New York)

When Hector sees Achilles coming, he turns and runs three times around the walls, then makes his stand. Achilles stabs his spear through Hector's throat, but misses the vocal cords (Figure 20.8). Hector begs Achilles for honorable burial. Achilles replies that he would rather eat Hector's flesh. Hector dies, prophesying that Achilles' death will follow soon.

Achilles ties Hector's body to his chariot and for days drags the corpse in the dust around the plain. Patroclus receives a splendid funeral. Achilles cuts the throats of ten Trojan captives over the pyre and many animals besides. When the fire dies down, the Greeks gather Patroclus' bones and place them in an urn, to await Achilles' own.

In the middle of the night, the grief-stricken Priam loads a wagon and, helped by Hermes, penetrates the Greek lines. To Achilles' astonishment, Priam appears at the door of his tent and offers ransom for Hector's corpse (Figure 20.9). Achilles sees in the aged, broken king the image of his own father Peleus, soon to be childless too:

[472]   Inside his tent was Achilles.
In back sat his silent friends, respecting his sorrow—two only,
Automedon the hero and Alcimus, scion of Ares,
475 stood by to care for his needs. He had just now finished his supper.
The table, not yet cleared, lay cluttered with wine cups and dishes.
Nobody noticed great Priam as he entered and knelt by Achilles,

FIGURE 20.9 The ransom of Hector, Attic cup, c. 480 BC. The dead Hector lies under Achilles' couch, his body pierced by wounds. Old Priam stands to the left leaning on his staff while Achilles, turning to a serving boy, asks that a meal be brought. Achilles' armor hangs from the walls of the tent.   (Kunsthistorisches Museum, Wien oder KHM, Wien)

embracing his knees and kissing his terrible murderous hands—
the very hands that had slaughtered so many sons of old Priam.

480   As when, in folly and rage, back home in his own dear country,
someone murders a man and is forced to go into exile—
he enters some rich man's palace, to the pity of all who behold him.
Just so Achilles felt pity at the sight of godlike old Priam,
and all the attendants as well, exchanging glances of wonder.

485   But Priam knelt by Achilles and spoke with a suppliant's meekness:
"Achilles, peer of the gods, reflect on your own poor father,
an old man, just as I am, on the verge of death and extinction.
Like me, he may be surrounded by those who make life a misery,
with no one there to defend him against his looming destruction.

490   But as long as he hears the report that you are alive and uninjured,
his heart can rejoice in the hope that some day soon he will see you,
his own dear son, returning from the war and tumult of Troy.

But for me no hope can remain. I fathered glorious sons
here in broad-streeted Troy. Not a single one now is left me.

495   They numbered full fifty back then, before the Achaeans attacked us.
No less than nineteen of my boys were born by only one mother,
and all the rest were the sons of women here in my palace.
Most of the others fell to the onslaught of furious Ares.
The only one to survive, the city's only defender,

500   was he whom you have just slain as he fought defending his homeland,
Hector. To ransom his body I have ventured among the Achaeans,
into the heart of their ships. I set no bound to his ransom.

O Achilles, out of respect for the clemency loved by the gods,
take pity on me, and remember in pity your own aged father.

505   Yet my lot is surely the sadder, for—a thing no human before me
has ever been humbled to do—I held the hand of the slayer
of my own son to my lips, in token of deep supplication."

He stopped. Achilles' heart was shaken with grief for his father.
Taking the old man's hand, he quietly moved it away,

510   and both men remembered their sorrow. Priam, groveling in silence,
could not erase from his grief the picture of man-slaying Hector.
Achilles sat openly mourning the helpless old age of his father,
but within him, the fate of Patroclus. Their misery filled all the camp.

But at last the noble Achilles, exhausted, lamented no further.

515   His sorrow ebbed from his mind and with it the pain from his body.
Quickly he jumped from his chair to raise the prostrate old ruler,
pitying his old gray head, his chin and his scanty gray beard.
To Priam he spoke these words like arrows that fly to their target:
"Poor man, what a load of troubles have stricken you to the heart!

520   How could you summon the courage to make your lone way to our beachhead,
to me, who have stripped as a trophy the armor of your dead sons,
so many, and all so brave? Your heart must be made out of iron!
Come now, sit here beside me. Now let us allow our resentment
to slumber in quiet within us, though we cannot forget the pain.

525   We will find no profit in tears, no comfort in heart-freezing sorrow,
for the gods have decreed a life of permanent grief to poor mortals,
while they themselves enjoy an endless freedom from troubles.

Zeus has disposed two jars on either side of his doorway,
full of the lots that he gives, one of blessings, the other of curses.
530   If He who Delights in the Thunder mixes the two for a human,
at one time his life will be painful, but equally often a pleasure.
But if a human's allotment is unmixed shame and derision,
then torturing madness dogs his steps all the days of his life,
and he walks on the glorious earth despised by gods and by mortals.
535   Thus, from his birth the gods gave glorious honors to Peleus.
In wealth he surpassed all others. The Myrmidons were his subjects.
To him, though only a mortal, the gods gave a goddess in marriage.
But with this some god mixed evil. No child was born in his palace
to follow him on the throne, save one, soon fated to die.
540   What comfort am I to his gloomy old age, so far from my country,
lingering here in the Troad, a curse to you and your children?
You too, poor old man, so they tell me, were once as blessed as he,
holding the mainland of Phrygia° from Lesbos, home of great Macar,
north to the Narrows of Hellê. Over all this land you were ruler,
545   and were blessed, moreover, with fortune and a mighty cohort of sons.
But since the gods on Olympus have brought this disaster upon you,
this endless war by your city, this endless bloodshed and slaughter,
all you can do is endure it. Do not grieve for what cannot be altered.
You will not accomplish a thing by endlessly mourning for Hector.
550   You cannot bring him to life. And worse things are still to be suffered."

HOMER, Iliad 24.472–551

543. *Phrygia*: That is, northwestern Asia Minor.

In a magnanimous gesture, forgetting that Priam is father to the man who killed his friend, Achilles gives up the body without ransom. Priam returns to the city. "And so they buried horse-taming Hector," reads the last line of the *Iliad*. **(For the complete *Iliad*, go to http://www.sacred-texts.com/cla/homer/ili/ili01.htm)**

Observations: Homer, Inventor of Plot and Character

Homer's great poems, the *Iliad* and the *Odyssey*, recorded in the earliest days of alphabetic literacy, have made stories about Troy some of the most widely known in the world. However, the *Iliad* is formally not the story of the Trojan War, but of a single episode of several weeks' duration in the tenth year of the war, the "anger of Achilles." When the poem ends, Achilles is still alive and the city yet to be taken.

Homer realized the need for a plot—a story describing a struggle that has a beginning, middle, and end. To some extent the earlier Mesopotamian poem *Gilgamesh* had a plot, but Homer immensely refined the device. Subsequent long poems, dramas, novels, and feature films are indebted to him. A good plot requires focus, and in the *Iliad*, Homer focuses on the turbulent emotions of a single man who allows his anger to run away with him, destroying alike those he hates and those he loves and, finally, preparing his own destruction.

Homer is also the inventor of character ("imprint") in literature, although his methods of portraying character are different from a modern novelist's. He never describes to us the inner life of his characters, but places them directly in the midst of events where they speak and act. He gives the sense that we are witnessing the lives of real men and women living in a real, although stylized, world. Helen is the lovely seductress, self-pitying but charming to every male. Odysseus is the clever man who can persuade through fine speech. Agamemnon is the blustering braggart, using political authority to swell his self-importance against the best interests of his people. Hector is the family man with much to protect, but doomed to a frightful end, like his family, whom he cannot save. Achilles is the warrior-intellectual, questioning the very foundations of his traditional culture when rejecting Agamemnon's offer of the rich gifts that Athena promised him would come. His successors in Greek culture will create philosophy, a rejection of traditional (and "mythical") explanations in exchange for a reasoned investigation into the natural laws that govern human behavior and the whole world. He is a man alone, pushing away the world around him and all it stands for, indulgent in self-destructive emotion, but fearless to act on his conviction regardless of consequence. In the final scene of the *Iliad*, when he sees his own father in his enemy Priam, he comes near to discovering "the brotherhood of man," a notion deeply alien to traditional Greek values.

Homer's figures are individuals, yet ideal types, images and models for all human beings, as capable of touching the heart of modern humans as they excited the admiration and attention of the ancient Greeks.

KEY NAMES AND TERMS

Pelops, 540	Clytemnestra, 545
Oenomaüs, 540	Oath of Tyndareüs, 545
Hippodamia, 541	Peleus, 547
Myrtilus, 541	Ajax, 547
Thyestes, 542	Hecabê, 550
Aegisthus, 542	Aulis, 551
Atreus, 542	Palamedes, 551
Menelaüs, 542	Calchas, 551
Agamemnon, 542	Iphigenia, 553
Tyndareüs, 543	Philoctetes, 554
Leda, 543	Chryseïs, 559
Polydeuces, 543	Briseïs, 561
Helen, 545	Andromachê, 563
Castor, 545	Astyanax, 563

SOME ADDITIONAL ANCIENT SOURCES

Stories related to the Trojan War permeate classical myth. Pindar set out to reform the myth of Pelops in his *Olympian Odes 1*. The Roman Seneca's play *Thyestes* is gruesome even for Seneca. The Dioscuri are the subjects of two *Homeric Hymns* (17, 33). The Sicilian poet

Stesichorus wrote a poem denying that Helen went to Troy (his *Palinode*, of which two lines survive). Lucian, of the second century AD, wrote an amusing parody of the Judgment of Paris in *Dialogues of the Gods 20*. The Roman Lucretius of the first century BC denounced religion on the example of the sacrifice of Iphigenia (*De rerum natura* 1.84–101). There is an excellent summary of the war in Apollodorus' "Epitome" 3–5.

FURTHER READING CHAPTER 20

Edwards, Mark, *Homer, Poet of the* Iliad (Baltimore, MD, 1987; reprinted Ithaca, NY, 1990). Readable, sensible, up-to-date analysis of Homer's poem of war. A fine introduction to the poem.

George, Margaret, *Helen of Troy* (New York, 2006). Lively recreation of Helen's life, from beginning to end; historical fiction.

Griffin, Jasper, *Homer on Life and Death* (Oxford, UK, 1980). Always interesting examination of major themes.

Latacz, J., *Troy and Homer: Toward a Solution of an Old Mystery* (Oxford, UK, 2004). Archeological evidence for the historicity of the Trojan War.

Page, Denys, *History and the Homeric* Iliad (Berkeley, CA, 1959; reprinted Berkeley, CA, 1972). A classic study of the relationship between historical records and the world of the poems.

Powell, Barry B., *Homer* (Oxford, UK, 2003; 2nd ed. 2006). Succinct study of philological, historical, and literary aspects of both poems. A readable short introduction to the poet and his poems.

_____ *The War at Troy* (Philadelphia, 2006). The author's own humorous take on the story of the Trojan War.

_____ and I. Morris, eds., *A New Companion to Homer* (Leiden, 1997). Up-to-date scholarly review of all aspects of Homeric studies.

Redfield, J. M., *Nature and Culture in the* Iliad: *The Tragedy of Hector* (Durham, NC, 1993; expanded edition of first edition, Chicago, 1975). Studies the relationship between the *Iliad* and the society that produced it.

Weil, Simone, *The* Iliad: *The Poem of Force*, trans. by Mary McCarthy and often republished. Insightful essay written against the backdrop of World War II.

Wood, Michael, *In Search of the Trojan War* (London, 2007). Based on a TV series, with excellent photos.

time + Geras
honor

Gifts

display your
honor

CHAPTER 21

THE FALL OF TROY
AND ITS AFTERMATH

"Aagh! I am hit—a blow—deadly and deep!"

AESCHYLUS, Agamemnon 1343

THE MANY LATER EVENTS of the Trojan War—how the city fell and what happened when the Greeks returned home—were told in the lost Cyclic Poems, of which only summaries survive. In this chapter we review the most important of these events, to which Homer sometimes refers in passing.

THE GREEKS AT TROY

The Judgment of the Arms of Achilles

After Hector's death, allies from far afield came to assist the Trojans. Penthesilea (pen-thes-i-lē-a), who led a contingent of Amazons, was cut down by Achilles. As she lay dying, he took pity on her, but the wound was mortal (Figure 21.1). A Greek scoundrel, Thersites, called by Homer "the ugliest man who went to Troy," derided Achilles for killing a woman, so Achilles killed him too.

Paris, assisted by Apollo, shot down Achilles as he fought near the Scaean gate. A great battle surrounded his body. At last Ajax got the corpse over his shoulder and fought his way back to the Greek lines through a rain of arrows. After a splendid

FIGURE 21.1 The death of Penthesilea, interior of Attic wine cup, c. 460 BC. Achilles, accompanied by another warrior, plunges the sword into the throat of the Amazon queen. Another Amazon lies dead at the right, supported by the rim of the cup. The artist seems to follow the tradition that Achilles fell in love with Penthesilea when their eyes met as he struck the death blow—alas, too late.   (Staatliche Antikensammlungen und Glyptothek, Munich; © Foto Marburg/Art Resource, New York)

funeral, the Greeks burned Achilles' body and mixed his ashes in the jar with those of Patroclus.

Achilles' armor was offered as a prize to the next-best warrior. Everybody knew this to be Ajax, son of Telamon, but Odysseus claimed them too. Each made a speech before the assembled Greeks. Odysseus' eloquence, and testimony from Trojan prisoners that Odysseus' intelligence had harmed them more than Ajax's brawn, won the armor for Odysseus. Sophocles tells the story in his earliest surviving play (the *Ajax*, written before 441 BC), how Ajax went mad with anger and grief at being denied the arms and how he attacked the Greek captains, Menelaüs, Agamemnon, Odysseus, and the others, cutting them to pieces with his relentless bronze sword— so he thought. When he recovered his senses, he saw himself standing in the midst

FIGURE 21.2 The suicide of Ajax, Attic jug, c. 480 BC. The lonely hero has stacked his cuirass and shield to the left; to the right, his quiver and club. He has fixed the sword in a mound of earth. His name is written above him.   (British Museum, London;
© Trustees of The British Museum / Art Resource, New York)

of a flock of dead sheep, covered in blood from head to foot. The Greek commanders shook with laughter at his folly. Shamed, Ajax walked to a secluded cave near the shore and threw himself on his sword (Figure 21.2), the only example of such a suicide in Greek myth (this form of suicide was common in the real world in Roman times). Agamemnon first ordered that the body be exposed to be devoured by dogs and birds, but later relented and allowed a proper burial.

When Odysseus was in the underworld on his journey home, he saw the ghost of Ajax and tried to appease him:

[541]   The other sad ghosts stood about me, heroes now dead and gone,
           asking news of the comrades they had loved in the regions above.
           But all by himself stood the spirit of Ajax, Telamon's son,
           nursing a grudge because I had received the arms of Achilles,
545   offered by Thetis, his mother, as prize to the bravest Achaean—
           I wish I had never presented a claim to so splendid a trophy!
           The children of Troy adjudged them, along with Pallas Athena.
           Because of that armor the earth soon covered Ajax, the hero,
           handsomest of all Greeks but Achilles and bravest in action.
550   Choosing my language with care, I spoke in words of appeasement:

"Ajax, great Telamon's son, even in death can you never
forget your quarrel with me, and the cursed arms of Achilles?
The gods indeed laid sorrow and pain on the host of the Argives.
We lost an impregnable tower when you died, and all the Achaeans
555   continue mourning your death, as deeply as that of Achilles.
Yet blame should not be imputed to any bronze-clad Danaän.
It was Zeus and his furious hatred that focused on you and your death.
So stand no longer aloof, my lord, but approach me and listen
to all that I have to tell, and calm your imperious spirit."
560   So I appealed, but he answered me never a word and departed,
along with the other ghosts, to the gloomy place of the dead.

HOMER, Odyssey 11.541–564

(For Sophocles' *Ajax*, go to http://bacchicstage.wordpress.com/sophocles/ajax/)

The Trojan Horse

Although the greatest heroes on both sides were dead, the war still dragged on with no end in sight. Calchas explained that various conditions would have to be met if the city were ever to fall: Achilles' son **Neoptolemus** (nē-op-**tol**-e-mus, "young fighter," also called Pyrrhus, "redhead"), conceived when Achilles lived in the women's quarters on Scyros, would have to join the army; a protective statue of Athena as city-protector, called the Palladium, which had fallen from heaven, would have to be taken from the city; and the bow of Heracles would have to enter the action.

Neoptolemus was summoned from Scyros; Odysseus and Diomedes, or Odysseus alone disguised as a beggar, sneaked into Troy and stole the statue; and Odysseus, in the company of Neoptolemus, sailed to Lemnos to recover the bow from Philoctetes, whom the Greeks had cruelly abandoned ten years before. Although consumed with hatred for the Greeks who had betrayed him, Philoctetes eventually gave up the bow; Sophocles tells the story in his play *Philoctetes*. A son of Asclepius healed his repulsive wound, and Philoctetes shot and killed Paris. But still the city did not fall. **(For Sophocles' *Philoctetes*, go to http://bacchicstage.wordpress.com/sophocles/philoktetes/)**

Odysseus instructed an ingenious artisan to construct an enormous wooden horse. Fifty warriors—among them Odysseus, Menelaüs, Diomedes, and Neoptolemus—concealed themselves in the horse's hollow belly (Figure 21.3). The Greeks burned their tents and sailed away, pretending to go home, but they hid behind the nearby island of Tenedos (see Map IX, Chapter 20). When the Trojans awoke the next day, they were astonished to see the plain empty of fighters, with only an enormous horse left behind. They went onto the plain, perplexed. A badly beaten Greek, Sinon (**sī**-non), emerged from the bush and explained that the Greeks, without hope of taking Troy, had sailed home. The horse was an offering to Athena, to ensure their safe return. He himself had been designated as a human sacrifice to the idol but managed to escape, he said.

A humorous scene in the *Odyssey*, set in Sparta ten years after the war, describes the episode of the Trojan Horse. Odysseus' son Telemachus has come to Sparta

FIGURE 21.3 The Trojan Horse, Cycladic storage jar, c. 670 BC. This relief from a large jar is one of the earliest surviving unequivocal references to myth in Greek art. The horse is on wheels, perhaps inspired by representations of Assyrian siege engines, and has openings through which we can see the heads of the heroes. From the portholes a shield, a sword, and a helmet are passed out. Some heroes have already come down and are striding off in full armor to the battle. Other scenes on the jar portray scenes of mayhem, the death of children, and the rape of women. (Archaeological Museum, Myconos; Erich Lessing/Art Resource, New York)

to seek news of his missing father and arrives in the midst of a wedding feast. To lighten their hearts, Helen offers Telemachus and Menelaüs a drugged wine and then in a calculated reminiscence praises the exploits of Telemachus' father, Odysseus, attempting to place her own role during the war in a favorable light. Menelaüs offers a less flattering version of events:

[220]
> To the wine poured into the crater
> from which they would drink she added a drug of mysterious power,
> narcotic of pain and calmer of anger and all kinds of sorrow.
> It was one of the most efficacious drugs in the keeping of Helen,
> shown her by Polydamna, wife of Thon, the pharaoh of Egypt,

225   a land whose nourishing earth is rich in herbs of great virtue.
Compounds of some bring health, but others are venomous poison.
Each man is his own physician, skilled beyond all other mortals,
for all of them come of the race of Paeëon,° greatest of healers.
So Helen mixed in her drug and, seeing the cups were replenished,
230   addressed the heroes again, urging them to go on with the story:
    "Zeus-favored Menelaüs, and all you children of heroes,
we know that good and evil are assigned to us mortals by Zeus,
whose power extends to us all. Very well. Recline at the banquet,
enjoying each other's adventures. My request is surely in reason,
235   for I myself could not list, even name, the trials of Odysseus.
But what an exploit was that, which he plotted and executed
in the very midst of the Trojans, at the lowest ebb of your hope!
He had himself lashed and beaten into bloody and shameful welts,
dressed in a dirty old cloak, and, disguised as a runaway slave,
240   got into the wide-streeted city. He changed his appearance again
to play the part of a beggar—how unlike the real Odysseus,
whom everyone knew as he was, encamped by the ships of Achaea!
    Like a beggar he entered the town. No Trojan offered a challenge.
I was the only person to pierce his disguise and address him.
245   He cleverly tried to elude me, but when I was washing his body,
rubbing his skin with oil and clothing his limbs in a garment,
I swore that until he was safe in camp by the swift-rowing ships,
no word would I utter revealing his entry into the city.
Then he told me in fullest detail the stratagem of the Achaeans.
250   On his way to the Argive camp to report what he had observed,
his sword had slain many Trojans, to the grief and despair of their women,
but my heart bounded in joy, for by now I was weary and homesick,
as I cursed the blindness and folly that Aphrodite injected,
bringing me into this land, so far from my dear native country,
255   carelessly leaving behind my daughter, my marriage, my husband,
a man who fell short in no virtue, either of mind or of body."
    Fair-haired Menelaüs replied with a smile of approval:
"Every word you have uttered, dear wife, is truthfully spoken.
I have traveled in many lands. I know the mind and the counsel
260   of many a hero, but never have I found the like of Odysseus.
Think of his quickness of wit and courage in moments of peril,
like that in the wooden horse, when all we bravest Achaeans
crowded together to bring destruction and death to the Trojans.
Some spirit, I guess, led you on to shower the Trojans with glory,
265   and behind you followed that godlike Deïphobus.°
Thrice you walked by the horse and stroked the hollow deception,
and spoke to the noble Argives, calling on each by his name
and simulating the voices of the wives of all the Achaeans.
Now I sat by Tydeus' son Diomedes, in the middle, with noble Odysseus,
270   hearing your voice as you called by name on each of our comrades.
Diomedes and I started up in a frenzy of eager desire
to burst from the horse, or at least to answer you from within.

228. *Paeëon:* That is, Apollo.   265. *Deïphobus:* The man that Helen took up with after Paris had
been killed.

But Odysseus grabbed us and checked our impulse to ruinous folly.
All the other Achaeans sat waiting in disciplined silence;
275   only Anticlus tried to make some reply to your wheedling.
But Odysseus firmly squeezed on his mouth with powerful hands,
thus saving all the Achaeans, till Athena took you away."

HOMER, *Odyssey* 4.220–289

A priest of Poseidon, **Laocoön** (lā-**ok**-o-on), also suspected that the horse held warriors. He came forward and declared Sinon, like all Greeks, to be a liar (hence the saying, "beware Greeks, even bearing gifts"). The horse was a trick, he said, and they should destroy it, and he hurled his spear into the horse's side. Two serpents suddenly arose from the sea, made straight for Laocoön and his two sons, and strangled them in their coils as the Trojans watched in horror (Figure 21.4). Obviously

FIGURE 21.4 The death of Laocoön, second–first centuries BC. One of the most famous works of sculpture to survive from the ancient world, this piece from the Hellenistic Period expresses unforgettably the anguish and terror of the Trojan priest and his sons.   (Vatican Museums; author's photo)

the serpents were a sign of the divine anger against a man so impious as to strike the sacred image (in fact Laocoön's death had a different cause: He had had intercourse with his wife within the temple precincts of Poseidon and now paid the price).

The Fall of Troy

To the sound of flutes, and in the midst of grand hilarity, the Trojans dragged the horse inside the citadel. That night a party of furious joy and abandon raged through the city. In the early hours of the morning, the Greeks descended to the ground from the horse's belly, opened the city's gates, and admitted their companions, who had returned from Tenedos. A blood-curdling cry pierced the night. Children clung to their mothers' robes and the slaughter began. The Greeks hunted down and killed the Trojan men. They took the women captive. The city burned.

In Euripides' antiwar play *The Trojan Women*, a chorus of Trojan captives sums up Troy's last agony. The play was produced in 415 BC just after the Athenians, in an especially nasty incident of the Peloponnesian War, had slaughtered all the male inhabitants of the island of Melos and sold their women and children into slavery. The play may therefore be read as a commentary on Athenian behavior (the play ran for more than ten years in New York City during the war in Vietnam).

[511]   *Chorus* Join with us, Muse, in our mournful dirge for Ilium.
      Sing through your tears her new song of sorrow.
      Mournfully sing the sorrows of Troy—
      how the four-legged wagon,° loaded with Greeks,
515   ruined the city, made me a slave.
      The Greeks left the horse outside the gates of the city,
      horse with a frontlet gleaming with gold,
      horse that would raise the war cry to heaven.
      The people of Troy from the citadel's top
520   raised a great shout: "Now freed from your toil,
      come, bring in the image of well-polished wood
      for Athena of Ilium, daughter of Zeus."
      What maid, what old man but emerged from the house at the call?
        With songs in their hearts, they set hands to the ropes
525   to drag in betrayal and ruin.
      Phrygians° old, Phrygians young ran to the gates of the city,
      ready to offer, as gift to the goddess,
      pine from the mountain, sleek ambush of Argives,
      destruction of Dardanus'° gullible race,
530   colt never broken, foal never to die.
      With ropes of spun linen, stout as a black ship's cables,
      they pulled the craft in, and up to its berth,
      the temple of marble, the floor soon to reek
      with worshipers' blood. They offered it there,

514. *four-legged wagon*: The Trojan Horse. 526. *Phrygians*: That is, the Trojans. 529. *Dardanus*: First ancestor of the Trojans (hence the alternate name Dardanelles for the Hellespont).

535 "to Pallas with thanks, on behalf of our country."
On joy and rejoicing descended the night
amid music of flutes, amid Phrygian songs.
The maidens' shrill song and quick-dancing feet spoke their joy,
    in every house the torch's dim beam
540   prevented the coming of slumber.
I was there with the rest. In the jubilant hall
I had joined in the dance to honor the maiden,
    the queen of the mountains, the daughter of Zeus.
When a blood-curdling cry rang out from the town and up the castle,
545 trembling children stretched little hands to their mother's lap.
        War sprang out of its ambush,
        the doing of maiden Athena.
Men were butchered beside the altar,
beheaded next to their brides
550   who were dragged away as a trophy,
as breeders of sons for the Argives, of bitter sorrow for Troy.

EURIPIDES, *Trojan Women* 511–567

Perhaps the most horrific death was that of old King Priam, whom Achilles' son Neoptolemus murdered at the altar of Zeus. Vergil gives the graphic details in the second book of the *Aeneid* (first century BC):

[506]   Perhaps you would like to ask me about the end of old Priam.
When he knew the town had fallen, the gates broken in by the foe,
the enemy storming each house in a frenzy of rapine and plunder,
he took down his rusty armor and fitted it over his shoulders,
510 trembling under the weight. His sword, too heavy to handle,
hung uselessly by his side as he stumbled out to destruction,
expecting to die in the thickest part of the enemy's phalanx.
    Now right in the central court of the palace, facing the sky,
stood a large and sacred altar, and beside it an ancient laurel,
515 shading the altar, where stood the household gods, the Penates.°
Like doves blown away as victims of a black and lowering tempest,
Hecuba° sat with her daughters, crowding closely around the altar,
clinging in desperate hope to the images of their protectors.
When Hecuba saw that Priam had donned his rusty old armor,
520 "Priam, my poor luckless partner, what desperate purpose is this?"
she screamed. "What frenzy spurs you to arm and hurry your fate?
Our condition no longer requires defense by armor like yours.
Even my Hector himself could afford us no comfort whatever.
Admit, then, that we are beaten. If anything now can protect us,
525 it must be this altar. If not, we two will perish together."
She drew the old man to her arms, and with him sat by the altar.
    Polites, a son of Priam, escaping the murderous Pyrrhus,°
fled down the endless halls, now ringing with enemy weapons.

---

515. . . . *the Penates*: Vergil's description fits a Roman household, not a Homeric palace. The Penates were protective spirits unique to Rome (see Chapter 23).   517. *Hecuba*: The Latin form of Hec-abê.   527. *Pyrrhus*: Neoptolemus, Achilles' son.

Reeling with wounds, he looked for safety in each empty chamber.
530 The rugged Pyrrhus, pursuing with spear poised ready to strike,
kept reaching out for the boy, who still eluded his captor.
At last he burst into sight, and under the gaze of his parents
he slipped and gasped out his life in a last outpouring of blood.
Priam, although now confronted by sure and immediate slaughter,
535 voiced his angry defiance in cries of embittered reproach:
"If heaven can recognize justice, if any gods can be bothered
to avenge outrages like yours, may they make you recompense fully
your wickedness. May they impose due penalty for your offenses
on you, who forced me to watch as you butchered my son before me,
540 spattering a father's face with blood poured out by his child.
You lie, hypocritically claiming to be the son of Achilles.
He never acted like that toward Priam, his deadliest foeman,
but sent back the mangled body of Hector for proper interment
and me to my city again, observing his word and his promise."
545 With that the old man threw his spear, feebly, doing no damage.
The bronze shield rattled a bit as it parried the useless spear,
which dangled harmlessly down from the edge of the knob in the middle.
Sarcastically Pyrrhus replied, "Bring your report to my father,
Peleus' son, and tell in detail the deeds of shame I committed.
550 Be sure he knows that his son is a weak and degenerate coward.
Now die!"
Feeble old Priam collapsed in a puddle of blood from Polites.
Neoptolemus wound his left hand in his hair and up to the altar
he dragged him, unresisting. His right drew his glittering sword,
555 and plunged it right to the hilt, deep into the bowels of Priam.
So ended the life of the king, a destiny long foretold.
This was the lot he had drawn: to live till the fall of the city,
till he saw Troy perish in flames, a city once monarch of Asia,
mistress of all her peoples. And now? a torso washed up on the seashore,
560 a head torn off from its body, a body without a name.

VERGIL, *Aeneid* 2.506–558

Menelaüs found Helen in her bedroom with her new husband Deïphobus, also a son of Priam, whom he killed and mutilated. Menelaüs was about to kill Helen too, but she bared her beautiful breasts to him and pleaded for her life. He hesitated, saying he would kill her later (in fact, they returned to Sparta and lived sort of happily ever after). The other Ajax, son of Oileus, raped Cassandra while she clung to an image of Athena (see Figure 21.7). This crime excited Athena's wrath, who caused much trouble to the Greeks as they returned home.

Of all the Trojan males, only a few escaped, the most important being Aeneas, who carried his lame father, Anchises, on his shoulders and led his young son, Ascanius (also called Iulus), by the hand out of the burning city. The victorious Greeks herded the captive women together outside the smoldering city, then distributed them among the heroes. At the command of Odysseus, Astyanax, Hector's son, was ripped from Andromachê's bosom and thrown to his death from the walls. "Only a fool kills the father and allows the son to live," Odysseus cynically remarked.

FIGURE 21.5 The sacrifice of Polyxena, on a Greek jug found in Etruria, c. 570 BC. Neoptolemus, son of Achilles, puts a sword into the throat of Polyxena, pouring the blood over his father's tomb. The three warriors holding the princess are named as Amphilochus, Antiphates, and Ajax, son of Oileus. Behind Neoptolemus stand Diomedes and Nestor. Phoenix is on the far right.   (British Museum, London; © Trustees of the British Museum)

Neoptolemus carried **Polyxena** (po-**lik**-se-na), youngest of Priam's daughters, to the tomb of his father Achilles and cut her throat over it, the blood pouring into the grave to quench the dead warrior's thirst (Figure 21.5). **(For a complete version of Euripides** *Trojan Women***, go to http://bacchicstage.wordpress.com/euripides/ trojan-women/)**

Observations: Was There Really a Trojan War?

Troy was built where the Hellespont meets the Aegean (Map IX, Chapter 20; Map XIII, inside back cover) on the only maritime passage between the Black Sea and the Mediterranean, a principal land route between Anatolia and Europe. The strait has been a zone of conflict throughout history, from the invasions of the Persian king Xerxes (480 BC) and Alexander the Great (334 BC) to Winston Churchill's catastrophic failed Gallipoli campaign (1915), and it remains heavily militarized today. Truly at the crossroads of civilizations, the Bronze Age citadel of Troy stood poised between large forces: the mighty Hittites to the east and the mighty Mycenaeans to the west.

There are nine phases of settlement at the archaeological site of Troy, one super-imposed on top of the next like a large layer cake (Figure 21.6). Settlement began

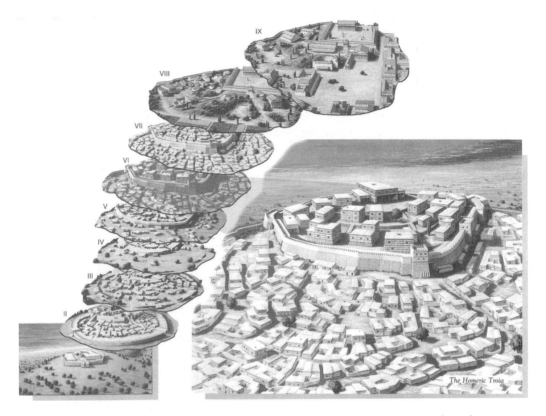

FIGURE 21.6 Conjectural reconstruction showing the superimposed settlements of Troy. Troy VI and VII, likely candidates for Homer's Troy, belong to the Late Bronze Age (c. 1700–1150 BC). Troy VIII is the Greek city (c. 800–133 BC) and Troy IX is the Roman city (c. 133 BC–AD 500). The reconstruction in lower right is Troy VII.   (By permission of the artist, Christoph Haußner)

about 3000 BC, at the start of the Bronze Age. The first seven layers are prehistoric, whereas cities VIII and IX are Greek and Roman. Archaeologists like to connect the two prehistoric phases of Troy VI and VII with the legend of the Trojan War.

Troy VI (1700–1250 BC) was the largest prehistoric city, when inhabitants fortified the citadel with astounding, huge, sloping walls of solid stone, twelve feet thick and thirty feet high (see Figure 1.2). Earthquake destroyed Troy VI around 1250 BC (perhaps why in legend Poseidon the earth-shaker was the enemy of Troy). The survivors rebuilt the town as Troy VII, but this town too was destroyed at about 1150 BC, this time by enemy action. Was the destruction of Troy VII the Trojan War of Greek legend?

In the 1870s the very successful and wealthy German businessman Heinrich Schliemann set out in search of Homeric Troy as a fulfillment of a childhood conviction in the historicity of the Trojan War. He first conducted major excavations at the place still known as Hissarlik (= Turkish "castle hill") and found amazing things. His finds were heralded across the globe: a city destroyed by fire deep within the mound and a cache of gorgeous gold and silver jewelry and other objects quickly dubbed "Priam's Treasure." However, we now know that the burned city Schliemann found belongs to the Troy II settlement (2500–2200 BC), far too early for the Late Bronze Age. There are doubts, too, about the integrity of the treasure and the real circumstances of its discovery, because Schliemann was not always truthful.

Schliemann's German architect, Wilhelm Dörpfeld, exposed the walls of the Troy VI citadel in the 1890s and quickly concluded that *these* walls, rebuilt by the inhabitants of Troy VII after the earthquake, were those that Homer memorialized. In the 1930s, the University of Cincinnati's Carl W. Blegen found signs of crowded housing inside the citadel walls of Troy VII, as well as installations for stockpiles of food, as if the inhabitants anticipated attack. Blegen also found sling stones and arrowheads and spearheads in destruction debris at the west gate, blocked after the earthquake. Blegen's final report on his work at Troy concluded that the Troy VII citadel yielded "actual evidence that the town was subjected to siege, capture, and destruction by hostile forces at some time in the general period assigned by Greek tradition to the Trojan War, and that it may safely be identified as the Troy of Priam and Homer."

Fieldwork by Troy's most recent excavator, Manfred Korfmann, who died in 2005, seems to have demonstrated that the citadel was only the upper city in a much larger settlement of perhaps 10,000 inhabitants. Immediately outside the citadel, a lower city was protected by a ditch and palisade that provided an outer line of defense far beyond the citadel wall, perhaps designed to inhibit the approach of a chariot-borne army.

Bronze Age Troy, then, constructed according to a common Anatolian design for a fortress, must have been an important commercial center, perhaps a royal residence, and must have had relationships with the great power of Bronze Age Hattussas, the Hittite capital in central Anatolia. If you travel inland from Troy over what today is a major commercial artery, first you come to the territory called Lydia, where coins were invented and Heracles was a slave to Omphalê; then you come to the territory called Phrygia, claimed as the haunt of Dionysus; then the long valley opens out onto a great plain, where the Hittites ruled from about 1600 BC. When a thousand years later the Persians ruled Anatolia starting in the sixth century BC, they called this route (really a trail) that joined the inland plateau with the coast "the royal road." The first piece of writing ever found at Troy, in 1995, is a bronze seal inscribed in a "hieroglyphic" syllabic script recording a Hittite dialect.

Hittite archives, furthermore, refer directly to Troy, calling it Wilusa (= Ilios) and Taruwisa (= Troia). Other names in the Hittite archives appear to give historical background to the Homeric epics. Around 1285 BC the Hittites made a treaty with one "Alaksandu of Wilusa," that is, Alexander in the Iliad, another name for Paris. *Priam* appears to be Hittite for "exceptionally courageous" (not "ransomed" as a false Greek etymology explained). The Hittite *Ahhiyawa* must be the Greek *Achaioi* (= Achaeans), who lived in a powerful place beyond the reach of the Hittite king, according to the Hittite archives. Homer's general picture of the political situation seems plausible: a powerful wealthy kingdom on the strategic shores of the Dardanelles and an overseas kingdom of Mycenaean Greeks who are not always on friendly terms with Asian powers.

But how could Homer have known about any such war? Not through writing, because Linear B was not used for literary or historical purposes, and it disappeared around 1200 BC. Most now believe that an oral poetic tradition preserved the memory of the war, the songs of figures like the singer Demodocus in the *Odyssey*. Whereas the specific issues of responsibility and behavior in the Homeric poems must belong to the eighth century BC, when a great poet named Homer composed our *Iliad* and *Odyssey,* the poet assumes that his audience is well acquainted with the traditions, the poem's personnel, and the background of the Trojan War.

In the Classical Period no one doubted the historicity of the war. We have seen how the Lesser Ajax, son of Oileus, from the district in central Greece called Locris, raped Cassandra at the shrine of Athena, a favorite scene among classical Greek vase painters (Figure 21.7). The classical Locrians every year

FIGURE 21.7 The Lesser Ajax, son of Oileus, attacking Cassandra as she clings to a statue of Athena, who carries shield and spear, on an Athenian red-figured wine cup, c. 430 BC. With his right hand Ajax seizes Cassandra from behind, her clothes disheveled. He is "heroically nude" and holds a shield with the emblem of a horse.   (Musée du Lourve, Paris; The Art Gallery Collection, Alamy)

sent two virgins from noble families across the sea to Ilium, now the hill at Hissarlik, to clean and maintain a sanctuary to Athena and so atone for the (mythical) crime of Ajax. The practice seems to have begun in the early Archaic Period, but the Locrians insisted it went back to the Trojan War itself. When Xerxes stopped at Ilium on his way to invade Greece in 480 BC, he sacrificed 1,000 cattle to Athena at the site of Troy. Alexander the Great claimed to find armor from the Trojan War inside Athena's temple there. From the classical settlement on the site of Ilium itself, Greek and Roman coins sought to connect Ilium to the heroic past. When the renegade Roman legate Fimbria captured Ilium in 85 BC, he boasted that in only eleven days he had captured a city that withstood Agamemnon for ten years. The Ilians replied: "Yes, but our city champion was no Hector."

AGAMEMNON'S RETURN

A genre of ancient epic told of the returns of the heroes from Troy and all that happened to them. These were called **Nostoi**, or "homecomings" (hence *nostalgia,* "homesickness"). Although the only extended epic account of a homecoming to survive is Homer's *Odyssey,* other literary works often refer to these stories. Agamemnon's return to Argos, his murder by Clytemnestra, and Orestes' revenge are known to us through Aeschylus' dramatic trilogy of 458 BC, the **Oresteia** (or-es-**tī**-a, "story of Orestes"). It is made up of three plays, each complete in itself but also contributing to the larger group: *Agamemnon, Choëphori* (ko-**ef**-o-rē, "libation bearers"), and *Eumenides* (yū-**men**-i-dēz; "the kindly ones" = the Furies). Whereas Homer in his *Odyssey* concentrates on the tribulations that Odysseus suffered while coming home and the difficulties he faced when he arrived, Aeschylus is concerned with bitter conflict within the family of Agamemnon and its resolution.

The Murder of Agamemnon

The subject of the first play is Clytemnestra's murder of her husband on the day that he returns from Troy. In the opening scene a watchman perches on the roof of the palace, waiting for the beacon fire that will signal from across the sea, by a sort of primitive telegraph, that Troy has fallen. The watchman's opening words reflect the gloom enveloping the palace. Clytemnestra has been having an affair with Agamemnon's cousin Aegisthus through the long years of the war. Suddenly the fire blazes up, a signal that Troy has fallen. A war-weary herald arrives, reporting the imminent appearance of the triumphant king Agamemnon. (Aeschylus has little interest in the sequence of events in real time.)

The herald describes the great storm that beset the fleet when it set out from Troy, a storm usually attributed to Athena's anger because of the Lesser Ajax's rape of Cassandra:

[646]   *Messenger*   Arriving in a city blessed and wealthy,
        reporting glorious news of its deliverance,
        how dare I mix such news with tales of horror,
        or tell of the raging storm that struck the Achaeans,
650   sent by the angry gods? For fire and ocean,
        enemies immemorial, conspired with an oath,
        to annihilate the unhappy Argive fleet.
           In the black of night the sea began to rise.
        A gale swept down from Thrace to smash our ships
655   one on another. Collision, screaming tempest
        with blinding squalls of rain forced us to run
        eyeless in darkness, helpless as driven sheep
        of a careless shepherd. When the pale dawn returned,
        we saw the Aegean dotted with Argive corpses,
660   floating like flowers among the shattered wrecks.
        We only and our ship escaped undamaged,
        saved by some god, who begged or stole our lives,
        ruling our helm with strong and practiced hand,
        a task too great for any mortal man.

                    AESCHYLUS, *Agamemnon* 646–664

Where Menelaüs was driven, no one knew, but Agamemnon's ship, at least, has survived.

Agamemnon arrives in a chariot, accompanied by his mistress and "prize" (*geras*), Cassandra. He greets the city and Clytemnestra, who comes out from the palace to greet him. She publicly complains of her suffering during her husband's absence, which nearly drove her to suicide, then invites her husband to enter the palace over a purple cloth, a central symbol in the play, a metaphor of the net by which Clytemnestra will trap and kill him: Deianira and Medea used cloth to destroy their enemies too (Chapters 15 and 19). At first Agamemnon refuses, saying this would be presumptuous, not befitting a mortal's place, but Clytemnestra urges him to put such thoughts from his mind. Persuaded, Agamemnon removes his sandals, steps from the chariot, and enters the palace across the purple cloth.

Cassandra, who remains outside in her own chariot, foresees Agamemnon's doom and her own. Over the lintel of the palace she has a vision of Thyestes' curse hanging heavy on the house, an image of the cannibal feast. Of course, no one understands her prophetic babble:

[1214]   *Cassandra*   O horrible! O horrible! Most horrible!
1215   Again the crushing weight of truth foreseen
        staggers my mind with visions I scarce dare speak.
        Do you see those children floating above the house,
        the sort of shapes one only sees in nightmares?
        Dead, dead! at the will of those who ought to love them!
1220   Why are their hands full of their own roast flesh,
        their own entrails—they hold it out as food—
        O horror! their father takes it, tastes it, eats.

For this, I tell you, a certain mangy lion
plots his revenge on my returning master
1225   (so I must name him; I bear the yoke of a slave),
keeping his house and reveling in his bed.

AESCHYLUS, *Agamemnon* 1214–1225

PERSPECTIVE 21.2

SHAKESPEARE'S *TROILUS AND CRESSIDA*

Shakespeare's play *Troilus and Cressida,* set during the eighth year of the Trojan War, revolves around many characters and incidents from ancient myth. But the central story of the play (Troilus' unhappy love for the fickle Cressida) proves, on close inspection, to have only a tenuous connection with the ancient sources. The play is a good example of the transformations undergone by ancient myth traveling through the Middle Ages and the Renaissance.

In the Middle Ages, all direct knowledge of Homer was gradually lost in Western, Latin-speaking Europe, and knowledge of the Greek language disappeared for about six hundred years. But the fame of the Trojan War lived on. It was known both from Vergil's account in the second book of the *Aeneid* and from the Latin translation of a Greek work by a certain "Dictys of Crete," the *Ephemeris belli Troiani,* "Diary of the Trojan War." Dictys claims actually to have been at Troy in the company of the Cretan commander, Idomeneus. Thus he was older than Homer and an eyewitness to the events of the war.

We now know the work of so-called Dictys to be a fake of the second or third century AD, but it was accepted as genuine by medieval scholars. So was the equally influential *De excidio Troiae historia,* "Concerning the Fall of Troy," by "Dares the Phrygian" (that is, a Trojan), a priest of Hephaestus, according to the *Iliad.* This Latin poem also is a fake, probably written in the fifth century AD.

In about 1160 a man named Benoît de Sainte-Maure, steeped in Dictys and Dares, wrote in French a *Roman de Troie,* "The Story of Troy," a classic of medieval romance. An Italian, Guido da Colonna, fashioned a prose version of Benoît's work, *Historia Troiana* (1272–1287), which was even more widely read because it was written in Latin, an international language. (The illustration of the Trojan Horse in Perspective Figure 21.1a comes from a translation back into French from Guido da Colonna's Latin version of Benoît's original French!) The story came to English readers through the *Troy Book* (1412–1420) of John Lydgate, based on Guido da Colonna, and William Caxton's *Recuyell of the Historyes of Troye* (1468–1471), which became the best-known version of the saga in English.

In Greek myth we learn only that **Troilus** was the youngest son of Priam and Hecabê and that Achilles killed him in an ambush at a spring. However, Dares portrays Troilus as a brave warrior fighting throughout the war. Benoît de Sainte-Maure and Guido da Colonna report the story of how the Trojan Troilus and the captive Briseida (= Briseïs) were lovers until the faithless Briseida forsook Troilus to take up with the Greek Diomedes.

Then Boccaccio (1313–1375) changed the name of Briseida to Griseida (in his *De casibus*), which eventually became the English Cressida (not therefore a distortion of Chryseïs, Agamemnon's prize). Boccaccio also made Pandarus, a bowman in the *Iliad,* into Troilus' dissolute companion. The English poet Chaucer depended on Boccaccio for his long poem *Troylus and Cryseyde* (1372–1386), which delicately portrays the frailty of human love.

By Shakespeare's day (1564–1616) Cressida had become a byword for a depraved woman—for example, "Fetch forth the lazar [leprous] kite [a scavenging bird] of Cressid's kind,/ Doll Tearsheet she by name" (*Henry V* 2.1.73–74). Pandarus had become a byword for a procurer (hence our word *pander*), and Troilus was now the innocent young man brought to grief through love for a bad woman. Shakespeare develops these central themes in his play *Troilus and Cressida,* probably produced in 1602 (just after *Hamlet*). Cressida is a giddy girl, a jilt, who first falls in love with Troilus, then thoughtlessly casts him aside for the sexier Diomedes. As background to the story, Shakespeare brings in Agamemnon, Ajax, Ulysses (Odysseus), Nestor, and Achilles from the Greek side and Priam, Aeneas, Hector, Andromachê, Paris, and Helen from the Trojans.

Although audiences had lost direct connection with Greek literature, the story of the Trojan War continued to entrance audiences in many countries throughout the European Middle Ages and later, when poets modified or built freely on inherited traditions to reflect contemporary literary styles and concerns.

Cassandra herself turns and goes into the palace. From within a cry rings out as Clytemnestra strikes the death blow (Figure 21.8). Clytemnestra comes forth, drenched in blood, looming over the murdered bodies of her husband and his mistress. Exulting, she declares how delicious was the murderous deed, which she prepared with her lover, Aegisthus:

[1378] *Clytemnestra*   My hatred was no sudden mindless growth.
          It rose from an old quarrel, which festered on.
1380   I stand here where I struck him. That work is finished.
          For it I offer no apology.
              To keep the man from dodging and eluding death,
          I spread a sumptuous net, like one for fishes,
          rich robes but deadly. He could only struggle.
1385   Once, twice, I chopped. He gave two retching groans,
          his knees collapsed, he fell. With one more blow,

FIGURE 21.8 The death of Agamemnon, Attic wine-mixing bowl, c. 470 BC. Aegisthus has stabbed Agamemnon, who is wrapped in a weblike garment. Behind Aegisthus, Clytemnestra runs up carrying a small ax (not visible). The woman behind Agamemnon is probably Cassandra, and the woman to the far right Electra.   (Photograph © 2011 Museum of Fine Arts, Boston)

> a coup de grâce, I sent him down to Hades,
> below the earth, comforter of the dead.
> So he gasped out his life, and, as he fell,
> 1390　a rain of crimson drops, from his bitter death,
> spattered upon me. My heart leaped up for joy
> exulting like a plot of budded wheat,
> which Zeus is ripening with his hoped-for rain.
> 　Elders of Argos, you have heard my story.
> 1395　Approve it or not. I glory in my deed.
> If piety permitted such libation,
> he would deserve it, more than any man.
> For it was he who filled the accursed cup.
> He has returned and drained its bitter dregs.
>
> 　　　　　Aeschylus, *Agamemnon* 1378–1398

Clytemnestra defends her treachery and murder, claiming as her motive Agamemnon's sacrifice of her daughter Iphigenia. Aegisthus joins her on the stage, and the play ends.

Orestes' Revenge

The second play of the trilogy takes place many years later. Agamemnon's son, **Orestes**, taken as a child to be raised near Delphi, has come to manhood. Ordered by the Delphic Oracle, he returns to Argos with his friend Pylades to avenge the murder of his father, even though this means killing his own mother. He goes to his father's grave and leaves a lock of hair upon it.

The night before, Clytemnestra had a horrible dream: She gave birth to a viper that sucked at her breasts and bit them. Thinking that the angry ghost of Agamemnon sent the dream, she sends her daughter **Electra** to his grave to make drink-offerings, in company with a band of women: the "libation bearers" who make up the chorus in the play. Orestes reveals himself to his sister Electra, who is bitter and filled with hatred toward the mother who killed her father. Together they plot the murder of Clytemnestra.

Pretending that he is a messenger come to report his own death, Orestes enters the palace. When Aegisthus arrives to hear the good news, Orestes kills him. Clytemnestra comes in to discover the corpse—and the truth. Orestes draws his sword, prepared to fulfill his mission. Clytemnestra, desperate for life, bares her breasts and pleads for mercy:

[896]   No, no, my child! Have pity on these breasts,
from which, still half asleep, your baby gums
so often sucked the milk that gave you strength.

AESCHYLUS, *Choëphori* 896–898

Orestes hesitates, but at the urging of his friend Pylades kills her, then exults over the body and that of her lover, both lying at his feet:

[973]   See, see the double tyrants of the land,
who killed my father and who wrecked my home!
975   In arrogance they mounted to his throne,
and even now they cling, these paramours,
still bound by oath—or so their end suggests.
Together they plotted Agamemnon's death.
They swore to die together and kept that promise.
980   Now look again, all you that hear these horrors,
upon the trap they set for my poor father,
like fetters and manacles for feet and hands.
Come, spread it out. Stand round it on all sides
and hold this winding-sheet in the plain sight
985   of the father—no, not mine, but Father Sun,
who oversees all things—that he may know
my mother's godless deeds, and stand by me
as witness when at last I face my judges,
to justify my compassing her death.
990   Killing Aegisthus bothers me not at all.
He has paid the penalty the law decrees
for such defilers. But as for her

who schemed the shameful death of such a man
as Agamemnon, who bore his children's weight
995　beneath her heart, a burden she once loved,
but which by now she loathed—how do you judge?
A snake, I tell you, an adder, whose poisoned bite,
at first unnoticed, brings death and quick decay,
fruits of her passion and malicious heart.

Aeschylus, *Choëphori* 973–1004

But already the **Furies** (or Erinyes, e-**rin**-i-ēz), the persecuting spirits of murdered kin, surround Orestes. They work their vengeance by disturbing the mind of their victim, and Orestes slips into madness.

The Trial of Orestes

The last play of the trilogy, in which the Furies make up the chorus, opens in Delphi. Orestes has gone there for Apollo's protection from the Furies, for it was Apollo who advised him to kill his mother. Apollo orders Orestes to go to Athens to seek justice from the Athenian law court presided over by Athena. The scene shifts (rare in Greek drama) to Athens, where Orestes falls down, a suppliant, at the statue of Athena. The Furies arrive and insist that the spilled blood of blood relatives must be atoned by more spilled blood, but Orestes claims that Apollo has purified him of pollution and appeals to Athena for help. The Furies claim that it is their divine prerogative to persecute those who murder their own blood kin, and that the upstart Olympians have no right to interfere with ancient privilege. Athena, seeing justice on either side, turns the case over to a jury of twelve Athenians, who hear the case on the Areopagus ("hill of Ares") below the Acropolis, the first trial scene in Western literature.

The Furies present their case. Without the ancient restraints, there will be no check on crime. Orestes asks why they did not persecute Clytemnestra for killing Agamemnon? Because, they reply, Clytemnestra and Agamemnon did not share the same blood. Apollo now takes up Orestes' case and claims the authority of Zeus, the protector of kings. King Agamemnon's death is not to be compared with that of an adulterous woman. As for the primacy of blood ties, the child's blood comes from the father who plants the seed, not from the mother who is but the soil in which the seed is sown. Athena herself is proof that the child is of the father—a modern twist to an old tale:

[657]　*Apollo*　Thus I declare, be sure I speak the truth.
She who gives birth to what we call "her child"
is not the parent of the new-sown growth;
660　rather, she is its nurse. Its parent is the man
who gives his seed to her, a stranger woman,
to keep for him, a stranger, as it swells,
if so the gods decree. Here is the proof:
A male can father children without a mother—

Stories from the Trojan War were important to Greek art from an early time. Perhaps one-fourth of the mythical subjects illustrated on Greek pots are related to the Trojan saga, and the tradition never stopped entirely. In *The Trojan Horse Disgorges Its Burden* (Perspective Figure 21.1a), from a late fifteenth-century French version of the Trojan story, three Greeks (perhaps Odysseus, Menelaüs, and Neoptolemus) emerge from the open hatch of the wooden horse to descend the ladder.

The horse stands by a breach in the wall beside a gate labeled *la porte dardane,* the "Dardanian Gate." The story is told as a sequence of pictures. Beyond the horse are the Greeks, now emerged from the horse, then medieval city towers and a moat. In the courtyard beyond, the Greeks are in massed formation and dead Trojans litter the grounds. In the sky appears the label *la ville de troie,* the city of Troy.

PERSPECTIVE FIGURE 21.1a *The Trojan Horse Disgorges Its Burden,* late fifteenth-century manuscript of Raoul Lefèvre's *Recueil.* (Bibliothèque Nationale de France, Paris; MS. Fr. 22552, fol. 276v)

In Book 24 of the *Iliad,* lines 25–30 refer casually to the judgment of Paris, but the lost epic poem the *Cypria* (perhaps = "myths about Aphrodite"), of which a summary has survived, fully treated the topic, along with the wedding of Peleus and Thetis and the Apple of Discord. The German Lucas Cranach the Elder painted several versions with the same general composition but different details (Perspective Figure 21.1b). He illustrated female anatomy by showing one woman from the side, one full front, and one from the back, a pose based on the ancient three Graces (see Perspective Figure 6.1). The middle figure may be Juno/Hera, because she points to heaven, where Juno/Hera is queen. The right-hand figure may be Venus/Aphrodite, who stares shamelessly outward at the person looking at the picture, her buttocks in plain view. The left-hand figure would be Minerva/Athena, placing her proposal before Paris.

Cranach's Paris is a perfect German knight (like Cranach's patrons), slouched against the tree, the Apple of Discord in his left hand. Behind him is Mercury/Hermes, with winged hat (peacocks!), holding a globe in his left hand (he travels the world) and a staff in his right (= caduceus). The landscape is a lively fantasy with a mountain citadel in the upper right, from which the knightly Paris has come, and Troy in the center background, a medieval town. In the upper left is a cupid with drawn bow, ready to give success to Venus/Aphrodite.

PERSPECTIVE FIGURE 21.1b Lucas Cranach the Elder (German, 1472–1553), *The Judgment of Paris,* c. 1528, tempera and oil on wood. (Metropolitan Museum of Art, New York; photograph by Schecter Lee © 1986)

The Roman encyclopedist Pliny the Elder, who lived in the early Roman empire (AD 23–79), tells us that the emperor Vespasian (AD 69–79), builder of the Coliseum in Rome, had in his palace the most marvelous work ever made, a sculpture that portrayed the death of Laocoön and his sons carved from a single block of stone. In January 1506, some workers unearthed it from a vineyard in the then sparsely populated city of Rome (see Figure 21.4). Pope Julius II, a warrior but patron of the arts, acquired it for the Vatican, where it is today one of the most famous works of art in the world. The Laocoön's vivid portrayal of suffering and its understanding of the musculature of powerful masculine physique deeply influenced Michelangelo and many others. Hundreds of adaptations (and parodies) of the sculptural group exist, but the *Laocoön* of the visionary El Greco (1541–1614) is one of the best known (Perspective Figure 21.1c). El Greco, "the Greek," migrated to Toledo, Spain, from his home in Crete, hence the nickname.

PERSPECTIVE FIGURE 21.1c El Greco (Domenikos Theotokopoulos; Spanish, born in Crete, 1541–1614), *Laocoön,* c. 1610–1614, oil on canvas. (National Gallery of Art, Washington, DC)

Here the Trojan priest, on the point of death, stares at the fangs of the serpent. The Trojan Horse is visible in the distance, above Laocoön's right thigh. One of his sons, on the left, holds with two hands a serpent about to bite his midriff. The two naked figures on the right, long thought to be either Apollo and Artemis or Poseidon and Cassandra, are now thought to be Adam and Eve (Adam gazes at the fateful apple in his left hand).

Thus El Greco compares the carnal sin of Laocoön, who had intercourse with his wife in the temple of Poseidon, with the sin of Adam and Eve, who disobeyed God's commandment and brought suffering, with the awareness of sexuality, into the world. In the background rises Troy, really the medieval town of Toledo. Flamelike lines, distorted faces, elongated figures, and full, vibrant color combine to give the painting a curiously modern air. El Greco's paintings were, in fact, neglected until the twentieth century.

In the nineteenth century, when the taste for suffering in literature was well developed, Frederic Leighton, president of the British Royal Academy and leader of the Victorian art establishment, took up a pathetic theme from the *Iliad* (see Chapter 20), the moment that Hector predicted to his wife Andromachê that one day, a slave, she would draw water from her master's well (Perspective Figure 21.1d). Leighton shows a forlorn Andromachê among the Greek women drawing water from the spring on the right. Perhaps the scene is set at the palace of Neoptolemus, whose captive she was. Most eyes turn to her, an object of pathetic interest, dressed in the black of mourning, her face covered and head bowed with sorrow. Even the water-carrier in the bottom middle stoops to stare. But the Greek women smile, and the happy family at the bottom right imitates, and bitterly mocks, Homer's description of Hector, Andromachê, and the baby Astyanax at the Scaean Gate. But that was in a former time.

PERSPECTIVE FIGURE 21.1d Frederic Leighton (English, 1830–1896), *Captive Andromache,* 1888, oil on canvas.   (Manchester City Art Galleries, Manchester, England)

665   as witness she who stands among you here,
Athena, daughter of Olympian Zeus.
She was not fostered in a darkling womb.
No goddess could give birth to such a child.

AESCHYLUS, *Eumenides* 657–666

Therefore, Orestes' murder of Clytemnestra was, strictly speaking, not the shedding of kindred blood. Orestes was obliged to avenge the murder of his father, a scepter-bearing king. The jury's vote is evenly divided. Athena, who always sides with the male, casts the deciding vote:

[734]   *Athena*   Mine is the last, mine the decisive vote.
735   This ballot, then, I cast—to acquit Orestes.
No woman ever labored through my birth.
My heartfelt fellow-feeling is for the man,
save in one thing: He is obliged to marry.
Thus siding with the father, I cannot place
740   an equal value on a woman's death,
who killed her husband, guardian of the home.

AESCHYLUS, *Eumenides* 734–739

Athena appeases the Furies, angry at the verdict, by assigning them a permanent place in Athens, but as beneficent spirits now, no longer malignant. Hence their new name the **Eumenides**, "the kindly ones," who will dwell in a grotto beneath the Areopagus (still visible today).

Apollo's argument, that the son is closer to the father than to the mother, strikes a modern as odd, but it is based on the ancient agricultural metaphor applied to human biology. The seed is planted in the earth, but is not of the earth. The rain from heaven, like semen, makes the seed grow, which otherwise would die. So the human female provides a soil in which the child may grow, but the child comes from the father.

The reasoning is typical of arguments offered in real Athenian courts of the fifth century BC, when conclusions based on the plausibility of evidence were first refined. A century and a quarter after the production of the *Oresteia*, Aristotle speculated on the roles of father and mother in producing children. Although he recognized that both sexes contribute, he assigned the generative force (which includes the form that the fetus is to assume) to the male contribution; the female contributes only its formless matter. In fact, the female's genetic contribution to human reproduction was not clarified until about two hundred years ago.

According to other sources, Orestes, after being freed from the Furies' persecution and regaining his sanity, ruled peacefully over Mycenae, Argos, and Sparta. He married his cousin Hermionê, daughter of Menelaüs and Helen. Earlier Hermionê was married to the cruel Neoptolemus, son of Achilles, but Orestes killed him when he was at Delphi (or the priests of Apollo did). **(For the complete *Oresteia*, see http://bacchicstage.wordpress.com/aeschylus-2/aeschylus/, http://bacchicstage.wordpress.com/aeschylus-2/choephoroi/, and http://bacchicstage.wordpress.com/aeschylus-2/eumenides/)**

Observations: A Parable of Progress

Aeschylus, born in 525 BC, grew up when the tyranny of Pisistratus and his sons was breaking down. He lived through the radical democratic reforms of Clisthenes and fought in the battles of Marathon, 490 BC, and Salamis, 479 BC. Alone of the major Athenian tragedians, he brought to his poetic vision the boundless optimism of the young democracy. In the *Oresteia* we see him refashion an old myth to proclaim this vision.

A leading theme in the trilogy is the question, "What is justice?" According to the ancient unwritten law of the clan, justice is revenge. Thyestes slept with Atreus' wife; Atreus gave Thyestes his own children to eat. Agamemnon killed Iphigenia; Clytemnestra killed Agamemnon; Orestes killed Clytemnestra. This is blood-vendetta, rooted in the ancient fear of ghosts who demand blood for blood, an eye for an eye, the old law that the Furies embody and execute. But the constant killing for revenge has no logical limit. Somehow the vicious cycle must end.

Earlier, at Delphi, an advance over the primitive blood-vendetta had appeared. In a rite of purification, pig's blood was dripped over a murderer to release him and those who had contact with him from persecution by a ghost (see Figure 7.5). The progressive Athenian system of civic law to settle homicide, which Aeschylus proudly celebrates, was a momentous improvement over the Delphic system of magical purification (but note that Aeschylus gives Apollo credit for inspiring this advance). We use a similar system of civic law in the West today.

In Athenian civic law, the authority of the state curtailed the juridical power of the family. Laws recorded in alphabetic writing record the will of the state. Many upper-class Athenian males could read alphabetic script, and from 621 BC onward Athenian laws were engraved on wood or stone and displayed in the agora, where anyone could examine them and argue over their meaning. Some written law had existed before in Mesopotamia (never in Egypt), but such laws were presented as handed down by gods, immutable, divine, and inexorable. The Hebrews, too, viewed law as divinely willed. In Athens, by contrast, the people drafted and approved the laws, constantly revised them, and interpreted them in open courts before a jury of fellow citizens.

There was nothing divine about these laws, and there were no lawyers in Athens to present a definitive interpretation. A defendant had to represent himself in court. Athenian females, who were never citizens, were excluded from this system of public governance and ordinarily were not allowed into court. When a woman was charged with a crime, a man would speak on her behalf. The system of Athenian popular democratic laws recorded in alphabetic writing, and interpreted in an open courtroom filled with one's peers, contributed greatly to the development of the arts of persuasion and led directly to the invention of logic and the elaborate philosophical speculations of Plato and Aristotle, on which modern science directly depends.

The Furies, on the other hand, stand for traditional, familial, and tribal ways. The avenging spirits of spilled blood take no interest in why familial blood was shed, but only that it was shed. These ancient powers of ghost vengeance, the children of Night (Nyx), are by nature opposed to the younger Olympians, Athena and Apollo. Although they cannot be cast out completely or destroyed, they can be tamed and transformed into propitious powers that will support the new order: the Eumenides. Thus Athens, the ideal *polis*, replaces the violent, archaic, and heroic world with one that looks to a brighter future in which human intelligence can resolve primitive, self-destructive fear.

Aeschylus incorporates numerous etiological details in *Eumenides*. He traces the institution of the Areopagus, a court with jurisdiction over homicide during Aeschylus' day, back to the trial of Orestes; the rule that a tie vote stands for acquittal (still true today in parliamentary procedure) begins with Athena's ruling; the cult of the Eumenides (which actually existed in caves beneath the rock of the Areopagus) is hereby explained; and the traditional political alliance between Argos and Athens in classical times is traced to Orestes' gratitude for being freed at Athens of the Furies' persecution. Aeschylus' *Oresteia* is another good example of how the Greeks modified and transformed ancient, traditional tales to reflect contemporary issues and justify contemporary practice.

KEY NAMES AND TERMS

SOME ADDITIONAL ANCIENT SOURCES

Ovid gives the story of the judgment of the arms at *Metamorphoses* 12.624–13.398. Homer's *Odyssey* (11.408–426) describes the murder of Agamemnon and Cassandra (also described by Menelaüs in *Odyssey* Book 4). Uniquely, three tragedies survive that tell of Orestes' murder of his mother—in addition to Aeschylus' *Choëphori*, Sophocles' *Electra*, and Euripides' *Electra*. Each play modifies the emphasis and details of the plot. Orestes is also important in Euripides' *Orestes, Iphigenia Among the Taurians,* and *Andromachê.* Apollodorus describes Orestes' adventures in "Epitome" 6.14 and 6.24–28 and Hyginus in *Fabulae* 123–127. Pindar's *Nemean Ode* 7.33–47 and *Paean* 6.98–120 describe the death of Neoptolemus.

FURTHER READING CHAPTER 21

Goldhill, Simon, *Aeschylus: The Oresteia* (Cambridge, UK, 1992). Introduction to the social and political background of the trilogy, with a lucid interpretation.

Herington, J., *Aeschylus* (New Haven, CT, 1986). Good general study.

Huxley, G. L., *Greek Epic Poetry: From Eumelos to Panyasis* (Cambridge, MA, 1969). Reconstruction of the lost Cyclic Poems on the basis of the fragments.

Lebeck, Ann, *The* "Oresteia"*: A Study in Language and Structure* (Cambridge, MA, 1971). A penetrating analysis of the sometimes desperate imagery and difficult themes in Aeschylus' tragedy, arguing that the central theme is a concern with causality.

Woodford, Susan, *The Trojan War in Ancient Art* (Ithaca, NY, 1993). Summarizes complex evidence for this very popular theme in ancient art.

Zeitlin, Froma, *Playing the Other: Essays on Gender and Society in Classical Greek Literature* (Chicago, 1996). Contains an excellent essay on the *Oresteia* (and much else of interest about Greek literature).

CHAPTER 22

THE RETURN OF ODYSSEUS

But I imagine that the story of Odysseus is greater
than what he actually did, through the sweetness of Homer's verse;
for by his winged song he gives to lies a certain dignity,
and his poetic craft deceives us, leading us astray by myths.

PINDAR, *Nemean* 7.20–23

THE POETIC GENIUS HOMER inherited a story about how Odysseus, one of the principal fighters at Troy, ran into great trouble trying to get home. After twenty years he returned, only to find his son's life threatened, his father living like a pauper, and his wife besieged in her own house by lascivious, greedy, and politically ambitious men. Without allies, except experience and high intelligence, Odysseus appeared in disguise among his wife's suitors and, on a feast day of Apollo, he killed them all in cold blood. Of this wonderful gory story of revenge Homer made a parable of the human journey from life into death and return again to life.

In ancient times the *Iliad* was compared to tragedy because of its somber themes and deep personal conflict; the *Odyssey*, by contrast, was compared with comedy because (like the folktales whose patterns and symbols Homer borrows) it has a happy ending in which the family is reunited and the promise of the future is affirmed. The *Odyssey* is a towering artistic achievement, admired and still imitated by artists today, one of the most influential myths in the Western world.

601

ODYSSEUS' JOURNEY FROM TROY

The Cicones and the Lotus Eaters

In the *Odyssey*, Odysseus recounts his adventures at a banquet on the island of Phaeacia in the court of King Alcinoüs (al-**sin**-o-us), where Odysseus came ashore after shipwreck in a violent storm. He has been away from home twenty years: ten at Troy, three lost at sea, and seven on the island of the mysterious nymph Calypso ("concealer"). Odysseus' first-person narrative of his travels occupies one-sixth of Homer's 12,000-line poem, the *Odyssey*.

When Odysseus and his twelve ships leave Troy, they stop at Ismarus in Thrace, land of the Cicones (**sik**-o-nēz), and sack the city. Against the advice of their commander, they pause to devour the stolen sheep, cattle, and wine. On the next morning the neighboring Cicones attack, killing six men from every ship (each ship seems to have a crew of fifty).

PERSPECTIVE 22.1

ULYSSES

The figure of Odysseus, the Roman Ulysses, has long fascinated the West. Although he takes on many meanings, he is always either glorified as the seeker of truth, the restless clever intelligence penetrating the secrets of the world, or damned as the treacherous deceiver, the exalter of intellect above the demands of the heart. Homer's Odysseus belongs to the first category, but the anti-Odysseus tradition appears as early as Sophocles' play *Philoctetes* (409 BC) and is refined by Euripides, Vergil, and others.

The Romans especially developed the tradition hostile to Odysseus because they claimed Aeneas, a Trojan, as their founder. In his *Divine Comedy*, Dante Alighieri (1265–1321) follows the Roman tradition, for he saw legitimate political power in his own world as descending from the Roman state, said to inherit Trojan power (according to the myth). Dante's is the first important portrayal of Odysseus in a nonclassical language.

In the twenty-sixth canto of the *Inferno,* the first of three parts of the *Divine Comedy,* Dante stands with his guide, Vergil, and looks down in the pit reserved for deceitful counselors. Dante and Vergil are near Hell's deepest caverns and beneath them see flames that look like fireflies in the darkness. Vergil explains that one flame, split at the top, is Ulysses, crafty inventor of the Trojan Horse, who through guile sneaked into Troy (with Diomedes) and stole the protecting statue of Athena, the Palladium.

Ulysses is condemned to Hell because of his successful stratagems against the Roman's Trojan forebears, but Dante also condemns him for the restlessness of his intellect and his search for truth, a sinful exploration that can lead only to destruction. The flame speaks and tells a tale never told in the ancient world: how Odysseus never reached home, but was lost, still searching, in the high seas beyond the Pillars of Heracles (= Strait of Gibraltar). The voice is prophetic, foretelling the age of discovery when restless Europeans, cultural descendants of Greece and Rome and dependent on ancient Greek geographers, crossed the Atlantic Ocean and sailed around Africa to discover new worlds. Although building his portrait of Ulysses on that of the Roman poet Vergil, Dante rediscovered the Greek Odysseus who scorns comfort to explore the unknown.

The pro-Odysseus tradition reappears in "Ulysses" of Alfred, Lord Tennyson (1809–1892), the most famous English poet of the Victorian age, who glorifies the very qualities that Dante condemns. The poem is set on Ithaca. Ulysses has grown old, but is determined to leave home again in pursuit of fresh adventure:

> It little profits that an idle king,
> By this still hearth, among these barren crags,
> Matched with an aged wife, I mete and dole
> Unequal laws unto a savage race,
> That hoard, and sleep, and feed, and know not me.
> I cannot rest from travel; I will drink
> Life to the lees . . .
> Old age hath yet his honour and his toil.
> Death closes all; but something ere the end,
> Some work of noble note, may yet be done,
> Not unbecoming men that strove with gods.
> The lights begin to twinkle from the rocks;
> The long day wanes; the slow moon climbs; the deep
> Moans round with many voices. Come, my friends,
> 'Tis not too late to seek a newer world.
> Push off, and sitting well in order smite
> The sounding furrows; for my purpose holds
> To sail beyond the sunset, and the baths
> Of all the western stars, until I die . . .
> We are not now that strength which in old days
> Moved earth and heaven; that which we are, we are;
> One equal temper of heroic hearts,
> Made weak by time and fate, but strong in will
> To strive, to seek, to find, and not to yield.

ALFRED, LORD TENNYSON, "ULYSSES"

A sympathetic perception also underlies the most celebrated recasting of Odysseus in the twentieth century in James Joyce's (1882–1941) novel *Ulysses* (1922). In this long and difficult work (768 pages), really a satire, Ulysses appears as Leopold Bloom, an Irish Jew, forever the outsider, who makes a modest living selling advertising for a newspaper. The book describes his wanderings on a single day through the streets of Dublin, whose humdrum everyday life replaces the exotic lands of Homer's story. Telemachus is replaced by Stephen Dedalus, whose name combines that of Stephen, the first Christian martyr, and that of Daedalus, the master artist of Athens.

Stephen Dedalus is a world-weary dropout whose mind is preoccupied with the relationship between Hamlet and his father (just as Homer's Telemachus goes in quest of his father). The princess Nausicaä, whom Homer's Odysseus compared to Artemis in beauty, is a crippled shop-girl who inspires Leopold Bloom to masturbate in his pants as he watches her on the beach. Penelopê, Leopold's wife, Molly, is conducting a torrid affair with Blazes Boylan (= the suitors), who in this case has succeeded in seducing the lady of the house. Although Leopold knows about her tryst on that afternoon, he can think of no way to prevent it. Yet Molly in her own way, in her heart, is truly like Penelopê, ever faithful to her beloved "Poldy."

The remaining Greeks escape by sea but are soon caught in a storm off the southern coast of the Peloponnesus. Violent winds blow them out of the everyday world into the mythical land of the **Lotus Eaters**. The local inhabitants consume a drug that makes men forgetful of their home and their purpose:

[94]   Once any of them had tasted the honey-sweet fruit of the lotus,
95   he lost his desire to return, to boast of his glorious exploits.
    All they wished was to stay in the land of the eaters of lotus,
    drowsily nibbling the fruit, and forgetting their hopes of return.
    Ignoring their tears, I frog-marched them back at once to the vessels,
    to lash them under the thwarts in the bilge of the hollow ships.
100   Then I ordered the rest of my crew, shipmates sober and trusty,
    to embark in the ships right away, lest, after tasting the lotus
    some of them might be tempted to give up all hope of return.
    Quickly they hurried aboard and took their place on the benches.
    Swinging together they caught at the foaming sea with their oars.

HOMER, *Odyssey* 9.94–104

Polyphemus

At sea again, the Greeks come to the land of the **Cyclopes** (sī-**klōp**-ēz, "round-eyes") and the cave of the Cyclops **Polyphemus** (pol-i-**fēm**-us, "much-renowned"). This story, one of the most famous in the world, surely had an independent existence before Homer adapted it to the story of Odysseus. From the evidence of art, the story seems to have been excerpted often from the longer poem for separate performance, once it was written down in the eighth century BC:

[105]   Forward we sailed, regretful of all we were leaving behind.
          In time we came to the land of the arrogant lawless Cyclopes,
          who sow no crops with their hands, nor harvest the ripened grain,
          but entrust all that to heaven; so all their needs are supplied—
          wheat and barley and vines which bear them wine in abundance,
110   fostered by Zeus's rain, without labor of seedtime or harvest.
          They never unite in assembly for common decisions or laws,
          but live in echoing caves on the highest peaks of the mountains,
          alone, each ruling his wife and children, ignoring all others.
              A little outside a harbor along the Cyclopean coastline
115   stretches a wooded island, a breeding place for wild goats,
          untroubled by wandering humans or hunters in search of game.
          No danger ever concerns them as they wander over the hillsides,
          no goat pens cumber the island, no plowland limits their range.
          No humans inhabit the region, unplowed and fallow forever,
120   unharvested through the ages, a pasture for bleating goats.
          For Cyclopes know nothing of ships with red-painted gunwales.
          They have no shipwrights to build vessels of well-fitted benches
          to sail to the cities of men and return with whatever they lack—
          crossing the sea in their vessels in search of something to trade.
125   Traders, indeed, might make of the island a prosperous city,
          a source of all that is good with nothing to threaten its safety.
          By the coast of the foaming sea lie rich and well-watered meadows
          that, planted with grapes, would yield almost perpetual vintage.
          Plowmen could easily harvest abundant crops in their season
130   from the island's soil, so easy to harrow, so deep and so fertile.
          The harbor, moreover, is perfect; a ship has no need of an anchor
          or hawsers at either end, to hold her fast in her place.
          Just beach her and leave her alone for as long a time as you fancy
          till the men are ready to sail and following breezes are rising.
135   Abundant fresh water runs from springs at the head of the harbor,
          rising deep in a cave whose mouth is surrounded by poplars.
              Some god was surely the pilot who guided us into the harbor
          through the dark of night, for the dawn had not begun to appear.
          Deep fog enveloped the ships, no moon was shining in heaven.
140   Clouds had covered her face. No one saw the loom of the island,
          nor did we see the long crests of the breakers rolling ashore
          till our vessels had already grounded and run on the sandy beach.
          We jumped out into the water, removed the gear from the vessels,
          then pulled our ships to safety and clambered up on the seashore
145   where we sank into deepest slumber to wait for the breaking of dawn.
              Rose-fingered dawn at last revealed the coming of morning.
          Gaping about in surprise, we wandered all over the island
          whose nymphs, the daughters of Zeus, the god adorned with the aegis.
          roused up herds of wild goats as breakfast for all my comrades.
150   From the ships we took curved bows and deeply socketed lances,
          split ourselves into three groups, and then set off to the hunt.
          The gods gave us wonderful luck. Nine goats were allotted to each
          of the dozen ships of my fleet, and ten to me as commander.
          So we spent the whole day till the sun was setting at evening,

155 feasting on endless fresh meat washed down with mellow old wine.
  For the wine in our ships as yet was not completely exhausted,
  wine that was part of our loot from the holy Ciconian city.
  This we had poured in great jars and distributed plenty to each.
  All that day we watched the land of the nearby Cyclopes,
160 seeing their smoke and hearing the sound of men and their flocks.
  But after the sun had set and darkness came over the heavens,
  we finally laid ourselves down to sleep by the edge of the water.
   Rose-fingered dawn at last revealed the coming of morning.
  I rose to my feet, called the men, and issued them these as orders:
165 "My comrades, stay here a bit while I and the crew of my vessel
  go out to spy on the natives, what sort of people they are.
  Uncivilized, maybe, and savage, having no vestige of honor,
  or possibly kindly to strangers with minds inspired by heaven."
   At this I climbed in my ship and ordered my comrades to follow,
170 to cast off the hawsers, board, and seat themselves at the oars.
  Quickly they hurried aboard and took their place on the benches.
  Swinging together they caught at the foaming sea with their oars.
  When we got to the nearby mainland, we could see the mouth of a cavern
  down by the edge of the sea, high-vaulted, shaded by laurels,
175 where sheep and goats liked to sleep. Its front was a sort of corral,
  fashioned of rough quarried stones piled up as high as the roof,
  braced by long slender firs and trunks of high-foliaged oak trees.
  Inside, there slept by himself a man of incredible stature,
  a hermit, watching his sheep, avoiding the rest of his fellows,
180 in solitude making up fantasy, dreaming his god-accursed dreams.
  His frame was enormous, atrocious, unlike that of bread-eating humans.
  Rather, he looked like a craggy spur of a desolate mountain,
  standing alone and apart, its trees all gnarled and contorted.
   The rest of my loyal crew I told to remain with the vessel
185 and to pull it up on the beach while I myself with a dozen,
  the best of the men, set out. With me I carried a goatskin
  of wine, black, potent, and sweet, which Maron, son of Euanthes,
  priest of Ismarean Apollo,° gave me when we protected
  him with his wife and son, out of reverence for Apollo.
190 For Maron lived in a tree-studded meadow, the property of the god.
  He had given magnificent gifts—seven talents of workable gold
  and a bowl of the purest silver. As crown to this he included
  fully a dozen double-eared jars, into which he decanted
  a sweet and powerful wine, a drink to delight the immortals.
195 Nobody knew it existed, not even the slaves of the household.
  Maron alone, his wife, and his stewardess knew of the secret.
  Whenever he drank of the crimson wine with a heart sweet as honey,
  he filled one cup and then added full twenty measures of water.°
  At once the bowl breathed out a bouquet of heavenly fragrance,
200 a scent which I knew full well no man would dream of resisting.
  With this I filled up a wineskin and hid it all in a knapsack,

---

188. *Ismarean Apollo*: The Apollo worshiped in Ismarus, home of the Cicones. 198. *water*: Ordinarily one mixed one part wine to two parts water; wine was never drunk straight.

for deep in my heart I suspected I soon would encounter a being
armed with invincible strength, but savage, barbaric, and lawless.
205   We quickly got to the cave, but did not find its owner within it,
for he was herding fat sheep and moving from pasture to pasture.
Into the cave we wandered and looked around in amazement:
baskets loaded with cheeses, pens crowded with kids and with lambs,
milling about, group by group, the oldest, middling, and weanlings;
containers—pans, bowls, and buckets—carefully fashioned for milking.
210   Uneasily then my companions began to urge me, suggesting
that we borrow a few of the cheeses and maybe a kid or a lamb,
driving them out from the sheepfolds. Then, hurrying back to the ship
we should depart at once and set off on the briny dark waters.
But I refused their advice (later on, how I wished I had listened!),
215   for I wanted to see the owner and see what gifts he might offer.°
(In fact, when he did appear, he was not at all nice to my comrades.)
   So we sat inside by a fire and nibbled bits of the cheeses,
offering some to the gods, while we waited for him to come back.
At last he returned from the pasture with a heavy load of dry wood
220   to give him light for his supper. He threw this down on the floor
inside the cave with a crash that frightened us off to a corner
while he himself went out, to return with the ewes and the nannies,
leaving the rams and the billies corralled outside in the forecourt.
He then picked up a great rock and set it to serve as a barrier.
225   Twenty-two four-wheeled wagons could not shift it up from its threshold,
yet he easily moved this towering rock to block up the doorway.
Then down he sat to milk the ewes and the bleating nannies,
setting their young under each, with everything neat and in order.
Half the white milk he collected to curdle in wickerwork baskets;
230   the rest he poured into bowls, to take and drink for his supper.
He busied himself at his task, but when at last he was finished
he blew up his fire, looked around, saw us, and thus he addressed us:
   "Gentlemen, who might you be? Whence did you voyage the waters?
Are you come hither to trade, or are you wandering at random
235   like pirates over the sea, cruising now this way, now that,
forever risking your lives and bringing destruction to others?"
   So he inquired and we felt our poor hearts shatter within us,
hearing his thundering voice and seeing the mass of his body.
Yet I managed to answer his question in these diplomatic words:
240   "We are Achaeans, returning home from our warfare at Troy.
Winds of all sorts have scattered and driven us over the surges,
some in the way they would go, but us by a far different journey.
No doubt the inscrutable mind of Zeus has determined our fortune.
Know you that we are the people of Atreus' son, Agamemnon,
245   whose fame is the greatest of all men living under the heaven
for the mighty city he sacked, the many peoples he conquered.
For our part, now we have met you, we beg you for only one thing:

---

215. *offer.* Odysseus hopes to receive the gifts appropriately given as an expression of *xenia,* "guest-friendship."

Grant us a kindly reception with a trifle to bid us good-bye,
the usual gift to a stranger, or show due respect to the gods.
250 Suppliants we kneel before you, whom Zeus, defender of strangers,
defends as fully as those to whom honor is owed to as guests."
From deep in his evil heart the Cyclops gave me his answer:
"Stranger, you really are stupid, or else live a long way off,
if you warn me to dread the gods or fear that they may be offended.
255 We Cyclopes pay no attention to Zeus or the other immortals
because we are stronger by far. And if a whim should possess me,
my fear of the anger of Zeus would not save you or your friends.
But tell me, where did you moor your stout and well-founded ship,
close by, or off at a distance? I really would like to know."
260 His clumsy attempt to trap me did not deceive my astuteness.
I innocently gave him an answer in lying treacherous words:
"Poseidon, Shaker of Earth, has smashed my ship on a reef
as a rising wind drove her close to a point we wanted to weather.
Only these men and I survived her utter destruction."
265 Even this tale did not soften the flinty heart of the Cyclops.
Springing erect, he grabbed with his hands, caught two of my sailors,
and smashed them down on the rock as you kill a superfluous puppy.
Their brains burst out from their skulls and ran all over the floor.
He twisted one limb from another (his way of preparing his supper),
270 and, crunching them down like a wildcat, left never a morsel uneaten,
not entrails or muscle, not even the bones and their succulent marrow.
What could we do but rage as we lifted our hands to the heavens
while watching this horrible crime? Despair crushed all other emotion.
When the Cyclops finally ended stuffing his monstrous great belly
275 with swallows of human flesh, washed down with milk by the bucket,
he stretched himself out in his cave, in the very midst of the sheep.
For a moment I planned to approach, to draw the sword by my side,
to feel for the lethal spot where the diaphragm covers the liver
and stab him under the chest. But second thought gave me pause:
280 We too would die in the cave and suffer a horrible ending,
for I saw no way human hands could budge his rock from the doorway.
So all night long we lay groaning and waiting for dawn to appear.
Rose-fingered dawn at last revealed the coming of morning.
The Cyclops rekindled the fire and milked his magnificent sheep
285 in smooth and efficient fashion, then set each lamb to its mother.
Next, this duty completed, he grabbed two more of my comrades
to gobble them up for his breakfast. Then he easily lifted the stone,
drove his fat sheep outdoors, and put back the boulder behind them,
just as one does when replacing the lid on a quiver of arrows,
290 and with many a merry whistle drove off his flock to the mountains.
There I was, left to brood and to fashion a terrible vengeance,
hoping Athena would grant my prayers and an opportune moment.
This plan suggested itself to my heart as by far most effective:
The Cyclops had cut a bludgeon of olive, still pliant and green,
295 and left it to dry by the pens. To us it looked fully as heavy
as the mast of a twenty-oared ship, black-sided, broad in the beam,
plodding its way through the surge, heavily loaded with cargo;

such was its length to our eyes, such was its cumbersome thickness.
From this I chopped off a piece, a length of fully a fathom,
300 and handed it on to my comrades to smooth it and taper it down.
They made the shaft of the weapon all smooth and easy to handle
while I first pointed the tip, then hardened it well in the fire.
This done, I carefully hid it by burying it under a dungheap,
plenty of which, of course, was everywhere piled in the cavern.
305 Lastly, I told the men to draw lots to decide who should join me
in the perilous job of lifting and twisting the ponderous timber
around in the Cyclops' eyeball when he drifted off to sweet dreams.
Four volunteers they chose, and I added myself to the number.
 At evening he reappeared, his wooly sheep going before him.
310 He drove the fat creatures onward into the depths of the cavern,
this time not leaving a one outside in the spacious forecourt.
Perhaps some deity moved him, or perhaps he suspected the truth.
Once more he lifted the boulder and set it over the doorway,
then sat him down to his milking of bleating nannies and ewes
315 in smooth and efficient fashion, then set each lamb to its mother.
Next, this duty completed, he seized two more of my comrades
and devoured them for his supper. At last I spoke to the Cyclops,
standing beside him and holding a large bowl of strong black wine.
 "Cyclops, drink up," said I, "now your cannibal orgy is over,
320 so you may learn what sort of drink we carried as cargo.
See, I have brought you a drop. I hope you will show me your mercy
and send me back to my home, giving up your boorish behavior
that I really can stand no more. How can you dream for a minute
that anyone ever will come, from any nation of mortals,
325 if they hear the way you have acted and the nasty way you behave?"
 At that he reached for the bowl and drained it all at a gulp.
The sweet wine delighted his heart, and thus he addressed me again:
"Give me another big drink. But tell me, what is your name?
I shall certainly give you a present, one you will surely enjoy.
330 Oh yes, our land, rich in grapes, yields us Cyclopes a vintage
good in its way, and fostered by showers sent us by Zeus.
But that with which you have plied me is truly a fountain of nectar!"
So he exclaimed, and I poured him a sparkling bumper of wine.
Three times I offered him more; three times he drank in his folly.
335 At last, when the fumes had addled the brain and wits of the Cyclops,
I spoke to him once again with words deceitful of purpose:
 "Cyclops, a moment ago you asked me to tell you my name.
I shall tell you, if you in return give me the present you promised.
'Nobody' is my name, for my dear mother and father
340 gave me this name at my birth, and since then all my companions."
 These were my words, and this the reply of his arrogant heart:
" 'Nobody,' then, will be last, after all his friends, to be eaten;
before him, the rest will go down. That will be my farewell gift!"°
 Collapsing, he sprawled on his back, his head drooping off to one side,

343. *farewell gift*: The gift of Cyclops parodies, by inversion, the custom of *xenia*—Odysseus will be eaten last!

345 and slumber, who conquers all mortals, received him into its charge.
The wine and the half-chewed flesh of humans spewed from his gullet,
vomited up by the drunkard. Then I thrust the stake in the embers
and, while it heated, inspired the hearts of all my companions,
hoping that no one would fail me or flinch in a spasm of terror.

350 Green though it was, the olive-wood stake was about to catch fire
and shone with a red-hot glare. Approaching, I lifted it out.
The others stood by me to help, and some god fired their courage.
They picked up the olive-wood log, red-hot and sharp at the tip,
and swung it into his eye. Against it I threw my whole weight

355 and spun it around, like a shipwright drilling a hole in a timber:
He guides the drill, while his helpers, standing on either side,
saw the thong back and forth as the drill° sinks deeper and deeper.
So I and my men rotated the stake in the eye of the Cyclops.
Hissing, his blood spurted out, and the heat singed eyelid and brow.

360 The eyeball, scorched to its roots, crackled and boiled in the fire.
As when a blacksmith is quenching a big bronze° adze or an ax-head,
he plunges it into cold water which makes it sizzle and scream,
but gives the temper required, the strength and toughness of iron;
just so his eyeball squealed as the stake of olive-wood entered [Figure 22.1].

365 He let out a horrible cry, which the rocky cavern reechoed,
scaring us back in terror. He plucked at the blood-smeared stake,
wrenched it out from his eye, and in torment hurled it away.
He shouted to other Cyclopes, who lived in the nearby caves
dotted about the wind-blown hillsides, to come to his rescue.

370 Hearing his call, they came at a run from every direction,
and standing before his cave, they asked him what was the matter:
"What troubles you so, Polyphemus, making you call us to help
and rousing us from our slumber, so late in the god-given night?
Perhaps some rascally mortal is trying to rustle your sheep,

375 or is somebody bent on your murder by treachery or brute force?"
The mighty Polyphemus replied from the mouth of his cave:
"Nobody wants to kill me by treachery, not by brute force!"
To this the others replied in words aimed right at the mark:
"If nobody's using force on a man alone and defenseless,

380 you must have an inescapable sickness, sent by great Zeus.
The best thing for you to do is to pray to your father Poseidon."
With this retort they departed. I laughed in my inmost heart,
gloating over my shrewdness and seeing them tricked by my name.
The Cyclops groaned in his pain and suffered spasms of torture.

357. *drill:* The auger described here is like a bow drill whose forward thrust comes from the weight
of the user as he leans against it. The twist of the drill came from a long thong wrapped in a single
turn around it. Men at each end pushed and pulled so it turned, now clockwise, now counter-
clockwise, like the drill of someone starting a fire by friction. But the simile is somewhat mixed:
How could Odysseus both guide the stake and twist it, especially if its weight was carried by four
other men?   361. *bronze:* When Homer was composing, iron was replacing bronze so the smith is
said to quench a bronze ax, which gives "the strength and toughness of iron." For centuries the
effectiveness of tempering iron (immersion does nothing for bronze) was thought to come from
substances dissolved in the water into which the hot metal was plunged, not from the sudden
cooling of the metal.

FIGURE 22.1 The blinding of Polyphemus, on a large Attic jug from Eleusis, c. 670 BC (the jar was used to bury a child). Odysseus and two companions, lifting the fire-hardened stake on their shoulders, blind Polyphemus. In this early mythic representation, the artist has experimented by painting Odysseus white, to distinguish him from the other figures; white usually meant that the figure was female. Note the cup in Polyphemus' hand, referring to the detail that Odysseus first got him drunk.   (Archaeological Museum, Eleusis; Erich Lessing/Art Resource, New York)

385   Groping about with his hands, he lifted the rock from the doorway,
meanwhile feeling around as he sat there at the entrance,
expecting to catch whoever might try to get out with the sheep,
and even hoping that I might be foolish enough to attempt it.
But I was pondering deeply, to make things turn out for the best,
390   and to find some way to avoid disaster for me and my comrades.
In this matter of life and death, in the face of imminent peril,
this was the method that seemed the best of all possible courses:
The cave held plenty of well-fed rams with thick shaggy fleeces
(big ones, handsome, all covered with heavy dark-colored wool),

395   which I quietly tied in threes with pliant shoots of the willow
      where the monster Cyclops slept, planning his criminal horrors.
      The rams in the middle each carried a man; the two on the outside
      trotted along beside them and thus protected my comrades.
      So three rams carried each man, but I myself was left over,
400   as also the noblest ram of the flock enclosed in the sheepfold.
      Approaching the beast from behind and stretching under its belly,
      I lay there, my hands holding tight to the animal's glorious wool.
      So we lay in discomfort and awaited the light of the dawning.
         Rose-fingered dawn at last revealed the coming of morning.
405   The Cyclops drove all the males of the flock away to the pasture,
      but the unmilked females remained, with udders swollen to bursting,
      bleating in pain, in the cave. Tormented by horrible anguish,
      their owner felt the back of each ram as it went out to pasture—
      dumbo! he never suspected my men were lashed under their bellies.
410   Last of all the bellwether approached and was nearing the doorway,
      slowed by the weight of his wool and of me, a man of resources.
      Gently caressing its back, the mighty Polyphemus addressed it:
         "My good old ram, how is it that you are last of my flock
      to hurry out of the cavern? The others have never outstripped you
415   as you proudly galloped along, the first to taste of the grasses,
      to get to the stream, and to hurry home to the fold in the evening.
      But today you are last of all. Is it grief for your master's eye,
      which Nobody blinded, the scoundrel, he and his evil companions,
      after getting me drunk? But I tell you, he hasn't yet gotten away
420   from the death he deserves. How I wish that you could stand here beside me
      and tell me in human speech how he managed to duck from my power!
      I'd smash him down on the floor, his brains would spatter all over
      in every part of the cave! And that would lighten the burden
      of all the sorrow I feel, which that no-good Nobody caused me."
425   With this he dismissed the ram to go free from the door and away.
      As soon as the ram and I were far enough from the doorway,
      I freed my hands from the wool and undid the bonds of my comrades.
      Turning the fat and shambling sheep away from their pasture,
      we drove them back to the ship and were greeted with great relief—
430   those of us who survived. For the rest they began to lament,
      but sorrow I could not allow and shook my head at each mourner.
      Instead, I told them to hurry and load the heavy-wooled sheep
      down in the bilge of the ship's timbers and set sail on the billowy ocean.
      At once they hurried aboard and took their place on the benches.
435   Swinging together they caught at the foaming sea with their oars.
      When we had gone as far as the sound of a man's voice will carry,
      I shouted back at the Cyclops in words of taunt and abuse:
         "Cyclops, your luck was bad. No coward was he whose companions
      you seized with violent hands in the hollow cave and devoured.
440   Your sin has found you out, your insolent treatment of strangers.
      Unscrupulously you killed and ate them, right in your dwelling!
      Revenge has fallen upon you from Zeus and the other immortals."
         So I jeered at the Cyclops, who raged even more in his heart.
      He broke off the topmost peak of a mighty mountain nearby

445   and flung it out at the ship. Flying over, it landed beyond us.
       The cresting sea swelled up where the rock fell into its waters
       in a surge which hurtled our vessel headlong back to the shore,
       a huge wave out of the deep, driving us in to destruction.
       Hastily grabbing a spar, I reached it down to the bottom,
450   fended her off, and in silence signaled the oarsmen to heave,
       to strain at the oars if they hoped to break away from the peril.
       They fell to their oars and rowed, until, by churning the sea
       we had opened a gap twice as wide as that we had earlier trusted.
       Again I taunted the Cyclops, while my sailors tried to restrain me,
455   assailing me from all sides with clever attempts at persuasion:
            "Why do you have to keep on infuriating this savage?
       Just now he hurled that great rock beyond us out into the ocean,
       washing us back to the shore, where we fully expected destruction.
       If you had made the least sound, or if he had heard what you uttered,
460   he would have smashed our bodies and ships into one bloody mess
       with the toss of one jagged rock at that incredible distance."
            So they attempted in vain to persuade my imperious spirit.
       Once more I called in an angry voice and showed my defiance:
       "Cyclops, if ever a human asks how you came by your blindness,
465   or who it was that disfigured your eye, just give him the answer:
       'Odysseus put out my eye, Odysseus, sacker of cities,
       the son of Laërtes, who dwells in Ithaca, lord of its palace.'"
            Hearing, he gave a great moan and sadly made this reply:
       "Alas, the words of a prophet have now returned to my mind.
470   There once was a seer among us, a prophet wise and sagacious,
       Telemus, son of Eurymus, a man who excelled at divining,
       grown old among the Cyclopes, for whom he practiced his science.
       Long ago he assured me I was doomed to loss of my eyesight
       at the hands of a certain Odysseus. This man, I assumed, would appear
475   big and impressive to look at, wearing the trappings of power.
       But the man who put out my eye is little, feeble, and sluggish,
       who could only do what he wanted by getting me drunk on his wine.
       Come back to me then, Odysseus, so I can give you a present
       fitting for your departure, by persuading the Shaker of Earth
480   to escort you off on your way and grant you a prosperous voyage.
       For I am his son and Poseidon is proud that he is my father.
       He himself, if he pleases, will escort you off on the journey,
       not leaving the task to another, be it human or blessed immortal."
            He tried to wheedle me so, but I quickly gave him my answer:
485   "I wish I were able to rob you of life and send you to Hades!
       Still, even the Shaker of Earth can never restore to you your vision."
            So I replied. The Cyclops then prayed to lordly Poseidon,
       lifting his suppliant hands to the star-studded heaven above:
       "Hear my prayer, Poseidon, thou dark-haired Shaker of Earth:
490   If I am truly your son, if you boast of being my father,
       grant that the sacker of cities, Odysseus, son of Laërtes,
       whose house is in Ithaca, never again may return to his home.
       But if Fate ordains that he must revisit the land of his father,
       that he look on his friends again and enter his well-built palace,

495 grant this: May he come as a beggar, a vagrant for long weary years,
  bereft of his comrades' lives, with no one left to support him;
  may he come in a ship not his own, and find his household a chaos."
   Such was his prayer, and the dark-haired god approved his petition.
  But the Cyclops seized on a rock, far bigger in size than before,
500 which he whirled up over his head, and exerting incredible force
  he threw it a little behind the stern of the dark-sided vessel,
  barely failing to reach the blade of the oar of the helmsman.
  The cresting sea surged up where the rock fell into its waters,
  making our dark ship yaw and plunge headlong right to the island.
505 We made our way to the shore, where our other well-fitted ships
  lay drawn up all in a group with their worried crews sitting alongside,
  always keeping a lookout and waiting till we should appear.
  Arriving, we beached the vessel, and pulled her up on the sand.
  We ourselves disembarked there by the side of the water,
510 brought the sheep of the Cyclops from out of the smooth-gliding vessel,
  and divided them up so no one should leave without a fair share.
  But to me as a special portion my well-armed comrades awarded
  the noble ram who had brought me out of the cave of the Cyclops.
  Of him I made an offering there on the shore of the ocean,
515 to dark-clouded Zeus, son of Cronus, ruler of all that has being,
  the animal's succulent thighs.° But Zeus ignored my offering
  and schemed to destroy my well-fitted ships and trusty companions.

HOMER, Odyssey 9.105–555

516. *thighs:* He burned the thigh bones in the fire, as was customary in Greek sacrifice.

Aeolus, the Laestrygonians, and Circê

Odysseus next tells how he came to the island of **Aeolus** (ē-o-lus), the wind-king (apparently unconnected with Aeolus, the ancestor of Jason), who spends his days dining with his six sons and six daughters, all married to one another. Aeolus feasts with Odysseus and his men and gives him a special gift in accordance with the customs of *xenia:* a sealed cowhide bag that contained the dangerous winds, which he warns him not to untie under any conditions (the motif of the folktale prohibition).

Favored by the good winds not enclosed in the bag, Odysseus and his men come so close to Ithaca that they can see men tending fires on the shore. In his exhaustion Odysseus falls asleep, and his men begin to murmur among themselves. Their commander probably has gold in the bag, they say, which he doubtless wants for himself. Greedily they untie the bag, the dangerous winds escape, and a storm catches the fleet. The Greeks find themselves back at the island of Aeolus. Observing that they must be bitterly hated by the gods to have suffered such a fate, Aeolus gruffly orders them away.

Next the Greeks come to the land of the **Laestrygonians** (les-tri-gōn-i-ans, perhaps "gnashers"). They park their ships in a long, narrow bay bordered by high cliffs and send out men to reconnoiter. The king's daughter meets them and leads the advance party to her father, but the king promptly gobbles one down. The Laestrygonians, like the Cyclops, are cannibals!

Other Laestrygonians run in from far and wide, take up position on either side of the fjord, and smash the ships below with giant boulders. They harpoon the men wiggling in the water like eels, pull them out, and eat them alive. Everyone is killed and every ship destroyed—all except Odysseus and his lucky crew, who cleverly moored their vessel outside the entrance to the harbor.

On they sail and come to Aeaea, land of **Circê** (**sir**-sē), daughter of Helius the sun and sister of Aeëtes, Medea's father. The island is heavily forested, surrounded by a mist so dense that one cannot see where the sun rises or sets. A wisp of smoke rises from the center of the island. Half the crew go inland to investigate, while Odysseus remains by the ship. Soon a crewmember, Eurylochus, returns in a panic. They came to the house of a beautiful woman, he says, who sang a beautiful song while she wove. For some reason he, Eurylochus, hung back and watched as the others sat down to drink a potion the woman prepared. She touched them with her wand and instantly they turned into pigs (Figure 22.2).

Odysseus says he will take care of the matter and sets forth alone along the path. In the middle of the forest Hermes appears and gives Odysseus a magic herb called *moly* (**mō**-lē) with a black root and a brilliant white flower (perhaps a mandrake root). When Odysseus reaches the hut, animals—enchanted men, evidently—fawn upon him. He hears Circê singing from within. He enters her

FIGURE 22.2 Circê enchants the companions of Odysseus, Attic wine cup, c. 550 BC. Seductive Circê stands naked in the center, stirring a magic drink and offering it to Odysseus' companions, already turning into animals—the one in front of Circê into a pig, the next to the right into a ram, and the third into a wolf. The figure behind Circê has the head of a boar. On the far left is a lion, beside whom Odysseus comes with sword drawn (but in the *Odyssey* they only turn into pigs). On the far right, one of the companions (Eurylochus) escapes.   (Photograph © 2011 Museum of Fine Arts, Boston)

house and sits down at a table. She offers him a drink, but nothing happens when she touches him with her wand; the *moly* protects him. You must be Odysseus, she observes: A prophecy foretold that a man would one day defy her magic (just as a prophecy warned Polyphemus of Odysseus' coming).

She then invites him to her bed, but Odysseus, remembering advice given by Hermes, draws his sword and forces her to swear a great oath: to do him no harm. If he did not extort this promise, she would castrate him, Hermes had warned. Circê swears the oath, and then they go to bed!

Afterward, Circê releases Odysseus' men from their enchantment. They remain on the island for a year, feasting and taking their pleasure. At last Odysseus' men remind the commander of their purpose: to return home. Circê agrees that they may go, but first they must cross the river Ocean to gather information from the ghost of Tiresias. They will need to survive the Sirens and Scylla (**sil**-la, probably "dog") and Charybdis (ka-**rib**-dis) too, and under no circumstances should they eat the Cattle of Helius.

Sirens, Scylla and Charybdis, the Cattle of Helius, and Calypso

And so they cross the river Ocean. Odysseus speaks with the ghosts of many, including Tiresias (Chapter 12). Again they embark and approach the island of the **Sirens**, whose song no man can resist. Odysseus, on Circê's advice, stops up the ears of his men—but not his own—with wax and orders himself bound to the mast. If he cries out when he hears the Sirens' song, they are to bind him tighter.

In art, the Sirens have the heads and breasts of women but the wings and bodies of birds (like the Harpies, an image taken from the Egyptian *ba*-bird, a picture of the soul; Figure 22.3). At their feet lie the rotting corpses of the many sailors who have heeded their sweet song, which draws all who hear it to their death. Odysseus, ravished by their song, begs his men to release him, but they only bind him more tightly until they pass in safety.

Next they come to a double evil, the origin of the proverbial saying for an impossible situation, to be "between Scylla and Charybdis." On one side of a narrow strait is **Charybdis**, an enormous whirlpool that sucks down and spits up a torrent of water three times a day, and on the other, beneath a cliff as sheer as glass, lives **Scylla**, a monster with twelve feet, all misshapen, and six long necks, each with its own head. In each head lie three rows of teeth. Up to her middle she is hidden in a cave, but she holds her head out to snatch passersby. Scylla seems to have no connection with the Megarian Scylla, daughter of Nisus, who fell in love with Minos. Because Charybdis promises certain death, Odysseus orders that they hug the cliff while he stands at the prow, sword drawn against the monster. Scylla, unimpressed, reaches down, seizes six men, and devours them gruesomely as the others row with all their might.

They come to Thrinacia, the island of Helius, where his cattle graze, which Circê had forbidden them to devour. Held on the island by contrary winds, the men soon begin to starve and are reduced to eating fish (real heroes eat red meat). While Odysseus reconnoiters inland, Eurylochus agitates against their commander, saying that he would rather die with a full belly than live like this. When Odysseus comes down from the hills, where he had fallen asleep, he smells the rich scent of

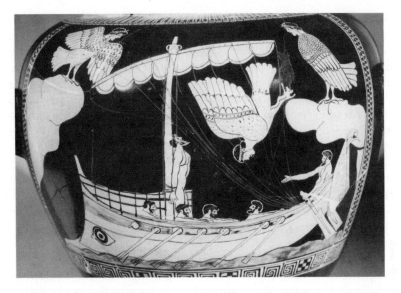

FIGURE 22.3 Odysseus and the Sirens, Attic jug, c. 450 BC. Odysseus, bound to the mast, hears the Sirens' song while his men, their ears plugged with wax, row past the island. Two stand on the cliffs, while the third falls to her death, evidently because Odysseus escaped their alluring song. Note the apotropaic eye on the prow of the ship and Odysseus' heroic nudity.   (© Trustees of the British Museum/Art Resource, New York)

beef roasting on spits and hears the mooing of the spitted cows (as a sign of divine displeasure). The damage is done.

When the winds blow fair, they set out again, but Zeus, acting on a complaint from the angry Helius, smashes the ship with a thunderbolt. Everyone drowns except Odysseus, who clings to a mast. He drifts back toward the straits of Scylla and Charybdis and feels himself sucked down, but at the last second seizes a fig tree growing on a cliff above the whirlpool. Charybdis rips away the mast as he hangs suspended, then whips round and round, exposing the sandy bottom of the deep sea. At last Charybdis spits up again, Odysseus drops back onto the mast, and again he is swept away. Days later he washes up on Ogygia, "the navel of the sea," Calypso's island.

Odysseus lives on Ogygia for seven years. **Calypso** is a beautiful nymph who loves him and even offers him eternal life, if he will only marry her. But Odysseus longs to go home and every day goes down to the shore. Looking across the sea, he weeps with desire for his beloved wife, Penelopê, and his home. Athena, his protectress, asks Zeus to release Odysseus at last from his suffering and the persecutions of Poseidon. Zeus consents, and Hermes descends to inform Calypso. Bitterly, she agrees.

Observations: Historical and Mythical Travel

About 800 BC Greeks from the long island of Euboea, which hugs the east coast of the mainland north of Athens, traveled in small open boats across perilous seas all the way to Italy, where they founded the earliest Greek colonies. Homer's *Odyssey*, by far the best known of the returns from Troy, seems to have been composed and written down on the island of Euboea at about this same time, between 800 and 750 BC, near the date of the alphabet's invention, which it may have inspired. Its natural audience was seamen who had actually traveled to the far West, and Odysseus' adventures were from an early time identified with specific geographic features in and around Italy: Calypso's island with Malta, Polyphemus' island with Sicily, Scylla and Charybdis with the Strait of Messina between Italy and Sicily, the island of Aeolus with the Lipari Islands north of Sicily, the Sirens' land with the promontory of Sorrento, and Circê's island with Ischia in the Bay of Naples.

Homer must have heard many sailors' tales about adventure in Italy, and he may have gone there himself. It is a mistake, however, to see in the *Odyssey* a sailor's log or to reconstruct a close identity between mythical and real locations. Homer fashions his narrative to appeal to an audience of wanderers, yet creates a symbolic voyage, a vision of moral purpose and national identity.

Sometimes Odysseus nearly forgets his purpose, as when he lies in Circê's arms. At other times he is the lonely Greek set in defiance against the alien outside world and its barbarous, sometimes disgusting customs. Cyclopes and the Laestrygonians are portrayed as cannibals, repulsive to the civilized Greek. The shepherd Cyclopes do not cultivate grains, have assemblies, respect the gods, or understand the responsibilities of *xenia*. They lack the arts of civilization (though they make a crude wine), very like the actual peoples with whom the Greeks struggled in Italy, Sicily, and further west. Such peoples are perceived as dangerous but stupid, and in the end no match for the wily Greek. A beautiful island, ripe for development, lies just off Cyclops' island, a perfect place for a colony, but Cyclopes have no ships to explore the world, preferring to live alone in their caves. That's the way it is with non-Greeks.

RETURN TO ITHACA

Phaeacia and Nausicaä

On Ogygia, the hero builds a raft and sets out to sea. After drifting many days, he comes near the shore of Scheria, island of the **Phaeacians** (fē-**āsh**-unz, identified by Thucydides, fifth century BC, with Corcyra, on the coastal route to Italy). As Odysseus is about to land, Poseidon, returning from the land of the blameless Ethiopians where he has richly dined, sees Odysseus on his raft. Still angry because Odysseus blinded his son Polyphemus, Poseidon sends a great storm. Caught in the violent waves and wind, the raft breaks up and throws Odysseus into the sea.

He swims for three days and nights and would have drowned had it not been for the sea-goddess Leucothea (lū-**koth**-e-a), who once was Ino, nurse of Dionysus and wife of Athamas. She rises from the waves and gives him her veil to tie around his chest; the veil has magical powers of protection. He comes ashore where a stream pours into the sea. Exhausted and scaly with brine, he climbs into the bushes, makes a dark nest, and falls asleep.

That night **Nausicaä** (nau-**sik**-a-a), adolescent daughter of the Phaeacian king Alcinoüs, has a dream. Athena appears to her in disguise and advises that she wash her clothes to attract a husband. Surely no man likes a woman who neglects her laundry! Next morning, Nausicaä receives her father's permission to go to the sea with her attendants, leading a wagon stuffed with dirty clothes.

Nausicaä and her friends, *parthenoi* all, spread the clothes on the shore to dry, then for relaxation throw a beach ball back and forth. The ball goes astray and falls into the stream, and the girls' excited shrieks wake up Odysseus. He staggers up stark naked out of the bushes, but modestly holds a branch before his private parts, so as not to be too frightening (Figure 22.4). The maidens, except for Nausicaä, flee down the beach. The tattered and weary but courtly wanderer praises her beauty in language reminiscent of Anchises' speech to Aphrodite (Chapter 9):

FIGURE 22.4 Odysseus and Nausicaä, Attic vase, c. 440 BC. A naked Odysseus, holding a stick in front of his genitals, with twigs in his hair, Athena at his side, speaks to Nausicaä, half-turned to run away. The princess's clothes hang from the tree behind the hero. In this case Odysseus' nudity is realistic, not heroic.   (Erich Lessing / Art Resource, New York)

[148]   "I drop to my knees, my lady. Are you goddess, or are you human?
        If in fact you are one of the gods who dwell above in the heavens,
150   to judge by your outward form you are Artemis, daughter of Zeus,
        whom in stature, bearing, and form I think you most closely resemble.
        But if indeed you are human, one of us who dwells on the earth,
        thrice blest in you are your father and the honored lady your mother,
        thrice blest also your brothers, whose hearts are warmed with delight,
155   watching your willowy movement as you come and go in the dance.
        But most blest of all is the lucky suitor who carries you homeward,
        offering the richest presents in the contest to make you his bride.
        I tell you, these eyes have never beheld your like among mortals,
        neither woman nor man, and I gaze at your every action in wonder.
160   Once, on the island of Delos, by the altar of Phoebus Apollo
        (I and my men had stopped on the way that would lead to such sorrow),
        I noticed a fair young sapling arising out of a palm tree,
        a shoot like no tree had ever made spring up out of the earth.
        As I looked on that, the same emotions arose in my spirit—
165   wonder, astonishment, fear—as strike me, kneeling before you.
        Yesterday I was cast ashore from the wine-colored ocean,
        on the twentieth day since first I was driven by wind and by wave
        from the isle of Ogygia. Doubtless some god directed me hither,
        to suffer, perhaps, even here. My troubles are surely not over.
170   Before my day of releasing, the gods will yet bring me more sorrow.
        But, lady, I pray you, have pity. To you I direct my appeal,
        for of others I know not a one who rules in this land and its city.
        Show me the way to the palace, and give me a rag like a beggar's,
        some cover, perhaps, from the linen you brought to wash on the seashore.
175   Lastly I pray that the gods may grant you a husband and home,
        a household of peace and love, for nothing is dearer or finer
        than concord of husband and wife who share their hopes for the family,
        the envy of all their foes and the glory of those who respect them."

HOMER, *Odyssey* 6.148–185

Nausicaä, flattered and unafraid, calls back her maids. They give Odysseus a
bath, from which he emerges shining like a young man, handsome and comely.
Wearing some of the laundry, Odysseus follows Nausicaä to the city, hidden in a
mist and keeping a certain distance (or the neighbors would gossip). In the court of
King Alcinoüs, Odysseus tells his famous adventures.

Ithaca, Argus, and Euryclea

The Phaeacians, who are marvelous seafarers, give Odysseus many gifts. Then, after
listening to his adventures, they transport him to Ithaca and, while he is asleep, put him
ashore in a fog. He awakes and cannot at first believe he has touched his native soil, but
Athena appears and reassures him. He makes his way to the hut of his own swineherd,
Eumaeus (yū-**mē**-us), who of course does not recognize his master after so many years.
Still, Eumaeus, who understands correct behavior, offers what hospitality he can.

Telemachus (tel-**em**-a-kus), Odysseus' only son and therefore in danger from the suitors, had gone abroad to Pylos and Sparta in hopes of finding some news about his father (where Helen drugged the punch and Menelaus told the story of the Trojan Horse). The suitors have laid an ambush, which he avoids by landing on the back side of the island. He comes up to the swineherd's hut. Odysseus reveals his true identity to his son, who describes the situation at the house. For many years the suitors have pressed their demand that Penelopê marry one of them. In the meanwhile, they devour Odysseus' wealth, sleep with the female slaves, and scorn the young Telemachus.

Disguised as a beggar, Odysseus makes his way inland to the palace. Just outside the gate his faithful dog **Argus** ("swifty") is asleep on a dung heap, old now and near death. As a pup he was Odysseus' favorite hound, before the hero went to Troy. Argus peers up, recognizes his master, cocks his ears, and drops over dead from excitement.

Inside the palace, Odysseus stands in the shadows of the great hall. The suitors, led by **Antinoüs** (an-**tin**-o-us), revile the beggar: One throws a stool at his head; another, a piece of bone. They complain how Penelopê had promised to marry one of them as soon as she finished weaving a burial robe for Laërtes, Odysseus' father, who lives in the countryside, sleeping on a bed of leaves, but each night she sneaked into the hall and undid as much of the weaving as she had done that day (Figure 22.5; compare Perspective Figure 22.2c). The suitors discovered the trick long ago, yet still she will not choose a husband.

Penelopê desires to speak to the beggar, whom she does not recognize as her husband in disguise. The beggar informs Penelopê that her husband is still alive. He has himself seen him, he says, and Odysseus will soon be home. Penelopê does not believe a word of it, but is thankful for the pleasant thought. She asks the old nurse **Euryclea** (yū-ri-**klē**-a), who suckled Odysseus when he was an infant, to wash the beggar's tired and dirty feet.

FIGURE 22.5 Penelopê before the web, from an Attic cup, c. 440 BC. Penelopê sits in a melancholy pose before her loom, the shroud partly done, while her son Telemachus stands before her with two spears, viewing her with skepticism. A griffin, a horse, and a man, all winged, are embroidered into the bottom band. (Museo Civico, Chiusi; University of Wisconsin–Madison Photo Archive)

Euryclea hauls out an enormous bronze cauldron and fills it with hot water. As she scrubs away, suddenly she feels a scar on the beggar's thigh. When Odysseus was young, a boar had sliced him there. Odysseus sees that she has recognized him and seizes her scrawny throat with his powerful hand. One sound out of her, he warns, and she dies!

Penelopê, Telemachus, and the Suitors

Penelopê, with a little help from Athena, suddenly decides that she will marry on the very next day. She arranges a contest to help her decide. She will marry whoever can string her husband's bow, stored all these years in a closet, and with the bow shoot an arrow through the holes of twelve aligned ax handles whose heads are buried in a long mound of dirt on the floor (if this is what Homer means; the language is unclear and there are many interpretations). The bow was a gift of Iphitus (son of the great bowman Eurytus), whom Heracles threw from the walls of Tiryns.

The suitors try to string the bow but are too weak from years of carousing. One suitor warms it at the fire, thinking this will make his task easier. A sneering Telemachus suggests that they let the beggar try his hand. He gives the bow to Odysseus. Ignoring the indignant noblemen, the beggar takes the wonderful weapon and easily strings it, like a poet who puts a string to his lyre. The beggar nocks an arrow and in a moment of high drama fires it through the aligned holes of the ax handles. Then:

[1]   Stripping himself of his rags, the shrewd foresighted Odysseus
sprang up to straddle the threshold, holding his bow and a quiver
loaded with swift-flying arrows, which he poured out, ready for use,
onto the ground at his feet. Then he turned and spoke to the suitors:
5   "So ends the meaningless contest, the silly purposeless pastime.
Now I shall shoot at a mark that no man has ever transfixed.
I shall know at once if I hit it. Apollo, grant me that glory!"
     Straight at a suitor he shot his arrow, bitter and deadly,
where Antinoüs sat, reaching out to receive a beautiful goblet,
10   twin-handled, golden, into his hands, to drink of its wine,
with no thought of death in his heart. Who indeed would ever imagine
that one single man, in the midst of banqueters crowded around him
(however strong he might be), could bring him death and destruction?
Odysseus' arrow, well aimed, struck its victim square in the gullet,
15   and its head sped on through the tenderest part of Antinoüs' neck.
His body slumped to one side. The cup in the hand of the dead man
clanged to the floor. From his nostrils spurted a jet of his blood.
In a dying spasm his legs jerked out and kicked back the table,
spilling the food in a dirty puddle of bread and hot meat.
20   From all the house the suitors ran with a shout to the body
of him who was murdered. Some jumped in alarm from their places,
peering around all through the well-built rooms of the palace.

HOMER, *Odyssey* 22.1–24

PERSPECTIVE 22.3

CAVAFY'S "ITHACA"

The Greek language has been encoded in writing longer than any other language still spoken on Earth, in Linear B script and a related script from Cyprus from about 1400 to 1100 BC and in alphabetic writing from about 800 BC up to the present. The oldest parts of the Hebrew Bible, once thought to be the oldest writing, date in their present form to about 500 BC. Although today the Greek language is restricted mainly to the borders of modern Greece, fine poets continue to appear who reinterpret for modern Greek speakers the traditions of ancient times. Such a poet was Constantine Cavafy (1863–1933).

Born in the Greek community in Constantinople (Istanbul), now almost nonexistent, he belonged to a prominent commercial family who moved soon after his birth to Alexandria in Egypt, founded by Alexander the Great. There he worked for most of his life as a clerk, but he knew and influenced the British writers E. M. Forster, T. S. Eliot, Arnold Toynbee, D. H. Lawrence, and Lawrence Durrell. Cavafy often celebrated erotic love between men, but in "Ithaca" (1894) he recreates Odysseus' homeland as a symbol for the journey that is itself the goal, the Odyssey of everyone's life:

Ithaca*

As you set out on your journey to Ithaca,
pray that your journey be a long one,
filled with adventure, filled with discovery.
Laestrygonians and Cyclopes,
the angry Poseidon—do not fear them:
You'll never find such things on your way
unless your sight is set high, unless a rare
excitement stirs your spirit and your body.
The Laestrygonians and Cyclopes,
the savage Poseidon—you won't meet them
so long as you do not admit them to your soul,
as long as your soul does not set them before you.
Pray that your road is a long one.
May there be many summer mornings
when with what pleasure, with what joy,
you enter harbors never seen before.
May you stop at Phoenician stations of trade
to buy fine things,

*Translated by Barry B. Powell from the Greek text in Cavafy, *Poiêmata: 1897–1933* (Ikaros, 1989).

mother of pearl and coral, amber and ebony,
and voluptuous perfumes of every kind—
buy as many voluptuous perfumes as you can.
And may you go to many Egyptian cities
to learn and learn from those who know.
Always keep Ithaca in your mind.
You are destined to arrive there.
But don't hurry your journey at all.
Far better if it takes many years,
and if you are old when you anchor at the island,
rich with all you have gained on the way,
not expecting that Ithaca will give you wealth.
Ithaca has given you a beautiful journey.
Without her you would never have set out.
She has no more left to give you.
And if you find her poor, Ithaca has not mocked you.
As wise as you have become, so filled with experience,
you will have understood what these Ithacas signify.

The suitors think it is some terrible mistake, but Odysseus tells them the truth:

[34]   Wily Odysseus, glaring, addressed the men in this fashion:
35   "You curs, you thought that I would never return to my homeland
        from Troy and seized on the chance to ravage my prosperous household.
        Your violence forced the women, my slaves, to give way to your lust,
        and while I was still alive you hoped you might marry my wife.
        You showed no fear of the gods, the mighty dwellers in heaven,
40   nor did you worry that human vengeance might strike you hereafter.
        But now—the crisis of death is waiting for you and your fellows."

                                          HOMER, *Odyssey* 22.34–41

Helped by Telemachus, Eumaeus, and another retainer, Odysseus massacres the 108 unarmed men (Figure 22.6). The hall reeks of blood and gore when Penelopê, awakened by Euryclea, descends from the upper chambers. She has just enjoyed the best nap, she says, since the day that Odysseus went to Troy! She sees the man drenched in the suitors' blood but refuses to believe that he is her husband. Nonetheless, she is grateful and, so that the man might rest, asks Euryclea to bring out her master's bed. Odysseus is amazed at her coldness—as his wife, she should be receiving him into her own bed:

[166]   "You're a strange woman all right. To you beyond
        all women have the Olympians given a hard heart.
        No other woman would harden her heart as you,
        and stand apart from her husband who after desperate suffering

FIGURE 22.6 Odysseus slays the suitors, Attic cup, c. 440 BC. Odysseus draws his bow as two serving girls look on. Below, on the other side of the pot, the suitors uselessly struggle to defend themselves. Two are on a couch, while a third crouches behind a table. Note the dapper mustache of the suitor on the far right.   (Antikenmuseum, Berlin; Bildarchiv Preußischer Kulturßesitz/Art Resource, New York)

170   had come to her in the twentieth year, to his native land.
　　　All right nurse, make up a couch so I may lie down alone,
　　　for her heart is iron." Then wise Penelopê answered him:
　　　　"Odd fellow, I am not proud, nor do I scorn you,
　　　nor yet am I so amazed, for well I knew you
175   when you went forth from Ithaca on your long-oared ship.
　　　Yet come, Euryclea, strew for him the stout bedstead

outside the well-built bridal chamber which he himself made.
Bring the stout bedstead from there and cast on bedding,
fleeces and shining coverlets." She spoke, testing her husband.
180   But Odysseus in anger spoke to his true-hearted wife,
and said, "Woman, you've spoken a bitter word.
Who has set my bed elsewhere? Hard would it
be to do, although highly skilled, unless a
god should easily by his will move it to
185   another place. But of men no mortal alive,
no matter how young and strong, could easily pry
it from its place, for a great token is set in the well-built
bed, and it was I who built it and no one else.
A long-leafed olive grew in the court, strong,
190   vigorous, thick and round like a pillar . . ."

HOMER, *Odyssey* 23.166–190

Odysseus goes on to describe how he built his bed with the tree stump as an immovable post.

So he spoke, and her knees went slack where she sat,
and her heart melted as she knew the sure tokens
that Odysseus told her. With a burst of tears she ran toward him
and flung her arms about the neck of Odysseus and kissed his head.

HOMER, *Odyssey* 23.204–208

Penelopê was only testing him, after all (as Odysseus had tested so many others). They go upstairs to make love and chat about all that has happened. Odysseus tells her everything, although he skims rapidly past the beautiful Circê and Calypso! So ends the twenty-third book of Homer's *Odyssey*. In the final book Odysseus goes to see his father Laertes, then battles briefly the relatives of the slain suitors. Athena interposes herself and the poem ends rather lamely, before more blood is spilled.

Curious tales from other sources report Odysseus' further career: how his restless nature carried him away again to the mainland, where he took another wife even while Penelopê was alive. He returned to Ithaca, there to meet his death. While living with Circê, he had fathered a child, Telegonus (tel-**eg**-o-nus, "begotten afar"), who grew up and came in search of his father. Telegonus arrived on Ithaca with some companions, but not knowing where he was, drove off some cattle. Telemachus and the aged Odysseus attacked the invaders. In the fight Telegonus stabbed Odysseus with his spear tipped with a stingray's poisonous tail. Thus was fulfilled Tiresias' prophecy in the underworld that Odysseus would "die a gentle death from the sea." According to a still odder tale, Telegonus then married Penelopê and carried her and Telemachus back to Circê's island, where Telemachus married the ageless witch. But such bizarre intricacies, popular in later antiquity and unfriendly to our expectations about a hero's career, are foreign to the spirit of Homer's timeless tale. (**For the complete *Odyssey*, go to http://classics.mit.edu/ Homer/odyssey.html**)

Observations: Symbols of Rebirth in the Folktale of the Man Who Came Home, Tested by Woman and the World

Homer's *Odyssey*, viewed as a whole, is the story of a hero who came home after a long absence, found his household in the hands of usurpers, and killed them to reestablish his ascendancy. The older generation—tough, smart, and wise in the need for just behavior—is triumphant over the younger generation—brash, indolent, and self-indulgent, taking what they want. Because the youthful usurpers threaten traditional property rights, the poem appears to be a simple tale of revenge, of human justice triumphant over wrong. Not the gods' enmity but their own thoughtless behavior brings about the suitors' destruction.

Zeus sets this powerful moral theme in the beginning of the poem when Zeus complains that humans blame gods for their troubles, when in fact their own recklessness brings them to grief. Zeus cites the example of Aegisthus: Warned not to sleep with Clytemnestra, he did so anyway. No wonder he paid the price! Similarly, Odysseus' foolish men dawdle in the land of the Cicones, eat the dangerous Lotus, open the bag of the winds, and devour the cattle of the Sun.

Justice is based on restraint, on the ability to hold back and not give in to one's animal appetite. Food is good, but when forbidden by gods, on Helius' island, or when it belongs to someone else, on Ithaca, you should not eat it. Sex is pleasurable, but when your husband is absent you must do without. Sometimes, however, these simple morals, typical of folktales, are contradicted by the story itself. Although Zeus explains that humans are responsible for their own troubles, it is Poseidon, a god, who harasses Odysseus in revenge for the blinding of Polyphemus, where the fault seems to lie heavily on the monster's side.

But the underlying structure of the story is much older than the moral posture Homer gives it. We noticed in Chapter 13 how the epic of Gilgamesh and Homer's *Odyssey* begin with nearly the same words. In these stories the hero goes on a journey where deadly dangers threaten, but eventually he returns. The hero must slay his dragon, even as Gilgamesh overcame Humbaba, and Odysseus overcomes many deadly enemies. Even the 108 suitors who besiege Odysseus' home are, in a realistic mode, a kind of dragon. Repeatedly they are described as voracious ("devouring his substance") and sexually threatening ("whoring with the maidservants"). They hope to have intercourse with Odysseus' wife.

In the same way, the mythical dragon devours everything in sight and sexually threatens a woman. In the myth of the dragon combat, the monster is often overcome by a trick, sometimes at a drunken banquet, and slain with a special weapon. Even so Odysseus tricks the beast with 108 mouths by entering the palace in disguise, surprising the suitors in the dining hall, then even as they drink killing them with a special bow that no one else can string. As the dragon-slayer receives a princess as reward, Odysseus too "marries" the woman.

In Mesopotamian cosmogonic myth and in Hesiod (see Chapter 4), such stories describe the triumph of the ordered world over the disordered, of life and progress over death and stagnation, even as a prominent theme in Homer's poem is the hero's victory over death—so closely interwoven are myths of creation, the epic hero, and the folktale hero. The enemies of Odysseus are death's allies: sleep

(Odysseus falls asleep at crucial junctions in the stories of Aeolus and the cattle of Helius), narcosis (the Lotus Eaters), darkness (the cave of Polyphemus, the shadowy land of the Cimmerians), or forgetfulness of purpose (Circê). Declared by all to be dead, Odysseus travels across water, the element separating this world from the next, to the land of the Cimmerians, where he interrogates the actual spirits of the dead and sees the torments of the damned (Chapter 12). Calypso, whose name means "concealer" and whose island is the "navel of the sea," offers him eternal life, but it is eternal death for the inquisitive man ever thirsting for experience: Death hovers in the still central point of the boundless water, "concealing" the dead from the living (Hades means "unseen").

Water is death and its god, Poseidon, is Odysseus' relentless enemy. Like Polyphemus and the Laestrygonians, death is a cannibal, devouring the living in the tomb's dark and hungry maw. Within the dark cave of the Cyclops, Odysseus is "Nobody"—nameless, without identity, nonexistent. As dragons of death are stupid, so Polyphemus is made drunk by wine, fooled by the trick of the name, then wounded by the special weapon of the pointed stake. The same pattern underlies the slaying of the suitors, but cast in a realistic mode. When Odysseus escapes from the cave, passing from darkness into light, from death into life, he takes his name back and shouts to Polyphemus, "I am Odysseus!" After he kills the suitors, Penelopê recognizes him and they retire to the wedding bed.

Triumph over death leads to rebirth. Odysseus, like a baby leaving the "navel of the sea," passes through waters to emerge naked on the shore of Phaeacia. He takes refuge in a womblike hole in the dark bushes, then is welcomed by Nausicaä, a *parthenos* who has dreamed of imminent marriage, like the marriage that will unite Odysseus and Penelopê at the end of the poem. Nausicaä's role as deliverer, as new mother, is explicit as Odysseus is about to depart for Ithaca. She says to him, "Never forget me, for I gave you life" (*Odyssey* 9.464).

In cosmogonic myth, the primordial being is female, like Tiamat or Gaea, who begets monstrous creatures that oppose the establishment of the ordered world; or she is herself the enemy. But the female is ambiguous and may also conspire with the hero to overthrow the monsters of chaos, as Gaea conspired with Cronus to defeat Uranus, or as Rhea conspired with Zeus to overthrow Cronus. The ambiguity of the female in such stories is paralleled in the extraordinary array of female types in the *Odyssey*, good and evil, who oppose or help Odysseus' efforts to return home and reestablish order.

At one end of the spectrum are the dangerous seductive females Calypso and Circê, so like the seductive but deadly Inanna/Ishtar. Calypso, although beautiful, is the "concealer." Circê, although beautiful, wants to castrate Odysseus, a symbolic death. She turns men into pigs by the irresistible female power that reduces the male to pure animal lust, snorting and groveling in the filth. The female Scylla eats them whole. The female Sirens, like perverted Muses, lead men to their deaths through the alluring promise of secret knowledge dressed in beautiful song.

On the positive end of the scale stand Athena, Odysseus' protector; Nausicaä, the uncorrupted *parthenos*, cast as both potential mate for Odysseus and symbolic mother; and Penelopê, who resists sexual temptation for twenty years. In Zeus's speech about human folly, Clytemnestra is cited as an example of humans

THE LEGENDS OF ODYSSEUS IN EUROPEAN ART

Fifteenth-century painter Dosso Dossi (1486–1542) worked at the court of Duke Alfonso d'Este at Ferrara where the duke's favorite poet, Ariosto Lodovico (1474–1533), composed his famous poem *Orlando Furioso,* which combined elements of classical tales with medieval romance. Ariosto's enchantress Alcina appears to be a blend of Homer's Circê and Morgan le Fay from legends about King Arthur. Dosso Dossi may have been thinking of Alcina when he painted this sensuous representation of the queen and enchantress who changed men into animals (Perspective Figure 22.2a). Homer's Circê used potions and a wand to wreak her

PERSPECTIVE FIGURE 22.2a Dosso Dossi (c. 1486–1542), *Circe and Her Lovers in a Landscape,* c. 1525, oil on canvas.   (National Gallery, Washington, DC; photograph by Lyle Peterzell)

magic, but Dosso Dossi's witch, in a European medieval tradition of magic, recites her spell from a tablet engraved with cryptic signs, having already consulted the book of magic still open at her feet. The peaceful deer, the fishing spoonbill, and the dogs at her feet may once have been men.

Claude Lorraine (1600–1682) was a classicizing painter who studied in Rome with a specialist in harbor scenes (Perspective Figure 22.2b). In this anachronistic setting he presents Odysseus' return of Agamemnon's concubine Chryseïs to her father Chryses, a priest of Apollo. Chryseïs herself is a diminutive figure in a blue dress seated on a hatbox just left of center in the foreground, her head turned to watch the cows for sacrifice arriving in a boat. The man in red beside her must be Odysseus, in charge of the prisoner's surrender. Three other Greek soldiers stand by and chat casually. Above them, to their left, arrive cattle for the sacrifice. Ransom is being stacked on the dock (lower center), and more goods arrive in the boat to the far right. The public building to the left is perhaps Apollo's temple over which Chryses presides. Boats and ships crowd the harbor, while others go about their business: In the lower left, a man repairs the dock

PERSPECTIVE FIGURE 22.2b Claude Lorrain (1600–1682), *Ulysses Returning Chryseïs to Her Father,* oil on canvas.   (Musée du Louvre, Paris; Scala/Art Resource, New York)

with a hammer and two men, one standing, play dice. The whole is suffused with the golden light of the setting sun.

The story of Penelopê's efforts to trick the suitors by promising to marry after finishing a shroud for Odysseus' father, then unraveling it at night, is represented in an early eighteenth-century painting by French artist François Lemoyne (1688–1737) (Perspective Figure 22.2c), known for his luminous sensuousness. Penelopê sits before her loom. Her trick discovered at last, she points to the finished shroud, which handmaids spread out for inspection. On the left, other handmaids bring yarn for Penelope's loom and a rug, apparently a gift from the suitors, tempting her to marriage. But Odysseus' ship even now draws into port, barely visible in the distance beyond the porch (to the right of the tree). Lemoyne was commissioned to paint this subject for the wife's room in an elegant private house in Paris. Thus he pays tribute to fidelity and the strength of the marriage vows to inspire the room's occupant.

The paintings of J. M. W. Turner (1755–1851) are among the outstanding artistic achievements of the nineteenth century. Known for his seascapes and misty landscapes, he is the first to isolate color apart from form, prefiguring the abstract painters of the twentieth century. Here (Perspective Figure 22.2d)

PERSPECTIVE FIGURE 22.2c François Lemoyne (1688–1737), *The Work of Penelope,* c. 1729–1737, oil on canvas.   (Musée Rodin, Paris; photograph by Adam Rzepka)

PERSPECTIVE FIGURE 22.2d J. M. W. Turner (1775–1851), *Ulysses Deriding Polyphemus,* 1829, oil on canvas. (National Gallery, London)

Odysseus, dressed in a scarlet cloak, stands beneath a red banner beside the left-hand mast of the eighteenth-century galleon to shout his defiance at Cyclops, a shadowy figure above the cliff (hard to make out!). At the bottom of the cliff gapes the cave of Cyclops, a fire burning within. The writhing Polyphemus, just blinded, invokes the vengeance of his father Poseidon. Some companions on the crowded galleon try to restrain Odysseus. Still others unfurl the sails to speed the boat away from danger. On the central mast the ship shows two flags, a red pennant at the top with Odysseus' name on it in Greek, and a white one below with a painting of the Trojan horse being dragged into the city (not visible here). The prow of the ship is a sea-monster with the anchor hanging from it like a great hook.

Beneath the prow mermaids play in the water. Another ship is visible to the right, its sailors cheering on Odysseus, and other ships are on the horizon, with the horses of the Sun visible in the lower right. For Turner the interest in this painting is the landscape/seascape, the misty colors of a never-never land satisfying to the Romantic taste for the picturesque and sublime. Painter John Constable described Turner's style as "airy visions, painted with tinted steam."

who act recklessly and pay the price. Throughout the poem Clytemnestra is the implied opposite to Penelopê. Clytemnestra is the wicked woman who gave in to sexual desire, betrayed the strict rules of wifely fidelity, and murdered her husband. Penelopê, by contrast, is the ideal woman, long-suffering, ever-faithful, and ingenious in preserving the honor of her home. Beset by a dangerous crisis, she courageously decides to take a second husband, thus setting up (unknowingly) the slaughter of the suitors. Clever like her husband, she cooly tests Odysseus with the token of the bed, in its immovability the symbol for their own marriage, as the olive tree from which it is made stands for the life of the family uncorrupted by adultery.

In the contrasting but parallel stories of the royal houses of Mycenae and Ithaca, Odysseus is like Agamemnon, each returning from Troy to find his house in the hands of enemies; Telemachus is like Orestes, fighting to restore family right and honor. The difference between the parallel legends lies in the character of the woman: Odysseus survives because Penelopê is woman as she should be, while Agamemnon is cut down like a dog. That, too, is a moral of the tale.

KEY NAMES AND TERMS

SOME ADDITIONAL ANCIENT SOURCES

Odysseus is an important character in Sophocles' *Philoctetes* and *Ajax*, and he appears in Euripides' *Hecuba*. Euripides' parodic *Cyclops* is the only surviving complete satyr play. Apollonius of Rhodes describes Scylla and Charybdis (4.788–832), as does Ovid (*Metamorphoses* 13.730–741, 13.898–14.74). Apollodorus has many references (e.g., 3.6–8, 3.22, 3.27–28) including a full account of the return in "Epitome" 7.

FURTHER READING CHAPTER 22

Atwood, Margaret, *The Penelopiad* (Edinburgh, UK, 2005). Novelistic reimagining of Penelopê's career.

Bloom, Harold, ed., *Homer's The* Odyssey (New York, 1988). Collection of modern essays.

Clay, Jenny Strauss, *The Wrath of Athena* (Princeton, NJ, 1983). Brilliant study of the goddess's role in the *Odyssey*.

Cohen, B., ed., *The Distaff Side: Representing the Female in Homer's* Odyssey (Oxford, UK, 1995). Essays with a contemporary theoretical, often feminist, perspective.

Finley, Moses I., *The World of Odysseus*, 2nd ed. (New York, 1978). Good on social background to the poem.

Louden, Bruce, *Homer's* Odyssey *and the Near East* (Cambridge, UK, 2011). Penetrating cross-cultural study.

Malkin, Irad, *The Returns of Odysseus* (Berkeley, CA, 1998). Stimulating study from myth and history of early Greek western colonization that places the *Odyssey* in the late ninth century BC.

Stanford, W. B., *The Ulysses Theme* (Ann Arbor, MI, 1968). Odysseus from Homer through the tragedians, Vergil, Dante, Tennyson, up to James Joyce and Nikos Kazantzakis's *The Odyssey: A Modern Sequel.*

_____, and J. V. Luce, *The Quest for Ulysses* (New York, 1974). Essays, lavishly illustrated, exploring the relationship of Homer's descriptions in the *Odyssey* to actual locations on Ithaca and elsewhere.

CHAPTER 23

LEGENDS OF AENEAS

When the age has come as the centuries glide their unhurrying path,
the royal line of the Trojans will enslave the home of Achilles,
with famous Mycenae as well, and will rule by conquest in Argos.
Caesar° will then be born, a Trojan of glorious lineage,
Julius, a name handed down from your son, the mighty Iulus,°
whose rule will end at the ocean, whose fame will end at the stars.

VERGIL, *Aeneid* 1.283–288

Caesar: Probably Augustus. Very little is made of his adoptive father, Julius Caesar, in the *Aeneid.*
Iulus: In fact, the name of the Julian *gens* ("clan") is not derived, as Vergil suggests, from the three-syllable name of I-ū-lus.

WE HAVE NOW LOOKED at a large number of Greek myths in a systematic way and some from the Near East as well. We have found in these rich and diverse stories a complex blend of religious symbol, national legend, and folktale. What of later developments in Rome, when a people of different language, culture, and geography adopted and modified the stories of the Greeks?

Roman religious and social patterns of thought were quite different from those of the Greeks, as were their economic and political institutions. This chapter deals with Roman foundation stories linked to Venus and Aeneas, especially as told in the *Aeneid,* a Roman epic poem inspired by the *Iliad* and *Odyssey.* The following chapter turns to the later foundation stories involving Mars and Romulus and to legends of Roman heroes.

In the native Roman tradition, there is no creation story and almost no divine myth as we have defined it in Chapter 1. Roman myth is Roman legend, intimately bound up with Roman history and equated with it by the Romans themselves. Nonetheless, there is little that is truly historical in these legends. Mostly they are myths in our modern sense, propaganda designed to elicit support for social patterns, and they did prove remarkably effective in maintaining Roman power.

The Romans knew that their legends worked as propaganda but nonetheless accepted their validity, just as American educators once taught children that George Washington cut down a cherry tree and, because he could not tell a lie, confessed the crime to his father. Even if George Washington never did this, he might have done so. The moral of the story is more important than its historical truth. Roman "myth," then, looks like traditional storytelling and is modeled after Greek myth, but moral and political purposes (as in Athenian myth) have become paramount.

The stories of early Rome have exercised a profound influence on Western civilization and continue to do so today. Whenever one is asked to suppress one's personal interests for the common good, the wonderful deeds of early Rome take on fresh meaning. Such has always been an important function of myth: to define a culture to itself, to inform a people what is real in their world and important in their personal and social lives, and to offer bases for the difficult decisions everyone must face.

EARLY ROME: MYTH, LEGEND, HISTORY

How did a small village on the Tiber become the center of one of the largest empires the world has ever known, and certainly the most successful? Many have speculated on this extraordinary and unparalleled development in human history, but we can be sure that the roots of Rome are based in the fortunes of its early neighbors. By the eighth century BC the metal-rich hills of Italy's western coast, inhabited by indigenous non–Indo-European Etruscans, had become a magnet for Greek colonists and Phoenician traders. Cultural exchange, especially of myth and language, was a by-product of commerce in mining and industry. One of the oldest known inscriptions (c. 740 BC) in the Greek alphabet is from the small island of Ischia in the Bay of Naples (early identified with the island of Circê). In dactylic hexameters, it already refers to a famous cup owned by Nestor in the *Iliad*. Evidently Homer's poems were known in the far West within a generation of Homer's having created them.

North of Rome in Etruria, at a town called Pyrgi, a local king set up golden tablets around 500 BC recording a dedication to the Phoenician goddess Astartê in both the Phoenician syllabary and language and in the Greek alphabet and Etruscan language. At Lavinium, south of Rome, where Aeneas was worshiped in Roman times, a bronze plaque from the same time inscribed in a hybrid of archaic Latin and Greek preserves a dedication to Castor and Pollux, the Dioscuri of Greek myth. Rome's insatiable appetite for territory and resources suited its voracious appetite for cultural forms, especially Greek and Etruscan, which Romans took over and remade as their own.

In its earliest days, Rome was ruled by kings. About 500 BC an alliance of wealthy land-owning Latin families, the *patricians*, "fathers," destroyed the foreign Etruscan monarchy (discussed in the following chapter). Thereafter the patricians met together in the Senate, "body of old men," to pass laws and decide on peace and war. Those excluded from this privileged class, the majority, were called *plebeians*, "commoners," who, especially in the fourth century BC, struggled to gain their own representation and voice in the affairs of the state, with real but limited success.

Under the *republic*, as modern historians call the period of Roman rule after the expulsion of the kings (from the Latin *res publica*, "business of the people"), elections, usually rigged, were held among the members of the ruling patrician oligarchy. There were never more than thirty or so ruling families at any time. Under the republic the legislative branch, we might say, normally held the power, whereas the weaker executive branch consisted of two *consuls*, elected annually. The power of the consuls was checked by their short term of office and the power of veto each held over the other. A consul possessed *imperium*, the "power" to command the army and enforce the law, including imposition of the death penalty, a vestige of royal power inherited by the new ruling patrician oligarchy. The symbol of *imperium* was the *fasces*, an ax surrounded by a bundle of rods carried by bearers called lictors, who preceded the consul wherever he went. The rods were for whipping and the ax for beheading. From this word comes the modern term *fascism*, because the twentieth-century Italian political leader Benito Mussolini claimed to be reconstructing the ancient Roman state (see Perspective 23).

Having set up a government controlled by small cliques belonging to a restricted social class, the patrician families fabricated legendary traditions about their ancestors to justify their monopoly of power. So successful was their form of government, wherein a self-sacrificing, idealistic oligarchy warred against much less efficient foreign constitutions, usually monarchical, that the rule—and the wealth—of Rome expanded enormously.

In the third to first centuries BC the Roman state took over virtually the entire Mediterranean world, not only the old Greek states, but what had once been great kingdoms of the East. The strain of expansion was too great, and by 30 BC the old patrician oligarchic republic gave way to a new quasimonarchy under Augustus (63 BC–AD 14). Modern historians call this new monarchy the Roman empire, when *imperium* resided permanently in the hands of a single man and not with the representatives of a privileged social class.

Julius Caesar (100–44 BC), a key figure in the disintegration of the republic, was in his enemies' eyes a man who placed personal ambition before the interests of the state, that is, the interests of the privileged patrician class. With brilliance and ruthless efficiency he destroyed the senatorial armies that opposed him. In defiance of Roman tradition he became sole ruler, but conspirators cut him down as he stood before the Senate to speak. As he fell—Shakespeare tells the story in his play *Julius Caesar*—Caesar cried out to the assassin Marcus Brutus, his good friend, *Et tu, Brute,* "You too, Brutus?" Not so coincidentally, this same Marcus Brutus claimed descent from an earlier tyrant-slayer also named Brutus, alleged founder of the patrician oligarchic republic five hundred years before.

Caesar's patrician enemies thought that his death would restore the power of the senatorial oligarchy, but Caesar's party rallied under Marc Antony, Caesar's general, and under Caesar's grandnephew and heir, Octavian, who after 27 BC was called Augustus, "greater than human." Octavian and Marc Antony conquered the senatorial armies and divided the world between them, Octavian taking the West and Antony the East. Antony's infamous affair with the Macedonian queen Cleopatra of Egypt, descended from a general of Alexander the Great, and other quarrels led in 31 BC to a war between the onetime partners, and to Octavian's final victory. The monarchy instituted by Octavian/Augustus was to last (in the East) until the fall of Constantinople to the Turks in AD 1453.

ROMAN RELIGION

The direct ancestors of the Romans were the *Latini* (la-**tīn**-ī) who may have entered the Italian peninsula as early as 1500 BC and occupied the site of Rome by 1200 BC. They gave their name to LATIUM (**lā**-shum), the territory west of the central Apennine range and south of the Tiber as far as the fertile plain of CAMPANIA behind the Bay of Naples (see Map X). Dominating Latium on the south and east rose the ALBAN HILLS, where many important Latin towns rose up in the sixth and fifth centuries BC. Among these were ALBA LONGA, at the western edge of the hills, and LAVINIUM toward the coast, which figure in stories about the early Roman state. These early Latin peoples had religious practices and attitudes rather different from those found in Greece.

Numina and *Sacrificium*

We noted in Chapter 1 that myths are stories, whereas religion is belief and the course of action that follows from belief. Religion is a system of assumptions about how external powers affect our behavior and the things we do to maintain good relations with these external powers. Greek myth was inextricably mixed with religion, as we have seen. Roman myth was too, but the profoundly different nature of the native Roman divinities created special conditions for the development of Roman myth.

Greek religion regarded its deities as endowed with superhuman powers and, in general, with immortality, but the Greek anthropomorphic gods also possess a human psychology. They lust, lie, cheat, fight, love, forgive, hate, and avenge, and many help the humans they favor. Native Roman deities, by contrast, seem to have been mostly personifications of various qualities and were strictly limited in their function, having only the right to refuse or assent to requests. The Latin verb *nuo* means "nod" and hence "assent," and from this word such deities are called *numina* (singular *numen*),

ANCIENT ITALY

Many of the place names are given in modern (Italian or English) forms if these are more generally familiar.

ALPS

TRANSPADANE GAUL

VENETIA

Verona

Padua

Mantua

LIGURIA

Modena

Apennines

CISPADANE GAUL

Po R.

Ravenna

Genoa

Lucca

Fiesole

Florence

Pisae

Rubicon R.

Arno R.

Volaterrae

Arezzo

UMBRIA

Cortona

PICENUM

ETRURIA (TUSCANY)

Clusium

Perugia

ELBA

CORSICA

SABINES

Tarquinii

AEQUI

Rome

See Inset

Ostia

LATIUM

Anzio

SAMNIUM

APULIA

Cannae

CAMPANIA

L. Avernus

Naples

Cumae

Mt. Vesuvius

Baiae

Misenum

Pompei

Brindisi

CAPRI

Paestum

Tarentum

CALABRIA

LUCANIA

SARDINIA

TYRRHENIAN SEA

ADRIATIC SEA

Sybaris

BRUTTIUM

IONIAN SEA

LIPARI (AEOLIAN) IS.

Messina

Palermo

Trapani

Mt. Aetna

Segesta

SICILY

Enna

Agrigento

Syracuse

MALTA

0 25 50

Miles

University of Wisconsin Cartographic Lab

Inset — ANCIENT LATIUM

Flaminian Rd.

Veii

Tiburtine Rd.

Aurelian Rd.

Collatia

Gabii

Rome

Mt. Algidus

Ostian Rd.

Alba Longa

Alban Hills

Corioli

Volscian Mts.

Lavinium

Appian Rd.

Ardea

Pomptine Marshes

0 5 10

Miles

MAP X Ancient Italy

635

FIGURE 23.1 A river *numen,* marble sculpture, c. second century AD. Almost everything had its indwelling spirit. This one was labeled "Marforio" evidently sometime in the medieval period. Most medieval and Renaissance paintings of the baptism of Christ have a figure representing the *numen* of the River Jordan. (Musei Capitolini, Rome; author's photo) (Musei Capitolini, Rome; author's photo)

"nodders." The *numina* are spirits that can inhabit almost any object or serve almost any function, petty or grand (Figure 23.1).

A good example is the *numen* called by some authors Robigus, grammatically masculine, and by others Robigo, grammatically feminine—that is, a spirit whose gender was unimportant. Robigus/o had one power, either to cause or prevent fungus disease in the grain crop. At a sacrifice called the Robigalia, held annually on April 25, the priest of Quirinus (kwi-**rīn**-us), a *numen* representing the Roman people (from Latin *co-viri,* "men together"), would ask Robigus/o to hold back the blight. In return, the priest offered him/her a sort of bribe of wine, incense, the gut of a sheep, and the entrails of a filthy red dog. The ceremony was called *sacrificium,* a "making sacred," the origin of our word *sacrifice.*

Sacrificium was a legal transfer of something into the ownership of the *numen,* who was then expected to fulfill his or her side of the bargain. Both parties to a contract gave something in order to receive something in return—*do ut des,* "I grant you this, so that you will give me that in exchange." Such a notion, applied to the gods, removed them from moral responsibility. The priest acted as a lawyer for the Roman people in fulfilling their side of the contract, and the *numen* was expected to fulfill his or her obligations as well.

The will of the *numina* was revealed through divination, at which the Romans were adept (thanks to their Etruscan teachers), and all proceedings required the "nod" of the invisible powers. There were many different procedures. On the brink of a naval offensive during the First Punic War (264–241 BC), the consul Appius Claudius Pulcher sought his favorable omen by feeding sacred chickens, but, seasick, they would not eat. With unwise impatience, he exclaimed, "Let them drink, instead!" and threw the chickens overboard. To no one's surprise he sailed into catastrophic defeat at the hands of the Carthaginians off northwestern Sicily. On trial for treason, he was found dead in his home.

The functions of *numina* could be subdivided and assigned to subdeities who had no temples or cult but were invoked on appropriate occasions. For example, at the Cerealia, a ceremony on April 19 in honor of Ceres (**sē-rēz**), *numen* of the grain harvest, and *Tellus Mater* ("Mother Earth"), a priest invoked the favor of First-Plower, Second-Plower, Maker-of-Ridges-between-Furrows, Implanter, Over-Plower, Harrower, Hoer, Weeder, Harvester, Bringer-In, Storer, and Bringer-Out. Such beings later excited the scornful mirth of the fathers of the Christian church, who had no use for such primitive pagan superstition.

Although the Roman *numina* were remote and colorless, some of them took on roles of service to the state and the family and enjoyed a central place in Roman civic and home life—roles that grew as Greek influence helped the *numina* to assume more personality. One of the best known was **Janus** (**jā**-nus), "gate," in origin a *numen* of bridges, hence of going forth and returning. He was represented as a man with two faces, one looking forward, the other back (Figure 23.2).

Janus came to be viewed as presiding over beginnings of all kinds, and the first month of our year was named after him. In the Roman Forum was a gate without a

FIGURE 23.2 Two-faced Janus, on a Roman coin, third century BC. A spirit of the doorway, he gave his name to the month of January, which looks forward to the new, backward to the old. Starting in 153 BC, the Roman year began in January. February was devoted to purifications (*februa*). Farming and war began in March, the month of Mars.   (Museum of Fine Arts, Boston; Photograph © 2007 Museum of Fine Arts, Boston)

building: Janus himself. His doors were opened when Rome went to war and closed when Rome was at peace. Until the final victory of Augustus in 30 BC, the doors of Janus had stood open for more than two hundred years. The emperor proudly proclaimed, "I closed Janus." From this *numen* seems to come the Roman triumphal arch (see Figure 24.4).

Roman Deities Equated with Greek

When the Roman poets fell under the influence of the Greeks living in southern Italy, they began to think of these bloodless abstractions, the *numina,* as being like the anthropomorphic gods of the Greeks. The Roman equivalents to Greek gods as named in Vergil, Ovid, and other poets (see chart "The Greek and Roman Pantheon" just before the Index) were largely a poetic invention with little basis in native Roman religion, although there were also important political motivations, especially during the reign of Augustus (27 BC–AD 14), for establishing such identifications (Figure 23.3).

The first syllable of the name of **Jupiter** (also called Jove, spelled Juppiter in Latin), originally *numen* of the bright sky, is etymologically identical to Zeus (see Chapter 6). He must descend from the common cultural, linguistic, and racial heritage shared by all speakers of Indo-European languages. Jupiter was worshiped in many manifestations, for example, as Juppiter *pluvius,* "Jupiter the rain." As Juppiter *lapis,* a sacred stone supposed to be a thunderbolt, he

FIGURE 23.3 The Hellenized Roman gods, marble relief from the Arch of Trajan at Beneventum (in southern Italy), AD 114–117. In the Greek anthropomorphic style, Jupiter stands in forefront with his staff and thunderbolt; to his right, Minerva with her helmet; to his left, Juno dressed as a priestess with cloak pulled over her head. Jupiter, Minerva, and Juno are called the Capitoline Triad. The great temple on Capitol Hill (to Jupiter Optimus Maximus) celebrated their cult. Behind the triad, left to right: Hercules (with his club), Bacchus (with vines in his hair), Ceres (with the torch), and Mercury (with winged helmet). The sculptural style goes back to the Athenian Parthenon.   (University of Wisconsin–Madison Photo Archive)

received pigs sacrificed with a stone knife, a rite descended from Neolithic times. Jupiter became the incarnation of the striking power of the Roman state, and his emblem, the eagle, appeared on the standards of the Roman legions. His magnificent temple sat on top of the Capitoline Hill, hence our word *capitol.*

Juno was the *numen* who presided over women as members of the family and was easily equated with Hera. She had close ties with the moon. **Ceres,** *numen* of wheat, was from an early time equated with Demeter. **Diana,** the Roman Artemis, shares the same Indo-European root *di-,* "shining," with Zeus, Jupiter, the Indian sky-god Dyaus, and the Norse war-god Tiu. Perhaps in origin a spirit of the wood, Diana, like Juno, was associated with women and childbirth.

Mercury has no ancient Italian heritage but is simply Hermes introduced to the Latins under a title suggestive of his commercial activities (*merx* is Latin for "merchandise"). **Vulcan**'s name is not Latin. Identified with Hephaestus, he may have come from the eastern Mediterranean through Etruria. The Etruscans may have come from the East and certainly had ties with Eastern cultures. Vulcan was a god of volcanic and other forms of destructive fire. **Neptune** was the *numen* of water, although not specifically the sea until identified with Poseidon. Apollo was never successfully identified with a Latin *numen,* but kept his ancient name as he came early to Latium through Etruria and the Greek colonies of southern Italy.

The origins of **Mars,** assimilated to the Greek Ares, are obscure. Closely associated with the wolf, he may once have protected flocks or been a primordial god of war (a spear kept in the Forum Romanum had the name *Mars*). He gave his name to the month of March, a good time for beginning military operations. **Minerva,** an Etruscan import, was *numen* of handicrafts, hence associated with the Greek Athena. Liber (**lē**-ber, "free"), *numen* of wine, was equated with Dionysus. According to the often fanciful etymologizing of the Romans, his name was a translation of a Greek epithet for Dionysus: *luaios,* "looser" from care. Liber had a female counterpart, Libera. **Faunus** (**fa**-nus), "kindly one," is named euphemistically: He was *numen* of the unreasoning terror of the lonely forest and so identified with Pan.

Venus seems once to have been a *numen* of fresh water, especially springs. An early inscription from the volcanic country in southern Italy is a dedication "to the Stinking Venus," the *numen* of a sulphurous spring. Water is, of course, essential for the cultivation of plants, especially in gardens, and the name of the *numen* may derive from the Latin word for "pleasant," *venustus.* From being a *numen* of vegetable fertility, Venus, under Greek influence, also took animal and human fertility under her protection.

A literary passage reflecting the transformation of Venus appears in the opening of the *De rerum natura,* "On the Nature of Things," a philosophical poem by one of Rome's finest poets, Lucretius, written about 60 BC. Venus, Lucretius writes, is a being "who stings every heart on land and sea and air, the leaf-laden trees and the birds, the green and flourishing land, with insistent desire that lures them on to propagate their kind." In these lines she functions still as *numen,* a natural force with a name. A few lines further, however, she becomes the Greek Aphrodite, in whose arms "reclines fierce Mars [= Ares] stabbed with love's undying wound. His head droops back; He feeds desire with gazing in your [Venus'] eyes, and his breath is locked to your responsive lips." The humanization of Venus presented by Lucretius in 60 BC, from *numen* to goddess, has much advanced forty years later in Vergil's *Aeneid,* in which Venus functions as would any Greek god in the poems of Homer, protecting her son Aeneas in his trials.

To **Hercules** belongs the earliest foreign cult at Rome. The form of his name reflects Western Greek pronunciation, as does Aesculapius, the Latin form of Asclepius, and Proserpina (pro-**ser**-pi-na), the Latin form of Persephonê, and Ulysses, the Latin form of Odysseus. Dis (dis), the Roman Hades, is an abbreviation of Latin *dives,* "riches," a translation of the Greek *Pluto* (which in Greek means "enricher"), a euphemism for Hades.

Observations: Gods and Men in the Roman Meat Market

The early cult of Hercules at Rome reflects the universal appeal of the most important Greek hero and Rome's voracious appetite for foreign novelties. Hercules had passed through Rome long before Aeneas, according to legend, and numerous special cults were dedicated to him in the area of Rome's ancient "cattle market," the Forum Boarium, a wide-open space along the Tiber river where fish and meat were sold (see Map XII, next chapter). Hercules was driving the cattle of Geryon back to Mycenae when he stopped at Rome and liberated the city from the ferocious cattle-rustler Cacus (**kā**-kus), who lived in a cave on the Palatine Hill (see Chapter 15). In a rather skewed chronology, one of Rome's first legendary settlers, the Greek king Evander, important in the eighth book of the *Aeneid* as host to the newcomer Aeneas, also welcomed Hercules. Later Evander built a great altar to Hercules (the Ara Maxima, "greatest altar") in the Forum Boarium as an offering of thanks for his liberating Rome from Cacus.

The altar still functioned as late as the fourth century AD as a site of large sacrifices and abundant feasts, as Hercules would have liked. Rome's first Greek athletic contests, in the early second century BC, were held in another sanctuary to Hercules in the cattle market, and military parades through the market passed by a statue of Hercules adorned in Roman triumphal garb. Several prominent Roman generals dedicated temples to him in the Forum Boarium, including one, to Hercules Victor ("conqueror"), that still stands.

As cleaner of the Augean stables, captor of the Cretan bull and the cattle of Geryon, and quintessential athlete, the imported Hercules became a versatile model in this rough-and-ready neighborhood of the world's greatest city, receiving the attention of Roman butchers, cattle-traders, athletes, and victorious generals. For centuries Roman emperors adopted the accoutrements of Hercules—the lion skin and the knotted club—for their portrait statues and erected them in the Forum Boarium (see Figure 15.7). Together with Hercules, the Greek god Apollo, who also sponsored athletics, and the Roman *numina* Fortuna ("good luck") and Portunus ("the river ford") received cultic statues in the Forum Boarium. The temple of Portunus (Figure 23.4), *numen* of the Tiber river crossing, was home to a famous market for flowers and garlands, one of the best preserved of Roman religious structures from the republican period. In the Forum Boarium came

FIGURE 23.4 Temple of Portunus, *numen* of the Tiber river crossing, in the Forum Boarium, Rome, first century BC (once thought to be the temple of Fortuna, *numen* of "good luck"). The Ionic architectural order of this temple is Greek in origin, but the high podium and frontal emphasis are of Etruscan temple design, intended to create a frame for priests to observe the flight of birds (augury). Also of Etruscan design are the frontal staircase, deep porch, and engaged columns along the back and sides of the cella.   (Photo Canali Photobank, Milan)

together the various strands of Roman religion and culture: Etruscan, Greek, and native, all mixed up together, all supporting the needs of Roman civic, economic, and military life.

Gods of the Family and State

The divinities associated with the Roman family always retained their own identities, despite Greek influence, either because the Greeks had no deities to correspond with these particular gods or because they were so embedded in Roman life that nothing could replace them. One such deity was the protective spirit called a Lar (plural **Lares**, lar-ēz), the name apparently derived from the Etruscan word for a spirit of the dead. The Lares probably began as protective ghosts of the fertile field, then came to protect all kinds of places: the household, streets, even whole cities (Figure 23.5).

FIGURE 23.5 Roman Lares, painting on plaster from Pompeii, c. AD 60. The master of the household, wearing a toga over his head in a ritual gesture, stands between his protective Lares, who hold horns of plenty and baskets of plenty. The serpent at the bottom, about to eat a honey cake, also protects the house, like the good-luck serpent in the House of Erechtheus on the Acropolis in Athens (called *agathos daimon,* "good spirit"). (House of the Vettii, Pompeii; author's photo)

The Lares were worshiped in small shrines at crossroads where the boundaries of four farms came together. There every year a doll was suspended for each member of the family and a ball of wool for each slave, perhaps a substitute for ancient human sacrifice. Similar to the Lares were the **Penates** (pe-**nāt**-ēz), who protected a household's things and especially its food. Penates and Lares were often confused, but Penates are portable and Lares were always fixed to a specific location. In origin the Penates were the *numina* of the storehouse—*penus* means "cupboard," the origin of our *pantry.* Later the Penates became identified with the welfare of the Roman state. The Trojan gods whom Hector's ghost entrusted to Aeneas as he fled the burning city of Troy were identified with the state Penates. The Romans also associated the Penates with the Dioscuri, Castor and Pollux, who protected the Roman state.

The religious activity of the family revolved around the *gens* (gānz, plural *gentes*), roughly "clan," and the *familia,* "household," including slaves. Citizenship meant membership in a *gens* and was confined to males. The head of the *familia,* at least in theory, had absolute power over all members of the *familia,* including the right to kill even his own sons (some instances are recorded). The *patria potestas,* "power of the father," invested in the *paterfamilias,* "father of the family," rarely was exercised to the full, but was always a real threat, especially for slaves.

One term from the Roman religion of the family, *genius* (**gān**-i-us), has passed into our own speech, although its meaning has changed. A man's *genius*, "begetter," was a sort of double, the part of himself that he inherited from his father and would pass on to his sons. Citizens throughout the Roman world worshiped the *genius* of Augustus, and later emperors. Not the man, but his *genius* was the object of adoration, the Romans insisted, but the distinction was lost on subject peoples, who came to view the Roman emperors as gods themselves.

The Romans felt that the state was a family writ large, a notion clear in the cult of the *numen* **Vesta**, whose name corresponds etymologically to the Greek Hestia. Like her, Vesta is protectress of hearth and home. Six Vestal Virgins served her, each chosen at the age of seven from the great families. The Vestals served for thirty years, after which they could marry, although few did. In their round temple in the Roman Forum (Figure 23.6) they served the state as unmarried girls served

FIGURE 23.6 The temple of Vesta, first century AD, near the center of the Roman Forum, near the building where the Senate met (*regia,* "king's house"). Within the temple burned the eternal flame of the Roman state. Its round shape, a Greek architectural convention, was perhaps inspired by primitive huts that once stood on the hills around the Forum.   (Photo John Heseltine; © Dorling Kindersley)

in a private home: baking, cleaning, tending the hearth, whose sacred flame, never allowed to go out, Aeneas had brought from Troy. If a Vestal was caught having sexual relations, she was buried alive in a tomb containing a loaf of bread, a jug of water, and a lighted lamp (some did meet their end in this way). Although Vesta was among the most sacred and revered deities of Roman religion, she had few myths (like the Greek Hestia), but remained an abstract *numen* throughout Roman history.

Perhaps the Romans' vision of the state as an enlarged family is most clear from the exaltation in myth and other propaganda of a set of duties called **pietas** (**pē**-e-tas). The term has little in common with its English derivatives *piety* and *pity*, but refers instead to the extraordinary devotion that one shows first to the *pater-familias,* then by extension to the abstraction of the state itself and its gods. The Roman exaltation of *pietas* as the highest virtue was prominent from an early time and was claimed in titles used by Roman emperors and the poets who wrote for them, especially Vergil, who calls his hero *pius Aeneas.* No doubt it was the native Roman predisposition to regard abstractions as divine that enabled them to trans-fer pious devotion from the head of a family to an invisible entity of great power, the Roman state. Greek religious anthropomorphism, by contrast, stood in the way of granting obedience to a divine abstraction, and the Greeks never did evolve a nation state.

THE LEGEND OF AENEAS

Augustus calmed the remains of the old senatorial party, which under the empire remained an advisory elite, by retaining the outward trappings of republican govern-ment. The religious, artistic, and literary program he sponsored, from which come most surviving accounts of Roman myth, was heavily propagandistic, with the aim of making the new regime appear to be a continuation of the old republic. In reality the old republic had ceased to exist. Two writers particularly important in Augustus' cultural program were Vergil (70–19 BC) and the historian Livy (59 BC–AD 17), but many other writers prominent under Augustus, especially Ovid, allude often to the tales of early Rome, linking the present political situation with a mythical past.

Vergil and the *Aeneid*

Vergil, in his immensely complicated and influential poem the *Aeneid,* used the legend of Aeneas, the founder of the Roman race, to create a literary document that might rival those of the Greeks, even Homer. Vergil was born in 70 BC near Mantua, in northern Italy. In 41 BC, if we can believe his own verses, he lost his farm in the political turmoil. Helped by Maecenas, a friend and minister of Augustus, he became a trusted member of Augustus' art council.

He wrote the *Eclogues,* graceful pastoral poetry celebrating the uncorrupted emotions and clever wit of imaginary shepherds, and the *Georgics,* a long poem ostensibly on farming, praising the physical beauty of Italy and the old-fashioned virtues of its peoples. During the last ten years of his life Vergil worked on the *Aeneid,* which he left not quite finished when he died in 19 BC. Although the poet ordered his poem to be burned, Augustus himself intervened to save it.

In Homer's *Iliad,* Aeneas was the son of Anchises and Aphrodite (see Chapter 9) and a cousin of Hector. He hoped to succeed Priam as king, although they were on bad terms. It is unusual for a hero to have a mortal father and a divine mother, yet the same was true of Achilles. Aeneas was destined to survive the Trojan War. One day his descendants would rule over the Trojans, as Poseidon explains to Artemis and Hera in the *Iliad* just as Achilles is about to kill Aeneas:

[300]   "Come, let us bring Aeneas away from the clutches of death,
          averting the fury of Cronus' son,° if he learns that Achilles
          has killed the man whom destiny calls to escape from this fate—
          all this so that Dardanus' line° may not perish in total oblivion,
          Dardanus, dearer to Zeus than all the rest of the children
305   born as the fruit of his loving embrace with the daughters of men.°
          You know how the son of Cronus now hates the household of Priam;
          know too that mighty Aeneas is to hold the rule of the Trojans,
          he and his children's children, for generations to come."

                                        HOMER, *Iliad* 20.300–308

301. *Cronus' son:* Zeus.   303. *Dardanus' line:* The Trojans.   305. . . . *daughters of men:* Dardanus was the son of Zeus and a nymph named Electra, a daughter of Atlas. Dardanus was the father of Tros and the grandfather of Ilus.

And so Poseidon saves him. Because the Romans had no native explanation for their origins, but were from the eighth century BC steeped in Greek litera-ture, as were the Etruscans, this passage from the *Iliad* suggested a possible illus-trious ancestor, complete with divine parent. Long before Augustus, a myth had evolved around this suggestion. Aeneas had fought valiantly for Troy, yes, but when the city burned, he escaped to the far West where his Trojan descendants, the Romans, were destined to rule all the lands around them. On his journey **Dido** (dī-dō, perhaps = "virgin" in Phoenician), queen of Carthage, attempted to hold Aeneas back from his goal, but driven by destiny he abandoned her and sailed to Italy, where he founded Lavinium in Latium (inset of Map X). His son **Iulus** (ī-ū-lus), claimed as ancestor by the Julian clan to which Julius Caesar and Augustus belonged, left Lavinium and founded the town of Alba Longa.

Hundreds of years later the descendants of Aeneas **Romulus** (rom-u-lus) and **Remus** (rē-mus), born in Alba Longa, founded the city of Rome. Aeneas was *pater-familias* of the whole race of victorious Romans and the direct ancestor of Augustus. The *Aeneid* is a modern poem, composed in writing and not orally, that makes self-conscious use of this mythical tradition to justify present conditions in the world. It is never just a story, but always an explanation of the problems that Romans faced and the moral and political solutions that gave Rome ascendancy over the world.

The *Aeneid* opens with an explanation, in mythical terms, of the ferocious and bitter rivalry that would one day exist between Carthage, a Phoenician col-ony in North Africa close to modern Tunis, and Rome. The name of Carthage is from Semitic *qart hadasht,* "newtown" (Naples too is Greek *Neapolis,* "newtown"). Although Vergil places the founding of Carthage at the same time as the burning of Troy, perhaps about 1200 BC, in fact Phoenicians settled the site about 800 BC, the same time as the Greek western expansion reflected in the *Odyssey.* Juno is the protector of Carthage, as Venus, mother of Aeneas and sponsor of the Julian clan, favors Rome:

[1]   I sing of ancient wars and an exile, by the order of Fate,
        who sailed from the seashore of Troy, pursued over land and sea
        by the might of the gods who heeded great Juno's implacable anger.
        To Italy's mainland he came, to the coast of the land of Lavinia.
5   Once more he fought to the death, as he tried to establish a city
        and settle his gods in Latium, whence rose the race of the Latins,
        the noble rulers of Alba, and the towering ramparts of Rome.
        O Muse, recall to my mind the insulted godhead of Juno:
        What did the queen so resent that she forced so pious° a hero
10   to suffer such trials and labor? Can divinity harbor such passion?
        There once was an ancient city, founded by Tyrian settlers,°
        far to Italy's south, but facing the mouths of the Tiber,
        Carthage, dowered with wealth, skilled and resourceful in warfare.
        Juno is said to have cherished this city more than all others,
15   Samos alone excepted.° Here she kept her weapons and chariot.
        Even as early as this the goddess was planning and helping
        to make—if fate should permit—of her city the ruler of nations.
        She heard that a race was arising from the conquered rulers of Troy
        that some day would dash to the ground the new-built Tyrian city.
20   From this race was destined to come a warlike imperial people,
        Libya's° bane and destruction. And the fated time was approaching.
        Saturnian° Juno trembled at this, but remembered the struggle
        that once she had waged at Troy at the head of the Argives she loved.
        The cause of that war and the bitter resentment it roused in her spirit
25   had never vanished away: Deep down in her heart she remembered
        the judgment of Paris, the wounding shame that her beauty was slighted,
        her rival's° hated descendants, and abducted Ganymede's honors.°
        Already embittered by this, she had blocked the way for the Trojans
        (survivors of war with the Greeks and the wrath of savage Achilles),
30   and driven them over the seas, far from the promise of Latium.
        Truly a mighty task was the founding of Rome and its people!

                       VERGIL, *Aeneid* 1.1–33

9. *pious:* The first reference to the *pietas* of Aeneas—his respect for family, country, and gods.   11. *Tyrian settlers:* That is, Phoenicians, from Tyre.   15. *Samos alone excepted:* On the island of Samos, just off the coast of Asia Minor, was an early cult to Hera and one of the earliest temples in Greece (eighth century BC).   21. *Libya's:* That is, North Africa. After a hundred years of war Rome destroyed Carthage in 146 BC.   22. *Saturnian:* Roman Saturn (a *numen* of the harvest) = Greek Cronus, father of Juno/Hera; hence Juno is "Saturnian."   27. *rival's:* The nymph Electra, on whom Zeus fathered Dardanus, ancestor of the Trojans.   27. *Ganymede's honors:* Ganymede, a Trojan prince brought to the Olympian court, was also rival to Juno's affections.

Aeneas and twelve shiploads of refugees have for seven years wandered across the Mediterranean, drifting ever westward. They have just left the south coast of Sicily when Juno persuades Aeolus, king of the winds, to raise a savage storm. The storm destroys some of Aeneas' ships, but others reach North Africa. Aeneas' mother, Venus, sends Cupid to breathe passion into Dido, queen of nearby Carthage and herself a refugee who left Phoenician Tyre after the treacherous murder of her husband Sychaeus (si-kē-us). She swore to his beloved ghost a vow of perpetual chastity.

At a banquet in honor of the newcomers, Aeneas tells Dido and her court the story of the fall of Troy: the wooden horse, Sinon, Laocoön, the death of Priam, his own escape through darkened streets, the disappearance into the shadows of his wife Creüsa. Carrying on his shoulders his lame father, Anchises, and his household gods, the Penates, he led his son Ascanius (as-kān-i-us, another name for Iulus) through the fire and carnage to safety, a striking image of the Roman patriarchal family (Figure 23.7).

He and other refugees managed to build ships and sail away. In a voyage deliberately reminiscent of Odysseus' travels, Aeneas describes how he and his companions stopped in THRACE, but a ghost warned them away (Map XI). From

FIGURE 23.7 Aeneas escaping with his father and son from the flames of Troy, painting on plaster from Pompeii, c. AD 60. On his shoulder Aeneas carries his father, who holds a special box, perhaps containing the Penates. He holds his son Ascanius/Iulus by the hand.   (Museo Archeologico Nazionale, Naples; University of Wisconsin–Madison Photo Archive)

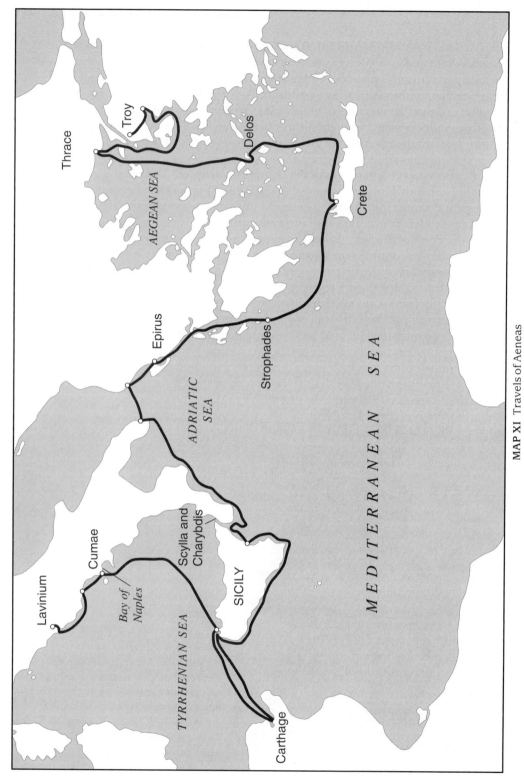

MAP XI Travels of Aeneas

Troy

Thrace

Delos

AEGEAN SEA

Crete

Epirus

Strophades

ADRIATIC SEA

MEDITERRANEAN SEA

Cumae

Lavinium

Bay of Naples

Scylla and Charybdis

SICILY

TYRRHENIAN SEA

Carthage

Thrace they sailed to the sacred island of DELOS, where Apollo's oracle told them to seek "the land of the founder of their race, Dardanus." This they supposed to be CRETE, but on Crete a plague beset them. Dardanus, Aeneas now learned, was not born in Crete, but in Italy. Sailing north, the Trojans put in at the island of the Harpies—one of the STROPHADES, small islands in the Ionian Sea—who make an unsettling prediction: They will travel until "hunger makes them eat their tables."

Disheartened, the Trojan refugees make their way up the coast to EPIRUS. Putting to land, they meet the Trojan prophet Helenus, himself a refugee and the last surviving son of Priam and Hecabê. Helenus describes the route to Italy and warns Aeneas to land on its western coast. He must found his city in a secluded valley by a stream, where he will find a white sow with thirty piglets.

They head west across the ADRIATIC, edge around the boot of Italy, and land in SICILY. An enraged and recently blinded Polyphemus attacks them—Odysseus had just been there. They continue west along the coast of Sicily. Aeneas' father Anchises dies and is buried. As they set out again, the great storm catches them that brings them to Dido's palace in CARTHAGE.

The setting for Aeneas' long retrospective tale is like that of Odysseus in the palace of Alcinoüs, and both recount adventures with the monstrous Cyclops; Vergil is imitating Homer. Dido, inspired with hopeless love for Aeneas (thanks to Cupid's arrows), listens to the story with fascination. A few days later, Aeneas and Dido (sworn to chastity) are out hunting. A thunderstorm bursts and the royal couple takes refuge in a cave. They fall into each other's arms. The rumor of their hot affair soon reaches the ears of a neighboring king whom Dido had refused to marry because of her vow to her dead husband Sychaeus. In anger the local king prays to Jupiter, who sends Mercury: Aeneas must abandon Dido and leave Africa. His destiny is to found the Roman race, not to idle away his life in the arms of a foreign queen.

When Dido hears of Aeneas' preparations to leave, she accuses him:

[305]   "Traitor, did you expect to conceal the crime you were planning,
          and quietly sneak away from my land? Was our love unable to hold you,
          or the mutual vows that we gave, or the thought of Dido abandoned,
          doomed to a piteous death? Pray, why pick the middle of winter
          for hurriedly readying ships to sail into a furious tempest?
310   Have you no heart?"
          So Dido poured out her pain, but Aeneas, by Jupiter's order,
          displayed no trace of emotion and repressed his anguish of heart.
          At last he muttered an answer: "If the choice were entirely mine,
          not a single word of the many which you so justly can utter,
315   O queen who deserved so much better of me, would I try to deny.
          As long as self-consciousness lasts, or body hearkens to spirit,
          never will I be ashamed to acknowledge my debt to Elissa.°
          Still, the plain truth demands a few words of exculpation.
          I never tried to conceal my hurried departure—no, never!

317. *Elissa:* Dido's real name. Dido ("virgin") is an epithet of the Phoenician goddess Astartê in her role as moon-goddess.

320   I never held the bridegroom's torch, nor acknowledged a marriage.
     If destiny so had allowed, I would live my life as I pleased,
     easing the cares that attack, in whatever way seemed to me best.
     I would cherish the city of Troy and whatever remained of my people.
     Priam's great hall would survive, and the Pergama° shake off its ashes,
325   raised up by my own hand, restored to a once beaten people.
     But now such a prospect is gone. The voice of Grynean° Apollo
     and the Lycian tablets of fate° have expounded Destiny's order:
     To Italy now must I voyage, to great Italy turn my endeavors.
     That is the land that I love, and that is the land of my fathers.
330   Mighty Carthage detains you, and the sight of your Libyan city,
     Phoenician though you were born. By what right, then, do you murmur
     if the Trojans at last find their promised home in Ausonia's° land?
     Surely we too are entitled to a kingdom in lands not our own.
     Night never covers the earth with misty shadows and darkness,
335   the stars never rise in the east to march on their fiery courses,
     but the troubled ghost of my father brings panic into my slumber,
     urging me on to my task. My son, too, appears in my dreams,
     reproaching me for my damage to the hopes of one so beloved,
     in cheating him of a kingdom, his destined Hesperian° acres.
340   And last, great Jove himself—I swear by your head and my own—
     has sent his herald to bring my orders down through the tempest.
     By the clearest light of the day I saw him enter the city,
     and when he addressed me I listened with all my closest attention.
     So please, give over inflaming both yourself and me with your protests;
345   though not by my own free will, to Italy I make my venture!"

VERGIL, *Aeneid* 4.305–361

324. *Pergama:* "Citadel," "stronghold," a word Homer uses to describe the walls of Troy.   326. *Grynean:* The epithet derives from Apollo's shrine in Mysia, south of Troy.   327. *Lycian tablets of fate:* That is, Apollo's oracles on Delos: Lycian is a common epithet of Apollo.   332. *Ausonia:* The borderland between Latium and Campania; here simply Italy.   339. *Hesperian:* That is, western.

Dido loses her self-control and threatens suicide. Aeneas sails anyway, just before sunrise. As he goes, he turns to see distant smoke rising from her funeral pyre spiraling into the sky. Dido has died by her own hand. With her last breath she curses Aeneas and all those begotten of him, a mythical explanation of the terrible wars one day to come between Romans and Carthaginians.

The Trojan fleet stops again in Sicily, now to hold funeral games for Anchises. The Trojan women rebel against their long wandering and attempt to burn the ships. Aeneas leaves them behind with the older, weaker men to found their own colony. The Trojans travel north toward what is today the BAY OF NAPLES, where the helmsman Palinurus falls overboard and is drowned, for Neptune had demanded a death before he would allow safe landing.

At CUMAE on the northern lip of the Bay of Naples, Aeneas consults the Sibyl, a local prophetess. From a magical tree he plucks a golden bough, sign of the elect, and he and the Sibyl penetrate the underworld (Chapter 12). On the banks of the River Styx, Aeneas sees the ghost of Palinurus, still unburied (as Odysseus encountered the unburied Elpenor). Charon allows them to enter his boat and ferries them over the gloomy water. On the other bank, the Sibyl drugs the ferocious Cerberus with a honey cake. Nearby, on the "mourning fields," populated by those who died for love, Aeneas espies the ghost of Dido in a scene reminiscent of Achilles' encounter with the dead Ajax (in *Odyssey*, Book 11):

[450]   Among them Phoenician Dido was wandering deep in the forest,
          still showing her wound. As Aeneas came, he peered through the shadow,
          like a man who sees or imagines the rise of the dim new moon,
          gleaming faint through the clouds. Unable to hold back from weeping,
          and touched by still tender affection, Aeneas spoke through his tears:
455   "So the word, poor Dido, was true, that reported that your life had ended,
          and that you had met your fate from a weapon in your own hands!
          Was I the cause of your death? I swear by the stars in the heaven,
          by the gods above, by whatever has force in the depths of earth,
          that I sailed away from your country, O queen, against my desire.
460   The orders of heaven forced me, and the gods' irresistible power,
          which forces me now to explore this region of darkness and mildew.
          How could I have foreseen what anguish my leaving would bring you?
          No, no! Wait for a while. Turn not away from my presence.
          This is the last time ever that fate will allow me to plead."
465   With words like this, with a flood of tears, Aeneas attempted
          to mollify angry Dido's scowling implacable specter.
          She fixed her eyes on the ground, and, silently turning her back,
          seemed no more moved by his pleading than would be a block of flint
          or a statue of Parian marble. At last she regained control,
470   and, still unforgiving, ran off to the shadowy depths of the forest,
          where at once her husband Sychaeus consoled her with mutual affection.
          Aeneas still watched as she went, deeply shaken by Dido's misfortune,
          shedding his tears of pity as long as she still could be seen.

VERGIL, Aeneid 6.450–476

Aeneas and the Sibyl pass Tartarus, where the worst sinners suffer, but the Sibyl will not allow Aeneas to enter there. Next they come to the Fields of Elysium, abode of the blessed dead. Aeneas vainly attempts to embrace the spirit of his father, Anchises. Nearby, ghosts drink from the River Lethê, "forgetfulness," and Anchises explains that these spirits will soon reincarnate, purified of crimes committed in earlier lives. Anchises points out to Aeneas the souls of Romulus, the other early kings of Rome, the great generals of Rome, and the spirit of Augustus himself. Anchises' words about Rome's destiny are central to this highly political poem:

[847]   "Others will chisel the bronze so subtly it seems to be breathing;
          others, no doubt, will extract a lifelike face from the marble.
          Tongues more fluent than ours will plead the rights of their clients;
850   sages will measure the heavens and tell of the rise of the stars.
          But you, Roman, never forget your duty to govern the nations.
          Your god-given skill will be this: to impose good conduct on peace,
          to thrust the proud from the throne, to forgive the beaten and humble."

VERGIL, Aeneid 6.847–853

After returning to the upper world, Aeneas and his followers board their ships and sail north to the mouth of the Tiber, in Latium. The Harpy's dread prophecy is harmlessly fulfilled when they eat breadcakes that, for want of dishes, they use as platters.

In Latium they encounter the local king, Latinus. His daughter, Lavinia, was betrothed to **Turnus**, king of the nearby Rutulians, but a prophecy directed Latinus to give Lavinia to a foreigner instead. When Aeneas accepts her, war erupts between the indigenous Italians and the Trojan invaders. The angry, jilted Turnus organizes a coalition of local warriors, including Camilla, a warrior-maiden from a neighboring tribe.

The river-god Tiber persuades Aeneas to form an alliance with King Evander, a Greek settled on the Palatine Hill, the future site of Rome. On the way to Evander, Aeneas sees a white sow with a litter of thirty piglets: Here he will found Lavinium, according to the prophecy of Helenus. Evander shows Aeneas sites near the Palatine later to be famous in Rome, and he agrees to support Aeneas in the war. He suggests that they also strike an alliance with a faction of the Etruscans led by the mighty Tarchon.

Meanwhile, Turnus has surrounded the Trojan camp. In a skirmish Ascanius kills his first man. In a glorious scene of battle, Turnus is trapped alone inside the walls of the camp (as once was Alexander the Great). Single-handedly he kills many Trojans, then dives into the river and escapes. In the company of Pallas, the son of Evander, Aeneas returns to the Trojan camp, but Turnus lies in wait and kills the young Pallas.

At last Aeneas and Turnus agree to settle the quarrel by single combat. The winner will marry Lavinia and rule over Latium. Aeneas wounds Turnus, who falls to the ground and begs for his life. Aeneas nearly shows mercy, but when he sees Pallas' sword-belt tied to Turnus' chest as a trophy, he angrily plunges his sword into the breast of the Italian warrior. So ends the *Aeneid*. **(For the complete *Aeneid*, go to http://www.theoi.com/Text/VirgilAeneid1.html)**

Observations: An Epic of National Rebirth

At first glance, the *Aeneid* and the *Iliad* or *Odyssey* look much the same: Both authors use an apparatus of gods to manipulate the action, set their poems in the days of the Trojan War, treat issues of honor and destiny, and present gory descriptions of death and physical violence. The first half of the *Aeneid* looks like the *Odyssey*, the tale of a hero's wandering as he tries to reach a home. The second part resembles the *Iliad*, a chronicle of warfare. Vergil's meter is the same dactylic hexameter of Homer, introduced into Latin about two hundred years before Vergil and by his time fairly well naturalized, although Vergil was the first Roman to write hexameters with true facility. All three poems use many of the same technical devices, such as fixed descriptive epithets like "swift-footed Achilles" and "pious Aeneas."

But the differences are profound. Homer was an oral entertainer in a boisterous, unlettered age that lacked political unity or great wealth. Vergil was highly literate, steeped in written Greek poetry and philosophy and in personal contact with the most powerful men in the world. Homer composed on the fly to entertain; our versions of the *Iliad* and *Odyssey* were (apparently) taken down by dictation. Vergil's poem was painstakingly learned, self-conscious, and created in writing with deliberate compression and elegant expression. Greek oral epic, usually complete in a single sitting, differed with every performance—our Homeric poems are snapshots of a single artificially extended performance. The *Aeneid*, composed in writing, was not finished even after ten years.

In Homer's stories people act: They become angry, do clever things, kill cruelly, or die nobly. The meaning of the story is in the action, and the characters are who they pretend to be. But Vergil's myths, like the Athenian myths of Theseus, are purposeful propaganda, to prove that Augustus deserved his place in the world and that Rome's destiny in history was willed by divine intelligence.

Characters and events in Vergil's myths have various levels of meaning; they stand for more than meets the eye. All events and characters are subordinated to his patriotic purpose of satisfying Rome's need for a tradition of national origin, a tale telling in the language of legend how this great empire was made. Its story of far away and long ago, when cows munched grass on the Palatine hill, satisfied contemporary literary taste for an escapist setting while making it possible for Vergil to proclaim, in symbolic form, the divine necessity of Rome's conquest of the world and of Augustus' ascendancy in it.

PERSPECTIVE 23

AENEAS, AUGUSTUS, AND MUSSOLINI

In the 1930s, Benito Mussolini (1883–1945), the ruler of Italy's fascist regime, joined forces with Nazi Germany in a failed bid to retake the Mediterranean by storm, just as imperial Rome had done 2000 years earlier. Roman legend and archaeology inspired the madcap scheme. Mussolini was called *il Duce,* "the leader," in Latin *dux* (*der Führer* in German had the same meaning). He sponsored excavations to recover evidence of Rome's heroic past, which he displayed prominently, and he built new monuments to promote continuity between Rome's imperial past and the fascist present.

When the famous Altar of Augustan Peace was discovered in the late 1930s, it was hastily excavated and restored (with fragments known since the 1500s), then exhibited inside a specially built glass enclosure near the Mausoleum of Augustus on the Campus Martius (see Map XII, next chapter). The altar consists of a central stone for animal sacrifice surrounded by a marble rectangular screen wall, decorated in high relief in a style reminiscent of the sculptures on the Parthenon in Athens. In 1939, Mussolini rededicated the restored altar on Augustus' birthday (September 23) in a grand gesture designed to inaugurate a new empire.

Apparently Augustus himself directed the design and erection of the ancient altar. Ovid tells us in his calendrical poem the *Fasti* (1.709–722) that Augustus dedicated it on the 30th of January, 9 BC, the birthday of Augustus' powerful wife, Livia. The altar was the site of annual sacrifices to celebrate the peace that followed Augustus' ascension to absolute power, called the *pax Augusta,* "the Augustan peace."

Some figures carved in the marble are unidentified, but numerous scenes are mythical. The general theme is to celebrate Augustus' military success, divine roots, extended family, heirs, and promise of a renewed "golden age," the *aetas aurea.* The *numen* Roma appears at rest atop a heap of captured weapons in a gesture of triumph and the peace that follows war. Mars, father of the Roman people, entrusts his sons Romulus and Remus to the shepherd Faustulus. In one scene (Perspective Figure 23a) a bearded Aeneas stands before a shrine

PERSPECTIVE FIGURE 23a
Aeneas about to sacrifice a sow before the sanctuary of the Penates, marble relief from the Altar of Augustan Peace (*ara pacis Augustae*), Rome, 13–9 BC.   (The Art Archive/Gianni Dagli Orti)

to the Penates and prepares to sacrifice a sow, whose presence, according to prophecy, marked the site of Lavinium (but here there are no thirty piglets). He wears a cloak over his head, as always with officiants at Roman sacrifice. A damaged figure behind him could be Iulus. Two attendants stand beside the sow. Thus does Augustus renew Rome with a fresh founding of the state. As Augustus cultivated continuity with the heroic age of Aeneas, Mussolini, in his patronage of the altar's recovery and display, sought legitimacy in his own bid for empire.

Augustus himself appears on the altar among members of the imperial family, with head veiled in the same manner as Aeneas: Augustus is the new Aeneas, as is Mussolini, whose Italian fascist state in 1930 published postage stamps with scenes from the altar to commemorate the two-thousandth anniversary of Vergil's birth. One stamp (Perspective Figure 23b) shows Tellus Mater (probably) with two suckling babes, probably Romulus and Remus, from the front panel of the Altar of Peace. Engraved beneath is a quotation from Vergil's pastoral poem (*Georgics* 2.173): *salve magna parens frugum, Saturnia tellus,* "Greetings, great mother of abundance, the land of Saturn [that is, Italy]." In the left-hand panel, *secondo millenario Virgiliano,* means "on the two thousandth birthday of Virgil." The panel on the right also contains a quotation from Vergil, *antiquam exquirite matrem,* the advice that Vergil received on Delos, that the Trojans should "seek your ancient mother."

Mussolini's other monuments in and around Rome included the Foro Italico, decorated with murals of Greek and Roman myth, and the Stadio dei Marmi

PERSPECTIVE FIGURE 23b Italian postage stamp with the scene of Tellus Mater (or some other fertility goddess) holding Romulus and Remus, from the Altar of Augustan Peace, 1930. In a panel beneath is a quotation from Vergil's *Georgics*.

("stadium of statues") for the 1944 Olympic Games (these were cancelled, but the stadium was used for the Games in 1960). A towering Egyptian obelisk rededicated in 1932 was inscribed "Mussolini Dux." Mussolini planned a gigantic new forum in the center of Rome with a colossal bronze statue of himself as Heracles, but in 1945 antifascist partisans placed him before a firing squad, then hung his corpse, and that of his mistress, upside-down in a gas station, for all to see and despise.

In order to provide justification for the new regime, Vergil needed a philosophy that could explain the whole sweep of Roman history, culminating in the achievement of Augustus. The old Roman *numina* lacked the authority to satisfy this requirement. Vergil needed a theory of destiny, an unchanging and inescapable plan laid down by immortal power, operating through all the ages.

He found this theory in the philosophy of Stoicism, which taught that the world is ruled by the divine *logos,* an untranslatable word that means something like "purpose," "structure," "intelligence," and "order" (the origin of our word *logic*). The Stoic *logos,* although it lacks personality, was close enough to the Judeo-Christian God to appear in the opening of the gospel of John (1.1): "In the beginning was the *logos,* and the *logos* was with God, and the *logos* was God, and without the *logos* was nothing made that was made." The usual translation of *logos* as *word* is inadequate.

A man named Zeno, from Citium in Cyprus, founded Stoicism about 300 BC, named after a colonnade (*stoa*) in Athens where Zeno taught. A central moral theme of this complicated philosophy is that one should live in harmony with nature, whose transformations reflect the underlying *logos.* The force of the *logos* permeates all history and predetermined Rome's ascendancy over all other nations. Rome's triumph is simply the working-out among mortals of divine will.

Vergil shows his hero as obedient to his country above all other obligations. Vergil may have had political motives for this attitude, but Stoic philosophy provided a convenient framework because the Stoics taught that one must always do one's duty, that is, follow nature. Aeneas is *pius,* placing duty above all, and he is not an independent agent. He is *fato profugus,* "driven by Fate," as Vergil says in the opening lines of the poem.

Fate is much the same as the *logos.* Latin *fatum* means "something spoken" or "decreed," as the Greek *logos* is derived from *legô,* "to say." The world of the *Aeneid,* and hence by implication the world of Rome under Augustus, is not controlled by a self-indulgent sky-god who squabbles with his wife and lusts after boys and young maidens. As Anchises reveals to Aeneas in the underworld, even Jupiter serves the impersonal *logos/fatum,* the divine order.

Aeneas may appear to be heartless for placing his duty to found Rome above his love for Dido, but the *pius* man must do his duty to the divine command, regardless of consequences to his personal life. He does what he must do, the only behavior that admits the possibility of human happiness, according to Stoic teaching. For the founding of empire, one must place personal interests behind those of the state. The Trojan women who tired of wandering and were left in Sicily are not worthy of empire. We must purge the weak before the great task can begin. Palinurus, the helmsman who fell from the ship off the Bay of Naples, is not just a member of the crew, but stands for every noble Roman who gave his life, at divine behest, that Rome might be great. The individual will perish, but empire grows.

Vergil's complex myth therefore places empire in the context of a divine plan for human history while glorifying the moral qualities necessary for the foundation of empire. The quality of *pietas,* devotion to duty, is the most important positive quality in a ruler. Vergil also shows what features a ruler should not have. Aeneas during his seven years of wandering has purged himself of material and sexual excess, which the exotic eastern city of Troy symbolized in ancient literature. He spurns the glorious new city that Dido is building and rejects his passion for her, so like that between Paris and Helen, who in placing personal desire above communal good gave rise to the catastrophic Trojan War.

In Dido, Vergil embodies many mythical and historical associations. Dido is not only like Helen of Troy, who gave in to her passion, but also like Circê and Calypso, enchantresses who would sway the hero from his purpose. She is also like Euripides' savage Medea, who represents all that is Eastern, foreign, and barbaric. In her the contemporary Roman reader would recognize Cleopatra, who seduced Marc Antony and turned him against Augustus and Rome.

Dido represents the moral failings of broken faith and Eastern passion. Although she swore to Sychaeus that she would have no other, she slept with Aeneas. Instead of transcending her heartbreak and pain (as a true Roman woman would), she took her life in an act of vindictive self-destruction. Dido also is an incarnation of Carthage, Rome's greatest enemy, who under the extraordinary general Hannibal (247–183 BC) nearly destroyed the Roman state. Such was the working-out of Dido's curse on Aeneas and his descendants.

The Romans were an amalgam of many clans and tribes whose primitive tribal identity was submerged in the greater being of the state. In Vergil's poem, Latinus the Latin, Tarchon the Etruscan, and Evander the Greek stand for the peoples fused into Rome. All work together toward the common enterprise. Brazen and hot-headed, Turnus is too like Achilles or Alexander the Great or Marc Antony to survive. Morally, he is not wrong; he may be right. After all, he was engaged to Lavinia before Aeneas appeared and carried off the bride already promised to Turnus. Still, Turnus must lose because he opposes the *logos,* the pattern of destiny. The personal and local pride that Turnus represents must succumb if empire will bestow its many benefits on humankind.

KEY NAMES AND TERMS

numen, numina, 634
Janus, 637
Jupiter, 637
Juno, 542
Ceres, 639
Diana, 639
Mercury, 639
Vulcan, 639
Neptune, 639
Mars, 639
Minerva, 639
Faunus, 639

Venus, 639
Hercules, 640
Lares, 641
Penates, 642
Vesta, 643
pietas, 644
Dido, 645
Iulus, 645
Romulus, 645
Remus, 645
Turnus, 652

SOME ADDITIONAL ANCIENT SOURCES

Ovid sketches a story similar to Vergil's, with many interruptions, in *Metamorphoses* 13.623–14.622. Apollodorus refers to Aeneas in "Epitome" 3.32, 3.34, 4.2, 5.21.

FURTHER READING CHAPTER 23

Bloom, Harold, *Virgil: Modern Critical Views* (New York, 1986). A good introduction to the poet through a collection of essays by leading scholars.

Cairns, Francis, *Virgil's Augustan Epic* (Cambridge, UK, 1989, reprinted 2007). The interrelation between poetry and politics in Vergil's Rome.

Feeney, D. C., *The Gods in Epic: Poets and Critics of the Classical Tradition* (Oxford, UK, 1991). Excellent synthesis of intellectual and literary history by a leading scholar.

Galinsky, G. Karl, *Aeneas, Sicily, and Rome* (Princeton, NJ, 1969). The origins of the legend of Aeneas, with much interesting evidence from art and archaeological finds.

Johnson, W. R., *Darkness Visible: A Study of Vergil's* Aeneid (Berkeley, CA, 1976). Influential reading of the *Aeneid* as an implicit criticism of Augustus and his policies.

Putnam, Michael C. J., *Virgil's* Aeneid: *Interpretation and Influence* (Chapel Hill, NC, 1995). A superior study on the achievement of Vergil, the character of Aeneas, and the legacy of the *Aeneid*.

CHAPTER 24

LEGENDS OF EARLY ROME

Foundations of cities are dignified by their antiquity, wherein mortal and divine affairs are allowed to mingle. If any people are entitled to consecrate their beginnings and trace them back to divine founders, these are the Roman people. So great is the glory of their military achievement that, when they lay claim to Romulus as city-founder and to his father Mars as parent, all humanity ought to accept it with the equanimity by which they endure our *imperium*.

LIVY, *History of Rome* 1.1

MARS, LIKE VENUS, WAS progenitor of the Roman people; he was the father of Romulus and Remus. Whereas Venus the mother of Aeneas was closely linked to peace in the Augustan worldview, Mars and the indigenous line of kings who followed gave legitimacy to Rome's military conquests. The 600-acre Campus Martius ("field of Mars," see Map XII), where troops were trained in early Rome, became in the Augustan period home to many institutions (the Altar of Augustan Peace was in the Campus Martius). Mars was invoked in the most important Roman ritual sacrifice, called the *suovetaurilia* ("pig-ram-bull-athon"), the bloody sacrifice of a pig, a ram, and a bull. Mars even presided over civil war. Augustus dedicated a great temple to Mars the Avenger (Mars Ultor) in the forum that he built to celebrate his victory over the assassins of his great-uncle Julius Caesar at the battle of Philippi (in Thrace) in 42 BC. Such behavior had good mythical precedent. The first Roman blood spilled on Roman soil belonged to Remus, cut down by his brother Romulus in the first of a thousand battles for primacy at Rome.

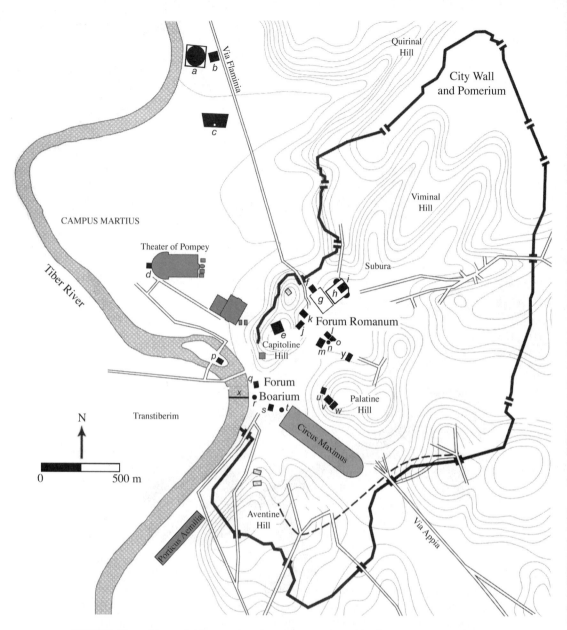

MAP XII Map of imperial Rome showing sites mentioned in the text. *a.* Mausoleum of Augustus; *b.* Ara Pacis Augustae ("Altar of Augustan Peace"); *c.* Horologium Augusti ("sundial of Augustus"); *d.* Temple of Venus Victrix ("conqueror"); *e.* Temple of Jupiter Optimus Maximus ("best, greatest"); *f.* Temple of Venus Genetrix ("begetter"); *g.* Forum of Caesar; *h.* Forum of Augustus; *i.* Temple of Mars Ultor ("avenger"); *j.* Temple of Saturn; *k.* Temple of Concord; *l.* Temple of the Divine Julius Caesar; *m.* Temple of Castor and Pollux; *n.* Temple of Vesta; *o.* Regia ("king's house"); *p.* Temple of Aesculapius; *q.* Temple of Portunus; *r.* Temple of Hercules Victor (? "conqueror"); *s.* Ara Maxima ("greatest altar"); *t.* Temple of Hercules Invictus (? "invincible"); *u.* Temple of the Magna Mater ("great mother"); *v.* House of Augustus; *w.* Temple of Apollo on the Palatine; *x.* Pons Sublicius; *y.* Arch of Titus. (James McConnachie © Rough Guides)

LEGENDS OF THE ROMAN MONARCHY

Romulus and Remus

Roman mythographers, "writers of myth," had to fill in the embarrassing gap of 450 years between the burning of Troy, traditionally placed at about 1200 BC, and the conventional date of the founding of Rome in 753 BC (according to a modern calendar). The usual story is that Aeneas founded the town of Lavinium, named after his wife Lavinia, then after three years died in battle. His son Ascanius/Iulus founded the nearby town of Alba Longa in the southeast of Latium, about twelve miles from the later site of Rome (archaeologists are not sure where Alba Longa was). There he was succeeded by a sequence of kings. In the twelfth generation after Aeneas—that is, about 450 years later—Romulus and Remus were born, who founded Rome on seven low hills on the banks of the Tiber river. In this way Roman mythographers brought together the legends of Aeneas and of Romulus and Remus.

Titus Livius or Livy (59 BC–AD 17) wrote an enormous history of the Roman people in 142 papyrus rolls, of which 35 survive, called *Ab urbe condita*, "From the founding of the city," after its first three words. Livy celebrated the political settlement of Augustus, who had personally encouraged him to write his history. Livy's prose version of the story of Romulus and Remus is a good specimen of how the Roman understood his early past. Livy has been describing the early kings of Alba Longa who succeeded Ascanius:

> The next king [of Alba Longa] was Proca. He had two sons, Numitor and Amulius. To Numitor, the older, he bequeathed the ancient throne of the Silvian dynasty.° But neither a father's intention nor respect for the claims of an elder son proved to be any match for violence when Amulius drove his brother out into exile. Then, piling crime on crime, Amulius killed all Numitor's sons, and stripped away all hope of male issue from his brother's daughter Rhea Silvia by giving her the empty honor of being a Vestal, and thus condemned to lifelong virginity.
>
> But surely the origin of so great a city, and an empire second only to the domain of the gods, must be ascribed to Fate itself. The Vestal presently gave birth to twins, the result, she claimed, of violent rape. She named Mars as their father, either because she really believed it, or because she felt that putting the responsibility on a god would lessen her own dishonor. Be that as it may, neither gods nor man defended the Vestal or her sons from the savagery of the king. She was chained and flung into a dungeon, and an order was given for the boys to be thrown into a running stream.
>
> By some piece of divine providence it happened that the Tiber had overflowed its banks and spread out into sluggish ponds, so that its normal bed could nowhere be approached. This led the men who were carrying out the babies to hope that they could toss them into any water that was moving, however slowly, and could thus feel that they were carrying out the royal command. So they abandoned the boys on the nearest mud bank, by the site of the present Ficus Ruminalis ["fig tree of the sucklings"], which, it is said, was then called the Romular ["of Romulus"].

Silvian dynasty: So called from Aeneas Silvius, grandson of Aeneas.

Now in those days there were wild areas all through the region. The story goes on that when the slow-moving water ebbed away, it left the basket that carried the boys stranded on the dry bank. Presently a thirsty she-wolf from the nearby hills came down to drink. Hearing a childish wail, she turned aside to the boys and offered them her teats so gently that, when a shepherd of the king's block found her a little later, she was licking them with her tongue. The shepherd's name is said to have been Faustulus ["lucky"]. He brought the boys back to his hut and gave them to his wife Larentia to bring up. True, some people maintain that Larentia was the local whore to whom the shepherds gave the nickname of Lupa ["she-wolf"], and that this was the source of the story—be it legend or miracle.

LIVY, History of Rome 1.3.10–1.4.7

The origin of the legend of Romulus and Remus, perhaps the best-known foundation story from all classical myth, is not clear. Some think it a genuine Roman tradition, but other scholars find in it a compendium of elements drawn consciously from Greek models. Native elements would include Romulus' name, an eponym of Roma, probably from the Greek word for "strength." No one can, however, explain the name of Remus. The detail about the Ruminal fig seems to be an etiological tag to explain a real tree venerated as the site of a *numen* called Rumina, "breast nourisher" (because the milk of the fig looks like milk from the human breast). Faustulus is perhaps related to the Roman woodland-spirit Faunus, identified with the Greek Pan. A *numen* with underworld associations, said to be mother to the Lares, was also called Larentia.

But the narrative details of the story recall Greek examples. The exposure of the children reminds us of Oedipus and other figures like Paris, exposed and suckled by a bear, and Zeus, suckled by a goat. Sargon of Akkad (c. 2500 BC), greatest ruler of Mesopotamia in the third millennium, the Hebrew Moses (c. 1200 BC), and Cyrus the Great, founder of the Persian empire in the sixth century BC, were all, like Romulus and Remus, abandoned in baskets on a river: So difficult is it to disentangle history from myth (Figure 24.1).

Royal brothers also appear in Greek myth, notably in the story of Amphion and Zethus, who founded Thebes. Danaë, a virgin like **Rhea Silvia**, was imprisoned in an underground cavern, but Zeus seduced her anyway and she and her child were set afloat on the sea. The rivalry between the colorless Numitor and Amulius may be consciously modeled on that between Eteocles and Polynices. The ancient motif occurs earlier in the biblical stories of Cain and Abel and Jacob and Esau and in the Egyptian story of Osiris and Seth. We cannot determine whether such elements were borrowed deliberately from Greek or even Eastern stories to concoct a Roman foundation myth or whether the story arose from a parallel native tradition.

When Romulus and Remus grew up, they became great hunters (like many traditional heroes), first of animals, then of bandits, whose loot they honorably divided with other shepherds. But one day bandits captured Remus and handed him over to King Amulius, who, oddly, gave him to his hated brother, the disenfranchised Numitor, for punishment. Numitor recognized his grandson. Romulus was brought into a conspiracy, and the father and brothers united to kill the wicked Amulius. Livy continues:

FIGURE 24.1 The Capitoline wolf, Etruscan bronze from the fifth century BC. The twins are not original but were added by a Florentine artist of the fifteenth century, probably Pollaiuolo (1431–1498). According to Livy the Ruminal fig tree grew up where the wolf suckled the twins. Rumina was a *numen* of nursing, connected with *ruma,* "a breast."   (Musei Capitolini, Rome; University of Wisconsin–Madison Photo Archive)

Thus the throne of Alba was restored to Numitor. But Romulus and Remus were eager to build a city in the place where they had been exposed and brought up. There were already too many people in Alba, both Albans and Latins, and beside them there were the shepherds—so many, all told, that it was quite reasonable to believe that Alba and Lavinium would look like little hamlets compared to the town now being founded.

But into these rosy dreams intruded the ancestral blight of ambition to be king, and a shameful quarrel arose from a trifling argument. Since Romulus and Remus were twins, respect for seniority could not determine whose name should be given to the new city and which of them should rule once it was founded. Romulus therefore occupied the Palatine and Remus the Aventine° to observe the signs by which the local gods might show them the answers. Remus, so goes the story, was the first to receive a portent, six vultures. But this sign had just been announced when twice that number appeared to Romulus. Both men were promptly hailed as king by their own henchmen, Remus on grounds of priority, Romulus on grounds of number.

Palatine . . . Aventine. The Palatine and Aventine were hills of Rome; see Map XII.

They began to argue, but their quarrel soon turned to violence, and in the fighting Remus was killed. There is a better known story that Remus contemptuously jumped over his brother's half-built wall [the *pomerium*]. Romulus, furious at the slight, killed him, adding the bitter jest: "This is what will happen to anyone else who tries the same!" Thus Romulus became sole ruler, and his name was given to the city he had founded.

LIVY, *History of Rome* 1.6.3–1.7.3

In later speculation the founding of Rome in fratricide was sometimes interpreted as foretelling the civil wars of the first century BC, but in origin the story of the two brothers may have advocated the sanctity of the consuls' dual rule in the state as the best refuge against kingship and tyranny. A recent theory suggests that the original story told of a foundation by Romulus alone, obviously the eponym of Rome, and that Remus was added to the story much later, in the fourth century BC, to represent the plebeians, who resisted the power of the patricians, represented by Romulus, in a prolonged struggle. That Rome claimed the murder of Remus by Romulus as the story of its founding is a tantalizing puzzle.

The Rape of the Sabine Women

Rome was founded and named, but there was no one to live in it except runaway slaves, bandits, and murderers who assembled from the hills. If the Romans were to grow in number, they needed wives. Romulus approached local communities and requested women for wives, but no man wanted his daughter to marry a Roman bandit. Romulus therefore conceived a plan.

During a festival large crowds flocked to Rome from neighboring Latin townships, including a people called the **Sabines** (sā-bīnz) who lived in the hills. As soon as the festival began, the Romans rushed into the crowd and seized the young Sabine women. The festival broke up in a panic, but the girls' parents, shouting curses, were forced to abandon their daughters.

The abducted women were angry and fearful, but Romulus assured them that everything would turn out well. They would enjoy the privileges of married women. Their children, when they came, would bind them closely to their new husbands, whom they would learn to love. The men spoke honeyed words and swore that passionate love had prompted their offense, a tactic, as Livy observes, that "touches a woman's heart." The women forgot their resentment.

No doubt Sabines did contribute significantly to the early Roman bloodline, but behind the story must also lie an early custom of the communal exchange of women, forced or voluntary; such practices occur in many societies. Even in classical Roman marriage the maid was pulled away from her mother in a mock show of force and her hair parted with a spear.

Titus Tatius, Tarpeia, and the Death of Romulus

The king of the Sabines, Titus Tatius (tī-tus tā-shus), promptly made war on the Romans. The struggle went on for years. Once the Sabines gained entry to the Capitoline Hill either by bribing **Tarpeia** (tar-pē-a), daughter of the Roman commander, or because she fell in love with Titus Tatius (Scylla, Medea, and Ariadnê also fell in love with their fathers' enemies). For her treachery she demanded in return "what the Sabines wear on their left arms," meaning their big gold bracelets. But once inside, the Sabines crushed the treacherous woman under the weight of their shields, which they also wore on their left arms. A cliff on the Capitoline Hill, where Tarpeia was supposed to have allowed the Sabines to enter the fortifications, was named after her, a place of execution down which traitors were thrown.

The day of the decisive battle arrived. The two armies drew up against each other, when between the lines ran the Sabine wives with their young children, begging fathers and brothers on one side, and husbands on the other, not to shed kindred blood. Seeing the insanity of war, both armies laid down their arms and united as one people.

Romulus died mysteriously. He was holding an assembly at the Campus Martius when the day went black. When it came light again, he was nowhere to be found. One tradition reports that senators, jealous of his royal power, murdered him, dismembered his body, and hid the pieces under their togas; another holds that he rose into heaven. In any event Romulus became a god and was ever after worshiped as the ancient *numen* Quirinus, who embodied the military and economic strength of the Roman people.

Observations: Becoming a God at Rome

Through **apotheosis**, the "process of becoming a god," the spirit not only of Romulus but of almost every Roman ruler after Caesar and Augustus, until Constantine's adoption of Christianity in AD 337, was elevated to godhead (Figure 24.2). Imperial apotheosis appears at the beginning of a new era of peace for Rome and also at the close of decades of horrendous bloody civil war. The emperor, with his inviolable power, could provide the peace and calm that traditional deities had not; he deserved divinity. Hercules, the Dioscuri, and Romulus offered mythical models for such elevation. Heroes were often semidivine (Romulus and Remus, the sons of Mars; Hercules and the Dioscuri, the sons of Zeus), and Julius Caesar and Augustus were the descendants of Venus. In the Eastern empire the temporal ruler was often already divine in some way, especially in Egypt, where the emperor simply became pharaoh, son of the Sun and incarnation of the hawk-god Horus. The Hellenistic kings, too, had long claimed divine status. Worship of the Roman emperor first appeared in Asia Minor in the old Hellenistic kingdoms.

Nonetheless, at first even a deified emperor was not officially a true god (*deus*), whatever the Egyptians might think, but could become *divus* (plural *divi*, feminine *diva*), "godlike," only by a vote of the Senate, and then only after he died. The title *divus* acknowledges divinity while not admitting the full supernatural power of an Olympian. Any cultic activity held in an emperor's honor while he lived was

FIGURE 24.2 Base for a funerary column of Antoninus Pius and his wife Faustina, Rome, AD 161 (the column is lost). Escorted by the eagles of Jupiter, deified spirits of the emperor and empress are shown as busts; he carries the imperial scepter with eagle, she is dressed as a priestess. They rise to heaven on the back of a nude, winged male spirit, perhaps *Aeternitas,* "eternity" (the fig leaf covering his genitals is modern). The spirit holds in his left hand a sphere surmounted by a snake, perhaps symbolizing endless time. On the right is the *numen* Rome portrayed like Minerva (Athena) seated beside arms captured in battle; the wolf suckling Romulus and Remus appears on her shield (lower right corner). On the left is a personification of the Campus Martius, where imperial funerals took place, shown as a man who cradles an obelisk in his lap: Augustus had brought one there from Egypt to serve as a gigantic sundial (Horologium Augusti), where the ritual of imperial deification took place.   (Vatican Museums; Scala/Art Resource, New York)

in theory directed toward his *genius,* "begetter," the *numen* that indwells a man but is beyond him and greater than he. In this way, Romans distinguished between the traditional pantheon of gods and goddesses and the deified imperial family.

Within these limits, *divi* in the Roman world were the recipients of cults, priesthoods, and even elaborate sanctuaries that rivaled those of the Olympian gods in expense and decoration. The Senate decreed a temple to the Divine Julius Caesar on the spot of his cremation in the Roman Forum. Many had witnessed his apotheosis as a comet, referred to repeatedly in contemporary literature. Similar temples to divinized emperors from later dynasties also rose in the Roman Forum.

Caesar and Augustus were wary of public claims to divinity and refused to be acknowledged as *deus*, at least in the city of Rome. Later successors, contemptuous of tradition, were less modest. The inexorable tyrant Domitian (AD 51–96) adopted the title *Dominus et Deus* ("lord and god") and set up statues of the Olympians in the reception hall of his Palatine home. Domitian even deified his son, who died an infant. The "good emperor" Trajan (AD 53–117) was called *Optimus*, imitating the divine head of the Roman state, Jupiter Optimus Maximus ("Jupiter best and greatest").

Wives of emperors were also deified, beginning with Augustus' highly influential wife, the *diva* Livia. The nefarious Caligula (AD 12–41) extended the honor to his sister Drusilla, with whom he was having sexual relations. In a bid for deification, the emperor Galba, who ruled for only seven months in AD 68–69, claimed descent from Jupiter on his father's side and Pasiphaë on his mother's side. Hadrian (AD 76–138) divinized his lover Antinoüs, drowned in the Nile on a drunken pleasure cruise. Even so, the rumor ran, had Osiris, god of resurrection, drowned in the Nile. Statues of Antinoüs were raised all over the empire.

Official legal apotheosis became a staged event with caged eagles, the embodiment of Jupiter, released into the sky on cue as flames consumed the imperial corpse on a monumental pyre (compare Figure 24.2). However, not every emperor was deified. Caligula, Nero, Galba, Domitian, and Commodus (see Figure 15.7) suffered the dreaded *damnatio memoriae*, "damnation of memory," decreed by the Senate—an erasure of the emperor's name and likeness throughout the vast empire.

The cult of emperor worship at Rome was more political than religious. As intermediaries between gods and men, the imperial family lent stability to an unpredictable world, and many Romans were happy to accept the emperor's "divinity." The cult helped unify the vast Roman state. Participation in the cult was a clear act of allegiance, whereas refusal to participate had the appearance of treason. Early Christians attracted intense suspicion and suffering, even death, from their refusal to burn incense on the altar of the emperor, which they considered a form of idolatry.

The Horatii and the Curiatii

After its foundation, supposedly in 753 BC (the days of Homer), Rome was ruled by seven kings, the first four Romano-Sabine (Romulus, Numa Pompilius, Tullus Hostilius, Ancus Marcius), the last three Etruscan (Tarquin the Elder, Servius Tullius, Tarquin the Proud). In an artificial schema, the odd-numbered kings were valiant and warlike, the even-numbered devoted to the arts of peace. Sometime during the Roman monarchy occurred one of the most celebrated examples of Roman valor.

The Romans were at war against their parent-city of Alba Longa. They agreed to decide the dispute by a duel between three Roman and three Alban brothers, the **Horatii and the Curiatii** (hor-āsh-i-ī,kur-i-āsh-ī; singular, Horatius/Curiatius). The fighting began, and almost immediately two of the Roman Horatii were cut down. The remaining Horatius, outnumbered three to one, turned and ran. As the Curiatii pursued, they became separated from one another. Suddenly, the surviving Horatius spun round and cut down the lead pursuer, then ran back to cut down the second. Now only one Curiatius remained, earlier wounded, and the single surviving Horatius killed him easily.

This inspiring lesson in Roman steadfastness was marred when the surviving Horatius, returning from the field, saw his sister weeping. She had been engaged to one of the Curiatii. In a rage at her sentimentality Horatius drew his sword and plunged it into her breast, crying, "Go to your lover, since you have forgotten your brothers, dead and living, and your country too! May every Roman woman die who laments an enemy!" Horatius was tried for the murder, but acquitted, compelled only to walk beneath a yoke with his head covered as a sign that henceforth he submitted to Roman law.

The Etruscan Dynasty and the Wicked Tullia

The jealous sons of the fourth king (Ancus Marcius) killed Tarquin the Elder, the fifth king of Rome, who had come to Rome from Etruria and captured the throne. However, the sons did not succeed in taking the kingship, which fell next to Servius Tullius, "Tullius the slave's son." His mother had been a slave in the royal house when the household Lar, taking the form of a phallus of ash on the hearth, leapt on her and conceived him. When Servius Tullius was a child, flames danced around his head, convincing Tarquin the Elder's wife, Tanaquil, a prophetess, that he was a man of destiny. After her husband's murder, Tanaquil conspired to place Servius Tullius on the throne.

Servius Tullius ruled long and well, and his daughters, both named Tullia, married sons of Tarquin the Elder, the murdered fifth king of Rome. (Roman women had no first names: They bore the name of their *gens* with a feminine ending—Julia, Cornelia—and, if necessary, a number—Claudia Quinta, "Claudia the fifth"; Antonia Minor, "Antonia the younger.") When Servius Tullius grew old, one of the Tullias, a woman as wicked as Clytemnestra, began a passionate love affair with her brother-in-law, soon to be the seventh and last king of Rome, **Tarquin the Proud**.

Tullia I urged Tarquin to murder his wife Tullia II (her sister) and his brother (her husband) and to get rid of her father, King Servius Tullius, so that together they could rule Rome. Soon Tullia II was dead, Tarquin's brother was dead, and Tullia I and Tarquin were married to one another. One day Tarquin, soon to be "the Proud," sat down in the king's seat in the Senate house. When the old king came to see what was happening, Tarquin picked him up and hurled him down the steps into the street. At that very moment the wicked Tullia I arrived in the Forum in her carriage. Livy tells the story:

> Everybody agrees that Tullia, driving her carriage into the Forum, paid no attention to the assembled crowd of men, but shouted to her husband to come out from the Senate House, and was the first to hail him as king. He told her to go away, because the crowd might become dangerous. But on her way home she had just reached the top of Cyprian Street (where the

LEGENDS OF EARLY ROME

Temple of Diana stood until a little while ago) and was turning right onto the Urbian Hill to get to the Esquiline Hill, when her coachman halted in terror, reined in the horses, and showed her the mutilated body of Servius Tullius as it lay in the road. The savage and brutal act Tullia then committed is commemorated by the place it occurred, which they now call Crime Alley (*vicus sceleratus*). For it was there that Tullia, crazed by the vengeful spirits of her murdered sister and husband, is said to have driven her carriage right over her father's corpse. She herself was spattered with his blood, and on the gory vehicle she brought back bits of his flesh to the household of herself and her husband.

LIVY, *History of Rome* 1.48.5–7

PERSPECTIVE 24.1

DAVID'S *OATH OF THE HORATII*

Little was known of ancient art and architecture until the mid-eighteenth century, when several publications by travelers who had visited the ruins of ancient cities in the Near East and Greece inspired an enthusiasm for all things ancient and classical. Between 1776 and 1788 appeared Edward Gibbon's long and learned *The Decline and Fall of the Roman Empire,* never since out of print. Sensational archaeological discoveries at Pompeii and Herculaneum, beginning in 1748, fed the admiration for classical antiquity, and in 1755 the founder of ancient art history, Johann Winckelmann, published (in German) his *Thoughts on the Imitation of Greek Art in Painting and Sculpture.* Such developments inspired an artistic movement called neoclassicism, which lasted well into the nineteenth century. Its central theory was that an unchanging eternal truth lies behind all appearance (in this respect, neoclassicism shared intellectual foundations with Renaissance Neoplatonism).

In France, Jacques-Louis David (da-vēd, 1748–1825) was a leading exponent of the movement, and his *Oath of the Horatii* of 1784 illustrates his political didacticism and admiration for classical geometric form (Perspective Figure 24.1).

The story was familiar to Parisian audiences not only through Livy but through a play by Pierre Corneille (1606–1684). The picture shows the three brothers as they swear on their swords to return with their shields or upon them, oblivious to the anguish of their sisters, one of whom is engaged to a Curiatius. The figures, enclosed by a rigorous architectural frame, are sculpted in the near foreground like ancient reliefs and posed almost like statues. The stiff, manly forms of the warriors contrast with the soft, grieving women: The

PERSPECTIVE FIGURE 24.1 Jacques-Louis David (1748–1825), *Oath of the Horatii,* 1784–1785, oil on canvas.   (Musée du Louvre, Paris; © Reunion des Musées Nationaux, France/ Art Resource, New York)

men embody the superior and virile qualities of patriotism, duty, and dedication to the state, while the women give in to love and sorrow.

David's hard-edged, glazed paintings reveal the painter-ideologist of the French Revolution. He was a friend of Robespierre and a member of the National Convention that voted for the execution of King Louis XVI. As Roman myth served as propaganda for the Roman empire, so did David's paintings exemplify ideals of the Napoleonic era. He believed that the "marks of heroism and civic virtue offered to the eyes of the people will electrify its soul, and plant the seeds of glory and devotion to the fatherland." The picture aroused a great commotion when placed on public view in 1785. Henceforth European art became increasingly political in its aims.

Surely in the days of Tarquin the Proud the patrician hatred of excessive power in one man's hands was fully justified. The king laid terrible burdens on his people and was feared by all.

Lucretia and the End of Monarchy

Several young army officers, including Tarquin's son Sextus Tarquin ("Tarquin the Sixth") were on military service near Rome. They were comparing the beauty and virtue of their wives, each boasting that his own wife was most virtuous. To settle the argument they visited Rome unannounced to see what the women were doing. They found most of the women drinking and gossiping, but **Lucretia** (lu-**krēsh**-a), wife of a Tarquin Collatinus, was virtuously spinning wool with her women servants. Sextus Tarquin, astonished by her beauty, virtue, and modesty, formed a vile plan.

Returning alone a few nights later, he was politely received, but as soon as the house was quiet he drew his sword, went to Lucretia's bedroom, and demanded that she yield to him. When she indignantly refused, he threatened to kill her and one of her slaves, then tell her husband that he had found the pair together in bed, thus joining shame to her death. Lucretia sadly gave in, but the next day summoned her family and a few friends, including Lucius Brutus, associate of her husband and a cousin of the Tarquins. His real name was Lucius Junius, but to ensure his safety he had carefully cultivated the appearance of a fool, and so received the nickname Brutus, "stupid":

> Shattered by such a horror, Lucretia sent the same message to her father in Rome and her husband in Ardea, to come to her, each with one trustworthy friend. Both speed and action were imperative. Something dreadful had happened. Spurius Lucretius came with Publius Valerius, the son of Volesus, and Tarquin Collatinus with Lucius Junius Brutus, with whom he happened to be returning to Rome when he met the messenger.
>
> They found Lucretia sitting dejectedly in her bedroom. Tears sprang to her eyes when her husband asked her, "Are you all right?" "Certainly not," she answered, "How can a woman be all right when her shame and modesty have been torn away? In your bed, Collatinus, are the marks of another man. But only my body has been violated. My soul is still guiltless—and this I shall prove by my death. But this you must promise: The adulterer shall not go untouched. He is Sextus Tarquin, who came last night in the guise of a friend, but in fact a bitter enemy, and made a plunder of this delight, a plunder deadly to me—and, if you are men, to himself."
>
> One after the other the men promised what she asked, meanwhile trying to console her sorrow by shifting the blame from the victim to the guilty man. Crime, they assured her, was a matter of the mind, not the body, and where there was no intent there could be no offense. But Lucretia only answered, "You must determine his punishment. As for me,

even though I acquit myself of guilt, I must still pay the penalty. From now on no adulteress can live with Lucretia as her model." She had hidden a dagger in her clothing. At this she plunged it into her heart and fell dying upon her wound.

LIVY, *History of Rome* 1.58.5–12

PERSPECTIVE 24.2

THE *LUCRETIA* OF REMBRANDT AND SHAKESPEARE

Rembrandt van Rijn (1606–1669) was a prolific painter and printmaker whose workshops produced some three thousand works of art. In 1664 he painted the first of two versions of the suicide of Lucretia (Perspective Figure 24.2).

PERSPECTIVE FIGURE 24.2 Rembrandt van Rijn (Dutch, 1606–1669), *Lucretia,* 1664, oil on canvas.   (National Gallery of Art, Washington, DC; © 1996 Board of Trustees)

He selected the moment just before Lucretia plunges the knife into her breast. Lucretia wears a red gown with white drapery in front, a style contemporary with the artist. She faces the viewer squarely but turns away her head in shame. Her face is deathly pale. She has just confessed the rape, demanded revenge, then drawn the hidden dagger. With her other hand she keeps her family at a distance.

Rembrandt may depend partly on Livy's account, but his more likely inspiration is a famous poem by Shakespeare, *The Rape of Lucrece* (1,855 lines), published in 1594 and influential throughout Europe. In the following selection, Sextus Tarquin has stolen into Lucretia's bedchamber:

[512]   Lucrece, quoth he, this night I must enjoy thee.
       If thou deny, then force must work my way,
       For in thy bed I purpose to destroy thee.
515   That done, some worthless slave of thine I'll slay,
       To kill thine honour with thy life's decay;
          And in thy dead arms do I mean to place him,
          Swearing I slew him, seeing thee embrace him.
       So thy surviving husband shall remain
520   The scornful mark of every open eye;
       Thy kinsmen hang their heads at this disdain,
       Thy issue blurr'd with nameless bastardy;
       And thou the author of their obloquy,
          Shalt have thy trespass cited up in rhymes.
525   And sung by children in succeeding times.
       But if thou yield, I rest thy secret friend.
       The fault unknown is as a thought unacted.

Lucretia yields but the next morning, dressed in mourning, calls her father and husband:

[1716] Here with a sigh as if her heart would break,
       She throws forth Tarquin's name. He, he, she says,
       But more than "he" her poor tongue could not speak,
       Till after many accents and delays,
1720 Untimely breathings, sick and short assays,
          She utters this, "He, he, fair lords, 'tis he
          That guides this hand to give this wound to me."
       Even here she sheathed in her harmless breast
       A harmful knife, that thence her soul unsheathed.

SHAKESPEARE, *The Rape of Lucrece* 512–527, 1716–1724

After much lamenting, the soldiers carry Lucretia's bleeding body through Rome, denouncing Tarquin for his dastardly deed. Seeing her thus, "The Romans plausibly did give consent / To Tarquin's everlasting banishment" (lines 1854–1855).

Brutus drew the gory dagger from her breast and on its hilt swore to drive out the Tarquins. He summoned the people, repeated the tale, and led them in the expulsion of the tyrant and his brood. A new order was established. Henceforth the Senate, presided over by two consuls, would rule the state, and there would be no more kings. The state was to be a *res publica*, a "public affair," not a plaything of kings. The first two consuls were Brutus himself and Tarquin Collatinus, the husband of Lucretia. According to a traditional, but entirely artificial, chronology, the expulsion of Tarquin the Proud took place in 510 BC, about the time of the foundation of the democracy in Athens.

Observations: The Etruscans

The tyranny of the Tarquins was vivid in Rome's memory of the Etruscans, but Etruria's cultural legacy at Rome has roots far deeper than stories of the monarchy's final years. From its city plan and decoration to its cult-places and social institutions, Rome owed an immense debt to its Etruscan past. According to legend, Tarquin the Elder first made the city livable by draining a malarial swamp below the Capitoline and Palatine hills, site of the later Roman Forum. Tarquin the Proud built the first temple to Jupiter on the Capitoline as a memorial to the Tarquin dynasty. Its Etruscan design influenced the materials and appearance of temples in the Roman republic for centuries, including those to the Dioscuri and to the *numina* Saturn, Fortuna ("good luck"), Concord ("peaceful harmony"), and Portunus ("crossing") (Figure 23.4). Even as late as the first century AD, over three centuries after Rome had subdued and assimilated Etruria, the emperor Claudius (ruled AD 41–54) could write twenty volumes on Etruscan civilization (now completely lost).

As with other foreign cultures, Rome adapted Etruscan religion to meet its own needs. Etruscan priests were expert augurs: A priest called the *fulguriator* ("lightning-examiner") scrutinized the sky for omens, as Romulus and Remus had done in t he contest for Rome's first kingship, and the *haruspex* (an Etruscan word) interpreted the entrails of animals at sacrifice (Figure 24.3).

The art of hepatoscopy ("liver inspection") was taught with bronze models of sheep's livers on which zones of the universe were marked out on specific nodules, along with the names of deities who ruled them. Similar models are known in clay from Mesopotamia.

The Etruscans fashioned a pantheon parallel to those of Greece and Rome. Thus Etruscan *Tinia* was Jupiter, *Sethlans* was Vulcan, and *Uni* was the Roman Juno. *Aita* was Hades, *Fufluns* was Bacchus, and *Aplu* and *Artimi* were Apollo and Artemis. Infernal demons populated the underworld of Etruscan religion, especially in funerary art and ritual. Charon and Hermes Psychopompus were transformed from Greek myth to satisfy Etruscan visions of the afterlife in which the Furies appear as horrific hybrid monsters, like *Tuchulcha*, winged with Gorgon-like hair and a vulture's face, and *Vanth*, a winged torch-bearing banshee who appears in Vergil's *Aeneid* as Allecto, bringer of war and wrath.

FIGURE 24.3 Calchas reading a liver, on an Etruscan mirror, c. 400 BC. Notice the esophagus and lungs of the sacrificed animal on the tabletop. The seer is labeled in the Greek alphabet and shown bearded and winged, as were gods, demons, and prophets in Etruscan art.   (Vatican Museums; Canali PhotoBank, Milan/SuperStock)

There are faint hints of Etruscan heroes, but nothing to match Greek and Roman ones. Achilles, Theseus, and others appeared in Etruria in scenes borrowed from Greek art, especially in tomb painting copied from painted vases imported from Greece by the thousands. Many of the Greek vases illustrated in this book were found in Etruria. Depictions of heroes like Eteocles and Polynices at the moment of death were popular in the decades leading up to Etruscan submission to Rome.

Overwhelmed by the Roman advance, the Etruscans may have instituted human sacrifice to alleviate the crisis. In the public square of a town called Tarquinia, three hundred Roman prisoners were sacrificed in 356 BC. During funeral games the Etruscans put prisoners to death to honor the dead, a form of human sacrifice and the evident origin of the Roman gladiatorial contest. Following the slaughter at Tarquinia, Rome retaliated with a sacrifice of 358 Etruscan captives.

HEROES OF THE EARLY REPUBLIC

Many patriotic tales, designed to inculcate traditional values, were told of early figures in the newly organized state.

Brutus and His Sons

Brutus, "founder of the Roman republic," allegedly the ancestor of Marcus Brutus, a leader in the conspiracy to murder Julius Caesar, had his own story. One day, before the revolution, a serpent appeared in the royal palace. Alarmed, Tarquin the Proud sent his two sons to ask the Delphic Oracle what he should do. For laughs the envoys took "stupid" Brutus along.

The oracle ignored their direct inquiry but reported, "He who first kisses his mother will succeed to the highest place in Rome." Returning to Rome, the sons ran to kiss their mothers. Brutus, who only feigned stupidity, saw the oracle's true meaning. As soon as they landed in Italy, he pretended to stumble, fell to the ground, and kissed the earth—the mother of all. Of course he became one of the first consuls.

For some reason Brutus' own sons were unhappy with the Tarquins' expulsion and plotted with the enemy to overthrow the newly founded republic. Their plot was discovered, the evidence incontrovertible. Brutus handed his sons over to the lictors, who threw the boys to the ground, whipped them with their rods, then beheaded them with the ax. Although others turned away, Brutus, as his office required, kept his eyes fixed on the execution: Criminals against Rome must pay the price. Sentiment has no place in measuring one's obligations to the state. Brutus fell in battle fighting the Etruscans, serving his country to the last.

Horatius at the Bridge

Tarquin the Proud fled from Rome north into Etruria, his homeland, and appealed to Lars Porsenna, an Etruscan king, to restore him. Porsenna raised a great army, marched on Rome, and ravaged the countryside, but could not reach the city until he captured the only bridge across the Tiber (the *pons Sublicius*; see Map XII, *x*), built of wood. **Horatius** Cocles (ho-**rāsh**-us kō-**klēz**, "one-eyed") and two others occupied the western end of the bridge until the rest of the Romans could chop it down behind them. Horatius' companions retreated just before it fell, but Horatius, wounded, was forced to swim back in full armor—a model of bravery for every good Roman. A statue in the Forum commemorated the hero's deed. A special college of priests (*pontifices*, "bridgebuilders") rebuilt the bridge and thereafter oversaw its maintenance and repair.

Mucius Scaevola

While the Etruscans lay encamped across the river, one of Rome's bravest men, Gaius Mucius (**mū**-shus), sneaked through the enemy lines, determined to kill the Etruscan king Porsenna. He approached where the king sat with his nobles, but, not knowing the king's appearance, Gaius Mucius killed the king's secretary by mistake. Brought before Porsenna, he announced that he was but the first of three hundred Romans who had sworn to kill him. To prove his determination, Mucius held his right hand in the fire on an altar until it turned red, then black, then caught flame, then fell, a chunk of ash, into the flame. Porsenna was impressed. He gave up the attack and sent Mucius in honor back to Rome, where he received the nickname **Scaevola** (sēv-o-la, "Lefty").

Thus the Etruscans were expelled from Rome forever and the republic firmly established.

Other Patriotic Heroes

In the early fifth century BC, Gnaeus Marcius had earned the name **Coriolanus** (ko-ri-ō-**lān**-us) by conquering a town called Corioli in northwest Latium. Despite his glorious service to the state, plebeian pressure forced the expulsion of Coriolanus from Rome because of his intolerable arrogance and contempt for men of common birth. In anger, he went over to the hostile city of Volsci (**vol**-skē) in south Latium and led them against Rome. Under his capable leadership his native Rome was in mortal peril. Although the senators begged Coriolanus not to destroy his own people, he was deaf to their plea, so offended was he by their rejection of him. Only when his wife, carrying their young sons, and his mother ran between the armies into the battlefield and begged him to relent did Coriolanus withdraw.

Shakespeare wrote an interesting play on the topic, *Coriolanus* (c. 1600). To preserve the memory of his mother and wife as fine examples of Roman womanhood, the Romans built a temple to the Destiny of Women but drove the treacherous Coriolanus into exile. When he returned to the Volscians, the disappointed rulers put him to death.

Cincinnatus (sin-sin-ā-tus), an ex-consul, was living and working with his own hands on his farm in Latium around 450 BC when word was brought that, to repel an enemy attack, he had been chosen dictator, a legal office of one-man rule used in extreme emergencies. Cincinnatus left his plow in the field to accept the special grant of *imperium*, led the Roman army to victory, and returned to his plow, still resting in the furrow—all within sixteen days! This inspiring tale of dedication to the simple life, constant readiness, and selfless devotion to the state gave the name to the Society of the Cincinnati, a fraternal and patriotic organization founded in AD 1783, after the American Revolution, by officers of the Continental Army, including George Washington. The society still exists and has given its name to the city of Cincinnati.

MYTH AND PUBLIC DISPLAY AT ROME

During Rome's great era of imperial expansion, chiefly in the second and first centuries BC, generals looked to such heroes as Horatius and Cincinnatus as models for virtue, even if vice too often prevailed in the real world. *Virtus*, "manliness," was best expressed in foreign conquest, but strict rules governed who could celebrate military victory in a great victory parade called a **triumph**. Like the imperial apotheosis, only the Senate could grant a triumph, a word probably derived from an Etruscan term, as may be its form.

The triumph was grounded in myths as old as Rome itself. According to Livy (1.10), Romulus was the first *triumphator*. After slaying a neighboring king, he attached the enemy's armor to a post cut from an oak and set it up on the Capitoline Hill—the origin of the Roman war-trophy. There he built a shrine to Jupiter Feretrius, "he who carries away [the spoils]," where all future triumphators would dedicate their spoils of war. Many triumphators followed the example of Romulus and vowed the construction of temples from the spoils of war.

To earn a triumph, at least five thousand of the enemy had to fall in battle, and the legions themselves had to proclaim the general "*triumphator*" on the field of battle. The celebration included feasting at public expense over several days, spectacles and contests in the arena, and an extravagant procession with prisoners of war dragged in chains and captured loot paraded through the streets. As the general came into the city, passing through the gate on the ancient sacred furrow protecting the city (the *pomerium*), he removed and set aside his armor as a symbolic rejection of civil violence. He put on a special painted toga, then returned to the parade. A slave stood behind the general and whispered in his ear, "you are not a god!" so that the victorious general might not forget his humanity in the midst of his glory. The parade ended at the temple to Jupiter Optimus Maximus atop the Capitoline Hill. There the general dedicated to Jupiter a laurel bough affixed to a bundle of *fasces* carried by lictors. The face of the general and the cult statue of Jupiter were both painted red—so highly valued was victory in battle, a mortal's highest achievement.

Aspiring for remembrance, generals paid for magnificent arches along the triumphal route through Rome. Such gateways, often with elaborate sculptural decoration, invoked the *numen* Janus. Inscriptions and statuary advertised the glory of the imperial family. Perhaps the most famous arch was built by the emperor Domitian (AD 51–96) in honor of his brother Titus (AD 39–81) near the Roman Forum, which names the emperor as *divus* on its inscribed face. Its interior represents the triumphal procession of AD 71 in celebration of total victory over the Jews and the destruction of the Jewish temple (Figures 24.4 and 24.5).

Augustus was a master of combining traditional myth with display to craft a public image for himself and the new imperial family. One component of his program was the *Aeneid*, which implicitly compared Augustus with Aeneas: war hero, city founder, defender of virtue, a man who did what he had to in obedience to the *logos* that rules the world. Another component of his program was to refurbish and reconstruct the city of Rome. "He found it in brick but left it in marble," according to a popular saying. Decorative themes for the new city's monuments included a careful mix of Greek and Roman legends to legitimize Rome as the inheritor of Greece's rich cultural patrimony and to establish the city, whose population of over two million was the largest in the world and the center not only of political, but also of cultural power (Map XII).

Augustus built a great forum ("marketplace") in his own honor, the Forum of Augustus (Map XII, *h*), whose centerpiece was a temple to Mars Ultor ("avenger,"

FIGURE 24.4 Arch of Titus, Rome, AD 81. The marble-clad arch stands on the route of the triumphal parade near the entrance to the Roman Forum. A bronze statue of the emperor riding in a chariot once crowned the monument. (Erich Lessing / Art Resource, New York)

Map XII, *i*), the god who favored Augustus in his war against the senatorial armies and the men who in shameless vice had killed Julius Caesar. In the sanctuary stood statues to Mars, Venus, and the deified Julius Caesar. "Mars the Avenger" not only brought success in war to Augustus, but in myth Mars was the father of Romulus and the lover of Venus, the ancestress of Julius Caesar.

Colonnades on either side bordered the open space in front of the temple. In one colonnade stood a statue of Aeneas carrying his father Anchises and leading Iulus by the hand in the flight from Troy (compare Figure 23.7). Other statues were

FIGURE 24.5 Marble relief from the Arch of Titus, Rome, AD 81. The monumental arch is a posthumous dedication, but this depiction of the triumphal procession of AD 71 shows the living emperor driving his chariot, crowned from behind by the winged Nikê ("victory"). A goddess, probably Roma, leads the chariot, and the half-clad *genius* of the Roman People stands beside it. Another allegorical figure may represent the *genius* of the Senate.   (Canali PhotoBank, Milan/SuperStock)

of early Roman kings, the descendants of Aeneas. In the opposite colonnade statues of famous Roman generals flanked a statue of Romulus. Both traditions culminated in Augustus—the new Aeneas, the new Romulus—represented in the middle of the open space in front of the temple as a bronze statue driving a gilded chariot drawn by four horses. A label on the statue proclaimed Augustus to be *pater patriae*, "father of the fatherland," the *paterfamilias* to all the Romans.

Augustus built his house on the Palatine Hill (whence our word *palace*), where, according to Vergil's story, Evander had entertained Aeneas. Close by stood an ancient primitive hut roofed over and venerated as "the hut of Romulus." Nearby, he built a Temple to Apollo (Map XII, *w*) with adjacent libraries and marble porticos. To the libraries he removed the books of the Cumaean Sibyl, once Apollo's beloved, who guided Aeneas through the underworld before he arrived at Lavinium. Apollo held special importance for Augustus because his victory over Antony and the Egyptian queen Cleopatra at Actium in 31 BC, off the northwest coast of modern Greece, took place beneath a promontory where stood a temple to Apollo.

Augustus' temple in Rome was a kind of thanks-offering to the god. In the porticoes he displayed statues of the fifty daughters of Danaüs and their fifty husbands, the sons of Aegyptus, killed on their wedding night, fitting theme for a temple financed by Augustus' victory over an Egyptian queen. The mythical recasting dulled the ugly reality: Antony and his Roman legions died in the conflict too. Decorative plaques on the temple depicted myths that celebrated Apollo's power: his struggle with Hercules for the tripod at Delphi and his slaying of the Niobids in company with his sister Diana. Perseus also appears, severing Medusa's head with Minerva's help, an exemplar of Augustus' righteous and civilizing violence directed against chaotic force. Augustan-era reliefs in other buildings portrayed the Roman myths of the rape of the Sabines and the punishment of Tarpeia.

In the Campus Martius, Augustus built three monuments related to his dominion and legacy: his own mausoleum, the Altar of Augustan Peace, and an enormous sundial called the Horologium Augusti (Map XII, *a, b, c*). The pointer on the sundial (called a *gnomon*) was an Egyptian obelisk from the seventh century BC that Augustus transported from Egypt (see Figure 24.2, lower left). The sundial allied Augustus with the forces that make the world the way it is, the *logos* that guarantees the equinox, the four seasons, and the bountiful harvest. On his birthday (September 23), the obelisk cast its shadow on the Altar of Augustan Peace. Augustus' nearby mausoleum was an enormous earthen mound, rather like the tombs of Etruscan aristocrats from the age of Etruscan glory or the tombs of heroes on the plain at Troy.

Observations: An Imaginary Past Preserves the Present

There was little change in Rome's system of government for five hundred years. The external world, by contrast, changed enormously, swiftly, and radically between the founding of the republic in the sixth century BC, when Rome controlled perhaps one hundred square miles, and the murder of Julius Caesar, when Rome controlled most of Europe, the Near East, and the Mediterranean world. Rarely in human history has a small power grown so large so fast, and never has a political power lasted so long. The Roman political achievement is unparalleled in history and is likely never to be equaled.

Roman violence was terrifying, but Rome was not a tyrant state, gobbling up everything in its path, taking what it wanted and offering nothing in return. Control by Rome was in most cases preferable to the dangers of freedom. Rome offered military protection in a cutthroat world, safe communication, free trade across the wonderful Roman roads, equal treatment (in theory) under written law, and relative freedom from religious and social persecution. Military superiority may grant any state an initial advantage over its neighbors, but only moral advantage can bestow permanence to conquest and rule. Moral advantage, according to the Romans' own understanding of their history, was in fact responsible for Roman victory where others failed. The ideal of selfless devotion appears again and again in Roman myth.

The Romans also wanted to know where they came from and how they got to where they were, but surviving traditions about the early days were unreliable. Greek historians of Sicily first suggested the Trojan ancestry of the Romans, which Romans readily agreed to after entering into close relations with Greeks living in the West. Perhaps building on a local story, the Romans claimed that the Trojan Aeneas' descendants, Romulus and Remus, had founded the city of Rome four hundred fifty years after Aeneas.

But the monarchy of Romulus concentrated power in the hands of one man, hateful to the ideals of the expanding Roman state and the powerful oligarchy within it. The republic, by contrast, spread power among this small class, which directed Rome's expansion and benefited from it. Thus did Roman myths support ideals of the Roman republic through examples of men—such as Coriolanus—who at first helped the city, then came to a bad end for "aiming at the kingship"; the enemies of Julius Caesar accused him of just this ambition. During the one-man rule of Augustus and his successors the challenge was to pretend that nothing had changed from the days of the *res publica*. For this reason Augustus called himself *princeps*, "first citizen" (hence our *prince*), never *rex*, "king." Few were fooled. Roman legend was an important force in stabilizing and conserving the Roman state, but in the end Time, the great devourer, swallowed that too.

KEY NAMES AND TERMS

Rhea Silvia, 662	Brutus, 676
Sabines, 664	Horatius, 676
Tarpeia, 665	Scaevola, 677
apotheosis, 665	Coriolanus, 677
Horatii and the Curiatii, 667	Cincinnatus, 677
Tarquin the Proud, 668	triumph, 678
Lucretia, 671	

SOME ADDITIONAL ANCIENT SOURCES

Livy is the principal source for these stories, but one of Plutarch's *Parallel Lives* is on Romulus.

FURTHER READING CHAPTER 24

Beard, Mary. *The Roman Triumph* (Cambridge, MA, 2007). A radical reexamination of the magnificence and the darker side of this ancient ceremony.

Bremmer, J. N., and N. M. Horsfall, *Roman Myth and Mythography* (London, University of London, Institute of Classical Studies, No. 52, 1987). A scholarly but readable and original study of several Roman myths, including those of Aeneas and Romulus and Remus.

Gardner, Jane F., *Roman Myths* (Austin, TX, 1993). Succinct review with good illustrations.

Grant, Michael, *Roman Myths* (New York, 1986). Good survey.

Livy, *The Early History of Rome*, trans. Aubrey de Sélincourt (Baltimore, MD, 1960). A principal source for Roman myth.

Pallottino, M., *A History of Earliest Italy* (Ann Arbor, MI, 1991). A general introduction to early civilization in Italy.

Wiseman, T. P., *Remus, A Roman Myth* (Cambridge, UK, 1996). Ingenious and learned attempt to explain why Romulus murdered Remus.

———, *Roman Drama and Roman History* (Exeter, UK, 1998). Brilliant and original study tying Roman myth to early dramatic performances.

———, *The Myths of Rome* (Exeter, UK, 2005). The best book on Roman myth, it emphasizes the importance of early drama in the promulgation of Roman myth.

CHAPTER 25

THEORIES OF MYTH INTERPRETATION

There are no facts; only interpretations.

FRIEDRICH NIETZSCHE (1844–1900)

WHERE DO MYTHS COME from? What do these stories handed down from the unknown past, often bizarre or mysterious, signify? Disturbed by the irrational and often immoral content of their traditional tales, Greek intellectuals had already posed these questions in ancient times, initiating a long tradition of theoretical inquiry into the nature and meaning of myth.

Some ancient Greeks rejected the traditional stories completely, but others developed elaborate theories to show that the myths contained profound truths, despite their initial implausibility. This tradition was developed further in the medieval period and the Renaissance. In the modern era, with the development of new fields of inquiry, the factual or philosophical truth of myth has ceased to be the only question considered. Anthropologists, for example, are concerned with the social function of myth, and psychologists develop theories about the emotional needs that myth reflects and satisfies. In the following pages we trace some of the major phases in the history of the interpretation of myth from ancient to modern times.

GREEK THEORIES

Through their **rationalism** the Greeks, assisted by the radical technology of the Greek alphabet, were the first people to become fully self-conscious and critical of their own traditions. The inquiry was closely bound up with Greek philosophy, which began partly in speculation about the nature of myth, then developed into a system of reasoning about causes and effects and about the nature of things that was independent of traditional—that is, mythical—explanations. The Greek philosophers wanted to reduce dependence on explanations that used the anthropomorphic categories of Greek religion so prominent in Greek traditional tales. They criticized the traditional stories for their implausible and irrational details or immoral content. Already in the sixth century BC **Xenophanes** (ksen-**of**-a-nēz) of Colophon (in Asia Minor) complained of the ethical weakness of the Olympians, insisting that popular notions about the gods must be wrong:

> In my opinion mortals have created their gods with the dress and voice and appearance of mortals. If cattle and horses had hands and wanted to draw or carve as men do, the cattle would show their gods in the form of cattle and horses would show them as horses, with the same form and appearance as their own. The Ethiopians say that their gods have snub noses and black skins, while the Thracians say that theirs have blue eyes and red hair.
>
> XENOPHANES, *fragment* 21 B 14–16 (DIELS-KRANS)

And

> One god is greatest among gods and men, but his appearance and thought are nothing like ours.
>
> XENOPHANES, *fragment* 21 B 23 (DIELS-KRANS)

Xenophanes, who lived about two hundred years after Homer, questions the very existence of the gods that populate Greek myth and, by implication, attacks the truth of the traditional tales cherished by the Greeks as their cultural heritage.

Plato, a friend of Socrates and founder of the immensely influential Academy during the fourth century BC in Athens, criticized such tales even more severely. He thought that the irrational stories of Homer and other poets had a corrupting influence because they presented to the untutored mind a false image of reality. In his ideal state, described in the *Republic,* Plato banned the poets and their lying tales. On the other hand, Plato was aware that some important truths lie beyond the grasp of human reason. In fact, the burden of his philosophy was to demonstrate the existence of timeless eternal realities that lie behind the transient and changing surface of the everyday world, realities Plato called "Ideas" or "Forms" (Greek *eidos* = "shape"). Hence our word *idealism,* belief in values not apparent in the material world.

Although opposing traditional myth, Plato considered mythlike stories to be an appropriate vehicle for giving expression to these truths. So he wrote his own "myths," dealing especially with the soul's fate after death, as in the "myth of Er" (see Chapter 12), but also with the nature of being and of the perfect political order. The "myth of Atlantis," a wealthy powerful city on an island that disappeared beneath the sea, was Plato's invention (see Perspective 1.1).

Other Greek thinkers went beyond Plato, asserting that even the traditional myths Plato had criticized so vigorously could be seen to contain a kernel of philosophical or historical truth. The task, they thought, was to interpret the myths so that this kernel would come to light. Despite their bizarre or immoral content, the traditional stories meant something other than what they appeared at first glance to mean. There was no need to dismiss the myths as errors, containing nothing that needs be taken seriously. They must be allegories, the Greeks argued, stories that look like one thing on the surface but are really something else inside.

Allegory is a Greek word that means "saying something in a different way" or "saying something different from what appears to be said." In allegorizing myth, the story is translated from its initial frame of reference into another that is more acceptable. For example, Daphnê's transformation into a laurel tree to escape the clutches of Apollo can be explained as an allegory about chastity. The story does not mean that a girl, pursued by Apollo, literally was changed into a tree but that abstinence from sexual intercourse can, at least for a woman, be desirable. Allegory is closely related to **symbolism**, "something put together with something else," because in both allegory and symbolism one thing points to and brings another thing to mind. Thus Daphnê can be interpreted as a symbol of virginity.

The allegorical or symbolic meaning found in a story depended entirely on the frame of reference that the ancient interpreter believed to be true. Because Greek philosophers were concerned primarily with "the truth" in such fields as cosmology, history, and—as in the case of Daphnê—morality, the meanings they found in myth generally originated in these spheres.

Physical Allegory

Theagenes (thē-**aj**-e-nēz), who lived in southern Italy during the later sixth century BC, is said to have been the first to use the allegorical method. None of his writing survives, but later commentators say that he explained mythical accounts of battle among the gods as representing conflicts among natural forces. In Theagenes' cosmology, dry is opposite to wet, hot to cold; water extinguishes fire, fire evaporates water. Such natural oppositions, Theagenes thought, must be embodied in Homer's story in the *Iliad* (20.54ff.) of Apollo who, armed with his arrows, faces Poseidon: Apollo stands for fire, Poseidon for water. The mythical conflict of the two gods is the allegorical expression of a basic cosmological principle concerning the opposition of fire and water. Other allegorists did not hesitate to apply allegory in psychological interpretations as well, making Athena personify rational thought; Ares, irrational violence; Aphrodite, desire; and Hermes, reason.

During the Hellenistic Period, the Stoic philosophers refined physical allegory into a powerful tool that could be applied to any myth. For example, they argued that the Greek creation myths contained profound truths about the origin of the universe. The story of Uranus' castration was explained as meaning that the original creative element of the universe, "fiery air" (= Uranus), begot its offspring spontaneously without the assistance of sexual union. Likewise, the Stoics identified Cronus with *chronos* = "time," and interpreted his role in creation to mean that all things are begotten by time. The children of Cronus are the ages, and the story that Cronus devoured them means that "time consumes the ages." The story that Zeus overthrew Cronus and bound him in the underworld means that time, although great in extent, is nonetheless limited.

The interpretation of Cronus as *chronos* illustrates how the Stoics used **etymology**, speculation about "the true meaning of a word," to reinforce allegory. They believed that the meaning of a word or name can reveal the meaning of a myth. The famous biographer Plutarch (c. AD 50–125) offers another example. He interprets the story of Demeter and Persephonê as an allegory conveying an important insight about life after death.

According to Plutarch, Demeter is the earth, Hades the shadow cast by the earth, and Persephonê the moon, which reflects the light of the sun. He proves this by reminding us that Persephonê's other name, *Korê*, means in Greek not only "girl," but also "pupil of the eye." As the eye (*korê* = "pupil") acts like a mirror reflecting little images of objects, so does the moon reflect the light of the sun. *Korê*, or pupil/Persephonê, is the moon, and the story of Persephonê's descent into the underworld and subsequent return refers to the waxing and waning of the moon, when the moon slips in and out of the shadow of the earth, Hades' realm. By extension, the story of Persephonê's descent and return means that after losing their bodies at death, human beings exist as souls and minds in Hades. If they are blameless, however, they may subsequently escape to the sun as pure minds. By adding a philosophical meaning, Plutarch's physical allegory turns the myth into a vehicle for deeper truth.

The etymologies offered by the Stoics, which depended on similarity in sound, must have seemed reasonable in a society in which myth was still part of the living, aural language. In reality, their etymologies were often quite fantastic because the science of linguistics was unknown in the ancient world. We now know that the name Cronus is etymologically unrelated to the word *chronos*. But through this false etymology arose the common picture of Father Time as the Grim Reaper, an old man carrying a sickle, because C(h)ronus/Time castrated his father with a sickle.

Roman writers who followed the Stoic philosophy also used Latin etymologies to interpret myths. For example, they argued that Juno (corresponding to Hera in Greek myth) was really air because the Greek (and Latin) word for air (*aêr*, *aura*) sounded like *Hera*. This etymology was supported by the belief that air lay just beneath the aether, or upper atmosphere, symbolized in myth by Jupiter. The position of air (= Juno) just beneath aether (= Jupiter, Juno's mate) was the true meaning of the story that Jupiter united with Juno in sexual embrace.

These physical allegorical interpretations attempted to explain a cultural inheritance from a distant, preliterate past in light of sophisticated philosophical thought about forces in nature. The allegorists had no notion that myths arose at different times and in different cultural conditions and for different reasons (a mistake easy to make!). Their explanations permitted the allegorists to maintain the respectability of the traditional tales, which might otherwise be rejected because of their patent factual errors or offensive moral content. In addition to protecting the decency and social utility of traditional stories, physical allegory was a philosophically respectable way of bringing to light hidden, even mysterious truths about the world.

Historical Allegory: Euhemerism

Allegorical interpretation of myth goes back to the sixth century BC, but about 300 BC the Greek mythographer Euhemerus (yu-**hēm**-er-us) offered a new approach, suggesting myth revealed historical rather than cosmological truth. Euhemerus wrote a book describing a journey to three fabulously wealthy islands in the Indian Ocean. On the main island, Panchaea (modeled after Plato's Atlantis), Euhemerus said that he had found a golden column on which was inscribed the history of the reigns of early human kings. This alleged history suggested a very different interpretation of Greek myth.

First to rule, according to Euhemerus' story, was Uranus, so called because he was learned in the study of the heavens. From union with his human wife, Hestia, Uranus begot the Titans and Cronus. The column gave further information about Uranus' successors, Cronus, Zeus, and their families. The war in heaven and Cronus' swallowing his children were explained as recollections of palace intrigues. During his reign, according to the column, Zeus traveled the earth teaching the arts of civilized life, banning such reprehensible religious practices as cannibalism, and founding temples. According to the story, he actually lived for a while on Mount Olympus, then, at the end of a long life, Zeus retired to Crete, died, and was buried near Cnossus. That is why the Cretans spoke of "the tomb of Zeus."

Although Euhemerus' story of the inscribed column is a fiction, his underlying theory is quite plausible and enters many modern interpretations of myth. By asserting that gods were in origin great men, so respected or feared that they were worshiped after death, he attempted to explain myth as a form of early history. From his book comes the modern term **euhemerism**, the thesis that gods once were humans.

Many features of the Greek mythical tradition lent themselves to explanation along these lines. After all, the gods were organized in a family on Olympus, and they looked and acted like Greek aristocrats. The god Asclepius shows many signs of having once been a real man, a famous doctor (but some think he was a healing god from the northern Levant). As for such deified heroes as Heracles, everyone always thought them to be real men anyway, who had actually lived, founded cities, and done great deeds.

Euhemerus' thesis derived convenient support from the politics of Hellenistic monarchs, especially in Egypt, who presented themselves to their peoples as gods incarnate and who included the native gods in their dynastic genealogies. The deification of dead Hellenistic rulers made more plausible the notion that great humans of the past had, with the passage of time, become more than human. Behind myth lay history.

An approach closely related to that of Euhemerus is found in a handbook on myth called *On Incredible Things*, of which an excerpt survives, written by one

Palaephatus (pal-ēf-a-us), a contemporary of Euhemerus. Palaephatus' special contribution was to explain myths as originating from a misunderstanding of language. According to Palaephatus, Actaeon, for example, was not really transformed into a stag and torn apart by his dogs; rather, he was ruined by spending too much money on his hunting dogs. The myth arose when neighborhood gossip began to tell of how "poor Actaeon is being devoured by his dogs."

Similarly, the Lernaean Hydra against which Heracles fought was not really a many-headed monster, although Palaephatus' interpretation of this myth is more complex. Lernus, he claimed, was a king in the Peloponnesus who went to war with the Mycenaeans. The myth originally told of a "General Heracles who destroyed Watertown ('Hydra'), defended by General Crabb, by using fire as an assault weapon against persistent defenders." The interpretation of myth as a "disease of language" was to undergo a surprisingly successful renaissance in the theories of the German-born Oxford scholar Max Müller in the nineteenth century AD (see later in this chapter).

Moral Allegory

The interpretation of myth as a system of advice on good and bad behavior, or moral allegory, was more highly developed than physical or historical allegory. We have already seen a crude example of it in the explanation of the story of Apollo and Daphnê as exhorting young women to remain chaste. So the Harpies who rob Phineus of his food are really prostitutes who ruin young men through their high fees. The goddesses in the Judgment of Paris represent three kinds of life: the active (Hera), the contemplative (Athena), and the amorous (Aphrodite), among which every man (Paris) must choose. The coupling of Leda and the Swan is an allegory for the joining of Power (Zeus) and Injustice (Leda, who is raped), whose fruit is inevitably scandal and discord (Helen).

PERSPECTIVE 25

APULEIUS' ALLEGORY OF CUPID AND PSYCHÊ

Sometimes allegory is an interpretation that the listener or reader teases out of the story, suggesting, for example, that the marriage of Zeus/Jupiter and Hera/Juno really refers to the upper air that lies upon the lower. At other times, the allegory appears to have been consciously in the mind of the storyteller.

The philosopher Apuleius of Madaura in North Africa (mid-second century AD) included one such story, a folktale much beloved in Europe after the Middle Ages, in a long Latin prose novel titled, like Ovid's work, the *Metamorphoses,* but usually called the *Golden Ass*. The story, told by an old woman to comfort a girl kidnapped by robbers, tells of the love between Cupid (= Greek Eros), "sexual desire," and Psychê (**sī-kē**), "soul," a Greek word almost as vague as the English.

Psychê was the youngest and most beautiful of three sisters, so beautiful that she aroused the jealousy of Venus. No one dared court her for fear of the goddess, and her father consulted an oracle, who ordered him to dress her as if for marriage, but then to expose her on a cliff to a winged monster of whom even Zeus was afraid. A wind picked up Psychê, left alone, and bore her to a garden of a beautiful palace.

A delicious meal was placed before her and heavenly music played, although she could see no one. She went to bed and in the black of night awoke to realize that someone was in bed with her. Her lover warned her that she must never see him or she would lose him forever. He visited her night after blissful night, but she never saw him by day. Reluctantly, he allowed her to have her sisters visit her. Fiercely jealous, they persuaded Psychê to kill her husband, who, they insisted, was the monster of whom the oracle had spoken.

Psychê therefore armed herself with a knife, lit a lamp, and entered her bedroom. So surprised was she to see the handsome, sleeping young man with wings that she let a drop of hot oil fall on him. Cupid—for it was he—leaped up, flew to the top of a tree, and bade poor Psychê farewell. The girl rushed off in despair to one of her sisters, told her the whole story, and added that her husband had announced that he much preferred the sister. The vain woman ran to a cliff and jumped off, expecting to be borne up by the wind, but was dashed to bits on the rocks below. The same thing happened with the second sister.

Cupid, tormented by the hot oil, could not protect Psychê from the anger of his mother, Venus, who, aided by her servants Convention, Worry, and Gloom, beat and tormented the girl. She was forced to sort a heap of mixed seeds in one night; she succeeded when a swarm of ants came to her aid. She had to bring golden wool from a flock of man-eating sheep by a river; friendly reeds plucked it for her. She had to bring Venus water from a stream that burst from a precipice; the eagle of Zeus himself fetched it. Finally, she had to go down to Hades to bring back in a box a day's supply of Proserpina's beauty ointment—a journey beset with traps laid by Venus. The girl evaded all these and obtained the box. Although forbidden, she opened it, hoping to make herself beautiful and win back Cupid. At once she fell into a profound sleep.

Cupid had by now recovered. He found Psychê, awakened her with a prick of his arrows, and appealed to Zeus to let him have his beloved. Zeus consented, Venus was appeased, they had a grand marriage feast, and Psychê became immortal.

The story contains many motifs familiar from modern folktales: the jealous sisters, like those of Cinderella, and miraculous assistance at an impossible task, like that of the dwarf who spun Rapunzel's gold. Like many of the stories of the Grimm brothers, an old serving-woman tells this tale too. On the other hand, the frame is that of an intentional allegory—a story with a further meaning obvious from the names of the characters: the longing of Soul (Psychê) for union with Desire (Cupid), who must overcome hindrances set up by Convention, Worry, and Gloom.

Such interpretations, like those of the physical and historical allegorists, fail to preserve myth, whatever the intentions of their practitioners, for they remove the charm of the original story and replace it with a truism or historical or physical incident. An intellectual movement linked loosely to Platonism dealt with myth more positively and gently.

In the final centuries of the pagan era (AD 200–500), a school known as **Neoplatonism** revived and developed many of Plato's theories and became the major philosophical movement of the day. Neoplatonists, like their founder, Plato, believed in a higher dimension of reality beyond the limits of time and space, where perfection and absolute truth—that which is always and everywhere the same—could be found. This higher world is accessible to us through our minds, if they are freed from our bodies and senses. The material universe, by contrast, yields only an inferior knowledge based on sense perception, at best imperfect and ultimately false because everything in the material world is always changing.

Yet this material world is somewhat modeled after the perfect rational world, having features that symbolize the eternal blueprint. Thus transient physical beauty, such as a sunset, symbolizes eternal beauty. In the same way, say the Neoplatonists, myths give us hints about the moral world beyond. Neoplatonism lends itself to allegory, although of a kind that does not reduce myth to literal fact but expands it into a vehicle for discovering profound truths, usually moral, about a higher domain hidden behind appearance.

Plotinus, the founder of Neoplatonism in the third century AD, held that myth describes timeless realities in the form of temporal events. He saw a correspondence between the sequence:

- **Uranus**
- **Cronus**
- **Zeus**

and the three great principles of reality:

- **Unity** (unchanging, the same in all parts = Uranus)
- **Intellect** (unchanging, but plural = Cronus)
- **Soul** (plural and subject to change and motion = Zeus)

Plotinus' student Porphyry produced an extremely complex interpretation of Homer's description of the cave of the nymphs on Ithaca, where Odysseus hides his treasure after returning from his wanderings (*Odyssey* 13.102–112). The cave, he argues, represents the universe because it is generated from matter and is natural. The nymphs, as spirits of water, represent the ceaseless flow of events within time. The looms of stone on which they weave represent souls descending to incarnation, as the flesh is woven on the bones (the stones of the body). The moral truths are obvious: The material world, including our bodies, is an illusion and unworthy of our aspiration.

The increasing interest of Neoplatonists in such allegories reflects an effort to rehabilitate myth and to establish its value for revealing higher truths in the face of the growing threat from Christianity. In the end Christianity swallowed Neoplatonism. St. Augustine (AD 354–430) began as a dualist (believer in two opposed principles), became a Neoplatonist, and ended as one of the greatest of Christian theologians.

MEDIEVAL AND RENAISSANCE THEORIES

Platonic modes of thinking exerted powerful influence on early Christian theology. Both myth itself and the various methods devised for interpreting it were part of the cultural heritage taken over by the Christian church. Although some church fathers rejected allegory on the ground that it was a way of holding onto pagan myth, most found allegorical interpretations a legitimate way to interpret pagan myth, especially when a moral encouraging righteous conduct could be found within the tale.

The allegorical method whereby moral meanings were drawn from old stories was also applied extensively to the Bible. For example, the frankly erotic content of the Song of Solomon, which tells of sexual love between a man and a woman, was explained as an allegory of God's love for the church (in fact, the poem descends from secular Egyptian love poetry). Euhemerism was a useful method of analysis for the Christians because it served to justify the authority of the church by proving that pagan religion was idolatry, just as Christians and Jews had always maintained.

The ancient methods of interpretation lived on, but direct acquaintance with classical culture and its literature declined drastically, especially in the Latin-speaking West. The myths were now known principally through handbooks, which became increasingly important and elaborate. One of the most influential was the *Mythologies* of Fulgentius (ful-**jen**-shus), a North African Christian of the sixth century AD. On reading his account of some god, the reader would find a succinct entry that included both the facts of the story and a moral based on an allegorical interpretation.

Fulgentius gives the allegorical interpretation of the Judgment of Paris mentioned earlier. In the story of Liber (the Latin equivalent of the Greek Dionysus) he sees an allegory in which Semelê and her three sisters represent four stages of intoxication: (1) too much wine, (2) the forgetfulness it causes, (3) lust, and (4) sheer madness. The interpretation is supported with typical etymological explanations. The first sister (and first stage of drunkenness) is *Ino,* linked to *vinum* and *oinos,* the Latin and Greek words for "wine." *Autonoë* is fancifully said to mean in Greek "ignorant of herself." *Semelê* is explained as a combination of *soma* = "body" and *luein* = "release"—a "release from bodily inhibitions," hence "lust." *Agavê* is insanity because she cut off her son's head, which only an insane person could do. Obviously one must avoid drunkenness.

Such material reappeared in other handbooks over the next centuries and for a long time made up the basic source of myths available in the West. Interpretation had become more complex and important than the myths themselves, whose telling might consist of little more than a few key details. Allegory continued to focus on acceptable moral meanings.

Ovide moralisé ("Ovid Moralized"), a text originally in French that went through many versions from 1300 on, listed interpretations of the often racy myths retold in Ovid's poetry. The story of Daphnê transformed into a laurel tree to escape the lustful Apollo is explained as an allegory for the moral that chastity, like the laurel, remains as cool as a river and always blooms, but never bears fruit. We may also understand the story as a botanical allegory (the warmth of the sun, Apollo, when combined with water, Daphnê, makes the laurel flourish) or even a medical allegory (chased by a rapist, she dies from exhaustion under a laurel tree). Such interpretations reached a wider public through Christian sermons, which could use Odysseus' encounter with the Sirens, for example, as an object lesson of the temptations posed by pleasure during a Christian's voyage through life (Figure 25.1).

Part of the renewed emphasis given to classical culture at the time of the Renaissance came from an interest in Platonism. The Platonic conviction that myth contains profound symbolic truth concerning higher spiritual realms was highly attractive to Christian culture and led to a vogue for even more elaborate allegory that combined pagan and Christian elements. Repeating arguments made earlier by the Neoplatonists, whom they admired, students of classical myth during the Renaissance maintained that bizarre, shocking features were actually the surest sign of truth in a myth. Only those who earnestly sought the truth would delve beneath the repulsive surface appearances to penetrate to the deeper riches hidden beneath.

For example, Hesiod's description of the birth of Aphrodite is a raw, even brutal account, beginning with a son's mutilation of his father's genitals. The foam that

FIGURE 25.1 Odysseus at the mast, relief from a fourth-century AD Roman sarcophagus. The story of Odysseus' journey was easily adapted to Christian allegory. Here the Greek hero is Christ on the cross, representing all believers who escape the Sirens' temptation to sin during the voyage through life. Above the boat an angel(?) blows the trumpet of resurrection. The Sirens are women with the feet of birds. A cupid strides off to the right, perhaps the redeemed soul of the dead Christian buried within.   (Museo Nazionale delle Terme, Rome)

gathers around the genitals suggests to Hesiod the false etymology for Aphrodite's name as "Foam-goddess" (because Greek *aphros* = "foam"), but the image is taken from actual intercourse. From these gory events and viscous fluids emerged a figure that is in appearance the opposite: lovely and lithesome, the object of desire. Yet within remains the blood and the foam, a woman's deceptive nature, occluded by the irresistible sweetness of always destructive passion.

From the same story Botticelli, a master artist of the fifteenth century, drew an entirely different lesson (see Perspective Figure 9a). Botticelli was a member of the circle of the rich and powerful Lorenzo de' Medici's Platonic Academy of Philosophy, whose guiding genius was Marsilio Ficino, an eminent Greek scholar. Ficino, following the Neoplatonists of the third to sixth centuries AD, taught that the universe was a hierarchy of descending spheres reaching from the oneness of God through angelic spheres to our own world of base matter. Before birth, the human soul (= Botticelli's Venus) was perfect and lived in the angelic spheres, then was caught at birth in the dark material world (the cloak in Botticelli's painting). Only through God's love, as expressed in the beauty of creation, could the soul regain its original perfection and be saved from vile matter. Through the contemplation of beauty (Botticelli's beautiful picture of the birth of Venus), the soul could perceive the abstract beauty behind the material expression, which would then restore the soul to its spiritual nature. Art, then, serves a philosophical function.

The medieval and Renaissance alchemists, who believed that knowledge of nature's secrets would allow them to transform common metals into gold or silver, found a different kind of truth in classical myth, reviving in new form Greek physical allegory. Accepting Neoplatonic theories about the relationship between matter and spirit, they put allegorical interpretation of myth to use in their description of secret physical processes. The figure of Hermes (= Mercury), for example, was taken to be a ready-made allegory of chemical facts about the element mercury.

In the alchemical work *Atalanta Fugiens* ("Atalanta Running Away"), published in 1617, Michael Maier provided his text with pictures and a musical score, "so that your eyes and ears may take in the emblems, but your reason searches out the hidden signs." Both text and pictures treat the mythical tradition as a treasure trove of alchemical allegory (Figure 25.2). Atalanta was identified with "volatile" mercury, which "flees," and her suitor Hippomenes is the sulfur that overcomes her, that is, effects a chemical reaction. The golden apples are another ingredient retarding the process.

Along with such specialized esoteric texts, handbooks continued to provide basic information for artists or writers along with interpretations. Myth had virtually become a language for talking about timeless truths, and in the seventeenth century the theory that pagan myth was a distorted version of biblical history reemerged with vigor. Scholars gathered evidence intended to show that many details in Homer were muddled versions of events in the Old Testament. The siege of Troy was explained as a recasting of Joshua's attack on Jericho. Odysseus' wanderings reflected those of the patriarchs. Nysa, the mountain where Dionysus was raised, becomes an anagram for *Syna* (= Sinai).

EMBLEMA XXXIX.   *De secretis Naturæ.*   165
Oedypus Sphynge superata & trucidato Lajo patre
matrem ducit in uxorem.

EPIGRAMMA XXXIX.

SPhyngem ænigmatico Thebis sermone timendam
    Oedypus ad propriam torserat arte necem:
Quæsitum est cui mane pedes sint bis duo, luce
    Sed mediâ bini, tres ubi vesper adest.
Victor abhinc Lajum nolentem cedere cædit,
    Ducit & uxorem quæ sibi mater erat.   X 3   BA-

FIGURE 25.2 Oedipus in *Atalanta Fugiens* by Michael Maier (1617) (Courtesy of the Library of Congress). The story of Oedipus was interpreted as an alchemical allegory. In clockwise order beginning at the top, the snaky-tailed sphinx besieges Thebes, Oedipus meets Jocasta, and Oedipus kills Laius. In the foreground is the riddle of the three ages, really about the laws of nature: the triangle on the old man's (= Old Age) forehead is body/soul/spirit, the hemisphere on the mature man (= Maturity) is the moon, and the square on the baby (= Childhood) is the four elements. At the left the sphinx is about to leap from a cliff in despair at her defeat. The Latin poetic text means

> While Thebes lies quaking in dread of the riddling monster's enigma,
>> Oedipus cleverly twists the Sphinx's word to its doom.
> The creature had asked, "Who, pray, has twice two legs in the morning,
>> at noonday only a pair; eventide sets him on three?"
> Oedipus, puffed up in triumph, bids Laius, "Get out of my way!"
>> kills him—then takes as his wife she who had given him birth.

THEORIES OF THE ENLIGHTENMENT

Such interpretations fell under serious attack in the eighteenth century as part of the profound cultural revolution called the **Enlightenment**. As the institutional power of the church waned in response to political and social changes in Europe, everything traditional was subject to reexamination, usually with a notable lack of sympathy. Because few things were so traditional as myth, the authority of mythical accounts (including the Bible) and the value of allegory for preserving their worth were increasingly questioned.

A book by Bernard Fontenelle (1657–1757), a nephew of the great French dramatists Pierre and Thomas Corneille, called *De l'origine des fables,* "Concerning the Origin of Fables" (1724), is a monument of the radical change in attitude taking place, initially in France. The book paved the way for many of the central themes of the Enlightenment. Fontenelle laid down new principles for dealing with myth. Instead of seeking deep, esoteric truths, he saw that myth was rooted in the ignorance of humans living at earlier stages of cultural development. Fontenelle shifted the emphasis of theory from interpreting myth to explaining the origin of myth, which, he asserts, develops in savagery and ignorance. Some scholars date the modern meaning of "myth" as a fanciful tale, or the notion that it exists as a discrete category at all, to Fontenelle's writings.

Information about the cultures of the American Indians and other preliterate peoples coming in from missionaries or colonial administrators was a source for Fontenelle's theories. Such information justified his distinguishing the "primitive" mind from the enlightened and his finding of parallels between the "primitive" cultures of his day and that of the early Greeks. Greek myth, too, he assumed, was the product of a "primitive" mode of thought. This radical, new, and dramatic approach, taking as its premise the notion of progressive evolutionary development away from an earlier condition of savagery to present conditions of civilization, was destined to shape Western thought for the coming centuries.

The Italian Giambattista Vico (jom-ba-**tēs**-ta **vē**-kō, 1668–1754), sometimes regarded as the first modern historian (*Scienza nuova,* "New Science," 1725), accepted this evolutionary approach to the understanding of the past. History, he thought, was the study of the origin and unfolding of human society and institutions. (His contemporaries regarded history as the biographies of great men or the record of the unfolding of God's will.) Vico argued that history moves in great cycles, each of which has three phases, the same in every cycle but modified by new circumstances and developments.

The first phase in each cycle is the Age of Gods. In our own cycle, this was the period immediately after the Flood. In the Age of Gods, human activity is limited to a struggle for physical survival. People live close to nature, whose power they understand only as a display of anger by a mighty god. From this phase comes the image of God and of gods as terrible and wrathful beings and what we have called divine myth. In the next phase, the Age of Heroes, nature becomes separated from humankind. Emerging social institutions are connected with personified gods and heroes about whom stories are told. From the Age of Heroes descend "legends." The third and last stage (we live in one now) is the Age of Man, in which reason replaces instinctive imagination and passion. Philosophy arises in this phase.

Vico's theory is one of the earliest of many efforts to understand myth as part of an all-embracing history of thought. Allegory, in his view, deals only with particular myths. What was really needed, Vico thought, was to discover a principle of myth itself in human consciousness. Myth originated in the earlier phases of culture, when humankind's thinking was highly concrete. At that time language, originally monosyllabic and versified, expressed a poetry and ritual more powerful than any we know today, a direct representation of reality. This is why myth is so personal and dramatic, so disconcerting to those who live in the "rational" Age of Man.

By recognizing that ways of thinking change fundamentally, Vico avoided two common pitfalls associated with evolutionary schemes: He did not simply idealize pre-literate culture, and he recognized that earlier forms of understanding, which cannot be fully grasped by the standards of rational thought, are valid in their own terms.

THEORIES OF THE NINETEENTH AND TWENTIETH CENTURIES

Romantic Theories

Although there have been many disagreements in emphasis, approaches to myth since the Enlightenment have either used an evolutionary perspective, which assumes that myths are the relics of savagery, or have studied myth with the methods of the social sciences, which assume that myth reflects ways of thinking different from our own. Both approaches are closely related, and their effect is to reduce myth to a cultural relic. However, the counterview of myth as valid and understandable in its own terms, which did not entirely disappear at the time of the Enlightenment, surfaced again in the Romantic movement during the late eighteenth and early nineteenth centuries.

Romanticism was a reaction against what many saw as the arrogance, superficiality, and outright blindness of the Enlightenment. Opposing the Enlightenment's confident rationalism, the Romantics saw the emotional side of experience as most distinctively human: intense feeling, awareness of powerful but obscure forces, abnormal states, and a direct intuitive relationship to nature. Whereas thinkers of the Enlightenment attacked myth as a product of primitive mental and emotional states, the Romantics returned to myth as a vehicle for regaining lost truths. Such ideals were expressed mostly in poetry, painting, and music, but ambitious philosophical theories, especially in Germany, argued for the timeless truth of myth and for its continuing vital role in the modern world.

An explanation of how this could be, that myth embodies timeless truths, was given by Friedrich Creuzer (1771–1858) in his long book (in German) *Symbolism and Mythology of the Ancient Peoples, Especially the Greeks* (1810). Creuzer studied recently discovered material on the myths of ancient India and interpreted all myth, in Neoplatonic fashion, as a set of symbols for universal truths. Indian religious texts, he argued, contained an ancient revelation of absolute truth. As the Aryans—that is, the Indo-Europeans—spread from their homeland, the once pristine truth became obscure, preserved only in symbolic forms by a priestly elite, refracted like white light broken into various colors by a lens. The different mythologies of the Indo-European peoples are those colors, each expressing in its own idiom a truth that was originally, Creuzer thought, symbolized visually by means of hieroglyphs like those of Egypt.

Creuzer considered myth to be a way of dealing with absolute, infinite truth in finite narrative form. Whereas truth is rational and abstract, myth is dramatic and concrete. For example, the golden rope by which Zeus could suspend sea and earth if he chose (*Iliad* 8.18–19) symbolizes the divine energy that supports the world. This is the same cosmic energy described as a thread of pearls in the Sanskrit classic *Bhagavad gita,* "Song of the Blessed One" (probably first century AD). Each mythic image—the golden rope and the string of pearls—descends ultimately from a single primordial revelation to humankind of truth about the nature of reality.

Another imaginative, partly Romantic theory was advanced by **Johann Bachofen** (1815–1887) in *Das Mutterrecht,* "Mother Right" (1861). Bachofen was a student of Roman law who noticed that women enjoyed considerable status in some ancient legal and social systems. All modern theories of a matriarchal phase in early human social development go back to Bachofen, who concluded that the patriarchal authority, which has dominated all present-day societies, was preceded by a stage during which women exercised great influence in their capacity as mothers.

Much of his evidence for this claim came from classical myth, which he considered to contain hidden truths about early human social structure. According to Bachofen's explanation, the earliest nomadic hunting phase was lawless, represented in myth by Aphrodite, who is unbridled lust. In this phase women were victims of violence. In a later phase, represented by Demeter, the institutions of agriculture and marriage were introduced, and values clustering around the mother encouraged peace and feelings of communal affection. On the other hand, the aggressive potential in woman's nature was reflected in myths about the Amazons.

Although Bachofen described favorably the early "mother right," he recognized a third, and higher, Apollonian phase, represented by Rome. Here the older, more primitive communal mother right was overthrown, and authority was invested in law that embodied the higher values of patriarchy, individuality, and rationality. His scheme, which influenced later Marxist theory, combined speculation about a happier, maternal past with a typically evolutionary pattern that moved through earthly and lunar phases to the present solar triumph of the patriarchal principle.

Friedrich Engels (1820–1895), one of the founding fathers of modern communism, took Bachofen's position in his book *The Origin of the Family, Private Property, and the State* (1883). Before the evolution of the state and the family, women ruled society and were free to have intercourse with whomever they pleased, so that no son ever knew his father. Eminent Russian folklorist Vladimir Propp (1895–1970), writing under the Soviet regime, pointed out that such was the situation of Oedipus: The myth must therefore be a historical reminiscence of the shift from a matriarchal to a patriarchal organization of society.

According to Propp, the shepherds in the Greek legend, who transported Oedipus to the wild and then to Corinth, stand for the foster parents who in a primitive matriarchy cared for the children. Oedipus' age-mates reflect some early collective, before the evolution of the family. Such teaching about a primordial primitive matriarchy replaced by an enlightened patriarchy is still official doctrine in the communist People's Republic of China.

Anthropological Theories

The flood of information about newly discovered cultures pouring into Europe from colonial outposts and journeys of exploration did seem to support the view that myth is a symptom of intellectual backwardness, and students of myth formulated many variations on the concept of "primitive" societies and "primitive" ways of thinking by which classical myth could be understood. During the second half of the nineteenth century, the process of integrating diverse data into general theories of development was further encouraged by Charles Darwin's (1809–1882) theory of biological evolution advanced in *The Origin of Species* (1859). From such studies emerged what is now called anthropology.

One of the most influential of these formulations was advanced by British anthropologist Edward Tylor (1832–1917), who presented his theory of universal cultural evolution proceeding through several stages in *Primitive Culture* (1871). Tylor explained the "quaint fancies and wild legends of the lower tribes" in terms of an original stage that he called "animistic." Animism is the belief that everything has a soul. Myth and religion, which are natural consequences of such a belief, do not ultimately come from inherently poetic language, as Vico thought. Instead, myth is a mistaken science or philosophy, rooted in fear or ignorance but designed to explain natural phenomena.

Other theories were advanced about the primitive state through which all human societies must pass. The model for the evolution of human societies was drawn from the biological evolution of a species. Thus societies that represent earlier stages can exist, although only in isolated backwaters, at the same time as more evolved societies. Technologically primitive communities still intact in Australia, or practices and beliefs of European peasants, were sources of information.

British author Andrew Lang (1844–1912) popularized this general approach in his *Myth, Literature, and Religion* (1887). Trained as a classicist, he was a prolific essayist, historian, poet, sportswriter, and critic, one of the leading intellectuals of his day. His retelling of traditional stories in the *Blue Fairy Book* and others, which he published with his wife, are still popular among children.

Deeply affected by the interest in evolution, he at first accepted Tylor's laws of cultural development, but as he examined the evidence more critically, he came to believe that there must have been more than a single pattern of development. Myth was indeed, as Tylor maintained, a protoscientific effort at explanation, but the primitive stage of culture was not always a time of confused theories about natural forces. Faced with examples of what seemed to be ethical monotheism among "savages," Lang argued that monotheism must in some cases have actually preceded animism and polytheistic myth, into which it subsequently degenerated.

To most scholars, then, myth essentially reflected an early, clumsy effort to do what science later did better: explain why things are the way they are. **Sir James Frazer** (1854–1941), a classical scholar and one of the founders of modern anthropology, accepted the validity of social evolution as an explanation with universal application. With immense industry Frazer gathered evidence from all over the world, from American Indians, from Africans, from Melanesians, as scientific evidence from which decisive conclusions about the meaning of myth could be drawn.

Frazer's celebrated book, *The Golden Bough,* is often ranked as one of the most influential works of modern times. It began as two volumes published in 1890 and reached twelve volumes in the 1911–1915 edition. Frazer started by inquiring into the ancient tradition that a "King of the Wood" at Aricia, a village near Rome, ruled over a grove sacred to the Italic god Virbius (once Hippolytus, son of Theseus, before being resurrected by Asclepius). If a runaway slave came into the wood and broke a branch, a golden bough, from a sacred oak, the priest was compelled to fight the man. Hence the title of Frazer's book (no connection, apparently, with the golden bough in Vergil's story of Aeneas' descent into the underworld; Chapter 23). If the priest was killed, the slave became the new priest. The priests of Virbius were always runaway slaves and always killed their predecessors.

Frazer searched the world over for evidence of his thesis that the story of the golden bough is a late survival of a primordial human social and religious institution in which the King of the Wood embodied and ensured the fertility of the realm. When his waning power threatened the well-being of the people, the king had to be killed and a young, vital successor placed on the throne. The king must die that the people might live. As embodiment of a "corn" or fertility-god, his life and death represent the fundamental vitality of nature. The stories of Attis, Adonis, Osiris, and Dionysus are mythical projections of this pattern.

On the basis of this hypothetical primordial rite, Frazer attempted to account for much that we find in myths and religions worldwide. An elaborate system of taboos hemmed in the king's life. If he broke a taboo, his ability to help his people would diminish. Here, Frazer argued, is the origin of the *dos* and *don'ts* in every religion and of the many violated taboos in myth. Because the old king must die, many myths tell of the death of kings and gods. These stories, he thought, arose as explanations for real rituals in which a king actually was killed. The origin of myth is thus closely tied to religious ritual. This is the **ritual theory of myth**.

Frazer's understanding of myth as a secondary elaboration of ritual exerted considerable influence. Like others influenced by evolutionary thought, Frazer wanted to formulate a comprehensive theory of cultural development. To that end he replaced Tylor's "animism" with "magic," understood as a mechanical operation used by primitive peoples as part of a ritual to coerce impersonal natural or supernatural forces to obey human wishes.

When humans realized that magic was often ineffective, religion was born. The propitiation of quasihuman gods replaced coercion through magic. Science, in turn, was destined to replace religion. Myth is associated especially with the religious phase of development because myth is characterized by a belief in personal forces that act in stories, whereas science and magic are concerned with impersonal forces.

The concept of progress preoccupied Europeans of the late nineteenth century. Especially in England, progress was considered a change for the better and, in fact, implicit in the principle of evolution. Like writers on myth during the Enlightenment, Frazer ignored the possibility that change may not always bring improvement. Frazer himself did no fieldwork. He integrated into his master scheme a vast body of data, often carelessly gathered, and manipulated it to fit his theory.

In the twentieth century, anthropological method was much improved by Bronislaw Malinowski (1884–1942) in his *Magic, Science, and Religion* (1948).

Malinowski was born in Poland but pursued his career chiefly in England. Influenced by French sociological thought, his own theory was based directly on fieldwork carried out between 1914 and 1918 among the Trobrianders, the people of a remote island complex southeast of New Guinea. Objecting to the evolutionary understanding of myth as protoscience, Malinowski held that its purpose was to serve as a "charter," a justification for the way things are. This is the **charter theory of myth**.

For example, a story might be told to justify someone's ownership of a certain part of the island—because that is where his ancestors sprang from the ground. According to Malinowski, myths justify and validate economic, political, social, and religious realities. We should not explain myth according to hypothetical patterns of cultural evolution at all, but from its social function, from how myth helps to deal with the practical problems of living. Malinowski usually is considered the founder of *functionalism,* the notion that the function of a practice determines the form it takes.

Linguistic Theories

The science of Indo-European linguistics, which made great advances in the nineteenth century, was the basis for another allegorical approach to myth in theories advanced by **Max Müller** (1823–1900), the leading Sanskrit scholar of his day and a vigorous rival of Andrew Lang. Müller, a German-born Oxford don, saw in nearly every myth, whether about heroes or gods, an allegory of the struggle between sunlight and darkness. Hence this method of interpretation is called **solar mythology**.

Müller's theory, like others inspired by evolutionary thought and the rapid growth of science, sought to understand myth as the effort of early peoples to explain prominent natural phenomena, such as storms or celestial bodies, but Müller's theory was unusually influential because of the linguistic support he provided for the central role assigned to the sun.

In the fairly obscure story of Endymion and Selenê, Endymion was a handsome youth whom Selenê ("moon") saw as he lay sleeping in a cave. She fell deeply in love with him and bore him many children. The two were separated when Zeus allowed Endymion to choose anything he wanted. He chose to sleep forever, never growing old. Because the Greek *endyein* originally meant "to dive," the name *Endymion* at first simply described the sun's setting ("diving") in the sea. The original meaning of *endyein* faded and was misunderstood to refer to a person, Endymion ("Diver"). The mythical story of the love of Selenê and Endymion, then, began with the words "Selenê embraces Endymion," that is, "Moon embraces Diver," which in the metaphorical "primitive" expression of early peoples was a way of saying "the sun is setting and the moon is rising."

Max Müller combined ancient physical allegory with the theories of Palaephatus about the distortion of language. Myth, he thought, begins through a "disease of language" whereby the original meaning of language, especially in observations about solar phenomena, was gradually misunderstood and reinterpreted. Müller and his followers were able in this way to argue that bloody death in myth was really the red-streaked sunset, that Odysseus' imprisonment in a cave was the waxing and waning year, and that Achilles' destruction of his enemies was really the splendid sun breaking through the clouds. Midas was the sun gilding everything it touches, and the story of Phaëthon describes how excessive heat (Phaëthon's ride) causes drought that is finally broken by a thunderstorm (the bolt hurled by Zeus to kill Phaëthon).

Müller did attempt to furnish a theoretical explanation for shifts in the meaning of the names of mythical figures. In this he differed from his many predecessors in the long history of allegory, who simply proclaimed, without justification, the truth of whatever came to their minds. Still, Müller and his followers found the sun in everything. Like many ambitious theories of myth, this one began to refute itself. Andrew Lang wittily parodied the theory in a learned article that proved, by Müller's methods, that Müller had never existed, but was himself a solar myth!

Solar mythology arose under the influence of one of the great intellectual discoveries of modern times, that most European languages (except Basque, Finnish, Hungarian, and Estonian) and many others spoken as far east as central India (including Armenian, Iranian, and Sanskrit, but not the Semitic languages) and even in China are descended from the hypothetical parent-language called proto–Indo-European. The discovery usually is credited to Sir William Jones (1746–1794), chief justice of India, founder of the Royal Asiatic Society, presented in a lecture in 1786. If it is possible to elucidate the origin and inner structure of modern European languages by comparing them with Greek, Latin, and Sanskrit, it should also be possible, according to the supporters of **Indo-European comparative mythology**, to elucidate European myths in the same way and to discover essential patterns and original meanings of myth.

For example, the Romans told a story about Mucius Scaevola ("Lefty"), who deliberately burned off his right hand to demonstrate Roman bravery to an enemy king. The Norsemen, Indo-European speakers like the Romans, told a story about the war-god Tiu (hence "Tuesday"), whose right hand the wolf Fenris, an enemy of the present order of creation, bit off. While the wolf was biting off Tiu's hand, Tiu bound the distracted wolf by an unbreakable chain. We could thus infer the existence of an original Indo-European story about a man who sacrificed his hand for the good of all. This story becomes a patriotic tale among the Romans, who emphasized civic duty, but among the Norsemen, concerned with the opposition between the cosmic forces of order and chaos, it became a tale of temporary world redemption (one day the Fenris wolf will escape its bonds and the world will end).

Indo-European comparative mythologists maintain that myths accompany language as language is passed on. They seek a common "grammar" or inner structure in the stories, which ought also to reveal something characteristic of Indo-European social traditions. In the mid-twentieth century French scholar Georges Dumézil (1898–1986) refined this sort of interpretation by correlating three hypothetical original classes in Indo-European society with the roles played by certain deities in Indo-European myth. These classes are rulers and priests, warriors, and food producers.

Consider, for example, the story of the Judgment of Paris. Why does Hera attempt to bribe Paris with an offer of royal power, while Athena offers him military glory and Aphrodite offers him Helen? Because the three choices represent the three fundamental activities in Indo-European society. Hera stands for royal authority, the ruling class; Athena stands for the warrior class; and Aphrodite, who sponsors reproduction and sustenance, represents the food producers. We might expect Demeter, because Aphrodite's concerns are preeminently with human sexuality; furthermore, Aphrodite is a goddess of Semitic origin. However, Dumézil must accept the story as it is given. In fact, the theory works poorly with Greek material.

Psychological Theories

New fields of study of the past century inspired corresponding new theories of myth. Sociology and anthropology led to functionalism; linguistics led to Indo-European comparative mythology. Psychology, too, has brought with it both a key myth—the story of Oedipus—and a variety of new psychological theories.

At the time when anthropological approaches were developing, **Sigmund Freud** (1856–1939) advanced a view of myth based in the individual rather than in society. Myth, he thought, was a by-product of personal psychological forces. Freud's theories of myth began with his thinking about the dreams of individuals. The mind of a sleeper works by different rules from the mind of the wakeful, although dream symbols can correlate with things in the waking world. Freud formulated rules by which translation from everyday reality to symbolism in dreams takes place.

For example, *condensation* occurs when several things from the waking world are fused together in a dream, perhaps with disturbing effect. *Displacement* occurs when something in a dream stands for something quite different in the waking world, even its opposite, as when an enemy represents a lover whom the sleeper does not entirely trust. Condensation and displacement are necessary to the dreamer because the true thought is morally or emotionally repugnant to the waking consciousness. Because the thought is still there, however, it must be dealt with, and the mind releases tension by dealing with the problem indirectly. Dreams are symptoms of psychological tensions that can affect the waking world of those suffering from mental disease, from neuroses.

How do the dreams of individuals result in myths, which belong to a whole people? They do, Freud thought, because myths are the collective and recurrent dreams of the race. An example in myth of dream condensation would be the mythical Centaurs or Sirens, made up of two separate beings fused together; an example in myth of dream displacement would be the upward anatomical shift of a woman's pubic region to create the face of Medusa.

Freud also held that neuroses and their symbolic expression in dreams go back to the infant's experience of his or her personal sexuality. He emphasized the **Oedipus complex**, first set forth in *The Interpretation of Dreams* (1900). From this story Sigmund Freud developed his notion that adult male psychology arises from the infant boy's sexual attraction to his mother and his hostility and jealousy toward his father.

Freud did not seek the origins of the legend in social history, as had Soviet folklorist Vladimir Propp, but in the incest dreams of his patients, which he took to represent suppressed desires of childhood. The son wishes sexual contact with his mother, from whose breasts he feeds and in whose warm body he is daily encompassed. He resents the father's sexual demands on the mother, which remove him from her embrace. He wants to kill the father, so that he might have the mother to himself. Only by overcoming such hidden, taboo, and obviously unspoken desires might one become an adult, Freud thought.

The myth of Oedipus, then, emerges from primeval dreams. To make his point Freud ignored inconvenient parts of the legend, above all the story that at the end of his life Oedipus may even have been taken up by the gods. Freud also ignores Oedipus' exposure as an infant and his great intelligence. Critics of Freud starkly complain that Freud's true intentions in his fantasies about human psychology were to denigrate human nature, to reduce it to raw and amoral animal impulse, a vision much in favor at the end of the nineteenth century. Like Oedipus, Freud says, we live in ignorance of our inner wishes that are so repugnant to morality, which Nature has forced upon us, but when we see them clearly, we seek to close our eyes. Freud was little interested in explaining the Oedipus story itself.

In Freudian interpretation, stories that describe heroes slaying dragons and marrying maidens are really forms of the Oedipus complex because they echo the son's repressed desire to kill his father (= the dragon) and have sexual intercourse with his mother (= the maid). Cronus castrated Uranus because sons want to deprive their fathers of sexual power, and they fear the same treatment from their own sons in turn. Mythical kings and queens represent parents. Sharp weapons are the male sexual organ, and caves, rooms, and houses symbolize the mother's containing womb. The imagery of myths can therefore be translated into that of sex, often in specifically anatomical ways.

Freud saw myths as arising among a race in the way that dreams arise in the individual, but he also argued that individual psychological development repeats the psychological history of the whole race. Sometime before Freud, embryologists had developed the notion that "ontogeny recapitulates phylogeny"—the development of the individual goes through the same stages as that of the race. This is an adaptation of evolutionary thinking. The individual's dreams reflect the same primitive mode of consciousness that we find in myth, which are collective dreams preserved from the primitive childhood of the race.

His theory is yet another that connects the mythical with the primitive and the irrational, an approach common since the Enlightenment. A Freudian reading of myth is allegory in yet another guise, translating mythical patterns and events into psychological patterns and events. But like Max Müller, and unlike earlier interpreters, Freud explained not merely how but also why shifts occur from one meaning to another.

Freud's associate **Carl Jung** (yunk, 1875–1961) continued to explore the notion of an unconscious part of human nature. Like Freud, Jung discerned a complex symbolism that both conceals the unconscious and, to the psychiatrist, furnishes access to it. Jung did not believe, however, that the symbolism of the unconscious mind was predominantly sexual in nature, nor even that dream symbolism ultimately belonged to the individual.

Jung's theory resembles Eastern religious teachings in some respects. For him the consciousness of the individual is like a bay or an inlet on a great ocean of psychic activity, which he called the **collective unconscious** (Freud had implied as much, with his notion of racial dreaming). Into the bay swim, from time to time, great beings that inhabit the deep. These are the *archetypes* (a Greek term also used by Neoplatonists), timeless recurrent images on which our emotional world and our myths are built.

Certain groups of archetypes may dominate the consciousness of entire cultures for periods of time. Jung spoke of such different archetypes as the Wise Old Man, the Earth Mother, and the Divine Child. Jung considered the *mandala,* a perfectly symmetrical, geometric visual figure used for focusing the consciousness in Buddhist meditation, to be an emblem of the total psychological integration that each person seeks and that myth reflects. In this sense myth can never be discarded from human life. Whether we know it or not, we live out myths in our own lives, a notion Joseph Campbell (1904–1987), deeply influenced by Jung, popularized in many books, especially *The Hero with a Thousand Faces* (New York, 1968).

Another follower of Jung, Erich Neumann (1905–1960), used Jung's method to explain the common myth of the dragon-combat. The myth, he argued, symbolizes the breaking-away of an individual's consciousness from the great collective unconscious of the world. The dragon represents the collective unconscious, always trying to swallow the hero, who symbolizes individual consciousness. The collective unconscious is also represented by the Great Mother-goddess, the mother of all things, a recurrent type in myth and in the history of religion. Although she is the source of individual consciousness and of life itself, she threatens to swallow her own progeny.

For this reason, evil female forces—witches like Circê or monsters like Tiamat— threaten the male hero. At some point the monster may actually swallow the hero (as the whale swallowed Jonah), but defeat is always temporary. The hero's ultimate victory over the dragon represents the emergence of personal identity, the victory of the individual consciousness over the threatening collective unconscious. The hero's reward—princess or treasure—represents the devouring collective unconscious in a tamed-down form, defeated, and now made fecund. The combat myth is really a description of an individual's psychological destiny.

Structuralist Theories

A highly influential theory of myth interpretation is **structuralism**, especially as propounded by French anthropologist **Claude Lévi-Strauss** (1908–2009). Meaning in a traditional story is not conveyed by the content, he maintained, but by the structural relations behind the content. In this most rationalistic and abstract of theories, the meaning of myth is its pure form.

Structural relations often are so subtle that they can be made clear only by means of diagrams, charts, and formulas, which resemble mathematical formulas. The meaning of a story, then, is independent of any particular telling of it, residing ultimately in all possible variants of the story taken together. Far from confining himself to "traditional tales," Lévi-Strauss declared that even the interpretation of a myth is to be considered part of the myth, including Lévi-Strauss's own analyses, which are simply additional variants!

Lévi-Strauss finds the origin of myth in the principle that "mythical thought always works from the awareness of oppositions toward their progressive mediation." Humans perceive the world in terms of sharp, intolerable dualities: hot and cold, bitter and sweet, raw and cooked, alive and dead. Because by nature we cannot tolerate opposition for which intermediaries do not exist, we bridge perceived contradictions by telling stories.

For example, the story of Cronus fathering his children but refusing to allow them to be born, and of Uranus' son Cronus swallowing his children after they were born, mediate between the opposites of birth and death. The irreconcilable opposites are brought together by telling a story in which the same creature both generates and consumes his progeny. Homer's *Odyssey,* the story of a man who went to the land of the dead and returned, brings together the irreconcilable opposites of life and death. Although life and death are opposites, in myth we can tell how a man journeyed to the land of the dead and returned. Our binary perception of the world derives, Lévi-Strauss thought, from the binary physical structure of our brains, which is supposed to make consciousness possible. Because of this binary structure, we can never be fully and finally reconciled with perceived oppositions— hence the dynamic quality of myth.

In 1955, Lévi-Strauss offered a celebrated interpretation of the myth of Oedipus. Despite its obscurity, his reading of the myth has attracted widespread comment. According to Lévi-Strauss, the myth has no message; it expresses the perception of irreconcilable claims about human origins. The Thebans claimed to be autochthonous, "sprung from the earth" (the teeth of the dragon). Thus Oedipus, "swollen-footed," is so called because creatures who spring from the earth, such as the snaky-footed Giants, have something wrong with their feet. On the other hand, the Thebans obviously sprang from their mothers' wombs, and Oedipus is certainly born from Jocasta. Therefore the myth of Oedipus is alleged to bridge, through story, what cannot be bridged through logic.

Lévi-Strauss's interpretations are difficult to assess, in part because of the obscurity of his expression. He summarizes his argument about the myth of Oedipus in this way: The "Overvaluation of blood relations is to their undervaluation as the attempt to escape autochthony is to the impossibility of succeeding in it."

It is also hard to know when we have found the true structure of a myth because different possibilities for analysis so often exist. As an anthropologist, Lévi-Strauss worked principally among South American Indians, through whose myths he wanted not only to discover the deep concerns, fears, and ambitions of these peoples but to lay open the inner workings of the whole human mind. In this he follows the ancient tradition of commentators wanting to prove that secrets about human nature and human destiny are hidden in traditional tales. More specifically, Lévi-Strauss echoed the Neoplatonists' program of discovering behind the stuff of myth an abstract pattern or code that explains the very nature of things.

In spite of its limitations, Lévi-Strauss's structural method of interpretation has had considerable exploratory power because it brings out hitherto unnoticed facets of myth by bringing together whole systems of myth and, beyond that, by relating myth to broader aspects of culture. A group of Lévi-Strauss's French followers has followed up the method for Greek myth, especially J.-P. Vernant (1914–2007) P. Vidal-Naquet (1930–2006) and M. Detienne (born 1935). These authors, together with Claude Lévi-Strauss himself, are often called the **Paris school of myth criticism**.

We can take as an example of their method their treatment of the Greek pantheon. The usual way (the method adopted in this book) of studying the pantheon is to examine each god in isolation, speculating on his or her origin and saying something about associated myths and rituals. According to Vernant, however, we can never understand any one god in isolation, any more than a single word; one must seek the "syntax," the complicated interrelations that bind together all the gods in myth. Only then can we understand the conceptual universe of the Greeks.

For example, the traveler Pausanias noted that on the base of Phidias' statue of Zeus in Olympia were linked the images of Hestia and Hermes. Why? Because, according to Vernant, Hestia and Hermes embody the contrary but complementary aspects of the Greeks' apprehension of space. Hestia is the fixed point, the hearth at the center of the household and of the city. Hermes represents transition, movement, change, the connecting link between oppositions.

Greek social life echoes the same polarity. As Hestia is to Hermes, so is woman to man. The woman stays at home, while the man travels abroad, conducts business, and wages war. Neither Hestia nor Hermes, then, can be understood in isolation because they constitute opposite poles of a single concept. To us the word *space* represents this single concept, but the Greeks, who lacked this abstract expression, represented the same notion by the different but complementary activities of Hestia and Hermes. (In fact, several words in Greek do roughly correspond to our *space*.)

By selecting and linking apparently disparate items taken from all aspects of culture, structuralist interpretations attempt to detect the rules shaping myth. The complexity of the enterprise points to both its possibilities and its hazards. Interplay between details and larger patterns yields fascinating insights, but the objectivity and significance of what emerges are a persistent difficulty. The universal claims of structuralist theory, professing as it does to be based on the very laws of human thought, permit it to be applied practically everywhere but encourage criticism on the familiar ground of attempting too much.

Contextual Approaches

German scholar Walter Burkert (born 1931) well describes such weakness in his book *Structure and History in Greek Mythology and Ritual* (1979), which has strongly influenced classical scholars. Burkert accepts the importance of structure in the study of myth, agreeing that the very identity of a tale is maintained by a structure of sense within it. The existence of this constant, partly invisible, internal structure makes it possible for us to say that Homer's story of Oedipus and Sophocles' story are both "the myth of Oedipus," despite their differences. However, Burkert opposes Lévi-Strauss's indifference to changing cultural and historical conditions, which constantly impart different collective meanings to a myth. Cultural and historical context must always be taken into account, Burkert insists.

Reviving in part the ritual theory of myth, Burkert argues that the structures that inform myth reflect biological or cultural **programs of action**. An example of a cultural program of action can be found in the hunting practices of Paleolithic man. Forced to kill his prey in order to survive but feeling a close relationship with and affection for animals, the hunter assuages his feelings of guilt through various ceremonies. After killing an animal, he makes a mock restoration by setting up its bones.

This program of action can explain details in the myth of the hunter Actaeon, who was turned into a stag by Artemis, a goddess of hunting, and torn to pieces by his own dogs. The story reflects a prehistoric ritual in which real animals were hunted by men in animal disguise—thus the dogs are personified in the mythical tradition to the extent of being given individual names. In one version of this myth, the dogs' grief-stricken howling at Actaeon's death is brought to an end when the Centaur Chiron makes an image of Actaeon, which the dogs mistake for their slain master. This making of the image of the slain man/animal, in Burkert's view, reflects the very old ritual reconstruction of the dead animal by the guilt-ridden hunter, actually practiced by tribal peoples.

Surely, Greek myth does preserve many ritual elements, including, no doubt, some drawn from Paleolithic hunting practice, and Burkert's remarks on religion and myth are always enlightening. However, his thesis that Greek sacrificial ritual, and the myths that reflect it, derive from ancient hunting practice leaves unexplained why Greek sacrificial ritual nearly always used domestic animals, not wild animals captured for the purpose. His conviction that ancient hunters felt "guilty" about killing their prey is also open to criticism. Although hunters undoubtedly respect their prey, we usually think of guilt as an emotion arising from violating the social mores; killing animals did not violate the mores of Paleolithic hunters. No doubt one reason that ancient hunters reconstructed their slain prey was to ensure, through magic, that there might be still more animals to kill.

Feminist critics may also apply a contextual approach, using myth to cast light on underlying social realities related to gender or show how myths may actually construct reality. Thus the myth of Demeter explained to Greek women their expected roles in marriage, childbearing, and religious cult, making such roles seem intrinsic and natural. Always, of course, such criticism must work with literary material generated by and for males.

The contextual approach to myth is complex, making use of insights from structural, historical, and comparative methods and appealing broadly to what we know about human biology, the history of religion, language, and anthropology.

CONCLUSION

What are we to make of this long development, the history of the interpretation of Greek myths, of which we have here given only brief highlights? We must be impressed by the abiding fascination that the Greek mythical tradition has exercised over the human mind. But what validity do these systems of interpreting myth have for our understanding of myth, if by "understanding" we mean placing something in a larger and more familiar context?

The ancient Greek theorists, puzzled by the strangeness of traditions taken from a preliterate and prephilosophic past, attempted to explain their own myths by assimilating them to "correct" models of reality as created by philosophy. They saw in myths allegories for philosophic descriptions of the physical world or, in euhemerism, a source for historical reconstruction of the human past, or a set of examples for how one should behave. Later methods have worked much the same way, adapting myths to new models of reality as they emerged from Christian to modern times. The scientific model of reality, which has increasingly dominated thought since the Enlightenment and especially since the nineteenth century, is only the latest in a long line of such models. Although the nineteenth-century theory of myth as a "disease of language" centering on natural phenomena was encouraged by scientific linguistics, it is remarkably similar to the interpretation proposed by Palaephatus in 300 BC. Modern psychological theories, especially those of Jung and Lévi-Strauss, offer explanations that in important ways repeat and refine approaches used by much earlier interpreters who sought in myth allegories of spiritual and psychological truths.

The strength of science lies in defining ideas precisely and treating them within strictly controlled guidelines. The power of humanistic studies, on the other hand, lies in their concern with the capacity of humans, as symbol-making beings, to create alternative worlds. Myth is one such alternative world, and the interpretation of myth is another; each is an expression of the same human capacity.

Historically, the interpretation of myth is fully as important as myth itself and in fact occurs on a far grander scale. The interchangeable use of the words *myth* (the story itself) and *mythology* (reflection on myth) in English usage unintentionally points to this critical confusion, a fact recognized by structuralists when they suggest that interpretations of myths are only the addition of new myths to old. If myth embodies the tensions, values, and intellectual currents of the society that produces it, myth interpretation embodies those currents no less faithfully. A sketch of the history of myth interpretation turns out to be a sketch of the history of ideas. In the history of myth interpretation we can watch and study ever-changing intellectual fashions in relation to an unchanging body of material.

The grand theorizers about myth like to pick out this or that story, this or that figure, make impressive observations, and then speak as if their conclusions were applicable to all myths from all times and all places. But myths are so different from one another, and even our definition of myth so vague and controversial, that any universal explanation is bound to be arbitrary and to serve the theoretical interests of the definer. The history of the interpretation of myth richly demonstrates this fact. The scope of Greek myth both invites and refutes the fatal tendency of comprehensive claims because Greek myth affords so rich a choice of test cases. With careful selection any theory will work well in particular instances, elucidating minor points with astonishing clarity. Applied to the next myth, the theory may be unable to deal plausibly with even obvious features.

Classical myth taken together is too complex, too many-faceted, to be explained by a single theory, as is fully recognized in the contextual approach, · which we have favored throughout this book. The complexity of myth is bound up with the complexity of human consciousness itself and with the special role that the Greeks, the inventors of the alphabet, played in the transition from an oral traditional culture to one that was alphabetic and self-critical. Greek myth therefore is a special case in the history of the human spirit. To understand it, we must make use of insights offered by different schools of interpretation. No one method of analysis will dissolve the endless mysteries of classical myth.

KEY NAMES AND TERMS

rationalism, 685
Xenophanes, 685
allegory, 686
symbolism, 686
etymology, 687
euhemerism, 688
Neoplatonism, 691
Enlightenment, 696
Romanticism, 697
Johann Bachofen, 698
Sir James Frazer, 699
ritual theory of myth, 700
charter theory of myth, 701

Max Müller, 701
solar mythology, 701
Indo-European comparative
  mythology, 702
Sigmund Freud, 703
Oedipus complex, 703
Carl Jung, 704
collective unconscious, 705
structuralism, 705
Claude Lévi-Strauss, 705
Paris school of myth criticism, 707
program of action, 708

FURTHER READING CHAPTER 25

GENERAL

Bremmer, Jan, and Fritz Graf, eds., *Interpretations of Greek Mythology* (London, 1987). A collection of essays on various topics by leading critics.

Buxton, Richard, ed., *From Myth to Reason?* (Oxford, UK, 1999). Problems in the history and reality of the myth/philosophy polarity, by several scholars.

Czapo, E., *Theories of Mythology* (Oxford, UK, 2005). The best comprehensive exploration of theories of myth interpretation in the modern period.

Dundes, Alan, ed., *Sacred Narrative: Readings in the Theory of Myth* (Berkeley, CA, 1984). Gathers important essays by major scholars on myth interpretation, edited by a leading folklorist.

Edmunds, Lowell, ed., *Approaches to Greek Myth* (Baltimore, MD, 1990). Essays on modern schools of myth interpretation, including myth and ritual, myth and history, Greek and Near Eastern mythology, Indo-European mythology, folklore, structuralism, psychoanalytic interpretation, and myth and Greek art.

Kirk, G. S., *The Nature of Greek Myths* (New York, 1974). Discusses "five monolithic theories"— nature myths, etiological myths, charter myths, myths that evoke a creative era, and myths that derive from rituals—and adds five additional theories that view myths as products of the psyche.

Segal, Robert A., ed., *Literary Criticism and Myth*, 6 vols. (New York, 1996). Essays by exponents of different critical schools.

GREEK THEORIES

Guthrie, W. K. C., *The Greek Philosophers, from Thales to Aristotle* (New York, 1960). Lucid condensation of how philosophy emerged in the Archaic and Classical periods, with bibliography for further exploration.

Kirk, G. S., and J. E. Raven, *The Presocratic Philosophers: A Critical History with a Selection of Texts* (Cambridge, UK, 1962). The earliest critics of traditional explanations of the world, including Xenophanes.

MEDIEVAL AND RENAISSANCE THEORIES

Allen, Susan Heuck, ed., et al., *Survival of the Gods: Classical Mythology in Medieval Art* (Providence, RI, 1987). Based on an exhibition, contains excellent essay on facets of the survival of classical myth, with excellent illustrations.

Bull, Malcolm, *The Mirror of the Gods: Classical Mythology in Renaissance Art* (London, 2005). Argues for the frivolous or pornographic use of classical myth in Renaissance art.

Bush, Douglas, *Mythology and the Renaissance Tradition in English Poetry* (Minneapolis, MN, 1932; New York, 1963). Good on the postclassical uses of mythology, with a list, chronologically arranged, of poems on mythological subjects.

Seznec, Jean, *The Survival of the Pagan Gods: The Mythological Tradition and Its Place in Renaissance Humanism* (New York, 1953; reprinted Princeton, NJ, 1994). Scholarly description of how the Greek gods were recast and reinterpreted in European literature and art after the triumph of Christianity—the most useful book on this topic.

THEORIES OF THE ENLIGHTENMENT

Marsak, L. M., trans. and ed., *The Achievement of Bernard le Bovier de Fontenelle* (New York, 1970). Introduction to Fontenelle, with selections from his works.

ROMANTIC THEORIES

Kamenetsky, Christa, *The Brothers Grimm and Their Critics, Folktales and the Quest for Meaning* (Athens, OH, 1992). Places the Grimms' collection in the Romantic movement; extensive review of theories of folktale interpretation.

ANTHROPOLOGICAL THEORIES

Fontenrose, Joseph, *The Ritual Theory of Myth* (Berkeley, CA, 1966; reprinted 1971). Argument against the theory that myth derives from ritual, by a leading scholar.

Frazer, J. G., *The New Golden Bough*, ed. T. Gaster (New York, 1959). A condensation of this seminal work.

Malinowski, Bronislaw, *Magic, Science, and Religion, and Other Essays* (New York, 1948; reprinted Prospect Heights, IL, 1992). The anthropologist sets forth his charter theory of myth.

Vickery, John B., *The Literary Impact of* The Golden Bough (Princeton, NJ, 1973). Résumé of Frazer's arguments and their influence.

LINGUISTIC THEORIES

Puhvel, Jaan, *Comparative Mythology* (Baltimore, MD, 1987; reprinted 1989). An up-to-date review of Indo-European elements in Greek myth, including the theories of Georges Dumézil (most of whose many publications are in French).

PSYCHOLOGICAL THEORIES

Jung, Carl G., et al., *Man and His Symbols* (New York, 1968). Jung and his followers expound the theory of unconscious archetypes.

_____ and K. Kerényi, *Essays on a Science of Mythology. The Myth of the Divine Child and the Mysteries of Eleusis* (Princeton, NJ, 1993). Classic study of Jungian archetypes.

Neumann, Erich, *The Origins and History of Consciousness,* trans. R. F. C. Hull (Princeton, NJ, 1954; reprinted 1970). A student of Carl Jung, Neumann analyzes the story of the dragon combat in terms of unconscious archetypes.

STRUCTURALISM

Detienne, Marcel, *The Creation of Mythology,* trans. Margaret Cook (Chicago, 1986). An important contribution of the "Paris school."

Gordon, R. L., ed., *Myth, Religion and Society. Structuralist Essays by M. Detienne, L. Gernet, J.-P. Vernant and P. Vidal-Naquet* (Cambridge, UK, 1981). Writings from the "Paris school."

Leach, Edmund, *Claude Lévi-Strauss,* rev. ed. (New York, 1974; reprinted Chicago, 1989). Excellent presentation of the Straussian analysis of myth.

Lévi-Strauss, Claude, *The Raw and the Cooked,* trans. J. and D. Weightman (Chicago, 1980). This is Volume 1 of his four-volume *Mythologiques* and a good introduction to his method and theories.

Propp, V., *Morphology of the Folktale,* 2nd ed. (Austin, TX, 1968; Russian original, 1928). English translation of the great Russian folklorist's seminal study of narrative pattern in folktale.

Vernant, J.-P., *Myth and Society in Ancient Greece,* trans. J. Lloyd (New York, 1990). Major statement by a leading member of the "Paris school."

CONTEXTUAL APPROACHES

Burkert, Walter, *Structure and History in Greek Mythology and Ritual* (Berkeley, CA, 1979). An influential modern contribution to theoretical approaches to Greek myth. Contains a lucid explication and criticism of the school of Lévi-Strauss.

_____, *Homo Necans: The Anthropology of Ancient Greek Sacrificial Ritual and Myth* (Berkeley, CA., 1983: German original 1972). Pioneering study that attempts to explain Greek cult practice in light of prehistoric culture.

Buxton, R., *Imaginary Greece: The Contexts of Mythology* (Cambridge, UK, 1994). Locates the stories within their originally peasant communities; analyzes narrative and social contexts.

Dowden, Ken, *The Uses of Greek Mythology* (London, 1992). Presents the diverse ways that Greeks used their myths.

Powell, Barry B., *A Short Introduction to Classical Myth* (New York, 2002). A condensation of this book with additional material on folklore and art.

REFERENCE CHARTS

CHRONOLOGY OF THE ANCIENT WORLD

10,000 BC	**Neolithic** ("New Stone") **Period** begins in the Near East with the development of agriculture and sedentary communities
4000 BC	Sumerian cuneiform writing is developed, c. 3400
	Egyptian hieroglyphic writing, Pharaonic civilization emerge, c. 3100
3000 BC	**EARLY BRONZE AGE** begins in Greece with introduction of bronze metallurgy, c. 3000–2000
	Sumerian cities flourish in Mesopotamia, c. 2800–2340
	Minoan civilization flourishes in Crete, c. 2500–1200
	Akkadian empire in Mesopotamia, c. 2334–2220
	Sumerian revival, c. 2200–2000
2000 BC	**MIDDLE BRONZE AGE** begins with arrival of IndoEuropean Greeks in Balkan Peninsula, c. 2000–1600
	Old Babylonian Empire in Mesopotamia, c. 2000–1550
	LATE BRONZE (or **MYCENAEAN**) **AGE** begins, c. 1600
	Hittite empire rules in Anatolia, c. 1600–1200
1500 BC	Phoenician syllabic writing appears, c. 1500
	Trojan War occurs, c. 1250 (?)
	DARK (or **IRON**) **AGE** begins with destruction of Mycenaean cities in Greece, c. 1200–1100
1000 BC	Greek colonies are settled in Asia Minor, c. 1000
	Greek colonies in Southern Italy and Sicily, c. 800–600
	ARCHAIC PERIOD begins with invention of Greek alphabet, c. 800
	Iliad and the *Odyssey*, attributed to **Homer,** are written down, c. 800–750
	Olympic games begin, 776
	Rome, allegedly, is founded, 753
	Hesiod's *Theogony* is written down, c. 750–700
	Homeric Hymns, c. 700–500
	Cyclic poets, c. 650–500

Age of Tyrants, c. 650–500

Cyrus the Great of Persia, c. 600–529

    Xenophanes, c. 570–460

    Pindar, c. 522–443

Alleged date of the expulsion of the Etruscan dynasty at Rome and the foundation of the "Roman Republic," 510

Cleisthenes founds the Athenian democracy, 508

500 BC   **Bacchylides,** fifth century

Persians invade Greece; battle of Marathon, 490

Persians invade Greece again; destruction of Athens; Greek victories at Salamis and Plataea, 480–479

CLASSICAL PERIOD begins with end of Persian Wars, 480

    Aeschylus, 525–456

    Sophocles, c. 496–406

    Herodotus, c. 484–420

    Euripides, c. 484–406

    Socrates, c. 469–399

Peloponnesian War, 431–404

    Thucydides, c. 460–400

400 BC Biblical book of *Genesis* reaches present form, c. 400

    Plato, 428–347

    Aristotle, 384–322

The Gauls sack the city of Rome, 390

Philip II of Macedon, Alexander's father, conquers Greece, putting an end to local rule, 338–337

Alexander the Great conquers the Persian empire and makes Greek culture world culture, 336–323

HELLENISTIC PERIOD begins with death of Alexander in 323

300 BC   **Apollonius of Rhodes,** third century

200 BC Punic Wars are waged between Rome and Carthage, 264–146

Greece becomes Roman province, 146

    Roman civil wars, 88–31

    Catullus, c. 84–54

    Vergil, 70–19

    Livy, 59 BC–AD 17

Julius Caesar rules as dictator, 46–44

    Ovid, c. 43 BC–AD 17

ROMAN PERIOD begins when Augustus defeats Antony and Cleopatra at battle of Actium and annexes Egypt, 31/30

Augustus Caesar reigns, 27 BC–AD 14

    Apollodorus' Library, first century AD (?)

    Plutarch c. AD 46–120

AD 100   **Apuleius,** second century

    Hyginus, second century

AD 200 Constantine, AD 280?–337;

AD 300 Edict of Milan freeing Christian church from persecution, AD 313

AD 400

MEDIEVAL PERIOD begins with fall of Western Roman Empire, AD 476

THE GREEK AND ROMAN PANTHEON

Greek Name (Roman Name)	Parentage	Origin	Concern	Attributes
Zeus (Jupiter, Jove)	Cronus + Rhea	Indo-European sky-god	kingship, law, weather	thunderbolt, scepter
Hera (Juno)	Cronus + Rhea	mother-goddess	marriage, family	peacock, scepter
Demeter (Ceres)	Cronus + Rhea	wheat-goddess	wheat harvest	grain, with Persephonê
Poseidon (Neptune)	Cronus + Rhea	god of fresh water	water, sea, earthquakes	trident, horses, dolphins
Hestia (Vesta)	Cronus + Rhea	the hearth	household	rarely shown
Artemis (Diana)	Zeus + Leto	fertility-goddess	hunting, wild things	bow, short dress, often with animals
Aphrodite (Venus)	Zeus + Dionê (or born from the foam)	fertility-goddess	human sexuality	nude, doves, with Eros (Cupid)
Hermes (Mercury)	Zeus + Maia	personified road marker	travel, trade, lies, oratory, thieves	winged shoes, caduceus
Hephaestus (Vulcan)	Hera (alone)	fire-spirit	metal crafts	skull cap, hammer
Apollo	Zeus + Leto	shaman's god	plague, healing, music, prophecy	beardless, lyre, bow
Ares (Mars)	Zeus + Hera	Thracian war god	war, violence	spear, shield, helmet
Athena (Minerva)	Zeus + Metis	city-goddess	civilization, crafts	helmet, aegis, other armor
[Dionysus]* (Liber)	Zeus + Semelê	dying god	ecstasy, the vine, wine	ivy, panthers, Maenads
[Pan] (Faunus)	Hermes + Arcadia	woodland spirit	cattle, terror	horns, hoofs, pipes
[Heracles] (Hercules)	Zeus + Alcmenê	deified hero	—	club, lion-skin, bow
[Asclepius] (Aesculapius)	Apollo + Coronis	deified hero (?)	medicine	staff with entwined snake
[Hades] (Dis)	Cronus + Rhea	underworld	the dead	rarely shown
[Persephonê] (Proserpina)	Zeus + Demeter	new crop; doublet of Demeter	the dead	torch; with Demeter

*Deities in brackets are not Olympians.

CREDITS

Figure 2.5 Two-handled cup, Greek, Attica, Late Archaic Period, about 520 BC 6th century BC Ceramic, black figure, Height: 11.4 cm (4 1/2 in.) , Diameter: 13.5 cm (5 5/16 in.). Gift of Edward Perry and Flake Warren, Museum of Fine Arts, Boston. 08.292.

Figure 2.6 Lewis Collection, The Parker Library, Corpus Christi College. Reproduced by permission of the master and fellows of Corpus Christi College, Cambridge, England, U.K.

Figure 2.10 Loutrophoros depicting a bridal procession, Greek, Classical Period, 430–420 BC, Attica, Athens. Ceramiic, red figure, height: 75.3 cm (29 5/8 in.), Diameter of lip: 25.3 cm (9 15/16 in.), Diameter of body: 18 cm (7 1/16 in.). Museum of Fine Arts, Boston, Francis Bartlett Donation of 1900, 03.802.

Figure 2.11 Deutsches Archaologisches Institut, Athens. Photograph: Eva-Maria Czako. Neg. D-DAI-ATH-NM 5127, DAI. All Rights Reserved.

Figure 2.13 Painter of Vatican 238, Hydria (Kalpis) about 510-500 BC Etruscan, Wheel-thrown, slip decorated earthenware with incised details. Ht. to top of handle 20 1/2 in. (52.1 cm. Toledo Museum of Art, Ohio, Purchased with funds from the Libbey Endowment, Gift of Edward Drummond Libbery. 1982.134.

Figure 3.4 Painter from Pistias Class "M", "White-Ground Footed Mastoid Skyphos," c. 515 BC Earthenware with slip and painted decoration. Chazen Museum of Art, University of Wisconsin-Madison, Cyril Winton Nave Endowment Fund Purchase, 1979.122.

Figure 5.5 Bell Krater, Red-figure terracotta, D. 30.5 cm. Greece, Apilia, 4th century BC (c) The Cleveland Museum of Art, 2002. Gift of J.H. Wade, 1924. 534.

Figure 8.3 The Pan Painter, Mixing Bowl (bell krater), Greek, Attica, Athens, Early Classical Period, about 470 BC Ceramic, Red Figure, Height: 37 cm. (14 9/16 in.), Diameter: 42.5 cm (16 3/4 in.). Museum of Fine Arts, Boston, James Fund and Museum purchase with funds donated by contribution, 10185.

Figure 9.5 The Pan Painter. Mixing bowl (bell Krater) (detail). Greek, Early Classical Period, about 470 BC Place of Manufacture: Greece, Attica, Athens. Ceramic, Red Figure. Height: 37 cm (14 9/16 in.); diameter: 42.5 cm (16 3/4 in). James Fund and Museum purchase with funds donated by contribution, 10.185.

Figure 12.1 The Lykaon Painter, Jar (pelike), Greek, Attica, Athens, Classical Period, about 440 BC Ceramic, red-figure, Height: 47.4 cm (18 11/16 in.), Diameter: 34.3 cm (13 1/2 in.). The Museum of Fine Arts, Boston, William Amory Gardner Fund, 34.79.

Figure 14.1 Deutsches Archaologisches Institut, Athens. Neg. D-DAI-ATH-Mykene 63, DAI. All Rights Reserved.

Figure 14.5 The Gallatin Painter, Water Jar (hydria), Greek, Attica, Athens, Late Archaic Period, about 490 BC Ceramic, Red Figure, Height: 41.7 cm (16 7/16 in.), Diameter: 27 cm (19 5/8 in.). Museum of Fine Arts, Boston, Francis Bartlett Donation of 1912, 13.200.

Figure 15.6 Deutsches Archaologisches Institut, Athens. Photograph: Hermann Wagner. Neg. D-DAI-ATH-NM 3397, DAI. All Rights Reserved.

Perspective 16.1 © British Library Board. All Rights Reserved. Harley 1766, f.39.

Figure 17.5 German Institute of Archaeology, Rome, Italy. Photo by Greifenhagen, negative no. D-DAI-Rom 1972.0261.

Figure 19.4 Circle of Antimenes Painter (Greek, Attic, active 530–510 BC). Dinos, c. 520–510 BC Black-figure terracotta; D. 50.8 cm. (c) The Cleveland Museum of Art, 2002. John L. Severancd Fund 1971.46.

Figure 19.6 Jatta Museum, Ruvo, Italy/German Institute of Archaeology, Rome, Italy. Negative no. D-DAI-Rom 1964.1045.

Figure 19.7 © Trustees of the British Museum / Art Resource, NY.

Figure 19.8 Erich Lessing / Art Resource, NY.

Figure 20.02 The J. Paul Getty Museum, Villa Collection, Malibu, California. Attributed to Painter of Louvre MNB 1148. Apulian Red-Figure Loutrophoros (Detail). About 330 BC Terracotta. Object: H: 90.2 × Diam. (rim): 26 cm (35 1/2 × 10 1/4 in.) South Italy, Apulia, Europe.

Figure 20.1 Museo Archeologico Nazionale Firenze.

Figure 20.4 © Trustees of the British Museum / Art Resource, NY.

Figure 20.8 © Trustees of the British Museum / Art Resource, NY.

Perspective Figure P21.1b Image copyright © The Metropolitan Museum of Art / Art Resource, NY.

Figure 21.8 The Dokimasia Painter. Mixing bowl (calyx Krater) with the killing of Agamemnon (detail). Greek, Early Classical Period, about 460 BC Place of Manufacture: Greece, Attica, Athens. Ceramic, Red Figure. Height: 51 cm (20 1/16 in.); diameter: 51 cm (20 1/16 in). Museum of Fine Arts, Boston. William Francis Warden Fund, 63.1246.

Perspective Figure 21.1c El Greco (1541–1614), Laocoon, ca. 1610–1614. Oil on canvas, 1.375 m × 1.725 m (54 1/8 in. × 67 7/8 in.). National Gallery of Art, Washington D.C., Samuel H. Kress Collection. Photo by Richard Carafelli.

Figure 22.02 The Painter of the Boston Polyphemos, Wine cup (kylix) depicting scenes from the Odyssey, Greek, Attica, Athens, Archaic Period, 560–550 BC Ceramic, Black Figure, Height: 13.2 cm (5 3/16 in.), Diameter: 21.7 cm (8 9/16 in). Museum of Fine Arts, Boston, Henry Lillie Pierce Fund, **99.518.**

Figure 22.3 © The Trustees of the British Museum / Art Resource, NY.

Perspective Figure 22.2a Dosso Dossi, Circe and Her Lovers in a Landscape, ca. 1525. National Gallery of Art, Washington, D.C., Samuel H. Kress Collection. Photo by Lyle Peterzell.

Perspective Figure 23.1a The Art Archive / Gianni Dagli Orti

Figure 24.02 Rembrandt van Rijn (Dutch, 1606–1669), "Lucretia", 1664. © 1996 Board of Trustees, National Gallery of Art, Washington, Andrew W. Mellon Collection.

Figure 25.1 Museo nazionale delle Terme, Rome, Soprintendenza Archeologica per l'Etruria Meridionale, Rome, Italy.

INDEX

Acastus (a-**kas**-tus. Akastos), son of Pelias and king of Iolcus, 506

Achaeans (a-**kē**-ans. Akhaians), a division of the Greek people, Homer's word for the Greeks at Troy, 25, 314, 359, 379, 550, 557–558, 561–569, 572, 579–582, 588, 591, 607

Acheloüs (ak-e-**lō**-us. Akheloos), river-god in northwest Greece, with whom Heracles wrestled for Deianira, 227, 405, 406

Acheron (**ak**-er-on. Akheron), "sorrowful," river of the underworld, 326, 331

Achilles (a-**kil**-ēz. Akhilleus), greatest Greek warrior at Troy, 1, 5, 11, 37, 78, 91, 459, 480, 502, 549, 551, 574, 576, 577, 584, 585, 597, 631, 645, 646, 651, 657, 675, 702; and Agamemnon, 556; and Alexander, 34; and Amazons, 394, 434; anger of, 68, 559–567; arms and armor of, 473, 578, 579; and Chiron, 389, 546, 552; death of, 48; epithets of, 39, 58, 516, 652; and Hector, 570; heel of, 552; and Patroclus, 305, 343, 545, 570, 571; and Medea, 529; and Peleus, 122, 506, 532, 533; and Priam, 226, 571–573; and Odysseus, 58, 314, 315; on Scyros, 553; and Telephus, 553; and Thetis, 157, 94, 49; tomb of, 306, 337, 586; and Troilus, 593

Acrisius (a-**kris**-i-us. Akrisios), father of Danaê, killed accidentally by Perseus, 13, 150, 351, 357, 359, 361, 368, 371, 380

Acropolis (a-**krop**-o-lis), hill in Athens on which the Parthenon is built, 22, 42, 129, 146, 160, 230, 232, 297, 298, 415–417, 419, 434, 448, 453, 483, 596, 642

Actaeon (ak-**tē**-on. Aktaion), son of Autonoë, torn to bits by his own dogs, 17, 227–230, 283, 427, 480, 536, 538, 690, 708

Admetus (ad-**mē**-tus. Admetos), king of Pherae, whose wife Alcestis died in his place, 392, 394, 505, 506, 532

Adonis (a-**don**-is), son of Cinyras and Myrrha, beloved by Aphrodite, killed by boar, 48, 129, 218, 265–270, 700

Adrastus (a-**dras**-tus. Adrastos), king of Argos, sole survivor of the seven against Thebes, 160, 446, 491, 494, 496, 497, 500

Aea (**ē**-a. Aia), "earth," land at eastern end of the Black Sea where Jason sought the Golden Fleece, 504, 511

Aeacus (**ē**-a-kus. Aiakos), father of Peleus, king of Aegina, judge in the underworld, 315, 452, 547, 548

Aeaea (ē-**ē**-a. Aiaia), "earthland," island home of Circê, 312, 615

Aeëtes (ē-**ē**-tēz. Aietes), "man of earth," king of Colchis in Aea, father of Medea, 476, 502, 504, 505, 511, 513, 514, 529, 615

Aegean (ē-**jē**-an) Sea, between Greece and Asia Minor, 23, 120, 203, 433, 468, 504

Aegeus (**ē**-jūs. Aigeus), father of Theseus, a king of Athens, 177, 428, 430, 432, 433, 445, 456, 529

Aegipan (**ē**-ji-pan. Aigipan), "goat pan," a form of Pan, saved Zeus in battle against Typhon, 99, 104

aegis (**ē**-jis), "goat skin," a shield with serpent border used by Athena and Zeus, 69, 70, 71, 97, 147, 193, 197, 218, 222, 230, 231, 232, 550, 562, 563, 605

Aegisthus (ē-**jis**-thus. Aigisthos), son of Thyestes, lover of Clytemnestra, murderer of Agamemnon, killed by Orestes, 542, 543, 590, 593–595, 627

Aegyptus (ē-**jip**-tus. Aigyptos), eponym of Egypt, brother of Danaüs, father of fifty sons, 357–359, 363, 379, 681

Aeneas (ē-**nē**-as), son of Aphrodite and Anchises, ancestor of the Roman people, 1, 52, 77, 222, 224, 325–329, 333, 334, 337, 396, 412, 585, 593, 602, 631, 632, 640–662, 678–680, 682, 700

Aeneid (ē-**nē**-id), poem by Vergil on founding of Rome, late first century BC, 69, 77, 235, 303, 325–333, 396, 397, 584, 585, 592, 631, 640, 644–646, 650–653, 656, 658, 674, 678

Aeolians (ē-**ō**-li-ans), a division of the Greek people, 27, 140, 141, 503

Aeolids (ē-**o**-lids), descendants of Aeolus in Thessaly, 503

Aeolus (**ē**-o-lus. Aiolos), (1) eponym of the Aeolians, son of Hellên, king of Magnesia, 140, 503, 504, 531; (2) king of the winds in Homer's *Odyssey*, 614, 618, 628, 647

Aëropê (a-**er**-o-pē), wife of Atreus, seduced by Thyestes, 542